OPERATIONS MANAGEMENT

CONCEPTS, METHODS, AND STRATEGIES

Mark A. Vonderembse
University of Toledo

Gregory P. White
Southern Illinois University–Carbondale

www.wiley.com/college/vonderembse

Dedicated with love to Gayle,
Our children, Leisje, Tosje, Anthony, Vanessa,
Talia, Elaine, and Maryke;
Gayle's parents, Bob and Pauline Bauer;
And in memory of Paul Edward Vonderembse
and Ruth Mary Vonderembse
—Mark A. Vonderembse

To Pat and our son, Eric;
Pat's mother, Marge Hendricks;
And in memory of Thomas White, Martha
White, and Earl Hendricks
—Gregory P. White

Acquisitions Editor *Beth Lang Golub*
Marketing Manager *Gitti Lindner*
Assistant Editor *Lorraina Raccuia*
Editorial Assistant *Ailsa Manny*
Production Manager *Lari Bishop*
Designer *Jennifer Fisher*
Illustration Editors *Jennifer Fisher and Kris Pauls*
Cover Design *Jennifer Fisher*
Cover Image Top and back: © Charles O'Rear/CORBIS; Bottom: © PictureNet/CORBIS

This book was set in Minion and printed and bound by R.R. Donnelly & Sons. The cover was printed by Lehigh Press, Inc.

This book is printed on acid free paper.∞

ISBN 0-471-39327-4

Printed in the United States of America

10 9 8 7 6 5 4 3 2 1

BRIEF CONTENTS

1   Introduction to Operations Management in a Global Environment   1

PART I
BUILDING CAPABILITIES TO COMPETE GLOBALLY   27

2   Gaining Competitive Advantage Through Operations   28

3   Enhancing Productivity: A Key to Success   51

4   Quality Management   71

5   Enterprise Integration and Supply Chain Management: A Strategic Perspective   92

PART II
DESIGNING THE SYSTEM TO PRODUCE SERVICES AND GOODS   115

6   Product Development: A Team Approach   116

7   Models and Forecasting   132

8   Process Selection: Volume Drives Costs and Profits   159

9   Capacity Decisions   192

10   Facility Location in a Global Environment   220

11   Facility Layout   242

PART III
PLANNING AND MANAGING OPERATIONS   285

12   Aggregate Planning   286

13   Planning for Material and Resource Requirements   312

14   Inventory Management   347

15   Just-in-Time and Theory of Constraints   373

16   Scheduling   405

17   Project Management   433

The following chapters are found on the companion Web site for this text at www.wiley.com/college/vonderembse

18   Time-Based Competition

19   Redesigning Business Processes

20   Quality Control

21   Supply Management

22   Job Design and Work Measurement

CONTENTS

Preface   xxii

About the Authors   xxxi

1 Introduction to Operations Management in a Global Environment   3

Defining Operations Management   3

Service versus Manufacturing Operations   5

Understanding Operations   7

Global Trade and Competition   11

Understanding the Systems Approach to Operations   12

The Organization as Part of the Economic and Government System   13

Legal and Ethical Issues in Operations   14

Operations as Part of the Organization   18

Strategy   18

Organizational Structure   19

Operations and Marketing Interface   19

Business Processes versus Business Functions   20

Operations as a Series of Related Subsystems   22

Summary   24

Key Terms   24

URLs   24

Questions   25

Internet Questions   25

PART I

BUILDING CAPABILITIES TO COMPETE GLOBALLY   27

2 Gaining Competitive Advantage Through Operations   28

Strategic Issues: Achieving Competitive Advantage with Operations   28

Customer Requirements   30

Competitive Capabilities   31

Flexibility **31**

Productivity **33**

Building Quality into Products **34**

Time **35**

E-business **36**

Designing Business Processes that Build Competitive Capabilities **38**

Strategy Development **38**

Product Development **38**

Developing Systems to Produce Services and Goods **38**

Order Fulfillment **39**

Strategy Development and Operations **39**

Linking Corporate Strategy to Operations **39**

A Changing Global Environment Offers Greater Competition **43**

The Role of Computer and Information Technology in Operations **43**

Expert Systems **44**

Decision Support Systems **44**

The Internet **44**

Virtual Reality **45**

The Role of Computer and Information Technology in Manufacturing **46**

The Role of Computer and Information Technology in Service Operations **47**

Summary **48**

Key Terms **48**

URLs **49**

Questions **49**

Internet Questions **49**

Chapter supplements are available online at www.wiley.com/college/vonderembse

Chapter 2 Supplement: Computer-Integrated Manufacturing

Introduction

Engineering Design with CAD

Flexible Manufacturing Systems

Production Planning and Control Systems

People, Technology, and Computer-Integrated Manufacturing

Soft Automation Enhances Flexibility and Improves Productivity

3 Enhancing Productivity: A Key to Success 51

Introduction **51**

Understanding Productivity **52**

Is Money More Important than Productivity? **53**

Productivity and the Nature of Work **54**

Productivity in Manufacturing versus Service Firms **54**

The Quality Condition **55**

Assessing Productivity **55**

The Inputs and Outputs of Productivity **56**

Multiple Factor Productivity **59**

Productivity: Where Do We Stand **60**

Productivity and Wage Rates **61**

Impact of Productivity Improvements on the Workforce **62**

Productivity and Leisure **63**

Enhancing Productivity **63**

Technology and Productivity Improvements **66**

Summary **67**

Key Terms **68**

URLs **68**

Questions **68**

Internet Questions **68**

Problems **69**

Chapter supplements are available online at www.wiley.com/college/vonderembse

Chapter 3 Supplement: Learning Curves

Using a Learning-Curve chart

Estimating the Learning Factor

Pricing Under the Learning-Curve Effect

4 Quality Management 71

Introduction to Quality Management **71**

What Is Quality? **71**

Internally Oriented Definitions of Quality **72**

Externally Oriented Definitions of Quality **72**

Dimensions of Quality **72**

Dimensions of Service Quality **72**

Dimensions of Quality for Goods **73**

Costs of Quality **74**

Six Sigma **75**

The Background of Quality Management **76**

W. Edwards Deming **76**

Joseph M. Juran **76**

Philip Crosby **76**

Genichi Taguchi **77**

Total Quality Management **78**

Focus on the Customer **78**

Quality Function Deployment **79**

Everyone Responsible for Quality   **81**

Team Problem Solving   **82**

Employee Training   **83**

Fact-Based Management   **83**

Philosophy of Continuous Improvement   **84**

Controversy Surrounding TQM   **85**

Quality Awards and Standards   86

The Malcolm Baldrige National Quality Award   **86**

ISO 9000:2000 International Quality Standards   **87**

Summary   **89**

Key Terms   **89**

URLs   **90**

Questions   **90**

Internet Questions   **91**

Notes   **91**

Chapter supplements are available online at www.wiley.com/college/vonderembse

Chapter 4 Supplement: Acceptance Sampling

Possible Sampling Errors

OC Curves

MIL-STD-105D

Multiple Sampling Plans

5   **Enterprise Integration and Supply Chain Management: A Strategic Perspective   92**

Introduction   92

Overview of Supply Chain Management   93

Information Sharing in the Supply Chain   94

The Bullwhip Effect   **94**

Electronic Data Interchange   **95**

Forecast Accuracy   **95**

Digital Loyalty Networks   **96**

Collaborative Planning Forecasting and Replenishment (CPFR)   **96**

Supply Chain Structure   97

Many Suppliers versus Few Suppliers   **97**

Insourcing versus Outsourcing   **97**

Vertical Integration   **97**

Virtual Organizations   **98**

Disintermediation   **98**

Types of Supply Chains   **99**

Responsive Supply Chains   **99**

Efficient Supply Chains   **99**

Supply Chain Strategies   100

Quick Response Programs   **100**

Vendor Managed Inventory (VMI)   **101**

Efficient Consumer Response   **101**

Postponement   **102**

Revenue Sharing   **103**

Cross Docking   **104**

3PL   **104**

E-commerce   104

B2C   **105**

B2B   **105**

Enterprise Resource Planning (ERP)   **106**

Performance Measurement   108

Measures Related to Competitive Priorities   **108**

Strategic Profit Model   **108**

Global Issues in Supply Chain Management   109

Principles of Supply Chain Management   110

Build a Competitive Infrastructure   **110**

Leverage the Worldwide Logistics Network   **110**

Synchronize Supply to Demand   **111**

Measure Performance Globally   **111**

Summary   **111**

Key Terms   **112**

URLs   **112**

Questions   **113**

Internet Questions   **113**

Problems   **114**

PART II

DESIGNING THE SYSTEM TO PRODUCE
SERVICES AND GOODS   **115**

6   Product Development: A Team Approach   **116**

Introduction   116

The Product Life Cycle   117

Development Stage   **117**

Growth Stage   **118**

Maturity/Saturation Stage   **118**

Decline Stage   **118**

The Increasing Importance of Product Development   118

Global Aspects of Product Development   119

Using Teams for Product Development   120

Overview of Product Development   121

   Initial Assessment Phase   121

   Engineering and Economic Analysis   123

   Development and Testing Phase   124

   Final Planning   124

   Launch Phase and Market Surveys   124

   Mortality in Product Design   124

   A Concurrent, Not a Sequential, Process   125

Product Development, Safety, and Liability   127

Allies in Product Development: The Role of Suppliers   127

Improving Product Quality and Costs through Product Development   128

   Product Development as a Determinant of Product Quality and Cost   128

   Quality Function Deployment   130

Summary   130

Key Terms   131

URLs   131

Questions   131

Internet Questions   131

Chapter supplements are available online at www.wiley.com/college/vonderembse

Chapter 6 Supplement: Roles of the Participants in Product Development

Introduction

Looking beyond the Firm: The Role of Marketing

From Consumer Needs to Product Ideas: The Role of Engineering

Product Ideas to Product Reality: The Role of Operations

Capital Formation and Evaluation: The Role of Finance

Information for Decision Making: The Roles of Accounting and Information Systems

7   Models and Forecasting   132

Introduction   132

Models and Decision Making   132

   Types of Models   133

   The Application of Models   134

Forecasting   135

   The Nature of Forecasting   135

   Forecasting Methods   137

   Qualitative Approaches to Forecasting   138

Analyzing a Time Series   139

Regression and Correlation Analysis   144

Measuring Forecasting Error   151

Summary   152

Key Terms   153

URLs   153

Questions   153

Internet Questions   153

Problems   154

8   Process Selection: Volume Drives Costs and Profits   159

Introduction   159

How Process Selection Relates to Product Design and Capacity   160

Relating Process Selection to Product Design   161

Process Selection and Capacity   161

Building Volume through Global Expansion   164

Understanding the Scale Factor   164

Modeling the Scale Factor: Cost-Volume-Profit Model   165

Process Selection and Economies of Scale and Scope   172

Ethical Issues in Process Selection   181

The Focused Factory   181

Mass Customization   182

Types of Customization   183

Containing the Cost-Side of Mass Customization   184

A Learning Organization: The Foundation of Mass Customization   185

Summary   186

Key Terms   186

URLs   187

Questions   187

Internet Questions   187

Problems   188

9   Capacity Decisions   192

What Is Capacity?   192

Why Is Capacity Important?   193

Estimating Capacity   193

Changing Product Mix   195

Adding People   196

Increasing Motivation   197

Increasing Machine Production Rate   197

Improving Quality   198

Increasing Product Yield   198

Points to Consider **199**

Determining System Capacity 199

Product Layout **199**

Process Layout **200**

The Product Layout and System Capacity **200**

The Process Layout and System Capacity **204**

Capacity Decisions for Service Operations **206**

Service Operations and System Capacity **206**

Making Capacity Decisions for Competitive Advantage 208

When to Add Capacity **208**

How Much Capacity to Add **210**

Where to Add Capacity **211**

What Type of Capacity to Add **211**

Adjusting Capacity to Meet Changing Requirements **211**

Summary **212**

Key Terms **213**

URLs **213**

Questions **213**

Internet Questions **214**

Problems **214**

Chapter supplements are available online at www.wiley.com/college/vonderembse

Chapter 9 Supplement: Modeling for Capacity Decision Making

Decision Trees

10 Facility Location in a Global Environment   220

Introduction 220

Location as a Strategic Decision 221

Factors Affecting the Location Decision **222**

Factors Affecting Service Operations **222**

Managing the Quantitative Factors **223**

Including the Qualitative Factors **228**

Analyzing Spatial Relationships **229**

The Location Decision's Effect on Other Operating Factors **230**

International Dimensions of the Location Decision 230

Why Locate in a Foreign Country? **230**

Japanese Automotive Industry Locates in North America **231**

Ethical Considerations in the Location Decision **232**

Location Analysis for Service Operations 233

The Location Decision Provides the Opportunity to Be Socially Responsible 233

Summary   234
Key Terms   235
URLs   235
Questions   235
Internet Questions   235
Problems   236
Appendix: Qualitative Factor in Location Analysis   238

Chapter supplements are available online at www.wiley.com/college/vonderembse

Chapter 10 Supplement: Analyzing Spatial Relationships

Introduction

The Load-Distance Method of Facility Location

The Transportation Problem

The Role of the Computer in Analyzing Spatial Relationships

11 Facility Layout   242

Introduction   242

Criteria for the Layout Decision   243
Overview of the Layout Question   244

Continuous Flow Processes   245

Continuous Flow Processes and Service Industries   246

Assembly Lines   246

Determining the Layout   246
The Role of Computers in Balancing the Line   257
Motivation   257
Integrating Product Design and Automated Assembly   258

Batch Processing   258

Using Group Technology to Organize Manufacturing Cells and Flexible Manufacturing Systems   259

Methods for Creating Families of Parts   259

Job Shops   261

Finding the Pattern and Determining the Layout   263
The Role of Computers in Job Shop Layout   269
Systematic Layout Planning   270

Using Layout for Competitive Advantage   271

Summary   272
Key Terms   272
URLs   272
Questions   272
Internet Questions   273
Problems   273

PART III

PLANNING AND MANAGING OPERATIONS 285

12 Aggregate Planning 286

Introduction 286

Medium-Range Operations Planning 287

Aggregation in Medium-Range Operations Planning 288

The Organizational Context of Aggregate Planning 288

Strategies for Meeting Demand 292

Proactive Strategies 292

Reactive Strategies 293

Cost Considerations 293

Aggregate Planning for Service Organizations 294

Techniques for Aggregate Planning 295

Three Pure Strategies 296

An Aggregate Plan for a Service Organization 298

The Graphical Approach 300

A Mathematical Procedure for Aggregate Planning 302

Summary 304

Key Terms 305

URLs 305

Questions 305

Internet Questions 306

Problems 306

Chapter supplements are available online at www.wiley.com/college/vonderembse

Chapter 12 Supplement: Linear Programming

Introduction

Formulating the Problem Mathematically

Solving the Mathematical Problem

Limitations and Extensions of Linear Programming

13 Planning for Material and Resource Requirements 312

Introduction 312

Master Production Scheduling 313

Planning Horizons 313

Developing the MPS 313

Matching the Master Schedule to the Aggregate Plan 314

Taking Customer Orders into Account 315

Master Scheduling in Practice 318

The Demand Management Process 320

Rough-Cut Capacity Planning 320

Calculating Requirements by Overall Factors 321

Handling Insufficient Capacity 322

Material Requirements Planning 323

Independent versus Dependent Demand 324

The Data Files Used by MRP 325

Determining Planned Order Releases for Level 1 Items 327

Determining Planned Order Releases for Lower Level Items 330

Combining Requirements 330

How MRP Coordinates Purchasing and Operations 331

Capacity Requirements Planning 332

The Ethics of MRP 334

Extensions of MRP 334

Closed-Loop MRP 335

Manufacturing Resource Planning 335

MRP in Service Organizations 336

The Role of MIS in Planning 339

Summary 340

Key Terms 340

URLs 340

Questions 340

Internet Questions 341

Problems 342

14 **Inventory Management** 347

Introduction 347

Purposes and Types of Inventory 347

Types of Inventory 348

Information Systems for Inventory Management 348

Perpetual Inventory Systems 349

Periodic Inventory Systems 349

Aggregate Performance Measures 349

ABC Classification 350

The Economic Order Quantity Model 351

Cost of Ordering 351

Cost of Holding Inventory 352

Assumptions of the EOQ Model 353

Mathematical Statement of the Model 354

A Variation of the EOQ Model 358

Quantity Discounts 359

Stockouts and Safety Stock 361

Order-Point Determination 361

Safety Stock **363**

The Fixed-Order-Interval Model **366**

Review Interval **366**

Order-Up-to Level **367**

Safety Stock for the Fixed-Order Interval Model **368**

Summary **369**

Key Terms **370**

URLs **370**

Internet Questions **370**

Problems **370**

15 Just-In-Time and Theory of Constraints **373**

Introduction **373**

Introduction to Just-In-Time (JIT) **373**

Fundamental Concepts of JIT **374**

The JIT "Pull" System **378**

Simplifying the Production Process **381**

Planning in JIT Systems **384**

The Role of MIS in JIT **387**

JIT in Service Operations **388**

Strategic Planning and JIT **389**

JIT II **391**

Lean Systems **391**

Theory of Constraints **391**

The Goal of Operations **392**

The Impact of Constraints **392**

Applying TOC in Operations **394**

The Drum, Buffer, and Rope **396**

Comparing TOC, MRP, and JIT **398**

Combining TOC, MRP, and JIT **398**

Summary **399**

Key Terms **399**

URLs **400**

Questions **400**

Internet Questions **401**

Problems **401**

16 Scheduling **405**

Introduction **405**

Overview of the Scheduling Process **407**

Data Collection **407**

Order Entry **408**

Orders Released for Production   409
Sequencing and Dispatching   409
Managerial Considerations in Scheduling   409
Ethical Issues in Scheduling   410

Techniques for Scheduling Line-Flow and Batch Processes   411
Scheduling Continuous Flow Processes   411
Scheduling an Assembly Line   412
Scheduling Batch Processes   412
Flexible Manufacturing Systems   413

Job Shop Scheduling   414
Sequencing Using Dispatching Rules   414
Sequencing Jobs Using Johnson's Rule   416

Dispatching in MRP   418
Machine Loading   418
Sequencing   422
Finite Capacity Scheduling   422
Input/Output Control   423
Simulation in Developing Schedules   423

Special Problems in Scheduling Services   424
When the Customer Is Waiting   424
Scheduling Strategies for Services   424
Workforce Scheduling for Services   425
Summary   427
Key Terms   427
URLs   428
Questions   428
Internet Questions   428
Problems   429

Chapter supplements are available online at www.wiley.com/college/vonderembse

W W W

Chapter 16 Supplement: Management Science Tools and Scheduling

Applications of Waiting-Line Models to Schedules
Simulation as a Scheduling Tool

17   Project Management   433

Introduction   433
The Beginnings of Project Management   434
Planning for Projects   434
Network Representation of a Project   435
Activities on Nodes   435
Activities on Arcs   436

Dummy Activities   **436**

The Critical Path Method   **437**

Calculating Start and Finish Times   **437**

Avoiding Late Completion   **439**

Project Management Is Used Throughout Organizations   **440**

Introducing Probability with PERT   **441**

Estimating Activity Time   **442**

Probability of Completion by a Given Time   **442**

Other Resource Considerations   **444**

Balancing Resource Requirements   **444**

Crashing the Critical Path: Time/Cost Trade-Offs   **445**

Critical Chain Scheduling and Buffer Management   **448**

Three Types of Buffers   **449**

Buffer Management   **451**

Summary   **451**

Key Terms   **451**

URLs   **451**

Questions   **452**

Internet Questions   **452**

Problems   **452**

The following chapters are found on the companion Web site for this text at www.wiley.com/college/vonderembse

18 Time-Based Competition

Introduction

Time: The New Competitive Battle Ground

Competing on Time

Achieving Time Reductions

Reducing Product Development Time through Early Involvement

Cutting Costs and Improving Quality with Time-based Competition

Innovative Product Development with Time-based Competition

Is Co-location Essential in a Global Environment?

Creating Time-Based Operations

Understanding the Order Fulfillment Process

Reducing Wait Time

Reducing Work Time

Using Teams and Early Involvement to Reduce Operating Time

Using Information Systems to Cut Time

Increasing Communication Capabilities Will Shrink the Globe

Ethical Issue: Squeezing Out Time May Generate Difficult Trade-Offs

Summary
Key Terms
Questions

 19 Redesigning Business Processes

Global Competition Is Driving Fundamental Change

Evolving From An Industrial to a Postindustrial Organization

Changing Characteristics from the Industrial to the Postindustrial Stage

Changing Premises and Patterns of Thinking

Reengineering Business Processes

Defining Business Process Reengineering

Determining When Business Process Reengineering Should Be Used

Steps in Reengineering

Keeping the Process Going after Implementation

Using Information Technology as an Enabler for BPR

A Word about Teams before We Move On

Summary

Key Terms

Questions

20 Quality Control

Introduction

The Concept of Variation

Two Causes of Variation

Process Capability

Taguchi Loss Function

Taguchi Methods

Tools for Controlling Processes

Control Charts for Attributes

Tools for Collecting Data

Check Sheets

Histograms and Graphs

Tools for Analyzing Data

Pareto Analysis

Cause-Effect Diagrams

Scatter Diagrams

Putting the Tools into Practice

Summary

Key Terms

Internet Questions

Questions

Problems

21 Supply Management

Introduction
Defining Terms
Materials: A Management Perspective

Material Flow and the Organization
Physical Flows
Information Flows

Purchasing
Defining Specifications
Obtaining Price Quotations
Developing Criteria for Supplier Selection
Classifying Suppliers According to Performance
Evaluating the Make-or-Buy Decision
Awarding the Contract
Expediting
Gathering Information for Follow-Up and Evaluation
Just-in-Time Purchasing versus Traditional Purchasing
How Purchasing Is Changing
Ethical Issues in Purchasing

Global Sourcing of Materials
Ethics and Global Trade

Inventory Control
What Is Inventory?
Why Maintain Inventory?
Inventory in Service Operations
The Role of Computers in Inventory Control

Material Handling and Storage
Receiving and Shipping
Storage Devices
Intelligent Warehouse Systems

Distribution Systems
Building a Production Chain
The Levels in a Distribution System
Distribution Requirements Planning
Changes in Distribution Systems
Summary
Key Terms
Solved Problems
Questions
Problems

22 Job Design and Work Measurement

Introduction to Job Design
Specifying the Tasks and Responsibilities of a Job
Ethical Considerations in Job Design

Methods Analysis to Improve Productivity
Flow Process Charts
Multiple Activity Charts

Measurement of Work
Historical Data
Time Studies
Predetermined Time Standards
Work Sampling

Compensation
Individual Rewards
Gainsharing
International Aspects of Employee Compensation
Summary
Key Terms
Internet Questions
Questions
Problems

PREFACE

Our approach to writing this textbook is based on four related ideas. First, a company should be viewed as a set of customer-facing processes that cross several functional areas. Operations plays an important role in these efforts as it interacts with marketing, research and development, and engineering to design new products; and with information system specialists to improve productivity and reduce lead-time. Operations managers are also building relationships with suppliers, who provide key components and services to the organization. Second, decisions made by operations managers are important to customers because they affect the value of the organization's products. Product quality, performance, availability, and costs are all directly influenced by actions taken in operations. As a result, operations has an influence on the organization's competitive position and should be part of the organization's strategy. Third, all business students, regardless of their major, should be brought to the cutting edge of operations management as practiced by successful firms. And fourth, quantitative methods should be integrated with the conceptual material and presented as tools for problem solving.

The book follows this sequence: Building Capabilities to Compete Globally, Designing the System to Produce Services and Goods, and Planning and Managing Operations. This sequence has been carefully chosen because it follows the logical top-down planning sequence most companies follow. Furthermore, it enables instructors to begin with an overview, then fill in the detailed pieces later. Students can see how the parts fit together, and are able to understand why the material covered in each chapter is important to the entire organization.

STREAMLINED, INTEGRATED APPROACH

This text is designed to be lean so that students and faculty can focus on the core topics in operations management. The text features integrative topics like supply chain management, product development, and productivity enhancement that are essential for managers in all disciplines. This cross-functional perspective provides students with a sound overview of operations management and its role inside the organization. The text also provides comprehensive coverage of traditional topics such as quality management, capacity, scheduling, and inventory management. The book achieves a balance between comprehensive coverage and comfortable size by covering material concisely and by using our Web site effectively. Additional material such as supplements, additional chapters, solved problems, and mini-cases are available on the Web site. This approach produced a leaner text, keeping the textbook cost lower for students while giving instructors the flexibility to bring in optional material from the Web as they see fit.

Intended Audience

The target market for the text is the introductory course in operations management for undergraduates and MBA students. The text is designed so that students in any business-related major will find it relevant. Thus, prior training in management science is not required to read and understand the text. However, it is assumed that students have had an introductory course in statistics.

Special Features

Cross-functional Approach

Woven throughout the text is the notion that operations is an important part of the organization and that to be successful organizations must integrate operations with the other functional areas. Each chapter attempts to demonstrate that to some extent. For example, Chapter 1 initiates this by defining operations, describing its role in the organization, and explaining how decisions made in operations impact and are impacted by the firm's external environment. Chapter 2 discusses how operations can be used to build a competitive advantage by satisfying customer needs. Chapter 3 describes productivity and explores avenues for enhancing it. Chapter 5 discusses enterprise integration and supply chain management, which are important organizational processes that involve relationships between companies. Chapter 6 describes product development as a process that is cross-functional in nature and requires teamwork for success. There are many other examples that illustrate this integrative theme, which is a critical component for success in business.

Services and Manufacturing

Operations exist in a variety of organizations, including aircraft manufacturers, banks, government agencies, hospitals, and computer chip producers. Service operations are a growing part of our world economy. In developed countries, service operations often exceed 50 percent of a country's gross domestic product. In the United States, services generate more than 75 percent of gross domestic product. In writing a text, it is essential to have a balanced coverage between service and manufacturing operations. Thus, we have been careful to include numerous examples and problems from both.

While striving to point out how services and manufacturing operations are different, we have also avoided covering them as totally separate topics. In fact, services and manufacturing operations have many similarities, and we have attempted to integrate this coverage. The result achieves an effective balance between the two.

Global and Ethical Issues

Global and ethical issues are important and will continue to grow in importance. We have attempted to weave these concepts into all of the relevant chapters. The introductory chapter clearly explains that operations and the organization are part of the global economic and government systems. The chapter introduces legal and ethical issues in operations, labor relations, the environmental impact of operations, and product safety. The remainder of the text elaborates on these concepts. For example, ethics in product design is an important element in Chapter 6. Designing processes that generate low levels of pollution and high levels of safety is discussed in Chapter 8 on process selection. Developing location policies and practices that do not exploit labor, especially child labor in third world countries, is discussed in Chapter 10.

Computer and Information Technology Applications

In today's rapidly changing environment, computer and information technology applications are essential to build effective operations and to achieve high business performance. Thus, we have devoted a significant effort to discussing these topics as they relate to the production of services and goods. For example, Chapter 2 provides an overview of the role of computers and information technology in services and manufacturing operations. The supplement to Chapter 2, which is available on the Web site, provides in-depth coverage of computer-integrated manufacturing. Chapter 3, on productivity, discusses the impact of computer and information technology on productivity improvements. An additional chapter on the Web site covers redesigning business processes, and describes how this technology provides the basis for process improvements. The foundation of enterprise integration and supply chain management is based on the effective gathering and communication of information to enhance decision-making.

The Role of Quantitative Methods

We understand the important role that quantitative methods, both statistics and management science, have in operations. Where deemed appropriate, these topics have been carefully woven throughout the text so their application can follow logically from, and be close to, the discussion of managerial issues. The result is that students are motivated to learn quantitative techniques because the managerial applications are readily apparent. Some faculty may wish to cover additional, more advanced, quantitative topics. These additional topics, which are available on the Web site, are linked directly to a chapter, so that they can be "pulled into" the text without losing continuity. From the perspective of material flow and integration, it would be as though the material on the Web site was contained in the text. The following tables indicate where quantitative material may be found in the text.

Quantitative Subjects in the Text Book	Chapter
Aggregate Planning	12
Assembly Line Balancing	11
Cost-Volume-Profit Model	8
Project Scheduling	17
Forecasting	7
Job Shop Layout	11
Lot Sizing Models	14
Material Requirements Planning	13
Modeling, An Introduction	7
Safety Stock Determination	14
Scheduling Production	16

Additional quantitative methods are available on the Web site. The second column in the following table indicates where the technique is located on the Web site. The location would be either a supplement to a text chapter or a stand-alone Web chapter. The third column links the Web material to a text chapter.

Quantitative Subjects on the Web Site	Web Site Location	Related Text Chapter
Acceptance Sampling for Quality Management	Chapter 4 Supplement: Acceptance Sampling	4
Decision Trees	Chapter 9 Supplement: Modeling for Capacity Decision Making	9
Learning Curves	Chapter 3 Supplement: Learning Curves	3
Linear Programming for Aggregate Planning	Chapter 12 Supplement: Linear Programming	12
Load Distance Method	Chapter 10 Supplement: Analyzing Spatial Relationships	10
Make versus Buy Decision	Web Site Chapter 21: Supply Management	5
Simulation of Waiting Lines and Machine Failure	Chapter 16 Supplement: Management-Science Tools and Scheduling	16
Statistical Process Control	Web Site Chapter 20: Quality Control	4
Transportation Method	Chapter 10 Supplement: Analyzing Spatial Relationships	10
Waiting Line Models	Chapter 16 Supplement: Management-Science Tools and Scheduling	16

Chapter Features

Many pedagogical features have been incorporated into this text as a means of achieving our overall objectives. These features include:

Learning Objectives

A list of performance-based Learning Objectives is provided at the beginning of each chapter so that students know what is expected of them after completing the chapter.

Examples

In order to help students understand the more quantitative material, we have provided numerical examples throughout the text. To facilitate the understanding of qualitative material, we have provided brief summaries of situations that real companies face, and have described how they cope with these issues. Companies such as Amazon.com, FedEx, Intel, SEGWAY, UPS, and others are used to illustrate important points.

Summary

Each chapter ends with a summary of key points that reflect the learning objectives listed at the beginning of the chapter.

Key Terms

Key terms presented in the chapter are included at the end of each chapter. A glossary of all key terms and their definitions is included at the end of the text, and on the Web site.

URLs

At the end of each chapter, Web addresses are provided for service and manufacturing firms that are described in the chapter or are referenced in the Internet questions. This provides an opportunity to investigate companies and learn about the services and goods they provide.

Questions

Each chapter concludes with an extensive set of review and discussion questions. Sample answers to the questions are included in the Instructor's Manual.

Internet Questions

Because the Internet represents a valuable learning resource, we have included a set of "Internet Questions" with each chapter. These questions require that students visit the Web site of a relevant organization and answer questions based on the information at that Web site. Such Web sites include those of the Supply Chain Council, FedEx, Travelocity, and the Harley-Davidson Supplier Network.

Problems

 We have provided a large number of numerical practice problems. Those problems that are especially appropriate for computer solution have been flagged with a special logo (shown here), although they can be solved by hand. Solutions to these problems are available in the Instructor's Manual.

The Web-Companion: http://www.wiley.com/college/vonderembse

The companion Web site offers several advantages. It allows faculty to customize coverage by including additional readings, optional topics, problems, and mini-cases. The additional topics include both chapter supplements and additional Web chapters.

Chapter Supplements

To streamline the book and to provide comprehensive coverage, some materials related to specific chapters are available on the Web site. This information can be pulled directly into the chapter without disrupting the flow. Supplements include:

Text Chapter	Web Site Supplement
2	Computer-Integrated Manufacturing
3	Learning Curves
4	Acceptance Sampling
6	Roles of Participants in Product Development
9	Modeling for Capacity Decision Making
10	Analyzing Spatial Relationships
12	Linear Programming
16	Management Science Tools and Scheduling

Additional Web Chapters

Additional topics are also provided in stand-alone Web chapters. These topics are not included in the printed text, because many instructors choose not to cover them. The dual benefit is that this saves space and therefore the cost to the students, while giving instructors the option of assigning these topics at no additional cost to the student. In the following table, we suggest where the Web chapters can be easily integrated with the text coverage.

Web Site Chapter	Associated Text Chapter(s)
18 **Time-Based Competition** Discusses time as an important dimension of competition and describes how to reduce time	2
19 **Redesigning Business Processes** Discusses why and how to redesign business process to improve performance	3
20 **Quality Control** Discusses quality management; It could also be covered later in the book with aggregate planning, inventory management, and scheduling	4
21 **Supply Management** Discusses material flow, purchasing, inventory control, and distribution systems	5, 14
22 **Job Design and Work Measurement** Discusses productivity enhancement, which is one reason for measuring work and designing specific jobs; also provides a framework for layout that links to designing individual jobs	3, 11

Another advantage of the companion Web site is that it enables the authors to add or update material more frequently. The entire business field, and operations management in particular, is rapidly and constantly changing. All textbooks contain some material that is dated or lack coverage of emerging topics. Through the companion Web site, students and instructors will have access to very current material without waiting for a new edition of the text to be published.

Web Site Features for Students

Many pedagogical features have been included on the Web site as a means of achieving our overall objectives. These features include:

Solved Problems

In addition to the examples located throughout the text, we have provided solved problems for chapters with quantitative material on the Web site. These should serve as models for students working the homework problems.

Data Sets for Computer Solution

To give students a feel for the real-world problems that can only be solved on a computer, we have provided separate problems with larger and/or more complex data sets on the Web site. At least two data sets are available in appropriate chapters. Solutions to these problems are available in the instructor's manual.

Mini-Cases

Each chapter has mini-cases on the Web site. These are more extensive problem situations that either rely more on subjective judgment or require considerable calculations. These may be assigned as extensive homework problems or used as the basis for class discussion.

Excel Templates

Excel templates are provided to solve problems in the text. Directions are provided so students can work through the data entry for each spreadsheet. The templates can be downloaded from the companion Web site.

Online Study Guide

A study guide will be available on the Web site at no charge to students. It includes an overview of the chapters' concepts and key terms, as well as sample questions with correct answers.

Glossary

Key terms have been highlighted in bold type through the book. These terms, along with their definitions, are provided in the text and on the Web site in alphabetical order.

Summary of Formulas

To help students find a formula without needing to recall in which chapter that formula appears, we have provided a summary of formulas on the Web site.

Selected Bibliography

Each chapter contains a list of books and articles that are related to the topics discussed in the chapter. This enables readers to research various topics.

Web Site Features for Instructor

Instructor's Manual

The instructor's manual, prepared by the text authors, includes teaching suggestions. It also includes answers and solutions to all end of chapter questions, problems, and mini-cases, whether they are in the book or on the Web site. The instructor's manual is available on the Instructor's Resource CD and on the Web site.

Test Bank

The test bank has been revised. A generous number of questions are provided. They are a mixture of multiple choice and true/ false questions, along with the answers. The test bank is available in hard copy and on the Web site.

PowerPoint Presentations

A PowerPoint presentation has been prepared for each chapter and is available on the Web site. It includes key concepts in each chapter as well as many exhibits. There are in excess of 400 PowerPoint slides, which you can customize to fit your specific needs. Students can be given access to the PowerPoint slides to minimize note taking.

Web-based Facility Tours

At the end of each chapter, links are provided that lead to company Web sites. Many of the companies offer a tour of their facilities over the Web so students can understand how their business functions.

Nightly Business Report Videos and Guide to the Videos

Students may view selected clips from the well-known business news program, *Nightly Business Report*. These selected clips relate directly to operations management material covered in the text. Some examples include Introduction to Operations featuring Amazon.com's Z-shop, Operations Strategy with Walt Disney, and Supply Chain Management featuring Cisco Systems. Accompanying the video is the NBR Video Guide, created by Ranga Ramasesh. This includes, for each video segment, a description of the segment, suggestions for use, discussion questions, and suggested answers to the discussion questions.

Acknowledgements

We wish to thank the following reviewers for their insights and helpful suggestions during publication of this edition. They are:

> Susanna Cahn, Pace University
> Anthony Inman, Louisiana Tech University
> Carol Markowski, Old Dominion University
> Satish Mehra, The University of Memphis
> Ajay Mishra, SUNY–Binghamton
> Ranga Ramasesh, Texas Christian University
> Maurice Reid, Ohio State University
> James Sisak, University of Wisconsin–Whitewater
> Enrique Venta, Loyola University of Chicago
> Nancy Weida, Bucknell University

We are also indebted to the reviewers of the previous versions of this text, whose input helped form the foundation for this project:

> Sal Agnihothri, SUNY–Binghamton
> Yasemin Aksoy, University of Florida
> Alireza Ardalan, Old Dominion University
> Sunil Babbar, Kansas State University
> Jeff Baum, SUNY–Oneonta
> F. Dean Booth, University of Missouri–Kansas City
> Jeremy J. Coleman, Fort Lewis College
> Lisa Houts, California State University at Fresno
> Tim Ireland, Oklahoma State University
> Birsen Karpak, Youngstown State University
> Taeho Park, San Jose State University

Peter Pinto, Bowling Green State University

Richard Reid, University of New Mexico

Richard Sandbothe, SUNY–Binghamton

Mandyam M. Srinivasan, University of Tennessee–Knoxville

Kerry Swinehart, East Tennessee State University

Fredrik Williams, University of North Texas

We also would like to thank the companies who allowed us to use information about their organizations in the Nightly Business Report Videos:

Air Transport Association

Amazon.com

Arcata-Halliday Printing

Aviation Consumer Action Project

Aviation Institute

Cisco Systems, Inc.

Lands' End and Sears

Mercer Management Consulting

Nordstrom

Office Depot

Roadway Express

UPS

Walt Disney Company

Xerox Corporation / PARC

In addition, we wish to thank the many people at Leyh Publishing, especially Rick Leyh and Lari Bishop for their support throughout the project, and Kris Pauls and Camille McMorrow for all their work. We would also like to acknowledge the support of a number of people at John Wiley & Sons: Susan Elbe, Beth Golub, and Gitti Lindner. We wish to thank Yunus Kathawala for his excellent work on the PowerPoint presentations, the test bank, and the student's study guide. Thanks also to R. Zheng and M. Sajid for their work on the PowerPoint presentations, and to M. Sajid for contributions to the test bank. We are appreciative of the fine work by Linda Stanley in her creation of the Excel problem-solving templates. We also would like to thank Ranga Ramasesh of Texas Christian University for developing the Nightly Business Report Video Guide. Finally, a special thanks to our wives for their understanding and patience as we took many evenings and weekends away from them while preparing this book.

Mark A. Vonderembse

Gregory P. White

ABOUT THE AUTHORS

MARK A. VONDEREMBSE

Mark A. Vonderembse is a Professor of Management at The University of Toledo and is currently Interim Director of the University's Intermodal Transportation Institute. He previously served as Chair of the Information Systems and Operations Management Department and Director of the M.S. and Ph.D. programs in Manufacturing Management. He earned a Bachelors of Science in Civil Engineering from The University of Toledo in 1971 and an MBA from The University of Pennsylvania in 1973. He earned a Ph.D. from The University of Michigan in 1979.

Dr. Vonderembse won the Research Award in the College of Business Administration in 1997. He has published in academic and professional journals including *Decision Sciences, Industrial Engineering Transactions, International Journal of Production Research, Journal of Operations Management,* and *Management Science.* His research interests are time-based competition, supply chain management, and manufacturing strategy.

GREGORY P. WHITE

Gregory P. White is a Professor in the Department of Management, Southern Illinois University at Carbondale, and is currently Chair of the Management Department and Director of the MBA Program for the College of Business and Administration. He has previously served as Associate Dean of that College. Before joining Southern Illinois University, Professor White taught at Loyola University of Chicago.

Dr. White, who was named Researcher of the Year in the College of Business and Administration for 2001, has research interests that include manufacturing performance measurement and operations strategy, and his publications have appeared in journals such as *Decision Sciences, Interfaces, International Journal of Operations and Production Management,* and *Journal of Operations Management.* He is an Associate Editor of the *Journal of Operations Management,* and was named Editor of the Year for 2001 by that journal.

Operations Management
Concepts, Methods, and Strategies

CHAPTER 1

Introduction to Operations Management in a Global Environment

LEARNING OBJECTIVES

After completing this chapter, you should be able to:

1. Discuss the role of operations in the organization.
2. Describe the differences and similarities between producers of services and producers of goods.
3. Explain why the approach to managing operations should grow from the organization's goals.
4. Discuss the growing impact of global competition on organizations and their operations.
5. Understand key ethical issues that impact organizations and operations.
6. Define systems theory and discuss the relationships between operations and the other functional areas in the organization.

DEFINING OPERATIONS MANAGEMENT

People who study business are often overwhelmed by details and terminology. They seldom stop to consider why organizations exist. Organizations exist to meet needs of society that people working alone cannot. With the cooperation and coordination that organizations provide, we can produce the tremendous array of services and goods in the vast quantities that are consumed each day. Transportation, food, entertainment, banking, shopping, fire protection, police protection, and housing are just a few of the goods and services that organizations provide. An individual working alone could never produce this combination of products because no individual has the skills or access to the equipment and technology necessary to do so many distinct jobs.

Operations play a critical role in organizations. Operations are the means by which organizations produce thousands of commercial aircraft, millions of software programs, billions of bank transactions, and all the other services and goods consumed in our global economy. Operations for a hospital involve determining the size of the facility, deciding the type and quantity of equipment to purchase, arranging the facility and equipment so the hospital is efficient, determining staffing levels and schedules to provide quality care, and managing inventories of food and bedding. A more clinical definition of operations would be: **Operations** are the processes within organizations that acquire inputs (people, capital, and material) and transform these inputs into outputs (services and goods) consumed by the public, as shown in Exhibit 1.1. Operations employ labor and management (people) and use facilities and equipment (capital) to change materials (steel and plastics) into finished goods (farm tractors) or to provide services (health care). To be successful, the outputs of the operation should be worth more to the consumer than the total cost of the inputs. In this way, organizations create wealth for society.

Operations are part of both private-sector (profit-driven) and public-sector (not-for-profit) organizations. **Services** are intangible products, and **goods** are physical products. According to classification schemes used by the U.S. Departments of Commerce and Labor, the service sector includes transportation, utilities, lodging, entertainment, health care, legal services, education, communications, wholesale and retail trade, banking and finance, public administration, insurance, real estate, and other miscellaneous services. Goods are defined as articles of trade, merchandise, or wares. **Manufacturing** is a specific term referring to the production of goods. Throughout the text, the term **product** is used to refer to services or goods. Exhibit 1.2 lists many services and goods produced by private- and public-sector organizations.

Service operations represent about 75 percent of the U.S. economy and continue to grow. The service sector is also an important and growing segment of the global economy. There are opportunities worldwide for organizations that offer services in banking and finance, transportation, health care, information systems, telecommunications, consulting, and others.

Operations should be viewed as a part of the total organization, which may also include such specialties as accounting, finance, marketing, information systems, engineering, and personnel. When relationships among operations, marketing, and engineering are strong, it is possible to design high-quality products that are well liked by customers, and cheaper and easier to produce. These capabilities enhance the competitiveness of organizations. Understanding these links among functions in an organization is critical to an employee's advancement beyond an entry-level position. Middle- and upper-level managers have broad responsibilities and a great deal of interaction with other disciplines.

EXHIBIT 1.1

Operations

INPUTS → Transformation process → OUTPUTS

People, Capital, Material → Transformation process → Products → Services, Goods

EXHIBIT 1.2

Examples of Goods and Services Produced by Organizations

Goods		Services	
Profit	Not-for-Profit	Profit	Not-for-Profit
Starter motors	Highways	Banking	Police protection
Electronics	Dams	Health care	Health care
Gasoline	Flood control projects	Stock brokerage	Public welfare
Air conditioners	Fabrication and assembly completed in workshops for the handicapped	Telephone services	Parks and recreation
Appliances		Repair services	Fire protection
Hair dryers		Education	Education
Furniture		Retailing	

Operations management is decision making involving the design, planning, and management of the many factors that affect operations. Decisions include which products to produce, how large a facility to build, how many people to hire, and what methods to use to improve quality. Operations managers apply ideas and knowledge to:

- Cut production time to speed new products to market.
- Improve flexibility to meet rapidly changing customer needs.
- Enhance product quality.
- Improve customer service.
- Increase productivity and reduce costs.

An organization that can achieve these advantages through operations can gain a competitive edge.

Service versus Manufacturing Operations

Much has been written regarding the relative importance of the service sector versus the manufacturing sector. Trying to isolate the impact of the service sector from the manufacturing sector is counterproductive because one depends on the other in so many ways. For example, in transportation, a trucking company purchases goods—tractors and trailers—from manufacturers that, in turn, buy services from consultants. Trucking companies run their tractors and trailers on public roads built by construction companies. What do trucks carry? They cannot carry services because services are intangible. They carry goods, so without a strong manufacturing sector, trucks and other forms of transportation would be severely hurt. The value chain of services and goods that brings products to customers is tightly woven.

In keeping with this close relationship between services and goods, most of the topics covered in this book can be applied equally to service operations and manufacturing operations. Examples from service and manufacturing operations will be used to illustrate key points. When there are important differences between the service sector and the manufacturing sector, explanatory sections, similar to the one below, are provided.

Comparing Services and Goods

The distinction between services and goods is not as clear as the U.S. Departments of Commerce and Labor indicate. Some operations classified as services actually provide both services and goods. For example, automotive repair facilities sell and install replacement parts, so customers are purchasing something tangible as well as the labor to install them. To carry this example one step further, the person installing a muffler on an automobile is classified as a service worker. The person who installed the original equipment muffler at the automotive assembly plant is classified as a manufacturing worker. Is there a difference?

At a restaurant, customers purchase not only food but also food preparation. In the abstract, is there a substantial difference between installing a muffler and putting together a pizza? In both cases, the ingredients (parts) should be easily available for the worker, proper tools should be provided to make the job fast and easy, training should be given, and a sequence of steps should be established.

When goods are purchased, services are part of the transaction; and when services are purchased, goods are involved, either directly or indirectly. When a consumer buys a dishwasher, the purchase price includes payments for retail services and audits of the manufacturer's books. When consumers pay for a taxicab or bus ride, a portion of the money is used to pay for the purchase of vehicles. A thriving economy and an increasing standard of living depend on strong and efficient service providers and manufacturers.

Comparing Organizations that Produce Services and Goods

Service-producing organizations and goods-producing organizations have many similarities. Consider the Lima (Ohio) Fire Department, which provides fire protection, and the Air-Temp Corporation, which produces air conditioning units for the home. Both are concerned with product improvements. For a fire department, product improvements are measured by response time, the quality of its fire-prevention program, and the dependability of the service. For Air-Temp, improvements are measured by the cooling power of the air conditioner and the unit's special features.

Managers at the Lima Fire Department should address many questions directly related to operations. What is the maximum time that should elapse between a fire signal and the arrival of the fire equipment? How many fire stations are required? Where should these stations be located to maximize effectiveness? What type of and how much equipment should be purchased? How many firefighters are required? What are their qualifications, and how will they be trained? The answers to these questions shape the service provided and determine the capital required to build facilities, purchase equipment, and train personnel. Operating decisions also determine the costs of providing the service.

Managers at Air-Temp Corporation have a similar set of questions. How is the product designed? What are its performance level and special features—thermostat control, multiple-speed blower, and so on? How many air conditioners should be produced? What type of and how much equipment are needed for efficient production? How many employees are required? What type of training will they receive? How many facilities are needed, and where will they be located? Answers to these questions have a significant impact on the company's ability to compete.

Although operating decisions for services and goods have many similarities, there is one important difference between the two products: A good is tangible, and a service is not. This has two important consequences. First, a service operation cannot inventory finished goods because a service is intangible and is performed on demand. (Most service organizations, however, do have supporting inventory. Hospitals have linens, drugs, and food; banks have forms, paper, and other supplies; telephone companies have spare parts and equipment.) Second, because a good is tangible, the product designer must deal with physical characteristics (height, strength, durability, etc.).

Managing Service Operations without Finished Goods Inventory

Not having inventory might seem to be an advantage because inventory is expensive to maintain and time consuming to manage. But the inability of service organizations to maintain finished goods inventory can be a disadvantage as well. Service organizations cannot separate production from consumption. A customer can buy a car on Saturday, even though the assembly plant is closed, because the dealer can sell one from inventory. But this is not so for services such as banking and telephone communications. The telephone company cannot perform services in anticipation of demand because it has no finished goods inventory. Banks cannot perform transactions before a request is made. Customers of service organizations must do without the service or wait until it can be performed.

Banks have reacted by installing computerized tellers and providing on-line banking services to extend service hours and relieve pressure on branch banks. Supermarkets may offer discounts to senior citizens who shop on slow business days. In contrast, Air-Temp can build air conditioners during the slow winter months to offset demand in the spring and summer.

Clearly, then, the planning implications of not having finished goods inventory can be significant. During the morning rush, if seventy people want to ride a public bus with a capacity of fifty, then twenty must wait or be turned away. The possible solution of adding another bus may not be cost effective because the extra bus will not be heavily used. The consequences of turning customers away are the short-term loss of revenue and the potential long-term loss of customers because of dissatisfaction with the service level.

Many bus lines try to relieve the capacity problem by shifting demand to off-peak periods. Discounts are often given to riders during late morning and early afternoon hours. The use of public transportation by high school students is scheduled so it will not conflict with the morning or afternoon demand peaks. Thus, when managers of service operations consider capacity, they should focus on maximum demand and variability in demand, not average demand. They cannot use inventory to smooth peak demand, not even the peaks that occur from hour to hour.

Some Service Operations Have Finished Goods Inventory

To further complicate these issues, some organizations that are classified as service providers act more like manufacturers. For example, restaurants sell a service, food preparation, and a good, the food itself. It has raw materials, work in progress, and finished goods. In many retail and wholesale operations, investments in inventory are substantial, and inventory management is a critical success factor. Restaurants, retail stores, and wholesale operations are classified by the U.S. Departments of Commerce and Labor as service operations, but have many points in common with producers of goods. These points are discussed in the chapters on capacity, material and resource planning, and inventory management.

Designing Products for Goods and Services

Designing goods requires consideration of physical properties because goods are tangible and services are not. Usually, designing goods requires training in engineering because strength, durability, and performance are important. A laser printer should be able to produce consistently high-quality documents with limited maintenance and near zero breakdowns. Size and shape of the product often influence the customers' perception of style and beauty. A laser printer's size or the style and grace of an automobile may influence the purchase decision.

When a service involves selling a good, such as food sold by a restaurant, the physical dimension is still present. Designing a hamburger may not require an engineer, and obviously a hamburger need not be strong or durable. However, size and shape, as well as other physical elements, are still important.

When a service, such as selling life insurance, does not involve a good, there are other elements of design that become important. The amount of the payout versus the premiums paid for the policy is based on statistical analysis of mortality rates and the age of the person when the policy is purchased. In some cases, lifestyle, such as smoking or career choice, is also considered. These decisions are evaluated by an actuary. Lawyers frame the contract so it is legally valid.

Understanding Operations

If an organization can produce and deliver high-quality, low-cost products that meet customer needs and if it can do so in a timely manner, its probability of success is greatly increased. Operations and operations managers play an important role in achieving these objectives because their effectiveness in organizing, planning, and managing operations shapes the firm's competitiveness. What factors influence the buying decision for most consumers? For most services and goods, price, quality, product features and performance, product variety, and availability of the product are important. All these factors are substantially influenced by actions taken in operations. When productivity increases, product costs decline and product price can be reduced. As better methods are developed for making the product, quality and variety may increase.

By linking operations and operating strategy with the overall strategy of the organization (including engineering, financial, marketing, and information system strategy), synergy can result. Operations become a positive factor when facilities, equipment, and employee training are viewed as a means of achieving organizational, rather than narrowly defined departmental objectives. The criteria for judging operations is expanding from controlling costs, which is a narrowly defined operating objective, to more global performance measures, such as product performance and variety, product quality, delivery time, and customer service. When flexibility is designed into operations, an organization is able to respond rapidly and inexpensively to changing customer needs.

To understand operations and how they can contribute to the success of an organization, it is important to understand:

- The value-added nature of operations.
- The impact that technology can have on performance.
- The importance of teamwork in achieving operating and organizational objectives.

Operations Add Value

Operations add value when consumers are willing to pay more for the finished good or service than the total cost of the inputs required to make it. In the private sector, the difference between the price a consumer pays for a good or service and the cost to produce it is profit that can be reinvested to build new and better products, thus creating wealth for society.

Without profits, a company cannot raise capital to continue its operations and will eventually become a casualty of competition. With profits, technology-based companies, such as Microsoft and Intel, and more traditional companies, such as Citibank and General Motors, are able to invest in new technology and new facilities, which lead to improved operations and lower prices. More efficient production of services and goods frees resources (people, capital, and materials) for new product development and innovation, which makes an organization stronger and more competitive.

In the public sector, which is not for profit, the value added to products represents improved wealth to society. For example, value-added fire protection saves more dollar value (in homes and businesses) than the cost of the service. The wealth created or preserved by such value-added operations contributes to economic growth and makes more resources available for other wealth-creating activities. This ultimately improves our living standard because more wealth is created than consumed.

EXAMPLE

Microsoft creates the software that drives most of the microcomputers in the world. Microsoft's impact is the result of designing and developing software that dramatically increases the productivity of secretaries, engineers, managers, etc. These people and the companies they work for see value in the software and are willing to pay more for it than the cost of development. When this impact is viewed in total, both sides of the transaction gain advantages. Microsoft, its founders, managers, employees, and stockholders gain through employment earnings and/or stock appreciation. The users gain by becoming more productive, which can lead to better job performance and more leisure time.

Technology and Operations

Technology is the application of knowledge, usually in the form of recently developed tools, processes, and procedures, to solve problems. Advances in technology make it possible to design and build better products using fewer resources.

Product design is the determination of the characteristics, features, and performance of the product. **Product technology** is the application of knowledge to improve the product. The change from cassette tape players to compact disks (CDs) is an example of using product technology to improve product design and enhance product performance. New products like digital video disc (DVD) players are changing the way people enjoy movies. In the future, CD and DVD players will be replaced by a new product technology that will provide better quality sound, more features, and a lower price. There are many other examples of product design improvements that are making our life better. A few are listed here.

Product Design and Technology

New Product	Enabling Technology	Outcome
Antilock brakes	Microprocessor	Safer automobiles
Lasik eye surgery	Laser	Faster recovery and fewer complications
Online banking services	Microcomputer, Internet, and telecommunications	Convenient, twenty-four-hour service from home or work
Nationwide reservation system for hotels, airlines, etc.	Large-scale database	Make reservations from anywhere in country
Plastic bottles versus glass bottles	Injection molding	Cheaper and lighter containers, as well as less breakage

Another major area to which technology can be applied is process. A **process** describes "how to." **Process design** describes how a product is made. **Process technology** is the application of knowledge to improve a process. Process technology affects how a product is produced but may have little, if any, impact on the product's features and function. Frying is one process for cooking a hamburger and grilling over an open flame is another. Both processes yield a cooked piece of ground beef. By contrast, a change in product design would directly affect the way a product functions and/or its features. Adding a second patty of ground beef, substituting ground turkey for ground beef, or adding bacon would involve a different product design. There are many examples of process improvements that are making life better. A few are listed here.

Process Design and Technology

New Process	Enabling Technology	Outcome
Creating a research paper with Microsoft Word	Microcomputer	Easy to change text and tables, many fonts, easy storage and retrieval of documents
Punching a hole in a steel plate versus drilling a hole	Punch press	Takes less time to make the hole
Using Power Point software for presentations versus overhead projector	Microcomputer and video graphic	Ability to deliver information with words and pictures, easy and inexpensive to update and to distribute
Delivering music via the Internet	Internet, digital processing, and communication	Easy to locate music and fast, low-cost downloads

Product design and process design are not necessarily independent decisions. A product design decision may dictate the process that should be used. For example, if a product specification requires a final report that presents key points with color graphics, then selecting word processing is the obvious choice because of the wide range of tools available on the microcomputer. In many industries, managers prefer that product design and process design be done simultaneously by the same group of people working in close collaboration. This approach, sometimes called **concurrent engineering,** has become more and more popular as organizations attempt to develop new high-quality designs quickly.

EXAMPLE

Technology can be a key to developing new ideas and implementing them successfully. eBay took an old process, the auction, and married it to new technology, the Internet, to create a new business model that is highly successful. An auction creates a market by bringing together buyers and sellers. Internet technology provides easy access to millions and eventually billions of people around the world. It allows sellers to provide detailed descriptions and pictures of the products to be sold. EBay has a wide variety of goods and services as well as collectables for auction. With eBay's approach, large amounts of information are easily and inexpensively available, transaction costs are low, and buyers and sellers can easily and quickly close a transaction.

Operations and Teamwork

In the late nineteenth and early twentieth centuries, labor and management in the United States treated each other as adversaries. At the time, management and labor believed a gain by one side meant a loss to the other. Today, we see a new era of cooperation between labor and management. Management and labor work together to solve quality and productivity problems with each side contributing to the solution. Where labor once opposed productivity improvements because it believed productivity increases meant fewer jobs, now labor often supports and encourages higher productivity because it means job security. Managers, who were reluctant to accept suggestions from labor, listen and learn. Well-managed, teamwork-oriented operations provide services and goods of high quality at prices that consumers can afford. This is good for the organization, labor, consumers, and management in the following ways:

- For the organization, the ability to meet the increasing demand for high-quality, low-cost products can lead to greater success in competitive world markets.
- For labor, well-managed operations provide continuing job opportunities. An inefficient operation drives prices up and makes services or goods subject to competitive pressure from efficient producers, both foreign and domestic. Increases in efficiency allow non-inflationary increases in wages, which leads to real growth in purchasing power.
- For consumers, a lower price means that more people will be able to buy the product. In addition, consumers will have money left for other purchases.
- For management, lower production costs can lead to increased sales and higher profit.

EXAMPLE

There are few better example of teamwork between labor and management than Southwest Airlines. Southwest is the most successful airlines in the United States, and possibly the world. During the downturn in airline travel following the

September 11, 2001 tragedy, Southwest was the only company that continued to do well. Southwest focuses on the basics of air travel and has an effective strategy and planning process. But, the key to its success is the way that its employees work for the company. Employees do the extras that help passengers have a nicer trip, work in ways that make company processes faster and more efficient, and look out for ways to improve operations through continuous improvement. Planes are on time, baggage is rarely lost, and passengers like the low fares. Part of this success is driven by the fact that all Southwest employees own a piece of the company.

Global Trade and Competition

It is impossible to ignore the impact of the global marketplace and free trade on organizations and their operations. The North American Free Trade Agreement (NAFTA) and the General Agreement on Tariffs and Trade (GATT) were designed to reduce or eliminate tariffs and other trade restrictions. They are increasing the opportunities for countries to focus on areas of trade and commerce in which they have a relative advantage. It is leading to mergers and acquisitions that bridge nations and continents. German-owned Daimler Benz and the Chrysler Corp. have formed DaimlerChrysler to unite the engineering and quality capabilities of Daimler with the product design capabilities of Chrysler. After some initial integration problems, the merger is resulting in better product quality in the Chrysler product lines.

Relative Advantage

A country that wants to enhance the living standard of its people will engage in global trade. The country will import those goods and services that are not available locally or cost more to make at home than their foreign-made counterparts. Even when a country is the most efficient producer of all goods and services, it can be demonstrated that the country would be better off engaging in global trade. The reason the country should trade is that its relative advantage in one product—for example, pitchforks—would be greater than its relative advantage in another product—say, furniture. **Relative advantage** is defined as the difference between the lowest cost producer and the next lowest cost producer. The country with the pitchfork production advantage should produce pitchforks for the global market and may import to meet some or all of its furniture needs.

As barriers to trade, such as import quotas and tariffs, decline and countries better understand the benefits of international trade, the level of trade between nations will continue to climb. Recently, global trade in goods and services reported by governments outpaced growth in the world's total production. This means that the percentage of world production moving between nations is increasing.

EXAMPLE

Before the trade agreements, DaimlerChrysler's Jeep assembly plant shipped unassembled Jeeps to some countries. The Jeeps had to be assembled there because these countries had laws that limited the amount of foreign content in imported products. Now, the Jeeps can be assembled in the United States and shipped abroad, thus adding jobs for domestic workers. Under NAFTA and GATT, it has become increasingly common for finished products to have components from many different countries. Global sourcing and production of goods and services will become even more common in the future.

Creating Global Markets

Markets for many items, such as those produced by the electronics, steel, automotive, textile, and photographic equipment industries, are world markets dominated by multinational firms. In order for firms to compete, they must be among the best in the world, not simply the best in the nation. These firms must compete with firms from other countries where the labor costs, material costs, material availability, culture, and sociopolitical environment are substantially different. These differences make a manager's job more difficult.

EXAMPLE

When Ford Motor Company's primary competitors were General Motors and Chrysler, Ford had the same workforce and labor cost per hour, virtually the same material costs, and the same set of government regulations as its national competitors. In many cases, these national firms traded executives back and forth so these organizations had similar ideas and approaches to management. Now, Ford faces global competitors that have substantially different cost factors and management styles. Organizations that are successful in the twenty-first century will develop an understanding of marketing, distribution systems, financial and capital markets, accounting, and operations that is global rather than national. Global competition has had, and will continue to have, a tremendous impact on operations and operations managers. Product performance, product quality, efficiency, and delivery lead time are all elements of competition affected by operations.

Job markets are also becoming global. Before NAFTA and GATT, it was common to see blue-collar jobs move from one country to another as firms moved production facilities in search of low-cost labor. Today, we are beginning to see a global job market for engineering, information technology, and management jobs. Some companies are outsourcing product design and information systems development activities to India and China to achieve lower costs and, in some cases, the capacity to get the job done.

UNDERSTANDING THE SYSTEMS APPROACH TO OPERATIONS

Today, leaders of most organizations recognize that substantial interdependencies exist between functional areas within the organizations, such as operations and marketing, between organizations that must cooperate to create and deliver innovative products to customers, and between organizations and government agencies. Within organizations, functional barriers to integration are being smashed as managers create cross-functional teams to tackle difficult problems such as product design, productivity improvement, and facility design. To encourage cooperation between organizations, managers are building strategic alliances with suppliers that increase the exchange of information and ideas for the benefit of both. Organizations are responding to concerns by government agencies regarding employee rights, environmental impact, and product safety. These social, legislative, ethical, and legal issues are growing in importance.

How do operations fit into this systems view of the organization and its environment? Operations management is only one part of the organization, which in turn is a part of the larger economic and government system. This section provides a brief description of what a system is and discusses how operations fit within this systems view of the organization and its environment.

A **system** is a group of items, events, or actions in which no item, event, or action occurs independently. Thus, no item studied in isolation will act in the same way as it would in the system. For example, a study that focuses on minimizing transportation costs might suggest that materials be ordered in larger quantities to reduce the number of trips and save transportation costs. However, larger shipments will require more storage capacity, and the increase in storage costs could be greater than the decrease in transportation costs. When making decisions, a manager should examine issues as they impact system level or organizational level outcomes.

In a system, all items, events, or actions are somehow related. A system can be divided into a series of parts or subsystems, and any system is a part of a larger system. Understanding the relationship among the various subsystems is an integral part of the study of operations management. We will examine relationships between the organization and its environment, relationships between operations and the rest of the organization, and relationships within operations.

Exhibit 1.3 illustrates that an organization is part of the global economic and government system. In turn, the organization is composed of several subsystems, one of which is operations. Operations managers work with managers in marketing, finance, accounting, engineering, and other areas to reach the goals set by top management.

Finally, because of the many functions it encompasses, the operations subsystem is itself divided into a series of subsystems. When studying the operations management subsystem, it is important to keep in mind the larger picture of operations, the organization, and the external environment. The systems approach is a central theme, which is reinforced at other points in the text.

In order to design, plan, and manage operations effectively, managers should be aware that:

- An organization is part of the global economic and government system.
- Operations are an integral part of the organization.
- Operations are composed of a series of related subsystems.

THE ORGANIZATION AS PART OF THE ECONOMIC AND GOVERNMENT SYSTEM

Organizations operate in an environment that includes several interest groups—stockholders, management, labor, consumers, and the general public. These groups are often called **stakeholders** because they are affected by (have a stake in) decisions made by management. Business leaders have realized that to achieve long-term success and to be good corporate neighbors, they should serve all of these interests. Thus, they should be responsive to issues

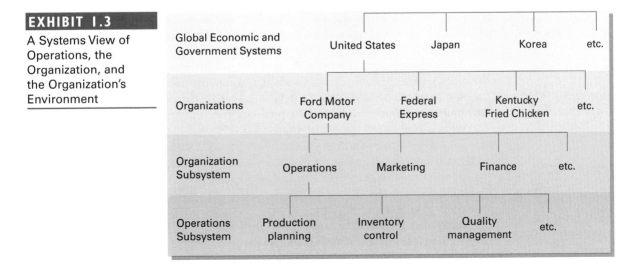

EXHIBIT 1.3

A Systems View of Operations, the Organization, and the Organization's Environment involving wage rates, working conditions, pollution, product safety, and global competition, in addition to the stockholders' return on investment. All of these factors are part of the larger economic and government system within which organizations operate. This larger economic and government system is broadly defined to include the legal, political, social, and educational subsystems as part of the environment.

The importance of these broader issues becomes clear as the following factors are discussed.

Factor	Interest Group	Impact of Operating Decisions
Wage rates and working conditions	Labor and middle management	Good working conditions and fair wages can be positive factors in employee performance.
Pollution	General public	Well-managed operations should not cause pollution.
Product safety	Consumers	When products are well designed, consumers are safer and more satisfied.
Global competition	Stockholders, labor, and middle management	When operations are well managed, costs are not excessive. If this is coupled with high quality, the organization becomes competitive.

Legal and Ethical Issues in Operations

Today, managers and organizations are facing a staggering array of problems that their predecessors largely ignored. These managers of the past often viewed labor relations and worker safety, environmental pollution, and product safety as outside of their area of concern. They often made decisions that were in the best interest of the organization's stockholders and detrimental to labor, to the environment, and even to the customer. For example, organizations have designed and built unsafe products and avoided taking corrective action even when the problem is obvious.

As a result of this neglect, organizations face labor unions, environmental advocates, and consumer groups that have been successful in passing legislation that defines labor management relations, regulates the safety of the workplace, shapes environmental programs, and protects consumers. In addition, the threat of a consumer boycott and the negative publicity associated with not responding as a "good" corporate citizen are causing companies to act responsibly. As a result, government plays a significant role in regulating organizations and their operations. Companies operating globally must understand the legislative and ethical requirements for competing in each country.

If you think about it, each of these areas of concern is directly related to operations. Normally, operations have the most workers and are often the focus of union activity, are the most likely place where workers can be injured, have the greatest potential for creating environmental pollution, and build the products that consumers purchase.

What is expected of "good" corporate citizens? There are no mathematical equations that allow us to derive an answer. It is necessary for organizations to develop a set of standards for ethical behavior that are in keeping with the expectations of the community. It is also reasonable to expect those standards to increase as the standard of living increases. Generally, product safety issues are less important when fewer products are available and the products are less sophisticated.

Today, managers need to search for solutions where all of the stakeholders—stockholders, management, labor, consumers, and the general public—can win. Fortunately, the new breed of managers has recognized the need to develop these approaches, and some impressive strides have been made.

Labor Relations

As late as the 1930s in the United States, many developing businesses required their production employees to work long hours for low pay. These businesses wanted to keep costs low and to increase their return on investment. In addition, many plants had poor or unsafe working conditions. In many cases, workers rebelled against management. They fought hard and often engaged in battles with management for better pay, better working conditions, and the right to form unions. Eventually, labor was able to unionize because the federal government passed laws in the late 1930s that permitted and protected unions. From these conflicts, labor unions and businesses developed an adversarial relationship that still exists today in some organizations.

Both groups should learn that their security lies in cooperative efforts, primarily in the effort to make better quality products with better performance at a lower unit cost. Such quality and productivity improvements will help secure jobs in the United States and make our products competitive in world markets. Many organizations are beginning to respond by working with labor to develop employee involvement teams. These teams, which include both management and labor, are often led by people from labor. The agenda is established by the group. It is not a vehicle for managers to control the labor force or to set direction for the group. It seems to work best when labor feels free to express ideas, suggest changes, and have a leadership role in implementation.

EXAMPLE

Shenandoah Life Insurance Company embraced the world of high technology by installing a new computer system to handle application processing and claims. After the investment, it still took the same length of time, about six weeks, to handle a routine policy application. The application wound its way through three different departments and was touched by more than thirty people. The problem was the design of its process, not the speed of its computers. Only by radically redesigning its processing system could the company take advantage of the new technology and achieve the dramatic improvements it needed. Shenandoah Life developed a cross-functional team approach that cut processing time from six weeks to two days and practically eliminated service complaints. The company took the same workers that were spread over three departments and created a series of work teams consisting of five to seven people. Now, a team is responsible for processing the entire claim from start to finish. When a situation arises that the team cannot handle, experts are available to help. This type of help is rarely needed. Team members have learned new skills, report greater job satisfaction, and are more productive. The company is processing 50 percent more applications and queries with 10 percent fewer employees.

Environmental Impact

In the 1920s and 1930s, many business leaders did not consider pollution a problem because few people fully understood its consequences. Waste from operations was something to dispose of at the least cost. When pollution problems began to surface in the 1950s and 1960s, some businesses were reluctant to change their position. As a result, businesses in this country operate under one of the most restrictive sets of environmental pollution laws and reporting procedures in the world.

Since the 1960s, concern for the environment has grown substantially in the United States and other developed countries. Today, many organizations take proactive steps to reduce emissions from facilities. Companies are discovering "win-win" opportunities in which an organization can actually cut costs and increase profits by recapturing pollutants and reducing solid waste. In other cases, organizations began to recognize that being good corporate citizens increased sales. Fast-food restaurants have begun recycling programs and changed packaging materials in response to concern from consumers. In other cases, being a good corporate citizen and protecting a company's renewable resources go well together. For example, many large forest product companies have major efforts underway to replant trees that have been cut for lumber and paper.

EXAMPLE

Making pollution prevention pay has benefited many organizations. These firms understand that environmental protection and economic progress can go hand-in-hand. Sauder Woodworking Company is left with about 300 tons of sawdust a day after workers craft ready-to-assemble furniture. The bulk of the sawdust was sent to a landfill at a cost to Sauder of $55 to $60 per ton. Today, Sauder operates a $15 million co-generation plant using that sawdust and produces enough power for 3,878 homes. The co-generation plant was conceived after Sauder and Toledo Edison Co. worked out a deal so the furniture company could supply power to the utility's grid. Ciba, a Swiss chemical company, has been able to eliminate up to 50 percent of the pollution from its operations and save $400,000 per year by changing its production process and recycling its wastewater and solvents. Only a small capital investment was required. A Japanese plant producing polypropylene as a by-product was able to implement a waste recovery system to capture the by-product. The value of the recovered product is 40 percent greater than the annual capital charges and the operating costs of the recovery system. In France, the food industry has been getting a 30 percent return on investment from the recovery of protein from slaughterhouse waste. A Minnesota Mining and Manufacturing Company's facility has expanded production by 40 percent and dramatically cut its annual pollution load. Its liquid effluent has gone from 47 tons to less than 3, its gaseous effluent from 3,000 tons to 2,400 tons, and its solid waste from 6,000 to 1,800 tons. The cleanup has resulted in an annual cost savings of $2.4 million.

Companies all around the world are discovering that recycling and recapturing of by-products, scrap, and even heat can be profitable. Companies are also finding that better results are achieved when environmental factors are considered during the design of the facility. Retrofitting facilities with pollution control equipment can be an expensive alternative to thoughtful analysis and careful design.

Product Safety

Because product design and production are part of operations, operations management decisions clearly play a significant role in determining product safety. Companies such as Black & Decker and Procter & Gamble owe their excellent reputations partly to their concern for product safety. These companies realize that high quality and safety are compatible with high profits and long-term success.

If global and domestic competition is not sufficient to keep out unsafe products, then consumer groups and legislative action will. The last forty years have seen the rising power of consumer advocates and efforts to protect consumer interest, evaluate products, and educate the consumer. Consumer groups have challenged organizations in the courts as they seek to force companies to remove dangerous products from the market.

The Ford Pinto, silicon breast implants, and asbestos are just three examples of consumer victories over unsafe products. The Pinto is a classic case from the 1970s that showed Ford's disregard for product safety. Evidence was brought forward that engineers at Ford understood the potential problem (the gas tank was too close to the rear bumper so an explosion might occur in a rear end collision). But, for a reason that will probably never be known (bureaucratic incompetence or callous disregard for safety), no action was taken until several people died and the case was taken to court. The lesson learned by Ford and others is that product safety is a key competitive dimension for producing and selling cars and trucks. Today, Ford is very concerned about product safety and the safety of its customers.

The silicon implant cases were recently settled with litigants receiving significant settlements. It is unclear whether the producers of the implants and the doctors who did the surgery were aware of the problem. Evidence seemed to indicate that they became aware of the problem, but did not respond quickly enough to address it.

Asbestos litigation has brought at least one company to bankruptcy (Owens Corning, maker of pink fiberglass insulation), and it has created significant problems for several others. In some cases, the companies, including Owens Corning, were unaware of the consequences of producing asbestos. Owens Corning stopped producing asbestos more than 40 years ago, but law suits running into billions of dollars are still pending. In other cases, the liability was assumed when one company purchased another. Halliburton, an oil service company, purchased Dresser and unknowingly bought its asbestos liabilities. Halliburton's lawsuits are pending.

Comparing the case of the Ford Pinto and asbestos liability, has the pendulum swung too far? Hardly anyone, even the staunchest advocates for business, can justify Ford's handling of the Pinto case. However, should a company like Owens Corning, which has not produced asbestos for more than 40 years and was unaware of the negative consequences of producing it until after it ceased production, be forced into a bankruptcy that damages management, labor, and investors?

Organizations must understand the implications of actions that are detrimental to the consumer and respond by demonstrating an honest concern for the customer. This approach creates a sense of trust between the consumer and the company, which can have substantial economic value.

Ethical Behavior

Ethics are a set of standards that are generally higher than legal standards. For example, if a representative of a company claims that a service or good is capable of something and it is not, this claim is illegal. If an individual is unaware of the true value of something and has set an asking price that is only a small percent of its value, the buyer faces an ethical dilemma. If the buyer knows the true value, should the buyer purchase the item and run or should the buyer let the seller know the true value?

Ethics are a sense of what is right and wrong that guide behavior. How far should a company go to ensure product safety and its safe operation? Should a Jet Ski contain a warning that all riders should wear life vests? Should a lawn tractor have a shut off device that disables the mower if the rider weighs less than 100 pounds? Should microwave ovens have a label that states that operators should not try to dry their cat in the oven? In product safety, what is sensible and what is silly? These are difficult decisions for which no "right" answer exists. Managers must continue to grapple with these issues as they develop a set of standards with which they feel comfortable.

Impact of Ethical Behavior on Performance

Is ethical behavior a corporate issue that affects the company's bottom line (profit)? The answer is complex, but it can be partially understood by reviewing our earlier points on labor relations, the environment, and the customer. Some organizations have attempted to maximize short-term earnings per share to the stockholder by minimizing costs. These actions have separated management from labor, the consumer, and the general public.

In the longer term, such actions alienated these interest groups and forced them to take action. The actions, often legislative, helped to create an adversarial environment that is not conducive to competition in today's world markets. Eventually, this environment forced costs up and made some industries vulnerable to global competition. In the authors' view, one reason that global competition has not hurt industries like paper and oil is that these industries have a balanced view, focusing on both long-term objectives and short-term performance. Over the years, companies in these industries have made significant efforts to deal with labor, environmental, and product safety concerns as part of their planning process.

A solution to the problem of world competition is difficult and will require significant time to implement. To meet this challenge, management should consider labor, the general public, and the consumer in decision making. Labor and management must work together to build better facilities and better products and to improve productivity. Organizations should use each employee's full range of physical and mental skills. The cooperation and mutual respect between labor and management will be a positive factor in improving operations and building better working relationships.

OPERATIONS AS PART OF THE ORGANIZATION

Exhibit 1.3 illustrates that although an organization is part of the larger economic and government system, it is also a system containing such subsystems as marketing, finance, accounting, personnel, and engineering, in addition to operations. These subsystems, often called **functional areas** or disciplines, should be linked by common organizational goals and a means of communicating these goals. These common goals are part of an organization's strategy. **Strategy** consists of the organizational goals and the methods for implementing the goals, called **key policies.** Strategy defines how the organization chooses to compete within the framework dictated by the external environment. The usual means of implementing and communicating strategy is the budgeting and planning process, which most organizations do annually.

Selecting a strategy and key policies leads to the creation of key business (organizational) processes that a firm uses to satisfy customer needs. A **business process** is a collection of activities or tasks that create value for a customer. A business process is cross-functional and leads to outcomes the customer desires, such as delivering quality products that meet specific customer needs in a timely manner.

Strategy

Operations should be linked to the organization by developing operating strategies consistent with the organization's overall strategy. Links between operations and the rest of the organization can be built into the planning process. A **plan** is a list of actions that management expects to take. A plan is a basis for allocating the organization's resources to deal with opportunities and problems present in the environment. Resources allocated by operations managers should help the organization achieve its goals.

The links between strategy and operations can be illustrated by comparing a fast-food restaurant with a four-star restaurant. Customers expect fast-food restaurants to deliver good-quality food at a low price, with a wait of only a few minutes. This implies a limited menu, some advance preparation, and a service operation with a smooth and simple means of communicating orders and delivering food. The training of counter workers and cooks should emphasize speed, efficient movement, and uniform performance of duties.

Compare these requirements with those of a four-star restaurant with a heavy tourist trade. Here, customers expect food of exceptional quality and variety; fine wine, imported beer, and the best liquor; higher prices; and a leisurely dinner. These expectations imply a wide selection on the menu, comfortable and pleasant surroundings, entertainment, and little or no advance food preparation. All operations, from training cooks to food procurement, are different from those in a fast-food restaurant. Four-star restaurants do not have counter help. The emphasis is on service to the individual customer rather than on uniformity and quick response. This comparison illustrates two different approaches to operating a restaurant successfully. Success in a fast-food restaurant is based on providing quality products at low prices and maintaining high customer volume. Success in a four-star restaurant is based on providing entertainment and atmosphere, as well as quality food. The allocation of resources in the design and planning of these restaurants should reflect the differences.

Organizational Structure

The development of strategy leads to the question of organizational structure. **Organizational structure** is the formal relationships among different functions or subsystems, such as marketing, finance, and operations. Organizational structure defines the lines of communication. Recently, many organizations have substantially reduced their administrative staffs and altered their lines of communication. IBM, General Motors, and Chase Manhattan Bank have cut hundreds of thousands of white-collar workers. In a few cases, the objective is simply to cut costs. In most cases, organizations are seeking a leaner, more competitive structure that will enable them to make better decisions and to respond more quickly to opportunities in the environment.

Accompanying this latter objective is often a move to decentralize decision making and to create less formal means of control. The resulting organization has fewer levels in its hierarchy and has more cross-functional teams. Eliminating the functional silos that traditional organizations often have enables teams to share knowledge and to understand the corporate-wide implications of a decision. Decisions are made based on corporate interests rather than narrow functional interests, and they are made with more knowledge and understanding of the consequences rather than in isolation. In this environment, organizations not only make better decisions, but they also make them more quickly because problems are uncovered early and resolved before becoming major points of dissension. Finally, all managers, including managers of operations, must be able to work on the critical cross-functional decisions that organizations face.

Operations and Marketing Interface

One of the most important groups of cross-functional decisions that organizations face spans the boundary between operations and marketing. The marketing function is responsible for investigating demand for services and goods and for establishing a distribution chain that delivers these products to customers. The operations function is responsible for producing these services and goods and managing the supply chain that provides the incoming resources. The operations manager's role is essential because without product (output), the organization has no means of achieving its purpose.

Exhibit 1.4 illustrates the operations and marketing interface. Let us begin with **market research,** which is an effort to measure customers' needs and preferences. The goals of market research are to determine new markets for existing products and to discover demand for new products. Market research leads to product designs that can satisfy consumers' needs at a reasonable cost and a high level of quality. As the product is being designed, the process for making the product should also be designed. After the process has been designed, it is necessary to acquire resources—material, trained people, and equipment. The production of the product includes concern for quality, cost, and on-time completion. Finally, marketing and distribution of the product take place. At this point, the customer's reaction to the product is measured, and another round of market research to monitor changing needs should occur.

Exhibit 1.5 illustrates how decisions in operations can affect marketing. Product cost must be covered by the market price with enough left over to cover overhead, administrative, and selling expenses and to provide the organization's profit. Effective scheduling helps the organization make timely delivery. Flexibility permits operations to deliver specially designed products at a low cost, making marketing's job easier. High-quality products pay dividends in repeat sales and new customers.

Business Processes versus Business Functions

Currently, a revolution is taking place in the world of business. This revolution is called different things by different people. Some call it reinventing business, others call it downsizing, and still others call it rightsizing. The core issue in this fundamental change is a shift from organizing by business functions, such as operations, marketing, finance, and information systems, to organizing by business process, such as strategy formulation, product development, and order fulfillment. Business processes span many functional areas. For example, product development requires inputs from marketing, engineering, finance, operations, and others.

Advocates of the business process approach argue that organizing by functions is inappropriate for today's fast-paced and fast-changing environment. Decision making is very slow as complicated decisions, such as product development, wind through the maze of functions and fiefdoms that exist in the functional organization. As a result, companies that are organized by function can be inefficient and slow to respond. Organizing by process tends to focus attention on activities that customers value and allows the organization to make decisions quickly.

Customers are not concerned about discipline- or function-related issues, such as how accounting values inventory, whether financial managers use internal rate of return or net present value to analyze investments in facilities, or whether an operation has the lowest transportation costs. Customers are concerned about how the outputs of the organization meet their needs. The customer requirements shown in Exhibit 1.6 include meeting specific needs (product variety), quick response, product performance and features, product quality (fitness for use), price, and service after the sale. The organization should develop

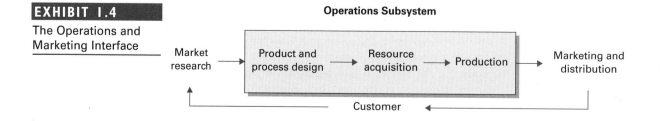

EXHIBIT 1.4

The Operations and Marketing Interface

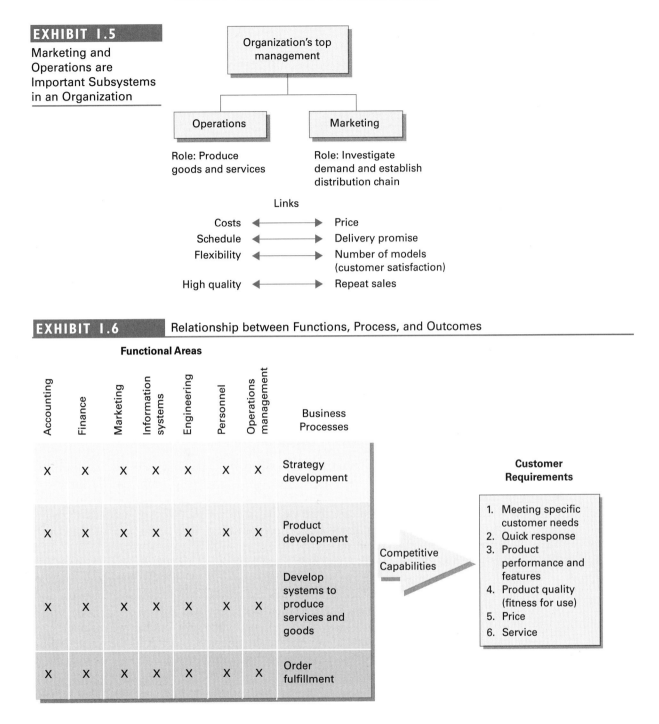

EXHIBIT 1.5

Marketing and Operations are Important Subsystems in an Organization

Organization's top management

Operations

Role: Produce goods and services

Marketing

Role: Investigate demand and establish distribution chain

Links

Costs ◄——►	Price
Schedule ◄——►	Delivery promise
Flexibility ◄——►	Number of models (customer satisfaction)
High quality ◄——►	Repeat sales

EXHIBIT 1.6   Relationship between Functions, Process, and Outcomes

Functional Areas

Accounting	Finance	Marketing	Information systems	Engineering	Personnel	Operations management	Business Processes
X	X	X	X	X	X	X	Strategy development
X	X	X	X	X	X	X	Product development
X	X	X	X	X	X	X	Develop systems to produce services and goods
X	X	X	X	X	X	X	Order fulfillment

Competitive Capabilities →

Customer Requirements

1. Meeting specific customer needs
2. Quick response
3. Product performance and features
4. Product quality (fitness for use)
5. Price
6. Service

competitive capabilities to meet these customer requirements. The capabilities are the result of organizational processes, such as strategy development, product development, design of systems to produce services or goods, and order fulfillment. Order fulfillment ranges from order entry through production to delivery and after-the-sale service. The processes listed here are illustrative and not exhaustive.

A business process is a set of work activities with a preferred order, an identifiable beginning and end, inputs, and clearly defined outputs that add value to the customer. As illustrated in Exhibit 1.6, business processes work across functions to create competitive capabilities. People trained in the disciplines work on teams to design, implement, and operate processes that produce the outcomes that customers want.

Customers don't care whether a company is organized by function or discipline. They care about value. For example, an organization that is the industry leader in sales and profit may have the highest distribution costs in the industry because it provides the shortest time from order to delivery. If that fast delivery adds value to the customer, then the customer may be willing to pay more for the product or to buy more of the product. A program that reduces distribution costs and increases the time from order to delivery reduces value to the customer. For more information, a chapter on redesigning business processes is available on the companion Web site for this text: www.wiley.com/college/vonderembse.

Operations as a Series of Related Subsystems

Early sections describe the relationships between the organization and its environment. These sections also describe the organization as a series of related subsystems with operations as one subsystem. As illustrated in Exhibit 1.3, operations, in turn, can be divided into different parts or subsystems, including quality management, inventory, and scheduling. To facilitate understanding of the subsystems, and to make the relationships between these parts clear, we provide the overview of operations shown in Exhibit 1.7. The three parts of the exhibit comprise the three major parts of the book.

1. Building Capabilities to Compete Globally
2. Designing the System to Produce Services and Goods
3. Planning and Managing Operations

The chapters in Part I, Building Capabilities to Compete Globally, discuss how firms use operations to gain a competitive advantage in a globally competitive environment, including the strategic importance of operations and the applications of computers and technology. These chapters describe the importance of flexibility, time, productivity, quality, and supply chain management as critical dimensions of competition and discuss how these capabilities can be obtained.

Part II, Designing the System to Produce Services and Goods, discusses the decisions necessary to design the services and goods that customers demand, to forecast demand, to select the process for producing the services and goods, to set capacity requirements, and to locate and layout facilities. These decisions are interrelated because the type of product that an organization chooses to produce will impact how the product will be made and how many are made. A pictorial summary of the approach to designing the system is provided in Exhibit 1.8. In addition, coverage of information systems and global and ethical issues are integrated into the text.

Part III, Planning and Managing Operations, describes how an organization expects to use its facilities, people, and materials to meet demand. It includes developing and executing production plans and coping with different planning horizons. Coverage of aggregate planning, material requirements planning, inventory management, just-in-time scheduling, and project management is provided.

Finally, the organization should close the loop by evaluating performance based on market feedback and reexamining the issues involved in design of the system.

EXHIBIT 1.7

Overview of the
Systems Approach to
Operations

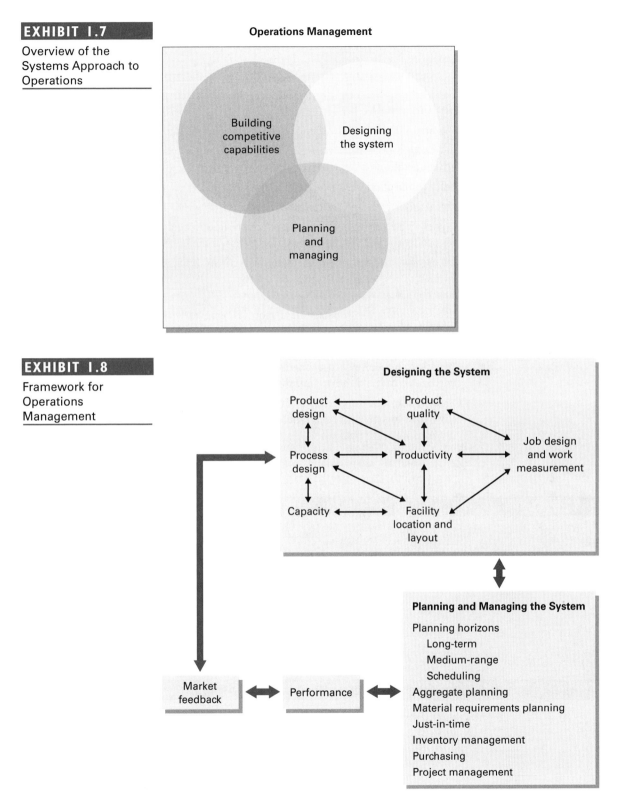

Operations Management

Building competitive capabilities

Designing the system

Planning and managing

EXHIBIT 1.8

Framework for
Operations
Management

Designing the System

Product design

Product quality

Process design

Productivity

Job design and work measurement

Capacity

Facility location and layout

Planning and Managing the System

Planning horizons
   Long-term
   Medium-range
   Scheduling
Aggregate planning
Material requirements planning
Just-in-time
Inventory management
Purchasing
Project management

Market feedback

Performance

SUMMARY

- Operations are the processes by which people, capital, and material are combined to produce the services and goods consumed by the public. Products should be value added, that is, the services and goods should be worth more to the customer than the cost of the inputs.

- Operations can be designed and used in a manner to gain competitive advantage.

- Service operations have many similarities with and some differences from manufacturing operations

- Global competition will strengthen organizations and increase living standards worldwide.

- Ethical issues are important business issues.

- A system is a group of items, events, or actions in which no item, event, or action occurs independently. The systems approach is a central theme that runs through this text.

- The organization must compete within the constraints presented by its external environment. These constraints include competitors, economic conditions, and government regulation.

- Successful operations management requires teamwork among operations and other functional areas (subsystems) within an organization. These areas include marketing, finance, accounting, engineering, and information systems.

- Operations are composed of many parts or subsystems, which should be effectively coordinated to build the organization's competitive position.

- Organizations should design business processes to achieve competitive capabilities rather than focusing on functional specialization.

 Visit our dynamic Web site, http://www.wiley.com/college/vonderembse, for extended chapter material, solved problems, mini-cases, computer software, and Web links.

KEY TERMS

business process
concurrent engineering
ethics
functional areas
goods
key policies
manufacturing
market research

operations
operations management
organizational structure
plan
process
process design
process technology
product

product design
product technology
relative advantage
services
stakeholders
strategy
system
technology

URLS

Microsoft: www.microsoft.com

General Motors: www.gm.com

Ciba Specialty Chemicals: www.cibasc.com

Black & Decker: www.blackanddecker.com

Procter & Gamble: www.pg.com

Sauder Woodworking: www.sauder.com

Halliburton: www.halliburton.com

Owens Corning: www.owenscorning.com

eBay: www.ebay.com

Southwest Airlines: www.southwest.com

QUESTIONS

1. What is the role of operations in the organization?

2. What does value-added operations mean? How would it apply to not-for-profit organizations?

3. Explain the major differences between producers of services and producers of goods? How do these differences affect operations?

4. Agree or disagree with the following statement and support your position: Operations management issues and problems should be narrowly focused on for-profit producers of goods, such as Microsoft, Ford Motor, and General Electric.

5. What impact has global competition had on operations?

6. What is meant by the systems approach to operations?

7. Why should an organization have a strategy? Should operating strategy be a part of this overall strategy?

8. What is the basic framework for operations management presented in this chapter?

9. What are the issues in designing a production system?

10. What are the issues in planning and managing a production system?

11. What are the issues in building a competitive base for operations?

12. How do ethical issues impact organizations and operations?

13. How is a business process different from a business function?

INTERNET QUESTIONS

14. Using the Internet, visit the Web site of Southwest Airlines and try to understand its approach to dealing with employees. Summarize the policy in one paragraph. In a second paragraph, describe why this policy is appropriate. Provide a copy of the information printed from the Internet.

15. Using the Internet, locate a manufacturing or service company and download its view of environmental responsibility. Summarize it in one paragraph. In a second paragraph, describe why this policy is appropriate. Provide a copy of the information printed from the Internet.

16. Using the Internet, download information on Owens Corning or Halliburton regarding the asbestos liability. Should they be responsible? What is the impact on all of the stakeholders (management, labor, customers, investors, and litigants)? Provide a copy of the information printed from the Internet.

17. Investigate the eBay auction site and examine the merchandise as well as the way that goods and services can be purchased. Summarize the reasons for the company's success in one paragraph. In a second paragraph, describe how the company can improve. Provide a copy of the information printed from the Internet.

18. Using the Internet, locate a manufacturing or service company and download its approach to global competition. Summarize it in one paragraph. In a second paragraph, describe why this policy is appropriate. Provide a copy of the information printed from the Internet.

PART I

BUILDING CAPABILITIES TO COMPETE GLOBALLY

Chapter 2: Gaining Competitive Advantage Through Operations

Chapter 3: Enhancing Productivity: A Key to Success

Chapter 4: Quality Management

Chapter 5: Enterprise Integration and Supply Chain Management: A Strategic Perspective

CHAPTER **2**

Gaining Competitive Advantage Through Operations

LEARNING OBJECTIVES

After completing this chapter, you should be able to:

1. Understand how business processes create competitive capabilities that enable organizations to satisfy customer requirements.
2. Describe some of the key business processes, including strategy development, product development, developing systems to produce services and goods, and order fulfillment.
3. Explain how operations management can maintain an organization's competitive edge through high-quality production, convenient delivery, effective customer service, and competitive cost.
4. Discuss why operations are strategically important.
5. List and define the steps necessary to link operations to corporate strategy.
6. Describe how operations managers are using information technology to increase productivity, improve quality, provide a safer environment, and reduce costs.
7. Discuss how computer and information technology affect operations.

STRATEGIC ISSUES: ACHIEVING COMPETITIVE ADVANTAGE WITH OPERATIONS

Operations present top management with many opportunities to develop competitive advantages. A **competitive advantage** is a capability that customers value, such as short delivery lead time or high product quality, and that gives an organization an edge on its competition. When properly used, operations can be an important tool for improving profits, increasing market share, and developing new markets. A firm's **market share** is its percentage of sales in a particular market, that is, its sales divided by total sales for all organizations competing in a market.

How can an organization create a competitive advantage? The simplest answer is to give customers what they want "better" than anyone else can. What do customers want or, in other words, what do they value? Exhibit 2.1 provides a model for understanding how an organization can deliver competitive advantage to its customers. An organization should know its external environment (threats and opportunities) and its internal environment (strengths and weaknesses), and it should have a clear understanding of the customers it is trying to serve. This is often called SWOT analysis, for strengths, weaknesses, opportunities, and threats. An in-depth understanding of customer requirements allows the firm to determine a set of competitive capabilities that will enable it to delight, rather than merely satisfy, the customer. These competitive capabilities are, in turn, the result of well-designed business processes.

A list of factors that customers value is provided in Exhibit 2.1. The list may vary from industry to industry and even from customer to customer, but it presents a good starting point. Exhibit 2.1 also provides a set of competitive capabilities that are affected, at least partially, by decisions made by operations managers. These competitive capabilities help the organization meet customer requirements, although there is not a one-to-one relationship between a competitive capability and a customer want. For example, flexibility in operations enables firms to meet specific customer needs quickly and may also affect product quality and price.

EXHIBIT 2.1	Model for Developing Competitive Advantage

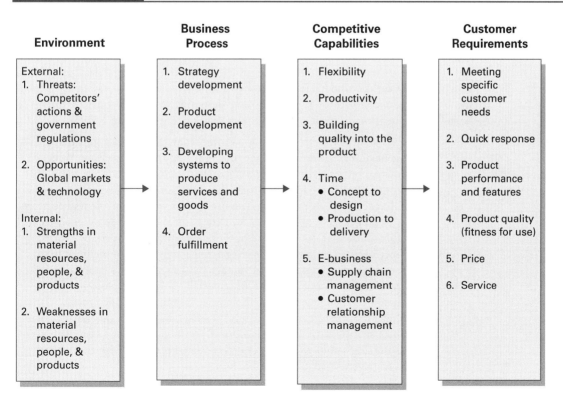

Environment	Business Process	Competitive Capabilities	Customer Requirements
External: 1. Threats: Competitors' actions & government regulations 2. Opportunities: Global markets & technology Internal: 1. Strengths in material resources, people, & products 2. Weaknesses in material resources, people, & products	1. Strategy development 2. Product development 3. Developing systems to produce services and goods 4. Order fulfillment	1. Flexibility 2. Productivity 3. Building quality into the product 4. Time • Concept to design • Production to delivery 5. E-business • Supply chain management • Customer relationship management	1. Meeting specific customer needs 2. Quick response 3. Product performance and features 4. Product quality (fitness for use) 5. Price 6. Service

Organizations should design business processes that enable them to achieve competitive capabilities. Exhibit 2.1 provides a list of business processes that are related to operations. This list may also vary from industry to industry and even from company to company within the same industry. Other processes not listed, such as those to recruit people or raise capital, are important, but they are not discussed in this text because of space limitations.

The sections that follow flow from Exhibit 2.1. They examine in more detail customer requirements, the competitive capabilities of the organization, business processes, and technology, one of the key environmental factors. Coverage of the environmental factors is often done in a course on business strategy or business policy and, with the exception of global competition and technology, will not be repeated here.

CUSTOMER REQUIREMENTS

Customers are at the heart of business operations. Exhibit 2.1 lists customer requirements that could lead to a competitive advantage if an organization can satisfy them better than its competitors can. If these requirements were equally valued by all customers, regardless of product or industry, assessing customer requirements would be easy. Unfortunately, there is no universal set of customer requirements for all industries or for all customers within an industry. For example, customers for gasoline buy based on convenience, price, and service because gasoline is, despite industry claims to the contrary, an undifferentiated product. On the other hand, many customers for automobiles buy based on product features, performance, quality, and price because automobiles are differentiated products. Some automobile buyers are unconcerned about price and buy for the status associated with a high-priced, high-performance luxury car with all possible features. Even for the same customer, requirements may change over time, so organizations must continuously measure and evaluate customer requirements.

To be successful at building competitive advantage, organizations should know who their customers are and what their customers want. By understanding their customers' requirements, organizations can build a competitive advantage that enables them to compete in global markets. Understanding these customer requirements is essential for focusing on the right competitive capabilities and designing the "best" business processes. Following is a brief description of the customer requirements listed in Exhibit 2.1.

- *Meeting specific customer needs*—A customer may have applications that are unique or different from most other customers of the organization. Value may be provided by precisely meeting a customer's needs. For example, computer firms provide software to do payroll. One approach may be to write a generic software package that many firms can use but does not fit any firm's needs precisely. This package is usually cheaper than a software package written specifically for a particular organization, but it may require extra work by the customer because certain parts of the payroll activity are not included in the generic software. A competitive advantage can be gained by customizing software to meet an organization's needs, especially if the price premium for customization can be made small. This approach, sometimes called mass customization, enables firms to design, produce, and deliver quickly products that meet specific customer needs at mass-production prices. Mass customization is the firm's ability to produce differentiated products with cost effectiveness, volume effectiveness, and responsiveness.

- *Quick response*—It is usually an advantage to customers to have products available immediately upon request. Late delivery may create delays, increase costs, and create other problems for customers. Early delivery often creates storage problems, creates the potential for theft or damage as the item sits in inventory, and increases the need for working capital to carry inventory. Long lead times force customers to commit to the purchase decision before they need the product. This situation can lead to mistakes because the environment may change during the lead time. For example, buying next summer's wardrobe at a clearance sale in September incurs substantial risk for the style-conscious consumer. Similar problems occur when organizations force their customers to have long lead times when placing orders.

- *Product performance and features*—Generally, high-performing products with many features are preferred by consumers, especially when acquired for little or no additional cost. Organizations that can be clever in the design and production of services and goods can achieve this. When it was first proposed that automobiles come equipped with air bags to increase safety, there was great concern that the cost of the air bag (estimated at about $1,200 each) would push the price of an automobile out of the reach of the average consumer. Today, air bags are touted as an important safety feature, and the cost of the air bags compared to other passenger restraints is very competitive.

- *Product quality*—To the customer, product quality means fitness for use. Does the product do what the customer wants, and does it do it well? Quality is broadly defined and can include product performance and features.

- *Price*—The amount paid for a service or good is still important to consumers. In fact, it is the other half of the value equation. Value is what a customer gets for the price paid.

- *Service*—Service is broadly defined. It includes companion activities, such as helping to arrange financing for a purchase or helping to install equipment. It also includes service after the sale—advice on operating a piece of equipment, providing repair parts, and processing warranty claims. If an organization can do this better than its competitors, it may achieve a competitive advantage.

COMPETITIVE CAPABILITIES

Competitive capabilities are the outcomes of well-designed business processes and, in turn, enable the firm to satisfy its customer requirements. They are outcomes that an organization has achieved, such as being flexible, so that a customer's needs can be precisely met or being productive so that costs can be kept low. The purposes of this discussion are to identify and define some of the most important capabilities required by most organizations and to describe how they might be achieved. The list of competitive capabilities in Exhibit 2.1 is not intended to be exhaustive. The emphasis is on operations and discussion focuses primarily on operating issues and concerns.

Flexibility

Flexibility, as defined for operations, is the ability to change between products or customers with minimal costs and delays. Flexible operations enable organizations to change from one product to another in response to customer requests quickly and inexpensively. Customer satisfaction increases, and delivery lead-time is reduced.

Flexibility in operations may be as simple as a barber's chair that can be adjusted for a customer's height. It may be an employee at Wendy's who can run the cash register, the grill, or the drive-up window. It may be a metal-bending press that can quickly be changed from producing a van door panel to producing a car hood. Consider how an organization can use flexibility to gain a competitive advantage.

- With a wide variety of products, marketing can meet specific customer demand more closely.
- Timely deliveries are possible because flexibility implies that inexpensive and quick changes can be made from one product to another.
- Changeover costs are reduced, thereby reducing operating costs as well.
- When sudden shifts in market preference occur, the cost of redesigning facilities and equipment is reduced because the system can more easily adapt to producing new and different products.

Using Flexibility to Satisfy a Variety of Customer Needs

Marketing would like to satisfy all demands made by customers because selling is part of its job. Sales can be more easily achieved when a wide variety of products is available for customer choice. Marketing would also like to avoid any unnecessary delays in delivering the service or good. One approach would be to request that operations keep adequate stocks of inventory for all items. Inventory, however, is very expensive. How can an organization maintain quick delivery and still keep finished goods inventory low? The answer is to reduce the time for changeover between products.

For service organizations, flexibility can be achieved through cross-training employees. Many service operations are labor intensive so if such an organization wants to deliver a variety of services, it is important to train employees to do more than one job. For example, an automotive repair firm may repair brakes, align wheels, and install batteries. If it has only one person to do each, it may have customers waiting for batteries, no work being done in brakes and wheel alignments, and two idle workers. Cross training can eliminate that problem.

EXAMPLE

Flint Auto Stamping uses flexibility to gain a competitive advantage. Stamping involves sending flat sheets of steel through a series of large presses that shape the metal by hitting it with dies (molds). The dies are formed to the shape of the finished product. Flint Auto Stamping produces left-front and right-front quarter panels (fenders) for cars. To change from left to right quarter panels, the press must be stopped, and the dies that shape the metal must be changed. At Flint Auto Stamping, it takes four to eight hours to change dies. How will management choose to operate? If it tries to change dies each day, there will spend four to eight hours each day with no production. Because of these delays, management will probably choose long production runs so the changeover times and costs will not be excessive. These longer runs will lead to greater inventory. Demand for the quarter panel not being produced must be satisfied from inventory because car assembly requires both front quarter panels at the same time.

If it takes only fifteen minutes to change the dies (typical of some producers), how will management choose to operate? It can afford more changeovers because they take less time away from actual production. More changes mean less inventory buildup because the time until the next change is short and less inventory is needed to supply the part that is not being produced.

Greater flexibility is a result of good planning and effectively organized changeover procedures that use written documentation and dedicated people—engineering, management, and labor—who are willing to work together. It can also be enhanced through the application of more recent technology.

Using Flexibility to Meet Sudden Market Changes

Flexibility in the production process also permits facilities to adapt to sudden market changes. Consider the U.S. automobile industry. Since 1973, the date of the first oil embargo, it has faced five major switches in market preference between large cars and small cars. These switches have dramatically changed the demand for eight-cylinder engines. If a transfer line, which machines engine blocks, is set up to produce eight-cylinder engines, can it easily be changed to produce six-cylinder engines? That is a function of the design of the transfer line. If it was designed to produce only eight-cylinder engines, then a major investment in time and money would be required to switch to six-cylinder engines. Flexibility has many facets and affects many different parts of the production system. In determining whether to have flexibility, the automobile industry should consider the tradeoff between the extra costs of designing and operating flexible machining centers for engine blocks and the costs of having to convert inflexible transfer lines each time crude oil prices change dramatically.

Productivity

Productivity is a ratio of the outputs achieved divided by the inputs consumed to achieve those outputs. As productivity increases, organizations can do the same work with less effort or can do more work with the same effort. Increases in productivity reduce costs, lower prices, and provide a basis for competing in world markets.

Productivity Improvements Free Resources for Innovation

Productivity improvements are beneficial to an organization, to consumers, and to workers (labor). In any situation, there are limits on resources, on capital and equipment, on material, and on energy and labor. Additionally, none of these resources are free. If an organization can produce more and better quality products with fewer resources, it will achieve two significant advantages. First, the unit cost of the product will decline because less labor and/or fewer materials are required to produce each unit. This makes the product price competitive. Second, there will be unused resources that can be used to develop and produce new and better products. When significant increases in productivity have been achieved, revolutionary changes in resource allocation have occurred.

The First Revolution   Increases in farming productivity have caused farm labor in the U.S. to decline from 95 percent of the labor force in the early 1800s to less than 3 percent today. This freed an army of workers for the task of creating and producing the vast array of consumer goods now available. At the same time, the prices consumers pay for food as a percentage of income have declined dramatically. Such consumer goods as automobiles, home appliances, and electronic gadgets were developed and produced by labor freed from farming tasks. These changes have improved business opportunities, created new jobs, and improved our living standards. They would not have been possible without the development of better methods and machinery that allowed companies to reallocate their human and physical resources from farming to the production of goods.

The Second Revolution   In the 1900s, improvements in manufacturing productivity freed resources for rapid expansion in service operations. Banking, health care, insurance, and other service industries have grown because of the labor freed by mechanizing operations. This explosion of opportunity for services is possible because improvements in labor productivity allow us to do more with fewer people and resources, which is how real improvement in living standards can be made.

The Third Revolution   The next wave of productivity improvements will be caused by the application of computer and information technology to create new "smart" automation systems. As this technology is applied to problems in decision making on the factory floor and in the office, the productivity of blue- and white-collar workers will increase. This technology allows fewer people, both labor and management, to do more work.

Although service industries may find it more difficult to apply robots and other equipment used in manufacturing, they are ahead of manufacturing in applying the soft side of automation. Service industries, such as airlines, insurance, and banking, are using information technology to improve service quality, lower costs, and make their workers more productive. Health insurers such as Blue Cross have developed sophisticated, computer-based information systems to process claims and handle subscriber inquiries.

Building Quality into Products

For firms to remain competitive in today's global markets they must produce high-quality products. To remain cost competitive, organizations must find ways to improve product quality without increasing costs. Technological advances can lead to reduced costs, improved product performance, and enhanced quality. Enhancements in quality can result from applying new technology (such as integrated circuits in DVD players), developing new materials (such as high-strength composites to replace steel), and improving operations through better management and training.

High Quality and Low Costs: The Ideal

At one time, many consumers took literally the old adage "You get what you pay for." As a result, consumers believed they had to pay more to get high quality. Although this statement has intuitive appeal, recent history has shown that improvements in quality can be achieved while costs are held constant or reduced. It is true that high quality can be achieved with high costs and that there will always be a market for exclusive products. But mass-market appeal requires the right blend of improved quality and lower costs, as illustrated in Exhibit 2.2. Organizations that can come closest to achieving this ideal product will have a tremendous advantage over the competition.

Moving toward the Ideal through Technology

To move toward the ideal of high quality and low costs, improvements in product and process technology should be considered. Product technology refers to the way the product functions, and process technology refers to the way the product is made.

A look back at the evolution of television provides a perspective on the potential impact of technology on quality and cost. In the mid-1950s, when color television was first introduced, a set cost over $600. Picture quality was poor and the useful life of a television set was only a few years. Refinements in technology have allowed producers to reduce costs and significantly improve quality. Today's televisions offer a vastly improved picture,

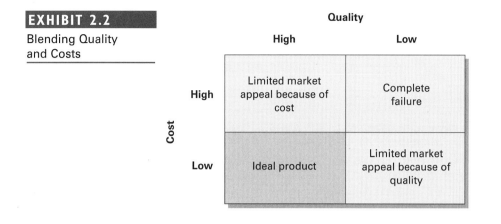

EXHIBIT 2.2

Blending Quality
and Costs

longer life, and more and better features, such as automatic fine-tuning and remote control. Today, a 25-inch television set can be purchased for about $200. To understand the magnitude of this decline, a typical worker in the mid-1950s earned a few thousand dollars per year. Today, this worker earns more than $25,000.

Process technology is the method of making a product. Improvements in process include the use of machines to do difficult and demanding jobs. Mechanized welding is an example of a process improvement. It is usually faster and cheaper than manual welding, and it produces stronger welds.

Moving toward the Ideal through Better Management

Higher quality and lower costs can also be achieved through better management practices, including quality and cost-management programs that trim waste from operations, better training and motivation for employees, and greater attention to machine maintenance. These improvements can have a dramatic impact.

Which should be first, new technology or improved management practices? Improved management practices come first. Full benefits from implementing new technology will result when existing operations are well understood and running properly. Placing new technology on top of poor management systems usually leads to little, if any, return on the organization's investment. If managers are having trouble coping with existing operations, it is unlikely that they will be able to understand and control more sophisticated technology and operations.

Time

Competing on time has become an important way to build competitive advantage because rapid market change places a premium on quick response. Time-based competition is a strategy of seeking competitive advantage by quickening the tempo of critical organizational processes, such as product development, order entry, production, distribution, and service. The emphasis is on end-to-end time (i.e., aggregate time) from the generation of new product concepts to the delivery of finished products, rather than the time to perform specific tasks or functions. Time is a fundamental business performance variable. In essence, time becomes one of the critical objectives as organizations redesign their business processes. Organizations like Hewlett-Packard, Marco's Pizza, L. L. Bean, and General Electric are competing on time. Each company is introducing new products quickly. For example, Hewlett-Packard has cut product development time from fifty-four to twenty-two months for their new printer and is working to reduce this even further. These companies and many others are shaving time from product development as well as order fulfillment. For more information, a chapter on time-based competition is available on the companion Web site for this text: www.wiley.com/college/vonderembse.

E-business

The concept of e-business (i.e., electronic business) often means different things to different people. For our purposes, **e-business** involves the use of electronic platforms to conduct company business. It means the application of computer and information technology to design, plan, and manage operations and to track transactions between your organization and its suppliers and between your organization and its customers. Two decades ago computer systems focused on reporting results and tracking performance. Today, this technology has become a proactive tool for working with suppliers and customers. The primary reasons for the differences between the e-business systems of today and the computer systems of twenty years ago are advances in software development and substantial improvement in the speed, power, and costs of hardware. Today, processing speeds, database capacity, telecommunications capability, networking, etc. have improved many times while costs have dropped dramatically. These are powerful forces that enable e-business solutions to make fundamental changes in the ways organizations, supply chains, and customers interact.

E-business can be divided into two elements: **business-to-business (B2B),** or supply chains, and **business-to-consumer (B2C),** or customer relationships. B2B refers to transactions between organizations in a supply chain, such as IBM selling computer services to Priceline.com or Boeing. B2C refers to transactions between an organization and its final customer, such as Amazon.com selling books or CDs to consumers via the Internet. E-commerce, another commonly used term, is a combination of e-purchasing and e-marketing, which involving buying and selling with suppliers and customers. To simplify, we will focus on B2B (supply chain management) and B2C (customer relationships management).

Supply Chain Management

Supply chains encompass all activities associated with the flow and transfer of goods and services from raw material extraction through use by the organization that sells to the final consumer. In oil refining, that would include locating and pumping crude oil to the sale of gasoline at the service station. Information flows in both directions along the supply chain while materials flow, at least ideally, in a consistent and orderly fashion toward the final consumer. Service providers play an essential role in helping organizations design, plan, and manage these information and material flows so that efficiency, speed, and on-time delivery are achieved. Engineering firms design and install material handling systems, transportation companies move materials between facilities, and computer-based companies design and implement information systems to help manage these activities.

Supply chain management is the integration of these activities through improved supplier relationships to achieve a sustainable competitive advantage for all members in the supply chain. It is an essential ingredient for competition. Progressive organizations have recognized that competition is no longer between individual firms, such as DaimlerChrysler and Ford or General Motors and Toyota, rather it is between the supply chains. The development, design, production, marketing, and delivery of a new car should be a coordinated effort that begins with extracting raw materials from the earth, continues through design, fabrication, and assembly, and ends with fit and finish in the dealer's showroom. When a customer buys a car from DaimlerChrysler, for example, the customer chooses the output of the entire supply chain and pays all the participants. To be successful, DaimlerChrysler must develop methods to manage the supply chain from its roots in basic materials, such as iron ore, sand, and crude oil, to the dealer. That does not necessary mean ownership or even direct control, but it does imply mechanisms that influence decision making and impact performance. These relationships should work to the benefit of all the participants.

EXAMPLE

Consider DaimlerChrysler's newest assembly plant in Toledo, Ohio. Modine Manufacturing Company has the exclusive contract to provide radiators/cooling modules to the facility. As a car exits the frame assembly area, an electronic signal is sent to Modine's facility, which is located less than five miles from the assembly plant. The signal tells Modine which vehicle is being built and which version of the radiator is needed. Modine has less than four hours to deliver the radiators to the assembly plant in the exact order requested. The radiators are loaded on the truck in reverse order so the first radiator loaded onto the truck is the last radiator needed at the assembly line. As a result, when the radiators are removed from the truck, they can be taken directly to the assembly line and installed in the car. This eliminates extra handling and simplifies product flow. Currently, Modine has a two-day supply of radiators at its facility, and it has plans to reduce that by at least half. To help Modine's suppliers, DaimlerChrysler sends Modine and its suppliers a tentative five-day build schedule so the suppliers can produce and deliver the correct component parts to Modine. The process is fast and efficient, and there is very little waste in the system.

Customer Relationship Management

Customer relationship management (CRM) is a process to create, maintain, and enhance strong, value-laden associations with people and organizations that buy products. CRM moves beyond creating short-term transactions to build long-term relationships with valued customers, distributors, and dealers. Firms using CRM attempt to build strong economic and social connections by promising and delivering high-quality goods and services, at a fair price, and in a timely manner. Increasingly, firms are attempting to build mutually beneficial relationships with customers, distributors, and dealers rather than to maximize the profit on a particular transaction. Firms can use the following ideas to develop stronger relationships with customers.

- *Financial benefits*—Firms can build value and satisfaction by adding financial benefits. For example, airlines offer frequent flyer programs, hotels give room upgrades to guest with a certain number of visits, and supermarkets give preferred customer discounts.
- *Social benefits*—Firms can build allegiance by increasing their social bonds with customers by learning individual needs and then personalizing service. Ritz-Carlton Hotel employees treat customers as individuals by attempting to learn their names and referring to them on that basis. The hotel records specific information about customer preferences in a database, and other Ritz-Carlton hotels around the world use this information at hotels. So, customers with a special request in one hotel should find that request met the next time they stay at a Ritz-Carlton hotel, even if it is in another city or country.
- *Structural ties*—Firms can add value by creating extra support services that make it easier to buy from one company than from another. A business might supply customers with special equipment or computer links that help them manage their

orders. For example, Dell creates personalized Web sites for its large commercial customers that provide most of the information and support the customer might need. In addition to handling purchases, the site also supplies tailored technical support, diagnostic tools, and other features designed for the customer.

DESIGNING BUSINESS PROCESSES THAT BUILD COMPETITIVE CAPABILITIES

Organizations do not control customer satisfaction directly. After all, the customer buys the product, and it is through the consumption of the product that customer satisfaction is achieved. As was shown in Exhibit 2.1, focusing on business processes is a critical factor in achieving competitive capabilities, which lead to customer satisfaction, which, in turn, leads to organizational success. An organization may have several different processes and many sub-processes within each process. The discussion here is limited to four key processes that most organizations have and that are substantially impacted by operations: strategy development, product development, developing systems to produce services and goods, and order fulfillment. Additional readings on redesigning business processes are available on the companion Web site at www.wiley.com/college/vonderembse.

Strategy Development

As described in Chapter 1, strategy should drive an organization toward its final objective. A strategy considers the threats and opportunities in the environment, and it measures the strengths and weaknesses of the organization. These represent inputs to strategy development. The strategic planning process provides a path toward the organization's objectives. This path includes setting goals, developing action plans for achieving the goals, and determining resource requirements. Developing a strategy requires a team with specialized knowledge from different functional areas or disciplines. When operational plans are linked to financial, marketing, engineering, and information systems development plans, synergy can result. Synergy involves cooperative actions (teamwork) in which the total effect of the actions is greater than the sum of the individual effects (i.e., the whole is greater than the sum of its parts). For example, the feat of putting a man on the moon required a cooperative effort that no one part of the team could have achieved, no matter how long and hard it worked. A description of the process for strategy development is provided later in this chapter.

Product Development

Product development is a teamwork-oriented process that begins with the organization's strategy and analysis of the markets as inputs. The team develops a product concept, generates a product design, and provides a process design for producing the service or good, which are the outputs. Knowledge regarding customer preferences, technology, operating capabilities, financial constraints, distribution systems, and so on should be available from specialists in accounting, finance, marketing, research and development, engineering, information systems, and operations. Product development is discussed in Chapter 6.

Developing Systems to Produce Services and Goods

Developing systems to produce the services and goods designed in the product development process requires firms to assemble resources—people, facilities and equipment, and material and energy. These resources may be part of the organization, or they may be contracted from another firm. Important knowledge inputs needed to develop an effective production system are the product and process designs created in the product development process. These designs help to guide decision making.

Traditionally, these topics fall under the discipline of operations management, but organizations that want to ensure success recognize the interdisciplinary nature of these tasks. Accounting and financial information is necessary for decision making, and human resources are necessary to make the system work. Engineering principles, especially industrial engineering, are an important foundation of this design for both services and goods. These topics are covered in Part II, Designing the System to Produce Services and Goods.

Order Fulfillment

This process involves all the steps required to satisfy a customer's order, from obtaining an order and entering it into the organization's information system to delivering the order. The primary inputs are from the customer, marketing, and the people responsible for designing the facility that will produce the service or good. The desired output is a satisfied customer, not the delivered product. While this difference may seem small, it is important to remember that an organization is only successful when customers are satisfied. Order fulfillment should be a highly integrative teamwork-oriented process that includes many disciplines and activities, such as sales, credit verification, analysis of working capital needs, and selecting shipping routes and transportation alternatives. An important part of order fulfillment is actually producing the services and goods intended to satisfy customer requirements. This execution is dependent on the organization's ability to plan and manage operations, including production planning, scheduling, inventory control, purchasing and material management, and project management. These activities both influence and are affected by activities carried out in other parts of the order fulfillment process. Details of the order fulfillment process from the operations management perspective are provided in Part III on Planning and Managing Operations.

STRATEGY DEVELOPMENT AND OPERATIONS

Strategy begins with the organization's goals and includes the key policies that are established to direct actions toward meeting those goals. As an organization defines its corporate strategy, a framework is created that enables the firm to develop a set of functional strategies consistent with and integrated to the corporate objectives. Research and development, marketing, engineering, operations, and other functional areas need to develop objectives, plans, and programs that are consistent with corporate goals.

Operating advantages should be pursued because they fit the organization's goals, not because they fit some narrowly defined operating objective, such as minimizing transportation costs. In fact, minimizing transportation costs may not be in the best interests of an organization if inventory holding or other costs would increase too much or if product quality or on-time delivery would be negatively affected. Operational goals should be important only when they help the organization reach its objectives. The following sections describe how corporate strategy is linked to operating strategy.

Linking Corporate Strategy to Operations

Corporate strategy and operating strategy must be carefully linked. Operations can become a positive factor that contributes to organizational success, rather than a negative or neutral factor. To make this happen, facilities, equipment, and training should be viewed as a means to achieve organizational, rather than operational, objectives. Consider the Midas and the

Genoa Ford examples. These organizations, both involved in car repair, have adopted different strategies and have tailored their operations to fit those strategies.

EXAMPLE

Midas is in the automotive repair business. Its strategy is to provide a narrow range of services at low cost. National advertising is used to develop wide geographical coverage. The company is not a full service repair shop, but concentrates on muffler repair, brakes, and shock absorbers. It is successful because it delivers quality service quickly and at low cost. How are operations important to Midas?

1. Limited service permits special design of the equipment and the shop so that the employees can be more productive.
2. Limited service requires a limited inventory that allows convenient storage close to the point where materials are needed.
3. Multiple shops and limited service permit careful engineering of the necessary hand tools and the work procedures. These special tools and work procedures make the shop employees more efficient. Midas can apply the same tools and methods to a large number of shops so that initial engineering costs are easily covered.
4. Because employees have few variations in service, they learn how to do these jobs more quickly.
5. Workers' skill levels and knowledge requirements focus on a limited area of service so they quickly become experts in a particular area.

As part of a Ford dealership, Genoa Ford's service operation provides a full line of automotive repairs. In contrast to Midas, this service operation competes without advertising or national appeal. It also has a different operating strategy. In order to maintain the dealership, Genoa Ford must be able to satisfy a variety of customer needs. It does wheel alignments, body repair work, engine overhauls, and other tasks in addition to working on brakes, shocks, and mufflers. How does Genoa Ford design operations to match its objectives?

1. The facility is adaptable to changing needs. For example, on one day a stall may be used to wash a new car, repair a door lock, fix an air conditioning leak, or tune an engine.
2. Genoa Ford has more tools than a specialist like Midas does because Genoa Ford does a greater variety of jobs.
3. There is some job specialization. Not everyone will be able to do everything, but employees still need a wide range of skills because Genoa Ford does not have enough of one particular job to allow everyone to specialize. Cross-training is necessary.
4. The workers' skill levels and pay rates are higher than workers at Midas.
5. A significant inventory of many different parts is maintained. These parts are physically separated from the repair stalls and controlled by specialists in parts.

As a result of its strategy, Genoa Ford has higher costs and charges higher prices than Midas does for comparable work. When your car needs routine exhaust system work, you will probably take it to a national chain like Midas. The generalists like Genoa Ford will do the more difficult jobs and warranty work.

How do organizations successfully link corporate strategy and operating strategy? Management needs a strategic, top-down view of operations. This begins with analyzing the competitive environment and ends with managing and controlling operations, as listed here.

1. Analyzing the competitive environment (external environment—threats and opportunities)
2. Appraising the organization's skills and resources (internal environment—strengths and weaknesses)
3. Formulating corporate strategy
4. Determining the implications of corporate strategy for operating strategy
5. Examining the limitations economics and technology place on operations
6. Designing systems for operations
7. Planning and managing operations

Each of these steps raises questions that should be addressed by management in the organization. Questions that should be asked about these steps are listed in the following sections.

Analyzing the Competitive Environment

All organizations operate within an environment that is shaped by external factors and forces over which they have limited control. These factors include the level of technology, labor supply, social and political environment, and array of competitors and potential competitors, both domestic and international. The application of technology to develop new products and/or processes can impact on an organization's ability to compete. Environmental legislation may dramatically alter an organization's cost of doing business in a way that leaves competitors unaffected. New entrants into the market may possess strengths that give them a competitive advantage over firms already in the market.

To be successful, an organization should know about the market in which it will compete and about its environment. In what market or markets is the organization planning to compete? Who are the present competitors, and what are their strengths? Who are the potential entrants? What changes in government regulations or business conditions might alter the competitive environment?

Appraising the Organization's Skills and Resources

What strengths does an organization possess? How might these be used to take advantage of certain opportunities in the environment? What technological expertise and production capabilities are available? What markets or channels of distribution are open?

Formulating Corporate Strategy

An organization should formulate a strategy by applying its skills and resources to the opportunities present in the environment. What are the goals and objectives of the organization? Suppose an organization wants to lead the state or region in providing financial services to the home via microcomputer connections. What are the key policies for achieving these goals? What policies will be set for minimizing security risks?

Determining the Implications of Corporate Strategy for Operating Strategy

What are the strategic operating decisions? For example, where should the facility be located to provide rapid response to customer needs at an acceptable level of cost? What process technology will be employed and at what capacity? What is the level of product quality? Is there really a trade-off between product cost and quality? What level of flexibility is required to produce services and goods for this market? Is the market likely to change, making flexibility important?

The corporate strategy should be the guidepost for production planning. It should set the stage for the short-term operating budget, which is a detailed annual plan for spending, and for the longer-term capital budget, which is a plan for facility improvements and expansion.

Examining the Limitations of Economics and Technology on Operations

What are the specific limitations of the existing operations? What resources need to be improved or obtained in order to meet organizational objectives? How large will a particular facility be? How should the production resources be distributed? Should there be only a few large facilities with their associated economies of scale? Or would several smaller facilities that are easier to manage be better?

Smaller facilities are part of the focused factory concept. **Focused factories** are smaller operations that produce fewer products. They do not attempt to achieve low costs through economies of scale (e.g., by spreading fixed costs over a large volume). Focused factories achieve low costs through better control (for example, by eliminating waste) and ease of managing a smaller operation (because fewer people are involved).

Designing Systems for Operations

How should operations be designed in order to meet the organization's objectives? To answer this question, management must consider product design, capacity, process selection, facility location and layout, productivity, and quality. How can flexibility be designed into the system in anticipation of changing needs? What are the information-processing capabilities necessary to provide management with useful information for decision making?

Planning and Managing Operations

How can the organization use the resources available to meet present and projected customer needs? These plans should move the organization toward its objectives as defined by the corporate strategy. How might those resources be changed through additional capital expenditures to satisfy changing demands? Planning for operations ranges from short-term decisions involving what products to make this week to long-term decisions regarding future changes in technology or shifts in customer demand.

How well has the operations function performed in meeting the established plans? Has it been successful at moving the organization toward its short- and long-term objectives? Has operations made the organization stronger and given it a competitive advantage by making better quality products, providing improved service and shorter delivery lead times, or reducing costs? Costs refer to total organizational costs, not just production costs.

A CHANGING GLOBAL ENVIRONMENT OFFERS GREATER COMPETITION

In 1992, Belgium, Denmark, France, Germany, Greece, Ireland, Italy, Luxembourg, the Netherlands, Portugal, Spain, and the United Kingdom joined to form the European Community (EC). The EC united these countries into a single international market that is designed to make trade between countries as easy as trade between California and Oregon. As a result, trade among the EC's member countries should increase as barriers to trade are eliminated. It also creates a powerful new force in the global marketplace. Currently, the EC represents about 350 million consumers while the United States has about 270 million and Japan has less than 100 million. With that kind of political muscle, the EC can offer serious competition to both the United States and Japan in the area of global trade.

This could have several effects on the production and distribution of services and goods in the growing global economy. Because of the EC's unified market and free trade within the market, multinational organizations may be more likely to locate new production facilities in EC countries. The pooling of resources and joint ventures are more likely to occur with the EC, making it a major force in developing, producing, marketing, and distributing products on a worldwide basis. The EC should stimulate international trade, making it more important for all organizations to think globally when developing strategies and plans for implementing those strategies.

The EC does not currently include eastern European countries. These countries represent hundreds of millions of consumers who are hungry for goods from the EC, Japan, and the United States. What might happen if some of these countries join the EC, or if they band together into a new trading block? There are substantial opportunities for new ventures in these developing countries. The continent of Asia, China in particular, is embracing principles of capitalism. These countries represent billions of new consumers for goods and services produced in the United States and are strong candidates for joint ventures.

Since the ratification of the North American Free Trade Agreement (NAFTA), countries in North, Central, and South America have been discussing creating a free trade zone in the Western Hemisphere. Leaders of several South American countries are aggressively pushing for the elimination of trade barriers.

THE ROLE OF COMPUTER AND INFORMATION TECHNOLOGY IN OPERATIONS

The use of computers in service and manufacturing operations is not new. In accounting, computers perform payroll, accounts receivable, and accounts payable functions. Computers monitor inventory levels and help to control quality. Airlines and hotels use them to take reservations and to schedule flight crews and housekeeping. Computers technology is used to monitor flow process in papermaking and oil refining and to control metal-cutting machines that shape parts needed in automobile engines and refrigerator compressors. In these situations, computers provide feedback on operations and can take corrective action.

Today, many organizations are expanding the use of computers and information systems in ways that could provide them with a competitive advantage. Organizations such as American Airlines have invested heavily in computer-based reservation systems that enhance their ability to serve customers and to maximize the use of their airplanes. Devilbiss Corporation has developed a computer-based expert system to help customers select the correct adhesive or paint for their specific application. This section discusses expert systems and decision support systems that can be widely applied in service operations or in manufacturing. It also discusses the impact of the Internet and virtual reality on operations.

Expert Systems

An **expert system** employs human knowledge that has been captured in a computer to solve complex problems. To be considered an expert system, the system must have (1) a method of acquiring knowledge, (2) a knowledge base (memory), and (3) an inference engine (brain) so it can reason. Knowledge acquisition is the accumulation, transfer, and transformation of problem-solving expertise from some source, usually a human expert. Often the human expert is overloaded or is close to retirement, so the idea of capturing the person's knowledge in a computer-based expert system is very appealing. Someone called a **knowledge engineer** helps the human expert structure the problem by interpreting and integrating human answers, drawing analogies, posing examples, and bringing out conceptual difficulties.

The knowledge base can be thought of as a powerful database that contains such facts as the problem situation and theory in the problem area, as well as special rules that direct the use of the knowledge. The inference engine is a computer program that provides a methodology for reasoning. This component makes decisions about how to use the knowledge in the system. The inference engine interprets rules, maintains control over the problem, and enforces consistency as the recommended solution emerges. There are many potential applications for expert systems from generating orders for inventory, diagnosing patients, troubleshooting equipment failure, advising on tax-sheltered annuities, and scheduling production.

EXAMPLE LaCourtier is a computer-based expert system in financial planning that was developed by Cognitive Systems, Inc. for a major Belgian bank. The system gives advice on stock purchases and portfolio distribution (how a client's money should be invested) and answers factual questions about the Belgian stock market. For a new customer, LaCourtier conducts an interview to collect information about the user's financial situation. According to the user's current portfolio and market conditions, the system gives advice about which stocks to buy or sell.

Decision Support Systems

A **decision support system (DSS)** is a model-based set of procedures for processing data to assist managers in decision making. A DSS allows managers easy access to information stored in a database and provides easy-to-use tools for analysis. With these supporting tools, management can more easily control complicated manufacturing and service operations. A DSS is different from an expert system because an expert system has a rule base and an inference engine for decision making and a DSS does not. Once an expert system has been constructed, it can make a decision. On the other hand, a DSS assists managers in making decisions; the manager provides the logic to structure the problem and ultimately makes the decision.

A DSS can help a manager relate the demand for a product to the correct quantities of materials to be ordered to make that product. If a manager has received an order for 10,000 hair dryers for next month, how does he or she know the number of electric motors, wire connectors, and plastic parts to order? How does the order fit into the production schedule? Does the organization have sufficient capacity? What are the impacts on cost and quality if the orders are processed on certain machines? It becomes necessary to link these decisions by using the computer as a tool to assist managers with information collection and organization.

The Internet

The Internet will soon link all households, businesses, government agencies, libraries, churches, etc. in the United States and will eventually connect these entities in all countries.

Developing this system is revolutionizing the ways businesses interact with each other as well as with customers. The more dependent an organization is on information transfer, the larger the impact. For example, publishing textbooks could change forever. Professors, sitting at computers in their offices, can design their own textbooks by mixing and matching sections from hundreds of published works in the area. Once created, these books can be downloaded to the universities' computer and printed with special printers that can handle digital transmissions. Printing presses and transportation could become less important. People could borrow books at the library without leaving their homes or offices. The publication and delivery of newspapers, book club offerings, and magazines are also changing, and the future holds even greater promise of change.

Shift to the areas of music and movies. Customers can select specific songs while sitting at their home computers. These songs can be sent over the Internet and captured by a compact disc recorder. Customers may have access to every song ever recorded, rather than the limited selection at the local music store. In addition, they could have the music almost instantly. Big film stars and other performers could bypass traditional movie studios and distribution centers by offering their movies directly to their fans through the Internet.

The impact on stock brokerage houses, banks, and insurance companies is equally dramatic. Even traditional manufacturing firms could be changed significantly. For example, purchasing departments should have electronic access to every imaginable service and good, with detailed pricing and delivery data. A supplier that is electronically linked to its customers' computerized production schedules could synchronize its production and delivery with its customers' needs. Companies could gather real-time information from individual customers and prepare customized orders without delay.

EXAMPLE

Amazon.com offers customers the opportunity to purchase a wide variety of products via the Internet. The firm's computer-based retail operation offers services that would be difficult to duplicate. Not only can you buy a wide variety of items from your home or office but you can also easily locate items that otherwise would be difficult to find. Suppose you are interested in locating a book that is no longer in print. Without Amazon.com, that would involve trips to many used bookstore plus searching the shelves until you find it. On Amazon.com, you can go to the Web site, enter either the author's name or the book title. Amazon.com can locate the book (which may be held by an individual or another company), complete the transaction, and have the book mailed in a few days. How long does the process take? If you know the title and/or the author, it only takes a few minutes. If you don't, but you do know the subject matter, the search function on Amazon.com should be able to locate this in a few minutes more.

Virtual Reality

When most people think of virtual reality, they think of computer games. Computer games use the most basic virtual reality system, where a user manipulates abstract objects by touching them in different ways. Users move their hand, and sensors in a glove pick up the movements and translate them into commands that control what is happening in the visual display. But unlike computer games, the real world needs virtual reality to move objects, objects that are too hazardous, heavy, distant, or delicate to be moved by hand. For precise maneuvers, a virtual reality system needs a sense of touch.

EXAMPLE

A construction crane's control levers are extremely complicated, and it takes years for an operator to become proficient. A doctoral dissertation at the Massachusetts Institute of Technology involved the design and construction of a device, called a

Dataglove, which controls a crane. The glove, developed by virtual reality scientists and worn by the crane operator, is fitted with position sensors and fiber optic cables. The glove responds to the operator's hand movements, which are similar to the hand movements that construction workers use to communicate with crane operators. In preliminary tests, the glove worn by the operator worked as well as or better than the crane operator pushing the levers. The operator can control the crane from a variety of locations, which provides the operator with a better view.

THE ROLE OF COMPUTER AND INFORMATION TECHNOLOGY IN MANUFACTURING

Computer-based control systems can be combined with manufacturing technology, such as robots, machine tools, and automated guided vehicles, to improve manufacturing operations. In this role, the computer can assist in integrating these technologies into a lean and efficient factory capable of competing in world markets. Organizations such as Allen-Bradley, Black & Decker, and Boeing have used information technology and factory automation to improve manufacturing operations. This combination of information technology and factory automation is often called computer-integrated manufacturing.

Computer-integrated manufacturing (CIM) blends developments in manufacturing with information technology to achieve competitive advantage. When properly organized, CIM offers the opportunity to automate design, manufacturing, and production planning and control. Each component is described briefly here. More information on CIM is available in the supplement to this chapter, which is available on the companion Web site www.wiley.com/college/vonderembse.

■ Engineering design through computer-aided design (CAD) allows an organization to make high-quality specialized designs rapidly. The designs can be tailored to meet individual customer needs.

■ Flexible manufacturing systems (FMSs) can quickly produce a variety of high-quality products efficiently. An FMS also allows an organization to produce highly specialized designs.

■ Computer-based production planning and control systems allow an organization to cope with the complexity of managing facilities that produce a wide variety of specialized products without losing efficiency.

When properly combined, these components can yield synergistic results. An organization can have more flexible and integrated operations, be better equipped to manage complex operations, and exercise better control than can a company that operates without CIM. To merge these components into one coordinated whole, staff from the information systems function needs to integrate engineering, manufacturing, and business databases into a cross-functional decision support system. Once accomplished, the flexibility to respond to customer demands with low-cost, high-quality specialized products becomes a powerful competitive advantage.

EXAMPLE

"A computer-integrated manufacturing facility was necessary to allow us to sell world-class products anywhere in the world and still make a profit," says the CEO at Allen-Bradley. Allen-Bradley is using automated assembly lines to capture a bigger share of the international market for contactors and relays used in electric starter motors for cars and trucks. With this facility, the company can produce 125 variations of these products in batch sizes as small as one. The only human intervention is provided by a handful of attendants. Product cost has declined, product quality has improved, and inventory has been reduced.

THE ROLE OF COMPUTER AND INFORMATION TECHNOLOGY IN SERVICE OPERATIONS

Service, by its definition, does not have a physical dimension. However, many organizations classified as service providers actually produce both goods and services. These hybrid operations include restaurants, which both sell food (a good) and prepare it (a service); department stores, which sell products as well as the retailing service; and shops that sell parts and offer repair services.

EXAMPLE

Kroger Supermarket's automated warehousing provides a competitive advantage. Retail food is a competitive business with low profit margins. To remain price competitive, Kroger must cut inventories and warehousing costs but maintain adequate supplies of thousands of products. To achieve these goals, Kroger and others have implemented automated warehouses and point-of-sale tracking of inventory. The process begins when an item is purchased by a customer. An electronic scanner reads the bar code on the product. The cash register, which is really a computer terminal, records the sale of that item in the computer's database. At the end of the day, or at any other time, a store manager can tabulate sales by product. Orders can be sent electronically to the automated warehouse. The orders are filled using automated stock pickers and shipped the next day. At the warehouse, computers help to track shipments to the stores and place orders to suppliers, so that inventory costs in the warehouse are low, yet product availability is high.

For many services, the tangible part of the product is not significant. With these operations, managers cannot buffer customer demand from the production process with finished-goods inventory. Managers in service operations must find other ways to provide better and faster customer service. This has led managers to implement information systems that provide up-to-date and accurate information about availability of the service and how customers can acquire it. As discussed earlier, the Internet offers substantial opportunities to change the way operations are conducted.

Many opportunities exist for using computers and information technology to improve service operations and to gain competitive advantage. In order to remain competitive, future managers should understand this technology and be capable of implementing it successfully. Tomorrow's managers will be expected to do more and better work with these improving tools. Consider the following examples where computer and information technology has been applied to improve performance.

EXAMPLE

USA Today is the first attempt at a national newspaper. It was made possible by the application of computer-based word processing and communication technology. The text of the paper is transmitted via satellite to geographically dispersed printing plants. Information technology allows an edition to be created, transmitted, and printed in color each day. *USA Today*'s use of technology allows it to publish a national daily newspaper, something that others have been unable to duplicate.

The U.S. Postal Service is moving quickly to automate mail sorting. Machines now read bar codes that are printed on envelopes by big mailers, such as banks and credit card issuers. Other equipment arranges presorted mail in the order of a carrier's delivery route, which eliminates much hand sorting.

The Montgomery County Court House in Norristown, Pennsylvania, uses an expert system to save big money on unneeded jurors. With two years of data on juror utilization and the next day's trial schedule, the system provides an immediate readout of the number of jurors required. The jurors, alerted thirty days ahead of time, are called and paid only if needed.

Mellon Bank is using an expert system to successfully battle credit card fraud, which is a multibillion dollar problem in the United States alone. The computer-based expert system examines 1.2 million accounts each day for many factors, such as an unusual number of transactions, charging large amounts, and changing patterns of expenditures. The system usually identifies about 100 cases that require more investigation. Mellon paid about $1 million for the software and predicted that it will pay for itself in six months.

Merck & Co., one of the largest drug companies in the world, decided to completely revamp its benefits system. To enroll over 15,000 salaried employees the old fashioned way using printed forms would have required Merck to double its personnel staff. The company spent $1 million to write computer software and install two dozen machines (similar to the automated teller machines at banks) to enroll its employees. Enrollment took just five weeks and not one person was added to the personnel staff. Merck is using similar systems to allow employees to adjust withholding allowances and reallocate their investment plan without speaking to anyone in payroll. Merck's software prevents employees from selecting options for which they are not eligible or from making obviously wrong decisions.

SUMMARY

- Satisfying customer requirements means building competitive capabilities, such as flexibility, productivity, quality, and time.

- Competitive capabilities are the results of good business processes.

- Operations should be viewed by top management as an opportunity to develop competitive advantage. When properly designed, operations can increase an organization's flexibility, reduce costs, enhance quality, and improve productivity.

- Operations are strategically important to an organization's success. Without this strategic view, an organization can never reach its full potential.

- Links that connect operations to an organization's strategy begin with analysis of the competitive environment and include an appraisal of the organization's skills, the implications of corporate strategy for operations, and the economic and technological limits of operations.

- Computer and information technology helps an organization to achieve a competitive advantage. These systems provide information to enhance decision making and improve control by integrating various parts of the production process.

- Applying information technology to service operations is a way to achieve a competitive advantage.

 Visit our dynamic Web site, http://www.wiley.com/college/vonderembse, for extended chapter material, solved problems, mini-cases, computer software, and Web links.

KEY TERMS

business-to-business (B2B)
business-to-consumer (B2C)
competitive advantage
computer integrated
   manufacturing (CIM)
customer relationship
   management (CRM)

decision support systems
   (DSS)
e-business
expert system
flexibility
focused factories
knowledge engineer

market share
productivity
supply chain management
supply chains

URLS

Allen-Bradley: www.ab.com

Genoa Ford: www.genoaford.com

Modine Manufacturing: www.modine.com

Midas: www.midas.com

USA Today: www.usatoday.com

U.S. Postal Service: www.usps.com

Merrill Lynch: www.ml.com

Merck & Company: www.merck.com

QUESTIONS

1. Describe what is meant by the phrase "operations for competitive advantage."

2. To be successful, organizations should focus on customer requirements. List the ways operations can help to satisfy customer requirements, and discuss each briefly.

3. How can the following attributes help an organization achieve competitive advantage?
   a. Flexibility
   b. Productivity
   c. Quality
   d. Time
   e. E-business

4. Why are the following business processes important?
   a. Strategy development
   b. Product development
   c. Systems to produce goods and services
   d. Order fulfillment

5. How and why are operations strategically important?

6. How can an organization link corporate strategy and operations? Describe the process.

7. How is the changing global environment altering the dimensions of competition?

8. Describe the role of computer and information technology in improving operations.

9. Describe some ways that manufacturing operations can use computer and information technology to gain competitive advantage.

10. Describe some ways that service operations can use computer and information technology to gain competitive advantage. Why are these means different from those used by manufacturers?

INTERNET QUESTIONS

11. Examine the Midas Web site and the Genoa Ford Web site, and describe how they have used this tool to their advantage. How do these companies differ in the use of their Web site? How does it help them to execute their strategies?

12. Using the Internet, locate a company that is implementing computer-integrated manufacturing. Summarize the company's approach in one paragraph. In a second paragraph,

describe how the company used one or more of these tools to improve operations. Provide a copy of the information downloaded from the Internet.

13. Using the Internet, locate a company that is implementing information technology for competitive advantage. Summarize the company's approach in one paragraph. In a second paragraph, describe how the company used one or more information technology tools to improve operations. Provide a copy of the information downloaded from the Internet.

14. Visit the Modine Manufacturing Web site and try to determine the company's manufacturing strategy. Does its manufacturing strategy fit with the overall strategy of the firm?

CHAPTER 3

Enhancing Productivity: A Key to Success

LEARNING OBJECTIVES

After completing this chapter, you should be able to:

1. Define productivity.
2. Describe why productivity is the key to an increasing standard of living.
3. Discuss how the relationship between productivity and the nature of work has changed over time.
4. Explain labor, capital, and material productivity.
5. Calculate productivity in single and multiple factor cases.
6. Discuss important trade-offs among the factors of productivity.
7. Explain the relationship between wage rate and productivity.
8. Describe ways to enhance productivity.

INTRODUCTION

Productivity is a term that is mentioned often in the news. It is one of those terms that we believe is important, but we are not sure why. Productivity is often associated with increasing efficiency and lowering costs, which have positive connotations. In fact, increasing productivity is essential for improving living standards.

Earlier, **productivity** was defined as the ratio of the outputs achieved from an activity to the inputs consumed to make those outputs.

$$\text{Productivity} = \frac{\text{output}}{\text{input}}$$

That definition, while accurate, does not convey the central role that productivity and productivity improvements have in determining our standard of living. To understand this impact, imagine that you and six of your friends are stranded on an island, completely cut off from outside contact. The island has abundant natural resources. The immediate problems are getting fresh water to drink and gathering fruits and vegetables to eat. Appropriate shelter and clothing come next. The amount of water the seven of you have to drink (the output) depends upon how much effort (the input) you place on locating, collecting, transporting, and storing it. As you become better at it—that is, gathering an adequate supply of water with less effort—you have more time for gathering food, building shelters, and making clothes. For example, rather than going to the stream or well whenever you need a drink of water, you could build buckets and barrels to transport and store large amount of water easily and quickly. Eventually, as you build shelters, you might design the roof so it collects rainwater and funnels it to a water barrel. This system substantially reduces the effort needed to collect water, which may provide more time for other activities, such as growing a large variety of food, building transportation devices, and devising forms of entertainment.

As the seven castaways become more productive, they meet their basic needs (outputs) with less time and effort (input). This provides free time, which can be used to create new products, develop better ways to make existing products, and enjoy leisure activities. Put in the simplest terms, the seven castaways can only consume what they produce. The more they produce, the more they have to consume.

UNDERSTANDING PRODUCTIVITY

As we advance from an island economy to a twenty-first century economy, the concept of productivity does not change significantly. Productivity still measures our ability to produce goods and services compared to the inputs or resources used in the process. The primary difference is that most work in our economy is done by groups of people working in organizations. Early in the book, we stated that organizations exist to meet the needs of society that people working alone cannot. It is through these organizations that we achieve the cooperation and coordination to produce the array of services and goods consumed each day. First, organizations allow individuals to specialize in work, such as production, engineering, and sales. Second, they support the development and implementation of technology and automation to achieve greater productivity in operations. Consider this important third point. Because organizations provide the mechanism to coordinate work toward a common set of goals, the productivity of these efforts is also important. So, examining and redesigning organizational processes and activities is another source of productivity improvement.

Productivity improvements are discussed later. For now, consider the following examples.

1. *Specialization*—Product design for life insurance requires an estimate of life expectancy. This effort is critical to setting the terms and conditions of the policy, including the premium. Actuaries are statisticians who specialize in making this estimate. Their productivity (ability to make the estimate quickly and accurately) is greatly enhanced by specialization. They are well trained in the techniques required to do the job. A general manager, sales manager, or accountant working for the life insurance company would require significantly more time and effort to do the same work, and the estimate would probably be much less accurate.

2. *Technology and Automation*—At most universities, students can pay fees via the Internet or over the telephone rather than standing in line at the cashier's office. Not only is this more convenient for the student (improves the student's productivity), but it also increases the productivity of the workforce at the university. From the university's perspective, each transaction that shifts from paying in person to paying via the Internet or telephone reduces the amount of time university employees spend accepting the payment and entering information into the computer system. This presents an opportunity to cut costs and to do more value-added work.

3. *Process Redesign*—In many organizations, marketing and sales are responsible for gathering information about customers and their orders. If a customer makes a request that requires specially processing (such as a special finish on a piece of steel or a major change to a software module), that information is relayed from the customer through sales to the people that do the work. Changing the process so the customer can communicate directly with the people doing the work increases productivity for all participants.

EXAMPLE

Sometimes, process improvements involve working across organizations. As an example, retailers are working with suppliers to develop innovative ways to improve the replenishment process and reduce the resources devoted to manage this relationship.

Procter & Gamble (P&G) supplies Wal-Mart with disposable diapers, a bulky, inexpensive, high sales volume and low profit margin commodity, so Wal-Mart must keep inventory low and product availability high. To accomplish this, Wal-Mart has fundamentally changed its replenishment process. Rather than placing orders with P&G, Wal-Mart provides sales data on a store-by-store basis. It is P&G's responsibility to track inventory, schedule production, and deliver the diapers.

How does this shifting of responsibility improve the process? P&G gets sales data from Wal-Mart each day. P&G uses the data, along with orders from other customers, to schedule its production processes more effectively and generate orders for its suppliers more quickly. P&G can more easily balance its production process to reduce spikes in production, which lead to higher costs through the need for overtime production and the like. P&G suppliers, in turn, can improve their response time and reduce their in-process inventory. As this responsibility shifts, overall costs decline, product availability increases, and the amount of communication and interaction at the boundaries between organizations is reduced.

Is Money More Important than Productivity?

In improving the standard of living, productivity is more important than money because productivity determines the output while money measures the value of the output. In essence, money is a way to keep score for organizations and individuals. Look back at the castaway example. Suppose the castaways landed on the island with $1 billion each in U.S. currency or, if you prefer, gold. The money does not create a single glass of water nor one bit of food. It is only through specialization of labor, automation, and technology that productivity can be improved and the wealth of society can be increased.

Initially, the economy would probably use a barter system in which the castaway gathering water would trade water for food. As the economy grows in complexity, a currency may be used to set the value of goods and services because bartering can be cumbersome. Suppose a currency is in place, and it is based on the gold that they brought with them. Now, the castaways find more gold on the island. So, each castaway now has twice as much gold and wants to buy more goods and services. The immediate impact is to increase the price for items because the quantity of goods and services has not changed. There would be no increase in the goods and services available unless productivity is improved or productivity is held constant and the castaways work more hours.

The key point is whether or not more gold is found, the castaways could do either of these activities, increase productivity or increase the number of hours worked. If the island economy develops into a capitalistic economy, income for each individual would be determined by the value of the work they do, as well as the balance between supply and demand.

So, if medical care is judged to be more valuable than education, and supply and demand are in balance, then doctors would make more than teachers.

Productivity and the Nature of Work

Many of us think that productivity applies exclusively or primarily to the blue-collar workforce. We tend to think of the number of laptop computers produced by workers on the assembly line or the amount of paper produced in the mill as key productivity data. While the productivity of blue-collar workers is important, blue-collar workers represent a small and declining portion of the workforce in developed countries.

During the last century, there was a substantial shift in the nature of work. Early in the twentieth century, nearly 80 percent of the workforce in the United States performed manual work, with the balance doing intellectual work, such as designing, planning, and managing. Today, that percentage has reversed. In addition, about 75 percent of the workforce in the United States is employed in service organizations. Of those employed in manufacturing, many work in management, sales, and other staff activities, such as quality control and engineering. Like the seven castaways, the productivity of everyone is important because each impacts the living standard of all. Because a large portion of our workforce does intellectual work, its impact on our living standards is very important.

Exhibit 3.1 presents some examples of people doing intellectual work, key measures of their productivity, and possible methods to improve that productivity.

Productivity in Manufacturing versus Service Firms

Part of the shift from an economy dependent on manual work to an economy dependent upon intellectual work is explained by a change from a manufacturing- to service-based

EXHIBIT 3.1   Productivity Growth Rate per Hour for Nonfarm Business

Worker	Activity	Measure	Method of Improvement
University faculty	Educate students and/or educate them better	Student credit hours taught. Problems with this measure are that it does not take into account what students have learned or other duties of faculty, including curriculum design, research, and service.	■ Increasing class size leads to more student credit hours ■ Assigning more sections per faculty also leads to more student credit hours ■ Distance learning provides access to education that might not otherwise be available ■ Innovative teaching methods can improve the quality and/or the quantity of what is learned
Postal worker	Oversee the operation of an automatic sorting machine	Number of pieces of mail sorted in an hour	■ Equipment improvements that speed up the sorting process ■ Job training
Case worker for children services	Manages the care of children in foster homes	Number of cases under management at any point in time. Problems with this measure are that it does not consider the degree of difficulty of the cases, or the quality of the service provided.	■ Information systems, including databases that support care ■ Communication technology that gives access to foster parents, service providers, and support services

economy. One problem presented by this shift is that productivity gains in the service sector have lagged behind gains in the manufacturing sector. Several explanations have been advanced to explain this lag, including ineffective measures for service sector productivity, fear of job loss by manufacturing workers, which motivates them to work harder and smarter, and macroeconomic factors, such as the low savings rate.

Biema and Greenwald contend that the problem is services sector managers who have not focused energetically and intelligently on putting existing technologies, the labor force, and capital stock to work. They cite examples from leading-edge service companies that have achieved dramatic improvements in productivity while other firms within the same industry have lagged. In many cases, these competing companies use the same basic technology, pay the same wage rates, and operate under the same basic labor agreement. For example, Northwestern Mutual has a processing cost of 6.3 cents for each dollar of premium collected from its policyholders while its competitors costs range from 15 to 20 cents. It is logical to argue that these companies have not managed their resources and technology effectively. U.S. West's cost per telephone access line declined by 18.0 percent over a four-year period while New York Telephone's costs increased by 6.2 percent over the same period.

The Quality Condition

While the importance of quality may be obvious, it is worth a brief comment. Productivity calculations are based on the assumption that quality levels are maintained. If an organization produces more output with the same level of resources, but the quality of the output is lower, then productivity may not increase. If you produce more computer software, but the software is defective and must be corrected, then you may have gained very little. In fact, productivity may have actually been reduced. If a lower quality product reaches the consumer, and the product's value to the consumer is reduced or the consumer must spend additional resources to prepare the product for use, productivity is certainly affected.

Conversely, quality may be another way to boost productivity. If firms find ways to make a product of higher quality, using the same or fewer resources, then productivity increases because the output has greater value. Following the software example, if a firm buys new software development tools that are easier to use and result in fewer errors, the productivity of its programmers and analysts increases.

ASSESSING PRODUCTIVITY

To calculate productivity, it is essential to define and measure the inputs and the outputs for the process or activity. In the simplest cases, measurement is a trivial problem. If we have a manufacturing operation making a single product on an automatic machine, calculating the productivity of that machine is simple. We measure output over a given period of time. It is usually better to measure a relatively long period of time, days or weeks rather than minutes or hours. The reason is that the outputs might be greatly affected by a short-term, random event, such as a machine breakdown.

PROBLEM   If the automatic machine can make 200,000 roofing nails in 40 hours, then productivity of the machine is 5,000 nails per hour.

$$\text{Machine Productivity} = \frac{200,000 \text{ roofing nails}}{40 \text{ machine hours}}$$

$$\text{Machine Productivity} = 5,000 \text{ roofing nails per machine hour}$$

This data point becomes a benchmark that the firm seeks to improve. Suppose the firm invests in a new piece of equipment that automatically feeds metal to the machine so the machine can run faster. Now, the machine is able to produce 210,000 nails in the same 40-hour period. Productivity has increased from 5,000 nails per hour to 5,250. Productivity has increased by 5 percent. Change in productivity is the productivity after the new equipment minus the productivity before the new equipment. Make sure that you keep the sign of that number so you can tell if productivity increases or decreases.

$$\text{Percent Increase in Productivity} = \frac{\text{Change in Productivity}}{\text{Productivity Prior to Change}}$$

$$\text{Percent Increase in Productivity} = \frac{5,250 - 5,000}{5,000}(100)$$

$$\text{Percent Increase in Productivity} = 5 \text{ percent}$$

The Inputs and Outputs of Productivity

While this example illustrates the method for calculating productivity, it does not consider that most operations have more than one input and more than one output. In an economic sense, the inputs are:

1. labor as managers, workers, and externally purchased services,
2. capital for land, facilities, and equipment, and
3. materials, including energy requirements.

The importance of these factors may vary widely for companies producing different products. For example, steel mills require large amounts of energy while Children Services, a social service agency, uses very little. In a steel plant, the significant inputs would include managers, laborers, land, facilities, equipment, energy, and raw materials. The inputs for Children Services would be management and case workers primarily. The investment in land and facilities would be small compared to labor costs. For Children Services, equipment investments might be relevant for information technology. Energy and raw material costs would be very small. Except for small quantities of supplies, such as paper clips and pens, material costs would be zero.

The outputs can be more difficult to define and measure. For example, how would we measure the productivity of a fast-food restaurant? Would we measure it in terms of customers served per hour? In that case, a problem occurs because customers may order different things. Measuring output as the number of items sold can also be misleading because these restaurants sell various items (such as drinks, sandwiches, and ice cream) that have different values.

This discussion has raised two important issues that can complicate how productivity is measured. (1) How can multiple inputs with different economic values be included? In the fast-food example, how does the productivity of labor relate to the productivity of capital or materials? (2) How can multiple outputs with different economic values be included? Continuing the fast-food example, a pizza shop may produce hot submarine sandwiches and bread sticks. How does it value those outputs compared to a pizza? Also, there are different sized pizzas with different toppings. In cases where there are multiple inputs and/or outputs with different values, dollars can be used to measure both inputs and outputs.

Labor Productivity   Labor is probably the most obvious input in the productivity equation. If fact, some businesses are concerned only with measuring labor productivity because it is easy to calculate and many managers believe it is one factor under their direct control. For many service operations, labor is by far the largest input. In pure service operations, such as banks, hospitals, and universities, labor is often 70 percent and more of total costs. For manufacturing firms, however, it is important to realize that direct labor usually accounts for a small percent of total input costs, 10 percent or less. If indirect labor, management costs, and outside services are added to direct labor costs, the total is usually below 50 percent of the cost of all inputs. Some service operations may be able to "get by" with labor productivity only, but a broader perspective on productivity may be relevant.

Probably the simplest way to determine labor productivity is to measure output per labor hour. This approach does not consider variations in pay rates among workers. To cope with this problem, many companies use labor costs as a measure of inputs. The equation for labor productivity is:

$$\text{Labor Productivity} = \frac{\text{units produced (or the value of units produced)}}{\text{labor hours (or labor cost)}}$$

The equation for any other individual factor of productivity would differ only by its title and its divisor. For example, material productivity would use material quantity or material costs as the divisor.

Capital Productivity   Another major component of the production is capital, which usually includes all money invested in land, facilities, and equipment as well as working capital, such as inventory. Capital productivity can increase when firms invest in new facilities and equipment that increase output to an even greater extent. Capital productivity can also be increased if a company can produce the same level of output as previously but reduce its inventory level or other working capital requirements. A word of caution, many firms invest in new facilities and equipment in order to reduce labor costs. So, the benefits in making a capital investment may be observed as greatly expanded labor productivity. In fact, capital productivity may actually decline. These trade-offs are discussed later.

Service and manufacturing firms often have very different capital requirements. Pure service operations have relatively small investments in capital. For example, insurance companies have office space, furniture, information systems, and working capital, which represent a small part of their input costs. Hybrid services operations, such as retail, often have major investments in retail outlets, distribution centers, and inventory in the system. Manufacturers usually have very large capital outlays to build production facilities.

Material Productivity   Materials and energy are often critical inputs to manufacturing processes, but may be insignificant in most pure service operations. For manufacturing concerns, materials usually represent more than 50 percent of the input costs. For universities, materials are purchased in the form of office and laboratory supplies. For hospitals, medicine, linens, and food for the cafeteria are the primary materials. For universities and hospitals, these represent a very small part of the inputs to the organization.

Important Trade-Offs   The ideal situation would be to increase productivity either by increasing output without increasing any input or by maintaining the level of output while decreasing all inputs. Of course, this situation is an ideal and difficult to achieve. In most cases, companies must be content with trade-offs among the various inputs in hopes of achieving increases in overall productivity, called multiple factor productivity. In this case, some individual factors of productivity may decrease while others increase.

- *Trading Capital for Labor.* For thousands of years, we have traded capital for labor. These trade-offs date back to the time when our ancestors first began using tools to make life easier. The wheel and axle allowed our early ancestors to carry heavy loads for greater distances. Instead of making many trips to move a certain load, a person could make one trip in a wheeled cart. This trade-off resulted in substantial productivity increases for centuries to come. This is why research and development activities are important for economic health and improving living standards. To develop the wheel and axle, someone or a group of people had to take the time to research the concept, create a design, build and test prototypes, and put the idea into production. This investment required a shift of resources from the labor associated with doing work to research and development. This meant that someone had to take a significant risk, but the benefits have been tremendous. The impact of this investment on living standards can be seen everywhere we look.

Trade-offs involving capital and labor have focused primarily on automating activities previously performed by people. In the construction business, trucks and bulldozers move large quantities of dirt and other materials on construction sites. In the automotive industry many boring, unpleasant, or dangerous tasks are performed by automation. In retail operation, checkout systems are becoming totally automated as customers check themselves out by scanning their items and paying by credit card or cash. The result is high capital costs and lower labor costs and greater overall output, which generate an overall productivity increase.

Some people would be concerned about the loss of cashier jobs. While these jobs are lost, jobs have been created to design the new checkout equipment, develop the software, manufacturing the equipment, and install the system. At the same time, our productivity increased, and the cost of doing business declined. New better paying jobs were created, and the economy continues to grow.

- *Trading Capital for Material or Energy.* It also has become common to make capital investments that improve material and/or energy productivity. The concept and issues are similar to those discussed in the prior section. For example, a plastic injection molding company produces parts for Hewlett Packard's laser printers. By investing in new injection molding equipment that reduces scrap, the company can produce the same number of plastic parts (output) from a smaller number of plastic pellets (inputs). In addition to leading to an increase in material productivity, the investment also reduces the amount of energy consumed because substantial energy is used to melt the pellets prior to injecting them into the molding machine. Because fewer pellets are used to make a given number of plastic parts, less energy is used and energy productivity increased. It is not always the case that both improvements can be achieved with a single investment, but it is not uncommon.

- *Substituting Materials for Labor.* In some cases, there may be advantages in spending more for materials in order to achieve a reduction in labor costs. Sometimes it makes sense to have the supplier do extra work, which is reflected in the price of the materials. The reasons for doing this may be to reduce labor costs or processing time for the manufacturer. Outsourcing work is becoming a common practice in both manufacturing and service operations. In the assembly of consumer electronics, it is a common practice for the supplier to produce the entire screen and mask subassembly that fits on the front of a television. The cost of the component purchased from the supplier is higher, but the in-house assembly costs are greatly reduced. The net impact for suppliers and manufacturers is greater productivity and lower costs. Many service operations will buy supplies that cost more, but increase the productivity of their workforce. In the medical field, more and more disposable medical supplies are being purchased to avoid, in part, their collection and cleaning.

Multiple Factor Productivity

To cope with the trade-offs that can occur when productivity improvement efforts are made, multiple factor productivity must be considered. **Multiple factor productivity** accommodates more than one input factor and more than one output factor when calculating overall productivity. For example, if the owners of a pizza shop want to increase the productivity of the ovens, they might consider decreasing the time that a pizza spends in the oven. To compensate for that, the heat in the oven is increased. A single factor productivity calculation based on oven utilization would show an increase in capital productivity because more pizzas are moving through the oven in a given period of time. However, there would also be an increase in energy consumption, which would not be captured. With multiple factor productivity, the outputs can be measured either in dollars or the number of units produced, provided the units all have approximately the same value.

$$\text{Multiple Factor Productivity} = \frac{\text{output (units produced or the value of those units)}}{\text{labor} + \text{capital} + \text{materials} + \text{energy} + \text{other (dollars)}}$$

Multiple Factor Productivity = 600 applications/$5,520

Multiple Factor Productivity = 0.109 applications/dollar of input

---

PROBLEM

Now, we can evaluate the following situation. Liberty Insurance Company processes applications forms. The average output in a week is 600 claims. Currently the staff includes six full time employees who work forty hours per week and earn $18 per hour including fringe benefits. Management has invested in computer technology, which has a weekly cost of $1,200. Materials and energy are not used in significant amounts. What is the productivity of the application process?

$$\text{Multiple Factor Productivity} = \frac{600 \text{ applications}}{(6 \text{ employees}) (40 \text{ hrs/wk})(\$18/\text{hr}) + 1{,}200}$$

In this case, the units of productivity are applications per dollar of input costs. That does have some meaning, but the real value of this number is comparisons with productivity when factors of production change. Suppose Liberty decides to invest in additional computer equipment that will drive the weekly cost of information technology to $1,800. One of the applications evaluators is retiring and will not be replaced. The remaining five processors should be able to do 650 applications per week with the new technology. What is the impact on productivity?

$$\text{Multiple Factor Productivity} = \frac{650 \text{ applications}}{(5 \text{ employees})(40 \text{ hrs/wk})(\$18/\text{hr}) + 1{,}800}$$

Multiple Factor Productivity = 650 applications/$5,400

Multiple Factor Productivity = 0.120 applications/dollar of input

With the new investment, productivity increased from 0.109 to 0.120 applications per dollar of input costs. The gain in productivity is 10.1 percent, which is a substantial gain. To give you a basis for comparison, 3 to 4 percent per year would be considered good productivity growth for a developed country.

$$\text{Percent Increase in Productivity} = \frac{\text{Change in Productivity}}{\text{Productivity Prior to Change}}(100)$$

$$\text{Percent Increase in Productivity} = \frac{0.120 - 0.109}{0.109}(100)$$

$$\text{Percent Increase in Productivity} = 10.1 \text{ percent}$$

PRODUCTIVITY: WHERE DO WE STAND

Over time, productivity growth in the U.S. economy is somewhat uneven. There was strong growth in the 1960s followed by low and in some cases negative growth in the late 1970s and early 1980s. See Exhibit 3.2. As the 1990s began, productivity growth began to accelerate. In the first two quarters of 2002, U.S. nonfarm productivity grew 8.6 and 1.5 percent per hour, respectively. This productivity growth is often attributed to the effective use of information technology in manufacturing and service operations and to the just-in-time efforts in manufacturing. The growth rate in manufacturing productivity in the last twenty years is even more dramatic. See Exhibit 3.3. In the first two quarters of 2002, U.S. manufacturing productivity grew 9.7 and 4.3 percent per hour, respectively. As explained later, productivity growth is often an indicator of expanding output and profits as well as an impending economic recovery

Increasing productivity tends to drive business performance. As organizations achieve more output with the same consumption of resources, the economy grows. Think back to the island example, more is produced so there is more to consume. At the same time, profits of the firm expand even if the selling price of the product does not increase. The cost

EXHIBIT 3.2 Productivity Growth Rate per Hour for Nonfarm Business (1962–2001)							
Year	Annual Percent Increase	Year	Annual Percent Increase	Year	Annual Percent Increase	Year	Annual Percent Increase
1962	4.5	1972	3.1	1982	-0.6	1992	3.7
1963	3.5	1973	-1.6	1983	4.5	1993	0.5
1964	4.2	1974	2.7	1984	2.2	1994	1.3
1965	3.1	1975	3.7	1985	1.3	1995	0.9
1966	3.5	1976	1.5	1986	3.0	1996	2.5
1967	1.7	1977	1.3	1987	0.4	1997	2.0
1968	3.1	1978	-0.4	1988	1.3	1998	2.6
1969	0.1	1979	-0.3	1989	0.8	1999	2.4
1970	1.5	1980	1.2	1990	1.1	2000	2.9
1971	4.2	1981	-0.6	1991	1.2	2001	1.1

EXHIBIT 3.3 Productivity Growth Rate per Hour for Manufacturing (1982–2001)			
Year	Annual Percent Increase	Year	Annual Percent Increase
1982	5.0	1992	5.3
1983	3.4	1993	1.9
1984	3.6	1994	3.0
1985	3.6	1995	3.8
1986	2.4	1996	3.5
1987	2.8	1997	4.2
1988	2.1	1998	4.9
1989	0.1	1999	5.1
1990	2.9	2000	4.1
1991	2.3	2001	0.9

structure of the firm (at least the labor portion) does not change, and there is more revenue from increasing sales. So, bottom line profits can expand dramatically. For example,
as Microsoft finds ways to produce and distribute more copies of its software while holding the resources used in these activities constant, it will generate greater revenue and
profit. Even if the selling price declines somewhat, the total revenue and profits usually
increase because more units are available for sale.

In many cases, productivity improvements are driven by investments in technology,
and these investments drive economic growth. For example, as retail companies such as
Sears invest in Internet applications for sales transactions, repair parts and service, and
advertising, demand for technology from companies such as Cisco Systems, Intel, and Dell
accelerates. As the U.S. economy continues to shift away from manufacturing toward services, investments in information technology for service operations become more important for productivity growth and economic expansion.

While it is clear that productivity is growing in the United States, how does it compare
to other countries? From 1990 to 2000, manufacturing productivity in the United States
has grown nearly as fast as France and faster than Canada, Germany, Italy, Japan, and the
United Kingdom. These six countries and the United States are the G-7 countries that meet
to discuss global economic issues. Exhibit 3.4 shows the productivity index for these countries with 1992 as the base year. Productivity improvements during that time show that the
United States is near the head of the pack.

Productivity and Wage Rates

Generally, wage rates and productivity are positively correlated. Positively correlated
means that organizations with high productivity can afford to pay their workers better
wages because their workers produce more output. This correlation has implications for
companies that are selecting locations for their operations. A country with a low wage rates
does not necessarily have low unit labor costs because workers in the country may have low
productivity. For example, if you were asked to move a pile of dirt from one point to
another and you were given a shovel and a wheelbarrow to do the work, your productivity would be relatively low. On the other hand, if you were given a bulldozer and proper
training, your productivity would be much higher. As the operator of a bulldozer, you
could be paid a higher wage because you do more work. As you see, wage rate is not the
sole determinant of unit labor cost. The other important ingredient is productivity or the
number of units produced.

Let's put some numbers with the dirt-moving problem. The person with the wheelbarrow and shovel is paid $2 per hour and can move 1 cubic yard of dirt in an hour. The
bulldozer operator makes $18 per hour and can move 20 cubic yard in an hour. The labor

EXHIBIT 3.4

Output per Hour in
Manufacturing

Year	United States	Canada	France	Germany	Italy	Japan	United Kingdom
1992	100.0	100.0	100.0	100.0	100.0	100.0	100.0
1993	102.1	105.8	100.6	101.4	101.7	101.7	103.9
1994	107.3	110.8	108.2	104.9	103.3	103.3	107.1
1995	113.8	112.4	113.9	108.0	111.0	111.0	104.9
1996	117.0	109.7	114.6	108.1	116.1	116.1	103.8
1997	121.3	113.5	121.7	109.9	121.0	121.0	105.2
1998	126.5	113.1	127.7	110.0	121.2	121.2	107.0
1999	135.3	116.0	132.7	109.9	126.9	126.9	111.6
2000	142.9	118.4	142.5	113.0	134.1	134.1	118.0
2001	145.6	116.1	146.3	115.0	128.1	128.1	119.8

cost to move the dirt by wheelbarrow is $2 per cubic yard ($2/hr.)/(1 cubic yard/hr.). The labor cost to move the dirt by bulldozer is $0.90 per cubic yard ($18/hr.)/(20 cubic yard/hr.). The owner of the construction company is able to pay much higher wages and achieve lower costs because the investment in equipment and training boosted productivity dramatically. Even after paying the higher wage, the owner is able to save enough labor cost to pay for the bulldozer, buy fuel to operate it, and pay to train the employee.

How does this hypothetical problem work in the real world? Among developed countries, the United States has a competitive unit labor cost when currency differences are ignored. Exhibit 3.5 shows the unit labor cost in manufacturing of the G-7 countries. The base year for the index is 1992, which means that the United States has experienced a decline in unit labor cost in manufacturing since 1992 of 8.6 percent. During this period, average hourly compensation in the United States has increased significantly, but this increase has been offset by an even larger increase in productivity.

When currency fluctuations are considered, the United States is at a significant disadvantage. Since 1992, the strong U.S. dollar has, in effect, increased the cost of U.S. produced goods to overseas consumers. With the exception of Japan, the strong U.S. dollar has boosted the cost competitiveness of our G-7 partners. See the third column in Exhibit 3.5.

In developing countries like China and Mexico, the impact of the strong U.S. dollar is further complicated by hourly wage rates that are extremely low. Even if U.S. productivity is twice or three times the productivity in these countries, their wage rate is often one-tenth or less of the rate in the United States This fact makes it very difficult for the United States to be price competitive for work that requires limited skill and/or technology.

Impact of Productivity Improvements on the Workforce

Some people would argue that productivity improvements such the one described in the previous section take jobs away from workers. Their claim is based on the fact that the construction company now employs one bulldozer operator who does the work of twenty laborers. While this is true, it is only part of the story. Remember the castaways; they can only consume what they produce. The same is true for our society. If we built highways by moving dirt with wheelbarrows and shovels, we would not have had enough labor to build the vast interstate systems and other road networks that we use regularly. In addition, they would have cost much more than we could afford. Productivity improvements, such as earth moving equipment, are essential for designing and building more goods and services at a lower cost. They increase our living standard.

The second point is that the net job loss is not nineteen jobs because new jobs are created to design and manufacture the bulldozer. Jobs are also created to sell and service the equipment. Workers and equipment are needed to transport the bulldozer from one job to another. Behind the scenes, new jobs are created, and most of these jobs require higher levels of education than moving dirt with a wheelbarrow. Will this substitution generate enough new jobs

EXHIBIT 3.5 Unit Labor Costs in Manufacturing	Country	Index of Unit Labor Cost (National Currency Basis)	Index of Unit Labor Cost (U.S. Dollar Basis)
	United States	91.4	91.4
	Canada	101.5	79.2
	France	86.5	62.5
	Germany	106.6	76.2
	Italy	115.4	65.7
	Japan	89.8	93.6
	United Kingdom	117.2	95.5

to make up for the nineteen lost? The question is easier to understand if we take a macro view of the situation. Society would not have a net productivity gain if the same or more work is required to design, build, sell, service, etc. the bulldozer than was saved by the substitution of capital (the bulldozer) for labor. Society benefits because we can do more work with fewer total resources. Also, remember that the remaining bulldozer operator is paid substantially more than wheelbarrow operators. The jobs created to engineer, manufacture, and sell the bulldozer are also likely to carry a much higher salary than the wheelbarrow operator. Those high wages must be covered by the savings generated from increasing productivity. As a result, we still have several displaced workers. What happens to them? As discussed in Chapter 2, these people are available to create new products that further expand our output. Just as advances in agriculture created the workforce for the factories of the industrial revolution, so these people have the potential to create new business opportunities.

Productivity and Leisure

It is not always the case that productivity increases result in more output. In the United States, as productivity increased over time, some of the benefits have been taken as less work time and more leisure time. In the United States the "nominal" workweek has stood at forty hours for several decades. In the first half of the twentieth century, however, the typical workweek was much longer—fifty to sixty hours or more with a six day workweek at many firms. During that period, holiday and vacation time were substantially less than they are today. Dramatic increases in productivity allowed the U.S. economy to experience an expanding living standard and a contracting workweek.

Today, many countries in Europe have shorter workweeks and more generous vacations than are available in the United States. This choice has implication for the people in these countries. If they want to work fewer hours, there is less for them to consume, unless they can find ways to increase productivity even more.

ENHANCING PRODUCTIVITY

Productivity increases sound wonderful, but the real issue is how to achieve them. Some managers view productivity improvements narrowly and attribute improvements to attention to the details of the production process. For example, changing the height of a desk so that a secretary has easy access to the word processing keyboard may increase productivity. This adjustment can be an important contribution in eliminating physical stress and reducing fatigue, which could lead to greater output. This narrow view, however, is far from the whole picture.

Productivity is affected by:

- Issues related to the structure of operations, such as the number, size, location, and capacity of the facilities providing the service or producing the good.
- The equipment and methods used in the activities.
- The detailed analysis of the individual jobs and activities.

The first issue is not as simple as saying that fewer, bigger facilities will result in higher productivity and lower costs, although that tends to be true and is what conventional economic theory tells us. It is matching these characteristics to the needs of the customer. For example, health-care productivity could be increased and quality could be enhanced if hospitals specialize. Currently, many hospitals are merging or forming alliances. These unions permit one hospital to specialize in some areas, such as pediatrics and obstetrics, while the other hospital specializes in other areas, such as neurology and psychiatry. In this way, they avoid duplicating expensive equipment, highly trained staff, and administrative overhead. The volume of patients using a particular service increases substantially because patients that once used services at either hospital now are treated at one hospital. The cost of the service declines, and the quality improves.

EXAMPLE

Shouldice Hospital in Ontario has specialized in the repair of hernias since 1945, when Dr. Shouldice needed to cope with a large number of hernia cases and a shortage of doctors and medical facilities. Specialization allowed the hospital and the doctors to find innovative ways to perform the surgery. The hospital reduced resource requirements and increased productivity.

The objective of the surgery is not only successful repair of the hernias, but also as little discomfort as possible for the patients so they can return to their normal life quickly. Patients frequently return to work in a few days; the average total time off work is only eight days.

The hospital's success has long been the benchmark for the medical profession internationally. The hospital has repaired more than 270,000 hernias with a greater than 99% success rate. Shouldice patients actually walk out of the operating room, and their postoperative recovery is fast. By the following morning, patients are participating in a gentle exercise program along with other patients. The process is fast and effective for the hospital and for the patient.

The equipment and methods (second level) used to provide the service or produce the good can also have a substantial impact on productivity. Suppose an employee were asked to move one million gallons of water from one point in a facility to another. The employee would have different levels of productivity if given a tablespoon, a bucket, or an electric pump and a hose. This rather simple example illustrates countless similar situations in organizations. The equipment and methods should fit the job. The pump and hose would not be appropriate for moving small amounts of water to make coffee at the corner restaurant.

EXAMPLE

The Segway Human Transporter (HT) is an example of a technology that could revolutionize work and dramatically increase productivity. It is the first self-balancing, electric-powered transporter and is designed to enhance the productivity of people by increasing the distance they can travel and the amount they can carry. It uses electronic gyroscopes for balance and microprocessors to "measure" the rider's intent (leaning forward or leaning backward) for forward and backward motion. It can travel at speeds up to 12.5 miles per hour. This innovation was inspired by Dean Kamen and a group of talented engineers and designers who approached old problems from new angles. The successful application of Segway HTs is currently under study.

National Park Service (NPS) staff have used the Segway HT to patrol Grand Canyon National Park. In this second NPS trial of the transporter, rangers, interpreters, and supervisors use the units on the South Rim of the Grand Canyon. The first trial demonstrated that productivity could be significantly increased and the mobility and accessibility of NPS staff could be enhanced with minimal environmental impact.

The U.S. Postal Service has purchased 40 Segway HTs and has evaluated them in a variety of terrains and climates. Mail delivery is one of the world's most demanding pedestrian-intensive businesses, and the Segway HT may lessen the physical demands while increasing productivity. In the

Photo provided courtesy of
Segway LLC

first phase of testing, the device reduced the physical stress of carrying up to thirty-five pounds of mail and decreased the time used to walk between delivery addresses.

Disney Cruise Line ships are the first location in the world where guests can ride and experience the Segway HT. The device can be experienced firsthand by guests 16 and older aboard the Disney Magic and Disney Wonder cruise ships. At other times, the Segway HT is used by the ship's captain and officers to travel around the 964-foot ship efficiently.

The Toledo Zoo is the first zoo in the world to deploy the Segway HT. The zoo expects to use the devices for security patrols and maintenance as well as moving animal-care specialists and managers around the grounds quickly. Management expects to increase productivity and provide better service.

Detailed analysis of individual jobs and activities (third level) focuses on making people more productive. Analysis might suggest a better way to do work. For example, most home dishwashers have a removable silverware rack so the rack can be moved to a convenient location and the silverware can be easily removed. When given this task, most people will use only their dominant hand. With only a small amount of training, a person can be taught to use both hands. This enables the task to be completed in about 70 percent of the time it takes for a person using only one hand. This may seem like a small improvement. But, think of the billions of tasks performed each day in service and manufacturing firms throughout the world, and visualize the impact of these kinds of improvements on productivity and costs.

This discussion leads to several approaches that can be used separately or in combination to increase productivity.

- *Technology Innovation*—Brings new ideas, methods, and/or equipment to the process of making a product. In banking, the advent of computers and information technology changed the process for reconciling checking account transactions and greatly increased productivity. Using technology in distribution centers and warehouses has enable retailers to increase productivity and reduce costs.

- *Automation*—Substitutes capital for labor. It is different from technological innovation because existing automation is merely applied to a new situation. Using conveyors to move parts between points in a packaging operation can increase productivity. Conveyor technology has been available for decades, but it is constantly finding new applications.

- *Economies of Scale*—Allows firms to increase productivity by making operations larger. Both service and manufacturing operations take advantage of this tactic to improve productivity and lower costs. Consolidation in the banking industry is being driven by the need to spread fixed costs, such as information systems, credit card processing, bank infrastructure, and management, over a broader base of operations. We also see this consolidation occurring in accounting firms, brokerage houses, and credit card companies.

- *Business Process Redesign*—Focuses on the understanding and redesign of processes that exist within and between companies. For example, how can a company streamline its product development process so it creates more and better product ideas in less time than the existing process? The Web site (http://www.wiley.com/college/vonderembse) contains a chapter on business process redesign that describes this process in more detail.

- *Learning and Experience*—Enable firms to achieve productivity improvements because the workforce gains knowledge about the product and work processes. From this knowledge, workers find better ways to organize work. This concept was first applied in the aircraft industry so firms could estimate the cost of future orders. The productivity improvements and the cost reductions were substantial. The Web site (http://www.wiley.com/college/vonderembse) has a supplement to this chapter that describes learning curves.

- *Job Design and Work Measurement*—Enable firms to examine work at a detailed level so that it can be investigated and improved. This examination often occurs at the level of the individual worker or the interface between a worker and a machine. The approach tends to examine individual movement to improve productivity. For example, the kitchen in a fast-food restaurant is laid out so the cook can make items on the menu with ease. This is the same overall objective used in a manufacturing firm to lay out the assembly area to put together a speaker or a keyboard. The Web site (http://www.wiley.com/college/vonderembse) contains a chapter on job design and work measurement that describes this process in more detail.

- *Human Resources*—Make possible productivity improvements without investing in facilities and equipment, buying high-quality materials, redesigning jobs and processes, or even spending for employee training. In many organizations, the rate of production is labor constrained. If labor is motivated to do more work, productivity can increase without additional investments or cost increases. For example, when faculty members sign additional students into their classes, they have increased productivity with no additional costs. When sales managers add another sales territory to their workload, their productivity increases without any increase in costs. Motivation is a powerful tool that can be used to increase productivity in any job that is labor intensive.

TECHNOLOGY AND PRODUCTIVITY IMPROVEMENTS

Developments in technology often drive productivity improvements. As organizations invest in technology, they can reduce time in the system, expand options, and reduce costs. Throughout this book we illustrate how technology is revolutionizing business and operations management by changing everything from the way products are designed to how inventory is managed and controlled. In general, the greatest benefit is in gathering, organizing, analyzing, and presenting data to managers for decision making. Because of the vast capabilities and low cost of computer technology, the amount of information that can be processed and shared is greatly increased. This means that better decisions can be made while taking less time from the people involved. This leads to real productivity increases.

Computer technology makes it possible for suppliers and manufacturers to share data and coordinate design and operating decisions. Better decisions are made faster and with fewer wasted steps and resources. In Chapter 2, we saw the potential impact of information technology on manufacturing performance through computer-aided design, flexible manufacturing, and other computer-based technology.

Information technology allows retail customers to place orders quickly and to verify that suppliers have the product on hand. Computer-based expert systems can make routine, rule-based decisions faster and with fewer errors than people. For example, when ordering product to restock the local clothing store, the computer can quickly scan current stock level, recent sales, and reorder points and make decisions about how much of each item to order. Chapter 2 also described several applications of information technology for service operations.

In spite of recent concerns about the viability of e-commerce, the potential of the Internet to fundamentally change business-to-business and business-to-consumer relationships is staggering. The productivity for distributing digital services, such as music, newspapers, books, and magazines, will be dramatically increased because they can be delivered over the Internet. There are still problems to be resolved, but the potential improvements in productivity are so large that they will be dealt with. Business-to-business relations are already taking advantage of the Internet to manage the flow of information and transactions between firms.

SUMMARY

- Productivity is the ratio of the outputs achieved from an activity to the inputs consumed to make those outputs.

- Productivity is a key to increasing our standard of living. Productivity is more important than money in driving economic growth.

- During the twentieth century, the nature of work shifted from primarily manual to primarily intellectual. As a result, the productivity of managers, designers, and planners is as important, and perhaps more important, than the productivity of blue-collar workers.

- Calculating productivity involves (1) assessing the outputs either by counting the number of outputs or by determining the economic value of the outputs and (2) assessing the inputs by determining their value. Single factor productivity is used when only one input factor changes. Multiple factor productivity is used when more than one input factor changes.

- The primary inputs are labor (managers, workers, and externally purchased services), capital (land, facilities, and equipment), and materials, including energy.

- In many cases, when firms seek productivity improvement, trade-offs between the inputs occur. Managers may be trading capital for labor, capital for energy, or material for labor in order to get an overall increase in productivity.

- Wage rates and productivity are positively correlated. Organizations with high productivity can pay higher wage rates.

- Productivity improvements have two impacts on jobs. First, they tend to shift jobs from hands-on labor to behind-the-scenes labor. The hands-on jobs are usually manual work, and the behind-the-scenes jobs tend to be intellectual work. Second, they free labor to seek opportunities to create new services and goods.

- Enhancing productivity can be done by technology innovation, automation, economy of scale, business process redesign, learning and expertise, job design and work measurement, and human resources.

- Computers and information technology can be applied to improve productivity in manufacturing and service operations.

 Visit our dynamic Web site, http://www.wiley.com/college/vonderembse, for extended chapter material, solved problems, mini-cases, computer software, and Web links.

KEY TERMS

capital productivity   material productivity   multiple factor
labor productivity   productivity   productivity

URLS

Amazon.com: www.Amazon.com

Barnes & Noble: www.bn.com

Citigroup: www.citigroup.com

Segway: www.segway.com

The University of Toledo: www.utoledo.edu

Bureau of Labor Statistics: www.bls.gov/home.htm

Shouldice Hospital: www.shouldice.com/

QUESTIONS

1. Define productivity and describe why it is important.

2. Describe why productivity is more important than money.

3. Explain how the nature of work has changed, and describe how that is affecting productivity.

4. What is the difference between single factor and multiple factor productivity?

5. Describe labor productivity. What are its components?

6. Describe capital productivity. What are its components?

7. Describe material productivity. What are its components?

8. What are the important trade-offs involving the inputs to productivity?

9. How are wage rate and productivity related?

10. What are the impacts of productivity on the workforce?

11. How does quality impact productivity?

12. Describe some ways that productivity can be enhanced.

13. How can computers and information technology increase productivity?

INTERNET QUESTIONS

14. Amazon.com offers a Web site and Internet access for purchasing a variety of products. How could the Web site be changed to increase your productivity? How could it be changed to increase Amazon.com's productivity?

15. Barnes & Nobel offers a Web site and Internet access for purchasing books. How could the Web site be changed to increase your productivity? How could it be changed to increase Barnes & Nobel's productivity?

16. Compare the Amazon.com Web site and the Barnes & Noble Web site. What do they have in common? How are they different?

17. Try finding an out of print book on the Amazon.com Web site. If you cannot think of one, try locating *The Battle of Leyte Gulf* by Adrian Stewart. Describe the process for finding the book, and give the price and delivery time. How easy or difficult was this process?

18. Get on the Web site for your bank. Check your account balance. Can you do transactions over the site? How can the Web site be more useful to you? How does this help the bank's productivity? If your bank does not have a Web site, log on to another bank.

19. Visit the Web site for your university. Can you use it to register for classes? How can the Web site be more useful to you? How does this site help the university's productivity? If your college of university does not have a Web site, log on to another university.

20. The Bureau of Labor Statistics provides a vast amount of data about labor costs and productivity. Visit the Web site, and examine productivity data that compares the United States to other countries. Describe how productivity impacts trade among countries. Provide data from the Web site that illustrates your point.

PROBLEMS

1. A junior accountant working for an accounting firm earned $40,000 last year in wages and benefits. The work this person performed was billed to clients at $200,000 for the year. What is the junior accountant's labor productivity?

2. A certain machine makes various-sized screws that have a market value of $50,000 per year. Materials used to make those screws cost $5,000 per year. The annual cost of owning and operating the screw-making machine are $25,000. What is the productivity of that machine? What is the productivity of the materials? What is the overall productivity?

3. A company that manufactures radios had sales last year of $3,750,000. Total labor costs for the year were $1,500,000, capital costs were $1,275,000, and materials costs were $750,000. What was the company's productivity based on this information?

4. The New City Hospital has kept track of its patient billings and labor costs during the last two years. How has the hospital's labor productivity changed?

	Two Years Ago	Last Year
Total billings	$10,230,000	$12,450,000
Labor costs	4,375,000	5,200,000

5. The Electro-Lite Electronics company has recently automated part of its production process. The labor and capital costs for the last two years are shown below, along with the value added by this process. Compare the productivity of labor and capital for these years.

	Two Years Ago	Last Year
Value added	$1,365,000	$1,425,000
Labor costs	870,000	375,000
Capital costs	160,000	924,000

6. The company mentioned in Problem 3 is considering substituting capital for labor by buying some automated equipment to perform an operation previously done manu-

ally. This new equipment will cost $200,000 per year to own and operate. What must the labor savings be to produce an increase in overall productivity?

7. Michael's Manufacturing wants to determine the overall productivity of its operations. The company has data for a month last year and good current data. The sales price of the product is $40.00, the wage rate including fringe benefits is $18.00 per hour, the resin cost $0.60 per pound, and the energy cost per BTU is $0.50. These costs can be applied to both years. What is the productivity then and now? At what rate is productivity changing?

	Last Year	This Year
Production (units)	2,000	2,150
Labor hours	600	550
Resin (pounds)	100	90
Capital (dollars)	20,000	23,000
Energy (BTUs)	6,000	5,700

8. Referring to Problem 7, suppose the company wants to increase productivity by 5 percent. How much labor savings must occur?

9. Witkowski Tax Services processes federal income tax forms. This year in April, the company's busiest month, the company prepared 4,500 income tax returns with an average revenue of $60 each. In April last year, they completed 3,750 returns with an average revenue of $55 each. Below are the average costs, adjusted for inflation.

	Last Year	This Year
Labor hours	$3,000	$3,200
Management costs	$25,000	$28,000
Computer technology	$15,000	$20,000
Rent for office	$2,000	$2,200
Office supplies	$3,000	$3,600

a. What is the productivity this year and last year for each factor and overall?

b. How has the productivity changed for each factor and overall?

c. What can be done to further improve productivity?

CHAPTER 4

Quality Management

LEARNING OBJECTIVES

After completing this chapter, you should be able to:

1. Define quality from both internal and external orientations.
2. List the dimensions of service quality
3. List the dimensions of quality for manufacturing.
4. Summarize the philosophies and contributions of W. Edwards Deming, Joseph Juran, Philip Crosby, and Genichi Taguchi.
5. List and explain the components of total quality management.
6. Describe the purpose and use of quality function deployment.
7. List the categories of Baldrige Award criteria and relate them to total quality management.
8. Explain the process and purpose of ISO 9000:2000 certification.

INTRODUCTION TO QUALITY MANAGEMENT

Look closely at almost any advertisement on television, in a magazine, or in a newspaper, and you'll notice that quality is probably mentioned at least once. Quality is often the first factor customers consider when making a purchase decision. In fact, some people have even suggested that companies can no longer use quality to differentiate their products from those of competitors because all companies emphasize quality. And yet, some companies, such as FedEx, Motorola, or Four Seasons Hotels, have been able to develop a very strong reputation for high quality while others have not. What makes the difference? Simply put, companies that have a strong reputation for quality have been able to integrate quality throughout the organization, adopting an approach often referred to as quality management.

The purpose of this chapter is to teach you about quality and how an emphasis on quality can be spread throughout the entire organization. Later chapters will build upon your understanding by showing how other operations activities contribute to quality. But first, we must define quality.

WHAT IS QUALITY?

Most of us tend to define quality rather vaguely. We may be able to indicate what we think is a quality hotel or a quality automobile and perhaps even explain why. But, beyond that, we often get stumped. In fact, even experts do not agree on a definition of quality. In general, definitions can be divided into those that take an internal orientation—approach quality from the company's perspective—and those that adopt an external orientation—approach quality from the customer's perspective.

Internally Oriented Definitions of Quality

Most definitions of quality that adopt an internal orientation focus on measuring some characteristics of the service or product, such as the number of packages delivered before 10:00 A.M. by an air express company or the thickness of an engine part manufactured by a car maker. Two examples of such internally oriented definitions of quality are:

1. Quality is the degree to which a specific product conforms to a design or specification.
2. Differences in quality amount to differences in the quantity of some desired ingredient or attribute.

One possible shortcoming of such internally oriented definitions is their assumption that the company's product specifications match what the customer wants—an assumption that may not be correct.

Externally Oriented Definitions of Quality

Definitions of quality that take an external orientation focus on the customer in some way. Two definitions that adopt such an approach are:

1. Quality is fitness for use.
2. Quality consists of the capacity to satisfy wants.

Although it may appear that such externally oriented definitions of quality are still rather vague, most companies known for high quality today define quality in the following terms:

> **Quality** is consistently meeting or exceeding the customer's needs and expectations.

In fact, if organizations relied only on the preceding definition as a way of determining quality, it would be a trial-and-error process. Instead, quality begins with an external process that identifies the customer's needs and expectations. Then, those needs and expectations are translated into an internal process to guarantee they are met or exceeded. One way of formalizing that translation is called quality function deployment, which is discussed later in this chapter. First, we must look more closely at quality itself.

DIMENSIONS OF QUALITY

An important step in translating customer's needs and expectations into internal processes is understanding the dimensions of quality. In Chapter 1, we discussed the differences between goods, which are manufactured, and services. Those differences have some significant impacts on the way we determine and measure quality. For example, because services are intangible, the quality of services will be based much more on perceptions. As a result, the dimensions of service quality are somewhat different than those of quality for manufactured products.

Dimensions of Service Quality

Valarie Zeithaml, Leonard Berry, and A. Parasuraman have studied service quality extensively. Their studies have identified five dimensions in customers' judgment of quality:

EXHIBIT 4.1	Reliability	Did the express package arrive on time?
		Was my VCR repaired correctly?
Examples of Service Quality Dimensions	Responsiveness	Did the florist deliver the flowers as ordered?
		Does the hotel send up an extra pillow when requested?
		Does the credit card company respond quickly when I have a question about my statement?
		When an employee says he will call me right back, does he?
	Assurance	Can the salesperson answer my questions about the computer on sale?
		Does the car mechanic appear to know about my car?
		Does my physician politely and knowledgeably answer my questions?
	Empathy	Does someone in the restaurant recognize me as a regular customer?
		Is the salesperson willing to spend the time to understand my particular needs?
		Does my advisor work with me to develop a program of courses for my specific career goals?
	Tangibles	Is the hotel room furniture clean and modern?
		Does the auto repair shop appear neat and tidy?
		Is my bank statement easy to understand?

1. *Reliability*—The ability to perform the promised service dependably and accurately.
2. *Responsiveness*—The willingness to help customers and provide prompt service.
3. *Assurance*—The knowledge and courtesy of employees and their ability to convey trust and confidence.
4. *Empathy*—The provision of caring, individualized attention to customers.
5. *Tangibles*—The appearance of physical facilities, equipment, personnel, and communication materials such as brochures or letters.

Some examples of these five dimensions are shown in Exhibit 4.1. Note that the dimensions are listed in order of importance. Zeithaml, Berry, and Parasuraman found that customers place more value on the human dimensions, such as empathy and responsiveness, than on tangibles when evaluating the quality of a service. In other words, it doesn't matter how nice the furniture in your hotel room looks if the staff is rude, unfriendly, and uncaring. Furthermore, reliability appears to be at the core of customer evaluation of service. If a company fails on reliability, it is more likely to lose a customer than if it fails on any of the other dimensions. As demonstrated in the following example, Southwest Airlines is one company that combines reliability with the human dimensions for a winning combination.

EXAMPLE

The dire situation for many airlines has been highlighted recently by bankruptcy filings and record losses. But, while other airlines have been losing both money and customers, Southwest has stayed profitable and has remained at the top of customer satisfaction rankings. Southwest does this by maintaining a clear focus on the customer and meeting the customer's needs. Customers want low fares, and Southwest provides fares that are consistently below the competition. Customers also want to be treated like humans, not numbers. Again, Southwest excels at that by empowering any employee to do whatever they can to solve a customer's problem.

Dimensions of Quality for Goods

David Garvin has examined eight dimensions of product quality for manufactured goods. Goods are tangible, and interaction with employees is usually not part of the product. Therefore, these dimensions are much more focused on specific attributes of the product and do not include human factors. The dimensions identified by Garvin are:

1. *Performance*—The primary operating characteristics of a product.
2. *Features*—Those secondary characteristics that supplement the product's basic functioning.
3. *Reliability*—The length of time a product will function before it fails or the probability it will function for a stated period of time.
4. *Conformance*—The degree to which a product's design and operating characteristics match preestablished standards.
5. *Durability*—The ability of a product to function when subjected to hard and frequent use.
6. *Serviceability*—The speed, courtesy, and competence of repair.
7. *Aesthetics*—How a product looks, feels, sounds, tastes, or smells.
8. *Perceived Quality*—The image, advertising, or brand name of a product.

You should notice that of the above, the last three are very subjective. Also, the dimension of serviceability includes various aspects of service quality that apply when the customer wants to have a tangible good, such as an automobile, repaired. Overall, though, the dimensions of quality for manufactured goods are much more concrete and quantifiable than those of services.

Costs of Quality

One last general aspect of quality worth some discussion is the **cost of quality.** Traditionally, companies thought of quality costs only as those that were necessary to produce higher quality. In fact, as many companies have discovered, higher quality can actually mean reduced costs because of savings from reduced scrap, rework, and customer warranty claims. This realization motivated one author to write an entire book on the premise that "quality is free."

In general, we can identify three categories for the costs of quality:

1. Failure costs (internal or external)
2. Appraisal costs
3. Prevention costs

Failure Costs

Failure costs are incurred whenever any product or component of a product fails to meet requirements. Such costs can be divided into two categories, internal or external. **Internal failure costs** are those associated with defects found before the product reaches the customer. Examples of such costs include the costs of correcting errors in a customer's bank account, discarding food that was improperly cooked, scrapping defective parts, or reworking products that contain defects. In some cases internal failures can even be dangerous to employees, as when a building collapses while under construction because of defective materials.

External failure costs are incurred after a product has reached the customer. Such costs can include the cost of warranty repair work, handling complaints, or replacing products. Even more considerable than these are the costs of lost goodwill and possible liability if anyone is injured or killed because of an external failure. The costs of external failure can be especially devastating in terms of lost customers. One expert has estimated that if a customer is happy, he or she will tell three other people about it but if a customer is unhappy, that person will tell eleven others.

EXAMPLE

The huge costs that can be associated with external failures are well demonstrated by the recent problems with tread separation in Firestone tires that were mounted on Ford Explorer automobiles. Several people were killed or injured when tread separation caused their Ford Explorers to roll over, resulting in expensive lawsuits. Both Ford and Firestone had to recall many of the tires, incurring several million dollars in costs, and both companies suffered severe blows to their reputations because of these problems.

Appraisal Costs

Appraisal costs are the costs incurred to measure quality, assess customer satisfaction, and inspect and test products. Such activities are designed to determine the current level of quality or to uncover defects. Appraisal costs could include the cost of conducting a customer satisfaction survey, hiring an individual to visit and inspect each property in a hotel chain, or "burning in" newly manufactured computers to be sure they will operate as intended.

EXAMPLE

Marriott Hotels take customer satisfaction seriously. To assess that satisfaction, questionnaires are mailed to customers a short time after they stayed at a Marriott property. Customer satisfaction surveys left in hotel rooms get some responses, but most customers are too busy to fill them out. By mailing questionnaires to customers' homes, it is more likely that customers will find time to complete the questionnaire. This does cost more, but Marriott believes the extra cost is worthwhile because of the additional information received. These costs are part of the appraisal costs of quality.

Prevention Costs

Prevention costs result from activities designed to prevent defects from occurring. Prevention costs can include such activities as employee training, quality control procedures, special efforts in designing products, or administrative systems to prevent defects. One example is the cost of modifying a bank's computer system to request confirmation whenever teller entries are unusually large or unusually small.

EXAMPLE

Poka-yoke is an approach adopted by many companies to prevent defects. The term is a rough approximation of Japanese words that mean mistake proofing. For example, Dell computers use color coding of connections so that when customers are setting up their computers at home, they are less likely to try plugging the printer cable into a slot for the monitor connection. This results in a better experience for the customer and higher customer satisfaction.

At one time there was a philosophy that companies should trade off the costs of prevention against those of failure. It resulted in the belief that there was some nonzero optimum level of defects that companies should be willing to accept. Fortunately, that philosophy has now been debunked as companies find that a reputation for high quality has benefits that far outweigh any additional prevention and appraisal costs associated with achieving high quality.

Six Sigma

Motorola, although a world-recognized quality leader, has set for itself a goal of six sigma quality. **Six sigma** quality relates to the variability in quality and represents only 3.4 defects per million, units, or 99.9997% error free. However, the term six sigma actually refers to a broader range of defect prevention strategies. For example, General Electric in its six sigma program trains employees in advanced statistical techniques for preventing defects. Once an employee passes a high level of training, he or she is designated as a "six sigma black belt" and is empowered to train other employees in those techniques.

THE BACKGROUND OF QUALITY MANAGEMENT

The groundwork for today's philosophies about quality was laid over a long period by many people. Some of the best known individuals here have been writing, teaching, and lecturing in the quality area for many years. In fact, two, Deming and Juran, are credited with teaching the Japanese about quality.

W. Edwards Deming

Until his death in 1993 at the age of 93, W. Edwards Deming was probably the most influential individual in the area of quality. Deming began his career as a statistician and became involved in quality when he worked with Walter Shewhart, the founding father of statistical process control. After World War II, Deming went to Japan under the auspices of the U.S. government as part of an effort to rebuild Japan's economy. His influence on the Japanese was so great that today Japan's highest prize for quality is The Deming Prize. Surprisingly, Deming was largely ignored in the United States until the 1980s. From that time on, though, he lectured extensively to large audiences throughout the country. In fact, during his final year, Deming taught thirty four-day seminars, collapsing during one in Rochester, New York. But he came back and continued, giving his last seminar only ten days before his death.

Deming's philosophy is contained in his well-known fourteen points, shown in Exhibit 4.2. To this day there is still confusion and disagreement about precisely what is meant by some of Deming's points. However, Deming's basic premise, which comes across loud and clear in his lectures, is that *the system* causes defects, not the employees. Management is responsible for changing the system and must accept that responsibility instead of blaming the employees when defects occur. Because of his background, Deming also stressed the use of statistical process control and encouraged training all employees in its use.

Joseph M. Juran

Joseph M. Juran, who was an active lecturer until 1995 when he retired to spend more time on writing, was also involved early on with Walter Shewhart and lectured and taught in Japan after World War II. In fact, some have argued that Juran's contribution to Japan's quality efforts was even greater than Deming's. Like Deming, Juran emphasizes management's responsibility for quality. Juran, however, shifts the focus of quality to the customer by defining quality as "fitness for use." He also emphasizes the need for continuous improvement and stresses that quality must be built on the three bases of quality planning, quality control, and quality improvement.

Philip Crosby

Philip Crosby became internationally recognized with the publication of his 1979 book, *Quality Is Free.* In that book, and later ones, he argues that failure costs are much greater than most companies had thought, often equaling at least 20 percent of the value of sales. By reducing failure costs, companies can actually end up saving money, thus justifying the title of Crosby's book. Because of that book, Crosby is most generally recognized for emphasizing the importance of considering all costs of quality. However, he is also responsible for promoting the idea that all errors must be eliminated through his slogan "do it right the first time" and the concept of zero defects.

Genichi Taguchi

Japanese companies were among the world's first to place a strong emphasis on quality, so it is not surprising that several people from Japan have made significant contributions to the field of quality. Genichi Taguchi's ideas are particularly important. Taguchi first gained prominence shortly after World War II when he was involved with research facilities established to develop Japan's telephone system. After noticing that considerable time and effort were expended in experimentation and testing, Taguchi developed procedures for designing experiments so more information could be obtained with fewer experiments. Today those procedures are known as **Taguchi Methods,** which are discussed in supplemental material located on the companion Web site for this text. More significant, however, is the fact that Genichi Taguchi has also contributed an entire philosophy about how products should be designed. That philosophy forms an important part of quality management.

Taguchi argues that quality must be designed into a product, that it cannot be inspected in later if the design is not good. Thus, an important part of Taguchi's philosophy is based on the concept of **robust design,** in other words, designs that guarantee high

---

EXHIBIT 4.2

Dr. W. Edwards Deming's 14 Points for the Transformation of Management

1. Create constancy of purpose toward improvement of product and service. Aim to become competitive and to stay in business, and provide jobs.
2. Adopt the new philosophy. We are in a new economic age. Awaken to the challenge. Learn the responsibilities, and take on leadership for change.
3. Cease dependence on inspection to achieve quality. Eliminate the need for inspection. Build quality into the product in the first place.
4. End the practice of awarding business on the basis of price tag. Instead, minimize total cost. Move toward a single supplier on any one item, on a long-term relationship of loyalty and trust.
5. Improve constantly and forever the system of production and service, to improve quality and productivity and thus constantly decrease cost.
6. Institute training on the job.
7. Institute leadership.
8. Drive out fear, so everyone may work effectively for the company.
9. Break down barriers between departments.
10. Eliminate slogans, exhortations, and targets for the workforce asking for zero defects and new levels of productivity.
11a. Eliminate work standards (quotas) on the factory floor. Substitute leadership.
11b. Eliminate management by objective. Eliminate management by numbers, numerical goals. Substitute leadership.
12a. Remove barriers robbing the hourly worker of his right to pride of workmanship. Change the responsibility of supervisors from sheer numbers to quality.
12b. Remove barriers that rob people in management and in engineering of their right to pride of workmanship. Abolish the annual or merit rating and management by objective.
13. Institute a vigorous program of education and self-improvement.
14. Put everybody in the company to work to accomplish the transformation. The transformation is everybody's job.

Source: Deming, W. Edwards. *Out of the Crisis.* Cambridge, Mass.: MIT Center for Advanced Engineering Study, 1986.

quality regardless of variations (such as employee errors) that might occur in the processes that produce the product and provide it to the customer. For example, McDonald's designed a ketchup dispenser that puts precisely the right amount of ketchup on each burger, eliminating variations in product quality that might result from employees putting on too much or too little.

A related concept is **design for manufacture and assembly (DFMA),** which emphasizes that products should be designed so they are simple and inexpensive to produce. This concept has also been applied to service operations under the term "**design for operations**" **(DFO).**

TOTAL QUALITY MANAGEMENT

Total quality management (**TQM**) is an approach to quality management that originated in Japan and was adopted successfully by many companies throughout the world, including American Express, Motorola, and General Electric. TQM is an organization-wide philosophy that embodies the following components:

- Focus on the customer
- Everyone responsible for quality
- Team problem solving
- Employee training
- Fact-based management
- A philosophy of continuous improvement

Each of these components will be discussed in detail. It should be stressed, however, that they apply to all aspects of a company's operation, from design of products and processes to distribution and after-the-sale service. Further, all parts of the company must be involved, even accounting or finance, which do not usually deal directly with external customers, but serve other parts of the company, that is, internal customers.

Focus on the Customer

We most often think of the customer as someone outside a company, such as the final consumer. However, it is also possible to think of internal customers, other parts of an organization that utilize information from an area such as accounting. In a hospital, the laboratory could think of the physician who requests lab work as its customer. Thus, a customer can be anyone, whether inside or outside an organization, who receives the output from an activity or process.

Juran's definition of quality as fitness for use provides the groundwork for focusing on the customer. Unfortunately, many companies in the past have tended to identify what they thought the customer wanted without actually asking the customer. Companies that use TQM rely on what they call the voice of the customer.

The **voice of the customer** means finding out exactly what the customer wants and what he or she likes and doesn't like. To do this, many companies actually get to know their customers personally. For example, some companies hold focus groups, in which customers are brought in to discuss their wants, needs, and expectations and to respond to proposals about changing the good or service produced. The more a company understands its customers, the better it will be at meeting or exceeding their needs and expectations.

Quality Function Deployment

The quality of a product, whether that product is a manufactured good or a service, is largely dependent on how well the product and the processes for producing it were designed. Listening to the voice of the customer provides a company with valuable information. That information, however, is usually in terms of the customer's needs or expectations, such as the need for transactions at a bank to be handled quickly and accurately or the expectation that the room you reserve at a hotel will be available when you arrive. Those needs and expectations must be translated into design characteristics for the product and process. **Quality function deployment (QFD)** is one method that can be used to make that translation by relating customer needs and expectations to specific design characteristics through a series of matrices.

Exhibit 4.3 shows the basic form of the matrix used in QFD, which is often referred to as the **"house of quality"** because of its shape. The customer needs, or WHATs, are listed along the left-hand side of the matrix. Design characteristics related to these needs are listed along the top as HOWs. The relationship matrix in the middle (WHAT vs. HOW) indicates the nature of the relationship between each customer need and each design characteristic. For example, Exhibit 4.4 shows the house of quality for a limited set of customer

EXHIBIT 4.3

The House of Quality

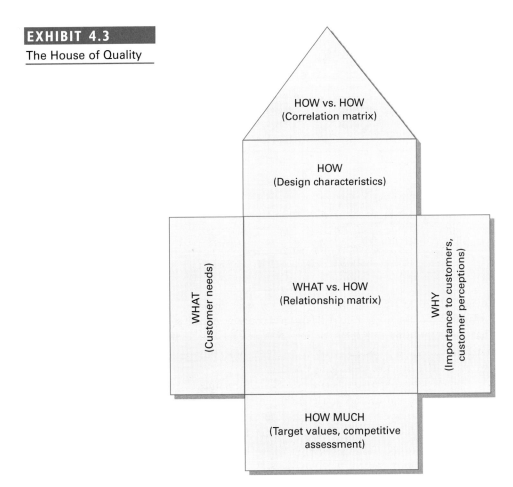

EXHIBIT 4.4

House of Quality for an
Automobile

EXHIBIT 4.4
House of Quality for an Automobile

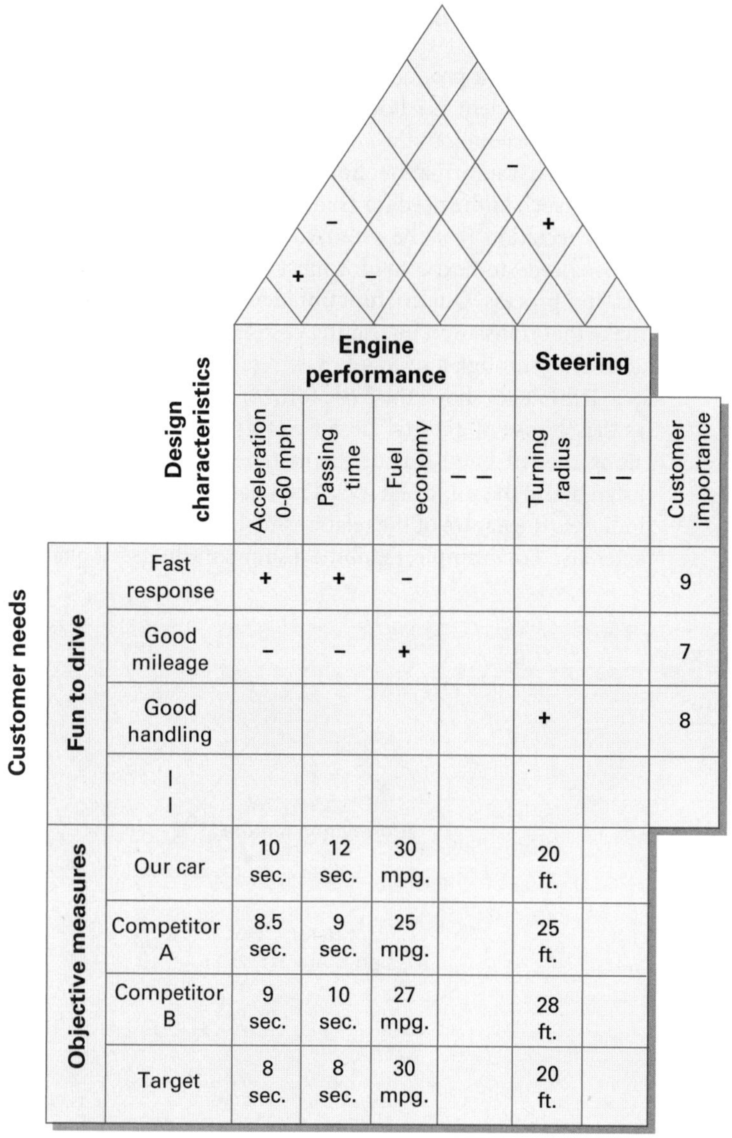

needs related to an automobile. As you can see, the need of good mileage is positively related to the design characteristic of fuel economy, negatively related to acceleration, and has no relationship to turning radius. In some cases the simple plus or minus signs used in Exhibit 4.4 are replaced by other symbols indicating the strength of the relationship, from strongly negative to strongly positive.

When designing products and processes, companies often face trade-offs, such as that between fuel economy and acceleration. The house of quality can also help a company evaluate trade-offs. The roof part of the house shows how each design characteristic affects other design characteristics. The right-hand side of the house shows the importance of each customer need and can also indicate customer perceptions about how well the company is performing relative to competitors. Performance on each design characteristic can be compared against competitors along the bottom. Thus, less emphasis might be placed on a customer need that is not very important to customers or on a design characteristic in which the company already outperforms the competition.

The house of quality shown here is only a simple example; those actually developed by companies can be extremely complex. For example, a survey by Van Fossen, Vonderembse, and Raghunathan found that chart size ran from a low of 24 cells in the relationship matrix to a high of 62,500, with 100 cells the most common size. They also found, however, that those companies using QFD believed it had significantly improved product design, product documentation, and customer satisfaction.

This first house of quality translates the voice of the customer into design characteristics, but characteristics by themselves will not tell us how to make a car. Those characteristics must be translated into parts characteristics, as shown in Exhibit 4.5. Parts characteristics define how the engineering characteristics will be achieved.

But, the parts characteristics cannot be achieved unless the process is planned to do so. Thus, another chart is required to convert the parts characteristics into process details, describing how the parts are to be produced with the required characteristics. Finally, production requirements are developed that specify inspection details, measuring methods, operator training, and so forth.

Using the four steps shown in Exhibit 4.5, the voice of the customer has been deployed throughout the entire organization. Further, all parts of the organization have had to work together to achieve that deployment.

Everyone Responsible for Quality

In the past, many companies utilized quality control (QC) departments that were responsible for ensuring quality. Unfortunately, everyone else in the organization assumed that since quality was the QC department's responsibility, it was not theirs. Organizations that embrace TQM have realized that everyone must accept responsibility, from the company CEO to the person who cleans the parking lot. Each of those individuals contributes to quality (or lack thereof) in some way. In fact, company suppliers must also accept responsibility for their role in quality. It is essential, however, that TQM have top management support and commitment in order for it to succeed.

EXAMPLE

The recent experiences of one person who stayed at the Ritz-Carlton in Buckhead, Georgia, (consistently named as one of world's best hotels) demonstrate this concept. One night she wanted a newspaper, but the gift shop was closed. During her late dinner (the hotel employees insisted on keeping the kitchen open past its closing time to serve her), she asked if any customer had left a newspaper behind. The waiter was back in three minutes with copies of the *Atlanta Constitution*, *USA Today*, *New York Times*, and *Wall Street Journal.* Of course, there was no charge for the papers.

This attention not only to meeting the needs of the customer but also to delighting the customer comes directly from the head of Ritz-Carlton Hotels. Such top-level commitment has resulted in the company winning the Malcolm Baldrige Award, a national quality award discussed later in this chapter. Quality, however, extends to every activity at the hotel, even opening the door for someone.

EXHIBIT 4.5

Successive Houses of Quality Deploy the Voice of the Customer throughout the Organization

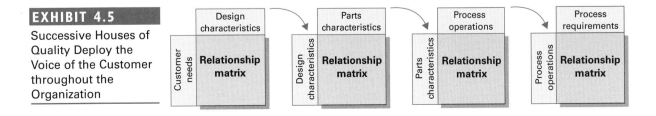

EXAMPLE

When the guest mentioned in the preceding example stayed at the Ritz-Carlton in Buckhead another time, the hotel's concierge had located a special store for her. When she got ready to take a taxi there, one could not be found. So, a doorman was summoned to drive her in a hotel car. Along the way the doorman explained he had just gone through three days of training before being allowed to open the door for customers. Of course, once again, there was no charge for the service of driving this guest to the store and back. As you might expect, she was delighted by this service.

Team Problem Solving

Companies that utilize TQM often find that problems are encountered when attempting to meet or exceed customers' needs and expectations. For example, a hospital might find that emergency room patients with problems that are not life threatening complain they have to wait too long for service, or an automobile manufacturer may find that its customers want an increasing number of product options but want prices to remain low. Problems like these, and many others, can be solved better by a team than by one individual. Having a team attack the problem not only allows for different viewpoints but also enables the team members to split the work and to brainstorm possible solutions with one another.

EXAMPLE

Motorola, a large global company that manufactures electronic products, such as pagers and cellular telephones, is one company that has led the way in team problem

EXHIBIT 4.6

Motorola's Criteria for Judging Team Problem Solving

Teamwork
- Team structure that recognizes scope of the problem
- Team skills and experience that support the goals
- Meetings and participation that demonstrate commitment
- Significant contributions by all members
- Use of expertise from outside if needed
- Mutual respect, good communication, and use of methods for reaching consensus and resolving conflict

Project Selection
- Specific criteria and methodology used to select the project
- Identification of the customer and customer's needs
- Specific and aggressive goals

Analysis Techniques
- Benchmarking of best practices
- Mapping of the "as is" condition and the "should be"
- Appropriate use of analytical tools
- Growth of team's knowledge and skills in using tools

Remedies
- Pros and cons of alternative solutions considered
- Development of a permanent solution
- Thoroughness and innovativeness in the solution
- Addresses customer's needs

Results
- Results reflecting goals
- Results documented and verified

Institutionalization
- Sustainable improvement through written procedures
- Communication to others

Presentation
- Clear and concise presentation
- Appropriate use of presentation aids

solving. In fact, Motorola in the past has held an annual team competition at which over 2,000 teams from its worldwide operations competed. Exhibit 4.6 lists the criteria upon which these teams are judged.

Employee Training

Deming emphasized the importance of training employees to use the tools of statistical process control. As organizations have adopted a team approach to problem solving, they have also found that employees need training to work effectively in groups and to use group problem-solving tools. Some of these problem-solving tools are discussed in supplemental materials located on the companion Web site for this text.

Fact-Based Management

As we mentioned when discussing quality function deployment, companies that use TQM must find out what their customers' needs and expectations really are, not what the company thinks they are. This philosophy of basing decisions on facts, data, and analysis—instead of intuition—extends to other areas of the TQM company. In supplemental material at the companion Web site, we demonstrate some of the tools that can be used to collect, organize, and analyze data. The results of that analysis can be used to make decisions about which quality problems to tackle first or the best way to solve those problems.

There is not only an increased emphasis in TQM companies on using data to make decisions, but the methods of measurement are also different. Companies today are beginning to operate with a new saying: "What gets measured gets attention." This has always been true as employees concentrated on the criteria they knew would be used to judge them. But now companies are realizing that those criteria must tie into the company's competitive strategy. As a result, some of the most important measurements today are those related to quality. These measurements of quality include not only internal measures, such as the number of customer complaints received or the percent of products reworked, but also external measures, such as customer satisfaction.

Benchmarking

Competitive benchmarking is a process by which a company compares its performance to that of others. Those other companies need not be competitors or even in the same industry. Instead, the purpose of benchmarking is to set a standard based on the company that is recognized as being best at a certain activity. As an example, many companies that are not even in the mail-order business use the mail-order company L.L.Bean as a benchmark for order fulfillment.

EXAMPLE   Xerox was especially hard hit by competition from Japanese companies that were able to provide higher-quality products at lower cost. To fight back, Xerox began a quality improvement program, but soon realized it needed some measures to use in judging its progress. Such measures came from other companies.

As part of benchmarking, companies also study the products of other companies and the processes for producing those products. For example, in benchmarking L.L.Bean, we would not only set its order fulfillment time as a goal to achieve, but we would also study how it achieves that time to determine whether some of its procedures could be used to improve our company's performance. Xerox benchmarks against its competitors' products by examining every individual part of each product, comparing it to Xerox's, and determining whether any ideas incorporated in a competitor's product can be used to improve Xerox's products.

Broader Measures of Performance

Companies have traditionally measured their performance using the accounting standards of cost and profit. Today those standards alone are insufficient. Quality, for one, is an important performance measure that must be used, especially by companies using TQM. But as the customer's needs may include other factors such as delivery speed, flexibility, or innovativeness, then the performance measurement system must also include such factors.

Philosophy of Continuous Improvement

The philosophies of Deming, Juran, and Crosby all include the concept of **continuous improvement.** No matter how good a company is it must always work to do better. This concept of continuous improvement can, once again, be credited to the Japanese who use the term **"kaizen"** to describe their continuous improvement philosophy.

This philosophy of continuous improvement is an extremely important part of TQM. In fact, some individuals differentiate between TQM and business process reengineering (BPR) by arguing. that TQM focuses on continuous change while BPR stresses a quantum leap. Regardless, continuous improvement is itself an important concept.

Key Components of Continuous Improvement

Companies adopting continuous improvement as an organizational philosophy have found the following are key components needed to make it work:

- Standardize and document procedures.
- Assign teams to identify areas for improvement.
- Use methods analysis and problem-solving tools.
- Use the Plan-Do-Check-Act cycle.
- Document improved procedures.

Some of these components require considerable explanation, so they will be discussed separately in later chapters of this book. However, the components of standardizing and documenting procedures as well as the Plan-Do-Check-Act cycle can be presented quickly and are discussed briefly here.

Standardizing and Documenting Procedures

Standardization and documentation form the basis of continuous improvement as you can see from the preceding list, which begins and ends with documentation. Standardization involves developing a preset procedure for performing an activity or job. Documentation is the act of putting that procedure into writing. Standardization and documentation are necessary for continuous improvement so that we can know exactly how something is done now (the "as is" condition). After that process has been improved, we need to document the new procedure (the "should be" condition) so that it becomes the new standard procedure. Documentation and standardization are especially important for companies that want to become registered under ISO 9000:2000, described later in this chapter. It should be noted, however, that the purposes of documentation and standardization are not to prevent change, but to ensure that everyone performs a task the same way every time. As better ways are found, the documentation and standardization are changed to promote continuous improvement.

EXAMPLE

Service organizations rely extensively on documentation and standardization to ensure consistent service. For example, fast-food restaurants, such as Burger King or McDonald's, have established procedures for everything from cooking hamburgers to taking orders. Airline pilots follow a prescribed checklist every time they land or take off. This procedure ensures a high level of customer safety and consistent service.

The Plan-Do-Check-Act Cycle

The **Plan-Do-Check-Act Cycle,** shown in Exhibit 4.7, is also often referred to as the Deming Wheel or Shewhart Cycle. By being in the shape of a wheel, it embodies the philosophy of continuous improvement; the cycle is repeated over and over without ending. Each part of the cycle is explained as follows:

- *Plan*—Before making any changes, be sure everything is documented and standardized. Use appropriate tools to identify problems or opportunities for improvement. Develop a plan to make changes.
- *Do*—Implement the plan, documenting any changes made.
- *Check*—Analyze the revised process to see if goals have been achieved.
- *Act*—If the goals have been achieved, standardized and document the changes. Communicate the results to others that could benefit from similar changes. If the goals have not been achieved, determine why not and proceed accordingly.

Controversy Surrounding TQM

TQM has received somewhat of a black eye recently. In fact, many companies have stopped using the term TQM, even though what they are doing is actually TQM. Instead, the term "quality management" is often used. The problem began when TQM was seen by some companies as a panacea for all their problems. Instead of taking the time to carefully and completely implement TQM, these companies often adopted a TQM façade. When their problems did not go away, they started saying that TQM doesn't work. From these failures, we have learned a number of key points about implementing TQM:

- Successful TQM implementation requires complete top-management support and understanding.
- TQM is not a quick fix. It takes time and resources to implement.

EXHIBIT 4.7

The Plan-Do-Check-Act Cycle

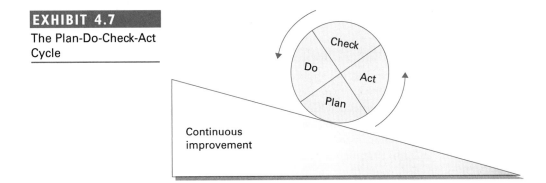

- Employees must be empowered and given resources to correct quality problems.
- TQM must be integrated appropriately into the company's strategic plan so that quality receives neither too much emphasis nor too little.

QUALITY AWARDS AND STANDARDS

To promote the adoption of quality concepts and techniques by companies and to recognize those companies that have excelled, several awards have been developed. One of the first of these was Japan's **Deming Prize,** named after W. Edwards Deming. It is awarded annually to companies that achieve a certain level of quality. The award has a category open to non-Japanese companies. Florida Power and Light was the first U.S. company to win in that category; AT&T won in 1994. In 1987 the United States government established its own award, known as the Malcolm Baldrige National Quality Award after a former secretary of commerce. The Baldrige Award's merits have been hotly debated, and the number of applicants for the Baldrige Award has decreased markedly in recent years. Nonetheless, it is still regarded as an important award and its criteria, which are often recognized as an important basis for TQM, are discussed here. Several states have also installed their own quality awards, such as New York's Excelsior Award, that require less burdensome and expensive application procedures than the Baldrige.

The International Organization for Standardization (ISO), to which many nations throughout the world belong, has established an international standard for quality management systems. That standard, known as ISO 9000:2000, is rapidly becoming a requirement for companies that do business internationally, especially those that operate in European Union (EU) countries.

The Malcolm Baldrige National Quality Award

Following the lead of Japan's Deming Prize, the U.S. government established, in 1987, the **Malcolm Baldrige National Quality Award (MBNQA).** In establishing this award, the U.S. Department of Commerce had three purposes in mind:

1. To promote awareness of quality as an increasingly important element in competitiveness.
2. To improve understanding of the requirements for quality excellence.
3. To foster sharing of information on successful quality strategies and the benefits derived from implementation of these strategies.

Originally, the award applied to business organizations, and awards were given in the three categories of manufacturing, service, and small business. In 1999, separate awards and criteria were developed for health care and educational organizations.

The Judging Criteria

The criteria used in evaluating applicants in the business category are shown in Exhibit 4.8. Similar criteria, with some minor adjustments, are used for health care and education.

Past winners have included Ritz-Carlton Hotels, AT&T, Universal Card Services, and, in the award's first year, Motorola. In 2001, the first winners were announced in the education category and included Chugach School District in Alaska, Pearl River School District in New York, and the University of Wisconsin-Stout.

The Baldrige Award has come under some criticism because of the extensive investment of time and money required to apply, especially when so few organizations can

EXHIBIT 4.8	Categories/Items	Maximum Points
Malcolm Baldrige Award Criteria and Points	1.0 Leadership	120
	2.0 Strategic planning	85
	3.0 Customer and market focus	85
	4.0 Information and analysis	90
	5.0 Human resource focus	85
	6.0 Process management	85
	7.0 Business results	450
	Total Points	1000

receive the award each year. Many thousands of copies of the award criteria and other information are, however, requested each year, indicating that companies may be using the criteria as a guideline in developing their quality management systems—even if they do not enter the competition.

Results for Baldrige Finalists

The similarity between the Baldrige Award criteria and the components of TQM is not completely accidental, as the Baldrige Award was established to foster the kinds of activities that make up TQM. But do such activities really pay off?

The U.S. government's General Accounting Office performed a study using data gathered from twenty of the MBNQA finalists during 1988 and 1989. The results of that study, which are presented graphically in Exhibit 4.9, found that increases in quality favorably influenced other aspects of the companies' operations, leading to increased competitiveness, which resulted in increased market share and larger profits. The solid lines and arrows in the exhibit represent direct results that were produced by improving quality (arrowheads alone within boxes represent direction of change). The dashed lines show feedback paths for collecting information to motivate further improvements.

ISO 9000:2000 International Quality Standards

In spite of the Baldrige Award and Deming Prize, there is no generally accepted standard that can be used to determine whether or not a company provides high quality. However, the International Standards Organization (ISO), which is made up of standards organizations representing ninety-one countries, has taken a first step in that direction through its ISO 9000 series of standards, which were established in 1987 and significantly revised in the year 2000 as **ISO 9000:2000.** The revised standards are based upon the following principles:

- Customer focus
- Leadership
- Involvement of people
- Process approach
- System approach to management
- Factual approach to decision making
- Mutually beneficial supplier relationships

The original ISO 9000 standards provided for companies to be certified under three different standards as follows:

EXHIBIT 4.9

Results for Baldrige
Award Finalists

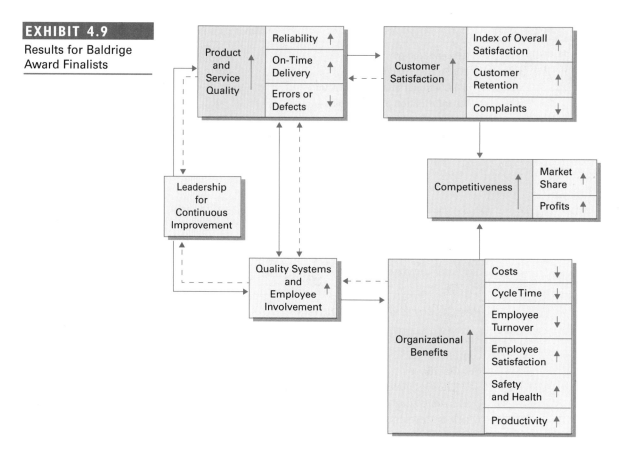

ISO 9001: Pertains to companies involved in the design, development, production, installation, servicing, inspection, and testing of goods or services.

ISO 9002: Pertains to companies that are involved only in producing, installing, servicing, inspecting, and testing.

ISO 9003: Pertains to companies not involved in production, such as distributors.

However, the revised ISO 9000:2000 standards eliminate the separate designations and leave only the ISO 9001 certification, which will apply to all companies regardless of the breadth of their activities.

The original standards have been criticized previously for requiring excessive amounts of documentation, for guaranteeing only consistent quality—not high quality—and for not having a provision for continuous improvement. The revised standards appear to answer these criticisms by reducing the documentation requirements, requiring that customer satisfaction be measured and monitored, and by emphasizing continuous improvement.

The Certification Process

In order to become **certified,** a company must undergo a two- to three-day audit by an outside **registrar.** That registrar must itself be accredited, and often accreditation is granted only to a specific company within each country. For example, in the United

Kingdom the British Standards Institute (BSI) is the accredited registrar, while in the United States one accredited registrar is the well-known Underwriters Laboratories (UL). Fortunately, agreements among these registrars allow one to operate as a subcontractor for another. Thus, a U.S. company can be audited by Underwriters Laboratories and receive certification under ISO 9000 to do business in the United Kingdom.

After a company has passed an audit, it is certified and then **registered** in a directory of certified suppliers. To maintain registration, a company must continue to pass unannounced yearly site visits by inspectors and to be reregistered every three years. Because the ISO 9000:2000 series is the only international standard, it is likely that registration will become more important, even for companies that do not do business in the EU.

SUMMARY

- Quality has many definitions, both internal and external. Today, most companies define it as consistently meeting or exceeding the customer's needs and expectations.

- The dimensions of service quality include reliability, responsiveness, assurance, empathy, and tangibles.

- The dimensions of quality for goods include performance, features, reliability, conformance, durability, serviceability, aesthetics, and perceived quality.

- Individuals who have had a significant impact on the field of quality include W. Edwards Deming, Joseph Juran, Philip Crosby, and Genichi Taguchi.

- The components of TQM include a focus on the customer, everyone responsible for quality, team problem solving, employee training, fact-based management, and a philosophy of continuous improvement.

- Quality function deployment is used to translate the voice of the customer into product and process design characteristics.

- The Baldrige Award criteria are divided into the categories of leadership, strategic planning, customer and market focus, information and analysis, human resource focus, process management, and business results.

- ISO 9000:2000 is an international standard that certifies companies that have quality management systems in place to benefit all parties through sustained customer satisfaction.

 Visit our dynamic Web site, http://www.wiley.com/college/vonderembse, for extended chapter material, solved problems, mini-cases, computer software, and Web links.

KEY TERMS

appraisal costs	house of quality	quality function
certified	internal failure costs	deployment (QFD)
continuous improvement	ISO 9000:2000	registered
cost of quality	kaizen	registrar
Deming Prize	Malcolm Baldrige National	robust design
design for manufacture	Quality Award	six sigma
and assembly (DFMA)	(MBNQA)	Taguchi Methods
design for operations	Plan-Do-Check-Act cycle	total quality management
(DFO)	prevention costs	(TQM)
external failure costs	poka-yoke	voice of the customer

URLS

American Express: www.americanexpress.com/homepage/mt_personal.shtml

AT&T: www.att.com/att/

British Standards Institute: www.bsi-global.com/index.xalter

Burger King: www.burgerking.com/CompanyInfo/index.html

Chugach School District: www.chugachschools.com/

Dell: www.dell.com/us/en/gen/corporate/access.htm

FedEx: www.fedex.com/us/about/

Florida Power and Light:
www.fpl.com/about/quality/contents/fpls_commitment_to_quality.shtml

Firestone: mirror.bridgestone-firestone.com/corporate/profile_fr.html

Ford: www.ford.com/en/default.htm

Four Seasons: www.fourseasons.com/about_us/company_information/index.html

General Electric: www.ge.com/en/commitment/quality/

ISO: www.iso.ch/iso/en/ISOOnline.frontpage

L.L. Bean: www.llbean.com/customerService/firstTimeVisitor/index.html

Marriott: www.marriott.com/corporateinfo/default.asp?WT_Ref=MI_corpInfo_homlnk

McDonald's: www.mcdonalds.com/corporate/index.html

Motorola: www.motorola.com/content/0,1037,1,00.html

Pearl River School District: www.pearlriver.k12.ny.us/quality.htm

Ritz-Carlton: www.ritzcarlton.com/corporate/about_us/default.asp

Southwest Airlines: www.iflyswa.com/about_swa/

Underwriter's Laboratories: www.ul.com/

University of Wisconsin—Stout: www.uwstout.edu/mba/

Xerox: www.xerox.com

QUESTIONS

1. Are there any similarities between any of the internally oriented definitions of quality and any of the externally oriented ones?

2. List the dimensions for service quality and those for manufacturing quality. What are the commonalities and differences?

3. What assumptions about the relationship between our standards and those of the customer are made by internally oriented definitions of quality?

4. What are the differences and similarities among the philosophies of Deming, Juran, Crosby, and Taguchi?

5. Find out which companies won the Baldrige Award this year and identify some aspects of their operations that conform with the components of TQM.

6. Is it possible for a company to implement TQM by having top management delegate responsibility to middle managers? Why or why not?

7. Do standard accounting measures of performance support or inhibit the implementation of TQM? Why?

8. Find a company that is working toward or has received ISO 9000 certification. Determine what benefits the company derived or is deriving from that process.

9. List the components of quality management and briefly describe a few of the ideas, concepts, or techniques that are included in each.

10. List some customer needs associated with home theater equipment, and group these together by categories. Suggest some possible engineering characteristics that could measure achievement of these attributes.

11. One quality myth is that increased quality means increased costs. Use your own personal knowledge or experiences to show this may not be true.

12. One argument against quality teams says that they will not work in the United States because the culture is different from that in Japan. Discuss this argument in terms of your knowledge about the Japanese management system.

13. List the three categories of quality costs, and briefly define each.

14. Explain how the idea of quality function deployment might be applied to a service organization that is not providing a tangible good as its product.

INTERNET QUESTIONS

15. Visit the Baldrige Award Web site (www.quality.nist.gov) and find the award criteria for health care and education. Identify how these criteria differ from the business category.

16. Visit the ISO Web site (www.iso.ch/iso/en/ISOOnline.frontpage) to identify the individual standards that make up the ISO 9000 "family."

17. Determine how quality is integrated into the competitive strategies of various companies based on information obtained through the Web site links to company pages for companies mentioned in this chapter.

NOTES

1. Harold L. Gilmore, "Product Conformance Cost," *Quality Progress* (June 1974): 16.
2. Lawrence Abbott, *Quality and Competition* (New York: Columbia University Press, 1955): 126–127.
3. Joseph M. Juran (ed.), *Quality Control Handbook*, Third Edition (New York: McGraw-Hill, 1974): 2-2.
4. Corwin D. Edwards, "The Meaning of Quality," *Quality Progress* (October 1968): 37.
5. Leonard L. Berry, Valarie A. Zeithaml, and A. Parasuraman, "Five Imperatives for Improving Service Quality," *Sloan Management Review* (Summer 1990): 29–38.
6. Based on Mary Baechler, "Tom Peters Ruined My Life," *The Wall Street Journal* (Oct. 25 1993): A18.

CHAPTER 5

Enterprise Integration and Supply Chain Management: A Strategic Perspective

LEARNING OBJECTIVES

After completing this chapter, you should be able to:

- Define supply chain management.
- Explain the consequences of not sharing information, and describe some of the information that can be shared in a supply chain.
- Define Digital Loyalty Networks and CPFR.
- Discuss various options in supply chain structure.
- Compare insourcing, outsourcing, and vertical integration.
- Compare responsive supply chains to efficient supply chains.
- Describe some supply chain strategies.
- Discuss the impact of e-commerce on supply chain management.
- Explain how ERP facilitates e-commerce.
- Describe some supply chain performance measures and use the Strategic Profit Model.
- Discuss global issues in supply chain management.
- Explain the four principles of supply chain management

INTRODUCTION

Earlier chapters introduced the concept of a **supply chain.** Recall that a supply chain encompasses all activities associated with the flow and transfer of goods and services, from raw material extraction through use by the final consumer. A supply chain may include different parts of one company as shown in Exhibit 5.1 or, more likely, different companies as shown in Exhibit 5.2. For example, suppose you purchase a DVD player from a retailer. The retailer obtained that DVD player through a distributor, which originally purchased the player from the manufacturer. All of those different companies, as well as you as the consumer, are part of the supply chain. However, the supply chain does not end there. The manufacturer purchased component parts from various tier 1 suppliers, such as companies that make plastic parts. Those **tier 1 suppliers** may have also purchased materials from **tier 2 suppliers,** such as companies that produce the chemicals for making plastic. Finally, those tier 2 suppliers could have also purchased the raw materials to make those chemicals from **tier 3 suppliers** who extract petroleum from the earth. In addition, the supply chain includes the companies that move these items, such as trucking companies, railroads, and shipping companies, as well as warehouses or distribution centers where items may be temporarily stored during movement from one location to another. This latter component is referred to as **logistics.** Finally, it may be necessary to return defective products to the manufacturer for repair or replacement. The activities that perform that function are known as **reverse logistics.**

It is important to be aware that, in addition to materials, information also flows through a supply chain. Suppose, for example, that the DVD player model you purchased is selling extremely well and the retailer wants to stock more of them. That retailer needs to provide information to the distributor to ship more of that model, the distributor needs to inform the manufacturer to make more, and the manufacturer needs to notify its suppliers to provide more of the necessary component parts. Ideally, though, the information from the retailer, as well as other information from other members of the supply chain would be shared among the entire supply chain, not just with those companies each member deals with directly. This global approach to having all members of the supply chain work together, coordinate their activities, and share information is known as **supply chain management.**

Some companies such as Wal-Mart, Dell, Toyota, and The Home Depot have fine-tuned their supply chains to the point that the supply chain provides a very strong competitive advantage both in terms of service and price. This chapter discusses how these companies and others have used supply chain management to their advantage.

OVERVIEW OF SUPPLY CHAIN MANAGEMENT

In the past, the separate companies, and even separate parts of one company, in a supply chain acted in their own best interests, not those of the entire supply chain. Information

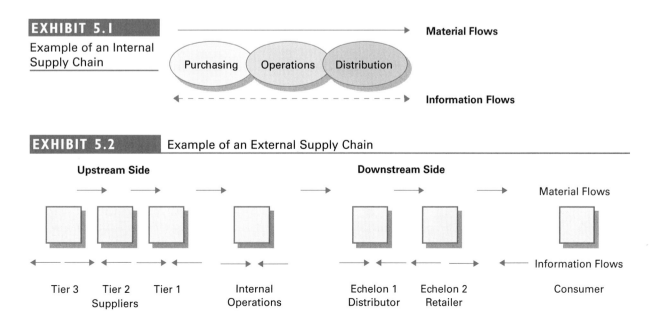

EXHIBIT 5.1

Example of an Internal Supply Chain

Purchasing   Operations   Distribution

Material Flows

Information Flows

EXHIBIT 5.2   Example of an External Supply Chain

Upstream Side   **Downstream Side**

Material Flows

Information Flows

Tier 3   Tier 2   Tier 1   Internal   Echelon 1   Echelon 2   Consumer
         Suppliers   Operations   Distributor   Retailer

was not shared among members of the supply chain, and only limited information was provided to the other members of the supply chain that a company dealt with directly. Several factors, however, have emerged that now require companies to use supply chain management as part of their competitive strategy. Those factors are:

- Globalization
- Increased competition
- Information technology
- Shorter product life cycles

Globalization has led to new markets, but also to more companies producing and selling the same products. Even established markets have become more competitive as companies identify new ways of winning market share. One way of winning market share is introducing new products, leading to shorter product life cycles. Finally, information technology has opened up new ways of buying and selling through the Internet and has also allowed companies to obtain and disseminate information much more rapidly than before.

Because of these changes, companies have been forced to be more competitive. One way to be more competitive is through supply chain management. By coordinating all supply chain activities, companies can ensure that the customer obtains the desired product at the desired time for a competitive price. Furthermore, companies in the supply chain can minimize costs over the entire supply chain, thus benefiting all the members. Supply chain management is, therefore, defined as the integrated coordination of all components of the supply chain—from raw materials to the final customer—so that information and materials flow smoothly.

INFORMATION SHARING IN THE SUPPLY CHAIN

Traditionally, information has been shared only between adjacent supply chain pairs, and that information has been very limited. For example, a retailer may order a certain number of units from a distributor, informing the distributor only of the number of units wanted at that time and, perhaps, when those units should be delivered. Very little, if any, other information, such as expected future changes in demand, possible trends, or planned promotions, would be shared between the retailer and the distributor. And, even the small amount of information that was shared would probably not go beyond those two members of the supply chain. This limited approach to information sharing does not optimize the performance of the supply chain, and can even lead to detrimental results such as the "bullwhip effect."

The Bullwhip Effect

The **bullwhip effect** is an example of what can happen when information is not shared in a supply chain. It is caused when a retailer experiences a slight increase in demand and increases its order quantity to avoid running out. The distributor also notices the increased order from its customer (the retailer) and, also to avoid running out, increases its order to the factory by an even larger amount. The factory, in turn, will further increase its orders to suppliers of raw materials. The end result is that a slight increase in demand at the retailer level gets magnified into a huge jump in demand at the raw material supplier level—a possible four-fold increase above usual demand, as shown in Exhibit 5.3.

Instead of succumbing to problems such as the bullwhip effect, successful supply chains use a hub and spoke approach to sharing information. Each spoke represents a connection to a member of the supply chain. All members of the supply chain transmit information to

EXHIBIT 5.3
The Bullwhip Effect

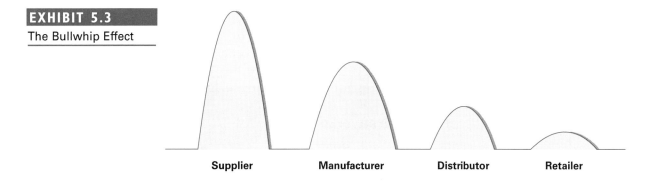

Supplier   Manufacturer   Distributor   Retailer

a central hub, and each member has access to all information provided by the other members. By sharing this information, all supply chain partners will be able to see changes occurring anywhere in the supply chain, and respond to those changes accordingly. The following sections indicate some ways for data to be shared.

Electronic Data Interchange

Electronic Data Interchange (EDI) has been around for a long time. But, now it is an important part of supply chain management. EDI connects the databases of different companies. In one early use, EDI allowed companies utilizing material requirements planning (MRP) to inform suppliers of upcoming orders by providing them with access to the database of planned orders. Although this approach was innovative at the time, it still represented only limited sharing of information between adjacent links in the supply chain. In supply chain management, EDI is a means of sharing information among all members of a supply chain. Additionally, shared databases can ensure that all supply chain members have access to the same information, providing visibility to everyone and avoiding problems such as the bullwhip effect.

Forecast Accuracy

One problem with sharing information is that some of that information may not be accurate. For example, a retailer may forecast future sales of a particular clothing line. When demand actually occurs, it may differ from the forecast by quite a lot, either higher or lower. If the forecast was too high, then the retailer may be left with excess inventory that must eventually be sold at a loss. On the other hand, a forecast that is too low can mean unmet demand and lost sales.

By sharing forecast information, risk can be spread across the entire supply chain rather than being borne by the retailer. Information sharing can also lead to improved forecast accuracy. For example, if one retailer is projecting low sales while others are projecting high sales, information about the forecasts from other retailers may lead the one retailer to revise its forecasts to be more in line with the consensus.

Simply realizing that forecasts will always be inaccurate can lead to improving supply chain management. For instance, Quick Response programs, discussed later in this chapter, are one technique the fashion industry has developed to deal with demand uncertainty. Furthermore, historical information about forecast accuracy can be used to develop a confidence interval for demand. Thus, the supplier may be able to say that there is a certain probability that demand will not vary from the forecast by more than a specific amount. This information can help the supplier to plan for a certain range of possible demand values.

Wal-Mart is one company that has used EDI to improve forecast accuracy. Vendors who provide products to Wal-Mart can use Wal-Mart's satellite network system to directly access real-time, **point-of-sale (POS)** data coming in from the cash registers at Wal-Mart stores. This up-to-the-minute information can then be used by those vendors to improve forecasts by spotting trends the moment they occur.

Digital Loyalty Networks

The term **"Digital Loyalty Networks"** was coined by Deloitte Research to describe links between a company's supply chain and its customer management operations, such as marketing and sales teams. The idea is to customize the supply chain to meet the needs of a company's most important customers or market segments. This customization is achieved by sharing information between the supply chain and customer management operations. By sharing information, the supply chain, the customer management operations, and the customer can all benefit through improved service and reduced costs.

Collaborative Planning Forecasting and Replenishment (CPFR)

In theory, information is shared easily among all partners in a supply chain. In actual practice, however, the process often does not work that smoothly. As a result, members of the supply chain may make assumptions about future actions of other supply chain members. For example, each supplier must forecast the demand of its customers. **CPFR** seeks to minimize this guessing game through collaboration among supply chain partners to jointly develop a plan that specifies what is to be sold, how it will be marketed and promoted, where, and during what time period. Furthermore, sharing of information is facilitated by utilizing a common set of communication standards. Thus, all partners are involved in the development of plans and forecasts for the entire group. Because these plans and forecasts have been jointly agreed upon, considerable uncertainty is removed from the process.

Eroski operates supermarkets and hypermarkets in Spain and France. Henkel, a German company, is one of the suppliers for Eroski stores. Although Henkel had utilized EDI with its customers to improve inventory reordering, Eroski stores continued to run out of Henkel products on a regular basis. The two companies decided to pursue CPFR, beginning with joint demand forecasting. Before implementing CPFR, half of Henkel's forecasts of sales to Eroski had been off by more than 50 percent, accounting for the stockouts of Henkel products. After implementation of CPFR, 75 percent of forecasts were within 20 percent of actual demand, and Henkel products were in stock at Eroski stores 98 percent of the time.

CPFR (pronounced C-P-Far) requires that all supply chain parties be committed to the plans developed jointly and that they be committed to replanning on a regular basis. Thus, for example, a retailer will share information about demand forecasts and planned product promotions with its suppliers. Likewise, the suppliers share information about possible limitations on supply or periods during which production facilities may be shut down. Once a plan is developed, suppliers can begin production knowing that their customers in the supply chain have committed to those orders. Still, those plans also must be revisited on a regular basis to ensure that adjustments are made when appropriate.

SUPPLY CHAIN STRUCTURE

As shown in Exhibit 5.2, the upstream supply chain includes suppliers, which may be tier 1, tier 2, or tier 3. Each tier of the upstream supply chain may include multiple suppliers for the same good or service. The **upstream** side of the supply chain also includes production planning and purchasing, which are part of the **internal supply chain,** as well as logistics, which is responsible for moving materials between supply chain members. On the **downstream** side, supply chain partners are divided into echelons. For example, **echelon 1** includes organizations, such as distributors, importers, or exporters that receive the product directly from the organization that produces it. Echelon 2 organizations would then receive it from those at echelon 1. **Echelon 2** might include retailers, dealers, or even final consumers.

It is important to realize that Exhibit 5.2 is a greatly simplified diagram of a supply chain. In reality there are a whole host of organizations that provides goods and services that are required either directly or indirectly for making the product and for moving materials and information between supply chain partners. How these numerous organizations are arranged and relate to one another is what determines supply chain structure. This section will briefly discuss only the most basic ideas related to how supply chains are structured.

Many Suppliers versus Few Suppliers

At each tier of the upstream supply chain, companies can decide whether to use many suppliers for a particular good or service or few suppliers. By using many suppliers, a company can often take advantage of competition among those suppliers to meet the company's demands for cost, quality, delivery, and so forth. Furthermore, if one supplier goes out of business or is unable to provide the good or service as requested, it is a simple matter to use another supplier.

On the other hand, there are some advantages to having only a few suppliers. Chief among these is the long-term partnership arrangements that can be developed. Such relationships enable both parties to work together for greater integration of the supply chain and for development of methods that can improve quality and lower costs. Having fewer suppliers can also have negative consequences. For example, such a close relationship may make each member too dependent on the other, stifling change and creativity. For this reason, some companies do not deal with suppliers if their business would account for more than 50 percent of the supplier's total sales.

Insourcing versus Outsourcing

Organizations must utilize a wide range of goods and services in making products and getting them to the customers. If those goods and services are provided by the organization itself, they are **"insourced."** Goods and services obtained from outside suppliers are **"outsourced."** One basic reason companies decide to outsource is that the goods or services can be obtained less expensively from outside suppliers. Outside suppliers may specialize in producing that good or service, enabling them to maintain high quality while keeping costs low. Other reasons for outsourcing and calculations that can be used to compare costs of insourcing versus outsourcing can be found in the additional supply chain material available through this book's companion Web site.

Vertical Integration

Supply chain management requires close coordination with suppliers, but if those suppliers are separate organizations, then there may be some question about how much coordination can occur. One way of promoting coordination is for a company to own its suppliers. This is called **backward vertical integration.**

> **EXAMPLE**
>
> The early Ford Motor Company provides a classic example of backward vertical integration. Henry Ford believed that owning his sources of supply was the best way to guarantee an uninterrupted supply of component parts and raw materials to build his Model T. As a result, he owned iron mines, rubber plantations, and shipping companies. Unfortunately, Ford may have been ahead of his time. Information channels necessary for coordination had not been developed to the extent they are today. Ford's massive system eventually became unwieldy and inflexible, resulting in severe problems when competitors began offering product variety that Ford was unable to provide.

If companies own the distribution systems and retail outlets that sell their products, then that is **forward vertical integration.** For example, many grocery chains have their own private-label brands, which are distributed through systems they own and sold through the grocery chains' retail stores. Vertical integration has both advantages and disadvantages, as shown in Exhibit 5.4.

Virtual Organizations

Today, outsourcing is gaining in popularity because of cost advantages and the opportunities for greater coordination that have been provided by the improved communication technologies of e-commerce. This system has even led to some **"virtual corporations,"** that is, companies that exist only as an administrative shell, with all other functions outsourced. Outsourcing provides a great deal of flexibility because the company can change sources of supply as the requirements of its products or markets change.

> **EXAMPLE**
>
> One virtual corporation is Mr. Coffee Concepts, which provides in-room coffeemakers for hotel chains, such as Marriott. The company itself provides only the administrative and coordination functions, while it contracts with other companies to perform the actual manufacturing, shipping, and distribution of the product. Mr. Coffee Concepts has no production facilities of its own and, if everything works correctly, it never even touches the product, which is shipped directly to the final destination.

Disintermediation

An intermediary is a business entity that exists between two other parts of the supply chain. For example, travel agents are an intermediary between the travelers who buy airline tickets and the airlines that sell those tickets. A growing trend today is to achieve efficiencies in the supply chain by eliminating some intermediaries. This process is known as **disintermediation.** For example, many airlines now have their own Web sites through

EXHIBIT 5.4 Advantages and Disadvantages of Vertical Integration	Advantages	Disadvantages
	Better coordination	Higher overhead
	Lower cost	Mismatch of business types
	Greater control over supply	Lack of flexibility
	Utilize excess capacity	Capacity mismatch

which travelers can purchase tickets directly from the airline, without using the services of a travel agent. From the traveler's viewpoint, this process may be advantageous because he or she can readily compare all different flight times and routing options, see what special promotions are currently being offered by the airline, and even compare prices among different airlines by visiting other Web sites. Getting that information from a travel agent in a form the traveler can readily utilize may be much more difficult.

EXAMPLE   Travelocity is one company that has succeeded by utilizing the Internet to provide travelers with easily accessible information from airlines, hotels, and car rental companies. The advantage of Travelocity is that it enables a customer to compare prices offered by different travel service suppliers without having to visit the Web site of each one. However, a group of major airlines has now begun competing directly with Travelocity through their own Web site, Orbitz. Orbitz is owned by American Airlines, United Airlines, Continental Airlines, Delta Air Lines, and Northwest Airlines and promises to provide airfares that are lower than those through Travelocity, thus seeking to eliminate Travelocity as an intermediary.

Types of Supply Chains

Supply chains are not only described by their structure, but also by their competitive focus. This section discusses the two major types from a competitive focus perspective—responsive and efficient. The type of supply chain that is most appropriate in a particular situation will be determined by the characteristics of products that move through the supply chain.

Responsive Supply Chains

Some product groups, such as fashions or technology, are characterized by frequent innovation. These innovations can make product demand unpredictable and require the entire supply chain to respond quickly as new products are introduced and as demand changes. At the same time, the supply chain must be able to transmit information quickly among its members. That information may include not only information about customer responses to new products but also information about what customers would like to see in future products.

A particular type of supply chain, known as a **responsive supply chain,** is needed to meet these requirements. Members of such a supply chain are selected based on their speed and flexibility and their capacity to provide information from the marketplace to supply chain members. For example, responsive (also called innovative) supply chains are frequently used in the fashion industry.

Efficient Supply Chains

A very different type of supply chain is needed for products that are standard functional items, such as commodities. These products have long product life cycles and stable, predictable demand. They are also often characterized by low profit margins. For these products, the supply chain must focus on operating efficiently to minimize costs. Such supply chains are known as **efficient supply chains,** and the members are chosen based on their ability to keep costs down and to minimize inventory in the system. The grocery industry is one group that is characterized by efficient (also called functional) supply chains. Exhibit 5.5 compares the two types of supply chains.

EXHIBIT 5.5	Responsive Supply Chains For Innovative Products	Efficient Supply Chains For Functional Products
Responsive vs. Efficient Supply Chains	Closely integrated in production planning and control, quality management, service, after-sales support.	Use traditional criteria for evaluating suppliers.
	Track work-in-process and finished goods inventory.	Place high value on integrity, commitment, reliability, and consistency.
	Share more information.	Value suppliers for ability to provide cost savings, reduce downtime, and reduce inventory.
	Use systemwide measures of end-use-customer satisfaction.	
	Suppliers are evaluated based on product development time, geographic proximity, lead time, and cycle time.	

Source: K. Ramdas and R. Spekman, "Chain or Shackles: Understanding What Drives Supply-Chain Performance," *Interfaces,* Vol. 30, No. 4 (July–August, 2000) pp. 3–21.

SUPPLY CHAIN STRATEGIES

Various approaches to managing supply chains have been developed. Many of these strategies can be used together, although some may be more relevant to certain types of supply chains or certain structures.

Quick Response Programs

Quick Response (QR) programs were initiated by the retail industry, particularly those that sell fashion apparel, as a means of reducing the difference between amounts produced and customer demand for an item. Historically, lead times required companies to produce fashion items far ahead of the typical selling season.

EXAMPLE

Sport Obermeyer, a maker of fashion skiwear, traditionally had to begin its design process two years in advance of sales. Actual production of those designs began about one year ahead of sales. Obviously, when production began, the company could only estimate how many units of each product would actually be sold. With the long lead time, companies often ended up with too many units of products that did not sell well and not enough of high-demand products. This resulted in high costs for carrying excess inventory, losses associated with selling that inventory at a discount, and lost sales for items with insufficient supply. Such costs have been estimated to be 25 percent of total retail sales.

The original idea behind quick response programs was to reduce costs by reducing the lead time, enabling producers to adjust inventory levels after some initial demand figures have been obtained. Thus, one key component of quick response systems is lead time reduction throughout the supply chain, which can be done through methods such as cross docking, discussed later in the chapter. The second major component of quick response systems is EDI. In order to take advantage of the early demand information, companies need fast access to that information. Thus, the data must be collected through point-of-sale (POS) systems such as bar code (UPC code) scanners and then made available to other members of the supply chain via EDI.

QR has now evolved beyond its beginnings and has expanded outside the apparel industry. Furthermore, although QR began in North America, it has now spread to Europe and Australia. A subset, known as Quick Response Manufacturing, focuses on identifying ways of modifying the manufacturing process so that manufacturers can quickly change products to meet changes in customer demand. Another advanced form of QR is Vendor Managed Inventory.

Vendor Managed Inventory (VMI)

Instead of a retailer following the traditional approach of placing inventory replenishment orders with suppliers, those suppliers can use demand and inventory information from the retailer to determine when they should replenish the supplier's inventory.

EXAMPLE

Wal-Mart, in conjunction with suppliers such as Procter & Gamble, has implemented **VMI.** Under VMI the vendor, or supplier, can better coordinate its own production with the replenishment of supplier inventory, thus reducing costs and improving delivery performance between the supplier and the retailer. To make this work, the supplier receives daily POS data from Wal-Mart stores and has access to Wal-Mart's inventory files.

Some companies such as Bose, which manufactures audio components, have carried this idea one step further by having personnel from their suppliers work within Bose's own purchasing department. Bose has called this approach **JIT II.** In the past, Bose's own purchasing personnel handled all purchasing from suppliers. But, because the Bose personnel worked with many different suppliers, they might not be fully knowledgeable about the full range of products offered by each supplier and they definitely were not aware of the inventory levels and production plans of those suppliers. Under JIT II, employees of major suppliers work right in the Bose purchasing department and handle all purchases from their companies. These employees are aware of all products offered by their companies. Thus, they are often able to suggest better alternatives. Furthermore, because these people are employees of the suppliers, they are kept aware of all supplier information, such as current inventory levels of products and plans for future production. This knowledge enables them to spot possible future shortages and avoid problems before they occur.

Efficient Consumer Response

Efficient Consumer Response (ECR) is a supply chain management approach originally used in the grocery business, but has now expanded into retail, health services, and even the automotive industry. Traditionally, the grocery industry has relied upon discounts by the manufacturers to push products through the system. Retail stores would engage in what is known as "forward buying" whenever manufacturers offered discounts. This forward buying meant that the retailer grocery store might buy a year's worth of supply of one particular item. Unfortunately, this approach did not work to anyone's benefit as retailers incurred huge inventory carrying costs to store the large inventory until it could be sold. The manufacturers experienced large bursts in demand whenever discounts were offered. To meet this increased demand, they often had to schedule overtime or add extra shifts, incurring additional costs.

Under ECR, material is pulled through the supply chain by consumer demand. Instead of offering special promotions and discounts, manufacturers offer "everyday low pricing." Thus, there is no advantage for the retailer to engage in forward buying. Once again, EDI and efficient supply chain management are important parts of the process. Information about consumer demand comes directly from the POS information provided by UPC scanners at checkout counters. This information is used by suppliers to match their production to demand, thus reducing inventory throughout the system.

EXAMPLE

Procter & Gamble has used ECR extensively, resulting in several changes in the way P&G operates. First, in line with the original ECR model, value pricing replaced the use of promotions and trade discounts. Second, the range of package sizes was reduced. Finally, some marginal product lines were dropped completely. These actions reduced costs and increased efficiency.

ECR has spawned a number of related initiatives, all of which utilize technology to increase efficiency and reduce costs:

- *Efficient assortment*—Category management software is used to stock more of those items that consumers want the most.
- *Efficient promotion*—Product promotion is related to customer need and usage, eliminating forward buying, etc.
- *Efficient product introduction*—New product development and introduction are a joint effort between producers, distributors, and retailers.

Postponement

A common problem in supply chains is that many different possible options on an individual product may be available to consumers. For example, a particular model of automobile may theoretically be built in two million combinations of paint color, trim package, engine, transmission, and interior colors. Because of this large number of possibilities, manufacturers find it extremely difficult to accurately forecast demand for each possible combination of options. Inaccurate forecasts mean that they may end up with large inventories of unsold products the consumer did not want while running out of the products the consumer did want. On the other hand, waiting to produce a product until the customer actually wants it may entail very long lead times. For example, the lead time to produce an automobile with the specific options desired by a customer may approach two months.

To overcome these problems, companies may use either product or process postponement. For example, electronics manufacturers such as Hewlett-Packard use **product postponement,** also known as delayed differentiation, by producing a generic product at the central manufacturing facility, then adding specific components needed to customize the product for the final consumer at the latest possible point in the distribution system. Thus, in product postponement, the final configuration of the product is delayed until the last possible step in the supply chain. This is done to some extent by automobile manufacturers located outside the United States. Certain options are added to their automobiles, customizing them for the U.S. market, after those cars are received in the U.S. In fact, some options may even be installed by the dealer.

In **process postponement,** certain steps in the production process are delayed until the last possible moment. Thus, instead of maintaining inventory of finished products, a company will maintain inventory of component parts. Ideally, the finished product will be produced only after customer orders have been received. Because there are usually fewer possible configurations of component parts than there are of finished products, less inventory must be held. For this approach to work effectively, however, the lead times for making finished products must be short enough that they will be acceptable to customers. If not, then either finished goods inventory must be held or ways must be found to shorten the process lead times.

EXAMPLE

With process postponement, companies may sometimes follow a hybrid approach. For example, pizza parlors usually do not assemble and bake pizzas until the customer places an order. However, at lunch time, when some customers may not want to wait for their pizza, the restaurant may produce commonly ordered pizzas, such as cheese or pepperoni, and put those in inventory so customers may order slices from those prebaked pizzas. At dinnertime, when customers have time to wait, all pizzas may be produced only to customer order.

Revenue Sharing

Revenue sharing is a supply chain approach in which the retailer's revenue is shared between it and its supplier, in return for the supplier providing the product at a lower cost. This approach has been used by Blockbuster video stores. Blockbuster purchases videos from movie studios, and then rents those videos to customers. For popular movies, the peak demand for video rentals occurs immediately after the video is first released. This peak demand period, however, usually lasts only a few weeks. If video rental stores purchase enough tapes (at a cost of $60 or more per tape) to cover peak demand, their profits during the two-week peak demand period will be drastically reduced. Thus, the video rental stores have traditionally purchased only enough tapes to maximize their expected profit during the peak demand period. Unfortunately, this often meant that when a customer went to rent a popular video, all available copies had been checked out. Not only was the customer frustrated, but the video rental store lost the revenue of that additional rental.

EXAMPLE

In 1998, Blockbuster implemented revenue sharing as a way to increase its profits by making more tapes of popular movies available for rental. Movie studios agreed to sell tapes to Blockbuster for $9 per tape instead of $60. In return, Blockbuster agreed to share its video rental revenue with the movie studios, with half of those revenues going to Blockbuster and half going to the movie studio that sold the video. Because Blockbuster could afford to purchase more videos, its rental income increased. Even though the movie studio's income from video sales decreased, the revenue received

EXHIBIT 5.6

Revenue Sharing
Example

	Traditional Pricing	Revenue Sharing
Retailer		
Number of tapes purchased	8	30
Price per tape	$75	$10
Total purchase cost of tapes	8 x $75 = $600	30 x $10 = $300
Number of rentals	200	400
Total rental revenue ($4/rental)	$4 x 200 = $800	$4 x 400 = $1,600
Retailer's share of revenue	@ 100% = $800	@ 50% = $800
Retailer's profit	$800 − $600 = $200	$800 − $300 = $500
Supplier		
Number of tapes sold to retailer	8	30
Revenue per tape	$75	$10
Total revenue from tape sales	8 x $75 = $600	30 x $10 = $300
Supplier's share of rental revenue	@ 0% = $0	@ 50% = $800
Supplier's total revenue	$600 + $0 + $600	$300 + $800 + $1,100
Supplier's production and distribution costs ($10/tape)	8 x $10 = $80	30 x $10 = $300
Supplier's profit	$600 − $80 = $520	$1,100 − $300 = $800

from video rentals more than offset that decrease. As can be seen in Exhibit 5.6, revenue sharing produces an increase in profits for both the retailer and the supplier.

Cross Docking

One objective of supply chain management is to reduce inventory throughout the supply chain. Distribution centers, which receive shipments from a factory, then break down those shipments into smaller quantities that are shipped to customers, often represent a major investment in inventory. The reason is that receipt of shipments from the factory is not coordinated with shipments to suppliers. Thus, a large shipment of a product may be received from the factory, then placed into inventory until separate small shipments to suppliers gradually decrease it.

Cross docking seeks to coordinate inbound and outbound shipments so that little, if any, inventory must be kept at the distribution center. As a shipment is received from the factory and broken down, each unit of the inbound shipment is immediately moved to a location awaiting outbound shipment to a customer. After each outbound shipment is fully assembled, it is sent on to the customer. Consequently, the distribution center serves primarily as a location for breaking down incoming shipments from the factory and redistributing the items into outgoing shipments to customers. Unlike the traditional approach, the distribution center used for cross docking does not serve as a site for storing inventory. Wal-Mart is one company that has used cross docking very effectively to decrease its costs by reducing inventory in the supply chain.

3PL

In order to maximize the use of cross docking, some companies have developed what are known as 3PL partnerships. In this case, **3PL** stands for third-party logistics. In other words, an outside supplier handles all the logistics activities between supplier and customer. These logistics activities can include inventory control, material handling, and transportation.

EXAMPLE   Penske and Ford Motor Company have formed a 3PL partnership under which Penske is responsible for all logistics from many of Ford's part suppliers to many of Ford's assembly plants, an arrangement that includes cross-docking activities. Through this 3PL arrangement, Ford has probably saved tens of millions of dollars in inventory costs per year.

The advantage of 3PL is that companies such as Penske can specialize in optimizing logistics efficiency because, unlike Ford, they are not also responsible for manufacturing a product. Furthermore, Penske is able to combine shipments from many different suppliers and many different customers, taking advantage of opportunities for cross docking and reduced transportation costs.

E-COMMERCE

When you hear the term e-commerce or e-business, don't just think of dot-com companies that sell over the Internet. The Internet is now an important part of the supply chain management and communication strategy for many companies. For example, Dell Computer Company did not realize substantial profits until it began selling its product directly to the consumer, with much of that business being done over the Internet. That particular aspect of the Internet, transactions between businesses and consumers, is referred to as **B2C** (business to consumer). However, B2C transactions over the Internet are dwarfed by the much larger volume of **B2B** (business to business) transactions. For example, Cisco, a manufacturer of computer software, and Oracle, a software company, have now transferred nearly all of their purchasing functions to the Internet. Furthermore, the Internet now serves as a fast, low-cost way for companies to communicate information throughout the supply chain. This section will briefly explore all three aspects of e-commerce as they relate to supply chain management.

B2C

It is now possible to buy nearly anything over the Internet. Some companies, such as Amazon.com, operate only on the Internet. Other companies that have been traditionally "bricks and mortar" retailers, such as J.C. Penney, now follow a "clicks and bricks" approach by also offering their products over the Internet.

From a supply chain management perspective, B2C transactions have both advantages and disadvantages. On the advantage side, customers can be given a much wider choice than would be possible in a traditional retail establishment. For example, Lands' End now offers, through its Web site, jeans customized to a buyer's exact specifications. Furthermore, the customer takes care of the order entry process by entering his or her own credit card number, address, measurements, and so forth. This information can be captured and used to simplify subsequent transactions. Information about the transaction has already been entered into the Internet and can be easily shared with other supply chain partners. Finally, some products, such as computer software or e-books, can also be distributed over the Internet.

At the same time, B2C transactions can make things more difficult, especially for the logistics component of the supply chain. For example, suppose a Dell Computer customer orders a computer, which is produced in Dell's plant near Austin Texas, and a monitor, which is purchased from a manufacturer in China. The customer would prefer that both items be delivered at the same time, not separately. Making sure that occurs can be a logistical nightmare.

EXAMPLE

Christmas in 1999 was the first big sales season for dot-com companies, and it was a disaster for many. While these companies had systems in place to take incoming orders, they were not well prepared to assemble those orders or to get them shipped out on time. The result was that many customers did not receive their orders until after Christmas. While orders peaked on December 10, shipments did not peak until December 21. That long delay left many dot-com companies holding the bag with a lot of unhappy customers. One company, Toys"R"Us, ended up offering a $100 coupon to each one of its dissatisfied customers.

B2B

B2B (business-to-business) transactions account for more than 80 percent of all transactions on the Internet and are projected to reach $3 trillion by 2003. To understand where all that transaction volume is coming from, it's worthwhile to look at the different types of B2B Internet companies that are developing to service those transactions listed below:

  ■ *Exchanges*—Allow purchaser to smooth peaks and valleys in demand by rapidly exchanging items required for production. One example of a B2B exchange is e-steel, which is an online marketplace for steel buyers, sellers, and processors.

- *MRO Hubs*—Increase efficiency by providing access to many suppliers of items used for maintenance, repair, and operations (MRO), such as oil and pencils. For example, Ariba provides online access to a worldwide group of suppliers.
- *Yield Managers*—Create spot markets for common operating inputs, such as electricity or labor. One such company, Employease, provides resources that can help companies optimize their human resource management operations, including hiring and training.

Enterprise Resource Planning (ERP)

The philosophy behind supply chain management is better integration, coordination, and communication among members of the supply chain. These efforts, however, are often stymied by the separate databases used by the individual members of the supply chain. The idea behind **ERP** is to eliminate this roadblock either by allowing access to one another's databases or, ideally, the use of one common database.

To understand the problems that can be engendered by separate databases, let's begin with a company that sells directly to the final customer. Suppose one of those customers calls up the marketing department to inquire about the status of an order. The marketing database will probably show only information specific to marketing, such as the date the order was entered. If that order is in production, then either someone from marketing or the customer will need to contact production to find out the status of the order because that information would ordinarily not be in the marketing database. Suppose the order has been completed and shipped. The production database would probably show only completion of the order, but no shipping information. To obtain that information someone would have to contact distribution or logistics. Because of the separate databases, no one in any area of the company has access to all company information. Thus, the customer is bounced from one department to another to get the answer to a simple question about order status.

A second problem with separate databases is that they may contain conflicting information. For example, suppose the customer order described above has been shipped, and the logistics database indicates so. But, the production database has not yet been updated, so it shows the order is still at the last processing operation. Thus, the customer might be told by production that the order is still in processing when, in reality, it was already shipped. So, the order might show up on the customer's doorstep unexpectedly.

The purpose of ERP is to avoid these problems by combining all these separate databases into one common database for the entire organization, and possibly even for the entire supply chain. The advantage of that approach is that anyone anywhere within the organization has access to all information. For example, someone in marketing would be able to tell if the order was held up in production awaiting a component part from a supplier. Furthermore, if the ERP system integrates the entire supply chain, then that marketing person could even determine where the part is in the supplier's production system. By using one common database, there is no problem with conflicting information among separate databases.

Extending this idea to an entire supply chain, the advantages become obvious. All members of the supply chain have access to the same information and utilize the same information for purposes of planning and execution. For example, some companies report reducing inventory levels throughout the supply chain by 50 percent or more. Microsoft expected to save $18 million annually by using ERP to replace 33 different financial tracking systems.

Exhibit 5.7 shows part of a typical ERP system configuration. All data are stored centrally in the database servers, which are accessed by individual application servers. Users access information via the application servers using front-end servers, which are usually PCs running Microsoft Windows.

EXHIBIT 5.7   Part of a Typical ERP System

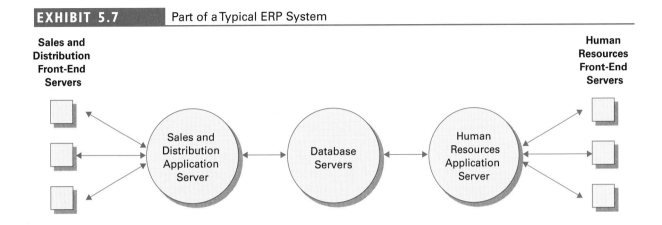

The latest configuration of ERP is Internet-based. The database servers shown in Exhibit 5.7 can be accessible to members of the supply chain via the Internet over secure connections, with information also being entered into those databases over the Internet. For example, the German company SAP, which has the largest share of the ERP market, now offers mySAP.com as its e-business version.

In spite of its advantages, ERP is not inexpensive, either in terms of purchase cost or in terms of the disruption that such a major change can have on an organization. It took Owens Corning two years to install an ERP system at a cost of $100 million. A recent survey found that the average cost of an ERP system was $15 million, although companies in that survey spent a low of $400,000 to a high of $300 million. There have also been some high-profile ERP failures.

EXAMPLE   Hershey Chocolate spent $112 million only to find that the ERP system ended up delaying shipments to customers. Allied Waste Industries stopped implementation of its ERP system after spending $130 million when the company decided the system was too expensive and too complicated to operate.

One complication from ERP implementation results from the fact that using a common database often requires that things be done differently than before. For example, in the past, people in the marketing department might have seen their function as selling product and then entering orders into the computer system. It was up to production to worry about meeting the promised delivery data, and finance was responsible for deciding whether to offer the customer credit. With an ERP system the marketing people may find that they now are not only responsible for entering orders but also for determining whether the delivery date can be met and whether the customer's credit rating is sufficient to justify offering credit. Such changes may require extensive retraining and a long break-in period until people get used to doing things the new way.

Some other criticisms of ERP center on the idea that it does not necessarily add value to the supply chain. For instance, ECR can greatly reduce costs and increase speed. Critics of ERP argue that it only perpetuates historical systems that are based on outdated approaches to supply chain management.

The main provider of ERP systems is a German company, SAP AG, whose ERP product is known as R/3. SAP has about 26 percent of the global ERP market, with the remainder split among such companies as i2 Technologies, PeopleSoft, Baan, and J.D. Edwards.

PERFORMANCE MEASUREMENT

Any organization must measure its performance, and a supply chain is no different. Measurement of supply chain performance, however, requires a different approach than has traditionally been used for individual companies. This section explores some current philosophies regarding supply chain performance measurement.

Measures Related to Competitive Priorities

Before the concept of supply chain management became popular, each company—or even each part of a company—would often focus on measuring its performance in terms of its own objectives, without regard to the rest of the supply chain. However, as discussed earlier, what is good for one part of the supply chain often is not good for the entire supply chain. Therefore, performance measures should focus on the entire supply chain and emphasize the objectives of that supply chain, not individual members. The list in Exhibit 5.8 indicates some possible supply chain performance measures related to various supply chain competitive priorities.

Strategic Profit Model

One popular tool for measuring overall supply chain performance is the **Strategic Profit Model.** The major advantage of this tool is that it aggregates many other measures into the one common measure of return on assets, which can be understood and appreciated by all components of the supply chain. Exhibit 5.9 shows the Strategic Profit Model and indicates how return on assets is calculated. Return on assets indicates how well each part of the supply chain, and the entire supply chain itself, is using its resources.

This model is also useful because it indicates the relationships among various measures. For example, it shows that return on assets can be improved by increasing either net profit margin or asset turnover, or both. Relative to supply chain management, suppose the company indicated in Exhibit 5.9 is considering an inventory reduction of $500. Such a reduction will increase asset turnover to .89. At the same time, an inventory reduction will reduce the variable expenses (for reasons that will be discussed more thoroughly in Chapters 12–14). For now, suppose variable expenses will be reduced by $100. This will increase net profit margin to 22.5 percent. The combined increases in asset turnover and net profit margin will increase return on assets to slightly over 20 percent. As this example shows, reducing inventory throughout the supply chain can have a significant impact on profitability measures.

EXHIBIT 5.8	Competitive Priority	Performance Measures
Supply Chain Performance Measure	Delivery Reliability	Percent on-time delivery Percent of demand satisfied from stock
	Responsiveness	Lead time
	Flexibility	Volume flexibility Product flexibility
	Cost	Cost of goods sold Supply chain costs Warranty/returns processing costs
	Asset Management	Days of inventory Inventory turns

EXHIBIT 5.9   Strategic Profit Model

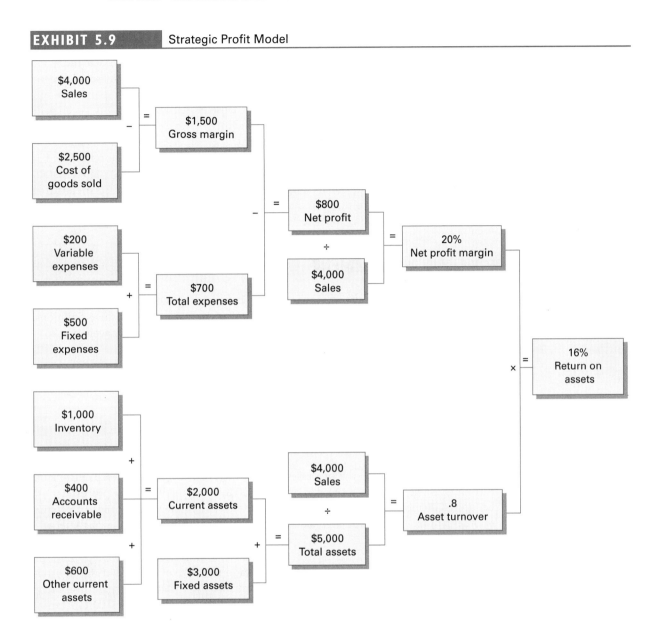

GLOBAL ISSUES IN SUPPLY CHAIN MANAGEMENT

Operating in today's global economy, companies have increased opportunities and challenges for managing their supply chains. Worldwide sourcing of materials and services means that companies may be able to reduce labor costs significantly by producing or purchasing products from countries such as China that have low labor costs. However, doing so may mean longer lead times and less control over quality. Additionally, higher shipping costs may offset the lower labor costs.

As mentioned earlier, decisions about supply chains must focus on the type of product and a company's competitive strategy. For example, a company that sells a standard functional product and competes on the basis of low cost may find it beneficial to source materials and products from low-cost countries because cost minimization is most important. The fact that long lead times may exist is less important because product demand is fairly constant, so it will not be necessary to respond quickly to changes in demand.

On the other hand, demand for an innovative product may vary considerably, and the supply chain must respond rapidly to such changes. For this situation, a responsive supply chain may seek to keep production and supply in close proximity to retail outlets, in spite of higher labor costs, so that lead times are kept short.

> **EXAMPLE**   Maintaining control over the supply chain can also be an important global issue. For example, McDonald's is very concerned about consistently high quality in its restaurants and the products they sell. Placing restaurants in far-flung locations means that McDonald's must ensure that the suppliers for meat, lettuce, and buns are able to provide the level of quality that McDonald's seeks consistently.

PRINCIPLES OF SUPPLY CHAIN MANAGEMENT

William T. Walker, who is the architect of supply chain management for Hewlett-Packard's Power Products Division, and Karen L. Alber, Vice President, Integrated Business Solutions, Quaker Oats Co., identify four principles associated with supply chain management:

1. Build a competitive infrastructure
2. Leverage the worldwide logistics network
3. Synchronize supply to demand
4. Measure performance globally

Build a Competitive Infrastructure

Infrastructure includes all the processes for ordering, delivery, inventory replenishment, accounts payable, accounts receivable, and returns. To be competitive, these processes must be focused on meeting the customer's needs. The easier a company makes it for a customer to order a product, pay for it, and take delivery, the more likely it is that the customer will buy from that company.

> **EXAMPLE**   Southwest Airlines now does a large percentage of its ticket sales over the Internet because the company has made it easy for customers to find and select the flight they want, use a credit card to purchase the ticket, then receive an e-ticket instantaneously. This may be one more reason Southwest has remained profitable while other airlines have filed for bankruptcy.

Leverage the Worldwide Logistics Network

Logistics includes those activities associated with moving and storing materials. Such activities, although they may appear superfluous, can often offer opportunities for cost reductions. For example, a company may be able to increase shipment volumes and reduce costs per unit by working with a smaller number of preferred carriers and shipping companies.

> **EXAMPLE**   The automaker Saturn has developed a relationship with Ryder trucking to provide carrier services from Saturn's suppliers to its assembly plant in Spring Hill, Tennessee. Even though the trucks are owned by Ryder, they are painted with the Saturn name and logo.

A further advantage of this relationship is that Ryder has on-board computers inside its trucks that provide useful information to Saturn about its incoming shipments.

Synchronize Supply to Demand

One objective of supply chain management is to minimize inventory in the supply chain, which is best done if supply is matched to demand throughout the supply chain. Such synchronization requires close cooperation and sharing of information among the members of that supply chain. Ideally, a new unit of product should be produced and moved through the supply chain only after the retailer has sold a unit of that particular product. Furthermore, the supply chain must be able to respond to surges in demand caused by special promotions or sales. In such cases, the retailer planning a sale or promotion must ensure that all parts of the supply chain are prepared and able to respond, without an increase in costs, to the increased demand.

Measure Performance Globally

In the past, each member of a supply chain sought to maximize its own performance without regard to other companies in the supply chain. Today, under the concept of supply chain management, the emphasis is on optimizing over the entire supply chain. Some global performance measures were discussed in the preceding section.

SUMMARY

- Supply chain management is an approach in which all members of the supply chain work together, coordinate their activities, and share information.

- The bullwhip effect, in which disruptions in demand are magnified through the supply chain, is one of the consequences of not sharing information. Some of the information that can be shared in a supply chain includes demand information, forecasts, planned orders, and sales.

- With vertical integration a company owns various components of the supply chain. Under outsourcing, those components of the supply chain are provided by independent companies.

- Responsive supply chains focus on quickly getting innovative products to market. Efficient supply chains emphasize reducing supply chain costs for functional products.

- Supply chain strategies include Quick Response Programs, Efficient Consumer Response, postponement, revenue sharing, cross docking, 3PL, and vendor-managed inventories.

- E-commerce now serves as a part of the supply chain by promoting business-to-consumer (B2C) and business-to-business (B2B) transactions.

- Supply chain performance measures should be ones that are applicable to the entire supply chain and relate to competitive priorities. The Strategic Profit Model translates sales, inventory, and other measures into the overall measure of return on assets, which is relevant to the entire supply chain.

- Globalization provides additional opportunities, but also additional challenges for supply chain management.

- The four principles of supply chain management are: Build a competitive infrastructure, leverage the worldwide logistics network, synchronize supply to demand, and measure performance globally.

Visit our dynamic Web site, http://www.wiley.com/college/vonderembse, for extended chapter material, solved problems, mini-cases, computer software, and Web links.

KEY TERMS

backward vertical integration
bullwhip effect
business to business (B2B)
business to consumer (B2C)
collaborative planning, forecasting, and replenishment (CPFR)
cross docking
digital loyalty networks
disintermediation
downstream
echelon 1
echelon 2
efficient consumer response (ECR)

efficient supply chain
electronic data interchange (EDI)
enterprise resource planning (ERP)
forward vertical integration
insourced
internal supply chain
JIT II
logistics
outsourced
point-of-sale (POS)
process postponement
product postponement
quick response (QR)
responsive supply chain
revenue sharing

reverse logistics
strategic profit model
supply chain
supply chain management
third party logistics (3PL)
tier 1 suppliers
tier 2 suppliers
tier 3 suppliers
upstream
vendor managed inventory (VMI)
virtual corporations

URLS

Allied Waste: www.alliedwaste.com

Ariba: www.ariba.com/company/company_overview.cfm

Baan: www.baan.com/home/aboutbaan/

Blockbuster: www.blockbuster.com/bb/about/0,7710,,00.html?

Bose: www.bose.com/company/

Deloitte Research: www.dc.com/obx/pages.php?Name=AboutResearch

Eroski: www.eroski.es/eroski/visor/main.jsp?idioma=5

Employease: www.employease.com/

e-Stee: exchange.e-steel.com/

Ford: www.ford.com/en/ourCompany/partnersAndAlliances.htm

Henkel: www.henkel.com/int_henkel/company/index.cfm

Hershey: www.hersheys.com/about/profile.shtml

Hewlett-Packard: www.hp.com/

i2 Technologies: www.i2.com/Home/

J.D. Edwards: www.jdedwards.com/

Lands' End: www.landsend.com/cd/frontdoor/

McDonald's: www.mcdonalds.com/corporate/index.html

Microsoft: www.microsoft.com/mscorp/default.asp

Mr. Coffee Concepts: www.mrcoffeeconcepts.com/

Owens-Corning: www.owenscorning.com/acquainted/

Penske http://www.penskelogistics.com/services/llp.html

Peoplesoft: www.peoplesoft.com/corp/en/about/index.asp

Procter & Gamble: www.pg.com/about_pg/sectionmain.jhtml

Quaker Oats: www.quakeroats.com/qfb_AboutUs/ThisisQuaker.cfm

Ryder: www.ryder.com/supply_chain.shtml

SAP: www.sap.com/company/

Saturn: www.saturn.com/company/

Southwest: www.iflyswa.com/

Sport Obermyer: www.obermeyer.com/home.html

Toys "R"Us: www1.toysrus.com/about/

Travelocity: www.travelocity.com/

Wal-Mart: www.walmart.com/cservice/aw_index.gsp

QUESTIONS

1. List the factors that now require companies to emphasize supply chain management.

2. Explain how the bullwhip effect might occur for a fashion retailer.

3. How could CPFR prevent the bullwhip effect from occurring?

4. Describe the supply chain that might exist for an automobile manufacturer and discuss some information that might flow through the supply chain. Do the same for a fast-food restaurant.

5. Identify some organizations that you think are vertically integrated and some that you think use extensive outsourcing.

6. Is Amazon.com a virtual organization? Find as much information as you can about the company, then use that information to support your argument.

7. List some products that would probably be most appropriate for a responsive supply chain. Do the same for an efficient supply chain.

8. Compare and contrast QR, ECR, VMI, and CPFR with regard to degree of integration of the supply chain and use of technology.

9. Explain how postponement might be used by companies that make material used in the apparel industry (e.g., denim).

10. Explain how ERP could either facilitate or block some of the most recent supply chain collaboration efforts such as CPFR.

INTERNET QUESTIONS

11. Visit the Web page for the Supply Chain Council (www.supply-chain.org) and describe how the SCOR model may be used.

12. Visit the Web site for Amazon.com. Explore the set of services that Amazon.com can offer its customers. How do these compare with the services offered by the traditional bricks and mortar bookstore?

13. Visit the Web site of covisint.com (www.covisint.com). Which type of B2B organization is covisint.com?

14. Go to the supplier network Web site for Harley-Davidson (www.h-dsn.com). Highlight the "Public Menu," then "General Business Information," then click on "Electronic Commerce Information." What approaches has Harley Davidson implemented for using e-commerce with its suppliers? Based on this information, how closely integrated is Harley-Davidson with its supply chain partners?

PROBLEMS

1. Referring to the information in Exhibit 5.6, suppose that the number of rentals with revenue sharing is expected to be 500, but that revenue will be split so that 60 percent goes to the retailer and 40 percent to the supplier. Recalculate the profit for each under this revised scenario.

2. In Exhibit 5.9, suppose the value of sales increases by $500 but all other figures remain the same. What would be the new value of return on assets?

3. In Exhibit 5.6, calculate the results if the supplier sells tapes to the retailer for $15, instead of $10 under the revenue sharing plan, but everything else remains the same.

4. Using Exhibit 5.9, how much would sales have to increase by so that return on assets would become 20 percent if cost of goods sold is 62.5 percent of sales? How much of a reduction in inventory would be required to produce the same result, assuming that variable expenses equal 20 percent of inventory?

DESIGNING THE SYSTEM TO PRODUCE SERVICES AND GOODS

Chapter 6: Product Development: A Team Approach

Chapter 7: Models and Forecasting

Chapter 8: Process Selection: Volume Drives Costs and Profits

Chapter 9: Capacity Decisions

Chapter 10: Facility Location in a Global Environment

Chapter 11: Facility Layout

Product Development: A Team Approach

LEARNING OBJECTIVES

After completing this chapter, you should be able to:

- Describe how product development and design determine the product's characteristics, performance, and function.
- Explain that product development is a cooperative effort that requires input from many parts of the organization, including marketing, engineering, operations, finance, and accounting.
- Illustrate how product development can be used to gain a competitive advantage.
- List the steps involved in designing and developing new products.
- Explain why product development requires a team effort.
- Discuss the role of suppliers in product development.
- Describe how product development is a determinant of product quality and costs.

INTRODUCTION

Product development is a process to generate product concepts, designs, and plans for new services and goods that an organization can provide for its customers. It usually includes analyzing the market to assess customer needs, designing the product to meet those needs, designing the process or methods for making the product, developing a plan to market the product and a plan for full-scale production, and analyzing the financial feasibility. The challenges to an organization are to create a product that customers demand, to produce it at a competitive cost, to attain the best level of quality possible, and to deliver it on time.

EXAMPLE | For air couriers such as FedEx, product design is a critical issue. FedEx, the largest of the air couriers, has positioned itself strategically by paying close attention to its product and how it was designed. FedEx has a vast network that can deliver overnight to most locations. When a FedEx operator gets a call to pick up a package, he or she puts the information into a computer. The order travels to a courier by radio and is displayed on a hand-held computer. Within an hour or two, the package is picked up and shuttled off to the airport. At each step from pickup to delivery, employees scan packages into a computer terminal that is linked to the central computer at the company's Memphis headquarters. Customers can track packages using the Internet. Because of its product design, FedEx can guarantee delivery by 10:30 the next morning. It also guarantees to track down the location of a package for a customer within thirty minutes. The company has gained a strategic advantage through its product design and has positioned itself well in the market.

THE PRODUCT LIFE CYCLE

Product development is a recurring process because all services and goods have a life cycle. In a **product life cycle,** a product passes through a series of stages that include development, growth, maturity/saturation, and decline, as displayed in Exhibit 6.1.

Development Stage

The development stage includes product design and testing. During this period, sales are usually very slow. For marketing, it is a time to gain acceptance for the product among wholesale distributors, retailers, and consumers. For operations and engineering, it is a time to work out remaining problems with the production process. For example, a product, currently in development, allows anyone (recreational boaters, commercial fishermen, truckers, and others on the move) to get an up-to-the-minute, radar-generated picture of weather anywhere in the world on a computer screen or other display device. This on-demand service allows users to avoid bad weather whether boating or driving. After spending many months building relationships with the right government agencies and industry groups, developing potential markets, and creating computer software, the product is ready for launch.

EXHIBIT 6.1

Development Stage

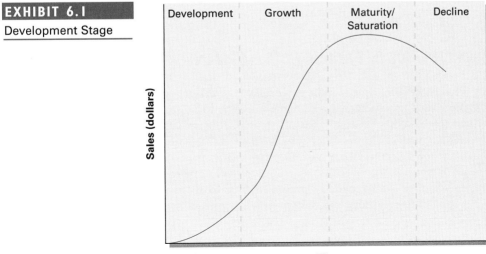

Growth Stage

The growth stage is characterized by a rapid increase in sales. In this stage, marketing managers strive to increase market share by competitive pricing, aggressive promotion, and intensive distribution. Operations are trying to find ways to increase production volumes to keep pace with increasing demand. Large volumes allow operations to apply mass-production techniques that lower costs. Operations are also striving to maintain quality and delivery schedules as the pace of sales quickens. For example, compact disc players have recently had a period of very high sales growth and are passing into the maturity stage of the product life cycle.

Maturity/Saturation Stage

Maturity/saturation occurs when sales and distribution have reached their peak. Volume, which reflects the number of customers, the quantity purchased, and the frequency of purchase, is stable. In this stage, price competition can become intense as existing firms try to maintain or increase sales in a market that has little or no growth. Firms begin to specialize (i.e., segment markets) and look for market niches. Pressure continues for further cost reductions. For example, the automobile is in the maturity/saturation stage. The increase in specialty vehicles, such as Jeeps, minivans, and four-wheel drive vehicles, is the automotive industry's way of segmenting the market in an effort to reignite sales growth. In this stage, operations should be able to cope with increasing product variety while keeping costs low.

Decline Stage

The decline of mature products is caused by changes in consumer preferences, product technology, competitive activities, and other environmental factors. In this phase, sales decline and firms take actions ranging from drastic reductions in profit margins to withdrawal from the market. For example, the steel industry is losing market share to plastics in the automotive market and to concrete in construction. These two industries have been major users of steel, and both markets are mature and experiencing limited growth.

The length of the product life cycle differs widely among products. For example, it has taken more than seventy years for automobiles to go from development to maturity and saturation. On the other hand, the compact disk, which was introduced a little more than ten years ago, is now a mature product.

THE INCREASING IMPORTANCE OF PRODUCT DEVELOPMENT

Product development is more important than ever because customers are demanding more product variety and are willing to switch to products with new technology more quickly than they have in the past. Customers are also demanding products that fit specific needs. For example, the number of toppings available on a pizza has increased substantially; the different flavors and other characteristics of toothpaste have increased to the point that even within the same brand there may be more than a dozen different possibilities; and the number of different printers available for microcomputers is staggering. The impact of this on product development is illustrated in the following example.

PROBLEM The impact of increasing product variety and shortening product life cycles is having a multiplicative effect on the need for product development. In the industrial era, a firm may have produced three different products and each product may have had a life of ten years. A firm would have had to develop three new products every ten years. That would be one product every three-and- one-third years. Today, in order to be competitive, the firm may have to produce six different products with a life cycle of only five years. This firm has to introduce six new products in five years to replace the existing products. That is a total of twelve new products in ten years or one product every 0.833 years, about ten months.

	Industrial Era Firm	Postindustrial Firm	Equations
Number of products per firm (NP)	3	6	
Product life cycle for each product (LC)	10	5	
Average years available to develop each product	3.33	0.833	$= \dfrac{LC}{NP}$
New products developed in ten years	3	12	$= \dfrac{(NP)(10)}{(LC)}$

The equations provided in the third column are used in calculating the last two rows of data. The variables *NP* and *LC* are defined in the first two rows.

In this example, the postindustrial firm has four times as much product development activity as the industrial firm. If a firm takes one year to develop a new product in the industrial stage, then product development is an intermittent activity. It will occur in only three out of ten years. Delays, problems, and confusion during the product development process are annoying but may not be life threatening for the organization. If the firm takes one year to develop a new product in the postindustrial stage, then product development is probability occurring all the time and two or more projects will overlap. In this case, delays, problems, and confusion in the product development process may be life threatening for the organization. As the need for product variety accelerates and product life cycles continue to shorten, the importance of product development will expand.

GLOBAL ASPECTS OF PRODUCT DEVELOPMENT

After World War II, developments in air and sea transportation and advances in communications technology made it clear that nations could no longer exist as isolated states, ignoring activities outside their borders. Even China shrugged off its isolationist tradition and began to pursue partnerships with foreign countries and companies. Initially, the activities of many companies were limited to international trade—that is, producing products in the home country and shipping a portion of the output to another country. Many companies took the next step, which involved locating production facilities in a foreign country and producing products for that country. As top management's level of sophistication in the international arena grew, it became evident that building a facility in each country to cater to local markets might not be effective.

Many organizations are designing and developing products that can be produced in more than one country and sold in many different countries. Timken advertises that its bearings are interchangeable no matter where they are produced. This approach to product design provides Timken with increased flexibility. If there is a problem in one plant, another can easily and quickly take up the slack. Where differences exist among the markets in several countries, it is necessary to accommodate those differences in the product design. For example, electric utilities in the United States and Europe supply different levels of current (voltage). Appliances designed for the U.S. market cannot be used in Europe unless they are modified. In today's environment, managers need to know the world market for their products and potential products.

USING TEAMS FOR PRODUCT DEVELOPMENT

Many organizations have seen the advantages of the team approach to product development. How does that approach work? Earlier, the chapters on quality and productivity described the use of teams and the positive impact that teams can have on performance. Rather than repeat the material contained in those chapters, the key points are summarized here:

- Build teams that include participants from all areas within the organization and first-tier suppliers at the beginning of the new product development efforts.

- Charge the team with responsibility for the successful completion of the new product development effort.

- Strive for solutions that meet the objectives of the organization, not for solutions that satisfy the objectives of a functional area. This means that no participant or group of participants can have veto power.

- Encourage participants to think not only about the task on which the group is presently focused, but also about the impact of their decision on other aspects of product design that the group has considered and will consider. This is the systems approach to product development.

EXAMPLE   Ford Motor Company has applied many of these concepts to product design. Ford studies customer wants and needs as it never has before and has made quality a top priority. Ford put aside its traditional approach to product development. Previously, product planners developed a general concept and then passed it on to a design team. They, in turn, passed it on to engineering, manufacturing, and, finally, the company's suppliers. In this highly sequential process, each group worked in isolation, there was little communication, and no one had overall project responsibility. In contrast, the team approach brings together representatives from each area, and the team takes final responsibility. Because of early involvement by all parts of the design team, problems are resolved before they become crises. With the team approach, manufacturing has been able to make several design suggestions that have resulted in higher productivity and better quality.

Ford forgot the "Detroit knows best" attitude and set out to identify the world's best design features from different models. Ford launched market studies to determine customer preferences. An "ergonomic group" did elaborate testing on seat design, dashboard instruments, and controls. People were timed pushing buttons, flipping switches, and adjusting dials in order to find ways to make the car easier to use.

Ford asked assembly-line workers for advice even before the design of the car was complete. Many of the suggestions were used. Simple ideas, such as making all bolt heads the same size so the worker is not constantly reaching for a new tool, were implemented. More complex suggestions, such as making doors with fewer pieces in order to improve assembly, were also used.

Even suppliers were brought into the design process. They were given long-term contracts and invited to have input on product plans. This involvement allowed Ford to incorporate suggestions that saved money for the supplier as well as Ford, improved quality, and improved productivity.

OVERVIEW OF PRODUCT DEVELOPMENT

Developing new products is a key factor for success because it shapes how organizations compete. Product development offers the opportunity to determine product costs, product quality, and the ability to serve customers. These factors are extremely important in establishing an organization's competitive position.

Product development and the design that results have a direct impact on costs because the design defines:

- How the product will be made
- What materials will be needed
- What machines and processes will be used

The procedures and the machines required to make the product affect the labor costs and the investment required. The quantity and type of raw materials specified influence material costs. The organization that can design a product of equal or better quality using methods, machines, and materials that have a total cost lower than its competitors can obtain a competitive advantage.

Product quality has become a critical factor for successful competition in the global marketplace. Successfully managing quality includes:

- Designing the product to achieve high quality while keeping costs in line
- Designing production processes that transform the design into a quality product at a competitive cost
- Developing sound training programs aimed at improving employee performance
- Inspecting the product to determine if Steps 1 through 3 have been successful

Organizations produce quality services and goods by designing and building them with care, not merely by inspecting them.

Customer service can be an important competitive advantage because meeting specific needs and providing rapid, on-time delivery are important to customers. A customer may have specific needs that are different from the needs of the typical customer. Have the products and processes been designed to be flexible enough to adjust to specific needs? Can flexibility be achieved without significant increases in costs? If the answer to both questions is yes, then the system gives the organization an advantage in competing for new customers and markets.

Product development starts by examining markets for new, modified, or existing products. Recognizing a customer's special application may raise a series of questions that determine the product's cost and quality as well as an assessment of how close the organization can come to satisfying those needs. Based on these inputs, someone or some group makes a decision to move forward with the product. For an overview of the decision-making process for product development, see Exhibit 6.2.

Initial Assessment Phase

An organization should continually monitor customer preferences to get ideas for new products. New product ideas may also come from engineering, operations, top management, or other parts of the organization. For example, an engineering breakthrough may trigger new product ideas, as the microchip did for electronic calculators and computers. Market analysis may indicate the need for upscale fast foods, such as rotisserie chicken. A market analysis for a rotisserie chicken dinner might include the following steps:

EXHIBIT 6.2

Overview of Product
Development

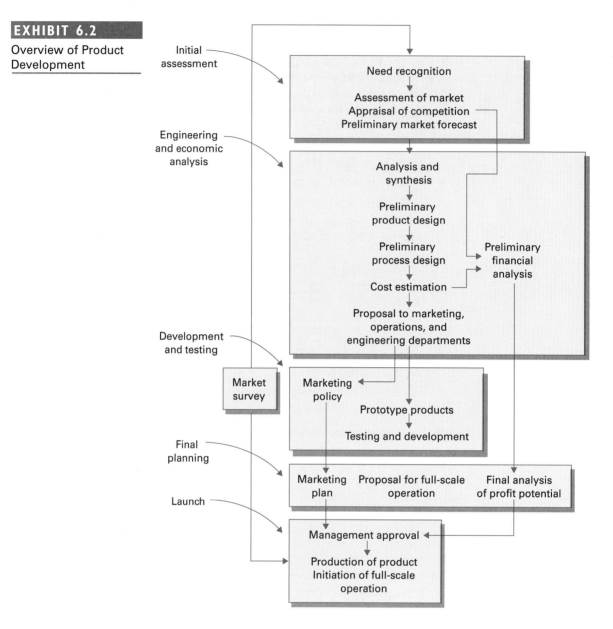

- *Assessment of the market*—What taste and texture are desired by customers? How large is the potential market? What are the long-term and short-term opportunities if the organization enters the market?

- *Appraisal of the competition*—Who are the present competitors in the market? What will their reaction be to a new entry? Who are the other potential entrants to the market? What strengths does the organization possess to gain an edge in this market?

- *Preliminary market forecast*—How many units can be sold in the first year, second year, and so on? What prices are customers willing to pay?

Many product ideas are discarded after such a market analysis because the expected sales are not sufficient, the estimated market price is too low to make operations profitable, or the competition is too great. Ideas that meet the criteria are given further consideration.

Engineering and Economic Analysis

A new product idea requires careful engineering, which involves analysis and synthesis. **Analysis** is separating a whole into its parts to determine their nature, proportion, function, and relationship. An analysis of the rotisserie chicken dinner involves breaking it down into its various components and examining each component, as follows:

- *Chicken*—How large should the chicken be? Should the skin and fat be removed before cooking? How long should it be cooked? What type of seasoning should be used?
- *Whipped potatoes*—What will be the consistency of the potatoes? How much butter, milk, and salt will be used? Will they be served with butter or gravy?
- *Coleslaw*—What type of cabbage will be used? How fine will the cabbage be cut? Will mayonnaise or salad dressing be used? What seasonings will be added?

Synthesis is putting the parts or elements together to form a whole. In analysis, each part is examined, and answers to questions are determined. In synthesis, the parts are combined in a way that addresses the interaction between those parts. The concept behind synthesis is to make the best decision for overall product performance, not to optimize one part. This may involve trade-offs. For example, leaving the skin on the chicken, using whole milk and butter in the potatoes, and blending the coleslaw with real mayonnaise may result in a very tasty meal, but one with too much fat. The designers feel pressure to reduce the fat because of the organization's pledge to provide healthy meals, so the skin is removed from the chicken and skim milk is used in the potatoes.

Based on the results of analysis and synthesis, a preliminary product design is prepared. For the rotisserie chicken dinner, the design team specifies the food, cooking instructions, and equipment needed for preparation. For example, the design would specify the size and breed of the chicken along with the type of potato. Ideas gathered in marketing investigations are solidified in the engineering phase.

A production proposal follows the preliminary product design. It addresses the broad problem of how to produce the product, that is, the process design. The following list describes some of the many decisions to consider:

- *Capacity*—What is the long-term potential demand for the product? How much food should a store be able to produce and store to meet anticipated demand?
- *Process*—What equipment, facility layout, and production system are required to support this level of production? How will this equipment be arranged?
- *Facility*—Can an existing building be used? If so, what modifications are necessary?
- *People*—What jobs are required for the new product? What skills are required? What training programs need to be developed?
- *Materials*—What are the sources of the materials? What are the costs?

From the production proposal, cost estimates are prepared. Costs are based on operating data that are available through accounting records. If such records are not available, then experience with similar products can be used to estimate costs. Preliminary financial analysis requires estimates of investment and revenue as well as costs. The capital required to build facilities and buy equipment is estimated from the preliminary engineering design and the preliminary production proposal.

Financial analysts compare the estimated profit (revenue minus cost) with the investment to determine if the product has a sufficient return (profit) for the amount invested. If this financial hurdle is crossed, a proposal for the development of marketing policies, operating plans, and prototypes can be prepared.

Development and Testing Phase

Engineering and operations combine to develop models of the product, called **prototypes.**
These may be working models, models reduced in scale, or mock-ups of the product.
Where traditional prototype development often took weeks or months, the technology for
rapid prototyping is becoming available. Some companies are using the same technology
that creates virtual reality to develop three-dimensional prototypes. Other firms are using
lasers to make prototypes by solidifying plastic in only a few minutes. This process can
produce prototypes with complex shapes.

Developing a prototype for the rotisserie chicken is a relatively simple and fast
process. In this case, different spices, cooking temperatures, and cooking processes would
be tried, and the results would be taste-tested.

Marketing is charged with formulating policies and developing plans for the advertising, promotion, distribution, and sale of the new product. Plans may be made for advertising campaigns, point-of-sale promotions, and the types of retail and wholesale outlets
to be used. Marketing may decide to test-market the chicken in a limited area before full-
scale introduction.

Final Planning

During development and testing, a proposal for full-scale production is prepared. This proposal is similar to the preliminary production proposal, but includes more details about each
of the areas within the business and more accurate estimates of costs. The full-scale proposal
obviously includes any changes and new information discovered in the development phase.
The marketing plans are finalized, and a final analysis of profit potential is made. The operating and marketing plans and the financial analysis are presented to top management for
approval. Many projects never reach the next phase because of poor profit potential.

Launch Phase and Market Surveys

Management approval begins the implementation of the marketing and operating plans.
Facilities are constructed, equipment is purchased, people are hired and trained, and materials are acquired. All these actions are aimed at producing the rotisserie chicken.

Market surveys are used to monitor customer satisfaction, detect changing customer
needs, and provide this feedback to the organization so the design process can begin again
if needed.

Mortality in Product Design

Product design and development do not always or even usually lead to the introduction of
a new product. Products can be eliminated at any point in design and development. For
example, products can be eliminated for any of the following reasons:

- Lack of sufficient customer demand
- Excessive production costs
- Inability to solve certain technical or engineering problems
- Insufficient profit potential

The mortality rate of new products is very high, as shown in Exhibit 6.3. Experts vary
on how many ideas are required to generate one commercially successful product. The
ratio of sixty ideas to one successful product, shown in Exhibit 6.3, is a typical estimate.
The key to success in new product development is to eliminate untenable new product
ideas as soon as possible in order to bring the best new products to market quickly.

EXHIBIT 6.3

Mortality Rate of New Products

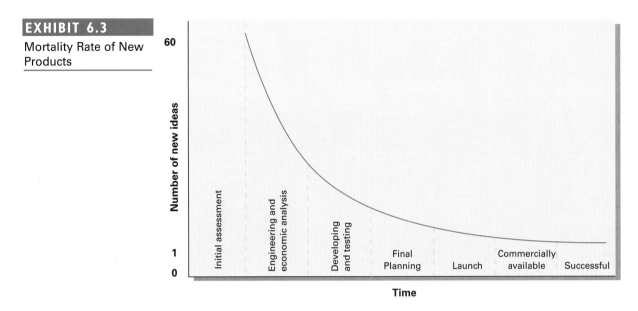

Discarded ideas should be carefully filed for several reasons.

- When a similar idea is later proposed, the product design questions can be handled quickly by referring to previous attempts.
- As conditions change in the marketplace, such as an increase in demand for the product, the design and development activities can be resumed.
- As technological improvements allow ways to reduce production costs, increase quality, or reduce the needed capital investment, the discarded product idea can be reintroduced. For example, improvements in microelectronics and computer technology have made possible many consumer products, such as fax machines, that had previously been too expensive to manufacture for home use.

A Concurrent, Not a Sequential, Process

The overview of product development described in Exhibit 6.2 illustrates it as a sequential process beginning with initial assessment and concluding with final planning and product launching. While this is a logical flow for the purpose of providing an overview of product development, it should be viewed as a concurrent process when applied in a real situation. It should be clear that not all decisions made in the initial assessment phase can or should be made before any decision is made in the engineering and economic analysis phase. Within the engineering phase, not every decision regarding product design can be made before a decision can be made about designing the manufacturing process. A significant amount of overlap among the phases of product development and a significant amount of information exchange among participants are not only necessary, but also desirable, to achieve a high-quality product design that meets customer expectations.

Previous chapters emphasize the importance of treating product development as a cross-functional process utilizing teams and early involvement to achieve exceptional new products. To better understand the team approach to new product development, examine Exhibit 6.4. It describes the roles of the participants during the various phases of the product development cycle. These roles are discussed in more detail in a supplement to this

EXHIBIT 6.4   Relationship between Product Design and the Functional Areas of an Organization

Phase of Product Development Cycle	Participant						Management Information Systems
	Marketing	Engineering	Operations	Suppliers	Finance	Accounting	
Initial Assessment	Market investigation Estimation of volume and price	Interpretation of technical data and participation in technological forecasting	Understanding of production economics and environmental issues		Description of the financial status of the organization		Classification, organization, and tabulation of information at all levels of product development
Engineering and Economic Analysis	Initial formulation of a marketing strategy	Analysis of needs Initial product and process design	Preliminary feasability study for production	Input to the design of product and process	Preliminary financial analysis: return on investment, payback	Data for cost estimation	
Development and Testing	Refinement of marketing strategy	Design changes Prototype construction Final product design changes Process selection	Preliminary production plans	Assistance in prototype construction	Continued updating of investment requirements Capital formation	More detailed information on cost and productivity	
Final Planning	Final marketing strategy Development of a distribution system	Machine selection Layout Supervision of equipment installation	Proposal for full-scale production	Planning to acquire resources for full-scale production	Final analysis of return on investment Capital formation	Review of feasability of final plans	
Launch	Initiation of marketing	Continuing product and process improvements	Initiation of production	Initiation of production	Follow-up evaluation of profit performance	Collection of actual cost data	

chapter, which is available on the Web site that accompanies this text www.wiley.com /college/vonderembse. Once again, let's get together on the Web site.

PRODUCT DEVELOPMENT, SAFETY, AND LIABILITY

Product development should consider product safety and product liability. The company that produces the service or good is ultimately responsible, not only for the product's performance, but also for its safe use. Designing a ceiling fan that is appealing to the eye and easy to install is important, but designing it so the mounting device will not break and cause it to come crashing down from the ceiling is as important. Even a hint of a problem with airline safety could be disastrous for an airline. An airline crash often results in customer apprehension about flying as well as a series of lawsuits. In nearly every case involving an airline crash, there is no criminal liability, that is, no one deliberately caused the accident. The requirements for civil liability are much less severe. It is not necessary to prove intent; it is only necessary to demonstrate that an error was made. A pilot was not properly trained, a maintenance procedure was not followed, or the design of the aircraft was flawed. Product design, process design, and training are essential for creating products that are safe to use and have limited product liability.

EXAMPLE

The eBay auction site offers a wide variety of products for sale. In some cases, the products offered are collectibles that have great value. Suppose an unscrupulous individual decides to take advantage of the situation and offers to sell an item, like a baseball card or figurine, that is a cheap copy of the original. Who is responsible? The person attempting to make the sale has committed a crime because he/she knew it was a fake and attempted to pass it off as authentic. There is criminal intent.

In this example, eBay can claim that it did not know what was happening, and it may not. The company did not commit a crime. Does that mean it is not liable? EBay is offering an auction site and has some responsibility to make sure that what is offered for sale is the real thing, just as the airline has the responsibility to do all that is reasonable to ensure flight safety. What is reasonable? Often, that is settled in court.

ALLIES IN PRODUCT DEVELOPMENT: THE ROLE OF SUPPLIERS

Why are suppliers playing an increasingly important role in product development? The most important reason for this is the increase in outsourcing. **Outsourcing** is contracting with another company to do work that was once done by the organization itself. It is common for both manufacturing and service operations to subcontract major components of a job to another company. IBM has established relationships with other companies to provide software support for some of its products. Dana Corporation and Pilkington North America are large suppliers to the automotive industry. If suppliers participate in product development, they can:

- Share design expertise. A supplier such as Pilkington North America may have more expertise in manufacturing flat glass than automotive producers do.
- Change their approach to production to better meet the objectives of the new product development team. A software contractor working on a project for IBM may have to hire and train staff in networking and telecommunications to meet specific requirements of a project.
- Indicate ways the overall product design can be altered so the component that the supplier is producing can have better quality or cost less. A supplier may

suggest moving a mounting bracket that supports a motor that it provides. Shifting the bracket may reduce manufacturing and assembly costs.

■   Suggest additional ways suppliers can participate in the project so that overall objectives of the new product development are met. A supplier may have capabilities or know of other suppliers that have capabilities that will improve the quality of the product.

If suppliers are involved after the product design is in place and all the product specifications are set, their ability to help improve quality, reduce cost, and enhance performance is greatly reduced.

In order for suppliers to be effective in product development, they need freedom to make decisions; yet the parts and components that one supplier designs and builds must work well with other parts and components designed by other suppliers. Coordination can be achieved via two mechanisms. First, when major suppliers are part of the design team, they have the opportunity to interact with other suppliers. Second, by assigning an entire component to a supplier, such as the accounts receivable package on an information system or the drive assembly on a washing machine, that supplier can approach this component as a module. Modular design provides the freedom for the supplier to make decisions about the component and how the component will function internally. At the same time, the supplier is required to meet certain overall parameters, such as computer language and computer hardware for accounting software development and size, strength, and connecting points for the drive assembly.

IMPROVING PRODUCT QUALITY AND COSTS THROUGH PRODUCT DEVELOPMENT

As discussed earlier in this chapter, product development is a key factor in organizational success because it helps to determine product cost, product quality, and the organization's ability to serve the customer. In today's competitive global marketplace, high quality and competitive pricing have become the tickets that give the organization a chance to compete. This section discusses why product development is so important in determining product quality and cost and describes how quality function deployment can be used to achieve these objectives.

Product Development as a Determinant of Product Quality and Cost

The quality and cost of any service or good is determined by (1) how it is designed, (2) the equipment and methods used (process design), and (3) the training and skill of the people doing the work. For example, if several people are interested in starting a hairstyling business, they should be concerned with offering hair styles that are designed to show off the best features of their clients, providing equipment that allows the workforce to achieve the effect desired in the design efficiently, and training the workforce in the skillful and courteous execution of the task. Product quality and costs are determined by actions taken prior to production (product and process design) and by actions taken when the service is being rendered or the good is being produced. Inspection of the finished product provides feedback on product quality.

Product Design

Product design shapes the product's quality. It defines the way in which the good or service will function. Quality has at least two components. First, the product must be designed to function with a high probability of success, or reliability. Reliability is the probability that a product will perform a specific function without failure under given conditions. When product reliability increases, the organization can extend the warrantee on a product without increasing customer claims for repairs or returns. Warrantees for such complex and expensive items as cars and appliances are important decision points for customers. Second, quality is affected by improved operating or performance characteristics, even though reliability may not improve. The goals of product design should be greater performance, greater reliability, and lower total production and operating costs. Quality and costs should not be viewed as trade-offs because improvements in product technology can enable better quality at lower costs.

Product design also helps to define the product's cost by focusing on production issues while designing the product. Ask questions. For example, what would it cost to implement a particular feature or capability? For a computer maker, like Dell, that could be a decision to include a combo DVD/CD-Write drive or upgrade the clock speed of the microprocessor. For a charter school, that could be adding special services or extracurricular activities. For a fast-food restaurant, that might mean specifying chicken breast versus reprocessed chicken for some of its products. In each of these cases, the product design decision should be made while considering both the increase in value to the customer and the increase in costs for these enhancements.

Process Design

Product quality and costs are important criteria for selecting the process to produce goods and services. A thorough design of the process contemplates the progression of product from assembling resources through final production. The process designer should be familiar with innovations in process technology that will improve quality and lower costs. The equipment used in production should be tested to ensure that it meets or exceeds minimal performance standards. The process designer is responsible for following the product specifications and tolerances described in the product design.

Process design has two major components—a technical or engineering component and a scale economy or business component. The technical side of process design requires that decisions be made regarding the technology, the sequence of operations, and the methods and procedures to be used for performing the operations. The business components involve economies of scale issues that are discussed in the chapter on process selection.

At McDonald's, the production engineer describes the basic flow of materials, the equipment used to produce the quantity of food needed, and arranges the equipment to provide fast and convenient service. Because of the well laid out facility, the service is not only fast, but it is low cost because no time is wasted. Manufacturing engineers at Intel try to do similar things for the facilities that produce microcomputer chips.

Work Execution

To be successful, the product and process designs must be well executed on the shop floor. At this point, employee training, skill level, and motivation are critical. The people operating the machines, assembling the good, or performing the service should have the necessary skills. They should have training sessions in which the function of the product and process and the roles they play are explained. They should feel involved in the production process so they are motivated to suggest improvements and to perform the job according to the design. Unless all relevant information is effectively communicated to the workforce, it is unreasonable to expect quality performance. Whether your organizations makes laser printers or rents automobiles, work execution is essential for good quality and low costs.

Inspection and Testing

Inspection determines whether the product meets the standards set by the company. For example, in making a door, an inspector might measure the width of the door to determine if it meets the specifications. Inspection alone does not improve the quality of any individual product. It merely identifies a substandard item. It is only when the source of the substandard product is identified and corrective action taken that inspection has an impact. Inspection is useful when the information gathered during the inspection is made available to the people doing the product design and process design as well as the people actually doing the work. This feedback should be as direct as possible so that information is not distorted or lost. Many organizations are having the people who do the work carry out the inspections so the feedback is both direct and immediate.

Product testing usually involves overall product characteristics, such as product performance and product life. Shaw Industries, one of the largest producers of carpet in the world, has groups of people walk on their carpets eight hours per day five days a week to test carpet life. They figure 20,000 steps represents one year of wear. This does not make the carpets any better, but it does provide information for designing and manufacturing better carpets.

Quality Function Deployment

We have discussed the determinants of product quality and costs, and we have described why they are important in achieving quality. Two things, however, are missing. First, managers need a way to implement what they have learned. Asking people to design a better product at a lower cost does not provide sufficient direction nor bring coordinated actions to the task. An organized approach is needed that focuses the attention of all members of the organization on the quality and cost objectives. Second, management must be assured that the product produced by the organization is one that the customer wants.

Quality function deployment is being used by some organizations to provide these missing links. Sometimes referred to as the "house of quality," **quality function deployment (QFD),** is a set of planning and communication routines that focus and coordinate actions and skills within an organization. The foundation of the house of quality is the belief that a product should be designed to reflect customers' desires and tastes. The house of quality is a framework that provides the means for inter-functional planning and communication that improve product quality and performance while keeping cost in line with customers' expectations. Additional information on QFD is available in the chapter on quality.

SUMMARY

- Product development is a strategic level decision that substantially impacts the future success of the organization. Operations play a key role in product development.

- Products move through a life cycle that has different impacts on operations at different stages.

- As product life cycles are getting shorter and product variety is increasing, product development is becoming more frequent and, therefore, more important.

- Product design requires the expertise and decision-making skills of all parts of the organization. Marketing, engineering, operations, finance, accounting, information systems, and personnel all have important roles in the team approach to product design.

- Product development moves through a series of stages that include initial assessment, engineering and economic analysis, development and testing, final planning, launch, and market survey. Based on the market data, a new wave of product development may begin.

- Suppliers play an increasingly important role in new product development.

■ Product development determines the product's characteristics and performance. As a result, product development becomes a competitive weapon for an organization. It is a major determination of the product's quality and costs. If an organization's product is superior, then it can realize a competitive advantage.

 Visit our dynamic Web site, http://www.wiley.com/college/vonderembse, for extended chapter material, solved problems, mini-cases, computer software, and Web links.

KEY TERMS

analysis
early involvement
outsourcing

product development
product life cycle
prototypes

quality function
   deployment
synthesis

URLS

FedEx: www.fedex.com

UPS: www.ups.com

Ford Motor Company: www.fordmotorcompany.com

Aetna: www.aetna.com

Toyota: www.toyota.com

Volkswagen: www.vw.com

Pilkington North America: www.pilkington.com

Owens Corning: www.owenscorning.com

QUESTIONS

1. What is product development?

2. Why is product development a critical determinant to an organization's success? Would you consider it to be strategically important?

3. What is the product life cycle, and how does it impact operations?

4. Explain the following statement: "Product development requires teamwork in order to be successful."

5. Provide an overview of the product development process.

6. Comment on the following statement: "Training programs will not be critical in future operations because organizations are continuing to substitute capital for labor."

7. Describe the relationship between product development and quality.

INTERNET QUESTIONS

8. Learn as much as you can about Ford Motor Company's, Toyota's, and Volkswagen's products and product development process. How are they similar and different? What are the advantages of each?

9. Pilkington North America supplies glass to the automotive industry. As a major supplier, how does Pilkington help the automakers design better vehicles?

10. Access the Web site of one or more law firms that specialize in product liability? Describe how errors in product design can lead to legal problems and damages that can ruin a company. Examine the case of at least one company that is facing bankruptcy because of product liabilities. Owens Corning is one example.

CHAPTER 7

Models and Forecasting

LEARNING OBJECTIVES

After completing this chapter, you should be able to:

1. Define a model and describe how models can be used to analyze operating problems.
2. Define forecasting and discuss the nature of forecasting.
3. Explain how forecasting can be applied to various problems in operations and in the organization.
4. Describe methods of forecasting, including judgment and experience, time-series analysis, and regression and correlation.
5. Construct forecasting models and estimate forecasting error.

INTRODUCTION

The previous chapter described the product development process and the key role that product development plays in organizations that produce both services and goods. In order for an organization to design, build, and operate a production facility that is capable of meeting customer demand for these products, it is critical for management to obtain an estimate or forecast of that demand.

A **forecast** is a prediction of the future. It often examines historical data to determine relationships between the key variables in a problem and uses those relationships to make statements about the future. Once a forecast of demand is obtained, it is possible to make final decisions regarding the volume of product that needs to be produced. Volume, in turn, drives product costs and profits.

The purposes of this chapter are to discuss models and describe how they can be applied to business problems and to explain forecasting and its role in operations. A **model** is an abstraction from the real problem of the key variables and relationships in order to simplify the problem. The purpose of modeling is to provide the user with a better understanding of the problem and with a means of manipulating the results for what-if analyses.

MODELS AND DECISION MAKING

Organizational performance is a result of the decisions that management makes over a period of time: decisions about what markets to enter, what products to produce, what types of equipment and facilities to acquire, and where to locate facilities. The quality of the decision is a function of how well managers do the following:

- *Define the problem and the factors that influence it.* If a hospital is having difficulty maintaining high-quality, low-cost food service, it should define that clearly and describe what factors might affect it, such as the quality and cost of incoming food and the training of staff.

- *Select criteria to guide the decision, and establish objectives.* The hospital may select cost per meal and patient satisfaction as the criteria. The objectives could be to reduce meal cost by 15 percent and to improve patient satisfaction to 90 percent, based on the hospital's weekly surveys.

- *Formulate a model or models that help the manager understand the relationships among the factors that influence the problem and the objectives that she or he is trying to achieve.* Develop mathematical relationships (one type of model) that indicate how materials (food) and labor are converted into meals. This model could include analysis of the amount of food wasted and the standard amount of labor required to prepare a meal.

- *Collect relevant data.* Data on food costs, the amount of food consumed, the number of meals served, and the amount of labor would be collected. Also, patient preferences would be investigated so that meals would not only meet nutritional requirements, but also taste good.

- *Identify and evaluate alternatives.* There may be many alternatives, including subcontracting food preparation, considering new food suppliers, establishing better training programs for the staff, and changing management.

- *Select the best alternative.* One of these alternatives, another alternative, or some combination of alternatives would be selected.

- *Implement the alternative, and reevaluate.* The selected alternative(s) would be implemented, and the problem would be reevaluated. This reevaluation would include monitoring the accounting cost reports and the patient survey data to see if the objectives have been achieved.

A model is a very important way of thinking about a problem. Decision makers use models to increase their understanding of the problem that they are considering. A model helps managers simplify the problem by focusing on the key variables and relationships in the problem. The model also allows managers to try different options quickly and inexpensively. In these ways, decision making can be improved.

Types of Models

Most of us have seen model airplanes, models of dams, or models of other structures. These models can be used to test design characteristics. Model airplanes can be tested in wind tunnels to determine aerodynamic properties, and a model of a hydroelectric dam can help architects and engineers find ways of integrating the structure with the landscape. These models have physical characteristics similar to those of the "real thing." Experiments can be performed on this type of model to see how it might perform under actual operating conditions. In today's hi-tech environment, many of these modeling activities can be performed with computer software. The aerodynamic properties of an airplane can be tested in a virtual wind tunnel that exists only inside the memory of a computer. Models also include the drawings of a building that display the physical relationships between the various parts of the structure. All of these models are simplifications of the real thing and help designers make better decisions.

On the other hand, managers and others use mathematical abstraction to model important relationships. The break-even point calculation that many of you performed in accounting is an example of applying a mathematical model. The use of drawings and diagrams is also modeling. The computer-aided design system that describes product features on a computer screen is a model. The newspaper graph that illustrates stock market price changes in the last six months is a way to help the reader see trends in the market. Models do not have to be sophisticated to be useful. Most models can be grouped into four categories, and computers play a critical role in the development and use of each type.

1. *Mathematical models*—Include algebraic models such as break-even analysis, statistical models used in forecasting and quality control, mathematical programming models, such as linear programming, and calculus-based models, such as the economic order quantity. Mathematical models are widely used in all areas within an organization.

2. *Graphs and charts*—Are pictorial representations of mathematical relationships. They include a graphical representation of break-even analysis, a pie chart that illustrates market share in an industry, a graph of an organization's stock price over the last six months, and a bar chart that indicates the demand for energy for the last five years.

3. *Diagrams and drawings*—Are pictorial representations of conceptual relationships. They include a precedence diagram that represents the sequence required to assemble a building, a drawing of a gear that is part of a transmission in a car, a diagram that represents the logic of a computer program, and a drawing of an aircraft carrier.

4. *Scale models and prototypes*—Are physical representations of the item. They include a scale model of an airplane and the first part produced (prototype), which is normally used for testing purposes.

The Application of Models

You use models frequently without realizing it. If you invite friends over for pizza, you will probably determine how much pizza to order by multiplying the number of people you anticipate are coming by the amount of pizza you expect each person to consume, on the average. You will probably take that one step farther and multiply the anticipated cost per pizza by the number of pizzas required to determine if you have enough money. This is a simple mathematical model that can be used to plan a simple party or expanded to plan a major social event.

In mathematical models, symbols and algebra are often used to show relationships. Mathematical models can be simple or complex. For example, suppose a family is planning a trip to Walt Disney World in Orlando, Florida. To estimate gasoline costs for the trip, family members check a road atlas (one type of model), or they go online to get directions and a map from the Internet (another representation of model). They determine that Orlando is approximately a 2,200-mile round trip from their home. From records (a database) kept on the family car, the family estimates that the car will achieve 23 miles per gallon (mpg) on the highway. The average cost of a gallon of gasoline is estimated at $1.20 cents. Using the following model, they make an estimate of gasoline cost.

$$\text{Cost} = (\text{trip miles})(\text{cost per gallon})/\text{miles per gallon}$$
$$= \frac{(2{,}200 \text{ miles})(\$1.20 \text{ per gallon})}{23 \text{ mpg}}$$
$$= \$114.78$$

Using Models to Answer What-If Questions

A mathematical model can be used to answer what-if questions. In the previous example, costs could be estimated for a side trip to Tampa or for a 30-cent increase in the price of a gallon of gas, as shown in the following.

$$\text{Cost} = \frac{(2{,}200 \text{ miles})(\$1.50 \text{ per gallon})}{23 \text{ mpg}}$$

$$= \$143.48$$

The model could also be used to estimate the cost of the trip if the car averaged only 20 miles per gallon, as shown in the following.

$$\text{Cost} = \frac{(2{,}200 \text{ miles})(\$1.20 \text{ per gallon})}{20 \text{ mpg}}$$

$$= \$132.00$$

Building Models That Are Easy to Understand

Models cannot include all factors that affect the outcome because many factors cannot be defined precisely. Also, adding too many variables complicates the model without significantly increasing the accuracy of the prediction. For example, on the trip to Florida the number of miles driven is affected by the number of rest stops made, the number of unexpected detours taken, and even the number of lane changes made. The number of miles per gallon is influenced by the car's speed, the rate of acceleration, and the amount of time spent idling in traffic. These variables are not in the model. The model builder should ask if adding them would significantly improve the model's accuracy.

FORECASTING

Forecasting is an attempt to predict the future. Forecasts are usually the result of examining past experiences to gain insights into the future. These insights often take the form of mathematical models that are used to project future sales, product costs, advertising costs, and so on. The application of forecasting is not limited to predicting factors needed to operate a business. Forecasting can also be used to estimate the cost of living, housing prices, and the average family income in the year 2020. For organizations, forecasts are an essential part of planning. It would be illogical to plan for tomorrow without some idea of what might happen.

The critical word in the last sentence is "might." Any competent forecaster knows that the future holds many alternatives and that a forecast is only one of those possibilities. The difference between what actually happens and what is predicted is forecasting error, which is discussed later in this chapter. In spite of this potential error, management should recognize the need to proceed with planning using the best possible forecast and should develop contingency plans to deal with the possible error. Management should not assume that the future is predetermined, but should realize that its actions can help to shape future events. With the proper plans and execution of those plans, an organization can have some control over its future.

The Nature of Forecasting

The forecasting process consists of the following steps: determining the objectives of the forecast, developing and testing a model, applying the model, considering real-world constraints on the model's application, and revising and evaluating the forecast (human judgment). Exhibit 7.1 illustrates these steps.

Determining the Objectives

What kind of information is needed by the manager? The following questions should be considered:

1. What is the purpose of the forecast?
2. What variables are to be forecast?
3. Who will use the forecast?
4. What is the time frame of the forecast—long or short term?
5. How accurate should the forecast be?
6. When is the forecast needed?

Developing and Testing a Model

A model should be developed and then tested to ensure that it is as accurate as possible. Moving average, weighted moving average, exponential smoothing, and regression analysis techniques for developing forecasting models are discussed later. Often, the help of a technical analyst is needed at this point.

Applying the Model

After the model is tested, historical data about the problem are collected. These data are applied to the model, and the forecast is obtained. Great care should be taken so that the proper data are used and the model is applied correctly.

EXHIBIT 7.1

Steps in Forecasting

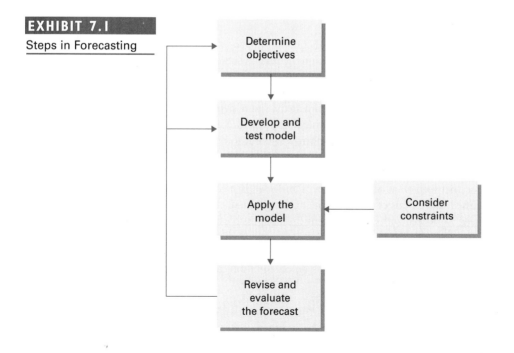

Considering Real-World Constraints

Applying any model requires consideration of real-world constraints. For example, a model may predict that sales will double in the next three years. Management, therefore, adds the needed personnel and facilities to produce the service or good, but does not think of the impact this increase will have on the distribution system. For example, a software company expands it product offerings by hiring additional programmers and analysts, but it does not provide the capability to install the software on customers' systems. What about raw-material availability, actions such as price cutting taken by competitors, or the availability of skilled labor? Application of the forecast should be grounded in reality. These factors are within management's control, and management action is required if a workable solution is to be obtained.

Revising and Evaluating the Forecast

The technical forecast should be tempered with human judgment. What relationships might have changed? In the case of the electric utility industry, a fundamental change in the rate of growth greatly affected the accuracy of estimates for future consumption. In 1973, the first oil embargo hit the U.S., and energy prices climbed substantially in only a few weeks. The price of gasoline doubled from about 30 cents per gallon to near 60 cents. Eventually, the costs of all forms of energy climbed, including natural gas and electricity. The embargo caused a nationwide effort to conserve energy. The demand for fiberglass insulation soared; fiberglass manufacturers did not have sufficient capacity because their planning models were based on much lower growth rates. On the other hand, the growth in demand for electricity dropped from about 3 percent annually, to near zero. In a relatively short time it rebounded to about 1 percent per year. The embargo changed the pattern of growth in the industry. Electrical utilities had planned for a significantly higher growth rate and did not react quickly enough to the change. Many utilities continued to build new power plants. The results were a surplus of electrical generation capacity and the cancellation of orders for many nuclear power plants. As we moved into the 1990s, the growth rate for electricity rebounded. Once again, the forecasting models, this time using the slower growth rates of the late 1970s and 1980s, underestimated the need for electricity. Today, in some parts of this country, we face shortages as electric utilities scramble to add more capacity.

Forecasts should not be treated as sacred or static. Revisions should be made in light of changes taking place within the firm or the environment. The need for revision may be occasioned by changes in price, product characteristics, advertising expenditures, or actions by competitors. Evaluation is the ongoing exercise of comparing the forecast with the actual results. This control process is necessary to attain accurate forecasts as we move forward.

Forecasting Methods

Before becoming immersed in the details involved with actually preparing a forecast, it is important to know that there is more to forecasting than developing the model and doing the analysis. The results from the model should be tempered with human judgment. The future is never perfectly represented by the past, and relationships change over time. Thus, the forecast should take into account judgment and experience.

Many techniques exist for developing a forecast. It is impossible to cover all the techniques effectively in a short time. Entire books are devoted to forecasting, and some students major in forecasting as others major in marketing, accounting, or operations. In the following sections, qualitative, time-series, and regression analysis methods of forecasting are discussed. Regression analysis can be used to project time series and cross-sectional data. There are several variations of these methods:

- Qualitative methods
  - Buildup method
  - Survey method
  - Test markets
  - Panel of experts (Delphi Technique)
- Time-series methods
  - Simple moving average
  - Weighted moving average
  - Exponential smoothing
- Regression and correlation analysis (simple and multiple regression)

Qualitative Approaches to Forecasting

Although mathematical models are useful in helping management make predictions, qualitative approaches can also be helpful. In fact, qualitative forecasts that are based on subjective interpretation of historical data and observations are frequently used. A homeowner who decides to refinance his or her home has made an implicit prediction that home mortgage rates have hit the bottom and are likely to increase in the future. Similarly, a manager who decides to purchase extra materials because of uncertainty in supply has made an implicit prediction that a strike or other action may disrupt the flow of materials. There are many different qualitative methods for making forecasts. We discuss briefly the buildup method, surveys, test markets, and the panel of experts.

Buildup Method

The **buildup method** involves starting at the bottom of an organization and making an overall estimate by adding together estimates from each element. For example, a brokerage firm could use this approach to forecast revenues from stock market transactions. If the buildup method is used for predicting revenue, the first step is to have each representative estimate his or her revenue. These estimates are passed on to the next level in the organization for review and evaluation. Estimates that are too high or too low are discussed with the representative so that management can understand the logic that supports the prediction. If the representative cannot convince the supervisor, a new prediction based on this discussion is made. The prediction is then passed on to the next level in the organization.

As these subjective judgments are passed up the organization, they are reviewed and refined until they become, in total, the revenue forecast for the organization. It is top management's responsibility to make the final judgment on the forecast's validity. One option is to also make an aggregate forecast using one of the mathematical methods discussed later. Then the aggregate forecast can be compared with the buildup forecast, and the differences between the two can be discussed and reconciled. Once top management has decided on the forecast, it becomes an input used in making capacity, production planning, and other decisions.

Survey Method

In some cases, organizations use surveys to gather information externally. A **survey** is a systematic effort to elicit information from specific groups and is usually conducted via a written questionnaire, a phone interview, or the Internet . The target of the survey could be consumers, purchasing agents, economists, and the like. A survey may attempt to determine how many consumers would buy a new flavor of toothpaste or consider a maintenance service that comes to your home or business to change the oil and do other minor repairs on your car or truck. Currently, surveys of purchasing agents are conducted to assess the health of the economy. Surveys are often used to prepare forecasts when historical data are not available, or when historical data are judged not to be indicative of the future. Surveys can also be used to verify the results of another forecasting technique.

Test Markets

Test marketing is a special kind of survey. In a **test market,** the forecaster arranges for the placement of a new or redesigned product in a city or cities believed to be representative of the organization's overall market. For example, an organization wanting to test the "at-home" and "at-work" market for the oil change service could offer the service in one or two cities to determine how customers might react. The analyst examines the sales behavior in the test market and uses it to predict sales in other markets. When done for an extended period of time, test marketing can be expensive. The results, however, tend to be more accurate than those of a survey because the consumers in a test market actually use the product.

Panel of Experts

A **panel of experts** is made up of people who are knowledgeable about the subject being considered. This group attempts to make a forecast by building consensus. In an organization, this process may involve executives who are trying to predict the level of information technology applied to banking operations or store managers who are trying to estimate labor cost in retail operations. The panel can be used for a wide variety of forecasts, and with this method, forecasts can often be made very quickly.

The **Delphi Technique** uses a panel of experts and surveys in a particular manner. The members of the panel provide a sequence of forecasts through responses to questionnaires. This sequence of questionnaires is directed at the same item or set of items. After each forecast, results compiled, and the individuals are given the 50th or the 75th percentile of the item or items being forecasted. This provides a reference point for the participants, who can decide whether to change their estimate based on this information. Because response is by questionnaire rather than by group interaction, domination by a few individuals, undue conservatism or optimism, and argumentation are avoided. The Delphi process assumes that as each forecast is conducted and the results disseminated among the panel members, the range of responses diminishes and the median moves to a position representing the "true" consensus of the group.

Analyzing a Time Series

The historical data used in forecasting can be cross-sectional data, time-series data, or a combination of the two. The simplest way to illustrate their differences is with an example. The First National Bank of Oakland wants to project usage of its automated teller service. It has collected data from similar systems in Stockton, San Jose, Santa Cruz, and Berkeley for the last two years. The study has both time-series and cross-sectional elements, as shown in Exhibit 7.2. The time-series part of the data is the two years of data that are available for the banks. The cross-sectional element is represented by the data from more than one bank.

Forecasting sales, costs, and other relevant estimates usually involves time-series data, and the techniques discussed here are useful in predicting such data. See Exhibit 7.3 for the time line and notation used in forecasting. Each point on the time line has associated with it an actual value, which is represented by x and a subscript. Each point on the line also has a forecasted value, represented by f and a subscript. Every period has a forecasted value when it is in the future; as time passes, it will have an actual value.

Simple Moving Average

One approach to forecasting would be to use only the most recent time period to project the next time period. This system, however, can introduce a significant error into a forecast because any odd occurrence in the previous period will be completely reflected in the prediction. Suppose that in one month a company had a strike that severely restricted the availability of its product and thereby affected sales or that a temporary price cut caused sales to be significantly greater than normal. If these actions are not repeated in the next month, then using the previous month's sales as the forecast will give a biased prediction.

The purpose of the moving average is to smooth out the peaks and valleys in the data. In the data set shown in Exhibit 7.4, the data fluctuate significantly. Basing a projection on the prior quarter's result could give a significant error. A moving average will smooth these peaks and valleys and give a more reasoned prediction. In the moving average model, the forecast for the next period is equal to the average of the most recent number of time periods.

$$f_{t+1} = \frac{\sum_{i=0}^{n-1}(x_{t-i})}{n}$$

where

f_{t+1} = the forecast for time period $t + i$, that is, the next time period.
x_{t-i} = the observed value for period $t - i$, where t is the last period for which data are available and $i = 0, ..., n - 1$.
n = the number of time periods in the average.

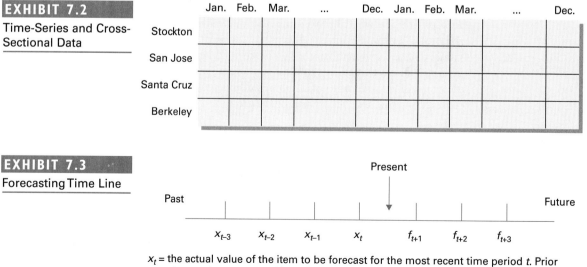

EXHIBIT 7.2

Time-Series and Cross-Sectional Data

EXHIBIT 7.3

Forecasting Time Line

x_t = the actual value of the item to be forecast for the most recent time period t. Prior observations are noted by subtracting 1 from time period t.

f_{t+1} = the forecasted value for the next period. Following periods are designated by adding 1 to time period $t+1$.

EXHIBIT 7.4

Graph of Imports

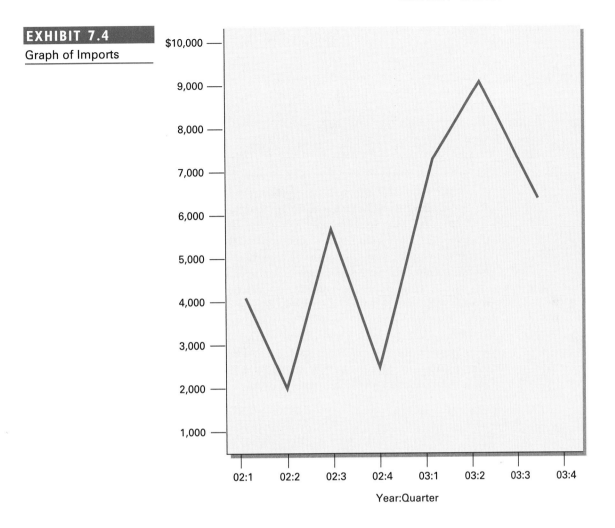

The longer the time—that is, the greater the n—the more smoothing that will take place. The selection of n is a management decision based on the amount of smoothing desired. A small value of n will put more emphasis on recent predictions and will more completely reflect fluctuations in actual sales. In fact, if $n = 1$, then the most recent time period's actual results becomes the next period's forecast.

PROBLEM

Following are the data shown in Exhibit 7.4:

Year:Quarter	Imports ($000,000)
2002:1	4,100
2002:2	2,000
2002:3	5,700
2002:4	2,500
2003:1	7,300
2003:2	9,200
2003:3	6,300

To calculate a seven-quarter moving average for imports, sum the most recent seven quarters, and divide by seven. Please observe that the notation year:quarter is used in the subscript here. The fourth quarter of 2003 would be 03:4.

$$f_{03:4} = \frac{(4{,}100 + 2{,}000 + 5{,}700 + 2{,}500 + 7{,}300 + 9{,}200 + 6{,}300)}{7}$$

$$= 5{,}300$$

A three-quarter moving average is calculated as follows:

$$f_{03:4} = \frac{(7{,}300 + 9{,}200 + 6{,}300)}{3}$$

$$= 7{,}600$$

Which estimate is likely to better represent the future? Which prediction should be used? It depends on whether the forecaster feels the last three quarters are a better predictor of what is to come than the prior seven months. If so, use the three-month moving average. If the last three months reflect some unusual conditions that are unlikely to recur, then use the seven-month moving average to smooth the high values in the last three quarters. Forecasting models do not give answers to questions. Managerial judgment plays a critical role.

This technique is called a moving average because to forecast the next quarter, the most recent quarter's actual imports are added and the oldest quarter's actual imports are subtracted from the total. In a sense, the average moves. For the import example, assume that actual imports for the fourth quarter of 2003 are $7,500 million. A three-quarter moving average for the first quarter of 2004 would drop the $7,300 million, which is the actual value for the first quarter of 2003, and add the most recent quarter. The following illustrates the calculation for the first quarter of 2004:

$$f_{04:1} = \frac{(9{,}200 + 6{,}300 + 7{,}500)}{3}$$

$$= 7{,}667$$

Weighted Moving Average

In a simple moving average, each time period has the same weight. With a weighted moving average, it is possible to assign different weights to each period. The equation for determining the weighted moving average is:

$$f_{t+1} = \sum_{i=0}^{n-1}(w_{t-i})(x_{t-i})$$

where

w_{t-i} = the weight for period $t - i$, where t is the last period for which data are available and $i = 0, \ldots, n - 1$. The weights for all n periods must sum to 1.0.

PROBLEM

In this example, a five-period weighted moving average is calculated for the fourth quarter of 2003.

Year:Quarter	Weight	Imports ($000,000)
2002:1	—	4,100
2002:2	—	2,000
2002:3	.10	5,700
2002:4	.15	2,500
2003:1	.20	7,300
2003:2	.25	9,200
2003:3	.30	6,300

$$f_{03:4} = .1(5,700) + .15(2,500) + .2(7,300) + .25(9,200) + .30(6,300) = 6,595$$

If the weights for each period are set at .20, then the weighted moving average and the simple moving average will be equal. Try this for yourself.

The weights for each period need to be selected in some logical way. Usually the most recent periods are weighted more heavily because these periods are thought to be more representative of the future. If there is a trend in the data either up or down, a weighted moving average can adjust more quickly than a simple moving average. Still, this form of the weighted moving average is not as good as regression analysis is in adapting to trends. (Regression analysis will be discussed later in this chapter.)

Exponential Smoothing

Exponential smoothing is really another form of a weighted moving average. It is a procedure for continually revising an estimate in light of more recent data. The method is based on averaging (smoothing) past values. To start a forecast using exponential smoothing, the forecast for the first period, f_{t+1} would be based on the actual value for the most recent period, x_t. (See Equation 7.1.) The forecast for the second period, f_{t+2} is equal to the actual value of the previous period, x_{t+1} times the smoothing constant, A, plus $(1 - A)$ times the prior period's forecast, f_{t+1}. (See Equation 7.2.) Remember, the prior forecast, f_{t+1}, is simply the actual value from period t. The forecast in Equation 7.2 is A times the prior period's actual value plus $(1 - A)$ times the prior period's forecast, f_{t+1}.

$$f_{t+1} = x_t \tag{7.1}$$
$$f_{t+2} = A(x_{t+1}) + (1 - A)f_{t+1} \tag{7.2}$$
$$f_{t+3} = A(x_{t+2}) + (1 - A)f_{t+2} \tag{7.3}$$

$$\vdots \qquad \vdots \qquad \vdots$$

$$f_{t+n} = A(x_{t+n-1}) + (1 - A)f_{t+n-1}$$

where

$n =$ some number of periods in the future
$0 \leq A \leq 1$

Let's examine one more equation in detail. Equation 7.3 uses the prior period's actual value times the weighting factor, A, plus $(1 - A)$ times the prior period's forecast. Exponential smoothing carries along all the historical actual data in the prior period's forecast.

How should the smoothing constant A be selected? First, A must be greater than or equal to zero and less than or equal to one. Within this range, a manager has discretion. What will happen if a manager selects a smoothing constant at an extreme? If $A = 1$, then according to Equation 7.2, the forecast will be based solely on the actual value from the prior period. In this case, no smoothing takes place. If the smoothing constant is set to 0, then the prior period's actual value is ignored. Once the forecasting pattern gets started, the forecast is so smooth that it will not change. No actual amounts can enter the equation because $A = 0$. Neither of these alternatives is acceptable.

There are no specific rules about picking the value of A. If the forecaster wants to put more weight on the most recent time period, then A should be set closer to 1. If the manager desires a smoother forecast that will not react violently to short-term change, A should be set closer to 0. Values between .1 and .3 are most commonly used.

PROBLEM

Use exponential smoothing to forecast imports from the previous example. To illustrate the impact of the smoothing constant, use $A = .1$ and $A = .6$. To begin, there can be no forecast for the first quarter of available data because no history is available.

The forecast for the second quarter is the prior quarter's actual value because no forecast is available for the first quarter. The third quarter's forecast can follow the equations described previously because an actual value and a forecasted value are available for the prior quarter.

For $A = .1$
$$f_{02:3} = A(x_{02:2}) + (1 - A)f_{02:2}$$
$$= .1(2,000) + .9(4,100)$$
$$= 3,890$$

For $A = .6$
$$f_{02:3} = .6(2,000) + .4(4,100)$$
$$= 2,840$$

Year:Quarter	Imports ($000,000)	Forecast $A = .1$	Forecast $A = .6$
2002:1	4,100	—	—
2002:2	2,000	4,100	4,100
2002:3	5,700	3,890	2,840
2002:4	2,500	4,071	4,556
2003:1	7,300	3,914	3,322
2003:2	9,200	4,253	5,709
2003:3	6,300	4,748	7,804
2003:4	—	4,903	6,902

The forecasts are significantly different. The forecast with $A = .1$ does not react abruptly to sudden changes. This can be seen graphically in Exhibit 7.5 where the actual value and the two forecasts are plotted.

Regression and Correlation Analysis

Correlation analysis measures the degree of relationship between two variables, and **regression analysis** is a method to predict the value of one variable based on the value of other variables. The **coefficient of correlation** is a measure of the strength of linear relationship between variables. If there is no relationship, then the coefficient of correlation is 0. Perfect positive correlation is 1.0, and perfect negative correlation is –1.0. (See Exhibit 7.6.) Between the limits of perfect positive and perfect negative correlation, there are many levels of strength. Examples are shown in Exhibit 7.7.

Regression analysis can be used to forecast both time-series and cross-sectional data. With time-series data, regression analysis is often used to estimate the slope of a trend line. Regression analysis can be either simple or multiple. **Simple regression** involves the prediction of only one variable (the **dependent variable**) and uses only one variable for prediction (the **independent variable**). **Multiple regression** has only one dependent variable, but can have more than one independent variable.

Simple Regression Model and Correlation

The equation for simple regression follows. Y is the dependent variable, and X is the independent variable. The variable b is the slope of the line, which is estimated by Equation 7.4, and variable a is the Y-intercept, which is estimated by Equation 7.5.

$$Y = a + b(X)$$

EXHIBIT 7.5

Exponential
Smoothing Examples

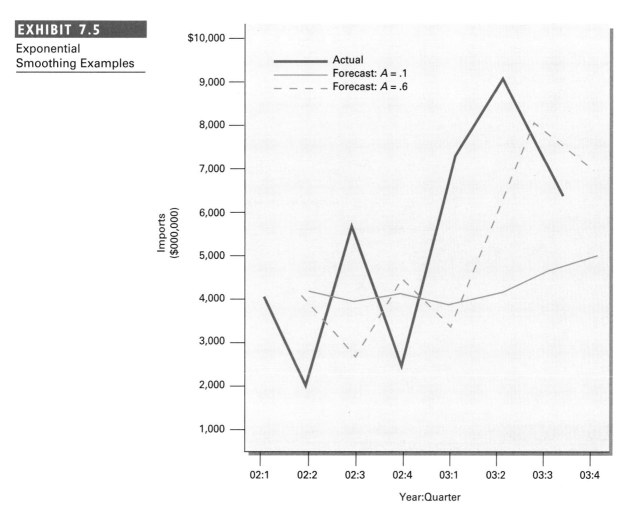

where

$Y =$ the dependent variable. It depends on the variable X and the model
parameters a and b.
$X =$ the independent variable
$n =$ the number of data points in the sample
$r =$ the coefficient of correlation

$$b = \frac{n\Sigma XY - \Sigma X \Sigma Y}{n\Sigma X^2 - (\Sigma X)^2} \qquad 7.4$$

$$a = \frac{\Sigma Y}{n} - b\frac{\Sigma X}{n} \qquad 7.5$$

$$r = \frac{n\Sigma XY - \Sigma X \Sigma Y}{\sqrt{\left[n\Sigma X^2 - (\Sigma X)^2\right]\left[n\Sigma Y^2 - (\Sigma Y)^2\right]}} \qquad 7.6$$

EXHIBIT 7.6

Scatter Diagrams
Showing Zero, Perfect
Positive, and Perfect
Negative Correlations

EXHIBIT 7.7

Scatter Diagrams
Showing Examples of
Correlation

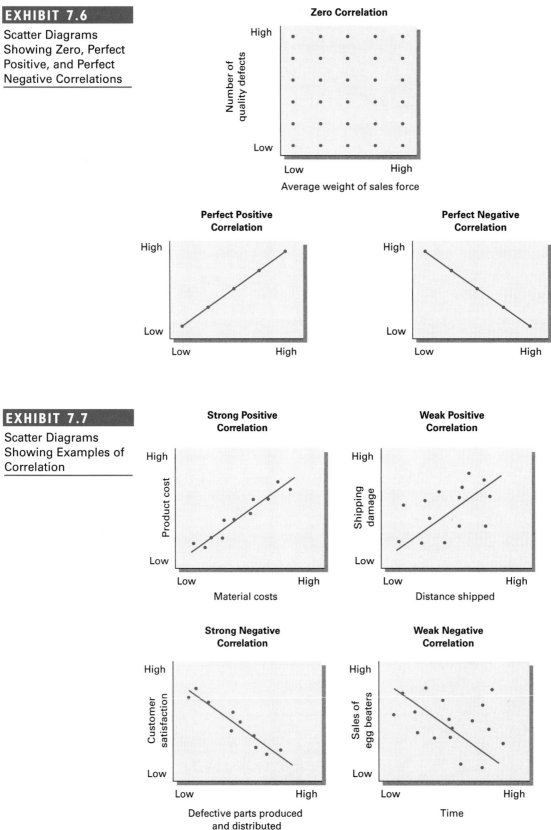

PROBLEM

When working with time-series data, it is usually easier to convert the time variable from the month/day/year format to simpler numbers. There are many possible ways of coding. Here, the number 1 is used to represent the first time period for which data are available. Following periods will be consecutively numbered. In this example, the assumption is that demand (Y) depends on time (X), the independent variable. The import data from an earlier example are used for analysis.

Year: Quarter	Coded Value for Year:Quarter (X)	Imports ($000,000) ($Y$)	XY	X^2	Y^2
2002:1	1	4,100	4,100	1	16,810,000
2002:2	2	2,000	4,000	4	4,000,000
2002:3	3	5,700	17,100	9	32,490,000
2002:4	4	2,500	10,000	16	6,250,000
2003:1	5	7,300	36,500	25	53,290,000
2003:2	6	9,200	55,200	36	84,640,000
2003:3	7	6,300	44,100	49	39,690,000
Sum	28	37,100	171,000	140	237,170,000

$$b = \frac{n\Sigma XY - \Sigma X \Sigma Y}{n\Sigma X^2 - (\Sigma X)^2}$$

$$= \frac{7(171,000) - 28(37,100)}{7(140) - 28^2}$$

$$= \frac{158,200}{196}$$

$$= 807.1$$

$$a = \frac{\Sigma Y}{n} - b\frac{\Sigma X}{n}$$

$$= \frac{37,100}{7} - \frac{807.1(28)}{7}$$

$$= 2,071.6$$

$$r = \frac{n\Sigma XY - \Sigma X \Sigma Y}{\sqrt{\left[n\Sigma X^2 - (\Sigma X)^2\right]\left[n\Sigma Y^2 - (\Sigma Y)^2\right]}}$$

$$= \frac{7(171,000) - 28(37,100)}{\sqrt{\left[7(140) - 28^2\right]\left[7(237,170,000)^2 - 37,100\right]}}$$

$$= \frac{158,200}{\sqrt{[196][283,780,000]}}$$

$$= 0.671$$

Interpreting the results of the model requires an understanding of the original units of the data as well as the slope/intercept method of representing a straight line. The code for the years has been explained. Because the quarters are consecutively numbered, the last quarter of 2003 is coded as 8. The imports are given in millions of dollars. As a result, the imports are projected to increase $807.1 million per quarter. The intercept is $2,072 million, and it represents the point on the regression line for the quarter prior to the first quarter of 2002. Project the imports for the last quarter of 2003 where the estimated value is represented by Y_e. The predictive model follows.

$$Y_e = 2,071.6 + 807.1X$$

$$= 2,071.6 + 807.1(8)$$

$$= 8,528$$

Thus, the projection for imports is $8,528 million.

Goodness of Fit

How well does the equation determined by regression analysis fit the data? The principles on which simple regression analysis and multiple regression analysis are constructed are similar. The regression model estimates the Y-intercept (a) and the slope of the line (b) that best fits the data. The criterion that is used to determine the "best fit" line minimizes the squared distance from each point to the line. This is often called the least squares method. These distances are labeled d_i in Exhibit 7.8, with i equal to 1, ... , n. The method used to derive the parameters of the best fit line is based on differential calculus and is not covered here. The equations that determine the parameters of the slope (b) and the Y-intercept (a) are 7.4 and 7.5, respectively.

The coefficient of correlation calculated in the prior example $(r = 0.671)$ indicates a high degree of relationship between the dependent and independent variables. The higher the coefficient of correlation, the more confident we can be that variation in the dependent variable (imports) is explained by the independent variable (time). This can be observed by looking at the scatter diagram in Exhibit 7.9. A measurement of this variation about the regression line is the **standard error of the estimate,** $s_{y/x}$. It is the difference between each observed value, Y_o, and the estimated value, Y_e. The equation for the standard error of the

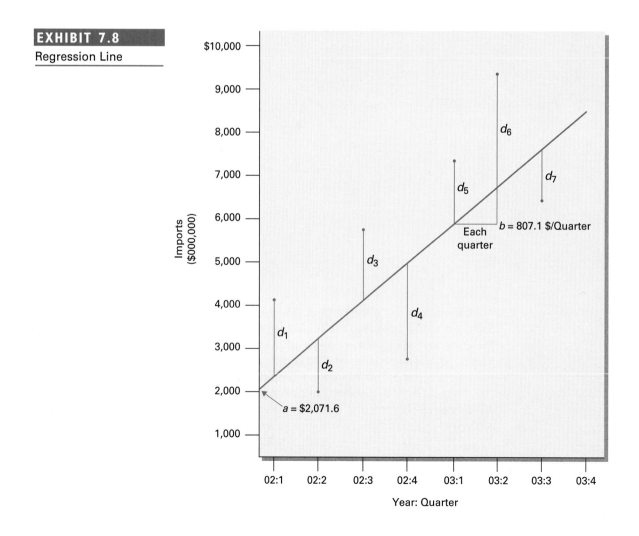

EXHIBIT 7.8

Regression Line

estimate follows. An alternative formula that is easier to use with a calculator is given in Exhibit 7.9.

$$s_{y/x} = \sqrt{\frac{\Sigma(Y_o - Y_e)^2}{n-2}}$$

Simple regression models can be constructed for cross-sectional data. The mechanics are similar.

Computer Application of Simple Regression Analysis

Many different computer software packages are available for doing both simple and multiple regression analyses. Exhibit 7.10 is the computer-based output for regression analysis.

EXHIBIT 7.9

Scatter Diagram and Regression Line for Import Problem

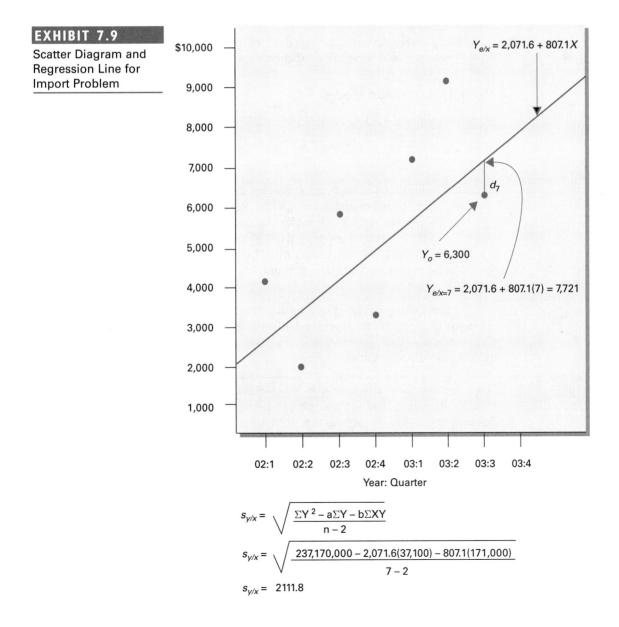

$$s_{y/x} = \sqrt{\frac{\Sigma Y^2 - a\Sigma Y - b\Sigma XY}{n-2}}$$

$$s_{y/x} = \sqrt{\frac{237,170,000 - 2,071.6(37,100) - 807.1(171,000)}{7-2}}$$

$$s_{y/x} = 2111.8$$

EXHIBIT 7.10

Regression Coefficients for Imports

Variable	Coefficient	Std Error	t Value	Two-sided Sig. Prob.
Constant	2071.42900	1784.8000	1.16059	0.298204
YRS/OUT	807.14290	399.09340	2.02244	0.099061

Standard error of estimate = 2111.804

The coefficients calculated by software are the same (with allowances for rounding) as the coefficients calculated by hand. The standard error of the estimate is also the same as the value calculated by hand. The computer output also provides additional information. The **standard error of the coefficients**, 1784.800 and 399.093, are standard deviations for the coefficients. They can be used to test the null hypotheses that the actual values of the coefficients are equal to zero. The **t-values** are the calculated t-statistics for the hypothesis tests. The two-sided significant probabilities are the levels that alpha or Type I error would have to be set at in order to fail to reject the null hypothesis. In this example, the trend coefficient would be significant if alpha error is set at 0.1 or higher. On the other hand, the coefficient for the intercept would be significant if alpha error is set at 0.3 or higher.

Multiple Regression Model

Multiple regression has only one dependent variable, but can have many independent variables.

$$Y = a + b_1X_1 + b_2X_2 + \ldots + b_kX_k$$

where

$Y =$ the dependent variable. It depends on the variables X_1 through X_k and the model parameters $a, b_1, b_2, \ldots, b_k$, where k is the number of independent variables. (Equations for the parameters are not given here. Rather, you are encouraged to use an available computer package, such as EXCEL, SPSSX, SAS, or MINITAB to do the necessary calculations.)

$X_i =$ an independent variable, with $i = 1, \ldots, k$. Each independent variable will have n observations or data points.

The concept of minimizing squared distances from each observed point to the best fit regression line is still useful. However, because multiple regression requires more than two dimensions, two-dimensional graphs cannot be used. Computerized statistical models are used to make the calculations.

PROBLEM

The prior examples use only one independent variable (time) to predict imports. Most relationships are not that simple because other factors will also affect the dependent variable. To expand the previous example, let's add disposable income and the consumer price index.

Imports ($000,000)	Year: Quarter	Code Value For Year:Quarter (X_1)	Disposable Income (Billions of $) ($X_2$)	Consumer Price Index (X_3)
4,100	2002:1	1	65	110
2,000	2002:2	2	60	111
5,700	2002:3	3	73	113
2,500	2002:4	4	61	113
7,300	2003.1	5	70	117
9,200	2003.2	6	77	118
6,300	2003:3	7	78	117

The multiple regression output is shown in Exhibit 7.11. The equation for predicting imports is

$$Y_e = -141,000 - 1,387.6X_1 + 206.35X_2 + 1,205.4X_3$$

To predict imports for the fourth quarter of 2003, assume that disposable income is $78 billion and the consumer price index is 118 for the fourth quarter.

$$Y_e = -141,000 - 1,387.6(8) + 206.35(78) + 1,205.4(118) = 6,232$$

The prediction is $6,232 million worth of imports in the fourth quarter of 2003.

Measuring Forecasting Error

Regardless of which forecasting model is used, it is important to have some means of determining the model's propensity for error. If an organization has been using a particular model to forecast sales for some time, has the model been performing well? How large is the error? One approach is to simply subtract the forecast for one time period from the actual value for the same time period. This can be repeated so that the forecaster has differences for many periods. Some of the differences are positive because the forecast is less than the actual value, and others are negative because the forecast is greater than the actual value. In raw form, these differences tell the forecaster little. A common method used by forecasters to measure forecasting error is to calculate the mean squared error. The **mean squared error (MSE)** is the average of all the squared errors. The differences are squared and added together, and then that total is divided by the number of observations. The following calculations help illustrate the method.

PROBLEM

Month	Actual Sales ($) (xt)	Forecasted Sales ($) (ft)	Error ($)	Squared Error
January	419,000	448,000	−29,000	841,000,000
February	480,000	481,000	−1,000	1,000,000
March	601,000	563,000	+38,000	1,444,000,000
April	505,000	525,000	−20,000	400,000,000
May	462,000	490,000	−28,000	784,000,000
June	567,000	519,000	+48,000	2,304,000,000
				5,774,000,000

EXHIBIT 7.11

Multiple Regression Output

```
THE REGRESSION EQUATION IS
Y = - 141000 - 1388 X1 + 206 X2 + 1205 X3

PREDICTOR        COEF
                 -141000
B1               -1387.6
B2                206.35
B3                1205.4

S = 534.6        R-SQ = 97.9%
```

S = standard error of the estimate
R-SQ = (coefficient of correlation)^2

$$MSE = \frac{\sum_{t=1}^{n}(x_t - f_t)^2}{n}$$

$$= \frac{5,774,000,000}{6}$$

$$= 962,333,333$$

Sometimes the square root of the mean squared error is used to measure the error. This is analogous to the standard error of the estimate, which is discussed in the section on regression analysis.

It is also possible to use **mean absolute deviation (MAD),** which is similar to MSE, to estimate forecasting error. MAD is calculated by adding together the differences between the actual and forecasted value once the negative and positive signs are removed. Otherwise, a large negative error would offset a large positive error, so the total error would be greatly underestimated. Try adding the ERROR column in this example with the signs included. The total error is $8,000 because the negative and positive errors tend to cancel each other. Once the signs are removed, the total error is $164,000, which is divided by the number of data points n, as was done for MSE. The MAD is $164,000/6, which equals $27,333. The MAD is easier to interpret then MSE because MAD is the average error for the prior six forecasts. As a result, MAD can be used to estimate future forecasting errors.

SUMMARY

- A model is an important way of thinking about problems. It is an abstraction from the real problem of the key variables and relationships in order to simplify the problem and improve understanding.

- There are many different types of models, including prototypes used in product design; scale models used in architecture; diagrams and drawings used by scientists, engineers, managers, and others; and mathematical models used in many disciplines.

- Models are used to assist managers and others in answering what-if questions by changing a parameter in the model.

- Forecasting is a type of mathematical model that can be used to predict the future. It is an important part of the planning process in an organization

- The forecasting process consists of determining the objectives of the forecast, developing and testing a model, applying the model, considering real-world constraints in the application of the model, and revising and evaluating the forecast.

- Forecasting techniques normally use historical data to develop the model that is used to make the projection. If the relationships in the data change over time, the model may no longer predict the future accurately.

- There are qualitative and quantitative methods for developing a forecast.

- Forecasters require a way to measure the amount of forecasting error.

Visit our dynamic Web site, http://www.wiley.com/college/vonderembse, for extended chapter material, solved problems, mini-cases, computer software, and Web links.

KEY TERMS

buildup method	mean absolute deviation	standard error of the
coefficient of correlation	(MAD)	coefficient
correlation analysis	mean squared error (MSE)	standard error of the
Delphi Technique	model	estimate
dependent variable	panel of experts	survey
forecast	regression analysis	t-value
forecasting	multiple regression	test market
independent variable	simple regression	

URLS

Dell Computer: www.dell.com

Gateway: www.gateway.com

NRG Energy: www.nrgenergy.com

FirstEnergy: firstenergycorp.com

QUESTIONS

1. What is model building, and why is model building important for managers?
2. Discuss the different types of models.
3. Describe how models can be used to answer what-if questions.
4. How are models used in business and operations?
5. What is forecasting, and why is it important to an organization?
6. Describe the forecasting process.
7. Discuss the qualitative approaches to forecasting.
8. How does the Delphi Technique work? What are its advantages?
9. How is regression analysis different from the moving average, the weighted moving average, and exponential smoothing?
10. What is forecasting error, and why should it be measured?

INTERNET QUESTIONS

11. Use the Internet to locate the annual reports for Dell Computer. What has been the trend for sales? What does the company expect for future sales? How does Dell compare to Gateway?

12. Enrollment at universities is critical because enrollment is a major driver of revenue. Locate the enrollment data for a college or university that you are familiar with. How is enrollment expected to change? What are the factors that influence enrollment?

13. NRG Energy generates electricity for residential and commercial users. Forecasts of demand are critical because the lead time for building a new power plant is quite long. What are NRG projections for demand? How do they compare to FirstEnergy's?

14. Merrill Lynch is a major brokerage firm. What has been the trend in sales? What does the company expect in the future? How does this compare with Paine Webber?

PROBLEMS

1. Blast-Away Housecleaning Service uses powerful water jets to clear loose paint from residential buildings and to clean aluminum siding. The company is trying to arrive at a fast and accurate way of estimating cleaning jobs. The following simple formula is its first attempt. It includes a fixed charge for coming to the job plus time requirements, which are a function of the exterior of the house measured in square feet (sf).

$$\text{Estimated cost} = \$15 + (\$0.06/sf)(sf)$$

a. How much should Blast-Away charge to clean a house that is a rectangle 40 by 28 feet? The distance from the roof line to the bottom of the siding is 9 feet.

b. Suppose Blast-Away's labor costs increase and the cost per square foot increases to $0.064. How much should it charge for the house in Part a?

c. What other factors might Blast-Away include in the pricing model to improve the precision of the model?

2. As a service to its customers, Turbo Natural Gas Company will estimate the amount of natural gas required (NGR) in hundreds of cubic feet (CCF) to heat your home. This is done by a mathematical model that considers the square footage on the first floor ($sf1$), the square footage on the second floor ($sf2$), and the temperature setting on the thermostat. The temperature setting you enter into the model should be the difference between the temperature setting in your home and 65 degrees (td). Make sure you keep the minus sign if the setting is less than 65 degrees. The model builder assumed that the homes have 8-foot ceilings, an average amount of good-quality windows, 3.5 inches of insulation in the wall and 6 inches in the attic, and a typical Midwestern winter.

$$\begin{aligned} NGR = \ &(0.50 \text{ CCF/sf})(sf_1) + (0.25 \text{ CCF/sf})(sf_2) \\ &+ (0.015 \text{ CCF/degree/sf})(td)(sf_1) \\ &+ (0.0075 \text{ CCF/degree/sf})(td)(sf_2) \end{aligned}$$

a. How much natural gas will an 1,800-square-foot ranch home (one floor only) use if the thermostat is set at 70 degrees?

b. How much natural gas will a two-story home with a total of 2,400 square feet use if the thermostat is set at 63 degrees? There is 1,000 square feet on the second floor.

c. What happens to the natural gas cost in Parts a and b if the model is revised and the usage for the first floor increases to 0.60 CCF/sf from 0.50 CCF/sf.

3. It appears that the imports of beef have been increasing about 10 percent annually on the average. Project the 2002 imports using linear regression.

Year	Imports of Beef (Thousands of Tons)
1993	82
1994	101
1995	114
1996	126
1997	137
1998	151
1999	164
2000	182
2001	189

4. Mighty-Maid Homecleaning Service has been in operation for eight months, and demand for its products has grown rapidly. The owner/manager of Mighty-Maid is trying to keep pace with demand, which means hiring and training more workers. She believes that demand will continue at the same pace. She needs an estimate of demand so she can recruit and train the workforce. The following represents the history of Mighty-Maid:

Time	Hours of Service Rendered
December	300
January	750
February	650
March	920
April	1,300
May	1,400
June	1,200
July	1,500

Estimate the trend in the data using regression analysis.

5. Use the regression model calculated in the Mighty-Maid problem to estimate the hours of service for December through July. Now that both the actual and the forecasted values are available, answer the following questions:

    a. What are the MSE and MAD for the forecast?

    b. Is the forecasting model a "good" model?

6. The figures below indicate the number of mergers that took place in the savings and loan industry over a twelve-year period.

Year	Mergers	Year	Mergers
1990	46	1996	83
1991	46	1997	123
1992	62	1998	97
1993	45	1999	186
1994	64	2000	225
1995	61	2001	240

a. Calculate a five-year moving average to forecast the number of mergers for 2002.

b. Use the moving average technique to determine the forecast for 1995 to 2001. Calculate measurement error using MSE and MAD.

c. Calculate a five-year weighted moving average to forecast the number of mergers for 2002. Use weights of .10, .15, .20, .25, and .30, with the most recent year weighted most heavily.

d. Use regression analysis to forecast the number of mergers in 2002.

7. Find the exponentially smoothed series for the series in Problem 6, (a) using $A = .1$ and then (b) using $A = .7$, and plot these time series along with the actual data to see the impact of the smoothing constant.

8. The time series below shows the number of firms in an industry over a ten-year period.

Year	Firms	Year	Firms
1992	441	1997	554
1993	468	1998	562
1994	481	1999	577
1995	511	2000	537
1996	551	2001	589

a. Find the five-year moving average for this series.

b. Find the three-year weighted moving average for this series. Use the following scheme to weight the years:

	Weight
Most recent year	.5
Two years back	.3
Three years back	.2

c. Determine the amount of measurement error in the forecast. Use the weighted moving average technique (with the weights from Part b to forecast for 1995 to 2001.) Then use that seven-year period to calculate measurement error (both MSE and MAD).

d. Find the exponentially smoothed forecast for this series with $A = .2$.

9. The quarterly data presented here show the number of appliances (in thousands) returned to a particular manufacturer for warranty service over the last five years.

	1st Quarter	2nd Quarter	3rd Quarter	4th Quarter
5 years ago	1.2	0.8	.6	1.1
4 years ago	1.7	1.2	1.0	1.5
3 years ago	3.1	3.5	3.5	3.2
2 years ago	2.6	2.2	1.9	2.5
1 year ago	2.9	2.5	2.2	3.0

a. Find the equation of the least squares linear trend line that fits this time series. Let $t = 1$ be the first quarter five years ago.

b. What would the trend-line value be for the second quarter of the current year—that is, two periods beyond the end of the actual data?

 10. The following are AJV Electric's sales of model EM-5V circuit assemblies over the last sixteen months (in thousands of units):

Month	Sales (Thousands of Units)	Month	Sales (Thousands of Units)
Sept. 2000	55	May 2001	63
Oct. 2000	53	June 2001	53
Nov. 2000	60	July 2001	51
Dec. 2000	49	Aug. 2001	60
Jan. 2001	48	Sept. 2001	58
Feb. 2001	61	Oct. 2001	52
Mar. 2001	61	Nov. 2001	51
Apr. 2001	53	Dec. 2001	63

Use the moving average technique to forecast sales of AJV's model EM-5V for January 2002 (use a three-month base). Does the model appear to be appropriate? Why or why not?

 11. Employ the single exponential smoothing technique to forecast sales of AJV's model EM-5V for January 2002 (use A = .8). Does the model seem to be appropriate?

 12. Utilize the single exponential smoothing technique to forecast sales of AJV's model EM-5V for January 2002 (use $A = .1$). How do the results compare with those in problem 11? Why is one better than another?

13. Using linear regression, forecast the sales of AJV's model EM-5V for January 2002 through June 2002.

14. Thrifty Bank and Trust is trying to forecast on-the-job performance by its employees. The bank administers an aptitude test to new employees. After the normal employee training plus six months on the job, the bank measures on-the-job performance. The following data have been gathered from the last eight people hired:

Employee Number	Score	Transactions per Hour
1	90	36
2	70	29
3	85	40
4	80	32
5	95	42
6	60	23
7	65	29
8	75	33

a. Fit a line to the data using regression analysis. What is the meaning of the parameters that were estimated by the regression analysis model?

b. How well does the model fit the data?

c.   How many transactions per hour would you expect from someone who scored 87 on the aptitude test?

15. The data in the following table were collected during a study of consumer buying patterns.

Observation	X	Y
1	154	743
2	265	830
3	540	984
4	332	801
5	551	964
6	487	955
7	305	839
8	218	478
9	144	720
10	155	782
11	242	853
12	234	878
13	343	940

a.   Fit a linear regression line to the data using the least squares method.

b.   Calculate the coefficient of correlation and the standard error of the estimate.

c.   How could the coefficient of correlation and the standard error of the estimate be used to make a judgment about the model's accuracy?

16. Perfect Lawns intends to use sales of lawn fertilizer to predict lawn mower sales. The store manager feels that there is probably a six-week lag between fertilizer sales and mower sales. The pertinent data are shown below.

Period	Fertilizer Sales (Tons)	Number of Mowers Sold (Six-Week Lag)
1	1.7	11
2	1.4	9
3	1.9	11
4	2.1	13
5	2.3	14
6	1.7	10
7	1.6	9
8	2.0	13
9	1.4	9
10	2.2	16
11	1.5	10
12	1.7	10

a.   Use the least squares method to obtain a linear regression line for the data.

b.   Calculate the coefficient of correlation and the standard error of the estimate.

c.   Predict lawn mower sales for the first week in August, given fertilizer sales six weeks earlier of two tons.

CHAPTER 8

Process Selection: Volume Drives Costs and Profits

LEARNING OBJECTIVES

After completing this chapter you should be able to:

1. Describe the process selection decision and how it is influenced by the volume of product demanded.

2. Construct a cost-volume-profit model of a firm and understand how the model can be used to evaluate risk in operations.

3. Calculate the break-even point for both single- and multiple-product cases.

4. Explain why mass production does not necessarily mean products with inferior quality or shoddy workmanship.

5. Define the different process types: line flow, batch flow, flexible manufacturing system, manufacturing cell, job shop, and project.

6. Examine mass customization and the focused factory.

INTRODUCTION

There is a strong relationship among process selection and three critical elements in business: volume, cost, and profit. **Process selection** is a series of decisions that includes technical or engineering issues and volume or scale issues. The technical or engineering issues include the basic methods used to produce a service or good. For example, deciding to use computer-based electronic analysis to diagnose engine malfunctions is a technical decision for an automotive repair service. This computerized process replaced a process for diagnoses that was based on how the engine sounded to the mechanic, the mechanic's experience, and trial and error. The electronic process helps to eliminate guesswork. On the other hand, deciding whether the automotive repair service should be large enough to serve two cars per hour or twenty cars per hour is a volume or scale decision. In general, the technical aspects of process selection are beyond the scope of this course, so the focus is on the volume or scale issues.

The volume or scale decision involves applying the proper amount of mechanization to leverage the organization's workforce. **Leverage** means making the workforce more productive through the use of better tools. For example, one person working alone with a few simple tools may be able to build an automobile, but he or she cannot build it at a cost that will allow that person to compete with organizations that provide their employees with sophisticated tools for producing automobiles. That person and others like him or her cannot build enough cars to satisfy demand without significant automation and an organization to leverage their time and talent. More sophisticated tools allow the workforce to produce more with the same commitment of time and effort. This productivity improvement lowers the unit cost of the product and raises the capacity of the workforce.

In general, as more sophisticated tools are provided to the workforce, productivity gains will be achieved, and greater costs will be incurred to buy the tools. This presents an interesting trade-off between efficiency and costs in the process selection decision. As more sophisticated tools are applied to the production process, productivity and capacity increase, and labor cost per unit declines. On the other hand, as tools become more sophisticated, the cost of acquiring them tends to increase, which translates into increased fixed costs. The analysis of these trade-offs is based on the quantity demanded by the customer.

HOW PROCESS SELECTION RELATES TO PRODUCT DESIGN AND CAPACITY

Product design, capacity, and process selection are decisions that should be considered simultaneously. The way the product is designed affects how many people will buy it, and that affects the producer's capacity planning decision, which affects the process and the costs to produce the product, which affects how many people can afford to buy it. This logic can be represented as a circle with customers at the center, as illustrated in Exhibit 8.1. Because a circle has no beginning or end, it should be considered as a whole. If these decisions are not viewed as a whole, a decision in product design that might offer the best technical solution could cause the product to fail because it makes the product less attractive to the customer or increases the cost of the product beyond the reach of most consumers. Process selection should be integrated with decisions

EXHIBIT 8.1

Product Design, Process Selection, and Capacity Decisions Are Closely Related

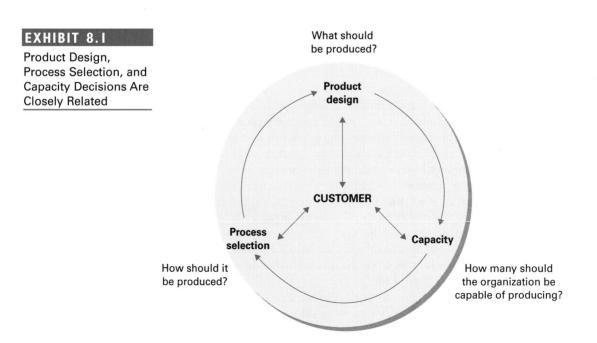

What should be produced?

Product design

CUSTOMER

Process selection

Capacity

How should it be produced?

How many should the organization be capable of producing?

about product design and capacity. This reinforces a major theme of the book: operations are part of a system, and decisions made in one area have a significant impact on other areas.

Relating Process Selection to Product Design

Decisions made in designing the product clearly have an impact on the process. For example, if a bed is described as brass, there is no need for woodworking equipment. Process selection, in turn, influences the product design. Product design should be undertaken in an environment that is defined by the available process technologies. Digital watches and electronic funds transfers are examples of products that were significantly affected by improvements in technology.

Relating the design of the product to process selection goes beyond the examples listed in the preceding paragraph. The teamwork concept is changing how organizations approach product design and process selection. In service organizations, such as fire departments, teams of managers from various disciplines design the services, which might include fire prevention programs for homes and business, fire safety for school-age children, and firefighting. While doing product design, the team examines various process selection decisions, including the types of equipment and facilities needed, the techniques used in fighting fires, the methods used to develop education programs, and the type and level of training needed by employees who deliver these services.

Manufacturing firms are combining design engineers with process engineers (sometimes called manufacturing engineers) to create a design team. This team, like the team at the fire department, is charged with doing what is best for the customer, rather than finding the best product design or the best process design. Because the design engineers and the process engineers work together, the lead time required to bring a new product from an idea to a reality is reduced significantly. This effort, called concurrent engineering, enables the organization to participate in time-based competition. By doing what is best for the customer, the organization hopes to be rewarded with increased demand for its products and high profit margins. These teams also improve communication between these two important groups, which decreases the number of engineering change orders, avoids unnecessary delays and gets the product to market more quickly, and avoids mistakes that could increase costs.

Process Selection and Capacity

Process selection is also related to the volume demanded in the marketplace. If the market for the product is estimated at only 1,000 units per year, it may be difficult to justify expensive specialized equipment that produces 100 units per hour. Such equipment would be required to operate only ten hours each year. It is unlikely that the cost of this specialized equipment could be supported by the 1,000 units demanded unless a very high price is charged for each unit.

PROBLEM Quick-as-a-Blink Printing Center is growing rapidly, and many of its customers are demanding that their documents be professionally bound. Management could purchase a manual binding machine that requires continuous operator attention or an automatic machine that requires only periodic operator attention. The following data are available for analysis. Note that the costs of materials can be ignored because we are assuming that the cost of the printed documents and the binding material are the same regardless of the machine used.

Machine	Annual Fixed Costs	Variable Labor Costs	Production Rate
Manual	$1,000	$18/hour	10 units/hour
Automatic	$9,000	$2/hour	100 units/hour

The total-cost equation is as follows:

$$TC = FC + (VC)(X_p)$$

where

TC = total cost
FC = fixed costs
VC = variable cost per unit
X_p = number of units produced

Comparing Costs

What is the cost to produce 1,000 units per year on each machine? From the following calculations, it is clear that the manual machine has lower costs. Dividing the total cost by the volume produced gives a unit cost that includes the variable cost and a share of the fixed costs.

Manual:

$$TC = \$1,000 + \frac{\$18/hr}{10\ units/hr}(1,000\ units)$$

$$= \$2,800$$

$$\text{Unit Cost} = \frac{\$2,800}{1,000}$$

$$= \$2.80 \text{ per unit at a volume of 1,000}$$

Automatic:

$$TC = \$9,000 + \frac{\$2/hr}{100\ units/hr}(1,000\ units)$$

$$= \$9,020$$

$$\text{Unit Cost} = \frac{\$9,020}{1,000}$$

$$= \$9.02 \text{ per unit at a volume of 1,000}$$

What happens if 10,000 books need to be bound? The marginal labor cost of binding each additional book on the automatic machine is only $.02 because the labor cost is $2.00 per hour and the output is 100 units per hour. On the manual machine, the marginal cost of binding a book is $1.80.

Manual:

$$TC = 1,000 + \frac{18.00}{10}(10,000)$$

$$= \$19,000$$

$$\text{Unit Cost} = \frac{\$19,000}{10,000}$$

$$= \$1.90 \text{ per unit at a volume of 10,000}$$

Automatic:

$$TC = 9{,}000 + \frac{2.00}{100}(10{,}000)$$

$$= \$9{,}200$$

$$\text{Unit Cost} = \frac{\$9{,}200}{10{,}000}$$

$$= \$.92 \text{ per unit at a volume of 10,000}$$

For binding 10,000 books, the unit cost for the automatic operation is significantly lower. As demand increases, the automatic process becomes more and more attractive.

The Indifference Point

At what production volume is the costs of the manual and the automatic machines equal? The variable X represents the volume produced. To check the accuracy of the following calculations, substitute the computed value of X into the total-cost equation for each machine to see if the two total costs are equal. Except for differences caused by rounding, they should be:

$$\text{Total cost manual} = \text{Total cost automatic}$$

$$(\$1{,}000) + \frac{\$18.00}{10 \text{ units}}(X) = (\$9{,}000) + \frac{\$2.00}{100 \text{ units}}(X)$$

$$(1{,}000) + (1.80)(X) = (9{,}000) + (.02)(X)$$

Solve for X:

$$(1.80 - .02)(X) = 9{,}000 - 1{,}000$$

$$X = \frac{8{,}000}{1.78}$$

$$X = 4{,}494 \text{ units}$$

The Power of Volume to Reduce Costs

This problem illustrates how unit costs can be decreased by purchasing high-speed equipment and producing large numbers of parts. The following table lists the unit costs for various volumes. Verify the unit cost for binding 100,000 books as an exercise.

Volume	Manual	Automatic
1,000	$2.80	$9.02
10,000	1.90	0.92
100,000	1.81	0.11

This example makes many simplifying assumptions, such as unlimited capacity, no increase in maintenance costs, and no increase in the failure rate of the machine as volume increases. These and other relevant factors could be estimated and considered in the analysis. In any case, the impact of volume on unit cost is very clear.

EXAMPLE   Sam Walton, the founder of Wal-Mart, demonstrated that volume drives profits, which, in turn, drive expansion in retail operations as it does in manufacturing. Best

Buy, a consumer electronics retailer, has followed Mr. Walton's example. Best Buy developed a way to price these products lower than retailers such as Kmart and Sears and substantially lower than the specialty retailers. Best Buy offers a wide selection and has a knowledgeable sales staff that can answer questions and provide support. The strategy is to sell consumer electronics in large volume, much larger than the specialty stores and other retailers. By pushing higher volume across the fixed costs associated with marketing and distributing these products, Best Buy is able to achieve economies of scale.

Building Volume through Global Expansion

If volume is an important factor in lowering the costs of goods and services, having a business expand globally may enhance its ability to compete. On the surface, this seems to contradict the common notion that competing globally is more difficult than competing nationally. If a company is running its operations at half capacity, say 50,000 units, it must charge a high enough price to cover all of its fixed costs plus its variable costs and profits. By expanding its marketing and distribution efforts into other countries, it may be able to increase volume to 70,000 units. This may allow a company to cut its price and be more competitive because the same fixed costs are allocated over 70,000 rather than 50,000 units. With a lower price, it may be possible to capture even more of the market, which could, in turn, lead to an even lower price.

In theory, this argument works even when the volume gained by a company in one country is lost by a company in another country. For example, suppose country A and country B both have companies that produce watches and ribbons for internal consumption. If the watch producer in country A could increase its volume by satisfying demand for watches in country B, the price of watches in the world would likely decline. Jobs would be lost in the watch industry in country B and would be gained in country A. If the ribbon producer in country B could increase its volume by satisfying demand for ribbons in country A, the price of ribbons in the world would likely decline. Jobs would be lost in the ribbon industry in country A and would be gained in country B. There is no guarantee that the job losses and gains will offset each other within the countries. There are many assumptions that underlie this discussion, but the example still makes a strong point about the potential of global trade to build volume and reduce costs.

EXAMPLE   Citibank is a dominant force in banking in the United States and around the globe. Through mergers and acquisitions domestically and internationally, Citibank has been able to examine overlaps in operations and eliminate redundant layers of costs. With greater transaction volume over the same fixed cost base, it has been able to increase profitability. With more customers, it can develop and offer new high-quality services at competitive prices. A large bank has the resources (deposits and fees) to support the increased organizational structure required to offer a full range of financial services around the world.

UNDERSTANDING THE SCALE FACTOR

For more than three hundred years, business leaders have recognized the advantages that can be gained by having high-volume operations. The tremendous increase in prosperity in the United States and other developed countries was driven by making large quantities of the same or similar products on the same equipment, that is, the same fixed cost base. This approach, often called mass production, is based on the concept of economies of scale. The **economies of scale** doctrine states that there is a most efficient size for a facility and a most efficient size for the firm. In practice, the doctrine has been used both to justify building larger facilities for the production of goods and services and to justify purchasing more automated equipment to speed production and lower costs.

An organization can use both or either of these approaches to leverage the time and talents of the people who create the large volume of services and goods demanded by its customers. If organizations and society are to progress, investments in equipment and facilities (fixed costs) must be made to increase the productivity of labor and management.

The critical issue in achieving economies of scale is putting a large volume of product across the same equipment or fixed cost base. In the past, it was necessary to have the stipulation that the products be the same or very similar because equipment was not flexible enough to cope with different products. With technological advances such as computer-integrated manufacturing, manufacturing cells, and flexible manufacturing systems, it is possible to achieve economies of scale by making different products on the same equipment, and it can be done without suffering the extra costs of machine changeover. Economies of scope is the term that describes this situation. **Economies of scope** are economies of scale across products. For example, Allen-Bradley has a facility that can produce a wide variety (100 different designs) of printed circuit boards in production lot sizes as small as one. The facility can produce them at a rate and cost that rivals mass producing standard circuit boards. The facility produces customized designs with ease.

Modeling the Scale Factor: Cost-Volume-Profit Model

To understand scale or volume issues, it is helpful to construct a simple model of the organization. A model is an abstraction of the key variables and relationships in a real problem and is used to simplify the problem and increase understanding. The **cost-volume-profit (C-V-P) model,** a simple model of an organization, uses estimates of costs, revenues, volume sold, and volume produced in order to estimate profit.

C-V-P Model Formulation

The C-V-P model is formulated by determining total revenue and costs, as shown in the following equations:

$$TR = (SP)(X_s)$$

where

TR = total revenue
SP = selling price per unit
X_s = number of units sold

$$TC = FC + (VC)(X_p)$$

where

TC = total cost
FC = fixed cost
VC = variable cost per unit
X_p = number of units produced

The profit (P) equation is:

$$P = TR - TC$$

By substituting the *TR* and *TC* equations into the equation for profit, the following mathematical model can be used to calculate profits, given sales and production volumes. This is the cost-volume-profit model.

$$P = SP(X_s) - [FC + VC(X_p)]$$

This model can also be manipulated to determine the volume required to earn some targeted value for profit. In order to do this, we assume that the number of units sold equals the number of units produced.

If $X = X_s = X_p$, then

$$P = SP(X) - [FC + VC(X)]$$
$$P = SP(X) - VC(X) - FC$$
$$P + FC = (SP - VC)(X)$$

Solve for *X* as follows:

$$X = \frac{(P + FC)}{(SP - VC)}$$

If *C* is defined as **contribution per unit,** then $C = (SP - VC)$. Thus, the equation becomes

$$X = \frac{(P + FC)}{C} \qquad (8.1)$$

The **profit point** is the number of units *(X)* that must be produced and sold at the contribution *(C)* in order to cover the fixed costs *(FC)* and profit *(P)*. Exhibit 8.2 represents the model graphically and illustrates the profit point. If the profit is set to zero, Equation 8.1 is recognizable as the so-called break-even formula. The **break-even point (BEP)** is the volume that must be produced and sold so that profit is zero.

PROBLEM

The mechanics of applying the C-V-P model are relatively simple. To calculate the profit point, you must know the selling price, variable costs, and fixed costs. Management can determine the projected level of profit to be used in the model. In this example, the fixed cost and profit are for a one-month period.

SP = $8.00/unit
VC = $4.50/unit
C = $3.50/unit
FC = $25,000/month
P = $8,000/month

In this case, the number of units that must be produced and sold to make $8,000 profit in a month is 9,429 units; that is the profit point.

$$X = \frac{FC + P}{C}$$
$$= \frac{\$25,000/\text{month} + \$8,000/\text{month}}{\$3.50/\text{unit}} = 9,429 \text{ units/month}$$

Managers can use this number in many ways. Here are two examples. First, if the organization has a capacity of only 5,600 units per month, then achieving an $8,000 profit is not possible. Second, if the sales forecast is for 9,000 units, then that profit level cannot be achieved because not enough units will be sold. Changes can

EXHIBIT 8.2

Cost-Volume-Profit
Model

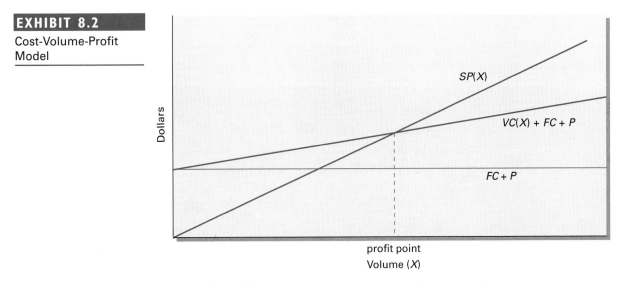

If profit (*P*) is set equal to zero, then the profit is equal to the break-even point.

be made to the model for the purpose of doing sensitivity analysis and answering what-if questions. For example, what if the variable costs increased from $4.50 to $5.00 per unit? Under these circumstances, the profit point becomes 11,000 units per month.

$$X = \frac{\$25{,}000/\text{month} \ + \ \$8{,}000/\text{month}}{\$3.00/\text{unit}} = 11{,}000 \ \text{units/month}$$

C-V-P Assumptions

The C-V-P model, like any other model, makes several assumptions. The assumption that sales volume equals production volume has already been mentioned. The model also assumes that total cost and total revenue are linear functions of volume. The model is based on historical data for costs and revenue. Any changes in these relationships caused by changes in technology, demand, or strategy may invalidate the use of this or any other model. Users of models should understand these assumptions, or they may apply the model ineffectively and thus obtain misleading results.

The Multiple-Product Case of the C-V-P Model

Our discussion of the C-V-P model has considered only single-product firms. But many organizations produce more than one product, using the same set of fixed costs. How can this firm be modeled? In this case, another set of variables, product mix, is added to the revenue and cost relationships. To solve the problem, a weighted contribution based on the mix of each product is calculated. Consider the following problem.

PROBLEM

A company repairs small appliances. The table that follows gives the average selling price, variable cost, and contribution for each service. The product mix and profit target are also listed. The fixed costs are shared by all three products.

	Coffeepot	Mixer	Blender
Product mix	45%	20%	35%
Selling price/unit	$12	$16	$9
Variable cost/unit	$6	$7	$4
Contribution/unit	$6	$9	$5

Profit target = $20,000/yr

Fixed costs = $30,000/yr

The mix is the number of each product repaired divided by the total number repaired. The weighted contribution is calculated as:

$$WC = \sum_{i=1}^{n} M_i (SP_i - VC_i)$$

where

WC = weighted contribution per unit

M_i = product mix as a percentage of total sales for product i, where $i = 1, ..., n$ for n different products or product lines

SP_i = selling price for product i

VC_i = variable cost for product i

Thus, the weighted contribution for the product mix shown above is:

WC = .45($12/unit – $6/unit) + .2($16/unit – $7/unit) + .35 ($9/unit – $4/unit)

= $6.25/unit

In the multiple-product case, the weighted contribution per unit substitutes for the contribution per unit in equation 8.1.

$$X = \frac{P + FC}{WC}$$

$$= \frac{\$20,000 + \$30,000}{\$6.25/\text{unit}}$$

$$= 8,000 \text{ units}$$

(8.2)

Interpreting the Results

The variable X is measured as a composite unit—that is, a unit consisting of 45 percent coffeepot, 20 percent mixer and 35 percent blender.

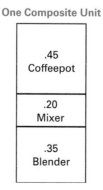

One Composite Unit

Weighted contribution = $6.25

Product	Mix	No. Required
Coffeepot	.45	3,600 units
Mixer	.20	1,600
Blender	.35	2,800
		8,000 units

The number of units, 8,000, represents the total number of coffeepots, mixers, and blenders that must be repaired to make a $20,000 profit. The number of coffeepots required is (.45)(8,000 units), or 3,600 units.

What Happens to the Profit Point if the Mix Changes?

In this model, the mix affects the profit point. If the estimated mix is different from the actual mix, then the profit point will change. Assume the mix changes to 50 percent coffeepots, 10 percent mixers, and 40 percent blenders, and the total number of units repaired remains 8,000. How is profit affected?

	Coffeepot	Mixer	Blender
Product Mix	50%	10%	40%
Selling price/unit	$12	$16	$9
Variable cost/unit	$6	$7	$4
Contribution/unit	$6	$9	$5

Profit Target (P) = unknown

Fixed costs = $30,000 yr.

Equation 8.2 can be restated and used to calculate profit.

$$X = \frac{P + FC}{WC}$$
$$WC(X) = P + FC$$
$$P = WC(X) - FC$$

We know the fixed costs are $30,000, and the volume is given as 8,000 units. First, we have to calculate the weighted contribution based on the new mix.

$$WC = \sum_{i=1}^{n} M_i(SP_i - VC_i)$$
$$= .5(\$12/\text{unit} - \$6/\text{unit}) + .1(\$16/\text{unit} - \$7/\text{unit}) + .4(\$9/\text{unit} - \$4/\text{unit})$$
$$= \$5.90 \text{ unit}$$

Now profit can be calculated.

$$P = \$5.90(8,000 \text{ units}) - \$30,000 = \$17,200$$

The profit is only $17,200 dollars because demand shifted away from mixers, which have a higher contribution per unit, to the lower-contribution coffeepots and blenders. Profit is not only a function of the volume produced and sold, but also a function of the product mix.

The C-V-P Model and Operating Leverage

The C-V-P model has uses in addition to calculating profit points. It also illustrates a fundamental concept in process selection. The volume of product demanded by customers and the organization's share of that market determine the organization's cost structure. To have large demands, a product must be priced so that large numbers of people can afford to buy it. If fertilizing services cost $250 for a typical lawn, the market would be much smaller than it would be if they cost $50. A small unit price forces the development of automated production systems in order to reduce total costs. How is this achieved? Capital in the form of equipment is substituted for labor to improve labor productivity and to utilize materials more efficiently. (Recall the example with the automated versus the manual binding equipment.) Larger volumes will support the engineering time necessary to make changes in product design and material specifications, thus reducing costs and improving performance. Volume is a key to the process selection decision.

- *Low-Volume Option.* When demand for a product is low, whatever the reason, it is difficult to support expensive specialized equipment for production. In such cases, more hand labor is used, and labor costs per unit of production are generally greater. Also, material costs are not as carefully scrutinized. A dollar of material savings on each unit cannot command much engineering and management time when only a few units, say 200 per year, are required. This low-volume producer has a cost structure like the one shown in Exhibit 8.3.

  For example, people fertilizing a few lawns as a sideline would buy a small manual application system. They would probably use the vehicle that they drive to their full-time job as their transportation to and from the fertilizing jobs. This decision keeps their fixed costs low. Variable costs are high. Their labor costs are high because it takes substantial time to push the manual equipment around the lawn. Because they have only a few jobs, they may pay retail price for their chemicals.

- *High-Volume Option.* The case for more specialized equipment is much stronger if 20,000 units per year are required. As volume grows, management is forced to change its operating philosophy because competitive pressure on price forces cost reductions. Cost reductions are achieved by shifting to an operation with high fixed costs and low unit variable costs, as shown in Exhibit 8.4. The variable names are subscripted with an M to indicate mass production. The products tend to be more uniform and are priced for the mass market.

  For example, a lawn fertilizing company with thousands of customers would purchase high-volume application systems that spread liquid fertilizer drawn from a large tank carried on the back of a heavy-duty truck. This equipment

EXHIBIT 8.3

Cost Structure of Low-Volume Producer (Low Fixed Costs and High Unit Variable Costs)

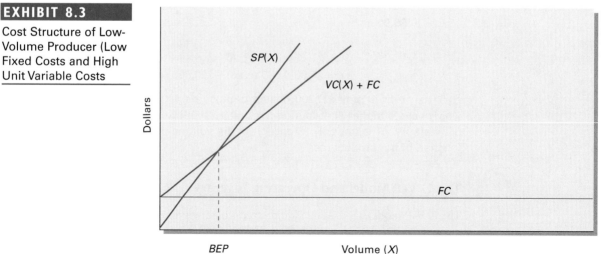

causes the company's fixed costs to be much higher than the low-volume option. It enables the worker to complete the lawn in less than one-quarter of the time. Because of the high volume, the company can buy chemicals directly from the producer at less than half of the retail price.

- *Moving from Low Volume to High Volume.* The change in operating position from low to high fixed costs brings greater risk and greater reward. This trade-off is referred to as operating leverage. The greater risk is evident in Exhibit 8.5, which shows the low-fixed-cost alternative as solid lines and the high-fixed-cost alternative in dashed lines.

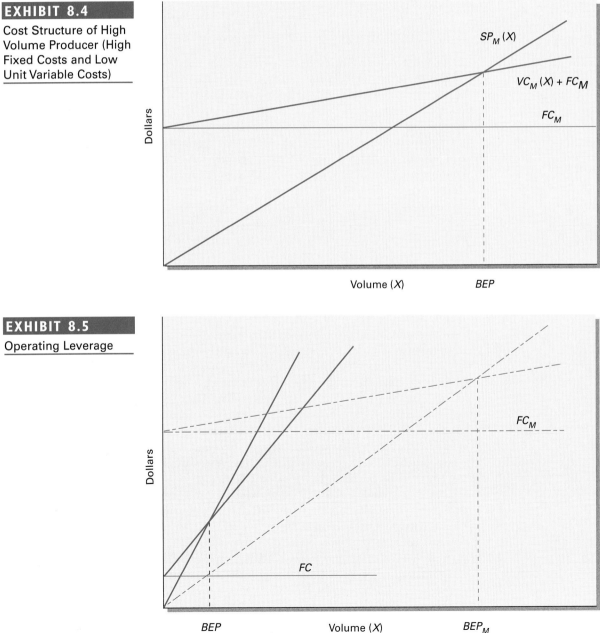

EXHIBIT 8.4

Cost Structure of High Volume Producer (High Fixed Costs and Low Unit Variable Costs)

EXHIBIT 8.5

Operating Leverage

The low-fixed-cost operation has a substantially lower break-even point, and variable costs can be reduced significantly as volume drops below the break-even point. The losses incurred can be small. The opposite is true for mass production. As volume drops below the zero profit point, the losses mount rapidly because most of the costs are fixed.

An increase in volume favors the mass producer because greater volume adds only small unit variable costs. The fixed costs do not change. This rapid increase in profits is stopped only by the capacity limits of the existing asset base. That is why mass producers prefer to operate at their capacity. This high operating ratio leads to high profits in the well-managed organization. The mass-producer is leveraging operations by adding fixed costs in the form of specialized equipment. The reward for this risk is greater profit potential.

Process Selection and Economies of Scale and Scope

From the perspective of economies of scale or economies of scope, process selection focuses on the volume of product demanded in the market. Organizations can influence that volume by increasing advertising, providing better service, and producing higher quality products. Regardless of how that volume is generated, an organization needs to respond to higher demand with an appropriate process.

When does an organization have sufficient volume to justify specialized, high-speed equipment? Is a demand of 50,000 units per year sufficient? It is not possible to give specific answers to these questions because the answers depend on what the organization produces. For example, if it produces space shuttles, then an annual demand of 50,000 would certainly be large enough to support specialized facilities, and even 5,000 would be considered a large volume. If, however, the organization is processing checks for a bank, 50,000 a year is a very small number, and even 1 million per year is not large.

In process selection, Hayes and Wheelwright (1979, 133) have suggested that product and process can be viewed through two sides of a matrix. Exhibit 8.6 displays a series of process alternatives that can be matched with identifiable product characteristics so that efficient operations can be achieved. High-volume operations are usually referred to as **line flow processes.** One type of line flow is the continuous flow process. A **continuous flow** does not usually identify individual units; rather, the product is mixed and flows together in a continuous stream. Oil refining is a good example of a continuous flow process. Processing checks in a bank is another example. The term **assembly line** is used to describe the high-volume assembly of discrete products. A washing machine is a good example of an assembly-line product and making a fast-food pizza on a busy Friday night may be another. Continuous flow and assembly lines are usually dedicated facilities that produce large volumes with little, if any, difference in the products. Because the items produced within such a facility are the same or very similar, the process involves economies of scale. To increase volume, cut costs, and achieve economies of scale, organizations traditionally move up the shaded diagonal in Exhibit 8.6.

Batch is a term used to describe a production process that does not have sufficient volume from a single product to use the facility fully. In this case, the facility produces several products to build sufficient volume. When this resource sharing exists, a transition time **(changeover time)** is usually required to change the facility from being able to make one product to being able to make the next. An example of batch production would be production at a company, like Merck, that produces medicine. Merck has equipment that is designed to mix the ingredients and form the pills. Often this equipment can produce in a few weeks all the capsules of a particular medicine needed for an entire year. Because of shelf life considerations and inventory costs, making even a one-year supply in a single batch creates too

EXHIBIT 8.6   Matching Process Alternatives with Product Characteristics

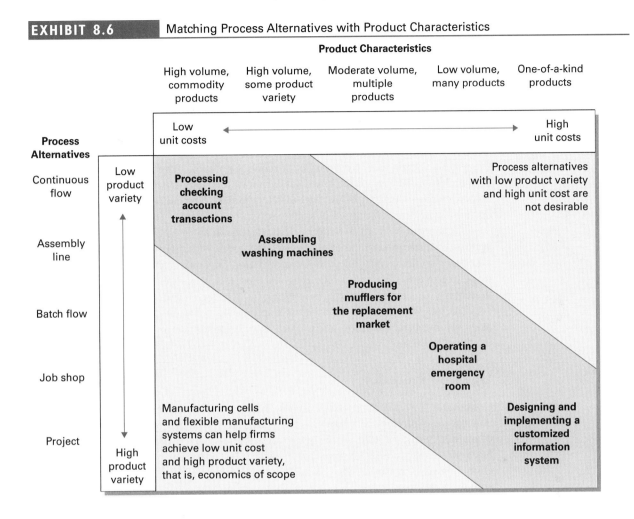

much inventory. So, companies like Merck produce different medicines in smaller batches using the same equipment. In between batches, the equipment must be thoroughly cleaned so the next batch is not contaminated. These changes take time and cost money, but are necessary to maintain enough volume to support the large investment in equipment.

As product volume declines, batching operations may no longer be possible. Here, only a few units of a product are required, and there may be no assurance that the order will be repeated. The differences between products can be significant. In this situation, usually called **job shop** production, the facility is general and flexible enough to meet a variety of needs. To achieve this flexibility, job shops generally have a much higher unit cost than line flow or batch processes for the same product. Fancy restaurants and hospital emergency rooms are examples of job shops. Both types of organizations offer great product variety and cater to individual customer demands.

At the bottom of the volume scale in Exhibit 8.6 are **projects,** which are usually one-of-a-kind operations. Each job is different from the rest. Most large construction jobs are projects, and many service operations can be categorized as projects. Installing new computer hardware, adding major new computer software, and implementing a new management planning and control system could all qualify as projects.

The relationship between product and process illustrated in Exhibit 8.6 indicates that there is a one-to-one relationship between product volume and the type of process. For example, Exhibit 8.6 indicates that one-of-a-kind products cannot be produced on an assembly line or in a continuous flow shop. In essence, Exhibit 8.6 implies that an organization's options are limited to product and process matches on the diagonal. The diagram implies that if an organization wants to achieve the low cost obtained in continuous flow or assembly-line operations, it must significantly limit product variety. An organization that wants to achieve the product variety obtained in a job shop or projects must incur high unit costs.

However, with the advances in information and manufacturing technologies, organizations have new process alternatives—manufacturing cells and flexible manufacturing systems. With these alternatives, the products produced within a facility are different and the volume is high, that is, economies of scope. This implies moving off the shaded diagonal in Exhibit 8.6 toward the lower left corner of the diagram where an organization can achieve both low unit costs and high product variety. The concept is often labeled mass customization and is discussed in a later section.

We may not be ready to build nuclear reactors on an assembly line, but we can create appliances, automobiles, and other services and goods with increasing variety, while maintaining or reducing the unit cost. As information and manufacturing technologies continue to expand, the shaded blue diagonal that represents the feasible product/process matches will expand as well.

The following sections describe the traditional process alternatives: continuous flow, assembly line, batch, job shop, and project, as well as manufacturing cells and flexible manufacturing systems.

Line Flow Processes

Continuous flow operations and assembly lines have some differences; yet both are high-volume, mass-production operations characterized by a standardized product with interchangeable parts. Because of this, the process is the same for each unit, and the product has a dominant product flow through the facility. Because there is little or no product variation, there is no reason to have more than one path through the facility. Furthermore, the equipment that processes the products should be arranged "around" the product so that material-handling and transportation costs are not excessive. This approach is called a **product layout.**

In terms of the cost structure, a continuous flow process or an assembly line has relatively high fixed costs and relatively low variable costs. The high fixed costs are, in part, a result of the substantial investment in specialized equipment.

There are some differences between a continuous flow process and an assembly line. In a continuous flow process, the product is often a commodity in which one unit is not distinguishable from another. In this case, the producer makes no attempt to track each unit separately. For example, in refining gasoline from crude oil, one gallon of unleaded regular gasoline is like another. Banks process checks one after another without changing methods. The production of fiberglass insulation is high volume and fast paced. It is not feasible to track and identify each piece produced. The emphasis is on measuring inputs and comparing them to outputs.

The traditional assembly-line process allows some variations among units. Options are usually selected from a list of possibilities, and the minor adjustments needed to cope with this variation can be made by workers on the production line. Adding green peppers to the standard pizza is easy to do. Adding power steering to a car or a temperature probe to a microwave oven is also easy to do. Customizing mass-assembled products generally takes place in a separate facility or in the aftermarket. For example, many customers buy vans from mass producers and have them customized elsewhere. The continuous flow and assembly-line characteristics are summarized in Exhibit 8.7, along with the other process types.

| EXHIBIT 8.7 | Characteristics of the Process Alternatives |

Characteristics

Process	Volume	Product variety	Product flow	Facility layout	Fixed costs	Variable costs	Equipment
Continuous flow	High	Standard	Dominant	Product	High	Low	Special purpose
Assembly line		Standard with minor modification	Dominant	Product	High	Low	Special purpose
Batch		Some variation	Dominant	Product	High	Low	Some flexibility
Flexible manufacturing system		Moderate variety	Dominant	Product	High	Low	Flexible
Manufacturing cell		Moderate variety	Dominant	Product	Moderate	Low to moderate	Flexible
Job shop	Low	Major differences	Random	Process	Low	High	Flexible
Project	One	One-of-a-kind	Not applicable	Fixed position	Low to moderate	High	Flexible

EXAMPLE

For Marco's Pizza, the busiest day of the week is Friday, and the busiest time of day is after 5:00 P.M. People going to football or basketball games, couples out for a relaxing evening, and parents who are too tired to make dinner order pizza from Marco's. Marco's meets this high volume by making pizza on an assembly line. We often think that an assembly line is a way to manufacture goods. Increasingly, high-volume service operations are learning that assembly lines and mass production can work for them.

At the first workstation, the dough is kneaded and spread onto the pan. At the second station, sauce is ladled onto the crust by another worker. At the third station, cheese is placed on top of the sauce. Extra toppings are added at the last station, where the pizza is placed in the oven. Each station is staffed by one or more workers, depending on the workload at that station. To organize production, as the order is taken, customer options are noted on the job ticket, which moves down the assembly line as the pies are created. In this way, the assembly line is able to cope with customer options, which include the size and type of crust, extra sauce, extra cheese, and additional toppings.

Because of the simplified flow of an assembly line, customers' pies are finished quickly. If fact, even though the volume is much higher on Friday night, customer waiting time on Friday night is about the same as any other night. The unit labor cost for each pie is actually lower on Friday night than on any other night because the high volume keeps everyone busy. There is little confusion and few mixed up orders because people and materials are moving in an orderly fashion.

If the assembly line works so well, why does Marco's use it only on Friday night? The answer is that the lower volumes on Monday night, for example, cannot support the staffing level needed to run the assembly line. On that night, one person might do all of the steps.

Mass Production and Quality

Mass production of goods and services does not necessarily imply inferior quality. A Rolls Royce could be made at the same quality level in quantities of five thousand or five million. The reasons that five million Rolls are not produced are (1) customers would not purchase that volume at the usual price and (2) the product would lose its prestige image if it were regularly seen on the highway.

It is the pressure on price that forces cost to be reduced. This pressure forces the substitution of less-expensive materials and less-expensive methods of production. Neither of these potential changes necessarily leads to lower quality. The organization that can find ways to make these substitutions and raise product quality at the same time will be rewarded with increasing sales and profits. The need to cut costs should not be an excuse for inferior design or shoddy workmanship. For example, in an effort to reduce costs and improve fuel efficiency, automotive engineers have replaced hundreds of pounds of steel parts, including exterior body panels, with plastic. Plastic is lighter and costs less than steel; it resists nicks and dings better than steel; and it will not rust. This kind of change is a winner for the customer and a winner for the company.

Evidence that high-quality products can be mass produced can be seen in many of the products we use every day. Automobiles, televisions, stereos, and dishwashers are a few examples. The old adage "They don't make 'em like they used to" is certainly true. Today's products are better.

EXAMPLE

EMC mass produces high quality disk drives to meet demands from the makers of personal computers, network servers, Web-hosting systems, and other products. EMC's ability to make disk drives in high volume allows the company to keep its costs low. As seen in Exhibit 8.5, high volume and low unit costs increase operating leverage and profits. High quality is essential for customer satisfaction. In addition to high-volume, high-quality, and low-cost products, organizations are seeking to achieve high product variety. This blend of capabilities is often called mass customization, and organizations such as EMC that can achieve it can gain a competitive advantage.

Batch Flow

When quantities are not sufficient to support dedicated production facilities, several groups or batches are produced using the same facility. These products are usually similar in design and have similar processing requirements. For example, glass containers come in a variety of sizes but are designed and built similarly. A key to understanding if the differences among products are meaningful can be found when the equipment is shut down to change from one product to another. If the time for these changes is not significant and the sequence of operations is similar, then it is like a line flow process. On the other hand, if the changeover time is significant, then these products should be built in batches.

Because of the similar processing requirements in batch operations, one or a few product flows dominate. For example, appliance manufacturers may produce several different models of refrigerators on the same assembly line. In cases where changeover time is significant, manufacturers may produce a batch—say, one week's production of a particular model—and then switch to another model. Although the models show some differences from batch to batch, these differences are not significant enough to change the product-oriented layout of the facility. If a producer is able to design the product and the process so that different models can be produced one after the other with zero or near zero changeover time, then the process is similar to an assembly line that is producing a standard product. The disadvantages of batch production are that (1) changeover time is nonproductive and (2) extra inventory must be maintained to satisfy demand for the products that are not being produced.

Firms that use batch processing tend to incur higher unit costs than mass producers because of equipment downtime for changeover, larger amounts of inventory, and increased labor costs due to the changeovers. The greater the time devoted to changing facilities, the greater the cost differential suffered by batch operations. The key to moving to lower cost production is to eliminate or at least greatly reduce the changeover time. One way to do this is to eliminate product variety. Henry Ford did this in the early days of automobile production when he said that customers could have cars of any color as long as they were black. Today, however, standardizing products does not often work because consumers are demanding greater product variety. Instead, companies are turning to group technology to build families of parts that can be produced using manufacturing cells or flexible manufacturing systems. This is part of the foundation for mass customization, which is discussed later in this chapter.

Management problems become more complex as production shifts from a line flow process and to a batch process. The following issues surface when batch processes are used:

- How are products to be sequenced in the facility?
- How many units of one product should be made before production is switched to another?
- How much inventory should be kept of the products that are not being produced?

These lot-sizing and scheduling issues are discussed later.

Manufacturing Cells and Flexible Manufacturing Systems

Manufacturing cells, sometimes called cellular manufacturing, and flexible manufacturing systems (FMS) are process options that offer the potential to produce low-cost products that meet varying customer requirements. Manufacturing cells rely on group technology to build a family of parts with similar design and processing characteristics. **Group technology** is a set of methods that enables firms to classify parts based on size, shape, use, type of material, and method of production. A **family of parts** is a collection of parts with similarities in these characteristics. In this way, a product-oriented layout (cell) can be designed that will reduce material-handling costs, increase machine utilization, and shorten production lead times. Because the processing is similar, less time is required to change from one product within the family to another. See Exhibit 8.7.

A FMS is similar to a manufacturing cell because it relies on group technology to build families of parts. Also, like a manufacturing cell, an FMS produces low-cost products with high variety. The major differences are that an FMS tends to have more automation, robots, and computer control than a manufacturing cell does, and it usually operates without people tending the machines.

FMSs grew from the need to cope with demand for increasing product variations. With an FMS, an organization can capture new markets by accumulating production requirements from several low-volume products. Higher-volume operations allow the arrangement of a set of machines in one layout to produce all the different products. The products, however, must be similar enough to have the same or a similar sequence of operations, and the machines must be flexible enough to handle the differences. This system is feasible with computer technology and robotics that can quickly be adapted to new products. Manufacturing cells and FMSs enable organizations to increase the volume of product moving across a group of machines and, thereby, reduce operating costs.

EXAMPLE

Badger Meters is located in Milwaukee and makes flow meters that range in size from household water meters to those for large water mains. The company produces 110 different meter housings in quantities that vary from 1 to 1,000 per year. The industry is very competitive and is plagued with overcapacity and price cutting. Many of the valves are purchased by public utilities through competitive bidding. An order can be lost for a few cents per meter.

Badger's first step to improve profitability was to take existing production equipment from the process-oriented job shop layout and rearrange it into a manufacturing cell. In one case, one person was able to operate three machines and produce a finished casting in six minutes. With the old system, the time, including delays for material handling and scheduling, was measured in days. The manufacturing cells reduced material-handling requirements, cut production time, and lowered costs. A picture that illustrates the differences in material flow is shown in Exhibit 8.8.

Applying Manufacturing Cells to Service Operations

The phrases "manufacturing cells" and "flexible manufacturing systems" both include the word "manufacturing." You might conclude, then, that these concepts only work when goods are to be produced. The concepts that underlie both manufacturing cells and flexible manufacturing systems can work equally well for service operations. The basic ideas behind these techniques are (1) to group products into one or more families that have similar processing

EXHIBIT 8.8

Process Flows Before and After Applying Group Technology to Achieve Manufacturing Cells

Job Shop: Jumbled Flow

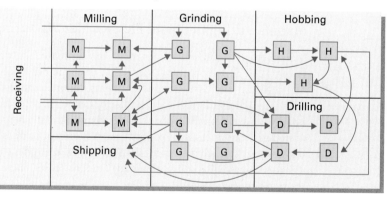

Families of Parts and Manufacturing Cells: Organized Flow

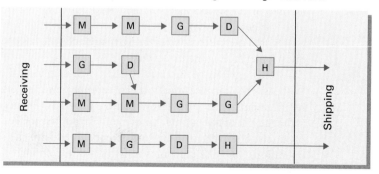

requirements and (2) to arrange equipment in close proximity that can meet those processing requirements. The major advantages of these techniques are that they:

- Reduce setup/changeover time and cost because similar products requiring similar setups are produced together
- Dramatically reduce material handling and material movement by locating equipment for performing the entire job in close proximity
- Increase the effectiveness and efficiency of people by focusing their attention on the product and its needs rather than on tracking material movements through the facility

The basic ideas of grouping products and grouping equipment, in abstract and in practice, can be applied to any service operation that has both a variety of products and equipment. A print shop is a good example because it often has a variety of different jobs with different processing requirements. The customer orders in a print shop could be grouped into families of jobs with similar processing requirements. The equipment could be arranged so that all the machines (e.g., two-color printing press, collator, and binder) needed to perform that family of jobs are in one location rather than scattered throughout the facility.

EXAMPLE

Hospitals are organizing into cells in order to focus patient care. How can cold and impersonal phrases like manufacturing cells and flexible manufacturing systems make hospital patients feel better cared for? The basic concepts that support manufacturing cells also support patient-focused care. They involve grouping patients with similar illnesses in the same location, providing nurses with special training to deal with the particular problems associated with that illness, and breaking apart centralized services and equipment and moving them into these areas.

As a result, the quality of the nursing care increases. Medicines commonly used to treat a particular illness can be kept close. Patients spend far less time traveling throughout the hospital and waiting hours for a blood test or respiration therapy. Services are more likely to be provided when needed, which can improve patients' qualities of life and hasten their recoveries. Patients feel better about the hospital and are more likely to return. When properly implemented, hospitals have found that patient-focused care can even reduce costs.

Job Shop

A job shop does not produce large quantities of the same or even similar products, but is dominated by a large number of different products produced in small volumes. Because the products are different, they do not follow the same path through the facility. In fact, the movement of products between work centers is best characterized as random. As a result, it is not possible to organize machines by product flow as in the line flow processes or even in batch operations. It is necessary to group machines by process or type of operation because a job is as likely to require work at one work center as at any of the other centers. The job shop is one of the process alternatives shown in Exhibit 8.7.

Because the products are very different, specialized equipment cannot be justified. Job shops use flexible equipment to meet the needs of the diverse product group. A job shop produces different products on general-purpose machines using skilled labor. The cost structure has low fixed costs and high unit variable costs. Gains in manufacturing and in computer and information technologies will permit more flexibility and thus allow products now made in job shops to be produced in families on manufacturing cells, as shown in Exhibit 8.8. In addition, as FMSs and the information systems that control them become capable of producing a wider variety of parts, the products once produced in job shops will become less expensive. These products will move up the volume scale in Exhibit 8.7 without losing their appeal to the market. Such a move can provide an organization with a competitive edge— low price, high quality, and product variety.

The differences among the hard automation that is often found in mass production; the flexible manufacturing systems that are now being applied; and the general-purpose equipment that is usually found in job shops are important to understand. These process alternatives affect several basic issues involved in production. The level of automation affects capital investment, unit costs, flexibility, and capacity. As FMSs become even more flexible, low-volume jobs will be grouped for production on them. As FMS technology becomes better understood and lower in cost, large homogeneous markets can be segmented because the FMS will provide customers with product variety and low costs. As shown in Exhibit 8.9, the area of application for FMSs will continue to increase as technology improves.

Project

Projects usually involve a one-of-a-kind product. Typical examples are found in the construction industry and include the construction of large ships, plants, and office buildings. In a project, cost structure is not the same as in other processes because there is only a single unit. In one sense, the cost for the project is all variable. Fixed costs in the form of overhead begin to make sense when a firm is engaged in more than one project and can spread certain major equipment costs and overhead costs over several different projects.

Product flow is not meaningful in projects because the end product of most construction projects is designed to remain stationary. The usual term that describes the layout is fixed position. A project-oriented operation is very flexible, allowing extensive customizing of the finished products.

EXHIBIT 8.9

Automation Systems

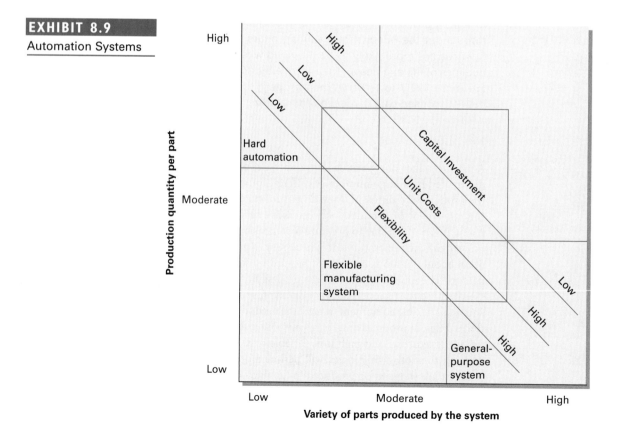

EXAMPLE

Projects are common in service operations, for example, Seibel Systems develops and installs software systems that control banking operations. These software systems can monitor each transaction, keep a history on it, and assist in reconciling the transaction to the account. To design these systems, software companies draw the needed talent from a pool of experts and form a project team. Because each system is different, different groups may be used to develop each system. These companies provide a service and use project management to successfully complete the work.

Ethical Issues in Process Selection

Some religious leaders have argued that organizations should move away from automation and return to manual labor to reduce worldwide unemployment. The argument is that a reduction in automation would provide more jobs, thus more people would have income and could consume more. On the surface, the argument seems to have some merit, but closer examination reveals fundamental flaws.

Consider the following statement, which is true by definition. People living in the world can only consume what they produce. Any reduction in world output caused by reducing automation would provide fewer services and goods to be consumed. If fewer services and goods are available for consumption, the amount of money available does not matter. People would consume less, not more, because there would be less to consume. People would simply bid the prices of the products higher until the law of supply and demand stabilized prices. Adding government-mandated price controls may keep prices artificially low, but would create no new services or goods. Price controls could actually cause businesses to reduce output because the price an organization received for its products might be less than the costs of production, thus exacerbating the problem.

The most effective way to increase the standard of living is to select the process that best fits the volume, cost, and quality characteristics of the product. Striving to increase worker productivity is the best recipe for increasing the standard of living in the world. This statement is true because productivity increases usually lead to more output, which means more can be consumed. Allowing free market economies to judge what to produce and how to produce it has been shown to be the most effective way of creating prosperity. Until something better is developed, automation and productivity increases driven by a free market economy will have to do.

EXAMPLE

An issue of growing importance is the use of children as production workers. In the United States, it is against the law for children to work in factories. In a global context, the International Labor Organization prohibits the employment of children under the age of fourteen. This has not stopped independent contractors, who are operating in other countries and are seeking to keep costs low, from employing children under the age of fourteen. These subcontractors often produce products for large national and international companies. While this may not represent a legal liability for the large corporation, if it was not aware of the practice, it certainly does present an ethical dilemma. In addition, the negative impact on public relations may be substantial and may offset the benefits from lower labor costs.

THE FOCUSED FACTORY

Previous sections have illustrated how investing in specialized equipment to attain high volume can reduce unit costs. For many years, it was accepted procedure for operations to produce more and more units in order to lower costs. This procedure created two problems. First, facilities grew larger and larger as more capacity was added. More levels of management had to be added to cope with the increasing numbers of people. Facilities with three or four thousand employees were common; and in some cases, facilities had ten thousand or more employees and covered many acres. Buildings with more than one million square feet (about twenty-four acres) were common, and more than one building could be at a location. The sheer size of these facilities made them difficult to manage. Coordination and communication of activities were major problems. Second, faced with rapid market changes and shorter product life cycles, facility managers wanted to keep volume high and costs low. So, they added the production of different products to facilities that were designed to have limited flexibility. The results were increased downtime for equipment changeover and overloads on information systems that were designed to manage homogeneous products and processes.

In many cases, management's response was to add staff personnel and indirect labor to handle these problems. It created a "hidden factory" of overhead costs. In some cases, the costs of handling materials, maintaining equipment, and coordinating operations exceeded the cost savings from increasing volume.

One approach to dealing with the increasing complexity caused by divergent customer needs is to build smaller, **focused factories.** These smaller facilities often have fewer than five hundred employees and concentrate on making a few products. These simplified factories not only limit the number of different products made but also limit the scope of operations to include only a few process technologies. Focused factories do not attempt to produce several different quality levels; they strive for the highest quality at all times. What the focused factory may give up because it does not take full advantage of economies of scale, it makes up by simplicity in management and control. In essence, the focused factory reduces product variety, which reduces total production volumes and may result in idle equipment. The positive side of this decision is that the facility avoids the complexity induced when another product is added to the production schedule and inventory control system.

MASS CUSTOMIZATION

Mass customization offers a different perspective on dealing with product variety than the focused factory. Firms that seek mass customization find ways to quickly design, produce, and deliver product that meet specific customer needs at close to mass-production prices. These firms develop close relationships with their customers, which depend on frequent information exchange.

From an operations perspective, mass customization is the low-cost, high-quality, large-volume delivery of individually customized goods and services. Put simply, mass customization combines the pursuit of economies of scale/scope, quality improvement, and flexibility. Economies of scale/scope imply achieving high-volume operations and low costs, as illustrated in Exhibit 8.5. Quality improvement efforts, discussed in an earlier chapter as well as in the Web site material, are techniques and processes for meeting customer's quality expectations.

When pursuing flexibility, there are three attributes of to consider:

1. *Range/variety*—The number of viable states for the production system and the degree of difference in those states. From the perspective of range, the greatest variety is when a large number of very different products can be produced.

   a. How many different products can the production process make? For example, can an automotive service center do only brakes on General Motors' vehicles or can it do brakes, exhaust systems, engine tune ups, tires, batteries, and wheel alignments on all makes and models? This would help us to count the number of different products.

b. The second part is how different is the work? Two different products may have many similarities or they may be quite different. There is very little difference in skills or equipment needed to do a brake job on a Ford versus a Chrysler. The difference between a brake job and an exhaust system repair is still fairly small. As the skills and equipment needed to do a job become more differentiated, the range needed to provide those goods and services increases. At an extreme, the difference between automobile repair and hand surgery are substantial even though they both require a certain amount of manual dexterity.

2. *Mobility/responsiveness*—The ability to change quickly from producing one product to producing another. High mobility minimizes the need for long production runs. How long does it take for the service center to shift from doing brake work on a Ford to doing exhaust work on a Chrysler?

3. *Uniformity*—The ability to attain similar performance across the entire range of outputs. Will the quality on the brake job for the Ford be at the same high level as the quality on the exhaust system for the Chrysler?

Clearly, flexibility is the highest when all three elements of flexibility are at the best level. That is, the firm can produce a large number of products that are very different, can change over between them quickly, and can maintain a high level of performance.

Flexibility is clearly an important issue for the service industry. Hospitals face this problem every day as they attempt to treat patients with a wide variety of needs. With the deregulation of financial markets, the differences between banks and brokerage houses have blurred. Banks are doing much more than taking deposits and making loans. Universities are attempting to cope with an expanding number of majors, specialized degree programs, and individualized study programs. When this expansion occurs, universities must have faculty who have the capabilities to teach and conduct research across disciplines. Otherwise, the capabilities of the faculty may not match the changing needs of the organizations that hire the graduates.

Types of Customization

Customization can occur at more than one level. Indeed, there are three types:

1. *Customer-Contact Customization*—Organizations conduct dialogues with individual customers to determine their needs and create offerings that fit those needs. This system is general considered the "traditional" view of mass customization. Bicycles and golf clubs designed to precisely meet the needs of their users are available today. Services such as hair care and medical procedures can be designed to meet special needs. In these cases, customization often begins with product specification and design and flows through to production and distribution.

2. *Adaptive Customization*—Organizations offer a standard but customizable product in which each customer can independently derive value from the product because it has many possible offerings. The base elements of the design are standard, but their selection and arrangement can be specified individually. Customization begins at production rather than at design. The automotive industry is a good example because options can be selected to provide a certain

degree of customization. Many customers still buy what is available on the dealer's lot, but a growing number are ordering vehicles with specific options or are using search programs at the dealerships to locate their specific vehicle at a nearby dealer. An Internet link that gathers order data and sends it to the factory so lead times between order and delivery are reduced should help increase the frequency of made-to-order cars.

3. *Presentation Customization*—In this case, organizations present standard products differently to different customers. These differences could be in:
   a. Packaging—size, shape, characteristics
   b. Marketing materials—such as video tapes or CDs
   c. Placement—delivery channel and display
   d. Terms and conditions—warrantee, payment terms, and financing
   e. Stated use—claims and benefits to users

This level of customization begins after the product is produced.

EXAMPLE

Dell Computers' marketing strategy is computers-your-way. Go online, customize your personal computer, have it delivered in a matter of a few days, and pay less than the price of the computer from the retail outlet. That sounds nice, but how does Dell make it work? At its heart, Dell is a manufacturing innovator, not a technology innovator. The company's newest U.S. factory boasts more than triple the output of its previous facility, which was shut down. By the way, the new facility is less than half the size of the old one. At the new plant, workers turn out 700 personal computers an hour on each of three assembly lines, compared to about 120 an hour at the old facility.

A wall full of patents inside the new facility illustrates that Dell is a manufacturing pioneer in mass-producing customized products. What makes it work at Dell is the information flow, and coordination with suppliers. With these advances, Dell has reduced by about 50 percent the number of times a computer is touched by workers during assembly and shipping. This new system speeds up the process and cuts down on damage. Dell is taking advantage of these improvements by squeezing the price and grabbing market share from its competitors.

Containing the Cost-Side of Mass Customization

One of the most important challenges of mass customization is producing a large volume of product while keeping costs low. Each level has different factors to consider in achieving customization. Presentation customization is the simplest. Product design and process design are standard so flexibility is not required in these activities. A company that fertilizes your lawn offers a standard product, which allows them to achieve economies of scale in both designing the service and applying it to your lawn. The company may market differently or offer different terms and conditions to tailor the service to the customers.

Adaptive customization takes the cost issues one step further because production of the finished product can be customized. In this case, production may require a substantial amount of flexibility to produce what is needed. In the automobile example, everything from paint color to engine size to seat options can be selected by customers from a list of options. This level of choice requires assembly operations to be flexible in order to accommodate customer preferences.

Customer-contact customization requires the customer and the company to interact to produce precisely what customers want. This interaction has always been the case for companies, such as many software designer, construction, or consulting firms that have one-of-a-kind products and use project management. What is new is the ability to customize and keep production volumes high. The development of information and management systems that interact with the customer during product design, as well as production, is necessary. These systems require the exchange and processing of large amounts of information as well as design and production systems that are both fast and flexible.

The keys to cost containment are:

- *Adaptive customization and presentation customization*—Allow the base product to be undifferentiated, as in the example with lawn fertilization or automobile assembly.

- *Modular product design (some times called platform products)*—Facilitates economies of scale in design. Software design companies can pull together software modules to develop new software that meet specific applications.

- *Modular process design*—Allows firms to put processes together in different ways to make different products. Financing companies like IBM Commercial Credit can bring together experts in law, credit, and finance to configure plans to fund the purchase of software.

- *Postponement*—Permits firms to delay product differentiation until the latest possible moment. Hewlett-Packard decided to customize its printers at local distribution centers rather than at the factory.

- *Flexibility in product design and production systems*—Allows the firm to meet changing customer needs. Flexible works, machines, and information systems allow companies to respond to change.

- *Information system planning and technology*—Enable data, information, ideas, and decisions to be shared instantly among participants that need the information. Real-time information provides the basis for fast and accurate decision making.

EXAMPLE

Hewlett-Packard is confronting the pressure to provide differentiated products at competitive prices by postponing customization until the last possible moment. Instead of customizing its DeskJet printer at the factory in Singapore before shipping the units to Europe, it had the distribution center do the job. The company designed the printer with a country-specific external power supply, which is plugged into the printer at the distribution center. Power characteristics such as voltage are not standard throughout the world. With this approach in place, manufacturing costs are slightly higher, but manufacturing plus shipping plus inventory costs are down by 25 percent. Separating the power supply reduces product variations in the Singapore operations, reduces worldwide inventory, and allows Hewlett-Packard to shift printers around the globe to meet sudden changes in demand.

A Learning Organization: The Foundation of Mass Customization

The ability of organizations to acquire and apply knowledge, sometimes called absorptive capacity, provides the foundation for mass customization. Organizational learning is the ability to identify, communicate, and assimilate external and internal knowledge and technology. Its components are:

- *Prior relevant knowledge*—Understanding of job skills, technology, and management practices possessed by the workers and manager in the organization.

- *Communication network*—Scope and strength of structural connections that bring flows of information and knowledge to different organizational units.

- *Communication climate*—Atmosphere within the organization that defines accepted communication behavior.
- *Knowledge scanning*—Mechanism that enables firms to identify and capture relevant external and internal knowledge and technology.

These components of mass customization are essential to acquire and disseminate information about customers, competitors, and technologies. They are essential for sharing information within the organization about product design, process design, and capacity. Flexibility, modularity, postponement, and information system planning depend on knowledge acquisition and sharing.

SUMMARY

- Process defines the way that the products should be produced. Does the product have sufficient volume to justify large investments in plant and equipment to leverage the worker output? If not, then much highly skilled, high-cost labor must be used.
- Process selection is closely related to the product design and capacity decisions. Products with widespread appeal to the consumer will require a process that can deliver these products at competitive prices and in large volume.
- The cost-volume-profit model of the firm is one way of viewing the processing options. This model allows the organization to examine the risks associated with selecting the right processing option. Mass-production alternatives involve greater risk, but have the potential for greater return.
- Process selection is a function of volume demanded. The different process types include line flow, which includes continuous flow and assembly line, batch, job shop, and project as well as manufacturing cells and flexible manufacturing systems. Each of these process types is summarized in Exhibit 8.7.
- Focused factories and mass customization are two alternatives for coping with demand for an increasing variety of products. The focused factory strategy embraces small facilities with a limited range of products. Mass customization attempts to develop systems that are flexible and can make the various products.
- In the future, flexibility in the production process will play an increasingly important role as firms build volume by making different services and goods on the same equipment, that is, economics of scope. Changing consumer demand and specialized designs will give a competitive edge to producers who have flexibility.

 Visit our dynamic Web site, http://www.wiley.com/college/vonderembse, for extended chapter material, solved problems, mini-cases, computer software, and Web links.

KEY TERMS

assembly line	economies of scope	line flow process
batch	family of parts	manufacturing cell
break-even point (BEP)	flexible manufacturing	mass customization
changeover time	system	operating leverage
continuous flow	focused factory	process layout
contribution per unit	group technology	process selection
cost-volume-profit	hard automation	product layout
(C-V-P) model	job shop	profit point
economies of scale	leverage	project

URLS

FirstEnergy: www.firstenergycorp.com

Citigroup: www.citigroup.com

Ford Motor Company: www.fordmotorcompany.com

Dell Computer: www.dell.com

U.S. Postal Service: www.usps.com

QUESTIONS

1. What is process selection, and how can the organization use it to gain competitive advantage?

2. How is process selection related to product design and capacity determination? What are some examples?

3. Explain how the cost-volume-profit model of a firm is derived. How is it useful to operations managers in making the process selection decision?

4. What is operating leverage, and how does it help to explain risk in the organization?

5. Support or refute this statement: "The quality of mass-produced goods and services must be inferior."

6. What are line flow processes, and what characteristics help to define them? Give examples.

7. What is batch flow, and what characteristics help to define it? Give examples.

8. What is a job shop, and what characteristics help to define it? Give examples.

9. What is a project, and what characteristics help to define it? Give examples.

10. How will flexibility help an organization achieve a competitive advantage?

11. How can computers be used in the production process, and how will their role change?

12. What is a focused factory?

13. What is mass customization

14. How can companies contain the cost side of mass customization?

15. How are manufacturing cells and flexible manufacturing systems affecting the process selection decision?

16. Define economies of scale and economies of scope. How are they different?

INTERNET QUESTIONS

17. Investigate the Web site of Dell Computer. Based on its product offerings and other available information, describe how Dell has designed its production process to provide users what they demand with a very short lead time.

18. The U.S. Postal Service processes and delivers millions of letters and parcels each day. Examine its Web site. Learn as much as you can about the services it offers and the processes it uses to gather, sort, and deliver mail. What type of production process is used by the Postal Service? Why was it selected?

19. Citigroup, one of the largest banks in the world, has organized its operations to meet a variety of needs in the United States and around the globe. From its Web site, learn as much as you can about its product offerings. How must the production process,

including computers and information systems, be organized to help the company achieve success?

20. Ford Motor Company is a global producer of passenger vehicles. From the company's Web site, learn about its extensive product offerings and how the company has organized itself to produce them. Is this system different from that of Toyota?

PROBLEMS

1. Nelson, Neddel, and Nickersen Stockbrokers are planning to invest in automated equipment that will process stock transactions. The equipment requires a $12 million annual investment. The operating costs are $120 per hour. The equipment can generate 5,000 transactions per hour.

   a. What is the unit cost of a transaction if 1 million are required?
   b. What is the unit cost if 10 million are required?
   c. What is the unit cost if 100 million are required?
   d. Why would NNN want to keep the level of transactions high?

 2. George's Mold Shop is planning to bid on a plastic part for automakers. If George's gets the bid, the manager is planning to buy a new semi-automatic machine to speed up the production process. The annual fixed cost of the machine is $45,000. The machine requires only part- time supervision, and the labor cost is estimated at $1.50 per hour. This has been calculated as 0.08 hour of labor at $18.75 per hour. On the average, the machine can produce 140 pieces per hour and is expected to operate for 2,000 hours per year.

   a. What is the unit cost of a plastic part if 10,000 are required?
   b. What is the unit cost if 100,000 are required?
   c. What is the unit cost if 200,000 are required?
   d. What is the unit cost if the machine operates at capacity for the entire year?

 3. Slimline Manufacturing makes briefcases. It is considering the purchase of new stitching machines for its final assembly. Following are the data for analysis:

System	Annualized Fixed Costs	Variable Costs
Spurance	$3,500	$1.25/unit
Yamamoto	$8,000	$0.85/unit

   a. If Slimline's demand is for 8,300 briefcases per year, which system should the company use?
   b. If Slimline needs to stitch 19,800 cases per year, which system has the lower cost?
   c. At what volume do the two alternatives have equal costs?

 4. Finn Bank and Trust is comparing a manual system for processing checks with a highly automated system. Presently, the bank processes about 10,000 checks each workday, and it operates 250 days per year. In the near future, it is planning to sell check-processing services to other small rural banks in the area. The bank's management has collected the following data:

System	Annualized Fixed Costs	Variable Labor Costs
Manual	$50,000	$0.045/check
Automatic	$350,000	$0.005/check

a.   At its present volume of checks, which system should Finn use?

b.   If Finn can process checks for other banks and boost its volume to 100,000 checks per day, which system has the lower cost?

c.   At what volume do the two alternatives have equal costs?

 5.   The X-ray machine at Marchal Medical Center was purchased and installed nearly four decades ago. Medically, the machine functions very effectively, but requires excessive time to adjust for each patient. A new X-ray machine is available that will reduce the time required to serve a patient.

System	Annualized Fixed Costs	Variable Labor Costs
Old X-ray	$40,000	$4.00/X-ray
New X-ray	$120,000	$1.00/X-ray

a.   Which system would give lower costs if the annual patient demand is 15,000?

b.   If volume could be boosted to 20,000 patients per year, which system would give the lower cost?

c.   At what patient volume do these alternatives have equal costs?

 6.   Quill Pen Company sells pens that are often purchased as graduation presents. The pens sell for $5.50 each and cost $1.50 per unit to produce. Fixed costs total $40,000 per year.

a.   How many pens must Quill sell to cover fixed costs?

b.   How many units must Quill sell to make $50,000 profit per year?

c.   If fixed costs increase $10,000 per year, then what are the answers to Parts a and b?

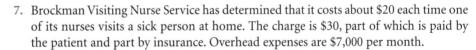 7.   Brockman Visiting Nurse Service has determined that it costs about $20 each time one of its nurses visits a sick person at home. The charge is $30, part of which is paid by the patient and part by insurance. Overhead expenses are $7,000 per month.

a.   How many calls does the service have to make to cover overhead expenses?

b.   How many calls must it make to ensure a $3,000 profit per month?

8.   A. J. Electronics produces monitors for microcomputers. It has a one-shift operation with fixed costs of $25,000 per month. The cost of purchased parts is $20 per unit, and the standard labor cost is $15 per unit. The company sells the monitors for $55 each to customers who sell them under their own brand names.

a.   How many monitors does A. J. have to produce and sell each month to cover costs?

b.   How many monitors must be produced and sold to meet a $5,000 target profit?

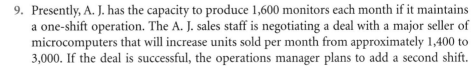 9.   Presently, A. J. has the capacity to produce 1,600 monitors each month if it maintains a one-shift operation. The A. J. sales staff is negotiating a deal with a major seller of microcomputers that will increase units sold per month from approximately 1,400 to 3,000. If the deal is successful, the operations manager plans to add a second shift.

Adding a second shift will increase fixed costs by $10,000 per month and increase production labor costs to $16 per unit for those units produced on the second shift. This increase is due entirely to paying a premium (shift differential) for second-shift labor. The unit price for purchased parts will drop by $.50 for units produced on both shifts because of discounts for buying larger quantities. The addition of a second shift will add 1,600 units per month to capacity.

a. Graph A. J .'s cost-volume-profit relationship for one shift only.

b. Graph A. J .'s cost-volume-profit relationship for two shifts.

c. How many units must A. J. produce and sell to cover its costs when the second shift is in place?

d. At what volume does A. J. make a $24,000 profit per month?

e. What happens to the company's profit if the selling price of monitors drops by $5 per unit? Be specific, using calculations to support your answers.

10. Carder Kitchen Utensil Production makes steak knives and salad forks in the same facility.

	Steak Knives	Salad Forks
Product mix	0.7	0.3
Selling Price/unit	$.80	$.40
Variable cost/unit	$.50	$.25

Annual fixed costs are estimated at $250,000

a. At what volume will Carder cover its costs, given the present mix?

b. At what volume will Carder report a $150,000 annual profit, given the present mix?

c. If the mix changes to 0.6 for steak knives and 0.4 for salad forks, recalculate the answers to Parts a and b.

d. If the price of a steak knife is raised $.05, what is the impact of this new mix on the volume required to make a $150,000 profit?

11. Junge Hardware Products makes nuts, bolts, and washers in the same facility.

	Nuts	Bolts	Washers
Product Mix	0.4	0.4	0.2
Selling price/unit	$.07	$.09	$.03
Variable cost/unit	$.03	$.06	$.0001

Annual fixed costs are estimated at $2,500,000.

a. At what volume will Junge cover its costs, given the present mix?

b. At what volume will it report a $1,500,000 annual profit, given the present mix?

c. If the price of a bolt is raised $.01, what happens to the volume required to make a $1,500,000 profit?

12. Winken, Blinken, and Knod, Inc., is considering three different machines to grind contact lenses. The annual costs and operating costs are listed below.

System	Annualized Fixed Costs	Variable Operating Costs
Manual grinder	$9,000	$5.00/lens
Automatic grinder	$30,000	$2.50/lens
Computer-controlled automatic grinder	$50,000	$0.75/lens

a. If 10,000 lens are needed, which option has the lowest cost?

b. If 20,000 lens are needed, which option has the lowest cost?

c. At what volume(s) of lens production do the alternatives have equal costs?

d. How would you explain these options to management?

CHAPTER 9

Capacity Decisions

LEARNING OBJECTIVES

After completing this chapter, you should be able to:

1. Define capacity as a measure of the organization's ability to provide customers with the requested service or good.
2. Explain that capacity estimation is difficult because many management decisions affect capacity.
3. Describe how overall capacity of the system is dependent on the capacities of the departments and machines that form the production system.
4. Determine the bottleneck in a system and demonstrate how that information can be used for managerial decision making.
5. Describe the important capacity decisions, such as how much capacity to add, when to add capacity, where to add capacity, what type (process) of capacity to add, and when to reduce capacity.

WHAT IS CAPACITY?

Capacity is a measure of an organization's ability to provide customers with the demanded services or goods in the amount requested and in a timely manner. Capacity is the maximum rate of production. An organization marketing rotisserie chicken should be able to produce and deliver chicken in sufficient quantities to satisfy consumer demand. Meeting customer demand requires the acquisition of physical facilities, the hiring and training of qualified people, and the acquisition of materials to achieve the desired production level.

The following important questions about capacity are discussed here:

- How can management estimate capacity?
- What is system capacity, and why is it important?
- How can capacity decisions be made to gain a competitive advantage for the organization?

EXAMPLE

Meijer superstores provide the consumer with a full range of food products as well as a diverse range of other products, such as sporting goods, automotive supplies, clothes, and lawn care equipment. Meijer's concept is twofold: to build big stores that have high sales and to expand the number of stores aggressively. In addition to the advantage of one-stop shopping, Meijer's large capacity stores offer other advantages.

The average purchase made by each customer should be higher because of the wide product variety. Although most traditional grocery items such as bread, rice, and milk have very low profit margin, products like microwave hamburgers, frozen yogurt, and in-store bakery goods have higher margins and should boost profits.

Larger capacity allows Meijer to spread the fixed cost of each store over a greater sales volume, thereby reducing costs and increasing profits. Even though the fixed costs of a superstore are greater than those of the typical discount store or supermarket, these fixed costs do not rise in proportion to sales. In essence, Meijer is attempting to take advantage of economies of scale offered by increasing capacity.

Meijer is also spreading the fixed costs of corporate operations over more stores by rapidly expanding the number of new stores. In addition to cutting the per-store share of these corporate-level fixed costs, expansion gives Meijer's more buying power, which enables it to negotiate better prices and delivery schedules from suppliers.

WHY IS CAPACITY IMPORTANT?

The importance of capacity planning decisions is easy to understand because significant capital is usually required to build capacity. Millions of dollars are required to build a brewery, a hospital, or an assembly plant for washing machines. These expenditures are usually for fixed assets (plant and equipment) that are expensive to maintain and even more expensive to change. Capacity decisions require careful consideration of an organization's long-term objectives and the market demand. They should not be based solely on the principle of minimizing production costs.

To meet future as well as present capacity requirements, facilities should be flexible. Flexible facilities allow managers to:

- Change production volume to respond to customer demand
- Produce different products on the same equipment (product mix) to respond to changing customer needs
- Alter product technology and process technology to maintain or improve an organization's competitive position

ESTIMATING CAPACITY

Before estimating capacity, it is necessary to recognize the difference between theoretical or ideal capacity and achievable capacity. Theoretical capacity is what can be achieved under ideal conditions for a short period of time. Under ideal conditions, there are no equipment breakdowns, maintenance requirements, material problems, or worker errors. While organizations strive to eliminate these unproductive delays, allowances for these elements must be made in order to develop realistic estimates of capacity.

To estimate capacity, managers must first select a yardstick to measure it. In some cases, the choice is obvious, for example, tons per hour of steel or kilowatt-hours of electricity. A hospital can use beds as a measure of capacity. Thus, a hospital with 100 beds that are available 365 days per year has a capacity of 36,500 patient-days each year. Hospitals measure the number of patients admitted and how long each stays so they can calculate patient-days consumed. A comparison of patient-days consumed and patient-days available gives the operating ratio shown below.

$$\text{Hospital's operating ratio} = \frac{24{,}000 \text{ patient-days consumed}}{36{,}500 \text{ patient-days available}} \times 100$$

$$= 65.8\%$$

In general, the operating ratio is calculated according to the following equation:

$$\text{Operating ratio} = \frac{\text{capacity consumed}}{\text{capacity available}} \times 100$$

Finding a yardstick to estimate capacity is more difficult in a restaurant than in a hospital because there is no uniform product on which the measurement can be based. Capacity could be measured in terms of people served, meals prepared, or the ability to generate sales dollars. It is management's responsibility to select the appropriate measure and apply it.

Once the measure has been selected, estimating capacity appears to be straightforward, involving the following steps. First, determine the maximum rate per hour of the production equipment. Second, determine the number of hours worked in a given time period; and third, multiply those two numbers.

$$\text{Capacity/period} = (\text{maximum production rate/hour}) \times (\text{number of hours worked/period})$$

$$\text{Production rate} = \frac{\text{number of units produced}}{\text{amount of time}}$$

Capacity can be changed by changing the number of hours worked in a time period or by changing the production rate. The number of hours worked per time period is affected by several factors, including overtime, multiple shifts, downtime for preventive maintenance, and allowances for unplanned equipment failure.

PROBLEM   Given the following information on maximum production rate and hours worked for an oven that cooks pizzas, determine the capacity per week.

Maximum production rate = 40 pizzas/hour
Number of hours = 84 hours/week
Overtime = 0 hours/week
Preventive maintenance (performed after closing) = 0
Equipment failure (unplanned downtime) = 2% of planned hours
Capacity/week = (40 pizzas/hour)(84 + 0 − 0 hours/week) (1 − .02)
= 3292.8 pizzas/week

The hours worked per week must be reduced from 100 percent to 98 percent of the available hours because of the 2 percent downtime anticipated for equipment failure.

Management decisions affect capacity. In this example, increases in the amount and quality of preventive maintenance could increase capacity by reducing equipment failure. Other decisions affect capacity by changing the production rate. The following decisions are examined here:

- Changing the mix of products produced by the facility
- Adding people to the production process
- Increasing the motivation of production employees
- Increasing the operating rate of a machine
- Improving the quality of the raw materials and the work in process
- Increasing product yield

Changing Product Mix

An organization's **product mix** is the percentage of total output devoted to each product. An agency may sell life, house, and automobile insurance. How does product mix affect capacity? In the insurance example, it may take more of an agent's time to sell life insurance than automobile insurance. Consequently, a shift in demand toward life insurance policies reduces an agent's capacity.

PROBLEM

Type	Mix 1	Mix 2
Life insurance	0.20	0.40
House insurance	0.30	0.40
Automobile insurance	0.50	0.20

Assume that each contact for life insurance takes 3 hours, house insurance takes 2 hours, and automobile insurance requires 1 hour. What are the capacities of an agent that works 40 hours per week under Mix 1 and Mix 2? Let's begin by calculating the production rate for each type of insurance. These production rates represent what an agent could do, if he or she sold only that type of insurance.

$$\text{Production Rate} = (\text{hours worked per week})/(\text{hour required per unit})$$
$$\text{Production Rate}_{Life} = (40 \text{ hrs./wk.})/(3 \text{ hrs./unit}) = 13.33 \text{ contacts per week}$$
$$\text{Production Rate}_{House} = (40 \text{ hrs./wk.})/(2 \text{ hrs./unit}) = 20 \text{ contacts per week}$$
$$\text{Production Rate}_{Auto} = (40 \text{ hrs./wk.})/(1 \text{ hr./unit}) = 40 \text{ contacts per week}$$

Now calculate the capacity for one week if Mix 1 is assumed. Now, the agent's time is divided among the various types according to the mix.

$$PR = (13.3 \text{ contacts/wk.})(.2) + (20 \text{ contact/wk.})(.3) + (40 \text{ contacts/wk.})(.5)$$
$$= 28.67 \text{ contacts/wk.}$$

On your own, calculate the capacity if Mix 2 is assumed. (Your answer should be 21.33 contacts per week.) Thus, as the mix shifts away from automobile insurance to life and house insurance, which require more time per contact, the capacity of an agent as measured by the number of contacts declines.

Product mix issues are also relevant in manufacturing. A steel company produces steel of many alloys, shapes, and sizes, and these differences require different production processes and times. For example, the sheet steel that forms the body of an automobile is produced in many widths. A 60-inch piece may be needed for the hood, but the 40-inch piece may be needed for a door panel. The mill that rolls these widths takes about the same amount of time per linear foot regardless of width. Therefore, a mill with a heavy mix of 40-inch pieces will be able to produce fewer tons per hour than will a mill with many 60-inch pieces. What then is the capacity of the processing equipment, and what are the units of capacity? Steel is measured in tons per hour, but those who estimate capacity realize that capacity changes as the mix of steel changes because different products have different production rates. Therefore, product mix must be estimated before capacity can be estimated.

PROBLEM

Assume that a company uses steel that is one-eighth of an inch thick and has a density of .2833 pounds per cubic inch. The machines roll steel for 80 hours per week at an average speed of 30 inches per second. The company produces both 40- and 60-inch widths of steel and wants to determine the capacity of each of the following product mixes.

Size	Mix 1	Mix 2
40 inches	80%	50%
60 inches	20%	50%

The company's production rate can be calculated as follows:

$$\text{Production rate (PR)} = (\text{production rate for 40-inch})(\text{mix for 40-inch})$$
$$+ (\text{production rate for 60-inch})(\text{mix for 60-inch})$$

The production rate for the 40-inch size (PR_{40}) can be determined as follows:

$$PR_{40} = (\text{width})(\text{thickness})(\text{processing rate inches/hour})(\text{density})$$
$$= (40 \text{ in.})(1/8 \text{ in.})(30 \text{ in./sec.})(3,600 \text{ sec./hr.})(.2833 \text{ lbs./cubic in.})$$
$$= 152,982 \text{ lbs./hr.}$$

This would be the production rate if only the 40-inch size were produced. Calculate the production rate for the 60-inch size on your own. (Your answer should be 229,473 pounds per hour.)

Now calculate the overall production rate if Mix 1 is assumed.

$$PR = (152,982 \text{ lbs./hr.})(.8) + (229,473 \text{ lbs./hr.})(.2)$$
$$= 122,385.6 \text{ lbs./hr.} + 45,894.6 \text{ lbs./hr.}$$
$$= 168,280.2 \text{ lbs./hr.}$$

Convert this figure to tons per hour.

$$PR = \frac{168,280.2 \text{ lbs./hr.}}{2,000 \text{ lbs./ton}} = 84.14 \text{ tons/hr.}$$

Next, convert the production rate into an estimate of capacity for a week.

$$\text{Capacity for mix 1} = (\text{PR of mix 1})(\text{hours worked})$$
$$= (84.14 \text{ tons/hr.})(80 \text{ hrs./week})$$
$$= 6,731.2 \text{ tons/week}$$

On your own, calculate the capacity if Mix 2 is assumed. (Your answer should be 7,649.1 tons per week.) Thus, as the mix shifts away from 40-inch to 60-inch steel, the capacity increases. Capacity is influenced by product mix.

Adding People

Adding people to an operation may increase the maximum production rate. This increase will occur when the operation is constrained by the amount of labor assigned to it. The capacity of both service operations and manufacturing operations is affected by adding or eliminating people. Organizations that are successful need to be willing and able to adapt to change. Part of being able to adapt is having flexibility to meet changes in demand volume. The following example illustrates the flexibility available to an organization in meeting varying levels of demand.

PROBLEM

To assemble the frames for twenty-five rocker/recliner chairs, each assembler takes his or her work order to the inventory clerk to pick the parts required to make the chairs. This takes about thirty minutes. After returning to the work area, each assembler completes twenty-five chair frames in 3 1/2 hours. To increase the capacity to assemble chair frames, a separate stock picker could be hired to gather inventory for all the assemblers. Then each assembler would be able to increase production by one-seventh because the thirty minutes out of every four hours formerly used to pick stock could be used to assemble chairs. One stock picker could serve eight assemblers.

The capacity improvement is calculated here.

$$\text{Capacity per assembler before stock picker} = (25 \text{ chairs/4 hrs.})(8 \text{ hrs./shift})$$
$$= 50 \text{ chairs/shift}$$
$$\text{Capacity per assembler after stock picker} = (25 \text{ chairs/3.5 hrs.})(8 \text{ hrs./shift})$$
$$= 57.14 \text{ chairs/shift}$$
$$\text{Capacity Increase} = \frac{\text{new capacity} - \text{old capacity}}{\text{old capacity}} \times 100$$
$$= \frac{57.14 - 50}{50} \times 100$$
$$= 14 \ 28$$

Increasing Motivation

Another way to increase the production rate for an operation with labor constraints is to increase motivation. Managers should realize that substantial increases in the production rate can be achieved when workers feel they are an important part of the operation. These productivity increases do not require additional labor costs or extra investment in equipment. The people work harder to accomplish more because they have a stake in the organization.

In the last ten years, there has been a growing awareness among both management and labor that communication and cooperation offer better opportunities for success than sharp-tongued rhetoric, lockouts, and strikes. Evidence of this willingness to cooperate exists in almost every industry as organizations fight for market share and workers fight for jobs in the increasingly global environment. In the automotive industry, labor has agreed to liberalize work rules so that productivity can be increased. For example, some facilities have reduced the number of job classifications from one hundred to a handful, making it possible to perform simple maintenance tasks with one or two employees rather than five or six. Management has agreed to profit sharing, which allows the workforce to share in the benefits of these simplified work rules. Management has also begun to recognize the talents of its labor force and has encouraged employee involvement in what used to be management domain, decision making.

Although skeptical at first, labor began to accept its new role when it felt that management's efforts were sincere. Labor is learning to accept more readily efforts to improve automation because workers see that cutting costs and enhancing quality can lead to the best kind of job security, that is, increasing sales. Shared decision making has not only caused increased cooperation, but it has created more motivated employees, thus providing the following benefits to organizations:

- Organizations can tap talents that already exist in their workforces.
- Workforces are more receptive to training and new ideas.
- People work harder and smarter.

Increasing Machine Production Rate

In an operation that is machine constrained, adding people will not increase capacity. **Machine constrained** means that the equipment is operating for all the available time at its best speed, while the operators have some idle time. For example, if a pizza oven can bake 40 pies per hour and the staff can assemble 60 pies per hour, then the process is machine constrained. To increase capacity, either new machines should be purchased or existing machines should be operated more efficiently.

One possibility that was suggested earlier is to increase preventive maintenance so that downtime due to machine failure will be reduced or eliminated. Another approach is to develop procedures that more efficiently utilize existing machines. The concept of continuing process improvements states that there is always a way to improve a machine's production rate and that if production engineers look hard enough, they will find it. Improvements caused by such procedures are not the same as increases in production rates caused by implementing new technology and equipment, but result instead from working smarter. A procedure could be as simple as increasing the heat in the oven to cook pizzas faster and without burning them.

Improving Quality

Improving quality can often increase the capacity of operations. Simply stated, if an operation produces a product of inferior quality and the product is rejected, the capacity used to produce that product is wasted. Poor quality not only gives the organization's customers a bad impression of its product, but also robs operations of needed capacity. Consider the following example.

EXAMPLE

Downey Carpet Cleaning is a family-owned business that cleans carpets, furniture, and drapes. It also performs general housekeeping services. For several years, Downey has offered a carpet service that thoroughly cleans high-traffic areas at one low price although some competitors charge extra for high-traffic areas. Why should Downey give away a service for which it could charge more? According to the owner/manager, it is a sound business decision.

A callback to re-clean a carpet for a dissatisfied customer takes as much time as making two regular carpet-cleaning stops because regular stops are scheduled to avoid as much nonproductive travel time as possible. Callbacks often require much longer drives. Each callback robs Downey of capacity and additional revenue. On the other hand, the extra time and money for the chemicals needed to clean the high-traffic areas right the first time are small.

The typical carpet-cleaning worker can perform ten jobs per day with an average revenue of $43 per job. One callback for which the company receives no additional revenue causes Downey to lose $86 in revenue. The company misses out on two regular jobs at $43 per job. Plus, the out-of-pocket costs for the chemicals to re-clean the carpet and the costs of operating the truck for the return trip are incurred. In one day, the extra costs of the chemicals and the time for the worker to do all ten jobs right the first time is less than $20. By avoiding callbacks, Downey is able to increase its capacity. In addition to being a financially sound decision, customers like the policy and frequently have Downey return for other services as well as for their next carpet cleaning.

Increasing Product Yield

In many operations, the quantity of output is less than the quantity of input. Yield is the ratio of the quantity of output to the input quantity.

$$\text{Yield} = \frac{\text{quantity of output}}{\text{quantity of input}}$$

The actual yield is a function of the characteristics of the process for producing the product. For example, an oil refinery begins with a barrel of crude oil, but when it is finished, there is less than a barrel of finished products. Small amounts evaporate, are spilled, or are otherwise lost in the process. Some is burned as waste gas. The yield is the percentage of the output that is useful product. A 96 percent yield means ninety-six barrels from every one hundred are made into useful products. If a refinery's engineers find methods to increase the yield by 1 percent, the refinery will have more product to sell, which increases effective capacity.

EXAMPLE

After Intel introduces new computer chips, it usually experiences a dramatic improvement in yield during production. Initially, the number of chips that meet standards may be only 60 percent. As the company learns more about the process the yield may increase to 90 percent or more. This 30-point increase in yield leads to 50 percent more product to sell. (Previously only 60 of 100 chips could be sold. Now 90 chips, that is, 30 more, are available.) So, capacity is increased. These 30 additional chips add no production cost, so most of the revenue from their sale falls directly to the company's bottom line. For Intel, moving up the yield curve as quickly as possible has a substantial impact on meeting customer demand and on increasing profitability.

Points to Consider

Capacity estimation is a necessary prerequisite to capacity planning. Without knowledge of the existing limits on capacity, meaningful capacity planning or production planning cannot take place.

Another point to remember is that capacity is not a fixed number below which organizations are forced to operate. Capacity is a function of management ingenuity. It can be influenced by good planning, good operating procedures, effective maintenance programs, and other management decisions. The role of operations managers is to investigate the possible methods to increase capacity before investing substantial capital in new facilities.

DETERMINING SYSTEM CAPACITY

Up to this point, our discussion of estimating and improving capacity has focused on only one machine or one operation. The system concept, which is an important theme of this text, makes us realize that operations are a combination of different machines/equipment and processes that make finished products. To plan effectively, management must know the capacity of the entire system, not just the individual parts. The term department is often used when referring to a portion of the production system.

Before beginning to analyze system capacity, you should know how departments are related. The two basic arrangements, product layout and process layout, are discussed in Chapter 8.

Product Layout

Product-oriented layout is characterized by high demand for the same or similar products. Examples include refining steel, making paper, and processing checks in a bank. In this arrangement, there are few, if any, product variations, and the layout fits the dominant flow of the product—thus, the name "product layout."

For example, to make paper, wooden logs are ground and chemically treated to produce a watery mixture called pulp. The pulp is pumped to the papermaking machine where excess water is gradually squeezed out, leaving a thin sheet of wet paper. The wet paper passes through a series of dryers that remove most of the remaining moisture. The paper is then rolled into logs that can be 30 feet wide and several feet in diameter. These huge logs are later cut into many different widths. Most types of paper are made using the same process and follow the same flow (see Exhibit 9.1).

Process Layout

The second type of layout is a process-oriented layout. This layout is characterized by low-volume production of any one product and the production of many different products with the same equipment. No single product has enough volume to support a dedicated set of machines. Each product has different production requirements that place different demands on the equipment. Examples include a machine shop that produces specialty automotive parts for racing engines and an automotive repair shop that offers a wide variety of services. In this arrangement, the layout is grouped by similar machine types because there is no dominant product flow—thus, the name "process layout."

An automotive center contains the equipment to analyze a variety of mechanical problems. As seen in the following list, customers desire a variety of services. The facilities are arranged by process because there is no dominant flow (see Exhibit 9.2).

Customer	Services Requested
A	Tires, shock absorbers, wheel alignment
B	Tires, brakes, tune-up
C	Brakes, tune-up, exhaust system
D	Tires, brakes, shock absorbers, muffler
E	Shock absorbers

The capacity of the product-oriented and process-oriented layouts is determined by analyzing the capacities of the individual departments. Approaches to determining the capacity of both layouts are discussed here.

The Product Layout and System Capacity

The capacity of a product-oriented system can be visualized as a series of pipes of varying capacity, with the smallest diameter or capacity holding back the entire system. Exhibit 9.3

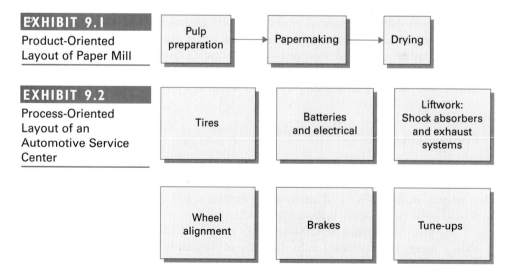

EXHIBIT 9.1
Product-Oriented Layout of Paper Mill

Pulp preparation → Papermaking → Drying

EXHIBIT 9.2
Process-Oriented Layout of an Automotive Service Center

Tires

Batteries and electrical

Liftwork: Shock absorbers and exhaust systems

Wheel alignment

Brakes

Tune-ups

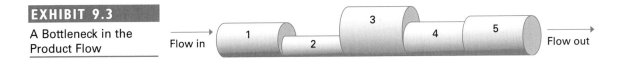

shows five pipes (departments or machines) with different diameters (capacities). The output from one pipe becomes the input to the next until the finished product exits pipe number five. In Exhibit 9.3, pipe number two cannot handle all the flow that pipe number one can deliver and, therefore, it restricts the flow. Because of pipe number two's limited capacity, it restricts the flow from upstream pipes and starves the downstream pipes. Pipes three, four, and five can work on only what pipe two can deliver. This restriction is called a **bottleneck,** and it determines the system's capacity.

Analysis of System Capacity

In a product-oriented layout, identifying the bottleneck is critical. The importance of this analysis cannot be overstated because the results are used not only in determining capacity, but also in planning and scheduling production, which will be discussed in Part III on planning and managing operations.

The approach to determining the bottleneck is illustrated in Exhibit 9.4. Start at the beginning of the system, and determine the capacity of the first operation or department. This is the system capacity so far. Use this capacity as the input to the next department in the sequence. Can that department take the total input from the previous department and process it completely? If it can, then the system capacity has not changed. If it cannot, then the system capacity is reduced to the capacity of that department. The procedure continues until the end of the process is reached and the system capacity is known.

Consider the example shown in Exhibit 9.5. The basic oxygen furnace has a maximum rate of 4,200 tons per day (tpd), while the continuous caster's rate is 6,000 tpd. Clearly, the capacity of that part of the system is limited by the capacity of the slower department.

Determining the Bottleneck

Now consider the entire system for making steel shown in Exhibit 9.6. The capacities are listed below each department. At two points in the steel-making process, outputs from two departments are inputs to a single department. The ratio of each input is listed on the arrow that illustrates the flow. For example, in the blast furnace, three pounds of iron ore are mixed with one pound of coke. In these cases, the inputs to a department should be combined in the correct proportion until at least one of the inputs is exhausted.

What is the system capacity? Follow along in Exhibit 9.6. Iron ore processing and coke ovens can deliver 3,000 and 1,000 tpd, respectively. (Only 3,000 tons can be used from iron ore processing because of the ratio requirements.) The combined 4,000 tpd is more than sufficient for the blast furnace, which requires only 3,000 tpd total. So far, the blast furnace is holding back production. The blast furnace and scrap handling, in turn, supply 3,000 and 1,500 tpd, which is more than adequate for the basic oxygen furnace capacity of 4,200 tpd. Because the basic oxygen furnace cannot process all available inputs, the blast furnace cannot be the bottleneck. The basic oxygen furnace cannot deliver sufficient output to the remaining departments. Therefore, the basic oxygen furnace is the bottleneck for the system, and the capacity of the system is 4,200 tpd.

To calculate the production rates that allow the system to produce 4,200 tpd, begin at the bottleneck department in Exhibit 9.7. Trace the product flow from the bottleneck to the beginning and the end of the process. In order to achieve 4,200 tpd of basic oxygen furnace

EXHIBIT 9.4

A Sequential Approach
to Bottleneck Analysis

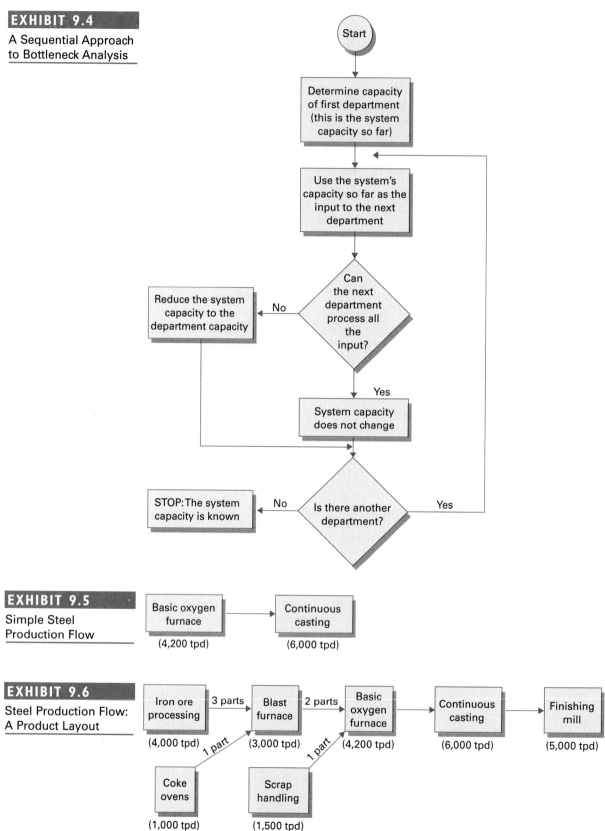

EXHIBIT 9.5

Simple Steel
Production Flow

Basic oxygen furnace (4,200 tpd) → Continuous casting (6,000 tpd)

EXHIBIT 9.6

Steel Production Flow:
A Product Layout

Iron ore processing (4,000 tpd) —3 parts→ Blast furnace (3,000 tpd) —2 parts→ Basic oxygen furnace (4,200 tpd) → Continuous casting (6,000 tpd) → Finishing mill (5,000 tpd)

Coke ovens (1,000 tpd) —1 part→ Blast furnace

Scrap handling (1,500 tpd) —1 part→ Basic oxygen furnace

EXHIBIT 9.7

Determining System
Capacity

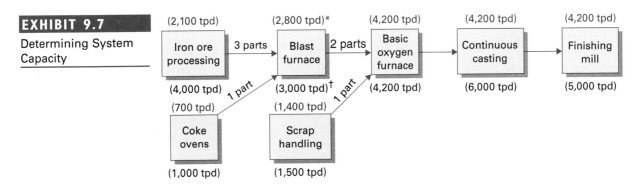

*Numbers above each department indicate the production rate required from that department to achieve a system capacity of 4,200 tpd.
†Numbers below each department indicate the individual department's capacity.

input, $(2/3)(4,200) = 2,800$ tpd comes from the blast furnace and $(1/3)(4,200) = 1,400$ tpd comes from scrap. The requirements are listed above each department. The blast furnace requires $(3/4)(2,800) = 2,100$ tpd of iron ore and $(1/4)(2,800) = 700$ tpd of coke. Moving from the basic oxygen furnace to the end of the process is simpler because there are no pairs of departments. The requirement for those departments is 4,200 tpd.

In actual production, each operation in this process would suffer yield loss, which we do not describe here in order to simplify discussion.

Rounding Out System Capacity

It is also important to know which department, machine, or step in the process restricts the system's capacity. An operations manager may be charged with increasing the system's capacity. If he or she tries to do so by increasing blast furnace capacity, there will be no increase in the system's capacity. This organization could spend millions on a new blast furnace and not get one additional ton of steel out of the system because the bottleneck constricts the flow.

The system capacity can be increased by applying resources to the bottleneck department. This approach is called **rounding out capacity** because resources are applied to the bottleneck to bring it into balance with other parts (departments) in the system. Rounding out capacity has a limit, however. Simply stated, if the operations manager doubles basic oxygen furnace capacity because it is the bottleneck, the system's capacity will not double. There is not enough capacity in other departments to absorb that large an increase. As a result of doubling basic oxygen furnace capacity, the bottleneck simply jumps to another department. Managers should understand this issue and carefully analyze the effect on the system of any increase in departmental capacity.

An important and useful piece of information to determine is how far the system's capacity can be increased before the next bottleneck appears. To answer, examine the requirements listed above each department in Exhibit 9.7. A quick review shows that scrap handling and the blast furnace will be bottlenecks as basic oxygen furnace capacity is increased. With a cushion of 100 tons per day in scrap handling, the capacity of the system could increase by only 300 tpd. (Remember that one part scrap and two parts hot metal from the blast furnace are required.) The scrap handling and blast furnace departments have insufficient capacity to handle an increase of more than 300 tpd in basic oxygen furnace capacity.

If this quick analysis is too confusing, simply set the capacity of the present bottleneck to infinity and rework the problem. The results are shown in Exhibit 9.8. The system's capacity is 4,500 tpd. There are two bottlenecks: blast furnace and scrap handling.

EXHIBIT 9.8

Rounding Out Capacity

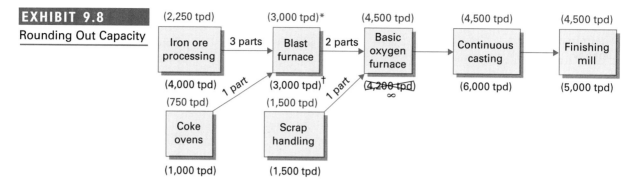

*Numbers above each department indicate the production rate required from that department to achieve a system capacity of 4,500 tpd.

†Numbers below each department indicate the individual department's capacity.

Remember, the basic oxygen furnace capacity was set to infinity. In reality, it must be 4,500 tpd or more if the system capacity is 4,500 tpd.

The analysis of system capacity and associated bottlenecks is extremely important for determining capacity. Rational decisions about capacity can be made only if these concepts are fully understood.

The Process Layout and System Capacity

The process-oriented layout is characterized as a multiple-product facility with low volume per product. The products are different from one another and usually require different methods and procedures in production. There is no dominant product flow to guide the arrangement of departments as there is in the paper or steel industry so similar operations are grouped together. The process-oriented layout does not have enough volume in any one product to dedicate specialized production facilities.

A medical center is an example of a process-oriented operation. Patients are screened at the reception desk to determine the nature and seriousness of their injuries and then usually proceed to a waiting room to be called by a nurse or physician. After an initial examination, the method of treatment for each patient is determined. Each treatment could be different and is based on the patient's individual needs. A patient in an automobile accident may be scheduled for X-rays, orthopedic surgery, and application of a cast. The next patient might have heart problems or have taken poison. Each would follow a different path through the medical center. The equipment should be flexible enough to handle a wide range of needs. For example, an X-ray machine should be able to photograph legs, feet, hands, and other areas of the body and should adjust to an infant or an adult.

Analysis of System Capacity

Determining system capacity in a process-oriented layout is more complex than doing so in a product-oriented layout. In the process layout, each product does not follow the same path through the system. The functions and machines are grouped into departments, and different products follow different paths. The layout shown in Exhibit 9.9 has six departments and four different patterns of treatment or products. The departments' capacities are given in patients per week (ppw) and are based on average time per treatment.

The determination of system capacity is not merely a search for the minimum department capacity because there is no dominant flow. The capacity of the system is a function

EXHIBIT 9.9

A Process Layout of a Medical Center

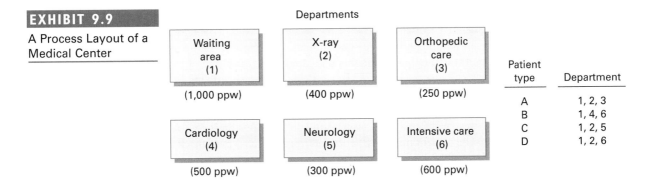

of the jobs presented. For example, if all the patients arriving at the medical center are type A patients (those needing orthopedic care), the capacity of the system will be 250 patients per week. This can be calculated by simply looking at the minimum capacity for departments 1, 2, and 3. If all patients are of type B, then the capacity will be 500 patients per week. For patients of types C and D, the system capacities are 300 and 400 patients per week, respectively. The following table shows the various capacities. The system's capacity is a function of the job types presented.

Mix	System's Capacity	Bottleneck Department
100% A	250 ppw	Orthopedic care
100% B	500 ppw	Cardiology
100% C	300 ppw	Neurology
100% D	400 ppw	X-ray

Product Mix and Capacity in a Process Layout

If the medical center only processed one type of patient, the system capacity could be easily and accurately estimated, as shown by the prior example. What would the system capacity be if the medical center processed all four types during the same week? To simplify the logic, assume that only type A patients arrive on Monday and Tuesday, type Bs on Wednesday and Thursday, type Cs on Friday and Saturday, and type Ds on Sunday. The system capacity per week for that mix would be calculated as follows:

$$\text{System capacity} = \frac{2}{7}(250 \text{ ppw}) + \frac{2}{7}(500 \text{ ppw}) + \frac{2}{7}(300 \text{ ppw}) + \frac{1}{7}(400 \text{ ppw})$$

$$= 357 \text{ppw}$$

The fractions in the preceding equation are the patient mix. A different assumption concerning the number of days per week assigned to each patient type would cause a different product mix and would result in a different system capacity.

In reality, not all orthopedic care patients (type A) will arrive on Monday and Tuesday. The method illustrated in the prior calculation is likely to underestimate the system capacity because we have assumed that no patient other than an orthopedic patient arrives on Monday or Tuesday. However, the system does have the capacity to process type B, C, and D patients on Monday and Tuesday in addition to $(2/7)(250 \text{ ppw}) = 71.4$ type A patients. How can managers of a medical center get an accurate estimate of system capacity and determine which department is the bottleneck? An often-used technique for estimating capacity in a process layout is simulation.

In this approach, an estimate of product mix (patient mix) is used to randomly generate arriving patients. A time to service each patient, which is based on historical data, is also randomly generated. The simulation is run for a long period of time, and statistics about the number of patients served and the utilization of each department are kept. (In fact, utilization data should be kept regularly for equipment in a process layout so that bottlenecks can be anticipated and corrective action taken.) Management can change the mix of arriving patients to determine how the system capacity and bottleneck department change. A different mix places different demands on the resources. Managers should plan for the present mix of patients and the associated bottleneck as well as for the mix possibilities that the future holds.

Capacity Decisions for Service Operations

Most of the concepts discussed here apply to producers of services as well as to producers of goods. It is important to note, however, that service operations are different from manufacturing operations in some respects. First, services are direct and cannot be inventoried. Whereas the consumption of goods can be delayed, as a general rule services are produced and consumed simultaneously. This means that service organizations must (1) build enough capacity to meet maximum demand, (2) manage demand so that people will use the services at off-peak times (allowing long waiting lines to occur is one way, usually a poor way, to manage demand, and offering monetary incentives to use the service at off peak times is another way), or (3) choose not to satisfy all the demand.

Each of these options has a cost. Building sufficient capacity to meet maximum demand can mean that a significant portion of the capacity is used infrequently. Having people wait in long lines for service may cause dissatisfaction that will result in a loss of business. For example, a hospital that has long lines in its emergency room is likely to lose business. Choosing to ignore demand means a loss of customers that may have long-term as well as short-term effects.

Second, there is often a high degree of producer-consumer interaction in the production of a service. This interaction frequently introduces a significant amount of uncertainty about processing time, and processing time is a determinant of capacity. For example, a person waiting in line at a bank may have one or many transactions to perform and may be skilled or unskilled at communicating his or her needs. This variation makes it more difficult to estimate the capacity required to meet customer demands.

Third, many services are not transported to the customer, the customer must come to the service delivery system. This has important implications for the location decision. It also means that capacity decisions should result in adequate space for the customer in the service delivery system. For example, many restaurants use a generous bar area to deal with excess demand in the dining area.

Service Operations and System Capacity

Despite their differences the concepts of determining system capacity and finding the bottleneck apply to service as well as manufacturing operations. The principles are the same, but in some cases, the application is different. In the following case, managers of an upscale restaurant chain are attempting to determine the capacity of their restaurant.

The flow of people through the restaurant follows this sequence. People arrive at the restaurant and park their cars. From records that the restaurant keeps, 20 percent of the guests spend time in the bar. The remaining 80 percent of the arrivals go to the dining area.

According to standards that management has developed over the years, each dinner served per hour requires about four square feet of kitchen space. Listed below are the resources of the restaurant.

Department/Area	Capacity/Size
Parking area	100 spaces
Bar area	80 seats
Dining area	200 seats
Cooking area	600 square feet

On the average, 2.2 people arrive per car, only 80 percent of the seats in the bar are normally available because tables for four are sometimes occupied by two or three people, and only 85 percent of the dining area seats are normally available for the same reason. The average stay is ninety minutes. Everyone in the restaurant orders a meal, and 40 percent of the people in the bar area order a meal. What is the capacity of the system? To begin, the capacity of each area can be calculated in terms of persons served per hour.

Department/Area	Capacity/Size	
Parking area	(100 spaces)(2.2 people/car)/(1.5 hrs.)	= 147 people/hr.
Bar area	(80 seats)(.8)/(1.5 hrs.)	= 43 people/hr.
Dining area	(200 seats)(.85)/(1.5 hrs.)	= 113 people/hr.
Cooking area	(600 square feet)/(4 sq. ft./meal)	= 150 people/hr.

If every customer spent time both in the bar and in the dining area, the system capacity would be easy to determine because each customer would place demands on each area, making the restaurant a product layout similar to the steel industry, and the system capacity would be the smallest of the four department's capacities. However, only a portion of the guests use the bar and the dining areas.

To calculate the capacity of the system and determine the bottleneck department in this case, the approach illustrated earlier could be used. That method, however, requires tracking two different flows, one involving the dining area and a second following the bar area. Another method will be used here to demonstrate that different approaches are possible. We will start by selecting a level of demand that we are fairly certain the restaurant can satisfy. If it cannot, the demand level is decreased, and another attempt is made. If it can, the demand level is increased. This trial and error method can quickly lead to the capacity if care is used in selecting the demand points. (In fact, this trial and error approach could be used to solve problems like the steel industry problem described earlier.) By inspecting the department capacities, it is clear that the system's capacity cannot exceed 147 people/hour because that is the capacity of the parking lot and the assumption of this model is that everyone drives. It is also clear that the capacity of the system is at least one hundred because all of the department capacities are at least one hundred, except for the bar area which only serves 20 percent of the customers.

We begin, therefore, by setting the arrival rate (demand) equal to one hundred people per hour. This means that during each hour one hundred people use the parking lot, twenty people use the bar, eighty people use the restaurant, and eighty-eight people order a meal. Everyone in the restaurant orders a meal, and 40 percent of the bar patrons order a meal. People in the bar that order a meal eat the meal in the bar. None of the individual departments is at capacity, so the analysis continues. The results are shown in the following table:

Department/ Area	Capacity (People/Hr.)	Set Demand Equal To			
		100 People/Hr.	125 People/Hr.	147 People/Hr.	113/.8 = 141 People/Hr.
Parking area	147	100	125	147	141
Bar area	43	20	25	29	28
Dining area	113	80	100	118	113
Cooking area	150	88	110	130	124

Next, we examine what happens if demand is set at 125 people/hour. Once again, none of the departments are at capacity. We now know that the system capacity must be between 125 and 147 people/hour. (Remember that the parking lot can hold no more than 147.) With demand set at 147 people/hour, the parking lot is at capacity, but demand in the dining area exceeds capacity. Bar demand is equal to $(147)(.2) = 29$. Dining demand is equal to $(147)(.8) = 118$. Cooking demand is equal to $118 + (29)(.4) = 130$. At this point, we are sure that the bottleneck is the dining area, but we are unsure of the system capacity because not everyone uses the dining room. To determine the system capacity, we divide the capacity of the dining area by 0.8, which is the percentage of customers that use the dining area. This calculation yields the system capacity, which is 141 people per hour. If the system capacity is set equal to demand and the department demands are calculated again, the excess capacities in the non-bottleneck departments can be identified. There is considerable excess capacity in the cooking area and in the bar, but the parking lot is near capacity. Expansion plans, if justified by demand, should be aimed at the dining area and the parking lot.

MAKING CAPACITY DECISIONS FOR COMPETITIVE ADVANTAGE

Informed capacity decisions can be made only when management (1) knows the ability of its present resources (capacity estimation), (2) knows the bottlenecks and what is causing them (system capacity), and (3) has an estimate of future demand (forecast of customer need). The first two topics have been the major thrust of the chapter to this point. Estimating demand is discussed on the chapter in forecasting and should be addressed in a course on marketing. Now, we can use this information to discuss the capacity decisions listed below:

- When to add capacity
- How much capacity to add
- Where to add capacity
- What type of capacity to add
- When to reduce capacity

When to Add Capacity

Many people argue that determining how much capacity an organization should have is not difficult. The real problem, they point out, is obtaining an accurate forecast of demand. These managers say that once an estimate of demand is obtained, it is simply a matter of setting capacity to meet demand. They would also say that the answer to the timing question is easy if an accurate forecast can be obtained. Management determines how long it takes to build additional capacity and adds an appropriate lead time to the point where demand exceeds capacity. In Exhibit 9.10, capacity is exceeded two years in the future. If it takes eighteen months to add capacity, then management should begin construction six

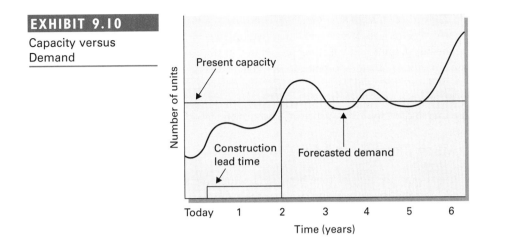

EXHIBIT 9.10

Capacity versus Demand

months from today. In reality, however, the answer to the question is not that simple. To avoid compounding the question of when to add capacity with forecasting error, let's assume, for the moment, that forecasts are guaranteed to be accurate.

Now consider the timing decision in Exhibit 9.10. Should the capacity be added by the end of the second year? The answer is probably no, for several sound reasons. Management could simply choose not to satisfy all the demand during the third year. The forecast shows that the really significant and long-term increase does not take place until the end of year five. It is possible that the organization has no long-term interest in the market and would choose to allocate resources to other products.

However, failing to satisfy demand fully may not be consistent with a company policy of building market share. If the sales force is told to increase market share, but operations cannot deliver the product, then long-term damage to the firm's reputation could result.

If ignoring the excess demand in the third year is not acceptable, then management must find a way to meet that demand. One possibility is to set the production rate higher than demand during the first and second years so that sufficient inventory is created to satisfy demand in the third year. Exhibit 9.11 illustrates this point. Obviously, this solution is limited to goods production because services have no finished goods inventory.

Other methods of dealing with the capacity shortfall in the third year can be understood by recalling the earlier sections on capacity estimation. From this discussion, you learned that

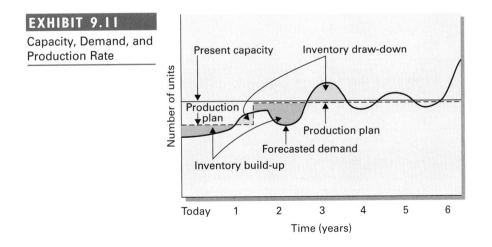

EXHIBIT 9.11

Capacity, Demand, and Production Rate

capacity is a variable that is subject to change through management innovation. If the operation runs two shifts five days a week, then overtime or another shift could be considered. Better scheduling, improved operating procedures, or improved quality of raw materials can increase capacity. Another important concept to remember is system capacity. To increase the capacity of a system, it is necessary to increase the capacity of only the bottleneck operation. It may be possible to buy production capacity to supplement the bottleneck operation and increase overall capacity. This practice of subcontracting work is very common.

How Much Capacity to Add

If additional capacity is built, then how much should be added? Again, assume that the forecasted demand is accurate, and consider the example in Exhibit 9.12. In this example, the decision of when to add capacity has been made. Construction will begin in the middle of the third year, and the new capacity will come on line at the end of the fourth year.

Option 1 is to add only enough capacity to handle the demand in the early part of the fifth year. Option 2 is to add enough capacity to handle the increase in the sixth year. Whether Option 1 or Option 2 is selected, the company should understand the importance of focusing on the bottleneck to increase system capacity. The financial versus operating tradeoffs of these options are summarized here.

Advantages of Option 1
1. Limits short-term investment and risk. Changes in technology will not find the organization with as much capital tied up in outdated technology.
2. Limits unused capacity for which no return on investment is provided.

Advantages of Option 2
1. May reduce long-term investment. Building capacity in one lump instead of two is bound to save total construction costs.
2. May reduce inflationary effects on construction costs by building now.

The major questions associated with Option 2 are:

- How long will it be before the capacity is needed?
- How likely is it that the forecasted need will occur?
- How stable is the technology?

EXHIBIT 9.12

How Much Capacity to Add

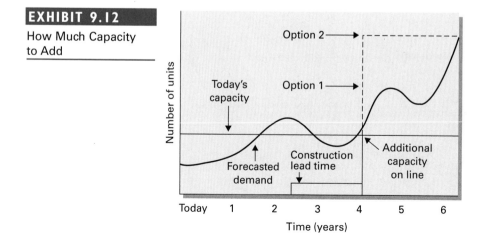

A firm producing products in an industry where the product or process technology is likely to change does not want to build plants that limit its long-term ability to compete.

The decisions about when to add capacity and how much capacity are critical capacity decisions that are complicated by the uncertainty in the estimates of future demand. Decision theory, which uses statistics and probability theory, can be used to model these decisions when forecasts are uncertain. The supplement to this chapter describes how to apply decision trees to analyze these decisions. This supplement is available on the Web site http://www.wiley.com/college/vonderembse.

Where to Add Capacity

The decision on where to add capacity (usually called the location decision) is complex and involves many factors. It is strategically important because it commits significant resources to a location. Great care and consideration should be given to the long-term implications. The location decision is addressed in another chapter.

What Type of Capacity to Add

In addition to determining how much capacity to add and when to add it, management should consider what type of capacity to add. Type of capacity can be separated into a technological or engineering question and an economy of scale or business question. The technological question is beyond the scope of this book.

The economy of scale question is a direct link among demand, capacity, and process selection. When demand exists for a product, the capacity will be supplied by one or more firms as long as the price customers are willing to pay is sufficient to cover costs and provide a reasonable profit. These and other related concepts are the focus of the chapter on process selection.

Adjusting Capacity to Meet Changing Requirements

Change is more prevalent today than ever before, and many organizations are closing facilities. Organizations are faced with (1) reducing capacity because demand for some products has declined, (2) shifting capacity to another location because of today's highly competitive global environment, and (3) building new facilities to replace existing facilities because technology has changed and the older facilities cannot keep pace.

In the first case, demand for products such as phonograph records has declined to zero and demand for cassette tapes is declining rapidly as substitute products capture demand. This situation requires organizations to close facilities or make major investments in retooling these facilities to make other products. The economic feasibility of retooling is a function of the size of the investment needed for conversion, the costs of constructing a new facility, and the attractiveness of the location of the existing facility.

In the second case, the relative attractiveness of locations in foreign countries versus the home country may cause an organization to relocate its facilities. Many factors can play a role in this switch, including better access to growing markets, lower labor costs, availability of raw materials or skilled labor, and access to capital. The North American Free Trade Agreement makes it much easier for companies to shift facilities around North America. Where is the fastest growing market for automobiles in North America? The answer is Mexico. Demand for cars is up by 17 percent, and the long-term growth potential is high and should increase as the United States and Canada, as well as Mexico, benefit from free trade. In response, General Motors is expanding production in Mexico.

Japanese and European automakers are quickly learning what GM knows, that Mexico is a good place to do business.

In the third case, firms are closing facilities not because demand for the product has diminished but because a facility's technology is no longer competitive. Many "old-line" industries such as automobile manufacturing are closing facilities built as long as 100 years ago and building new facilities to take their place. The new facilities are usually on a single level, are open and accessible for the worker, and allow the easy movement of parts from the truck docks, which are greatly increased in number, to the assemble line. Hospitals have been turning over their facilities for several years. Small, older hospitals that were designed primarily for inpatient care are closing, and larger hospitals designed for outpatient care and new technologies are taking their place.

EXAMPLE

The health care industry is struggling with too many hospitals competing for too few patients. Nationwide, more than 40 percent of the hospital beds are empty. Because a large percentage of a hospital's costs are fixed, a decline in the occupancy rate does not lead to a proportional decline in operating costs. With revenues tied to occupancy rates and a large base of fixed costs, hospital profits are squeezed by overcapacity.

How did the health care industry get into this predicament? After World War II, the baby boom caused substantial growth in the demand for health services. The health care industry, which was dominated by government-owned and private not-for-profit hospitals, expanded to meet this apparently ceaseless increase in demand. This expansion, however, was not coordinated, and inefficient hospitals often continued to operate by increasing their subsidy from the government or the private agency that supported them.

Two forces halted the growth in demand for hospital beds and then caused it to decline. First, dramatic improvements in medical procedures made trips to the hospital unnecessary in some cases and significantly reduced the time of confinement in others. Many medical procedures, such as knee surgery and laser surgery, are performed on an outpatient basis. For other procedures, such as back surgery, that still involve a hospital stay, the time of confinement has been reduced from weeks to a day or two. Second, there has been mounting pressure from insurance providers and the organizations that pay for the insurance policies to reduce the time of confinement.

SUMMARY

- Capacity is a measure of the organization's ability to provide customers with the demanded services and goods in the amount requested and in a timely manner.
- Capacity decisions are critical to the organization's success because they commit significant resources to assets that usually cannot be changed easily or economically. Capacity decisions should be based on the best estimate of the future and should be made so that as much flexibility as possible is retained.
- Capacity should also be obtained in the proper amount. Too much capacity means that money has been invested in resources that are not really needed. Too little means that potential sales and market share are escaping.
- Estimating an organization's capacity is not easy because capacity is affected by management decisions regarding changing the number of hours worked, changing the

product mix, adding staff, improving worker motivation, improving machine capabilities, enhancing quality, and increasing product yield.

■ Machine and departmental capacities are needed to determine the capacity of a system. A system can go only as fast as its slowest part, which is the bottleneck.

■ Increases in system capacity can be achieved by increasing capacity in the bottleneck department. This is called rounding out capacity.

■ Capacity decisions include the following: when to add capacity, how much capacity to add, where to add capacity, what type of capacity to add, and when to reduce capacity.

 Visit our dynamic Web site, http://www.wiley.com/college/vonderembse, for extended chapter material, solved problems, mini-cases, computer software, and Web links.

KEY TERMS

bottleneck	machine constrained	rounding out capacity
capacity	product mix	yield

URLS

Meijer: www.meijer.com

ProMedica Health System: www.promedica.org

U.S. Steel: www.ussteel.com

Nucor: www.nucor.com

Intel: www.intel.com

QUESTIONS

1. What is capacity, and why is it important?

2. Why is it difficult to estimate capacity? Isn't capacity a constant?

3. Should an organization always attempt to match its capacity to its estimate of demand? Why or why not?

4. Capacity decisions are strategically important. Agree or disagree with the statement, and support your position.

5. What factors influence the capacity of an organization? List any factors you can think of, and explain how they influence capacity.

6. Explain in detail the difference between departmental and system capacity.

7. What are the principles for determining system capacity in the product layout?

8. What are the principles for determining system capacity in the process layout?

9. How does a change in the product mix affect system capacity?

10. What are the important decisions for capacity planners?

11. What are the key factors in determining when to add capacity?

12. What are the key factors in determining how much capacity to add?

13. Why would an organization want to reduce its capacity?

INTERNET QUESTIONS

14. Meijer, a grocery and general merchandise retail chain, has been building stores at a rapid pace. Check the firm's Web site to see the geographic and product line diversity. Why are these important? How does this help Meijer achieve success?

15. ProMedica Health System manages hospitals and health care systems. Visit the company's Web site to determine where it has health care services. Why are large health care service providers replacing small independent hospitals? Are there economies of scale that justify this shift? If so, what are those? If not, why not?

16. The steel industry is making a fundamental transition from old-line fully integrated steel mills (U.S. Steel) to steel producers that specialize in specific steel applications (Nucor). Check the Web sites of each organization to examine how the companies are different. Describe the differences in one paragraph. Is there room for both types of companies in what appears to be a declining market for steel?

PROBLEMS

1. Determine the system capacity and the bottleneck department in the following line flow process. The capacities in pieces per hour for departments A, B, and C are 5,250, 4,650, and 5,300, respectively.

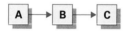

2. Determine the system capacity and the bottleneck department in the following line flow process. The capacities in tons per hour for departments A, B, C, and D are 2,200, 1,100, 1,600, and 2,500, respectively. For each ton of output from department B that is input to department D, two tons from department C must be added.

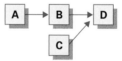

3. Answer the following questions using the information in Problem 2:
   a. How much can the system capacity be increased by adding capacity to the bottleneck department?
   b. How much capacity must be added to the bottleneck department to achieve this increase in system capacity?
   c. Which department is the new bottleneck department?

4. Examine the following line flow process:
   a. Determine the system capacity.
   b. Determine which department is the bottleneck.
   c. Determine how much capacity can be gained by adding capacity to the bottleneck.
   d. Explain your answers to a, b, and c.
   e. How would the analysis change if department A achieved an 85 percent yield? Recalculate a, b, and c.

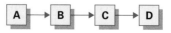

Department	Capacity (Parts/Hour)
A	120
B	110
C	140
D	160

5. Macro Galvanizing coats sheet steel for the appliance industry in its plant in Gary, Indiana. Macro has one production line that can coat steel up to 72 inches wide. The production line runs 80 hours per week. Regardless of width, the steel is processed at 200 feet per minute. Macro processes only the three widths of steel listed here.

Width (in.)	Product Mix
36	.30
50	.25
60	.45

   a. What is the capacity of Macro's production line in square feet of steel coated per week?

   b. What is the capacity in square feet per week if the mix changes from .30, .25, and .45 to .40, .40, and .20?

   c. What is the capacity in square feet per week if the mix does not change and Macro decides to use 10 percent overtime per week?

   d. What is the capacity in square feet per week if the mix does not change, there is no overtime, and Macro experiences 5 percent unplanned downtime?

   e. What is the capacity in square feet per week if the mix does not change, there is no overtime, and Macro's engineers find a way to run the line at 220 feet per minute?

6. Allen Bank and Trust processes checks at its Golden, California, Operations Center. The five steps in the process are listed here and must be done in the listed sequence. The listed capacity for each step is the total capacity for all work stations of that type.

Step	Capacity (Checks/Hour)	Number of Work Stations/Step
1	8,000	4
2	6,000	3
3	9,000	1
4	5,000	2
5	7,000	2

   a. What is the system capacity, and which is the bottleneck department?

   b. What is the capacity per work station for each step?

   c. How could Allen Bank and Trust increase its capacity to process checks to 6,000 checks per hour?

   d. How could Allen Bank and Trust increase its capacity to 10,000 checks per hour?

7. Pacific, Plumber, and Placid Investment Company processes thousands of stock transactions each day at its headquarters in Peoria, Illinois. Each transaction passes through four steps and must be processed in order. The steps are the same for all transactions except for step 3. In 50 percent of the cases, transactions are processed

only by an over-the-counter (OTC) clerk, while the other 50 percent are processed only in the normal manner.

Step	Capacity (Transactions/Hour)	Number of Work Stations/Step
1	10,000	1
2	12,000	2
3	4,000	1
3(OTC)	4,000	1
4	9,000	3

a. What is the system capacity, and which is the bottleneck department?

b. What is the capacity per work station for each step?

c. How could PP&P increase the system capacity to 9,000 transactions, assuming that the OTC requirements remain at 50 percent of the transactions?

d. How could PP&P increase the system capacity to 15,000 transactions, assuming that the OTC requirement shifts to 75 percent of the transactions?

8. Monique Food Processing Company produces light snacks that can be heated in a microwave. The following steps are included in the process:

Steps	Description	Capacity (Units/Hour)
1	Prepare food	200
2	Measure and place in plastic pouch	175
3	Prepare cardboard box	200
4	Insert pouch into box	300
5	Shrink-wrap box	200

a. What is the system capacity, and which is the bottleneck department?

b. How much slack (unused capacity) is available in other departments?

c. How much system capacity can be gained by adding capacity to the bottleneck?

9. Botkins Bicycle Shop manufactures ten-speed bikes. The assembly process requires the components listed below. Botkins can assemble about 350 bicycles per week without overtime. The labor contract allows Botkins' management to add up to 10 percent overtime to assembly operations.

Component	Quantity per Finished Bicycle	Source	Capacity (Units/Week)
Wheels	2	Internal	750
Tires	2	External	900
Frame	1	Internal	400
Brakes	2	External	950
Handle Bars	1	Internal	600
Pedal and drive sprocket subassembly	1	Internal	500

a. What is the capacity of the facility without using overtime? Which is the bottleneck department(s)?

b. What is the capacity of the facility with overtime? Which is the bottleneck department(s)?

c. What increases in department capacity would be required to increase system capacity to 450 units per week?

10. The Mills Brothers Cereal Company makes a wheat and raisin cereal on one of its production lines. One pound of raisins is required for four pounds of wheat flakes in order to make five pounds of cereal. The following steps are included in the process:

Step	Description	Capacity (Pounds/Hour)
A	Crush wheat	1,400
B	Form flakes	1,200
C	Toast flakes	1,600
D	Coat raisins	250
E	Mix cereal and raisins	1,200
F	Put mixture in box	1,100
G	Place boxes in shipping containers	1,400

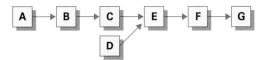

a. What is the system capacity, and which is the bottleneck department?

b. How much slack (unused capacity) is available in other departments?

c. How much system capacity can be gained by adding capacity to the bottleneck?

11. White Chemical has a problem with its operations. Analyze the following flow process:

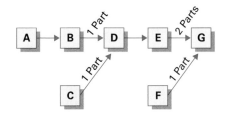

Department	Capacity (Gallons/ Hour)	Department	Capacity (Gallons/ Hour)
A	100	E	100
B	60	F	40
C	50	G	140
D	120		

The ratio for mixing the outputs from departments E and F is two to one. This means that getting three gallons out of G requires mixing two gallons of E's output and one gallon of F's output. The ratio for departments B and C is one to one.

a. What is the system's capacity?

b. Which department(s) is the bottleneck?

c. How much slack (unused capacity) is available in the other departments?

d. How much system capacity can be gained by adding capacity to the bottleneck?

12. Platinum Refining and Chemical Company is examining its pesticide plant. At this time, the company is unable to satisfy customer demand for a new insect spray. You have been asked to spend some time at the facility to determine how output can be increased. Analyze the following line flow process:

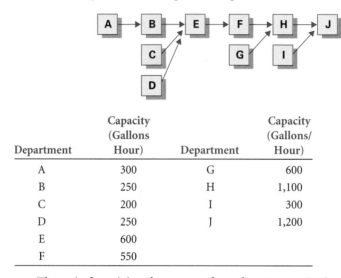

Department	Capacity (Gallons Hour)	Department	Capacity (Gallons/ Hour)
A	300	G	600
B	250	H	1,100
C	200	I	300
D	250	J	1,200
E	600		
F	550		

The ratio for mixing the outputs from departments B, C, and D is two to two to one, respectively. This means that getting five gallons out of department E. requires mixing two gallons of B's output, two gallons of C's output, and one gallon of D's output. The ratio for departments F and G is one to one. The ratio for departments H and I is four to one.

a. What is the system capacity, and which is the bottleneck department?

b. How much slack (unused capacity) is available in other departments?

c. How much system capacity can be gained by adding capacity to the bottleneck?

13. Bauer Electric makes integrated circuits for the computer industry. Currently, the process for making circuits yields 80 percent good parts. The facility has the capacity to produce 2,000,000 units per year including both good and bad units. The variable cost is $2.00 per unit. The annual fixed costs is $10,000,000. The selling price is $12.00 per unit. Currently, the market demand exceeds the units available.

a. If Bauer Electric works at capacity, what is the total amount of units produced in a year that meet specifications?

b. If the yield can be increased from 80 to 90 percent, how much does the unit cost for a circuit change?

c. If the yield can be increased from 80 to 90 percent and demand is unlimited, how much will profits increase?

d. If the yield can be increased from 80 to 90 percent and demand is 1,600,000 units, what is the impact on profits?

e. Why is there such a difference between the answers to c and d?

14. McComas Educational Service provides training to pass the bar exam. The company offers a money back guarantee if a student does not pass on the first try. Currently, 60

percent pass the exam. The company is working on some computer-based training that could increase the pass rate to 80 percent. The cost of the service is $800, and 10,000 first-time students enroll in the course each year. Demand has grown at about 5 percent per year. The variable cost is only $100, and the annual fixed cost is $2,000,000. For the current cost structure, capacity is 12,000 students per year.

a. Currently, how many first-time students pass the test each year?

b. If the pass rate increases from 60 to 80 percent, how much will profits increase?

c. Should McComas consider reducing capacity?

CHAPTER 10

Facility Location in a Global Environment

LEARNING OBJECTIVES

After completing this chapter, you should be able to:

1. Discuss location as a strategic decision.
2. Discuss the quantitative and qualitative factors influencing the location decision.
3. Integrate the qualitative factors with the quantitative factors in order to make effective location decisions.
4. Describe how the location decision influences other operating decisions.
5. Explain the international ramifications of the location decision.
6. Discuss special implications of the location decision for service operations.

INTRODUCTION

Facility location is the placement of a facility with respect to customers, suppliers, and other facilities with which it interacts. The decision usually commits substantial resources, and it cannot be easily changed. Many of the principles and techniques used in locating a facility are the same whether an organization is selling fried chicken or groceries, providing fire protection or health services, storing electronic parts or food, or making computer chips or paper. Managers making the decision should consider the costs of operating at a location, including costs to acquire the land and build the facility, as well as costs for labor, taxes, and utilities. They should consider the convenience of a particular location for customers as well as the cost to transport materials to the facility and move finished product from the facility. They should also consider access to banking, educational, and other activities that are important to the success of their organization. Thus, many factors, both quantitative and qualitative, influence the location decision.

What often differs from one industry to another are the weights assigned to these various factors. The size of the weight assigned to a factor indicates its importance. For example, a primary factor in locating a fire station is its response time to the buildings in that fire district. Thus, response time should be assigned a large weight. In locating a restaurant, easy access by customers is more important than the cost to transport raw material (food and beverages) to the facility. An organization producing solar cells may feel that it is very important to locate in an area close to a university or research park that specializes in silica science. Organizations that produce plywood, dimensional lumber, or paper need a readily available supply of wood so they usually locate near timber resources. Managers of labor-intensive operations may feel that low labor cost is the critical factor that determines the location of their facility.

The location decision usually involves commitment of a large capital investment that normally cannot be moved from one location to another. As a result, location should be viewed as a long-term, strategic decision because it has a major impact on the organization's ability to compete. The location decision should not be based solely on marketing issues, production factors, or transportation costs. Successful managers integrate the relevant factors and weigh them appropriately in order to make the best long-term decision for the organization.

This chapter discusses the factors that affect the location decision, including quantitative and qualitative factors, and how these factors can be integrated. Over the last two decades, the breaking down of barriers between countries has greatly accelerated the investment in new facilities by foreign competitors. The implications of global competition for the location decision are discussed. Special consideration is given to the location decision for service operations.

LOCATION AS A STRATEGIC DECISION

In addition to the quantitative and qualitative factors that affect the location decision, an organization must recognize that location is a long-term commitment of resources. This long-term commitment should fit with the organization's overall strategy, which should be linked to the organization's existing and potential customer base. How should an organization respond as population shifts from the Northeast and the Great Lakes areas to the West and the South? What new opportunities are created by the expansion of the population base in the warmer climates? More air conditioners and swimming pools are obvious answers, and many others exist. As population shifts across the United States, the center of any market is likely to shift. Should an organization have a strategy that moves facilities to deal with long-term population shifts?

Sometimes organizations develop marketing and operating strategies that have an impact on the location decision. We will discuss the regional facility strategy and the product facility strategy. The **regional facility strategy** means that each facility is assigned a market area and each facility produces a complete line of products for that area. This is often done when customer convenience and access are important, or when outbound transportation costs are very high. Fast-food restaurants, instant oil change operations, and branch banks are examples of operations located to provide maximum customer convenience and access. In fact, many customer-oriented service operations are located in this way. Bottle making, corrugated box production, and aluminum can making operations are examples of facilities that would be located by region to hold down outbound transportation costs. These products have high shipping costs because the finished products occupy a lot of space.

The **product facility strategy** means that one facility is responsible for producing one product or product line and shipping that product all over the country and the world. This approach is appropriate when the production process is complex and hard to control, such as making ceramic heat shields for spacecrafts. It can be used when a firm does not want to duplicate expensive equipment, facilities, and highly trained personnel. This approach is also popular when there are advantages to specialization and economies of scale and when transportation costs are not prohibitive. The production of igniters for jet aircraft engines, for example, would benefit from a product facility strategy. This item is small so shipping costs are low. An igniter is high in value so shipping cost, as a percent of purchase price, is also small.

EXAMPLE   Recently, Boeing, a maker of commercial and military aircraft, decided to shifts its headquarters from Seattle, Washington, to Chicago, Illinois. Engineering, design, and manufacturing operations will remain on the West Coast. Why did the company do this? When asked, Boeing's CEO responded that it was essential for corporate management, sales, and finance to get closer to customers and to the money centers. A trip to New York, Washington, D.C., Chicago, or St. Louis to meet with airline executives, the Department of Defense, or the financial community usually required at least two days. Even with an early morning flight out of Seattle, it was difficult to arrive in these cities in time for meetings because of the long flight time, potential plane changes, and time zone effect. From Chicago, flights in the early morning leave plenty of time for meetings in the late morning and afternoon. In effect, this decision allows Boeing to provide a higher level of service to its customers while increasing the productivity of its executives.

Factors Affecting the Location Decision

As described earlier, there are some potential differences in the location decision for manufacturers and service providers. Manufacturing firms consider a variety of items, some of which are qualitative and others quantitative. Quantitative factors for manufacturers include:

- Labor costs
- Material costs
- Transportation into and out of the facility
- Utilities, taxes, real estate costs, and construction costs
- Government incentives

In addition, manufacturing firms often examine qualitative factors such as:

- Labor climate
- Quality of life
- Proximity to customers and markets
- Proximity to suppliers and resources

To discuss these topics in an organized manner, they are grouped into three subsections. The first subsection describes managing the quantitative factors, including the impact of location on cost, the increasing importance of government incentives, the impact of location on revenue, and a way to analyze cost and revenue. The second subsection describes the qualitative factors and illustrates how these can be analyzed and then integrated with the quantitative factors. The third subsection discusses the effects of the location decision on other operating factors. Before we do this, however, consider how the factors impacting service operations might be different.

Factors Affecting Service Operations

In service operation, many of the factors identified with manufacturing are still relevant. Clearly, service providers would consider labor cost, taxes, real estate costs, construction costs, and government incentives as important elements in a location decision. Material cost and transportation costs would be relevant for service providers, such as restaurants and retail operations, that purchase, transport, and resell goods. Utility costs may not be a significant factor for service operations because consumption is generally low compared to manufacturing. The qualitative factors listed for manufacturers are likely to be relevant for service providers with the possible exception of proximity to suppliers and resources.

Where customers actually come to the service facility, being close to customers is more important for service providers than it is for manufacturing operations. Customers often place a high value on their time so convenience is essential. For warehousing and distribution, transportation costs are important, but response time may be even more important. If travel distance and time are short, total inventory in the system can be kept very low. In some cases, the trip from producers to the distribution center to the retail store can be one day or less.

Location of competitors may also be an important factor for service operations. In some services, like newspaper publishing, having competitors in the immediate area often has a significant negative impact on sales. In others, service providers tend to cluster together. In many cases, they advertise together. Nearly every medium-size town and large city has the "auto mile" or the "auto strip" where one of every dealer is located. The idea is to create a critical mass, so customers can quickly and easily compare the products from different dealers. You often see similar clusters of fast-food restaurants. These clusters are caused to some extent by the need to deal with customer choice. With a large group, some want pizza, some want burgers, and others want chicken. It also happens because the fast-food chains locate their restaurants near high-volume activities, such as large shopping malls, sport centers, and expressway exits in large urban areas.

Managing the Quantitative Factors

Quantitative factors include the costs associated with facility construction, production, overhead, and transportation to and from the facility. State and local governments offer incentives to attract and retain businesses and jobs. Such incentives include tax abatement, low-interest loans, help in cutting through red tape, low business taxes, and low rates for unemployment insurance and worker's compensation. Finally, the location can affect sales volume and selling price. The announcement of a new facility may initiate price-cutting or other costly product promotion activities by existing competitors in the area.

The Impact of Location on Costs

The location decision plays an important role in shaping the cost function. The total-cost equation is:

$$TC = (VC)X + FC$$

where

TC = total cost
VC = variable cost per unit
X = the number of units produced
FC = fixed costs

Variable costs are affected by prevailing wage rates, material costs, utility rates, and transportation costs for incoming materials and outgoing finished products. Fixed costs are affected by construction and land costs and the cost of administration, all of which are likely to be lower in rural areas. There also may be tax incentives or other special considerations for a site.

To prepare cost estimates for a site, data are collected and analyzed. To illustrate, Exhibit 10.1 contains data for a site in Indianapolis, Indiana, for a facility to build computer control panels. These data can be used to prepare a pro forma operating budget.

Exhibit 10.1 contains projected labor, material, and utility usage in addition to the rates. Utilities may have both fixed and variable components. Some utility costs are variable and directly linked to producing a product, such as the power required to run a drill press. In other cases, utility costs cannot be linked to a product. An example is the energy needed to heat a building. The amount of heat required is not related to the number of units produced. Exhibit 10.1 shows variable utility costs. The fixed component of utilities is included in overhead expense.

Transportation costs are a function of the quantity of materials shipped, the distance traveled, and the type of carrier used. Price quotes are usually easy to obtain.

Exhibit 10.1 also lists as a lump sum an estimate of facility overhead expenses, such as supervisors, material handling, and plant management staff. The value of the investments in the facility and the value of any special considerations are also listed as lump sums. The special considerations figure is shown as a savings that should be deducted from the initial investment.

EXHIBIT 10.1		**Variable Production Costs**		
Data for Site in Indianapolis, Indiana		Type	Rate	Projected Usage
	Labor	Welding	$10.00/hr.	0.5 hrs./unit
		Electrical	$12.00/hr.	0.3 hrs./unit
		General assembly	$9.00/hr.	1.1 hrs./unit
	Material	Sheet metal	$.40/lb.	100 lbs./unit
		Threaded fasteners	$2.00/100	20/unit
		Electrical wire	$.06/lineal ft.	70 lineal ft./unit
	Utilities	Natural gas	$4.00/1,000 cu. ft.	500 cu. ft./unit
		Electricity	$.06/kilowatt hr.	200 kilowatt hrs./unit
	Transportation*	In rail	$.03/lb. (sheet metal)	100 lbs./unit
		In motor carrier	$.04/lb. (fasteners)	5 lbs./unit
		In motor carrier	$.04/lb. (wire)	4 lbs./unit
		Out motor carrier	$20/unit (finished)	1
	Facility Overhead			$2,100,000
	Initial Investment			$175,000,000
		Land acquisition costs		
		Building construction		
		Plant start-up costs		
		Initial employee training		
	Special Considerations			$25,000,000
		Tax abatement		
		Low-interest loans		
		Supplementary training expenses		

*Rates are given from a specific origin to a specific destination, so distance has been accounted for.

Exhibit 10.2 shows a pro forma operating budget based on producing 45,000 units/year at the site described in Exhibit 10.1. An operating budget usually does not include capital costs for facilities.

The costs of making products at this facility can now be estimated. Considering only the variable costs, we can calculate the unit variable cost as follows:

$$\text{Unit variable cost} = \frac{\$4,520,700}{45,000 \text{ units}}$$
$$= \$100.46/\text{unit}$$

The cost including a share of the annual facility overhead is:

$$\text{Cost with overhead} = \frac{\$6,620,700}{45,000 \text{ units}}$$
$$= \$147.13/\text{unit}$$

The Rising Importance of Government Incentives

Many states and local governments have been very aggressive in their efforts to attract new businesses. One incentive offered by state and local governments is a significant reduction in property taxes. They have also offered low-interest loans, provided free training to workers, and subsidized wages for some period of time. In addition, many states and cities have established agencies that can help private industry slice through governmental red tape. In some

EXHIBIT 10.2		
Pro Forma Operating Budget for One Year Based on Estimated Sales of 45,000 Units		

Labor

Welding	($10.00/hr.)(.5 hrs./unit)(45,000 units)	$ 225,000
Electric	($12.00/hr.)(.3 hrs./unit)(45,000 units)	162,000
Assembly	($9.00/hr.)(1.1 hrs./unit)(45,000 units)	445,500
Total labor costs		$ 832,500

Material

Sheet metal	($.40/lb.)(100 lbs./unit)(45,000 units)	$1,800,000
Fasteners	($2.00/100)(20/unit)(45,000 units)	18,000
Wire	($.06/lin. ft.)(70 lin. ft.)(45,000 units)	189,000
Total material costs		$ 2,007,000

Utilities

Natural gas	($4.00/1,000 cu. ft.)(500 cu. ft./unit)(45,000 units)	$ 90,000
Electricity	($.06/kwh)(200 kwh/unit)(45,000 units)	540,000
Total utility costs		$ 630,000

Transportation

Sheet metal	($.03/lb.)(100 lb./unit)(45,000 units)	$ 135,000
Fasteners	($.04/lb.)(5 lb./unit)(45,000 units)	9,000
Wire	($.04/lb.)(4 lb./unit)(45,000 units)	7,200
Finished product	($20.00/unit)(45,000)	900,000
Total transportation costs		$1,051,200
Variable costs		$4,520,700
Facility overhead*		2,100,000
Grand total		$6,620,700

*Some overhead costs can be variable, but to simplify the discussion in this case, we will assume all overhead costs are fixed.

cases, they have put together parcels of land by using their powers of eminent domain. Simply stated, eminent domain means that an owner can be forced to sell property to the government at fair market value if it will be used for the good of all. Once obtained, properties are sold to private industry for development. Governments can acquire property more quickly and less expensively than private industry can. As soon as word leaks out that private industry is interested in developing an area, the land prices are sure to increase significantly. With the power of eminent domain, the government can avoid being held up by owners of key parcels.

These incentives were part of the packages used to attract a new DaimlerChrysler assembly facility to Toledo, Ohio. In combination, the City of Toledo, Lucas County, and the State of Ohio provided site acquisition assistance, tax abatement, training subsidies, and new expressway access points to attract the facility. The City of Toledo put together a team of local business people and engineers to help with site design and facility layout.

In some cases, businesses that have been in the state for years are grumbling about the preferred treatment given to newcomers, and some states are beginning to wonder if the jobs created are worth the costs of the incentives. Even so, the bidding wars among the states for the jobs these new developments bring are likely to continue. The pressure on elected officials to create jobs in the short term seems to mask the long-term impact that this treatment might have on future revenues and expenses of the state.

EXAMPLE

Over the last ten years, Alabama has won a significant piece of the automotive industry. Alabama persuaded Mercedes-Benz to build an assembly facility for making sport utility vehicles in Vance with more than $250 million in incentives. The facility opened in 1997 and employs about 1,900 people, with plans to go to 4,000. In 2001, Honda opened a facility in Lincoln that employs more than 2,000 people to make its Odyssey mini-van. Toyota is constructing an engine assembly facility in Huntsville that will employ about 350 people. Recently, Alabama earned a commitment from Hyundai Motor Co. of South Korea to build a final assembly facility near Montgomery that will employ about 2,000 workers.

These efforts cost Alabama nearly $700 million in incentives over nine years. Critics argue that the state has not gotten its money's worth and that these big handouts have taken money from schools and services and made it difficult to provide tax relief for its low-income residents. Proponents argue that these efforts are "Alabama's new day." In addition to the jobs and taxes associated with the new facilities, these efforts are giving Alabama the reputation as the South's hottest automaking center. This reputation has prompted dozens of companies, including key suppliers, to investigate the potential that Alabama has to offer.

The Impact of Location on Revenue

It is possible that a plant's location will influence the sales volume, as well as the selling price per unit, of a product. The revenue function is:

$$TR = (SP)X$$

where

TR = total revenue
SP = selling price per unit
X = the number of units sold

Any influence that location has on marketing efforts can affect sales volume. For example, if a location is selected that has a higher cost, then a higher selling price may be needed. This price can affect the volume sold. A location that is convenient for customers can increase sales volume.

Suppose an organization announces plans to locate a facility in a region where a competitor already has a facility making the same product. The competitor may feel threatened by the move. Increased competition, leading to vigorous price-cutting, may result. The foreign invasion into the U.S. car market has led to renewed efforts to improve quality and to lower prices. This threat has been amplified as foreign firms have located more and more automobile assembly plants in this country.

An Approach for Integrating Cost, Revenue, and Time

To make effective location decisions, management must organize the potential costs and revenues for each site in a way that allows them to be easily compared.

The discussion here can only begin to define the important factors to consider in developing such a model. Let's begin by examining the cost data for the Indianapolis site, which is detailed in Exhibits 10.1 and 10.2, and for an alternative site in Lexington, Kentucky. The new facility is scheduled to produce 45,000 units per year. The costs and revenues for both sites are listed below. (The incentives are to be subtracted from the initial investment.)

	Indianapolis	Lexington
Variable costs	$100.46/unit	$95.77/unit
Annual overhead	$2,100,000/year	$1,900,000/year
Initial investment	$175,000,000	$168,000,000
Incentives	$25,000,000	$10,500,000

Comparing Costs Using the Same Time Period   We make several assumptions in this comparison: (1) revenue is not affected by either choice, (2) sales volume per year, selling price, unit variable costs, and fixed costs do not change over the period in question, and (3) the time value of money is ignored. After this simple model is constructed, each of these assumptions will be relaxed to determine its effect on the model.

PROBLEM   We can compare the costs of the Indianapolis and Lexington sites over a five-year period, using the total-cost equation. (The subscript I stands for Indianapolis and the subscript L for Lexington.)

$$TC = (VC)X + TC$$
$$TC_I = (\$100.46/\text{unit})(45,000 \text{ units/year})(5 \text{ years}) +$$
$$(\$2,100,000/\text{year})(5 \text{ years}) + \$175,000,000 - \$25,000,000$$
$$= \$22,603,500 + \$10,500,000 + \$150,000,000$$
$$= \$183,103,500$$
$$TC_L = (\$95.77/\text{unit})(45,000 \text{ units/year})(5 \text{ years}) +$$
$$(\$1,900,000/\text{year})(5 \text{ years}) + \$168,000,000 - \$10,500,000$$
$$= \$21,548,250 + \$9,500,000 + \$157,500,000$$
$$= \$188,548,250$$

Over a five-year period, Indianapolis has a lower total cost.

At what point in time will the costs of these two sites be equal? In this case, X will represent the number of years until costs are equal. This information may be a very useful for managers in choosing between the alternatives.

$$TC_I = TC_L$$

$(100.46)(45,000)X + 2,100,000X + 175,000,000 - 25,000,000$
$= (95.77)(45,000)X + 1,900,000X + 168,000,000 - 10,500,000$
$\$4,520,700X + \$2,100,000X + \$150,000,000$
$= \$4,309,650X + \$1,900,000X + \$157,500,000$
$\$6,620,700X - \$6,209,650X = \$157,500,000 - \$150,000,000$
$\$411,050X = \$7,500,000$
$X = 18.25 \text{ years}$

Check the answer by substituting the time X into the cost equations for Indianapolis and Lexington and seeing if the costs are equal.

If we allow the amount sold per year to vary, the point of equal costs could be viewed in a different way. In the model, the number of years could be a constant, and the number of units sold per year could become a variable. If we assume that the time period is set at five years, how many units must be sold each year if costs are equal? Here, the variable X represents the number of units sold each year.

$$TC_I = TC_L$$

$(100.46)(X)5 + (2,100,000)5 + 175,000,000 - 25,000,000 = (95.77)(X)5$
$+ (1,900,000)5 + 168,000,000 - 10,500,000$
$X = 277,186 \text{ units/year}$

Allowing Revenue to Be a Variable   What happens if revenue is affected by the choice of a site? This means that the sales volume and/or the selling price could be different. In order to include these possible changes, the model must compare profits rather than costs. In addition to varying the number of units sold per year and the number of years, management can vary the selling price to see the impact that it has on profits. Because of the added complexity of the model, computerized spreadsheets can be applied. Managers could write a computer program that allows them to calculate profits under a variety of circumstances, or they could use one of the popular spreadsheet programs to lay out several alternatives quickly. Probabilities could be assigned to alternatives, and expected values could be calculated.

Applying the Time-Value-of-Money Concept   Enhancing the model to include the time value of money forces managers to separate costs and revenue by period. Then, they must apply the appropriate discount factors to make current and future expenses and revenue comparable in terms of today's dollars. To accomplish this, a spreadsheet is helpful.

We will not explain the details of discounting expenses and revenues here. However, a word of caution is appropriate. In many cases, the simple approaches described in this chapter may be all that is necessary. It is possible that differences in revenue are not significant or that one site is clearly superior to another. There are significant costs in developing and testing a sophisticated model so you should be sure there is something to gain by doing it.

Including the Qualitative Factors

Qualitative factors are also affected by the location decision. Although their direct impact on profits is usually not measurable, these factors need to be carefully considered and integrated into the decision by management. The appendix at the end of the chapter contains a list of many of the qualitative factors that could be considered.

To integrate qualitative factors into the location decision, managers should:

1. Decide which factors are relevant to the problem

2. Weight each of the factors—several factors may be relevant, but some might be far more important than others

3. Evaluate each site so that rational comparisons can be made

Unless a manager makes a judgment about the importance of each factor, all the factors are assumed to have equal weights. These weights are usually selected prior to determining the rankings or raw scores so that the weights are not biased by the scores. The weights are multiplied by the scores to determine the weighted scores. Then, the weighted scores are added to determine total scores.

PROBLEM

Let us continue the Indianapolis and Lexington example. A committee has determined that the following factors are relevant to the decision. Indianapolis and Lexington are ranked on a scale of 1 to 10, with 10 being most desirable. The rankings are subjective estimates of some of the factors contained in the appendix at the end of this chapter.

	Weight	Indianapolis Raw Score	Lexington Raw Score
Recreational activities	20	8	7
University research facilities	40	8	8
Union activity	40	4	7
Banking services	80	7	6
Available labor pool	60	7	5

So the rankings can eventually be added, 10 is considered "good" in all cases. For example, a 10 in university research activities is desirable and indicates high levels of research; a 10 in union activity is also desirable, but may indicate low levels of union activity.

Multiply the weight by the raw score for both Indianapolis and Lexington.

	Weight	Indianapolis Raw Score	Indianapolis Weighted Score	Lexington Raw Score	Lexington Weighted Score
Recreational activities	20	8	160	7	140
University research facilities	40	8	320	8	320
Union activities	40	4	160	7	280
Banking services	80	7	560	6	480
Available labor pool	60	7	420	5	300
Total			1,620		1,520

As long as the same weights are applied to each location, the weighted scores are comparable. The absolute value of each score does not have meaning, but comparing total scores is useful.

If Indianapolis is superior in terms of profits and investment, then the choice between the two is easy because Indianapolis also has a slight qualitative edge. If Indianapolis is not superior in profits and investment, then management should judge the impact of these qualitative factors on the long-term success of the organization. Even though a mathematical model can be used to analyze the data, the results still must be interpreted and a decision made.

Analyzing Spatial Relationships

In locating facilities for organizations that provide services and goods, it is often important to analyze the distance and the cost associated with customers traveling to a facility (hospital or retail outlet) or with suppliers shipping products or materials to a facility. Two techniques, the load-distance method and the transportation problem, are described in a supplement to this chapter, which is available on our Web site, http://www.wiley.com/college/vonderembse.

The Location Decision's Effect on Other Operating Factors

The location decision can have a significant impact on an organization's ability to compete. It can influence costs, selling price, demand, educational opportunities for employees and their families, and access to financial services. How can the location decision affect other factors in production?

Assume that demand for an organization's product exceeds present capacity. An organization can consider two options to increase capacity: the on-site option is to build additions to the existing plant, and the off-site option is to design and build a new plant. On-site expansion is more popular because it usually involves less capital investment. Many services, such as shipping, receiving, and administration, may not have to be expanded. Only the critical operations—that is, the bottlenecks—require capacity increases.

On the other hand, on-site expansion can create many problems, especially if it is a repeated practice. As more production space is added, material handling and storage become more difficult because inventory space is often converted to production. As new product variations are added, the once simple product flow becomes complicated by twists, turns, and backtracking because plant additions often occur over many years and no long-term planning for future additions is made. When on-site expansion is used to add capacity, intraplant transportation and communication can become strained.

Staying at the same site often postpones the introduction of new product and process technologies. Old equipment and old production methods are used longer than they should be. Future product innovation, productivity increases, quality improvements, and cost reductions can be negatively affected. On-site expansion can mean a growing number of workers, products, and processes that need to be managed. Such layering of expanded responsibilities creates real complexities for managers at all levels.

INTERNATIONAL DIMENSIONS OF THE LOCATION DECISION

In the last twenty years, the international dimensions of business and business operations have grown dramatically. Facility location is one of the most obvious results. During the 1980s, ten Japanese automobile assembly plants were built in this country. Today, a host of foreign suppliers has located manufacturing facilities in the United States. The British, Germans, and French have invested heavily in this country. Organizations headquartered in the United States have major production facilities in other countries. This section discusses some of the reasons for locating facilities in foreign countries and the ethical considerations that are involved.

Why Locate in a Foreign Country?

There appear to be several reasons why organizations decide to locate facilities in foreign countries. An organization may seek:

1. Comparative advantage in the quantitative aspects of producing goods or services
2. Closeness to a market that it serves
3. Improved political relationships
4. Resources that are scarce in the home country

Comparative advantage appears to be one of the major reasons to locate facilities in foreign countries. Some countries have lower labor, utility, transportation, or material costs than others do. These advantages are sometimes short-term advantages that disappear after several companies have made major expenditures for new facilities. The law of supply and demand works in all countries, not just the United States. There may also be good reasons for the differential in costs. If labor costs are low in a particular country, perhaps the labor force is not very skilled or perhaps the country has other disadvantages that offset the cost savings.

Organizations may locate in other countries to be close to their market. When a country exports a substantial amount of product to a particular country, locating a facility there may be appropriate. This decision allows the company to tailor products to the needs of customers in that country and to deliver products to customers quickly. It can also dramatically reduce the logistical problems and costs of moving products around the world.

There may be political advantages to locating a production facility in a country that accepts many imports from an organization. Job creation and contribution to the tax base are powerful political tools. This decision may also lower any trade deficit that exists between the two countries.

In some cases, companies actually have a shortage of labor or other resources in the home country. One possible solution is to import labor; the other is to build facilities in other countries. For example, one advantage that East Germany brought to the reunification of East and West Germany is surplus labor.

Japanese Automotive Industry Locates in North America

In Marysville, Ohio, in 1982, Honda Motor Company opened the doors to the first Japanese-owned facility to manufacture automobiles in the United States. Since then, there have been two major additions to the facility, capacity has grown to more than 500,000 units per year, and Honda exports cars from Marysville to Tokyo. Honda's move to the United States was quickly followed by transplants from Nissan, Toyota, Mazda, Mitsubishi, Isuzu, and Suzuki, bringing the total to ten plants with a total capacity of nearly 2.5 million units per year. What caused the Japanese to locate that much capacity in North America? Initially, the Japanese were responding to pressure from U.S. automakers and the UAW to build cars in North America, rather than relying 100 percent on imported cars. American automakers felt that if the Japanese manufacturers were forced to pay UAW wages and accept work practices in the union contracts, a level playing field would be created, and U.S. producers could compete. American automakers felt that poor quality and high absenteeism were part of doing business in this country.

Seven of the ten transplants have avoided union contracts by locating in rural or semi-rural areas of the Midwest and by hiring first-generation factory workers. As a result, they have enjoyed lower health care costs, less costly pension benefits, and lower wage rates. These seven facilities have also avoided work rules that restrict productivity and increase the number of labor hours required to build a car. The other three transplants are joint ventures with the U.S. auto makers and must accept the UAW as part of doing business. In each case, the joint venture has been very successful. The Japanese have been very particular about whom they select from the UAW workforce, and they have negotiated much more flexible work rules with the UAW.

In addition, locating facilities in the Midwest gave the Japanese credibility with the car-buying population in the Midwest. It was an area where the Japanese had not been as successful in attracting first-time buyers as they had been on the West or East Coast. It is much easier to explain that the Honda you purchased was made in Marysville or that the Camry you drive was produced in Georgetown, Kentucky. Locating in the Midwest also helped them to reduce transportation and distribution costs. Finally, it certainly helped in the political arena.

Ethical Considerations in the Location Decision

Ethics should be a part of all business decision making. The decision to locate operations in another country brings special ethical problems. For example, in the United States, paying government officials "extra" money, a bribe, to speed up the processing of applications or to obtain favorable ruling is not only unethical, but also a criminal offense. In other countries, it is sometimes considered a normal part of doing business. In the late 1970s, the United States passed laws designed to cope with what this country viewed as the unethical practice of bribery. However, these laws are not very clear. In response, some companies have decided to eliminate all "questionable payments," legal or illegal. Some of the companies have been surprised to find that their business has not fallen off as they expected. Their actions have been reinforced by a number of foreign governments that have passed stricter laws or have begun to enforce laws already on the books.

In the debate over the North American Free Trade Agreement (NAFTA), opponents believed that many U.S. companies would move their facilities to Mexico to avoid the more stringent U.S. pollution laws and regulations. Some people insisted that Mexico adopt the same or similar laws that exist in the United States in order to discourage organizations from moving facilities across the border. NAFTA was ratified, and Mexico did not adopt similar laws. Will we see a major shift in facilities from the United States to the Mexican side of the border?

In addition, many U.S. firms have looked to foreign countries for low labor costs. While there is nothing unethical or illegal about this, there have been situations where operations in foreign countries have created oppressive working conditions and/or employed children to keep cost low. The International Labor Organization prohibits the employment of children under the age of fourteen. The charge of running a sweatshop can damage greatly the appeal of certain popular brands. It also builds the argument for defining a living global wage and working conditions, which establishes another layer of costly regulation. Organizations must monitor the companies they subcontract with to make sure that they are engaged in legal and ethical practices. Even if there is no legal requirement to do so, these organizations may suffer significantly from adverse publicity, as well as product boycotts.

Other ethical issues ought to be considered when moving a facility from one city to another or from one country to another. What are the organization's responsibilities to the people who work at the facility and the local economy that depend upon that facility for economic development? Fifty to one hundred years ago, companies were much more paternalistic than the companies of today. Organizations often provided recreation for families, housing, and even health care, as opposed to health care insurance. These organizations were often criticized for these activities by social scientists and politicians who believed it made the workers too dependent on the company. The organizations viewed their commitment to the local community as being quite strong. Their willingness and opportunities to move were substantially less than they are today.

Today, firms competing in the global economy often seem to view state and local government as a source of funds through tax abatements and low-interest, guaranteed loans. Facilities close, and jobs move around the country and around the world in search of the "best deal."

In other cases, organizations move for tax purposes. Stanley Works, a long-time maker of hand tools in the United States, once planned to reincorporate in Bermuda, primarily to gain an income tax advantage. Even though its manufacturing operations would not have moved, its tax bill would have been reduced because it would have been a foreign company.

LOCATION ANALYSIS FOR SERVICE OPERATIONS

Location decisions for service operations have many points in common with the location of manufacturing facilities. The strategic issue of getting close to your customers is an integral part of location for service operations. The cost analysis, government incentives, and the qualitative factors are also essential for both.

Location analysis for service operations has some differences from location analysis for manufacturing operations. For instance, in many service operations, products do not move to customers; customers move to the product. Thus, the location of service stations, restaurants, supermarkets, and retail outlets depends on concentrations of demand and the location of competition. The load-distance method discussed in the chapter supplement may be useful in analyzing the location of service operations with respect to the potential client base.

To determine the potential client base that might use a proposed retail service facility, a manager may examine population, average income, number of competitors, traffic counts, and other information by census tract, zip code, or other classification. Public service facilities, such as post offices, schools, and welfare offices, should be located so as to be convenient to their client base. While public service organizations do not have the bottom-line, profit-driven motivation for providing convenient service, they should seek to provide the maximum benefit to the group they serve. Many times, cost-benefit analysis is used to make the location decision and other decisions for public institutions.

The location of emergency units, such as fire protection and ambulance service, is determined by minimizing response time, providing minimum coverage, and operating from a mobile location. Response time, the time from a request for service to the delivery of that service, is important when time is a critical factor. The objective is to locate a facility so that the maximum response time to any point served by the unit is minimized.

Minimum coverage implies that all customers have a minimum level of coverage. For example, no house in the city will be more than one mile from a fire station or an ambulance service. The number and placement of facilities required to provide minimum coverage can be determined by grouping customers into appropriate population centers and examining candidate facility locations to see if the minimum coverage is provided. This can be accomplished by listing the population centers in the columns of a table and listing the potential facility locations in the rows of the same table. Then, each potential facility can be judged to determine if the minimum coverage is achieved. In many cases, more than one candidate facility may be required to provide that coverage.

With mobile locations, some units might be directed from place to place without returning to base. One good example here is dispatching police cars. To deal with this problem, mobile units may be assigned a travel area. Simulation is one tool that can be used to analyze this type of problem.

THE LOCATION DECISION PROVIDES THE OPPORTUNITY TO BE SOCIALLY RESPONSIBLE

The location decision often provides a company the opportunity to build a new facility or to make a major addition to an existing facility. In either case, the company is faced with an opportunity to make a major investment and to make that investment in the best interests not only of the firm's stockholders but also of its stakeholders. In addition to creating jobs, the company can develop facilities that recapture and recycle their own waste, use materials that are recycled by the public, and reduce pollution in general. Designing these features into the facility when it is built generally provides a much better solution than trying to retrofit facilities.

EXAMPLE

The paper industry believes that recycling is not a passing fad, and to continue its success, it must be socially and economically responsible. For many years companies have had facilities that recycle paper and reduce pollution. A next step is to collect and recycle office waste to make high quality paper. This effort is out of the ordinary because recycled paper is normally used to make lower grade paper. New facilities should be capable of producing high-quality paper from low-quality waste, which would increase the opportunities for recycling and reuse.

To make this work, the recycling plant will wash the toner and ink particles from the office waste paper and will grind the paper into fibers. A pipe conveyer will carry the fiber pulp to the main plant where it will be mixed with virgin fibers. (Most virgin fibers come from trees so this process is not only reducing the need for landfills, it is also saving trees.) The recycling plant allows papermakers to take a low grade of office waste and make a fiber that is functionally and aesthetically equivalent to virgin fiber. In addition to the recycling efforts, the facility can use an ozone-based process to bleach the pulp. Ozone replaces chlorine, which is highly corrosive and dangerous.

SUMMARY

- The facility location decision should not be based entirely on production factors and transportation. It is a long-term strategic decision that can have a major impact on the organization's ability to compete.

- Locating a facility can have strategic implications. Some organizations employ a regional facility approach where one facility is responsible for producing all the products for that area of the country. Others employ the product facility strategy where one plant produces one product or product line and ships it all over the country.

- Both quantitative and qualitative factors influence the location decision. These factors should be integrated if the decision-making process is to work effectively.

- The location decision can have a significant impact on an organization's ability to compete. It can influence costs, selling price, demand, and access to financial services.

- Locating facilities in foreign countries has increased dramatically. Many of these organizations are attempting to gain some comparative advantages that one country may have or to be closer to their market. Others are relocating for political reasons or to remedy resource scarcity in the home country.

- Some service operations have to look at special considerations in making the location decision. The location of emergency units such as fire stations depends on response time, minimum coverage, and mobile location.

 Visit our dynamic Web site, http://www.wiley.com/college/vonderembse, for extended chapter material, solved problems, mini-cases, computer software, and Web links.

KEY TERMS

facility location　　　　product facility strategy　　regional facility strategy

URLS

The Home Depot: www.homedepot.com

Kohls: www.kohlscorporation.com

DaimlerChrysler: www.daimlerchrysler.com

City of Toledo: www.ci.toledo.oh.us

QUESTIONS

1. Why is the facility location decision important to an organization?

2. What factors are affected by the choice of locations? Which of these factors can be measured in dollars, and which cannot?

3. How can qualitative and quantitative factors be integrated to make a sound and logical location decision?

4. What hidden factors are influenced by on-site location, and how are they influenced?

5. Why are spatial relationships important in the location decision?

6. Why is location a strategic decision?

7. What are the international dimensions of the location decision?

8. What role do ethics play in locating new facilities in foreign countries?

9. What special problems are faced by service operations in locating new facilities?

INTERNET QUESTIONS

10. The Home Depot is opening new stores across the United States. Visit The Home Depot Web site and learn as much as you can about the company's plans for future store openings. (You may have to examine its annual report.) What is The Home Depot's approach to locating facilities?

11. Kohls, a retailer, is expanding store locations. Visit the company's Web site and learn what you can about its cost structure. How does this expansion help Kohls become more profitable?

12. DaimlerChrysler recently built a new manufacturing facility for the Jeep Liberty in Toledo, Ohio. Visit the Web sites of DaimlerChrysler and the City of Toledo to understand why that decision was made? Explain the reasons for the decision.

13. Pick a medium to large size city that you are familiar with and visit its Web site (It should have information related to economic development.) Describe the strengths and weakness of the city for locating a manufacturing plant, distribution center, and retail operation.

PROBLEMS

1. Drwal Developers specializes in analyzing facility location decisions. Presently, the company is looking at two locations, Orlando, Florida, and Olympia, Washington, for which it has determined the following cost information:

	Orlando	Olympia
Variable fixed costs	$14.70/unit	$16.45/unit
Annual fixed costs	$12,000,000	$11,000,000
Initial Investment	$166,000,000	$145,000,000

   a. At a volume of 800,000 units per year for a ten-year period, which facility has the lower cost?

   b. At what annual volume do these facilities have equal costs? Once again, assume a ten-year period.

   c. Graph the results of Part b.

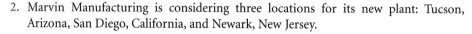

2. Marvin Manufacturing is considering three locations for its new plant: Tucson, Arizona, San Diego, California, and Newark, New Jersey.

	Tucson	San Diego	Newark
Variable costs	$1.60/unit	$1.45/unit	$1.50/unit
Annual fixed costs	$1,800,000	$2,000,000	$1,900,000
Initial investment	$14,000,000	$16,000,000	$15,000,000

   a. At a volume of 2 million units per year for a five-year period, which facility has the lowest cost?

   b. At what annual volume or volumes do these facilities have equal costs? Once again, assume a five-year period. (Hint: It is helpful to graph each of the cost equations before solving for the point where the costs are equal.)

3. Intensive Technologies does consulting for the aerospace industry. Corporate head-quarters is located in Washington, D.C., but the organization is planning to relocate on the West Coast. It is considering three sites: Seattle, Washington, Portland, Oregon, and Oakland, California. The full costs of operating at each site, which include initial investment, annual fixed costs, and variable costs, are approximately equal. A management team from Intensive Technologies has visited each city and has evaluated each site, using the following criteria. The evaluation uses a one-to-ten scale, with one being the best score. The criteria and the weight assigned to each were selected by top management.

	Weight	Oakland Score	Portland Score	Seattle Score
University research specializing in aerospace	50	4	2	2
Available pool of skilled engineers	50	4	3	2
Opportunity for advanced management education	40	2	3	3
Cultural activities	20	1	2	3
Recreational activities	20	2	4	3

a.   What is the weighted score for each city?

b.   Which city has the advantage in terms of the qualitative factors? Is this advantage significant?

c.   What is your recommendation to top management?

4.   Barrel City Health Care System is looking for a new location for its corporate headquarters. It is considering Atlanta, Georgia, and Danville, Illinois. The cities are rated from one to ten on each of the following factors, with ten the best score.

	Weight	Atlanta Score	Danville Score
Cultural activities	40	8	6
University research facilities	80	8	8
Union activities	60	8	4
Banking services	60	6	8
Available labor pool	20	6	8

a.   Determine the weighted scores for both cities.

b.   How can these scores be integrated with cost differences?

c.   Suppose the following costs apply:

	Atlanta	Danville
Operating costs	$1,400,000/year	$1,300,000/year
Initial investment	$22,000,000	$20,000,000

Over a ten-year period, Danville has a $3,000,000 advantage. To determine that, take the difference in operating costs per year, and multiply it by ten years. Then add the difference in initial investment. Under what circumstances might the company still choose Atlanta? How much would Barrel have to value each point of Atlanta's qualitative advantage to make it the new headquarters?

QUALITATIVE FACTOR IN LOCATION ANALYSIS

Many factors that cannot be measured in dollars should be considered in the location decision. The factors in the following list are often important.

LOCATION

Country _____

Distance in miles from:

Chicago _____	Los Angeles _____
Dallas _____	Memphis _____
Denver _____	Omaha _____
Kansas City _____	St. Louis _____

POPULATION

	2000	1990	1980
City	_____	_____	_____
Country	_____	_____	_____

MUNICIPAL SERVICES

Type of local government _____

Comprehensive city plan: Date completed _____

    Under way _____ Under consideration _____

City zoning ordinance in effect: Yes _____ No _____

County zoning ordinance in effect: Yes _____ No _____

Subdivision ordinance with design standards in effect: _____

Number of full-time fire department personnel: _____

Number of volunteer fire department personnel: _____

Fire insurance class: In city _____ Outside city _____

Number of full-time city police officers: _____

City engineer employed: Yes _____ No _____

Garbage service provided: Yes _____ No _____

Public library in city: Yes _____ No _____

EDUCATIONAL FACILITIES

Type	Number	Teachers	Enrollment	Grades
Elementary school	_____	_____	_____	_____
Junior high school	_____	_____	_____	_____
High school	_____	_____	_____	_____
Trade and technical school	_____	_____	_____	_____
Junior college	_____	_____	_____	_____
University	_____	_____	_____	_____

University research activity _____

_____

_____

COMMERCIAL SERVICES

Machine shop in city: Yes _____ No _____ Number _____

Tool-and-die service in city: Yes _____ No _____

Electric motor repair service in city: Yes _____   No _____
Type of newspaper in city: Daily _____   Weekly _____
Radio station(s):   Yes _____   No _____   Number _____

BANKING SERVICE

Number of banks in city _____
Assets of largest: $_____

TRANSPORTATION SERVICES

Train
    Community served by railroad(s):   Yes _____   No _____
    Distance to nearest loading point: _____ miles
    Number of freight train trips per day: _____
    Reciprocal switching available: Yes _____   No _____
    Piggyback ramp available: Yes _____   No _____
    Distance to nearest piggyback service: _____ miles
    Name(s) of railroad(s): _____
    _____

Motor carrier
    Highway bus service available: Yes _____   No _____
    Number of highways serving city: Federal _____   State _____
    Distance to nearest interstate interchange: _____ miles
    Number of motor freight carriers serving community: _____
Barge
    City adjoins navigable river: Yes _____   No _____
    Barge dock available: Yes _____   No _____
    Channel depth: _____ ft.
    Length of season: _____ mo.
Airplane
    Distance to nearest public airport: _____ miles
    Length of longest runway: _____ ft.
    Runway lighted: Yes _____   No _____
    Private aircraft storage available: Yes _____   No _____
    Private aircraft maintenance available: Yes _____   No _____
    Distance to nearest commercial air transportation: _____ miles
    Name(s) of airline(s) serving point: _____
    _____

Length of time goods in transit to:

City	Days by Railroad	Days by Motor Freight
Atlanta	_____	_____
Chicago	_____	_____
Cleveland	_____	_____
Dallas	_____	_____
Denver	_____	_____
Kansas City	_____	_____
Los Angeles	_____	_____
Memphis	_____	_____
Minneapolis	_____	_____
New Orleans	_____	_____
New York	_____	_____
St. Louis	_____	_____

UTILITIES

Water
    Water supplied by: Municipal _____ Private _____

    Name of supplier: _____

    Address: _____

    For rate information, contact: _____

    _____

    Source of city water: River(s) _____ Well(s) _____ Lake(s) or reservoir(s) _____

    Supply of river water available: _____ cu. ft./sec.

    Supply of lake or reservoir water: _____ gals.

    Water supply approved by State Board of Health: Yes _____ No _____

    Capacity of water plant: _____ gals./min.

    Capacity of water plant: _____ gals./day

    Average consumption: _____ gals./day

    Peak consumption: _____ gals./day

Sanitation
    Type of sewage treatment plant: _____

    Treatment plant certified by the State Board of Water Pollution: Yes _____ No _____

    Characteristics of waste treatment plant:

Measurement	*Capacity*	*Present Load*
Gallons per day	_____	_____
Population equivalent	_____	_____

Natural gas
    Natural gas service available: Yes _____ No _____

    Name: _____

    Address: _____

    _____

    For rate information, contact: _____

    _____

Electricity
    Suppliers: Municipal _____ Private _____ Co-op _____

    Name(s): _____

    _____

    Address(es): _____

    _____

    For rate information, contact: _____

    _____

LOCAL MANUFACTURING CHARACTERISTICS

Number of manufacturing plants in community: _____

Number of manufacturing plants with unions: _____

Number of manufacturing employees in community: _____

Strikes within last five years affecting 5 percent or more of the labor force: _____

Major manufacturers or other large employers in community: _____

Name of firm: _____

Employment: _____

Product(s) manufactured: _____

LABOR MARKET ANALYSIS

Date of last labor market survey: _____

Results of survey: _____

Estimated labor force available: _____

    This estimate can be documented: Yes _____ No _____

County labor data:
   Civilian work force (annual average): _____
   Unemployed: _____
   Unemployed as a percentage of work force: _____
   Total employment: _____
      Agricultural employment: _____
      Nonagricultural employment: _____
      Manufacturing employment: _____
      Nonmanufacturing employment: _____

HEALTH FACILITIES

Number of hospitals in community: _____
   Number of beds: _____
If no hospitals, distance to nearest facility: _____
Clinic in community: Yes _____   No _____
Medical personnel: MD(s) _____   DO(s) _____
Nurses: Registered _____   Practical _____

RECREATIONAL FACILITIES

Type of recreational facilities available in city or within ten miles:
   Public golf course(s) _____   Public park(s) _____
   Public tennis court(s) _____   Public swimming pool(s) _____
Country clubs available: Yes _____   No _____
Nearest public access to lake or river: _____ miles
Activities allowed:
   Swimming _____   Fishing _____
   Water skiing _____   Motor boating _____

LOCAL INDUSTRIAL DEVELOPMENT ORGANIZATION

Name of group: _____
Person to contact: _____
Address: _____
_____
Phone number:
   Home: _____
   Business: _____
   Area code: _____

CHAPTER 11

Facility Layout

LEARNING OBJECTIVES

After completing this chapter, you should be able to:

1. Illustrate the objectives of the layout decision for a continuous flow process, an assembly line, a batch process, a manufacturing cell, a flexible manufacturing system, and a job shop.

2. Explain the layout for a continuous flow process and why it is dominated by precedence relationships.

3. Explain the important issues in laying out an assembly line, and describe the need to balance workloads on an assembly line.

4. Describe the relationship between the capacity of an assembly line and its cycle time.

5. Balance a simple assembly line and understand the role of computers in assembly line balancing.

6. Explain the problems of motivating assembly-line workers and describe some possibilities for improving motivation.

7. Describe techniques for building families of parts used in manufacturing cells and flexible manufacturing systems.

8. Construct a model of the job shop layout problem and apply techniques for developing a layout.

9. Explain the role of computers in determining a job shop layout.

INTRODUCTION

In this chapter, we discuss facility layout for continuous flow, assembly line, batch, manufacturing cells, flexible manufacturing, and job shop processes. **Facility layout** is the arrangement of the work space. Broadly defined, it can involve questions at three levels of detail.

1. At the highest level, how should the departments or work groups be arranged? Which departments or groups should be adjacent, and which can be placed farther apart? For example, in a hospital, how close should the pediatrics department be to the X-ray department?

2. Next, within the departments or work groups, how should people, equipment, and storage be arranged? How large should the department be? Within an X-ray department, how much equipment should there be, and how should it be arranged? The department may need more than one machine, space for viewing X-rays, and storage.

3. Finally, how can the arrangement of each work space within a department be designed so that assigned tasks can be efficiently and effectively carried out? How should the workstation where the technician operates the machine be arranged? How should the space for viewing X-rays be designed for easy use by doctors and technicians?

These layout issues are all related. For example, the size of the facility is dependent on the size of each department, which, in turn, is dependent on the number of people, the amount of equipment, and the amount of storage space. The amount of space each person needs is a function of how well the individual's work space has been designed. It should be clear from this description that capacity and layout are related because the capacity a company is seeking to achieve determines the number of people and the amount of equipment used in its operations.

This chapter focuses on the first issue, arranging departments. However, the same concepts used for arranging departments can be applied to the layout within a department, which is available on the companion Web site, www. wiley.com/college/vonderembse. For example, within a department, the proximity of two pieces of equipment or two workers implies the same approach to managing spatial relations as positioning two departments. Proximity should be related to the level of interaction between the people or the equipment. The third issue, the arrangement of individual work space within a department, is addressed in the Web chapter on Job Design and Work Measurement.

Criteria for the Layout Decision

The objectives of facility layout are similar, regardless of whether the layout is for an office building, a steel mill, a hospital, or a ship. One objective is to provide convenient access between two groups or departments that interact heavily. It costs money to move people, information, and materials around a facility. Management would like to minimize that cost without reducing the organization's overall effectiveness.

In some cases, departments that depend on the same resource may have to be located physically close together even though they interact very little. This arrangement allows them to share expensive resources. For example, both shipping and receiving may require use of an overhead crane to load and unload heavy parts to railcars. Because both departments require access to the crane and the railcars, they are likely to be located close together even if they interact very little. In an office layout, two departments that interact very little may require access to expensive copying and printing capabilities that would be too expensive to duplicate.

In other cases, departments or functions that are potentially detrimental to one another should be separated to the extent possible. A sanding operation and a painting operation are not compatible because the grit from sanding may travel through the air and land on the fresh paint. These operations are likely to be physically separated unless special booths are built for painting.

In retail services operations, another dimension, the impact of layout on the customer, often dominates the layout decision. While layout cost and floor space utilization are important for discount retailers, customer access and convenience dominate the layout decision. Retailers like Wal-Mart, Meijer, and Kroger lay out their stores to make it easy for customers to find products they need. For upscale retailers like Victoria's Secret, layouts are conceived to entice customers to purchase high-profit margin items. These elements of the layout question are typically discussed in marketing textbooks and courses.

Overview of the Layout Question

The techniques and methods used to determine facility layout depend upon the process used in operations. Product-oriented layouts are used in continuous flow shops, assembly lines, batch operations, manufacturing cells, and flexible manufacturing systems to take advantage of a dominant product flow. In most cases, the layout is obvious once the production sequence is determined. Basing the facility layout on this flow allows the firm to reduce the cost of moving materials and people around the facility. In process-oriented layouts, products and people move around the facility in many different paths. Finding the layout that serves these different paths requires a different, more detailed, approach to facility layout. The methods and techniques for facility layout for each process type are discussed in the remainder of the chapter. A fixed-position layout, which is used for projects that make large one-of-a kind products, is discussed in the project management chapter. The following list provides some examples of companies for each process type.

Continuous flow shop
- *Sorting mail*—The U.S. Postal Service sorts millions of pieces of bulk mail daily.
- *Making paper*—Longview Fibre transforms trees into wood pulp, continuously.
- *Transaction processing*—Citibank processes checks, Amazon.com processes customer orders, the federal government processes FAFSA (financial aid forms).

Assembly lines
- *Automobiles*—DaimlerChrysler assembles automobiles.
- *Food preparation*—DiGiorno assembles frozen pizza for your supermarkets.
- *Microcomputers*—Gateway assembles personal computers.

Batch
- *Medicine*—Merck creates a variety of medicines in large batches using the same equipment.
- *Surgery*—Shouldice Hospital specializes in hernia surgery.
- *Lumber*—Weyerhaeuser cures lumber in specially design kilns (furnaces).

Manufacturing Cells and Flexible Manufacturing Systems
- *Metal forming operations*—Wyman-Gordon forges many different parts for the automotive industry.
- *Hospitals services*—Hospital wards group together patients with similar needs to improve service and lower costs

Job Shop
- *Offices*—Colleges of business strive to achieve a layout that locates colleagues with similar fields close together.
- *Medical services*—Emergency room layouts cope with a wide variety of medical problems.

CONTINUOUS FLOW PROCESSES

The layout for a continuous flow operation builds directly on the concept of minimizing the distance that people, information, and material move. An **activity matrix** for a continuous flow process is shown in Exhibit 11.1. This matrix organizes and displays the movement of people, parts, or other things between departments. The zeros in Exhibit 11.1 indicate no movements between those pairs of departments. The number ten represents ten items moving from one department to another. The items could be pieces of wood used to make furniture, stock purchase transactions, or even people moving from one point to another.

The matrix does not consider movements from department 1 to department 1, 2 to 2, and so on. These intradepartment moves would be considered as part of the layout within the department. As shown in the matrix in Exhibit 11.1, product movement follows the same sequence through the departments: 1–2–3–4–5. The flows between any other pair of departments or in any other sequence are zero. As a result, the layout that minimizes the costs of moving between departments is simple—it follows the product's sequence of operations. This is why a continuous flow process and assembly lines are said to have product-oriented layouts.

Even in cases where other minor product movement exists, the dominant flow will govern the layout. It is only when these other flows become significant that the process is no longer a continuous flow or an assembly line. When many different paths or sequences occur, the process takes on characteristics typical of a job shop.

Because the layout for continuous flow processes follows the product's sequence of operations, the technical aspects of the process selection ultimately dictate the layout. For example, when crude oil is refined to make various products, including gasoline, diesel fuel, kerosene, and heating oil, the process follows a sequence of steps. In the first step, distillation, crude oil is heated to 700 degrees F. A mixture of vapor and unvaporized oil passes from the heating furnace into a fractioning column that contains perforated trays. The vapor condenses at different trays, which means that different products come out of the column at different levels. Gasoline is lighter than heating oil and therefore condenses at a different (higher) level. In the next step, alteration, the remaining heavy oils, which have little economic value, are processed so their chemical structure is altered. These elements are recombined to make high-value products such as gasoline. In the final step, impurities, such as sulfur, are removed from the products. The layout of the oil refinery should follow the processing requirements so the equipment for distillation is close to the equipment for

EXHIBIT 11.1

Activity Matrix for Continuous Flow Process

		To Department				
		1	2	3	4	5
	1		10	0	0	0
	2	0		10	0	0
From Department	3	0	0		10	0
	4	0	0	0		10
	5	0	0	0	0	

alteration, which, in turn, is close to the equipment for purification. In this way, material-handling costs are reduced.

Continuous Flow Processes and Service Industries

Many continuous flow operations are found in the production of goods because many service operations lack the volume required to support the large fixed investment in facilities necessary for continuous flow operations. There are some notable exceptions, however. The U.S. Postal Service handles billions of pieces of correspondence with thousands of expensive and sophisticated sorting machines and handling systems. FedEx handles packages and mail in the same way.

Large banks also have continuous flow processes. Most customers see only the small branch operations, which tend to be tailored to the individual customer's needs and thus are more like job shop operations. But the central processing area is a continuous flow operation that can handle hundreds of thousands of transactions each day. Here, checks written against deposits in the bank are processed and the information entered into the computer system.

The approach to facility layout for handling mail or processing checks is similar to the approach to facility layout for making steel or refining oil. Once the sequence of operations is determined, the layout will follow.

ASSEMBLY LINES

An assembly line is designed to arrange various components into a final product that conforms to standards set in product design. The purpose of an assembly line is to divide complex tasks into small, easy-to-learn segments that can be repeated over and over. An assembly line usually consists of a series of **workstations** or **work centers** at which individuals perform these tasks on each product. Most assembly lines are designed to produce large volumes of one product that have limited options.

Knoxville Auto Equipment is a major producer of automotive speedometers, tachometers, fuel gauges, and the instrument panels that hold these items. About 75 percent of its business comes from contracts with the automakers for the assembled instrument panels. Exhibit 11.2 lists the task descriptions and the estimated times for completion, and Exhibit 11.3 shows the precedence diagram.

Knoxville has an order for 50,000 of these units for next year. The company usually works a standard forty-hour week for fifty weeks per year. During those fifty weeks, there are ten paid holidays. How should the line be laid out? How should the tasks be assigned? These questions will be addressed in the following sections.

Determining the Layout

Like the continuous flow process, the assembly line has a product structure or precedence relationships that describe each task to be performed. In the Knoxville example, the light bulbs in the instrument panel (Tasks 11–15) must be installed before the case can be put over the speedometer (Task 16). How long will each of these tasks take? It is necessary to have an estimate of the time required to perform each task so that reasonable estimates of production rate and capacity can be made.

EXHIBIT 11.2	Task Descriptions and Times for Instrument Panel Assembly				
Task	Description*	Time (Min.)	Task	Description*	Time (Min.)
1	Case to line	.08	22	Turn filter	.05
2	Neck gasket to speedometer	.07	23	Hi beam filter	.05
3	Clip to speedometer	.08	24	Spring to slider to case	.25
4	Printed circuit to case	.08	25	Fasten seat belt filter	.06
5	Label to case	.08	26	Temperature gauge	.10
6	Clip to case	.09	27	Cable	.22
7	Clip to case	.09	28	Pointer	.10
8	Clip to case	.09	29	Battery charge and fuel gauges	.12
9	Clip to case	.09	30	Screw	.07
10	Clip to case	.09	31	Screw	.07
11	Bulb to case	.07	32	Screw	.07
12	Bulb to case	.07	33	Tachometer	.10
13	Bulb to case	.07	34	Screw	.07
14	Bulb to case	.07	35	Screw	.07
15	Bulb to case	.07	36	Screw	.07
16	Case over speedometer	.08	37	Screw	.07
17	Grommet screw	.08	38	Screw	.07
18	Grommet screw	.07	39	Screw	.07
19	Case up	.07	40	Retainer	.09
20	Brake and oil filter	.06	41	Lens	.20
21	Turn filter	.05	42	Inspect	.50

*Tasks cannot be further split due to the spatial arrangement of equipment and inventory.

Objectives

There are two major objectives in laying out an assembly-line process. First, to lower material-handling costs, the line should be positioned for a continuous flow of assembled products. This objective can be achieved by following the precedence diagram and positioning workstations so that distance traveled is reduced to the lowest level compatible with efficient operations. It is similar to the continuous flow process, which also has a dominant flow.

Second, the assembly line should have balance in the same way that the continuous flow process has balance. That is, each work center or workstation in an assembly line should be assigned an equal amount of work. If this is not done, then the stations that have less work to do and thus are faster will wait for the stations that have more to do (the bottlenecks). An imbalance in the work assigned reduces capacity and increases costs.

Once the tasks are assigned to workstations by observing all precedence relationships, the first objective, lower material handling costs, can be achieved by sequencing workstations to minimize material movement. The second objective, assigning an equal amount of work to each station, requires further discussion. Consider the following mailing service problem.

EXHIBIT 11.3   Precedence Diagram for Instrument Panel Assembly

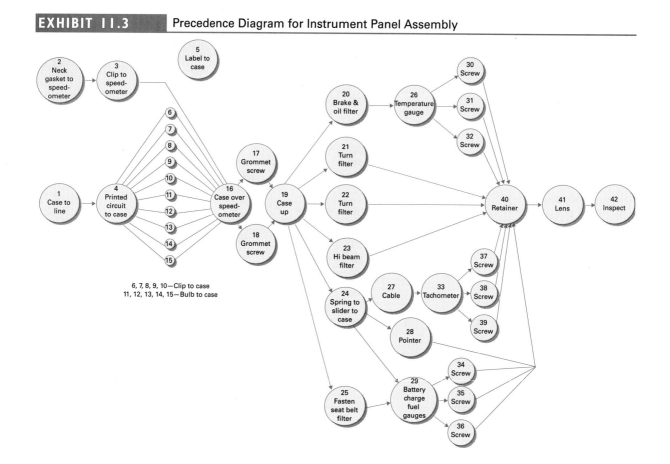

6, 7, 8, 9, 10—Clip to case
11, 12, 13, 14, 15—Bulb to case

PROBLEM   An organization uses computers and automation to process the large amounts of mail that are used in marketing campaigns to sell insurance or to raise money for charity. The time for completing each task, the precedence relationships, and the number of workstations are given. Assume that one person is assigned to each station. The times listed here are based on processing 1,000 pieces of mail contained in one packet.

This example demonstrates the impact on capacity and costs when an assembly line is improperly balanced.

Assembly-Line Work Stations	Precedence Diagram

Task	Description	Estimated Time (seconds)
A	Prepare for next packet	60
B	Prepare address labels	30
C	Sort material for stuffing	90
D	Apply address labels	45
E	Stuff envelopes	45
F	Seal envelopes and place in mailer	90
Total time required		360

To illustrate the impact of an unbalanced assembly line, we have deliberately assigned tasks to the stations so that the workload is uneven. Techniques for assigning tasks to workstations are discussed later.

	Workstation 1	Workstation 2	Workstation 3	Workstation 4
Tasks	A	B, C	D, E	F
Time	60	120	90	90

Results of the Assignment

How many seconds of work are required to assemble each packet? The sum of the estimated task times is 360 seconds. How much time is there between completed packets exiting the line? This time is determined by the station with the most task time assigned to it—in this case, workstation 2. After the line has produced the first packet, it will take 120 seconds for the next packet to exit the line because station 2 acts as a bottleneck, starving downstream stations and restricting flow from upstream stations. The 120-second time between completed packets will, thereafter, continue for each packet even though the last station takes only 90 seconds. The only way a packet can get to workstation 4 is to pass through station 2, and it takes 120 seconds to do all the tasks assigned at that station.

   Cycle time is the amount of time required to produce a unit (i.e., minutes per piece or seconds per piece). Cycle time is the reciprocal of the production rate. When viewed independently, each workstation has its own cycle time. Because station 2 has the longest station cycle time, its cycle time becomes the system cycle time for the entire assembly line. The **system cycle time** for the assembly line is the time between the nth unit (any unit) and the $n + 1$ unit (next unit) exiting the line when the bottleneck station is working to capacity. (When the term cycle time is used in reference to an assembly line, the authors are referring to system cycle time.)

The difference between the sum of the task times for the entire job (360 seconds) and the cycle time (120 seconds) is sometimes difficult to understand. Visualize the difference in this way. The sum of the task times would be like following a product from the beginning of the first station to the end of the last station. The trip takes 480 seconds, and it includes 360 seconds of work. Cycle time is like standing at the end of the line and watching consecutive products exit the line. A product exits the line every 120 seconds. These times are different because stations are working simultaneously on different units. Thus, station 1 is just starting a unit while station 3 is working on a different unit that is approximately half complete.

Calculating Production Rate from Cycle Time

There is a direct mathematical relationship between the cycle time in an assembly line and the line's production rate.

$$\text{Production rate} = \frac{1}{\text{cycle time}}$$

$$= \left(\frac{1}{120 \text{ sec./unit}}\right) 3{,}600 \text{ sec./hr.}$$

$$= 30 \text{ units/hr.}$$

Calculating Idle Time

It is important to know how much idle time there is at each workstation. The organization is paying for this time, but receiving no output. The sum of the idle times at each station is the idle time in the system.

In this system, there is a total of 120 seconds of idle time for each unit produced. Station 1 has only sixty seconds of work, and therefore the person at this station must wait another sixty seconds (idle time) before beginning work on the next unit. If the person continued to work without waiting, station 1's output would be sixty units per hour. This is twice the rate that the bottleneck station, station 2, can achieve. The unused thirty units per hour would accumulate as inventory. But this inventory buildup would not be acceptable because the bottleneck station could not catch up during normal operating time.

The bottleneck station, station 2, has no idle time. It allows only thirty units per hour to pass to stations 3 and 4. The present solution allows 120 seconds at each of these stations to complete ninety seconds' worth of work. Therefore, stations 3 and 4 each have thirty seconds of idle time.

Calculating Unit Labor Cost

What is the unit labor cost if each person at the station receives $20 per hour, including fringe benefits, for eight hours work? The total labor cost for eight hours is (8 hours/shift) (4 workers/shift) ($20/hour), or $640/shift. The total number of units produced is (30 units/hour) (8 hours/shift), or 240 units/shift. The unit cost is ($640/shift) (240 units/shift), or $2.67/unit.

A Balanced Assembly Line

We will now assign tasks so that the line is "perfectly" balanced—that is each station has the same task time. This is accomplished by shifting task B from station 2 to station 1. Note that the precedence relationships are not violated.

	Workstation 1	Workstation 2	Workstation 3	Workstation 4
Tasks	A, B	C	D, E	F
Time	90	90	90	90

The following table lists the total task time, cycle time, production rate, idle time, and unit cost for the unbalanced line and the balanced line.

	Unbalanced Line	Balanced Line
Total task time	360 seconds	360 seconds
Cycle time	120 seconds	90 seconds
Production rate	30 units/hr.	40 units/hr.
Idle time	120 seconds/unit	0
Unit cost	$2.67/unit	$2.00/unit

You can see that the balanced layout increases the system's capacity and reduces the idle time and the unit cost. It is far more efficient than the initial unbalanced layout.

Introduction to Balancing the Line

The importance of balancing the line is described in the preceding sections, but how is the balance achieved? There are many possibilities for achieving a balance, including some that are mathematically sophisticated. We will limit our discussion to a few possibilities that can easily be applied to even large line-balancing problems.

Remember that the objective of balancing is to assign tasks to workstations so that each station has a balanced load. For these discussions, we will assume that each workstation has only one person assigned to it. If a balanced workload is achieved, then the idle time at each workstation will be zero. The elements of the balancing equation are as follows:

C = cycle time for the balance
t_i = task time for element i, where $i = 1, ..., n$ tasks

$$\sum_{i=1}^{n} t_i = \quad \text{total task time required to assemble one unit}$$

N = theoretical minimum number of work stations
m = actual number of stations in the balance

There must be a target or goal in order to measure the efficiency of the balance. The theoretical minimum number of workstations (N) provides a gross measure of performance. It is the total task time divided by the cycle time, rounded up to the nearest whole number.

$$N = \frac{\sum_{i=1}^{n} t_i}{C}$$

Think of N as the minimum number of equal-sized time blocks required to cover the sum of the task time. The size of these blocks is the cycle time. Given a cycle time (C), a balance that achieves the minimum number of stations is the best solution in terms of minimizing worker idle time.

Selecting a Cycle Time Determines System Capacity

Balancing the line is a key factor in managing an assembly operation. The balance not only affects the plant layout and determines the unit labor cost but also determines the capacity of the system. Remember that the cycle time chosen for the balance is the reciprocal of the production rate. For an assembly line, this production rate is the maximum rate, and the maximum rate of production is the definition of capacity.

Cycle time and capacity are linked by the relationship illustrated in Exhibit 11.4. Capacity should be a function of the estimated customer demand. It is not necessary to set capacity exactly equal to demand. For example, in a fast-growing business, management may want to set capacity at a level higher than present demand to allow room for growth.

Are there theoretical or practical limits to the cycle time, or can any number be used? Theoretically, the cycle time must be equal to or less than the sum of all the task times (Σt_i). If the cycle time equals Σt_i then the solution to balancing the assembly line is trivial. All tasks are assigned to a single workstation, that is, one person does the entire assembly. The cycle time should be equal to or greater than the maximum of the individual task times (t_i). To achieve a cycle time that is less than the maximum of t_i, the longest task would have to be divided between two or more stations, or other special arrangements would have to be made. The following statement helps to define the theoretical limits on cycle time:

$$\text{Max.}(t_i) \leq \text{Cycle time} \leq \Sigma t_i$$

Practically speaking, when assembly lines are not automated, a cycle time of a few seconds or less is generally too short. Usually, too much time is lost when a worker has to start, stop, and move a unit to the next station every few seconds.

In some cases, it may be necessary or desirable to have more than one assembly line. The number of hours each assembly line operates per week is another important piece of information. By combining these two pieces of information with the desired capacity, it is possible to calculate the production rates for the assembly lines. Once the production rate is known, the cycle time can easily be calculated, as described in the previous section.

When there is only one assembly line, the following formulas can be used to calculate capacity. If hours worked per year is used in the formula, then annual capacity is calculated. In the equation, PR is the production rate, and H is the hours worked for the line.

$$\text{Capacity} = (PR)H$$

When cycle time (C) is substituted for PR, the equation becomes

$$\text{Capacity} = \frac{H}{C}$$

EXHIBIT 11.4

Relation of Capacity to Cycle Time

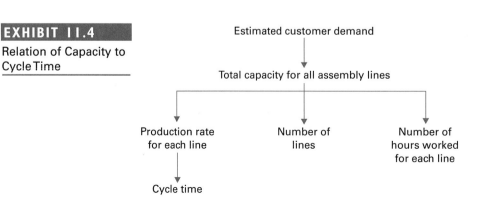

For situations with more than one assembly line, the capacity of the individual lines can be totaled.

If the required capacity and the available hours (H) are known, then the production rate can be calculated as follows:

$$PR = \frac{\text{capacity}}{H}$$

PROBLEM

Farmall produces irrigation systems for vegetable growers, distributing these systems primarily in the West and Southwest. Its Clarkson plant assembles a modulator to control water flow. This unit, which is used on most of Farmall's irrigation systems, has a forecasted demand of 15,000 units per month. Even though demand is highly seasonal, Farmall has decided to balance its assembly line to produce 400 units during a forty-hour week.

Periods of higher demand will be satisfied through overtime and from inventory built during nonpeak periods. Periods of lower demand will call for shorter work weeks and will allow for the annual two-week vacation and for a modest build up of inventory. The required cycle time is calculated as follows:

$$PR = \frac{\text{capacity}}{H}$$
$$= \frac{(400 \text{ units/wk.})}{(40 \text{ hrs./wk.})}$$
$$= 10 \text{ units/hr.}$$

Next, production rate is converted to cycle time as follows:

$$C = \frac{1}{PR}$$
$$= \left(\frac{1}{10 \text{ units/hr.}} \right) 60 \text{ min./hr.}$$
$$= 6 \text{ min./unit}$$

Now, let us assume that Farmall anticipates rapid growth and projects a need to produce 700 units per week. It is considering building another assembly line. What would the production rate per hour and the cycle time have to be if each line worked forty hours per week?

$$PR = \frac{\text{capacity}}{H}$$
$$= \frac{700 \text{ units/wk.}}{40 \text{ hr./wk} + 40 \text{ hr./wk.}}$$
$$= 8.75 \text{ units/hr.}$$

Next, convert production rate to cycle time.

$$C = \frac{1}{PR}$$
$$= \left(\frac{1}{8.75 \text{ units/hr.}} \right) 60 \text{ min./hr.}$$
$$= 6.86 \text{ min./unit}$$

This cycle time would be applied to each assembly line.

Techniques for Assembly-Line Balancing

How are tasks assigned to workstations to achieve a balanced load? Which tasks are available to be assigned at the first station? Consider the tasks involved in assembling medical care kits used in nursing homes. The medical kit comes in a small cardboard box with a lid and contains the basic items that any new patient would need when admitted to a nursing home. The precedence diagram in Exhibit 11.5 shows which task or tasks are available. In the example, only one task is initially available to be assigned to a worker on the assembly line. After task A is assigned, tasks B, C, and D are available to be assigned.

How is the task selected? Although one option would be to select a task at random by flipping a coin or rolling dice, this method would not necessarily lead to a good solution. What is needed is a systematic way of selecting a task that will move us closer to a good solution. Many articles and books discuss various decision rules. Automobile and appliance manufacturers spend millions of dollars investigating different methods of balancing their huge assembly lines. A few of the simplest choice rules are listed here:

- *Longest task time*—Select the task with the greatest task time that will fit in the remaining station time.
- *First in the list*—Select the task that has been in the list of tasks available for assignment for the longest time. This requires keeping track of when each task had all of its precedences assigned and entered the task-available list.
- *Most following tasks*—Select the task with the most tasks following. This is determined by counting those tasks on the precedence diagram.

	EXHIBIT 11.5			
	Medical Kit Example			

Task	Description	Estimated Time (seconds)	Preceding Task
A	Unfold cardboard container and place on assembly line	15	—
B	Place water pitcher in box	9	A
C	Place drinking glasses in box	7	A
D	Place bedpan in box	7	B, C, D
E	Insert cardboard separator	7	E
F	Fold dressing gown and place in box	18	
G	Place tissues in box	6	E
H	Place Band-Aids in box	7	E
I	Place lid on box	10	F, G, H
J	Shrink-wrap box	21	I
		107	

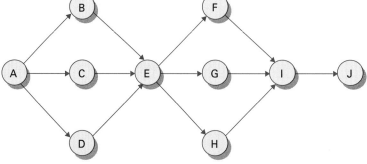

Each of these choice rules may lead to a different balance with different amounts of idle time (different labor efficiencies). Because it is possible for two tasks to tie based on any of these criteria, a tie-breaking method should be determined. For example, if the choice rule is longest-task-time first, another rule, such as first-in-the-list, could be used when two tasks have the same time. If there is still a tie, then the modeler could use another choice rule or select a task at random.

Do these rules produce good results? There is no guarantee that any of these rules will reveal the best answer or even a good answer. Research has been done on these and other rules, and the longest task time rule often performs well.

PROBLEM

Let's find a balance for the medical kit example in Exhibit 11.5. The facility manager has been directed to balance this single-line operation with one forty-hour shift. The line should produce 6,000 kits per week.

$$PR = \frac{\text{capacity}}{H}$$

$$= \frac{6{,}000 \text{ units/wk.}}{40 \text{ hrs./wk.}}$$

$$C = \frac{1}{PR}$$

$$= 150 \text{ units/hr.}$$

$$= \frac{1}{150 \text{ units/hr.}}$$

$$\left(\frac{1}{150 \text{ units/hr.}}\right) 3{,}600 \text{ sec./hr.}$$

$$= 24 \text{ sec./unit}$$

$$N = \frac{\sum_{i=1}^{n} t_i}{C}$$

$$= \frac{107 \text{ sec.}}{24 \text{ sec./station}}$$

$$= 4.46 \text{ or } 5.0 \text{ stations}$$

The preliminary calculations indicate that the cycle time needed to produce 6,000 kits per week is 24 seconds per unit. Given the data, the best balance will have five stations. Even if that can be achieved, the total system will have (5.0 – 4.46) stations, or 0.54 stations that are idle. This best balance will have (0.54 stations) (24 seconds/station), or 13 seconds of idle time for each unit produced. The only way to reduce this idle time is to reduce the sum of the task times (the numerator of N) or to change the cycle time (the denominator of N).

The balancing procedure is relatively simple, once the fundamentals of an assembly line are understood and the preliminary calculations have been made. Exhibit 11.6 shows a form that can be used to balance a line. The starting point is the list of tasks available to be scheduled. The longest-task-time rule is used to choose between these tasks because it is easy to use and often gives good results. In case of a tie, the first-in-the-list rule will be used to break it. If there still is a tie, a random choice will be made.

Task A is the only task available because of precedence, and it is assigned to the first station. The time remaining at the first station is 24 seconds minus 15 seconds, or 9 seconds. Once A is assigned, other tasks are available to be scheduled, including tasks B, C, and D. Of these tasks, B is the longest task and it will fit in the station time remaining so it is assigned to station 1. When the task time for B, 9 seconds, is subtracted from the time remaining at the first station, also 9 seconds, the time remaining at the first station is zero.

After task B is assigned, no new task can be entered into the available list because every other task required to assemble the medical kit can begin only after tasks C and D are complete. In selecting between tasks C and D, we observe that they each have the same task time. When the tie-breaking-rule, first-in-the-list, is invoked, these tasks tie again. In this case, we pick randomly, and task D is assigned to the second work station. The time remaining at station 2 is 17 seconds. After task D is assigned, only task C is available to be assigned, and it is assigned to the second workstation. At this point, 10 seconds are available at station 2. Now that tasks B, C, and D have all been assigned, task E is available. Task E, which requires 7 seconds, will fit in the station time remaining, which is 10 seconds. The result is that station 2 has 3 seconds remaining. Because no task is that small, this 3 seconds will become idle time. (This is based on the assumption that tasks cannot be split into two or more parts.) No more tasks can be assigned to station 2 so the process continues with station 3.

Once task E is assigned, tasks F, G, and H are available. The longest of these is task F, which is assigned to the station 3. This leaves only 6 seconds of time remaining at station 3. After task F is assigned, only tasks G and H remain. Task H is longer than task G but task H cannot be assigned to station 3 because it takes more than the 6 seconds remaining at station 3. We turn to task G, which can be assigned in the station time remaining. The rest of the balance is shown in Exhibit 11.6.

The resulting balance has five stations and a total of 13 seconds of idle time. The balance delay or percent idle time is calculated as follows:

$$\text{Balance delay (percent idle time)} = \frac{\text{idle time}}{\text{time available in the line}}(100)$$

$$= \frac{(m)(C) - \sum_{i=1}^{n} t_i}{(m)(C)}(100)$$

$$= \frac{(5\ \text{stations})(24\ \text{sec./stations}) - 107\ \text{sec.}}{(5\ \text{stations})(24\ \text{sec./station})}(100)$$

$$= 10.8\%$$

				Time Remaining
Task Available to be Scheduled	**Task Selected**	**Estimated Time (seconds)**	**Assigned to Station**	**at the Station (seconds)**
A	A	15	1	
B, C, D	B	9	1	0
C, D	D	7	2	
C	C	7	2	
E	E	7	2	3
F, G, H	F	18	3	
G, H	G	6	3	0
H	H	7	4	
I	I	10	4	7
J	J	21	5	3

EXHIBIT 11.6

Balanced Line for the Medical Kit Problem

Because the balance has the theoretical minimum number of workstations, achieving a better balance would require a change in the cycle time or the total task time. A change in the task time would involve engineering changes in the assembly procedure. A change in the cycle time would change the production rate, which would affect the balance between capacity and demand.

The Role of Computers in Balancing the Line

Balancing assembly lines by hand can be a long and tedious process when large problems are encountered. Consider the instrument panel example described earlier in this section. Although the process is simpler than the assembly of an air conditioner or a tractor, the number of tasks would make manual balancing difficult. Computer models have been developed that can perform assembly-line balancing. These models can keep track of all the details in the procedure and can be run quickly with a variety of cycle times and selection methods. In fact, one of the biggest advantages of computerized line balancing is being able to use more complicated procedures for selecting tasks from the available list.

The Computer Method of Sequencing Operations for Assembly Lines (COMSOAL) rapidly generates large numbers of feasible solutions that can quickly be evaluated to determine which one gives the best balance. Other computer-based solution procedures have been developed by industry to assist in the line-balancing process.

Motivation

Our discussion of assembly lines would not be complete without considering motivational problems. The repetitive nature of assembly lines often makes them boring places to work. The skills required to work on the line can easily be mastered, and any mental challenges to the job are quickly overcome. Historically, motivational problems often surfaced as high employee turnover and absenteeism, excessive use of drugs and alcohol, sabotage, and theft.

Solutions to motivational problems are not simple. How can a person be motivated to repeat the same task 350 to 400 times per shift for five days a week, fifty weeks a year? Most automotive assembly lines operate at about that pace. Money is not the answer. The average wage paid by the U.S. automakers is higher than the average wage paid by the Japanese automaker with facilities in the United States. In most cases, the motivation of the U.S. workers in the Japanese transplants is as high or higher than the motivation of the U.S. workers in U.S. facilities.

This increased motivation of assembly-line employees seems to be due to the environment of mutual respect and understanding that is developing between management and labor. It is critical for organizations to appreciate their employees' intelligence. Employees should be encouraged to think about ways to solve problems related to their job and to improve plant operations. They should be asked to consider how quality and productivity can be improved and if there might be better methods of production.

Labor-management relationships are a key to effective use of employees in problem solving. At facilities where workers are involved in decision making and where management and labor work together toward common goals, productivity and quality improve. Workers willingly contribute to improving the product, the production process, and the efficiency of operations because they recognize that the benefit for them is long-term job security. Why should management move or close down a facility when it is competing at world-class levels in terms of productivity and quality?

Integrating Product Design and Automated Assembly

Whirlpool Corporation, Benton Harbor, Michigan, is designing for automated assembly. Whirlpool sells more than $4 billion annually in appliances and operates eighteen U.S. plants and seven plants in foreign countries. In the early 1980s, it found that its washing machines were becoming overpriced. The major problems were that the basic washer design had not been changed since the 1950s and that manual assembly was slow and costly.

Whirlpool's basic model was a high-quality product that was well received in the marketplace, but the top-loading outside cabinet was a major structural part on which other parts were hung. So the cabinet went in place at the beginning of the assembly line, and workers had to reach down through the openings to attach parts. This was slow and costly and did not lend itself to automated assembly.

Now, several years and $162 million later, its 1.5-million-square-foot Clyde, Ohio, plant is the largest washer-producing plant in the world. The lower cost and better quality that automation made possible, plus Whirlpool's good name and modern marketing, have raised the company's share of the market. The plant has increased output by 80 percent, while increasing employment from 2,400 to 3,700.

Whirlpool redesigned the washer for automated assembly. Most parts are attached to the inside of the frame. It is put together from the bottom up and is accessible from all sides. The cabinet goes on last and is held in place by only a few screws. This helps to hold down repair and warranty costs.

BATCH PROCESSING

To operate economically, continuous flow and assembly lines, which are both line flow processes, require large volumes of the same or closely related products. However, many products do not have enough volume to support such mass production. To maintain low costs at lower volumes, products with some variations are produced on the same set of equipment. This requirement needs equipment that is flexible enough to deal with the increased variations.

For example, Composite Container Corporation produces containers for frozen orange juice and lemonade concentrate. These containers, holding six, twelve, or eighteen ounces, are constructed from two ends punched from sheet metal and a cardboard tube. All three sizes are made on the same machine. The machine must be shut down for several hours when sizes are changed. Composite Container's major advantage in using the same machine for all three sizes is to increase equipment utilization and to reduce product costs so the organization can remain competitive as a supplier to the frozen concentrate industry.

What principles guide the layout in batch operations? Efforts should be directed at (1) combining products with similar processing requirements (those that use the same equipment in approximately the same way) and (2) using the same or a similar sequence of operations. Capturing the same sequence and building on it is such a strong idea because material-handling costs can quickly get out of hand when materials are delivered all around the facility. The keys to layout in batch processing are to find as much similarity among the products as possible and to increase the facility's flexibility to handle product variation so that variation in material movement is reduced. This concept is similar to the concept used in group technology to organize manufacturing cells and flexible manufacturing systems.

USING GROUP TECHNOLOGY TO ORGANIZE MANUFACTURING CELLS AND FLEXIBLE MANUFACTURING SYSTEMS

Group technology (GT) is an approach to manufacturing that is based on the idea of grouping similar parts into families, which leads to economies in the manufacturing cycle. In design, it enables firms to organize existing designs so they can be easily retrieved, and it encourages standardization of designs. In process planning, it enables firms to simplify product flow and to organize equipment. In production, it enables firms to achieve mass-production efficiency where product variety exists. How does group technology establish the families of parts needed to organize manufacturing cells and flexible manufacturing systems? Many different methods exist. We will discuss visual inspection, product flow analysis, and coding and classification.

Methods for Creating Families of Parts

Visual inspection, sometimes called **tacit judgment,** involves the visual review of design drawings and specifications for similarities. This fairly simple process can result in good families of parts if relatively few parts are involved.

Product flow analysis (PFA) uses process plans to form families of parts. From the process routing for a part, a list of machine codes is determined. The process routing is a description of how the part is to be processed and on which machine the processing will take place. For example, a part could be processed on machines 01, 03, and 05. The numbers merely designate particular machines or types of machine. Parts with identical machine codes are grouped into "packs" for further analysis. A pack might contain many different parts, but all the parts are processed on the same machines. All the parts in a pack will be in the same family of parts. However, a family of parts may include several packs that have similar, but not identical process routings.

EXAMPLE

The following example applies product flow analysis to a facility with five different types of machines. The process routings for the company's parts have been analyzed, and the parts have been grouped into six different packs. A number 1 at the intersection of a particular row and column indicates that the pack is processed on the machine. For example, all parts in pack D are processed on machines 01, 02, and 03.

Machine Code	A	B	C	D	E	F
			Packs			
01	1	—	1	1	—	—
02	1	1	—	1	—	1
03	—	1	1	1	1	—
04	—	—	—	—	1	1
05	—	1	—	—	1	1

The idea is to group packs with similar machining requirements together. This is usually done by shifting rows and columns so that the 1s are as close as possible to a diagonal line that runs from the upper left-hand corner of the matrix to the lower right-hand corner. The following matrix shows one possible solution. Computer programs have been written to do this with the large problems that are often encountered in real companies.

Machine Code	Packs					
	D	A	C	B	F	E
01	1	1	1	—	—	—
02	1	1	—	1	1	—
03	1	—	1	1	—	1
04	—	—	—	—	1	1
05	—	—	—	1	1	1

One family of parts could include packs D, A, and C and would be processed in a manufacturing cell or flexible manufacturing system that includes machines 01, 02, and 03. The other family of parts could include packs B, F, and E and would be processed in a manufacturing cell or flexible manufacturing system that includes machines 02, 03, 04, and 05. In machining operations, a company may have more than one machine of each machine code or type. If this organization does not have two of the same machines coded 02 and 03, then it will have to purchase additional equipment or share existing equipment.

Another method for determining families of parts is coding and classification. In a coding and classification scheme, each part is given a code, which can be twenty digits or more. The code defines size, shape, metal type, machining requirements, and other factors. These codes can then be quickly scanned by a computer to determine which parts are similar. There are many commercially available **coding and classification** schemes on the market, including Opitz, Brisch, MICLASS, and CODE developed in West Germany, the United Kingdom, the Netherlands, and the United States, respectively. Specialty codes have emerged to deal with unique problems in some organizations.

Once the families of parts are organized, the facility layout can be determined by following the dominant sequence of the family. In this way, material handling is simplified, and costs are reduced.

EXAMPLE

Quadrum Corporation has applied group technology to improve operations. The company manufactures parts for transmissions used in medium- and heavy-duty trucks. One of the parts it produces is a power input shaft for the transmission. This piece is the major component for taking the power from the engine and distributing it through the truck's transmission.

The market for these trucks is not large, there are many models and options to choose from, and Quadrum is not the only supplier. As a result, the demand for any one input shaft is not large enough to support production in a line flow process. In fact, demand for the part is spread over ninety different part numbers. Presently, production takes place in a job shop that produces other transmission parts. Parts travel from department to department, and significant work-in process inventory clogs the facility, Exhibit 11.7 shows the existing job shop layout. The facility has approximately 54,000 square feet.

Quadrum has applied group technology to the production problem and has consolidated the ninety parts into ten families. It is planning to pull equipment from the job shop and dedicate it to the production of these families. The proposed layout, shown in Exhibit 11.8, is greatly simplified and will enhance productivity. This new layout will require only 8,000 square feet, and the total distance that work in process will travel is only 550 feet, including the return trip to receiving. This is clearly superior to the present job shop arrangement.

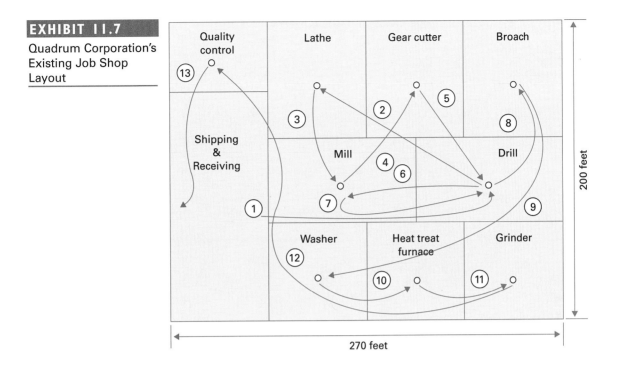

EXHIBIT 11.7

Quadrum Corporation's Existing Job Shop Layout

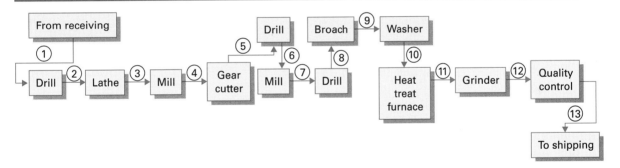

EXHIBIT 11.8   Quadrum Corporation's Proposed Layout for Transmission Parts

JOB SHOPS

Use of job shops should be limited to cases where the volumes are so low and the differences between products are so great that line flow processes, batching, and cellular manufacturing are not feasible. The techniques discussed here apply equally well to laying out a hospital clinic, government offices, an automotive repair facility, and a manufacturing plant.

The first step in approaching the job shop layout problem is to understand the fundamental difference between the job shop and the line flow processes. In a line flow, the movement of product is clearly defined. Exhibit 11.9 illustrates the point by showing an activity matrix for the line flow. In this case, 100 units of product are produced and move methodically through the work-stations (departments). As discussed earlier, the layout follows this dominant flow.

EXHIBIT 11.9

Activity Matrices for a
Dominant and a
Random Product Flow

Dominant Product Flow for Line Flow Process

		To Department					
		A	B	C	D	E	F
From Department	A		100	0	0	0	0
	B	0		100	10	0	0
	C	0	0		100	0	0
	D	0	0	0		100	0
	E	0	0	0	0		100
	F	0	0	0	0	0	

Random Flow for Job Shop

		To Department					
		A	B	C	D	E	F
From Department	A		20	20	20	20	20
	B	20		20	20	20	20
	C	20	20		20	20	20
	D	20	20	20		20	20
	E	20	20	20	20		20
	F	20	20	20	20	20	

The number in each cell of the matrices represents the number of units
moved from one department to another.

Now, consider the case at the other extreme. Here, the flow is random. This means that the chance (probability) of a unit in one department moving to any other department is equal for all possible departments. If the activity matrix for a facility is random, such as the one displayed in the lower half of Exhibit 11.9, then it makes little difference what the layout is. All departments interact equally, so one layout seems to be as good as another.

Fortunately, in most real job shop problems, the product flow is not completely random. Typically, the activity matrix would look like the one shown in Exhibit 11.10 for the offices and laboratories of the Rieselinger Research Institute. Although a dominant pattern is not as apparent as it would be in a line flow process, a pattern can be found. Finding this hidden pattern and using it to determine the layout should give a better solution than simply guessing at the layout.

EXHIBIT 11.10

Activity Matrix for the
Rieslinger Research
Institute

To Department

From Department	A	B	C	D	E	F
A		15	35	20	40	50
B	10		20	20	50	10
C	15	0		40	40	20
D	10	15	30		10	10
E	30	0	40	10		10
F	50	20	0	0	30	

(Trips measured in average number per day)

A Executive offices
B Stress laboratory
C Group dynamics laboratory
D Research report writing offices
E Marketing offices
F Word processing and mail room

Finding the Pattern and Determining the Layout

In order to model the layout question in a job shop and find the hidden pattern, the objective of the layout should be well defined. If significant amounts of supplies, materials, people, and information are transferred between two departments, then it is logical to conclude that they should be adjacent, provided other factors are equal. The amount of activity between two departments can be measured and considered directly in the layout. The distance between any two operations can be measured and the cost per unit distance determined.

Objectives

Now it is possible to evaluate any layout by multiplying the activity level by the distance by the cost per unit distance. The objective is to minimize the cost of movement between departments. The following model uses all department pairs except for $i = j$. Such movements would be within a department.

$$\text{Objective function} = \text{minimize} \sum_{i=1}^{n} \sum_{j=1}^{n} A_{ij} D_{ij} C_{ij} \text{ for all } i \neq j \qquad (11.1)$$

A_{ij} = the activity level from department i to department j, $i = 1, ..., n$, and $j = 1, ..., n$, where n is the number of departments
D_{ij} = the distance from department i to department j
C_{ij} = the cost per unit distance from department i to department j

The purpose of applying the model is to minimize the cost of moving people, products, and information among departments or work centers. Before using this model, the following information must be collected:

1. Activity data.

- ■ If this is an existing facility, records of past jobs and the movements between departments should be available.
- ■ If records do not exist, the present set of jobs and future jobs can be used to build the activity matrix.
- ■ If it is a new facility, estimates of the activity levels can be generated from the types of jobs expected in the facility.
- ■ What-if analysis can be done by changing the activity levels to reflect a different mix of jobs.

2. Estimates of the distance between all departments. To achieve these measurements, an initial layout of the facility is determined by the model builder.
   - ■ If an existing building is to be used, the analyst should work with a drawing that is to scale.
   - ■ If a new building is to be constructed, the analyst can work without boundaries to determine the building's shape. Still, working to scale is important.

3. Estimates of the costs per unit distance traveled.
   - ■ Estimates of transportation costs can usually be made from data available in accounting records.
   - ■ If they cannot be, there are at least two options for the analyst. First, information from other similar operations can be used to estimate costs. Second, the cost per unit distance can be assumed to be equal for all trips between departments. This is a very reasonable assumption if no other information is available.

Technique for Determining the Layout

The previous section defined the objective that management is trying to achieve in a job shop layout. How can the objectives of minimizing handling and transportation costs be achieved? One approach would be to evaluate every possible layout and pick the best one. However, like the assembly-line balancing problem, there are usually too many possible layouts to make this approach feasible for a large problem, even with the fastest computers. Instead, management's efforts are usually aimed at finding a "good" solution.

The following outlines the steps of such a procedure. These steps will be discussed in the next several sections.

Step 1.   Determine a feasible initial solution.

Step 2.   Evaluate the new solution(s), and keep the best one. Is the solution satisfactory? If so, stop. Otherwise, continue with Step 3.

Step 3.   Change the present solution in an effort to find an improved solution. Return to Step 2.

Our analysis will be based on the problem described in Exhibit 11.10.

Finding an Initial Layout   Finding an initial layout is a very important and difficult step. It is important because the small amount of time spent finding a "good" initial solution can greatly reduce the amount of work necessary in later steps. It is difficult because of the large number of options that should be considered. What happens if the departments are different sizes? How could the departments be shaped? A 1,000-square-foot department could be approximately 31.5 by 31.5 feet, 50 by 20 feet, 40 by 25 feet, or oddly shaped (see Exhibit 11.11).

EXHIBIT 11.11

Department Shape

31.5 feet by 31.5 feet   50 feet by 20 feet   25 feet by 40 feet   L-shaped

The designer of a new building must consider many different building shapes. What about multiple stories? Because the layout question is complex and full coverage cannot be given in an introductory course, we will make some simplifying assumptions. (Remember that models are used to simplify a complex problem, while retaining the key variables and relationships.) We will assume that an organization has a new facility with departments of equal size and shape. This gives us the freedom to arrange the departments in a wide variety of ways and to switch any department pair without affecting the positioning of the other departments. Exhibit 11.12 displays the layout for the problem described in Exhibit 11.10.

To complete the initial solution, one department is assigned to each of the six spaces. If the "goodness" of the initial solution is not important, the departments can be assigned in any way. Let's investigate a quick way of finding a good initial solution.

The Adjacent-Department Method   The adjacent-department method assumes that the cost per unit distance is equal for all trips, so that cost is not a factor. It also assumes that departments can be categorized as adjacent, one department away, two departments away, and so on. Thus, the distance between departments can be assigned as 0, 1, 2, and so on. This simplifying assumption permits the user to make quick judgments about the positioning of departments and to make relatively few calculations. This method is not as precise as the model described by equation 3.3, but it should give us a good initial solution.

To begin, add the return trips together so that the trips from A to B and B to A total 25, the trips from A to C and C to A total 50, and so on. This will simplify the calculations by cutting the number of cells in half. We can do this because the cost per unit distance has been assumed to be equal for all trips. Exhibit 11.13 contains the recalculated activity levels for the problem in Exhibit 11.10.

Now, we can begin to assign the departments to positions in the layout. The ranked activity levels shown in Exhibit 11.14 indicate that departments D and F have the least interaction and should be placed far apart, and that A and F have the highest interaction level. Exhibit 11.15 shows the layout to this point. Department A could have been located above F rather than to the left of F. Try the problem using this choice, and see if you achieve a better initial solution.

EXHIBIT 11.12

Facility Layout for Equally Sized Departments

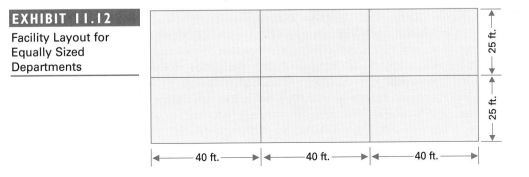

EXHIBIT 11.13

Job Shop Activity Matrix Representing Trips Between Departments Restated from Exhibit 11.10

		A	B	C	D	E	F
	A		25	50	30	70	100
	B			20	35	50	30
From Department	C				70	80	20
	D					20	10
	E						40
	F						

To Department

EXHIBIT 11.14

Ranked Activity Levels

Department Pair	Activity Level
A–F	100
C–E	80
A–E	70
C–D	70
A–C	50
B–E	50
E–F	40
B–D	35
A–D	30
B–F	30
A–B	25
B–C	20
C–F	20
D–E	20
D–F	10

EXHIBIT 11.15

Partial Layout

D	A	F

EXHIBIT 11.16

Layout

B	C	E
D	A	F

We can see from the ranked activity levels in Exhibit 11.14 that departments D and E also have limited interaction and should not be adjacent. Departments C and E have the second highest level of interaction. Consequently, we add departments C and E to the layout. This leaves the position of department B set by default. The resulting layout is shown in Exhibit 11.16.

How good is this solution? According to the method of assigning distances as 0, 1, 2, and so on, adjacent departments are given a 0 distance. Departments that are separated by another department are assigned a distance of 1. The value of the solution measured in trips between nonadjacent departments is 110, as shown in Exhibit 11.17. The smaller the number of trips between nonadjacent departments, the better the solution. All other department pairs are considered adjacent and thus have a distance factor of 0. This analysis treats such department pairs as A–C and C–F as adjacent. Although this simplifying assumption does make the model easier to work with, it may reduce its accuracy. For small problems like the one used in this example, this procedure will often yield a good final solution.

We could continue with the adjacent-department method to improve the initial solution. Instead, let's take the solution we have found so far and consider distances and costs.

Evaluating the Solution How good is the solution if actual distance and cost information are used? Using the initial solution displayed in Exhibit 11.16, it is possible to obtain distances from the center of each department to the center of all other departments. Exhibit 11.18 shows the layout with the center of each department plotted. The distances displayed in Exhibit 11.19 can be determined in two ways. First, if the departments and department centers are drawn to scale, the distances can be measured directly from the drawing. Second, because the departments are equally sized and organized into rows and columns, they can be easily calculated. For example, the distance from department B to department C is 40 feet because the center of each department must be 20 feet from the boundary. The distance from department A to department B can be found by applying the Pythagorean theorem. The line from A to B is the hypotenuse of a right triangle defined by the points A, B, and D.

$$(\text{Distance A to B})^2 = (\text{Distance B to D})^2 + (\text{Distance A to D})^2$$
$$\text{Distance A to B} = \sqrt{25^2 + 40^2}$$
$$= 47.2$$

Other schemes can be used for measuring distance if they more accurately represent reality or are easier to work with. This scheme is used because it is typical of the method used by computer-based procedures.

Exhibit 11.19 lists the cost per unit distance for each department along with the activity level and the distance. In the case where cost per unit distance is the same for all departments, the cost column can be bypassed by setting all values equal to 1. The activity level is multiplied by the cost per unit distance and then by the distance for each department. These values are summed to give the result for equation 11.1. Each new solution will be evaluated in this way, and the lowest value will indicate which solution is the "best." The

EXHIBIT 11.17			
Evaluation			

Department Pair	Activity Level (Aij)	Distance (Dij)	(A)(D)
B–E	50	1	50
B–F	30	1	30
D–E	20	1	20
D–F	10	1	10
			110

EXHIBIT 11.18

Facility Layout for Equally Sized Departments

EXHIBIT 11.19

Value of Layout

Department Pair	Activity Level (A_{ij})	Cost (C_{ij})	$(A)(C)$	Distance (D_{ij})	$(A)(C)(D)$
A–B	25	1 $/ft.	25	47.2	1,180
A–C	50	1	50	25	1,250
A–D	30	1.5	45	40	1,800
A–E	70	1	70	47.2	3,304
A–F	100	1	100	40	4,000
B–C	20	2	40	40	1,600
B–D	35	1	35	25	875
B–E	50	2	100	80	8,000
B–F	30	1	30	83.8	2,514
C–D	70	1	70	47.2	3,304
C–E	80	1	80	40	3,200
C–F	20	1.5	30	47.2	1,416
D–E	20	2	40	83.8	3,352
D–F	10	1	10	80	800
E–F	40	1	40	25	1,000
					37,595

absolute value of the number is not important, but how it compares with other solutions is important.

Generating a Better Solution   An initial solution and the value of that initial solution have been determined. The next task is to find a way to improve on the 37,595 figure shown in Exhibit 11.19. If we had unlimited time and patience, we could make many changes in the departments' locations and evaluate all the solutions, using a computer. To find a better solution when solving the problem by hand, we can examine the $(A)(C)(D)[(Activity)(Cost)(Distance)]$ column in Exhibit 11.19. We can try to find a large $(A)(C)(D)$ value for a department pair, and see if a switch can be made that will significantly reduce this value.

In this problem, the largest $(A)(C)(D)$ value is 8,000 units. This value is caused by one of the largest $(A)(C)$s, 100, moving nearly the greatest distance, 80 feet. To find a better solution, we switch departments C and E, as shown in Exhibit 11.20. The recalculated $(A)(C)(D)$ values are shown in Exhibit 11.21. The new value is 36,071, which is lower than the initial solution. This process is continued until the solution is satisfactory.

Stopping Rules   Stopping rules are more difficult to discuss in an introductory text because much theoretical work is required before full understanding can be achieved. The problem is to determine how good the present solution is when compared with the optimal solution. It is difficult to know when the solution is getting close to the optimal. In manually solved problems, there are two questions to ask. Have a significant number of attempts been made? Are improvements in the solution getting smaller and smaller? If the answer to both of these questions is yes, then consider stopping. Stopping rules for computer-based solutions are easier to define and will be discussed in a later section.

Modeling Layouts with Departments of Unequal Size   The mechanics of modeling layouts are largely unaffected by the size and shape of the departments. The only substantial change lies in how to arrive at an initial layout and then to revise this layout once a switch has been made. Two approaches are possible. The first is to draw the layouts to scale and then measure distances from center to center, using a ruler. The scale does not matter

EXHIBIT 11.20

Revised Facility Layout for Equally Sized Departments

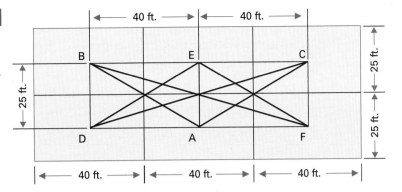

EXHIBIT 11.21

Value of Revised Layout

Department Pair	Activity Level (A_{ij})	Cost (C_{ij})	$(A)(C)$	Distance (D_{ij})	$(A)(C)(D)$
A–B	25	1 $/ft.	25	47.2	1,180
A–C	50	1	50	47.2	2,360
A–D	30	1.5	45	40	1,800
A–E	70	1	70	25	1,750
A–F	100	1	100	40	4,000
B–C	20	2	40	80	3,200
B–D	35	1	35	25	875
B–E	50	2	100	40	4,000
B–F	30	1	30	83.8	2,514
C–D	70	1	70	83.8	5,866
C–E	80	1	80	40	3,200
C–F	20	1.5	30	25	750
D–E	20	2	40	47.2	1,888
D–F	10	1	10	80	800
E–F	40	1	40	47.2	1,888
					36,071

because the absolute value of (A)(C)(D) is not important. Only the relative values are important, so in this case it makes no difference whether the measurements are in feet or in inches. The second approach is to cut pieces of paper to scale and quickly and easily move them around to make new layouts. Even if the edges of two departments overlap somewhat, this approach gives an accurate enough layout. Once the departments are in place, a ruler can again be used to measure distance between departments.

The Role of Computers in Job Shop Layout

Solving the job shop layout problem can be time-consuming and tedious. Several computer procedures exist for assisting with the layout. Computerized Relative Allocation of Facilities Technique (CRAFT) was developed by Buffa and Armour. It works much like the procedure described in the previous section. The user supplies an initial layout, an activity level matrix, and cost information. If certain departments must be located together to share a key resource, this can be specified. If departments cannot be adjacent, this can also be specified.

These computer procedures can calculate many alternatives very quickly. CRAFT reduces the cost by switching all department pairs and calculating values for (A)(C)(D) for each alternative. The lowest-cost alternative is selected for further analysis, and the switching of pairs continues.

Although the stopping rules for computer-based procedures are still somewhat arbitrary, they are easier to implement than those for a manual procedure. The brute power and speed of the computer allow it to investigate quickly far more alternatives than can be reasonably done by hand. The following approaches can be considered:

1. Specify a certain amount of computer time, and use the best solution found.
2. Allow the model to perform the switching of pairs only a certain number of times.
3. Specify an increment of improvement to be achieved with each evaluation. If this is not achieved, the procedure will end. For example, one could specify that at least a 2 percent reduction from the last solution must be achieved or the search ends.
4. Combine some of these rules. For example, the procedure can stop after a certain amount of time or after a specified number of switches, whichever is lower.

Other computer-based procedures, such as Computerized Facility Design (COFAD), Plant Layout Analysis and Evaluation Technique (PLANET), Computerized Relationship Layout Planning (CORELAP), and Automated Layout Design Programs (ALDEP), are also available. These procedures attempt to maximize nearness ratings. However, solutions generated by these computer models are not guaranteed to be optimal.

Systematic Layout Planning

In some cases, managers may want to summarize nearness on a subjective scale with factors other than activity levels and costs. **Systematic layout planning (SLP)** involves using the codes and matrix shown in Exhibit 11.22 to arrive at an appropriate layout.

We begin the solution procedure by positioning department pairs that are categorized as absolutely necessary and those that are categorized as undesirable. Once these pairs are positioned, it is possible to work on the very important, important, and somewhat important categories to locate the remaining departments in the layout. Exhibit 11.23 displays the layout using this approach. Departments R and F are positioned first. Then, A and T are positioned. Because T and D are undesirable, they are put at opposite ends of the facility. This gives the location of department W by default.

We can use a simple evaluation procedure to judge the effectiveness of this solution. First, we count the number of times each code appears in the matrix in Exhibit 11.22. Next, we count the number of times each condition is satisfied. For codes a, e, i, and o to be satisfied, the departments must be adjacent, as departments A and R are, or diagonally opposite, as A and W are. Any location satisfies code u because the relative location of that pair of departments is unimportant. Separation by one or more departments satisfies code x.

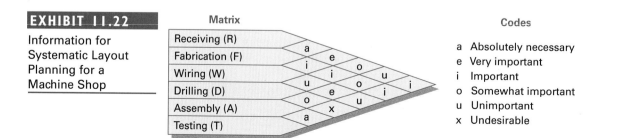

EXHIBIT 11.22

Information for Systematic Layout Planning for a Machine Shop

Matrix		Codes

Receiving (R)
Fabrication (F)
Wiring (W)
Drilling (D)
Assembly (A)
Testing (T)

a Absolutely necessary
e Very important
i Important
o Somewhat important
u Unimportant
x Undesirable

EXHIBIT 11.23

Solution and
Evaluation of Machine
Shop Layout

A	R	F
T	W	D

Evaluation codes	Number of Appearances in Matrix	Number of Times Satisfied in Layout	Percentage Satisfied
a	2	2	100%
e	2	2	100
i	4	3	75
o	3	1	33
u	3	3	100
x	1	1	100

The percentage satisfied column in Exhibit 11.23 indicates that the proposed solution is effective at meeting the nearness codes. This approach works well on problems with relatively few departments.

USING LAYOUT FOR COMPETITIVE ADVANTAGE

The impact of a good layout on an organization's performance may not be as obvious as good product design skills or superior capacity planning. The effects of layout are subtle, yet important. Efficient layouts reduce unnecessary material handling. Good layouts help to maintain low costs, which is a critical part of building and maintaining market share in a global environment. Good layouts also keep product flowing through the facility, which is important for providing good customer service. A facility choked with inventory is more likely to damage products and lose customers' orders.

Layout decisions should be made only after consideration of the long-term impact on the overall facility. Managers should ask themselves how organizational performance will be affected by a proposed change in layout. How will costs, as well as quality and delivery time to the customers, be affected? For example, an inefficient layout with many material movements may cause delays in processing because the transport system is overloaded. This problem can cause unnecessary idle time for equipment as departments wait for the next batch of products. It could also delay customer shipments.

If a change is made in layout, how will future options be affected? Will this change increase opportunities for making layout improvements, or will some opportunities be lost? Individual layout decisions may not seem important, but when added together over time, these decisions can be powerful determinants of an organization's success in the global marketplace.

EXAMPLE

In manufacturing, the inefficiencies of poor layouts surface as many other problems. The most obvious of these is a dramatic increase in inventory and material-handling costs because product flows are jumbled and discontinuous. Dell Computer has carefully organized its facility layout so that it can quickly and efficiently assemble personal computers.

In service operations like Pacific Bell, management costs are a substantial part of total costs. By paying careful attention to office layout, the company is able to get the most from its employees. In addition to office layout, the use of telecommunication technology helps to speed the flow of information and ideas between people.

SUMMARY

- Facility layout is based on easy access between departments or groups of people that interact heavily.

- Layouts for continuous flow processes are determined by the dominant product flow. The primary goal is to reduce material handling.

- Assembly-line layouts also attempt to reduce material handling. The assembly-line balancing procedure attempts to equalize the work assigned to each workstation, determines staffing levels, and sets the capacity of the line.

- Batch processing requires building parts in families with similar characteristics. This is necessary because the volume of a single product is not sufficient to support a dedicated system.

- Group technology involves building volume by combining parts with similar processing requirements. It is the basis for establishing manufacturing cells and flexible manufacturing systems.

- In a job shop, processes are usually grouped by departments because no product or group of products has sufficient volume to justify a layout with a single dominant product flow. Finding an effective layout requires working with activity levels between departments.

 Visit our dynamic Web site, http://www.wiley.com/college/vonderembse, for extended chapter material, solved problems, mini-cases, computer software, and Web links.

KEY TERMS

activity matrix	product flow analysis (PFA)	tacit judgment
coding and classification	systematic layout planning	visual inspection
cycle time	(SLP)	work centers
facility layout	system cycle time	workstations

URLS

Whirlpool: www.whirlpool.com

Wal-Mart: www.walmart.com

Sears: www.sears.com

Kroger: www.kroger.com

QUESTIONS

1. What is facility layout? What objectives does an organization try to achieve with facility layout?

2. Discuss the differences and similarities in the objectives of the layout for a continuous flow process, an assembly line, a batch process, and a job shop.

3. Briefly describe how to determine the layout for a continuous flow process.

4. Explain the significance of precedence relationships in determining an assembly-line layout.

5. What are the objectives of balancing an assembly line?

6. How does the cycle time used in balancing the line determine the capacity of the line?

7. What role do computers play in assembly-line balancing?

8. Motivation of assembly-line workers has been and will continue to be a problem. Describe some ways to address this issue.

9. Batch processing depends on combining several similar products that require the same or similar processing. How does this help management determine the facility layout?

10. Flexible manufacturing systems are an effort to produce products with greater variability on the same set of equipment with minimal changeover time. How can group technology help in this process?

11. Describe job shop layout. How is it different from the approach to assembly-line balancing?

12. Describe the solution procedure for job shop layout.

13. What role do computers play in job shop layout?

14. How can layout be used to gain a competitive advantage?

INTERNET QUESTIONS

15. Retail operations such as Wal-Mart, Sears, and Kroger spend considerable time and effort to find a layout that helps them to display more products and increase sales. How have these companies used layout to make shopping easier and more enjoyable? What can you find on the Internet? What can you learn from visiting these stores?

16. Access the Internet to get a view of the campus map and the long-term plan for campus expansion/development. What factors limit the future development of the campus? What appears to be the criteria used to organize and layout the campus?

17. The organization and layout of manufacturing facilities are critical to their success. What are the major benefits associated with layouts. Find some examples that help you to make these points.

PROBLEMS

1. Managers at Simpson Steel Machine Shop have analyzed all the parts the company produces for the purpose of building a manufacturing cell. Given the information below, recommend groupings for families of parts.

Machine Codes	Packs				
	A	B	C	D	E
21	1	—	1	—	—
22	—	1	—	—	1
23	—	1	—	1	—
24	1	—	—	—	—

2. For each of the following, determine whether the layout would be a product, a process, or a fixed-position layout:

a. The location of departments within a college or university

b. A hospital emergency room

c. A self-service cafeteria

d. Building a custom-designed home

e. A prefabricated factory-built home

 3. Firmtech has a projected customer demand that averages 480 items per working day. Firmtech's production has the following task times assigned to each station:

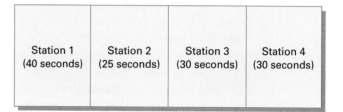

Station 1 (40 seconds)	Station 2 (25 seconds)	Station 3 (30 seconds)	Station 4 (30 seconds)

a. What is the cycle time? What is the production rate per hour?

b. What should the cycle time be to produce the 480 units per day demanded by customers if the production line works 7.5 hours per day?

c. If management chooses to run the line for 7.5 hours per day using a cycle time of forty seconds, what are the results?

d. How would you propose that management solve this problem?

4. Benskee Brokerage House has organized its stock transaction processing system into a line flow process with the following work assignments. To complete a transaction, steps A through F must be completed. The times listed are to process one transaction.

Work Station	Task Assigned	Task Times (Seconds)
1	A, B	40, 90
2	C	120
3	D	100
4	E, F	40, 40

a. Assuming that one person is assigned to each workstation, which is the bottleneck operation?

b. What is the hourly production rate for this operation?

c. If each clerical worker makes $11 per hour, what is the labor cost per transaction?

5. The following precedence diagram and times are given for the assembly of the pump on a washing machine. The times in seconds are listed by each activity.

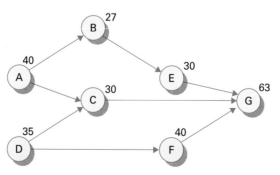

a.   Assuming a cycle time of seventy seconds, balance the assembly line using the longest-task-time rule. Break any ties using the first-in-the-list rule. Ties at the second level will be broken by picking at random.

b.   What is the balance delay for the pump?

c.   How many pumps can be built if the line is producing 7.25 hours per day?

6.   Pietro's Sandwich Shop has signed a contract to deliver a minimum of 2,000 and a maximum of 4,000 sandwiches to each home game of a major league baseball team. Even 2,000 is more than double its best sales day. The sandwiches need to be made each day. Pietro's does not want any holdovers. To make this many sandwiches, it will have to use an assembly line. Following are the precedence relationships and estimates of the time required for each step:

Task	Description	Time (Seconds)	Immediate Predecessors
A	Spread both buns with mayonnaise	15	—
B	Add green pepper	10	A
C	Add lettuce	5	A
D	Add meat	7	A
E	Add cheese	6	A
F	Add tomato	5	A
G	Wrap finished sandwich	10	B, C, D, E, F

Because most of the workers will be college students, the number of hours the assembly line can work is a variable. However, due to delivery-time constraints, management figures that nine hours of actual production time is all it can expect after allowing for breaks.

a.   What cycle time is required for Pietro's to deliver 4,000 sandwiches, using the full nine hours for production?

b.   Devise a plan that would allow Pietro's to build 4,000 sandwiches. Include in this plan the cycle time, the number of assembly lines, and the hours worked. Keep in mind that on some days it may only have to build 2,000 sandwiches.

c.   Balance the line using the cycle time determined in part b and the longest-task-time rule.

7.   Delphos Division has balanced its production line as shown here.

Work Station	Tasks Assigned	Task Times (Seconds)
1	A, B	40, 30
2	C	80
3	D, E	40, 40
4	F	60
5	G	50

a.   Which is the bottleneck operation, assuming that one person is assigned to each station?

b.   Assuming an eight-hour workday, what is the maximum daily output? What is the balance delay of the present balance?

c.   If each production worker makes $13 per hour, what is the labor cost per unit produced?

d.   If Delphos Division management assigned two people to stations 2 and 3, what would the maximum daily output become? What would happen to the unit cost of a product?

 8. Garfinkle Bank and Trust needs to balance its check- processing line. Following are the tasks required to completely process a check:

Task	Time (Seconds)	Immediate Predecessors
A	6	—
B	2	A
C	6	—
D	2	A
E	4	B, D
F	2	E
G	2	—
H	6	G
I	8	F, H

a.   If these tasks cannot be further divided, what is the minimum cycle time?

b.   Balance the line, using the longest-task-time rule and the cycle time determined in part a.

c.   Determine the percentage of idle time for the balance.

9. Cable Manufacturing's assembly line has the following requirements.

Task	Time (Seconds)	Immediate Predecessors
A	30	—
B	60	—
C	20	A, B
D	40	A
E	50	D
F	20	C
G	30	E, F
H	50	G

a.   What is the maximum daily output of the assembly line if it operates eight hours per day?

b.   Using the cycle time determined in part a, balance the assembly line, using the longest-task-time rule. What is the percentage of idle time for the line?

c.   Assuming the cycle time can be changed, how can the idle time percentage be reduced?

d.   Find a balance that is better than the one found in part b.

10. A small manufacturer has four departments. The following loads are transported between departments:

From	To			
	A	B	C	D
A	—	40	25	70
B	10	—	40	20
C	45	80	—	15
D	30	10	45	—

Assume that all departments are the same size and shape. Also, assume that material-handling costs per unit distance are the same for all trips. Calculate the distance between departments as described in the chapter. Use the following building layout:

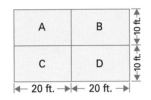

a. Evaluate the initial solution.

b. Try to find a better solution by switching department pairs. Evaluate the solution to see if it is better than the initial solution.

11. Quik-Grow Flower Shop is moving into new headquarters. The following information about the activity levels between departments has been collected over the past few months. This represents trips per day between departments.

From	To					
	A	B	C	D	E	F
A	—	0	100	40	20	10
B	—	—	0	70	10	0
C	—	—	—	140	50	60
D	—	—	—	—	80	10
E	—	—	—	—	—	20
F	—	—	—	—	—	—

New Building Design

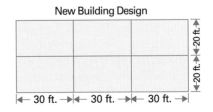

a. Using the adjacent-department method, find a good solution to the layout problem.

b. How do you know it is a good solution?

 12. Nashua Medical Center is considering a new location for department 4, Pediatrics. The center would like to switch it with department 5, Neurology. Activity levels are measured in movement of staff between departments.

| | | | To Department | | | |
From Department	1	2	3	4	5	6
1	—	35	50	100	20	0
2	—	—	30	20	10	15
3	—	—	—	10	30	0
4	—	—	—	—	10	15
5	—	—	—	—	—	15
6	—	—	—	—	—	—

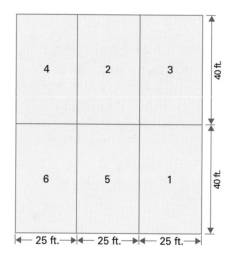

a. Given the layout and other information, what is the impact of this change? Use the adjacent-department criteria discussed in the text.

b. Can any further improvements be made? If so, what are they? If not, why not?

 13. Seeman Satellite Dish Company has a small manufacturing facility in Wyoming. Its present layout and an activity matrix showing trips per week between department pairs follow. The company wants to find an improved layout by trying to minimize activity level times distance. Cost per unit distance is assumed to be equal for all department pairs.

From Department	To Department					
	1	2	3	4	5	6
1	—	70	60	—	40	100
2	85	—	70	80	90	85
3	80	60	—	90	70	100
4	85	90	80	—	90	85
5	—	80	40	70	—	85
6	70	90	20	100	90	—

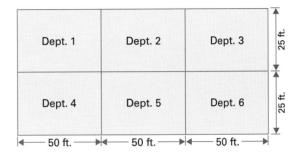

Improve on the present layout using the adjacent-department method.

14. Conway Cablevision Company is attempting to organize its new offices and has asked you to develop a new layout plan. The departments and the proposed building design are provided.

a. Develop the layout for Conway.

b. Evaluate the layout plan.

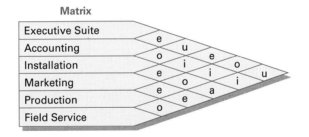

Code

a   Absolutely necessary
e   Very important
i   Important
o   Somewhat important
u   Unimportant
x   Undesirable

15. Medwich Urgent Care is building new facilities and has asked you to develop the layout. The departments and the proposed building design follow.

a.   Develop a layout for Medwich.

b.   Evaluate the layout.

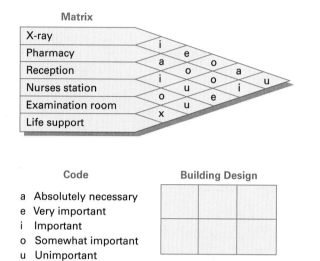

Matrix

- X-ray
- Pharmacy
- Reception
- Nurses station
- Examination room
- Life support

Code

a   Absolutely necessary
e   Very important
i   Important
o   Somewhat important
u   Unimportant
x   Undesirable

Building Design

16. Webster's Metal Working is attempting to organize its parts into families for production using a flexible manufacturing system. It has obtained the following information:

Machine Code	Packs								
	A	B	C	D	E	F	G	H	I
101	1	—	1	—	—	—	—	1	1
102	—	1	—	1	—	1	—	—	—
103	—	1	—	1	—	—	—	—	—
104	1	—	1	—	1	—	1	1	—
105	—	1	—	—	—	1	—	—	—
106	—	—	—	1	1	1	1	—	—
107	1	—	—	—	1	—	1	—	—

a.   How should Webster organize its families of parts?

b.   What are the advantages of organizing parts into families?

17. Bauer Drive Gear Company is preparing to balance its production lines located in Tipp City, Ohio; Warwick, North Dakota; and Breckenridge, Texas. Each line is to be balanced in the same way, and each has a 300-second cycle time.

Task	Time (Seconds)	Immediate Predecessors
A	300	—
B	125	A
C	100	A
D	200	B,F
E	250	C
F	50	—
G	225	D
H	125	A
I	175	H
J	150	E,G,I
K	225	I
L	75	H
M	100	K,L
N	175	M
O	150	M
P	125	N,O
Q	75	B

a.   Draw a precedence diagram for the tasks.

b.   What is the theoretical minimum number of workstations? How many units can Bauer produce if each line works forty hours per week?

c.   Balance the line using a 300-second cycle time and the longest-task-time rule

d.   What is the percentage of idle time for this balance?

e.   Rebalance the line with a 360-second cycle time. What effect does this have on Bauer's capacity and the percentage of idle time of the balance? Use the longest-task-time rule.

18. Gatsbee Electronics assembles microcomputers from top-quality components and sells them to students at about 60 percent of the price of a comparable computer purchased through a retail outlet. The following steps are required to assemble each microcomputer. The workers will be paid $9.00 per hour.

Task	Time (Minutes)	Immediate Predecessors
A	3	—
B	8	A
C	4	A
D	9	B, C
E	12	A
F	4	D, E
G	4	F
H	8	F
I	9	G, H
J	7	H
K	2	J
L	6	J
M	5	J
N	9	K, L
O	11	M
P	3	O

a. If the assembly line is expected to produce forty micro-computers per eight-hour day, what should the cycle time be?

b. Balance the assembly line with that cycle time.

c. What is the balance delay for that balance?

d. Is the assembly line efficient? If not, what would you do to correct the problem? Be specific. Rebalance the line, if necessary.

19. The International Institute for the Preservation of Goldfinches (IIPG) is moving from the 59th to the 69th floor of the Sears Tower. This gives it an opportunity to shift office space and reduce travel time between departments. The present activity matrix giving movements per month and the layout are shown below.

			To		
From	B	D	E	G	H
A	400	300	100	200	—
C	300	—	700	100	100
F	—	—	200	—	300
I	100	200	600	—	100

A	B	C	D
E	F	G	H
I	J	K	L

a. Assume that transportation costs per unit distance are equal for all trips. Evaluate the present solution, using the adjacent-department method described in the chapter. Assume that diagonal departments such as A and F in the present layout have 0 distance. Departments situated as A and C are a distance of 1, departments situated as A and G are a distance of 1, and so on. If you are unsure about a distance, like that between A and L, look at the distance assigned to other pairs, and make a reasonable assumption. Remember, you are the model builder.

b. Suppose that department F is the executive suite, and that the cost per unit distance for any trip starting or ending in department F is four times the cost per unit distance of any other trip: With these new conditions, solve the problem as described in part a.

 20. Able Print Shop is moving to a new building that is 120 by 165 feet. Department heads have submitted the following requests for space in the new building, and these have been approved. The requested sizes are as follows:

Department	Length (Feet)	Width (Feet)
Art (A)	60	60
Binding (B)	60	60
Cutting (C)	60	30
Layout (L)	30	30
Packing and shipping (PS)	30	30
Printing (P)	75	60
Storage (S)	60	45
Receiving (R)	60	30

The annual number of loads among departments is shown below:

| | | | | To | | | | |
From	A	B	C	L	PS	P	S	R
A	—	100	100	800	100	100	100	—
B	—	—	100	—	300	—	—	—
C	—	400	—	—	100	—	—	—
L	400	100	—	—	—	900	100	—
PS	—	—	—	—	—	—	—	—
P	—	400	500	—	200	—	100	—
S	200	600	—	100	300	10	—	—
R	50	100	—	100	200	50	1,400	—

What is your layout recommendation? The objective is to minimize activity level times distance.

21. The State University College of Business Administration is moving into a new building. The dean has asked you to suggest a layout. The square-footage requirements for each area are given, along with the number of trips made from one area to another in one month.

Department or Area	Space Requirement (Net Square Feet)
Dean's Area (D)	900
Graduate Studies (GS)	600
Undergraduate Studies (UG)	900
Business Research Center (BR)	600
Graduate Assistant's Area (GA)	1,200
Accounting (A)	2,400
Finance (F)	1,800
Information Systems and Operations Management (I)	3,000
Management (MG)	3,600
Marketing (MK)	3,000

					To					
From	D	GS	UG	BR	GA	A	F	I	MG	MK
D	—	20	5	40	0	100	120	200	150	180
GS	40	—	20	150	300	50	50	70	60	40
UG	10	30	—	0	0	100	40	200	120	80
BR	150	200	0	—	100	200	140	400	300	200
GA	0	150	0	300	—	70	40	100	40	50
A	50	80	10	50	10	—	200	300	80	40
F	40	100	5	40	5	150	—	100	60	30
I	100	200	10	50	5	250	120	—	600	100
MG	80	100	5	30	10	100	40	400	—	140
MK	50	50	10	20	10	60	50	120	120	—

a. Assume that the average graduate assistant is paid 20 percent of the salary of the average faculty member or administrator. What layout would you recommend? The objective is to minimize activity level times distance times cost for all trips.

b. What would you recommend if the building being designed has two stories of equal size?

PART III

PLANNING AND MANAGING OPERATIONS

Chapter 12: Aggregate Planning

Chapter 13: Planning for Material and Resource Requirements

Chapter 14: Inventory Management

Chapter 15: Just-In-Time and Theory of Constraints

Chapter 16: Scheduling

Chapter 17: Project Management

Aggregate Planning

LEARNING OBJECTIVES

After completing this chapter, you should be able to:

1. Explain how the process decision will constrain aggregate planning decisions.
2. Explain how order-winning criteria will influence the plan.
3. Define sales and operations planning.
4. Explain differences between aggregate plans for service organizations and those for manufacturers.
5. Define hierarchical production planning.
6. Explain yield management.
7. Develop aggregate plans using the three pure strategies and mixed strategies.
8. Calculate the costs of an aggregate plan.

INTRODUCTION

Planning is probably one of the most important, yet least understood, jobs that a manager performs. Poor planning can mean a company's inability to handle unexpected occurrences. But, good planning can place a company in an extremely strong competitive position, one from which the organization is prepared to deal with any event. However, all parts of the organization—marketing, operations, finance, and so on—must work together in the planning process to ensure that they are moving in harmony with one another.

Probably the most important planning activity is concerned with developing a competitive strategy. In today's extremely competitive global marketplace, organizations can ill afford to go forth without a well-planned strategy, which must include the operations function as well as every other part of the organization. As Chapter 2 stressed, operations can be an extremely valuable competitive weapon.

The rise of such Japanese companies as Toyota, Mitsubishi, and Sanyo has been tied largely to their effective development and execution of competitive strategies—and the integration of operations activities into those strategies. As more companies enter the world market, each one tries to capture its own share of that market. The ability of a company to do so will depend heavily on how well it has done its homework in developing a strategic plan and in using the operations function as a tool for implementing that plan.

Planning in an organization must begin at the top with strategic planning. The strategic plan is then converted into a business plan—a blueprint for actually implementing the strategic plan. Based on the business plan, each part of an organization must then develop its own plans that describe how the various parts will work to implement the business and strategic plans. This series of planning stages is shown in Exhibit 12.1. In this chapter, we discuss how operations develop its medium-range (aggregate) plan to meet corporate objectives and to serve the customer.

MEDIUM-RANGE OPERATIONS PLANNING

Medium-range planning is concerned with a time horizon that is generally from six to eighteen months in the future. While **long-range operations planning** deals with facilities and resources, medium-range operations planning develops ways to utilize those resources.

EXHIBIT 12.1

Operations Planning
Activities

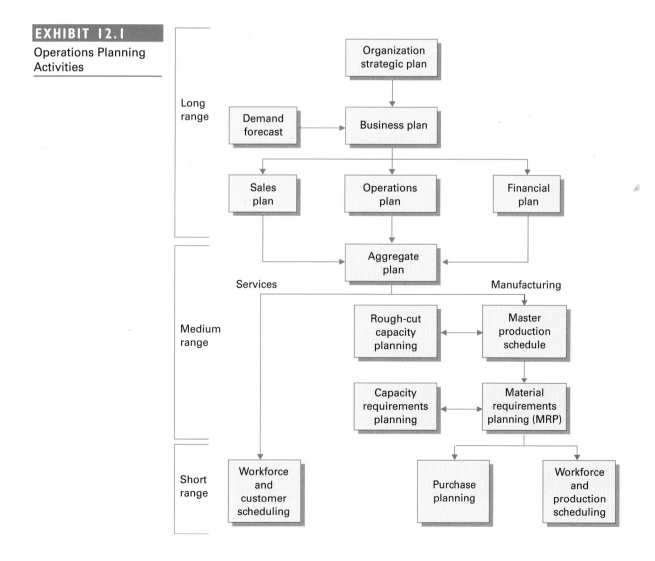

The decisions that are usually made as part of medium-range operations planning include the following:

- Workforce size
- Operating hours of the facilities
- Levels of inventory that will be maintained
- Output rates for the processes

While these decisions are much more specific to particular products than facility or resource decisions, medium-range operations planning is still quite general in nature. Aggregated groups of product type are usually considered, instead of specific product models.

Aggregation in Medium-Range Operations Planning

Aggregation refers to the combining of products into groups or families for planning purposes. For instance, an appliance manufacturer might begin medium-range planning by determining output rates for the broad product families of refrigerators, stoves, and dishwashers. Later on, as part of short-range planning, the appliance company would begin to break those output rates down into specific models, such as side-by-side, frost-free, or energy-efficient refrigerators. While this grouping by product seems logical, it is not uncommon for companies to group end items according to similar processing operations or production time needed, or by the level of labor skill required to make the product (see Exhibit 12.2). Thus, it could be possible for an appliance manufacturer to group dishwashers and washing machines together into one category for medium-range planning purposes because both products use the same production facilities. An airline might group together all routes in a given geographic area or routes that serve a particular hub. Inventory levels and planned size of the workforce are also considered only in aggregate terms, not by individual end product or by particular job descriptions. For this reason, medium-range operations planning is also often referred to as aggregate planning, a term that we will also use in this book. Aggregation allows for greater forecast accuracy and simplifies the planning process.

The Organizational Context of Aggregate Planning

Aggregate planning is a first rough-cut approximation at determining how existing resources of people and facilities should be used to meet projected demand for an organization's goods or services. For example, consider the demand forecast for a product group shown in Exhibit 12.3. In aggregate planning, a company must determine what workforce levels, overtime production, inventory, and so forth it will use to meet that demand.

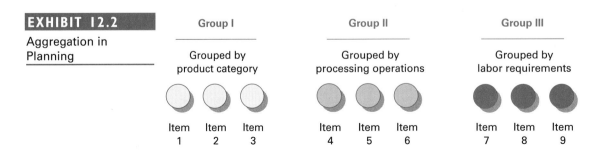

EXHIBIT 12.2

Aggregation in Planning

Group I	Group II	Group III
Grouped by product category	Grouped by processing operations	Grouped by labor requirements
Item 1 Item 2 Item 3	Item 4 Item 5 Item 6	Item 7 Item 8 Item 9

EXHIBIT 12.3

A Twelve-Month Forecast Showing Varying Demand for a Product Group

Month	Forecasted Demand
January	12,000
February	11,000
March	13,000
April	11,000
May	12,000
June	15,000
July	10,000
August	13,000
September	11,000
October	13,000
November	9,000
December	10,000

Although such decisions may seem innocuous, they can actually have a major impact on an organization's ability to compete successfully, and they can affect other functions. Consequently, aggregate planning decisions must be made with reference to the organization's competitive strategy. At the same time, however, earlier process selection decisions will limit the options available.

Although the aggregate plan relates primarily to the operations function, its results are also important to both marketing and finance. Because the aggregate plan indicates planned production versus projected demand, it will indicate to marketing how well expected demand can be met. Further, it can show periods when excess capacity might exist so that the marketing function can consider special sales promotions aimed at increasing demand during those times. Periods of tight capacity are also apparent, which might lead marketing to scale back advertising expenditures for those periods.

The aggregate plan also indicates planned workforce and inventory requirements, both of which have financial implications. Further, cash flow can be projected by comparing projected revenue from forecast sales against the costs of planned production.

Planning Constraints Caused by Type of Process

Chapter 8 has already discussed the process selection decision and how it relates to organizational strategy. Further, the manufacturing process alternatives, ranging from continuous flow and assembly line to job shop and project, were discussed. By the time a company approaches the aggregate planning problem, it will already have selected the type of process to be used.

Unfortunately, each type of process has major implications for changes in output level, as shown in Exhibit 12.4. For instance, continuous flow processes are represented by steel mills or oil refineries. The ability to change the output levels of such processes is extremely limited and usually requires a new facility. On the other hand, job shops are usually quite flexible, and output levels may be changed by hiring additional employees, scheduling more work hours, or utilizing alternative equipment. In developing aggregate plans, an organization must take into account the possible changes that can be made in the output levels of the processes being used. For services, this may depend on the type of service. For example, hotels or hospitals are limited by the number of rooms, a factor not easily altered. On the other hand, it is relatively easy for retailers to vary the number of salespeople.

	Process Type	Level of Output Change	Methods to Vary Output
EXHIBIT 12.4 Options for Changing Output by Process Type	Project	Incremental	Change working hours Change workforce size
	Job shop	Incremental	Change working hours Change workforce size
	Batch	Incremental to stepped	Change working hours Change workforce size Add or subtract shifts Shut down facility
	Assembly line	Stepped	Add or subtract shifts Shut down facility
	Continuous flow	Facility	Shut down facility Build new facility
	Service	Depends	Change working hours Change workforce size Add or subtract shifts Shut down or build new facility

Make-to-Order versus Make-to-Stock

A second area of concern in aggregate planning is whether the organization can produce to build up inventory and then use that inventory later to meet demand (known as make-to-stock). Service organizations, since they provide a service, cannot inventory that service and must meet demand as it occurs. Likewise, job shops produce custom products to customer order (make-to-order) and usually cannot produce for inventory. However, companies in the process industries, such as oil refining, make a standard product that can be kept in inventory to meet future demand. This ability to store inventory in anticipation of future demand opens up a larger number of options for the aggregate plan.

Reflecting Order-Winning Criteria in the Plan

Any company, to stay in business, must win orders from its customers. Any time you select a certain restaurant at which to eat, a particular car to buy, or a certain movie to see, the company providing that good or service has won your order, and its competitors have not.

Your ordering decisions will be based on certain criteria that you use, whether consciously or subconsciously. For example, your choice of a restaurant might be based on the price, quality of food, range of items on the menu, or speed of service. In fact, the decision you make about which car to buy could include many of the same criteria. These are called **order-winning criteria.**

Order-winning criteria include, but are not limited to, the following:

- Price
- Quality
- Delivery speed
- Delivery reliability
- Range of products provided
- Ability to meet customer specifications

The order-winning criteria with which a company decides to compete must also be taken into account in the aggregate plan. For example, a company stressing delivery speed must ensure either that it has inventory on hand to meet customer demand or that sufficient capacity is always available. In contrast, a company emphasizing price as an order winner will strive to keep costs low, which may mean minimizing workforce and inventory levels. Thus, the order-winning criteria will limit the aggregate planning alternatives available.

Sales and Operations Planning

As shown in Exhibit 12.1, the functional areas of sales (marketing) and operations develop their own plans based on the overall business plan. However, these two plans must be synchronized so that operations will be planning to produce what the sales force is planning to sell. To ensure that this synchronization occurs, many companies use what is called **sales and operations planning.** In this approach, the sales function and operations function agree upon a plan that will best meet the organization's objectives. Thus, if the sales function is planning a special product promotion, the operations function must plan to ensure that sufficient product will be available in a time frame and at a cost that conforms to the organization's order-winning criteria.

Hierarchical Production Planning (HPP)

As we begin thinking about aggregate planning for large companies that may have several divisions and several different plants that can manufacture the same product groups, you might realize that developing an aggregate plan in such situations can become an extremely large, complex problem. The aggregate plan must not only indicate which product groups will be produced at which plants, but also the quantities, inventory levels, and workforce levels for each product group during each time period.

Under **hierarchical production planning (HPP),** that large problem is broken down into smaller ones, with each smaller problem being solved at the appropriate organizational level. Thus, the question of which product groups to produce at each plant will be decided at the corporate level. Once that decision is made, then plant management can use it as the starting point for their decisions about production quantities, inventory levels, and workforce levels for those product groups they will be producing. This planning process can continue plans for individual products being developed by departmental managers, as shown in Exhibit 12.5

Aggregate Planning in an International Context

Chapter 10 discussed reasons for a company to locate its facilities in a foreign country. Among those reasons was an increased ability to serve foreign markets. However, there is often a tendency then to develop product designs that are unique to each market. While customization of products to particular markets can be desirable as a competitive strategy, it often makes aggregate planning more difficult.

For example, suppose a company operates production facilities for a given product in two different countries. If those two products are the same, then excess capacity at one facility can be used to meet demand that the other facility may not be able to serve due to capacity limitations. On the other hand, if the products produced are not the same, then

EXHIBIT 12.5 Hierarchical Production Planning	**Organizational Level**	**Decision**
	Corporate	Assign product groups to plants
	Plant	Production quantities, inventory levels, and workforce levels for product
	Department	Production schedules for individual products

excess capacity will go unused at one facility, and some demand will be unmet in the market served by the other facility.

To avoid this second scenario, many companies develop product designs that can be used in several different markets. As a result, aggregate planning can be done by the organization on a global basis, rather than on a facility-by-facility basis. Likewise, the idea of postponement, discussed in Chapter 5, allows a company to plan globally, while hierarchical production planning, discussed here, can make that planning process easier.

STRATEGIES FOR MEETING DEMAND

As a company begins developing its aggregate plan, there are two broad types of strategies available, either proactive or reactive. Using proactive strategies a company will attempt to modify demand so that demand is not so uneven.

EXAMPLE

Campbell's soup has traditionally been a product that sells best in the fall and winter months. However, Campbell would like you to think of soup as a year-round food item. Therefore, it has developed advertisements that highlight this idea by showing people enjoying soup during the warmer months of the year. Its hope is that this will lead to more uniform product demand throughout the entire year.

The other approach to meeting demand is reactive in that a company will not try to influence demand but will find ways of responding to variations in the pattern of that demand. For example, companies that make lawn mowers often produce throughout the year even though most lawn mowers are sold in the spring and summer months. During periods of low demand, such as fall and winter, the mowers are simply kept in inventory, then sold later when demand picks up again.

The following section describes some additional proactive and reactive strategies.

Proactive Strategies

Rather than reacting to variations in customer demand, many companies use **proactive strategies** in an attempt to alter that demand. Such strategies are aimed at smoothing demand and bringing it into line with available capacity. Some possible approaches follow.

Produce Products That Are Seasonal Complements

The idea behind this strategy is to find products with alternating demand patterns so that demand for one is high when demand for the other is low. For example, companies that manufacture both snow blowers and lawnmowers take advantage of complementary products. The same approach is used by state highway departments, which operate largely as service organizations. In northern climates, the same crews used for snow plowing during the winter do the mowing during the summer.

Offer Discounts and Promotions

The objective here is to increase demand during low periods through incentives to buy. Conversely, prices can be raised during high-demand periods. Hotels located in summer vacation spots often do this by cutting prices in the winter and raising them in the summer. The telephone company also does this with late-night and weekend telephone rates.

Increase Advertising in Slack Periods

Advertising can obviously have a great impact on demand. During periods when demand is ordinarily low, increased advertising can generate increased demand. Conversely, significant amounts of money can be saved by reducing advertising if demand is already sufficient to use available capacity.

Reactive Strategies

The second approach to aggregate planning is to treat the demand forecasts as given and to focus on ways of meeting that demand, whether through inventory or changes in workforce levels or both. The following are some of these **reactive strategies:**

- Vary the number of employees through hiring or layoffs.
- Schedule overtime work or allow employees to slack off.
- Add or eliminate second or third shifts.
- Schedule vacations or plant shutdowns.
- Build up or draw down finished-good inventory.
- Subcontract work to outside suppliers.
- Build up order backlogs during peak periods.
- Back-order items not available or incur lost sales.

Cost Considerations

Another factor to be considered in aggregate planning, and one that is often easiest to determine, is cost. The following are the major costs that must be included in aggregate planning. It is, however, important to keep in mind that the aggregate plan that minimizes cost may not necessarily be the best. The other organizational factors already mentioned will often take priority over cost.

- *Payroll Costs*—These are the costs associated with having a certain number of employees on the payroll. They usually include wages, health insurance, social security, retirement contributions, and vacation pay.
- *Hiring Costs*—Costs associated with hiring include those for advertising, interviewing, and training and those for productivity losses and scrap until the new employee becomes proficient at the job.
- *Layoff Costs*—These include severance pay, state-mandated payments into an unemployment fund, and productivity losses due to "bumping" by senior union employees.
- *Overtime Costs*—Overtime is usually paid at a rate equal to 150 percent of the regular hourly rate. Further, productivity and quality may drop for employees who have already worked a full day. All these factors should be considered in overtime cost.
- *Inventory Holding Costs*—These will include the cost of capital tied up in inventory, as well as the variable costs of insurance, taxes, obsolescence, theft, and spoilage. It is usually calculated based on average inventory
- *Subcontracting Costs*—When a company cannot meet demand with its own resources, it will subcontract with another to provide the good or service. Whatever cost the company pays its subcontractor must be included.

- *Back Orders, Stockouts, and Lost Sales*—If demand cannot be met when it occurs, it may be possible to convince the customer to accept later delivery through a back order. In this case, additional paperwork cost is incurred, and customer goodwill suffers. In other cases, the sale may be lost, meaning lost income and lost goodwill.

Aggregate Planning for Service Organizations

As we have already mentioned, service operations generally are unable to hold their product in inventory and must provide the service when it is demanded. For example, unoccupied hotel rooms cannot be saved up from periods of low demand to satisfy peak-period demands. Thus, in general, services are limited to proactive strategies and to those reactive aggregate planning strategies that do not involve inventory. However, services are often better able to use order backlogs as one way to meet peak demand.

Planning with Order Backlogs

There are now many service outlets that will change the oil and oil filter in your car on demand. Such facilities are designed to provide immediate service. However, if you want major repair work done on your car, you will probably have to schedule that for some time in the future, not necessarily when you want the work done. The reason is that major repair shops have limited capacity. When that capacity limit is reached, orders are backlogged by making appointments for future dates. The major cost of this strategy comes from lost sales when the customer goes elsewhere for service.

Proactive Strategies

Although limited somewhat in reactive strategies, service organizations quite often have more options for shifting demand than do manufacturers. In addition to those proactive strategies described earlier, service organizations can also take advantage of the following.

- *Fixed Service Schedules*—Many service organizations, such as airlines, buses, and railroads, maintain a fixed schedule. This schedule fixes capacity, which customers then use up when they purchase tickets. Ticket purchases also offer some opportunity for adding capacity, as railroads can put on additional cars or bus lines can schedule more than one bus if demand justifies doing so.
- *Appointments for Service Times*—Physicians and dentists use appointments to smooth out demand for their services. Customers know in advance when they will obtain service, rather than just showing up and having to wait for service. Appointments also help to eliminate slack time for the service facility.
- *Customer Involvement*—Self-serve gas stations, salad bars, and automatic teller machines all get the customer involved in the service process. To a large extent, this option enables the system to respond to its own demand.

Yield Management

Many service organizations that use reservation systems and have limited capacity, such as airlines, hotels, and car rental companies, have adopted an approach to revenue maximization known as yield management. The idea behind **yield management** is to change the price for a service based upon the level of demand at a particular point in time, with the objective of maximizing expected profit. For example, if a car rental company finds that reservations for full-size cars next Monday at its Denver Airport rental facility are running lower than usual, the company may reduce the price to increase demand. On the other hand, if demand is running strong, the company may raise the price. In either case, the objective is to modify demand by changing the price so that expected revenue will be maximized.

Although the preceding example provides the basic idea behind yield management, the reality of its implementation today is much more complex. Consider the airlines, which is where yield management originated. Airlines realized long ago that a certain percentage of those customers holding reservations on a particular flight would be "no-shows." If a customer with a reservation is a "no-show" and the airplane then flies with an empty seat, that revenue has been lost. To minimize lost revenue, the airlines first began overbooking flights based on the probability that a certain number of passengers would be "no-shows." However, overbooking can also produce added costs if an insufficient number of seats are available to accommodate the passengers who actually show up for a given flight. Passengers who are "bumped" may have to be re-booked on other airlines or receive free tickets or cash compensation.

With yield management, the airlines seek to avoid overbooking flights by enticing passengers to take less crowded flights. For example, Exhibit 12.6 shows hypothetical fares an airline might offer on three different flights from San Diego to St. Louis. As shown, the most desirable flight is only available at full fare while the less desirable flights offer lower fares. The least desirable flight even offers a promotional fare to attract passengers.

Under yield management, the number of seats available at each fare would be dynamically altered to maximize expected revenue. Thus, if demand appears strong for flight 908, the number of seats at the discount fare might be limited to just a few. On the other hand, demand for flight 1158 might be low, so more seats could be offered at the promotional fare. Such decisions are actually made by extremely sophisticated computer programs that look at aggregated groups of flights that have similar revenue potential. The objective is to sell as many seats at full fare as possible, but to offer discounted seats if necessary to fill the airplane. Overbooking is used to adjust for expected no-shows, subject to constraints that attempt to minimize the number of passengers bumped from a flight.

EXAMPLE   American Airlines has been very successful in its use of yield management. Over a three-year period in which the airline's net profits were $892 million, yield management saved $1.4 billion in revenue that would have been lost otherwise. Thus, this technique made the difference between profit and loss for the airline, which estimates that yield management will save $500 million every year.

TECHNIQUES FOR AGGREGATE PLANNING

Aggregate planning is largely a trial-and-error process and, therefore, most companies use manual trial-and-error techniques in developing the aggregate plan. However, several attempts have been made to develop mathematical procedures to solve the aggregate planning problem. We begin by showing trial-and-error approaches and then present a mathematical procedure that uses a special type of linear programming called the

EXHIBIT 12.6					Advance		
Example of Airfares for Yield Management	Flight	Departs	Arrives	Stops	Full Fare	Purchase	Discount	Promotional
	899	3:00 P.M.	5:00 P.M.	0	$400	X	X	X
	908	5:00 P.M.	9:00 P.M.	1	$400	$299	$250	X
	1158	9:00 P.M.	1:00 A.M.	1	$350	$299	$250	$199

transportation problem. The supplement to this chapter discusses linear programming in more detail.

Three Pure Strategies

There are many different ways to combine the various reactive strategies. However, three general **"pure strategies"** are often identified, each focusing on varying only one of the factors used to meet demand. In demonstrating each, we will use the twelve-month demand forecast presented earlier in Exhibit 12.3. However, we will also indicate how each pure strategy would be most appropriate for different types of processes and organizational competitive strategies. Later, a mixed strategy will be presented that varies several factors used in the pure strategies.

Strategy 1: Vary the Workforce Size

The basic idea of this strategy is to vary production to meet demand. If demand rises and falls, then production will have to rise and fall. But, under this particular strategy, the variations in production are achieved by varying the number of employees.

Usually this strategy means hiring more employees when demand is high and then laying off employees when demand drops. For example, retail outlets usually handle the Christmas rush by hiring additional salespeople on a temporary basis for the peak-demand periods. Afterward, the sales force returns to its normal size. Companies that provide a service, since they cannot inventory that service, most often follow this strategy. Manufacturing companies, however, may also follow the same approach because it minimizes the level of finished-goods inventories. It is not uncommon for auto manufacturers to utilize a variation of this strategy by completely shutting down several assembly plants for a week or more when production exceeds sales.

PROBLEM

Hickory Hill packages and sells gift boxes of fruit by mail. The company cannot carry any inventory of finished products due to spoilage. Further, the packaging operation is rather simple, and new employees can be trained quickly. The company is located near a large metropolitan area, and new employees are readily available. On the average, each employee can produce 1,000 gift boxes of fruit per month. Payroll costs, including wages and fringe benefits, average $1,730 per employee per month. It usually costs about $200 to hire a new employee and $300 to lay one off. The twelve-month aggregate plan used by Hickory Hill and its associated costs are shown in Exhibit 12.7.

Strategy 2: Hold Workforce Size Constant, But Vary Its Utilization

In some cases, it will be undesirable to vary the workforce size due to labor agreements or hiring costs, or for labor-relations reasons. Under such conditions, the workforce size may be held constant, but its utilization varied through the use of overtime or a shortened work week. In this situation, the hiring and layoff costs associated with Strategy 1 are avoided, but they are generally replaced by higher payroll and overtime costs. In addition, employees who must work overtime are generally less productive and more accident-prone due to fatigue. Second and third shifts are also usually less productive than first shifts are because these workers are usually newer, less skilled, and sometimes working another job during daytime hours.

A variation of this strategy involves **subcontracting,** or **outsourcing,** which is buying parts or subassemblies from outside suppliers whenever a company's capacity is insufficient to meet its needs from internal production. In this situation, a company would subcontract with an outside supplier instead of using overtime to meet production requirements. Instead of overtime costs, the company incurs the added cost of paying another company to make the parts.

	Month	Forecasted Demand	Planned Production	Required Employees	Employees Hired	Employees Laid Off
EXHIBIT 12.7	January	12,000	12,000	12	—	—
Varying Workforce Production Strategy for Aggregate Planning	February	11,000	11,000	11	—	1
	March	13,000	13,000	13	2	—
	April	11,000	11,000	11	—	2
	May	12,000	12,000	12	1	—
	June	15,000	15,000	15	3	—
	July	10,000	10,000	10	—	5
	August	13,000	13,000	13	3	—
	September	11,000	11,000	11	—	2
	October	13,000	13,000	13	2	—
	November	9,000	9,000	9	—	4
	December	10,000	10,000	10	1	—
			Total	140	12	14

Costs:

Payroll: 140 employee-months at $1,730/month = $242,200

Hiring: 12 employees at $200/hiring   =   2,400

Layoffs: 14 employees at $300/layoff   =   4,200

= $248,800

PROBLEM

Stemple-Hartley sells personalized stemware that has the customer's initials engraved in each piece. The company has ten highly skilled craftsmen who would be hard to replace. Further, because of the custom nature of its product, Stemple-Hartley does not maintain a finished-goods inventory. On the average, each employee can engrave 1,000 pieces per month. By union contract, overtime work is limited to 200 pieces per employee per month. However, a subcontractor is available to engrave up to 5,000 pieces per month.

Each employee is paid an average of $1,730 per month in wages and fringe benefits. Overtime work costs $2.60 per unit, and the subcontractor charges $3.00 per unit. The aggregate plan developed by Stemple-Hartley and its costs are shown in Exhibit 12.8.

Strategy 3: Produce a Constant Amount and Use Inventory to Absorb Fluctuations

Under this last strategy, a company will try to keep production constant, but meet demand fluctuations through inventory variations. In this case, inventory will build up during periods of low demand when the production rate exceeds demand. Then, when demand exceeds the company's ability to produce, this inventory will be drawn down to meet demand. Companies that produce products with seasonal demand, such as air conditioners or snow blowers, often follow this strategy. Its major disadvantage is that storage space and money will be tied up in maintaining the inventory. However, the positive side is that workforce size and hours worked remain constant.

Of course, this last strategy is not usually feasible for service organizations because their product cannot be stored as inventory. For example, an airline must be able to meet the demand that exists for its airplane seats whenever that demand occurs. Thus, service organizations are usually concerned only with strategies that involve varying either the workforce size or its utilization.

EXHIBIT 12.8

Aggregate Production
Plan Using Overtime
and Subcontracting

Month	Forecasted Demand	Employment Level	Regular-Time Planned Production	Overtime Planned Production	Units Subcontracted
January	12,000	10	10,000	2,000	—
February	11,000	10	10,000	1,000	—
March	13,000	10	10,000	2,000	1,000
April	11,000	10	10,000	1,000	—
May	12,000	10	10,000	2,000	—
June	15,000	10	10,000	2,000	3,000
July	10,000	10	10,000	—	—
August	13,000	10	10,000	2,000	1,000
September	11,000	10	10,000	1,000	—
October	13,000	10	10,000	2,000	1,000
November	9,000	10	9,000*	—	—
December	10,000	10	10,000	—	—
Totals		120	119,000	15,000	6,000

Costs:

Payroll:	120 employee-months at $1,730/month	=	$207,600
Overtime:	15,000 units at $2.60/unit	=	39,000
Subcontracting:	6,000 units at $3.00/unit	=	18,000
		=	$264,600

*Production rate is cut back, underutilizing ten employees who produce only 9,000 units.

PROBLEM

EMC manufactures memory upgrade chips for personal computers. Because computer owners don't want to wait when they order a memory upgrade, EMC always maintains an inventory of finished products. On the other hand, its employees are highly trained and difficult to replace. For these reasons, EMC prefers to maintain a constant workforce and build up inventory. Each employee can produce an average of 1,000 memory upgrade chips per month. Wages and fringe benefits average $1,730 per employee. Further, it costs $.17 to hold one memory chip in inventory for one month. The aggregate plan EMC would use and its costs are shown in Exhibit 12.9.

Mixed Strategies

As you review the preceding aggregate plans, you should notice that in each case, we used exactly the same demand and cost figures. However, each company used a different approach based on its unique circumstances and competitive strategy.

In actual practice, companies usually combine several of the preceding pure strategies to meet their own unique requirements. For example, Exhibit 12.10 shows a mixed strategy that combines hiring and layoffs with overtime and inventory. In this case, the company might have limited finished-goods storage space, but also wants to keep its workforce size fairly constant. Of course, many other mixed strategies could be developed.

An Aggregate Plan for a Service Organization

As mentioned previously, the type of service organization will often determine possible aggregate planning options. Those that are labor-intensive may have to follow the approach of hiring and layoffs. However, some, such as physicians' offices, may be able to utilize backlogs. The following example shows how backlogs are used by a company that provides an engine-rebuilding service.

EXHIBIT 12.9

Aggregate Plan with Varying Inventory

Month	Forecasted Demand	Planned Production	Required Employees	Beginning Inventory	Ending Inventory	Average Inventory
January	12,000	12,000	12	2,000	2,000	2,000
February	11,000	12,000	12	2,000	3,000	2,500
March	13,000	12,000	12	3,000	2,000	2,500
April	11,000	12,000	12	2,000	3,000	2,500
May	12,000	12,000	12	3,000	3,000	3,000
June	15,000	12,000	12	3,000	0	1,500
July	10,000	12,000	12	0	2,000	1,000
August	13,000	12,000	12	2,000	1,000	1,500
September	11,000	12,000	12	1,000	2,000	1,500
October	13,000	12,000	12	2,000	1,000	1,500
November	9,000	12,000	12	1,000	4,000	2,500
December	10,000	12,000	12	4,000	6,000	5,000
		Totals	144			27,000

Costs:

Payroll: 144 employee-months at $1,730/month = $249,120

Annual inventory cost: 27,000 at $.17/unit/month   =   4,590

                                                          = $253,710

EXHIBIT 12.10   A Mixed Aggregate Planning Strategy

Month	Forecasted Demand	Employment Level	Regular Time Production	Overtime Production	Employees Hired	Employees Laid Off	Beginning Inventory	Ending Inventory	Average Inventory
January	12,000	10	10,000	2,000	—	—	0	0	0
February	11,000	10	10,000	1,000	—	—	0	0	0
March	13,000	12	12,000	1,000	2	—	0	0	0
April	11,000	12	12,000	—	—	—	0	1,000	500
May	12,000	12	12,000	—	—	—	1,000	1,000	1,000
June	15,000	12	12,000	2,000	—	—	1,000	0	500
July	10,000	12	12,000	—	—	—	0	2,000	1,000
August	13,000	12	12,000	—	—	—	2,000	1,000	1,500
September	11,000	12	12,000	—	—	—	1,000	2,000	1,500
October	13,000	10	10,000	1,000	—	2	2,000	0	1,000
November	9,000	10	10,000	—	—	—	0	1,000	500
December	10,000	10	10,000	—	—	—	1,000	1,000	1,000
		134	134,000	7,000	2	2			8,500

Costs:

Payroll: 134 employee-months at $1,730/month = $231,820

Overtime: 7,000 units at $2.60/unit   =   18,200

Hiring: 2 employees at $200/hiring   =   400

Layoffs: 2 employees at $300/layoff   =   600

Annual inventory cost: 8,500 at $.17/unit/month   =   1,445

                                                         $252,465

PROBLEM   Midwest Diesel Service operates a rebuilding service for the diesel engines in large trucks. Each employee of Midwest Diesel can rebuild an average of ten engines per month. Payroll costs average $2,500 per month per employee. The company currently has twelve employees and cannot hire more due to space limitations. Further, the company does not want to lay off any employees due to the difficulty of replacing them. Based on past experience, each order backlogged from one month to the next will cost $300 in lost sales and lost customer goodwill. Overtime work is limited to one-fifth of regular time each month, and employees are paid a 50 percent premium for overtime work. Exhibit 12.11 indicates the aggregate plan Midwest Diesel has developed for the next six months.

The Graphical Approach

Another possible approach to medium-range, or aggregate, operations planning is a graphical one. This approach indicates cumulative demand for the product versus cumulative production and can be very helpful in developing a mixed strategy. Use the following steps:

1. Develop a graph that shows numbers of units on the vertical axis and time throughout the planning horizon on the horizontal axis.
2. Graph cumulative expected demand from the beginning of the planning horizon to its end.
3. Develop a production plan, and use the graph developed in the preceding steps to graph cumulative production throughout the planning horizon.
4. Compare cumulative demand to cumulative production. Areas where cumulative production exceeds cumulative demand indicate an inventory buildup. Whenever cumulative demand exceeds cumulative production, demand will not be met at that time.
5. Perform the above steps until a satisfactory production plan is developed.

PROBLEM

The Regal Toy Company has fifty employees who make and assemble various plastic toys. The aggregate plan for Regal is stated in terms of planned toy production each month, in number of toys, based on the following sales forecast:

Month	Jan.	Feb.	Mar.	Apr.	May	June
Sales Forecast	12,000	16,000	14,000	18,000	16,000	16,000
Cumulative	12,000	28,000	42,000	60,000	76,000	92,000

EXHIBIT 12.11

An Aggregate Plan for Services with Backlogs

Month	Demand Forecast	Regular-Time Production	Overtime Production	Beginning Backlog	Ending Backlog
January	100	100	—	—	—
February	110	110	—	—	—
March	130	120	10	—	—
April	150	120	24	0	6
May	130	120	16	6	0
June	120	120	—	—	—
		Totals	50	6	6

Costs:

Payroll: 12 employees × 6 months = 72 employee-months at $2,500/month = $180,000

Overtime: $50 \times \dfrac{\$2,500}{10}(1.50)$ = 18,750

Back orders: 6 at $300 each = 1,800

$200,550

Month	Jan.	Feb.	Mar.	Apr.	May	June
Sales Forecast	15,000	15,000	15,000	15,000	15,000	15,000
Cumulative	15,000	30,000	45,000	60,000	75,000	90,000

Exhibit 12.12 shows a graph comparing total cumulative demand (dashed line) with total cumulative regular-time production (solid line). The inventory level at any time is the amount by which cumulative production exceeds cumulative demand. As Exhibit 12.12 indicates, inventory will reach zero at the end of April. After that, production is insufficient to meet demand by an amount equal to 1,000 units per month.

Regal Toy might decide to schedule overtime in May and June so an extra 1,000 units could be produced each month. Under that mixed strategy, cumulative production and cumulative demand would coincide from the end of April through the end of June.

This graphical approach is best used for determining what the inventory level will be at any given time and whether demand can be satisfied from available inventory and planned production. If demand exceeds available supply, then the planner must decide whether production will be increased through assigning overtime, through hiring, or possibly by subcontracting with an outside supplier. The determination of which approach to follow is usually based on the costs associated with each strategy and any other relevant considerations, such as company policy or a union contract that limits overtime or hiring.

EXHIBIT 12.12

Graphical Aggregate Planning

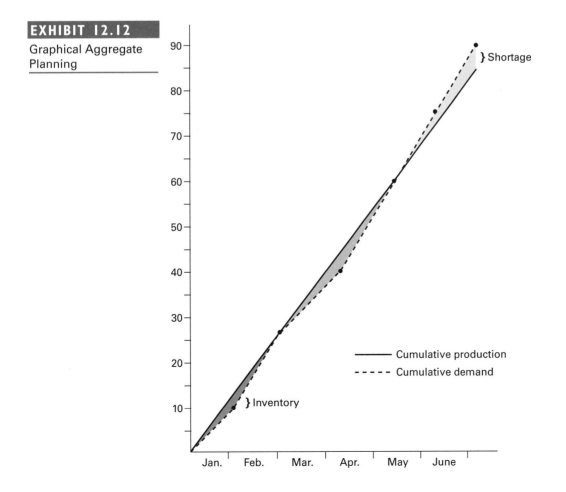

PROBLEM   The graph of Exhibit 12.12 can also be used to determine what constant level of production will be required to meet cumulative demand. Note that if a straight line is drawn from the origin of the graph out to the cumulative production that is farthest above the cumulative production, this line indicates a constant-production plan that will meet demand. Cumulative demand is farthest above cumulative production for June. Thus, a line is connected from the origin to that point, as shown in Exhibit 12.13. This line corresponds to monthly production of 15,334 units.

A Mathematical Procedure for Aggregate Planning

One mathematical method that attempts to simplify the aggregate planning problem uses a transportation problem tableau, as shown in Exhibit 12.14. Rows of this tableau represent possible product "sources," such as regular time, overtime, and subcontracting, for each month. Columns of the tableau correspond to "demand" each month. The last two columns to the right indicate capacity not used and available capacity from each source. The last row indicates demand requirements in each month.

Notice that production in January (the first three rows) may be used to meet demand for January. However, by carrying inventory from one month to the next, it can also be used to meet demand in successive months. In contrast, production in later months cannot be used to meet demand for January unless back orders or backlogs are allowed. In this example, we assume they are not.

EXHIBIT 12.13

Aggregate Plan to Avoid Shortages

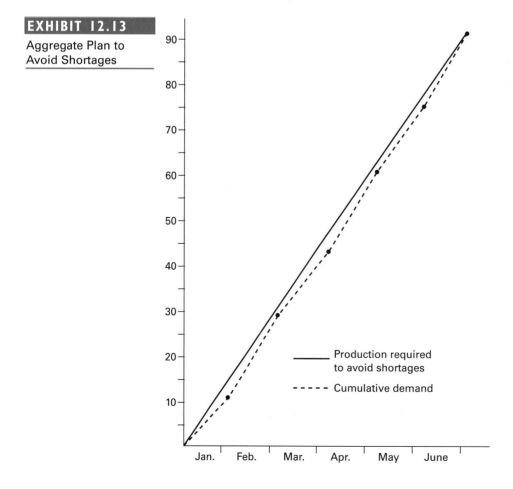

EXHIBIT 12.14

Tableau for Solving Aggregate Planning Problems

	Source	January	February	March	April	Unused capacity	Capacity available
January	Regular time	R	$R + H$	$R + 2H$	$R + 3H$		
	Over-time	T	$T + H$	$T + 2H$	$T + 3H$		
	Sub-contract	S	$S + H$	$S + 2H$	$S + 3H$		
February	Regular time		R	$R + H$	$R + 2H$		
	Over-time		T	$T + H$	$T + 2H$		
	Sub-contract		S	$S + H$	$S + 2H$		
March	Regular time			R	$R + H$		
	Over-time			T	$T + H$		
	Sub-contract			S	$S + H$		
April	Regular time				R		
	Over-time				T		
	Sub-contract				S		
	Demand						

In the upper right-hand corner of the cells are unit-cost figures, using the following symbols:

R = cost per unit of regular-time production
T = cost per unit of overtime production
S = cost per unit of subcontracting
H = cost per unit to hold inventory for one month

Thus, a unit produced on regular time in January and sold that same month will cost the producer R. However, a unit produced in January on regular time and not sold until April will cost $R + 3H$ because it must be carried as inventory for three months. To develop an aggregate plan using this tableau, use the following steps:

1. Copy all figures from the Capacity Available column into the Unused Capacity column.
2. Find the cell with lowest cost in the first month's column, and put the "minimum" of either unused capacity for that row or demand for that column into the cell. Adjust unused capacity accordingly.
3. Repeat the preceding step until all demand for the month is satisfied.
4. Proceed to the next month (column), and repeat Steps 2 and 3.

When the process is completed, all entries across a row, including unused capacity, must add up to the capacity available. Likewise, all entries in a column must add up to the demand for that column. The solution obtained by this method is shown in Exhibit 12.15.

When back orders are allowed, we can modify the tableau so demand in a given month can be satisfied by production in a later month. The associated cost will represent production cost plus back-order cost.

EXHIBIT 12.15

Tableau Solution to Aggregate Planning Problem

	Source	January	February	March	April	Unused capacity	Capacity available
January	Regular time	1.73 / 10,000	1.90	2.07	2.24	~~10,000~~ 0	10,000
	Over-time	2.60 / 2,000	2.77	2.94	3.11	~~2,000~~ 0	2,000
	Sub-contract	3.00	3.17	3.34	3.51	5,000	5,000
February	Regular time		1.73 / 10,000	1.90	2.07	~~10,000~~ 0	10,000
	Over-time		2.60 / 1,000	2.77 / 1,000	2.94	~~2,000~~ ~~1,000~~ 0	2,000
	Sub-contract		3.00	3.17	3.34	5,000	5,000
March	Regular time			1.73 / 10,000	1.90	~~10,000~~ 0	10,000
	Over-time			2.60 / 2,000	2.77	~~2,000~~ 0	2,000
	Sub-contract			3.00	3.17	5,000	5,000
April	Regular time				1.73 / 10,000	~~10,000~~ 0	10,000
	Over-time				2.60 / 1,000	~~2,000~~ 1,000	2,000
	Sub-contract				3.00	5,000	5,000
	Demand	12,000	11,000	13,000	11,000		

SUMMARY

- Processes will place constraints on output changes.
- The order-winning criteria will limit a company's choice of aggregate planning approaches.
- Sales and operations planning synchronizes the plans of marketing and operations.
- Hierarchical production planning solves aggregate planning subproblems at each level of the organizational hierarchy.
- Make-to-order companies and services cannot produce for inventory.
- Yield management is an approach for varying prices to maximize revenue in service organizations that use reservation systems.
- Three pure strategies for reacting to demand include varying the workforce, using overtime or subcontracting, and varying the inventory.
- Service organizations cannot carry inventory, but they can often use order backlogs or schedule orders.

 Visit our dynamic Web site, http://www.wiley.com/college/vonderembse, for extended chapter material, solved problems, mini-cases, computer software, and Web links.

KEY TERMS

aggregate planning
aggregation
hierarchical production
    planning (HPP)
long-range operations
    planning

medium-range planning
order-winning criteria
outsourcing
proactive strategies
pure strategies
reactive strategies

sales and operations
    planning
subcontracting
yield management

URLS

American Airlines: www.amrcorp.com

Black & Decker: www.blackanddecker.com

Campbell Soup Company: www.campbellsoup.com

Coffman: www.coffmanstairs.com

Expedia: www.expedia.com

Hershey Foods: www.hersheys.com

Mitsubishi: www.mitsubishi.com

Orbitz: www.orbitz.com

Sanyo: www.sanyo.com

Toyota: www.toyota.co.jp/en/

Travelocity: www.travelocity.com

QUESTIONS

1. What are the steps in converting organizational objectives into an aggregate plan?

2. What is the role of the aggregate plan in the planning process?

3. What changes in output level are possible for each type of process?

4. How will the aggregate plan differ in a make-to-stock company compared to a make-to-order company?

5. List and define the costs that are relevant to aggregate planning.

6. Describe how hierarchical production planning (HPP) might be applied by a company such as General Motors, which manufactures several different brands of automobiles (Cadillac, Chevrolet, etc.), with each brand being manufactured at several different manufacturing plants.

7. Develop a list of possible reactive strategies and a list of possible proactive strategies for meeting demand.

8. What reactive and proactive strategies are available to both service organizations and manufacturers? Which are available to only one or the other?

9. For automobile manufacturers today, what would you say are the major order winners?

10. Consider Wendy's and McDonald's. In what ways might their competitive strategies differ? How might the aggregate planning for each reflect those differences?

11. Suppose a company identifies quality as an order winner. Would this company want to have an aggregate plan with large workforce variations? Why or why not?

12. Find some recent articles that indicate various ways companies vary output to meet demand. Write a report summarizing those articles.

13. Airlines, hotels, and car rental companies are identified most often with yield management. List other possible industries that might benefit from yield management and explain why.

14. Black & Decker makes many different power tools and household products. Describe some possible ways these products might be aggregated for planning purposes.

15. Select an actual service operation, and describe some reactive and proactive strategies it uses to meet demand.

16. The XYZ Company produces a very standardized product and emphasizes immediate delivery. Its workforce is highly skilled. What reactive aggregate planning strategies would probably be used?

17. Describe some ways, reactive and proactive, in which colleges and universities meet demand.

18. What change would be made in the tableau method for aggregate planning to allow back orders?

INTERNET QUESTIONS

19. Visit the Web site for Campbell Soup Company (www.campbellsoup.com), and identify some proactive strategies they may be using for meeting demand.

20. Visit the Web site for Black & Decker (www.blackanddecker.com), and determine possible ways it might aggregate its various products for aggregate planning.

21. Using one of the airline travel Web sites (e.g., Travelocity, Expedia, Orbitz, etc.) select various air travel options and examine the fares being offered. Determine how day of the week, time of day, and number of connections might be factored into the yield management equation.

22. Visit the Web site for Hershey Foods (www.hersheys.com), and take its factory tour. Also visit the Web site for the plant tour of Coffman, a manufacturer of stairs, (www.coffmanstairs.com/tour). Based on the information provided, identify some ways in which the aggregate plans for these two companies might be similar and some ways in which they would be different.

PROBLEMS

1. Given the following forecasted demand, develop a production plan that uses a varying workforce in which each employee can produce 2,000 units per month.

Month	Forecasted Demand (Units)	Month	Forecasted Demand (Units)
Jan.	80,000	May	80,000
Feb.	90,000	June	70,000
Mar.	90,000	July	60,000
Apr.	80,000	Aug.	50,000

2. For the situation in Problem 1, determine the total cost of hiring and layoffs if it costs $500 to hire an employee and $1,000 to lay off an employee. There are forty employees at the beginning of January.

3. A fast-food restaurant performs its planning in terms of sales dollars. In the past, the restaurant has needed one employee per $10,000 of sales. Temporary help is readily available so that workforce size may be varied easily and inexpensively. How many employees should the restaurant plan to have working each month?

Month	Forecasted Sales	Month	Forecasted Sales
May	$100,000	Aug.	$120,000
June	120,000	Sept.	120,000
July	130,000	Oct.	100,000

4. A commercial laundry does its planning in terms of tons of laundry per month. The laundry's equipment has a maximum capacity of three tons of laundry per hour. Given the following forecast of demand, determine overtime hours that will be required each month:

Month	Forecasted Demand (Tons)	Regular-Time Hours
Aug.	500	184
Sept.	500	168
Oct.	550	192
Nov.	600	176
Dec.	650	184
Jan.	600	192
Feb.	500	160
Mar.	600	192

5. An electronics manufacturer maintains a constant workforce of forty employees. Each employee can produce ten units of the company's product per hour. Regular-time work is eight hours per day. Given the following demand forecast and working days, determine the number of overtime hours that will be needed each month for overtime work. Calculate the regular payroll cost and overtime cost for each month.

Month	Demand Forecast (Units)	Working Days
Jan.	70,000	24
Feb.	60,000	18
Mar.	75,000	25
Apr.	70,000	21
May	80,000	24
June	80,000	20

6. Refer to Problem 5. Employees earn an average wage of $12 per hour on regular time and a 50 percent premium for overtime work. Calculate the regular payroll cost and overtime cost for each month.

7. The Lee Key Boat Company manufacturers power boats. Obviously, spring and summer are its high-demand seasons. During fall and winter, the company builds up inventory in anticipation of the spring–summer peak. If Lee Key produces an average

of 2,000 boats per month, determine the company's expected ending inventory each month, based on the following sales forecast. The company expects to have 3,000 boats left in inventory at the beginning of August.

Month	Forecasted Sales (Units)	Month	Forecasted Sales (Units)
Aug.	3,000	Feb.	800
Sept.	1,500	Mar.	1,500
Oct.	1,000	Apr.	2,000
Nov.	1,000	May	4,000
Dec.	1,000	June	6,000
Jan.	1,000	July	4,000

8. For the Lee Key Boat Company, of Problem 7, determine the total inventory carrying cost for the year if it costs $30 per month to store each boat in inventory.

9. Referring to Problem 7, develop a graph that shows cumulative production and cumulative sales of the Lee Key Boat Company. (Be sure to include beginning inventory for August as the starting point for cumulative production.)

10. The Sunshine Dairy plans its production in gallons of product per month. A maximum of 1,000 gallons may be carried over from one month to the next; otherwise, spoilage occurs. If demand cannot be met in a given month, the company loses sales. Inventory carrying cost is $.10 per gallon per month, and the cost of a lost sale is $.30 per gallon. Sunshine's maximum production rate is 20,000 gallons per month. Using the following demand forecast, determine monthly production to minimize inventory and lost sales costs without exceeding the inventory limit.

Month	Forecasted Sales (Gallons)	Month	Forecasted Sales (Gallons)
June	15,000	Sept.	19,000
July	22,000	Oct.	18,000
Aug.	20,000	Nov.	22,000

11. Diamond Electronics is developing an aggregate plan for the first six months of the next year. The company expects to have capacity on regular time to produce 5,000 units per month at a labor cost of $3 per unit. Each month 1,000 units can be produced on overtime at a cost of $4.50 per unit. Back orders are not allowed, but the company is willing to carry inventory from one month to the next at $.50 per unit. Use the tableau method to develop an aggregate plan that will meet the following demand forecast for lowest total cost:

Month	Jan.	Feb.	Mar.	Apr.	May	June
Forecasted Demand	3,000	3,000	6,000	7,000	6,000	4,000

12. Suppose in Problem 11 that back orders are allowed at a cost of $1 per unit. Again, use the tableau method to develop an aggregate plan.

13. Norge Company manufactures washers and dryers. For aggregate planning purposes, each product is treated separately, although both require many of the same production facilities. The forecasted demand, in units, is shown as follows:

Month	Forecast For Washers	Forecast For Dryers
Aug.	100,000	80,000
Sept.	120,000	90,000
Oct.	100,000	90,000
Nov.	150,000	100,000
Dec.	170,000	110,000
Jan.	140,000	100,000
Feb.	100,000	80,000

The parts for each washer and dryer are machined on the same equipment, but there are separate washer and dryer assembly lines. Each washer requires .3 hour of machining time and .1 hour of assembly time. Each dryer requires .2 hour of machining time and .15 hour of assembly time. Calculate the total machining and assembly requirements for each month.

14. Referring to Problem 13, suppose that Norge has available 50,000 hours of machining time each month on regular time. An additional 20,000 hours is available on overtime. After that, a second shift must be added. Calculate overtime hours required each month, and indicate which months will require a second shift for machining.

15. Referring to Problems 13 and 14, suppose that regular-time pay is $10.00 per hour, overtime pay is $15.00 per hour, and second-shift pay is $10.50 per hour. Reevaluate your solution for Problem 14 to determine when it is less expensive to add a second shift instead of using overtime. The second shift must be paid for a minimum of 20,000 hours each month even if that much time is not needed.

16. Using the data from Problem 13, graph the total assembly requirements and the total machining requirements for each month.

17. The Branchville office of Eastern Bell Telephone Company is planning its requirements for telephone installers. Based on past experience, the following forecast of installation hours required each month has been developed:

Month	Forecast Of Installation Hours	Month	Forecast Of Installation Hours
Apr.	1,800	Aug.	3,500
May	2,000	Sept.	3, 000
June	2,800	Oct.	2, 200
July	3,000		

The company currently has fifteen installers who each work an average of 175 hours per month.

a. Draw a graph of cumulative installation hours available versus cumulative installation hours forecast.

b. In the past, Eastern Bell has had a policy of maintaining a sufficient number of installers to meet peak-period demand. If enough additional installers were hired before April to meet peak demand, graph cumulative installation hours available versus cumulative hours forecast.

18. In addition to the data given in Problem 17, suppose each installer is paid $7.50 per hour.

a. Calculate total payroll costs if enough additional installers are hired before April to meet peak demand over the planning horizon.

b. Eastern Bell is considering subcontracting work to an independent electrical contractor for periods when demand exceeds existing installation capacity. Determine how many installation hours would need to be subcontracted each month if the existing workforce of fifteen is maintained.

c. If the subcontractor charges $15 per hour, compare the costs of subcontracting with the costs of maintaining the peak-period workforce over the planning horizon. Which minimizes total costs?

19. The Itty Bitty Machine Company has just entered the pocket computer market. Although the company is starting with modest sales, it expects sales to grow before leveling off at 6,000 units per month, as shown in the following twelve-month forecast:

Month	Sales Forecast	Month	Sales Forecast	Month	Sales Forecast
Jan.	4,000	May	4,700	Sept.	5,700
Feb.	4,200	June	4,800	Oct.	6,000
Mar.	4,300	July	4,900	Nov.	6,000
Apr.	4,500	Aug.	5,300	Dec.	6,000

The company currently has fifty employees on its payroll, each of whom can assemble 100 computers per month. It costs $500 to hire a new employee and $1,000 to lay off an employee. Employees each earn $1,500 per month, but overtime work earns a premium of 50 percent above regular pay. It costs $10 per month to store one unit in inventory for one month. There are 400 units currently on hand for the beginning of January.

a. Calculate production plans for the twelve-months, using each of the three pure strategies.

b. Calculate the total costs associated with each of your production plans developed in Part a.

20. Referring to Problem 19, suppose that the Itty Bitty Machine Company does not want to lay off employees. Develop a production plan, using any pure strategy (without layoffs) or a mixed strategy, to minimize total cost over the planning horizon.

21. FyreGlow is a manufacturer of gas barbecue grills. As you might expect, demand for its product is highest during the warm months of the year and lowest during the cold months. The following indicates expected demand during the next year:

Month	Sales Forecast	Month	Sales Forecast	Month	Sales Forecast
Jan.	3,000	May	4,800	Sept.	4,000
Feb.	3,500	June	5,000	Oct.	3,500
Mar.	4,000	July	5,200	Nov.	3,000
Apr.	4,500	Aug.	4,500	Dec.	3,000

In the past, FyreGlow has produced a constant 4,000 units per month by maintaining a workforce of twenty employees, with each employee producing 200 units per month. As a result, the company has incurred large inventory carrying costs at $2 per unit per month. Now, however, FyreGlow is considering offering discounts during the cold months to level out demand. How much discount per unit would FyreGlow be willing to offer to offset its current inventory carrying costs?

22. Suppose the FyreGlow Company in Problem 21 has decided it wants to consider producing a complementary seasonal product during the cold months and chooses to make fireplace inserts. It is expected that each employee will be able to produce fifty fireplace inserts per month.

    a. How many employees will be needed to meet demand for barbecue grills without stockpiling?

    b. Based on the answer from Part a, what is the number of fireplace inserts that can be produced each month?

CHAPTER 13

Planning for Material and Resource Requirements

LEARNING OBJECTIVES

After completing this chapter, you should be able to:

1. Describe the relationships among aggregate planning, master scheduling, MRP, and capacity planning.
2. Show how a master schedule is developed from an aggregate plan.
3. Use the method of overall factors to estimate capacity requirements based on a master schedule.
4. Explain the difference between independent and dependent demand, and indicate the type of demand for which MRP is appropriate.
5. Use MRP to develop planned order releases for items at all levels of the bill of materials.
6. Develop a load report and load profile based on MRP output, routings, and labor standards.
7. Describe the characteristics of MRP II.

INTRODUCTION

The preceding chapter dealt with how a company moves from its strategic plan to a medium-range operations plan, or aggregate plan. The aggregate plan indicates how the organization intends to meet demand for the good or service it provides. Thus, the aggregate plan is a statement of planned output, inventory, and/or staffing levels, usually by product groups on a monthly basis.

Because of its broad, general nature, the aggregate plan cannot be implemented directly. Instead, another, more detailed, plan must usually be developed based on the aggregate plan. This latter plan is called a master production schedule.

In meeting the demand for its goods or services, an organization will need to use various resources and materials. However, if sufficient quantities of these resources and materials are not available when needed, customer service will suffer. Therefore, when developing a master production schedule, a company must ensure that the schedule is realistic in terms of its resource and material requirements.

In this chapter, we explain how to develop a master production schedule. Further, we indicate how an organization can determine the resource and material requirements of that schedule and then plan to have the appropriate quantity of materials and resources available at the right time. We then conclude by discussing how Enterprise Resource Planning (ERP) allows large organizations, or even entire supply chains, to better coordinate their activities through a shared database.

MASTER PRODUCTION SCHEDULING

The master schedule—or **master production schedule (MPS)**—is based on the medium-range operations plan discussed in Chapter 12. While that plan was "aggregated" in terms of product groups, the master schedule is "disaggregated." The master schedule is a specific statement of exactly what, usually stated in terms of individual end items or product models, will be produced in each time period. Usually these time periods are weeks, although they may be days or even hours. The master schedule is thus a detailed extension of the medium-range operations plan, or aggregate plan.

Planning Horizons

The aggregate plan is generally developed for a year or more into the future. The master schedule, however, usually does not need to go that far, especially since it becomes more difficult to manage as the number of time periods increases. As a general rule, companies use six months for their master schedule. However, the most important rule is that the master scheduling horizon must be at least equal to the longest cumulative lead time of any product and its component parts. In other words, enough time must be allowed from the time a master schedule quantity is entered for all parts and raw materials to be ordered from suppliers, component parts to be manufactured, and the final product to be assembled and shipped. Otherwise, the master schedule will be difficult to meet for those products with long cumulative lead times.

Developing the MPS

Because the master schedule is a statement of exactly what will be produced, the company must be sure of two things:

1.   The master schedule must satisfy the needs of marketing.
2.   The master schedule must be "doable" by operations.

Developing a master schedule that is close to the aggregate plan, yet still satisfies marketing and operations, is no easy task. The aggregate plan was developed based on a strategy that maintained acceptable inventory and workforce levels. The master schedule should still be based on that strategy, but must now do so for individual end items. In addition, the master schedule must not place more capacity demands on any machine or work center than can reasonably be met by existing capacity.

Due to the difficulties involved in developing a good master production schedule, the job is usually done by experienced individuals called master schedulers. But because it is likely you will someday have contact with a master schedule, we will show you how they are developed under two different situations. Following the approach taken by real companies, we will begin with the aggregate plan.

We will use the Maine Woods Company, which produces wooden toys, as an example. The company's production process is quite labor intensive and relies heavily on skilled woodworkers who use such equipment as saws, lathes, routers, and jointers to make most of the parts that go into the company's finished products. The company's medium-range, or aggregate, production plan is developed on a monthly basis for one year into the future. For planning purposes, the company's forty-eight different products are grouped by product characteristics into three product families: wheel goods, blocks, and baby toys. It is these families that are reflected in the aggregate plan. Exhibit 13.1 shows that plan for the wheel-goods products only.

As you can see, the company has developed an aggregate plan that emphasizes maintaining a constant workforce. Due to the high skill level required of its employees, Maine Woods does not want to use hiring and layoffs. Instead, inventory is built up in anticipation of high demand during late summer and fall when the retail stores that sell Maine Woods' toys order in preparation for Christmas. Overtime has been planned only as a necessity in October and November when no inventory will be available to draw on.

Matching the Master Schedule to the Aggregate Plan

Referring again to the Maine Woods aggregate plan shown in Exhibit 13.1, you can see that during the early part of the year, production exceeds demand, thus building up inventory. During that time period, the company's objectives for the master production schedule will be to:

- Produce quantities that will match the aggregate plan
- Produce each individual product in proportion to its expected demand
- Schedule production so available capacity is not exceeded

The wheel-goods product group consists of three products: tricycles, toy wagons, and scooters. Past experience indicates that orders for these will be divided so that about half are for tricycles and the remaining orders are equally divided between wagons and scooters. Thus, in January, the planned production of 2,000 units should be divided so that 1,000 tricycles, 500 toy wagons, and 500 scooters are produced. The same should also be done for February and March.

Exhibit 13.2 shows one possible master schedule that satisfies the preceding requirements. Notice that the total production of all three products in each month matches the aggregate plan for that month. Further, production of each individual product is spread out evenly so the production facilities will not be overloaded in some weeks and underloaded in others.

The master schedule shown in Exhibit 13.2 could be extended across the first nine months of the year because planned production in each of those months is the same. But, in October, planned production increases to 2,400 units. To meet this increase, we can

EXHIBIT 13.1	Month	Demand Forecast	Regular-Time Production	Overtime Production	Beginning Inventory	Ending Inventory
Maine Woods Co. Aggregate Plan, Wheel-Goods Product Group	January	1,800	2,000		0	200
	February	1,700	2,000		200	500
	March	1,800	2,000		500	700
	April	1,500	2,000		700	1,200
	May	1,800	2,000		1,200	1,400
	June	1,900	2,000		1,400	1,500
	July	2,000	2,000		1,500	1,500
	August	2,500	2,000		1,500	1,000
	September	2,500	2,000		1,000	500
	October	2,900	2,000	400	500	0
	November	2,400	2,000	400	0	0
	December	2,000	2,000		0	0

EXHIBIT 13.2

Maine Woods Co.
Master Production
Schedule,
Wheel-Goods Product
Group: Constant
Planned Production

Month		January				February				March			
Week		1	2	3	4	5	6	7	8	9	10	11	12
Product	Tricycle	250	250	250	250	250	250	250	250	250	250	250	250
	Toy wagon	250		250		250		250		250		250	
	Scooter		250		250		250		250		250		250
Totals		2,000				2,000				2,000			

simply spread the difference evenly across that month, keeping each product's proportion of the total the same as before. Exhibit 13.3 shows the master schedule with increased output for October.

Taking Customer Orders into Account

The master schedules just developed were based strictly on the aggregate plan and historical information about demand for each product. However, customer orders must enter into the process. Otherwise, we may be producing based on a plan that is no longer valid because actual demand has changed.

To show how a master schedule can be developed that takes demand into account, let's remove inventory buildup from the picture by concentrating on the company during November and December when no inventory is available and demand must be met from current production. We will also concentrate on just one product—the toy wagon.

Suppose we are in the last week of October, and our forecasts still indicate that 600 toy wagons (one-fourth of 2,400) will be ordered during November and another 500 (one-fourth of 2,000) during December. We can enter this information in Exhibit 13.4 in the Forecast demand row. Actual customer orders may, however, differ from the forecast. Therefore, the next row in Exhibit 13.4 indicates actual orders booked. Notice how the actual orders received decrease as we go farther into the future. As those time periods draw closer to the present, we will expect orders to increase, coming closer to the forecast.

Calculating Projected On-Hand Inventory

Because Maine Woods produces toy wagons only every other week, a key to meeting customer orders will be inventory on hand. For example, notice that the company has 100 toy wagons in on-hand inventory at the end of October. However, customer orders for the first week of November are 170. Therefore, unless more wagons are produced, demand cannot be met. To avoid this problem, Maine Woods has already scheduled another batch of 300 wagons for production during the first week of November, as shown in Exhibit 13.4.

To plan additional production of toy wagons, which will be scheduled in the Master schedule row of Exhibit 13.4, it will be necessary to calculate the projected on-hand inventory. We refer to this as "projected" because it is based on information currently available. As new customer orders arrive, the actual on-hand inventory each week may change.

To determine projected inventory on hand for a specific week, perform the following calculations:

EXHIBIT 13.3

Maine Woods Co.
Master Production
Schedule,
Wheel-Goods
Product Group

Month		September				October			
Week		37	38	39	40	41	42	43	44
Product	Tricycle	250	250	250	250	300	300	300	300
	Toy wagon	250		250		300		300	
	Scooter		250		250		300		300
Totals		2,000				2,400			

EXHIBIT 13.4

Maine Woods Co.
Master Production
Schedule Based on
Demand Forecast and
Booked Customer
Orders for Toy Wagons

On-hand inventory at end of October = 100

Month	November				December			
Week	45	46	47	48	49	50	51	52
Forecast demand	150	150	150	150	125	125	125	125
Customer orders booked	170	165	140	120	85	45	20	0
Projected on-hand inventory	230	65	−85					
Master schedule	300							

1. Add either actual inventory on hand from the preceding week or projected on-hand inventory from the preceding week to any quantity shown in the Master schedule row for the week being calculated.

2. Determine the larger of forecast demand or customer orders booked. This is done for two reasons. First, we must allow for actual orders exceeding the forecast. Second, additional orders could be received in the future for periods in which customer orders booked are currently less than the forecast.

3. Subtract the amount determined in step 2 from the amount in step 1. The result becomes projected on-hand inventory for the week in question.

PROBLEM

Refer to Exhibit 13.4 for Maine Woods. The projected on-hand inventory for weeks 45, 46, and 47 is calculated as follows:

WEEK 45:

1. Actual on-hand inventory from the preceding week (last week of October) is 100 units.

2. The master schedule amount in week 45 is 300.

3. Customer orders booked in week 45 are 170, which is larger than the forecast for that week (150).

Projected on-hand inventory = 100 + 300 − 170 = 230

WEEK 46:

1. Projected on-hand inventory from the preceding week (week 45) is 230 units.
2. The master schedule amount in week 46 is 0.
3. Customer orders booked in week 46 are 165, which is larger than the forecast for that week (150).

$$\text{Projected on-hand inventory} = 230 + 0 - 165 = 65$$

WEEK 47:

1. Projected on-hand inventory from the preceding week (week 46) is 65 units.
2. The master schedule amount in week 47 is 0.
3. Forecast demand in week 47 is 150, which is larger than the customer orders booked for that week (140).

$$\text{Projected on-hand inventory} = 65 + 0 - 150 = -85$$

Entering a Master Schedule Quantity

Whenever projected on-hand inventory becomes negative, as it has in week 47, the need for more production is indicated. Thus, a master schedule quantity must be entered for week 47.

The exact quantity to schedule will be determined on the basis of production capacity available, expected demand, and desired batch sizes. Following its procedure of producing toy wagons every other week, Maine Woods would plan to produce enough to meet demand for the next two weeks, which would be 300, based on the demand forecast shown in Exhibit 13.5. Notice that the projected on-hand inventory balance for week 47 has been recalculated, based on the new master schedule quantity.

Determining the Amount Available to Promise

We have just dealt with the problem of scheduling production to meet projected demand. You should keep in mind, however, that customer orders will constantly be coming in with

EXHIBIT 13.5

Calculation of Available-to-Promise for November and December for Maine Woods Co.

On-hand inventory at end of October = 100

Month	November				December			
Week	45	46	47	48	49	50	51	52
Forecast demand	150	150	150	150	125	125	125	125
Customer orders booked	170	165	140	120	85	45	20	0
Projected on-hand inventory	230	65	215	65	190	65	190	65
Master schedule	300		300		250		250	
Available-to-promise	65		40		120		230	

requests for completion of each order in a desired week. For example, suppose a customer has just contacted Maine Woods and requested fifty toy wagons to be shipped in week 46. Will the company have enough toy wagons available to meet this new order plus the existing orders for 335 already entered in weeks 45 and 46?

To determine whether new orders can be accepted within a given time period, companies calculate an **available-to-promise** quantity. This quantity represents the number of units that can be promised for completion any time before the next master schedule quantity.

The available-to-promise quantity is calculated as follows:

1. In the first time period of the planning horizon, add actual on-hand inventory from the preceding time period to any master schedule quantity and then subtract the sum of customer orders booked before the next master schedule quantity.

2. For subsequent weeks, calculate available-to-promise only for those weeks when a master schedule quantity is indicated. Subtract the sum of customer orders booked before the next master schedule quantity from the master schedule amount for the given week. *Do not* include projected on-hand inventory, as that amount could be used in preceding weeks if more orders are booked.

PROBLEM

Referring to the Maine Woods example shown in Exhibit 13.5, we will determine available-to-promise quantities for November.

WEEK 45:

Actual on-hand inventory from the preceding week (end of October) = 100. The master schedule quantity for week 45 = 300. The sum of customer orders booked before the next master schedule quantity (week 47) = 170 + 165. The available-to-promise quantity = (100 + 300) − (170 + 165) = 65.

WEEK 46:

There is no master schedule quantity in this week, so it is skipped.

WEEK 47:

The master schedule amount = 300. The sum of customer orders booked before the next master schedule quantity (week 49) = 140 + 120. The available-to-promise quantity = 300 − (140 + 120) = 40.

This indicates that Maine Woods can promise another sixty-five units to its customers for completion in week 45 or 46. However, based on current information, only forty more units may be promised for week 47 or 48.

Although the preceding example has related to a manufacturing environment, master scheduling is used extensively by service organizations. For example, the appointment systems used by physicians' offices are actually a form of MPS. Knowing which patients are coming in on a given day and why they are being seen can help office staff in planning the time that will be required for each patient.

Master Scheduling in Practice

Our discussion of master production scheduling thus far has been designed to give you the basics. In actual practice, the job is much more difficult and involved. In this section, we will briefly survey a few key points of which you should also be aware.

Integration with Other Functional Areas

Although the master schedule relates primarily to production, it also has significant implications for marketing and finance. The number of units produced during each time period will often determine whether demand can be met for that time period. Further, this production will generate significant costs for labor and materials, while also determining the inflow that comes from sales. Consequently, both marketing and finance must not only be aware of the master schedule, but also must give it their approval.

In the past this was often an iterative process, frequently involving only marketing and operations. But with today's emphasis on elimination of functional barriers, some companies have formed interfunctional teams with representatives from operations, marketing, and finance. Such a team works together to develop a master schedule that meets all their needs. As a result, the schedule is completed more quickly. Further, through their face-to-face discussions, each individual on the team can better understand the challenges and constraints faced by the functional areas other team members represent.

An Iterative Process

The steps we followed in the preceding section would generally lead to a "trial" MPS, not necessarily the final one. As Exhibit 13.6 indicates, after this trial master schedule is developed, a determination must be made as to whether sufficient capacity is available. Although the aggregate plan was developed to ensure that adequate overall capacity would be available, the specific mix of products and timing of production can mean that there will not be sufficient capacity in every week. This check is performed using rough-cut capacity planning, which will be discussed in the next section of this chapter.

Next, marketing must approve the master schedule. Marketing may have special promotions or other plans that must be reflected in the master schedule. If the trial MPS does not satisfy marketing's requirements, then it must be redone. Meeting the various internal and external demands with available resources is what makes master scheduling so difficult. However, many companies have gone to using a joint team from operations, marketing, and finance to develop the MPS.

EXHIBIT 13.6

Iterative Process for Developing a Master Production Schedule

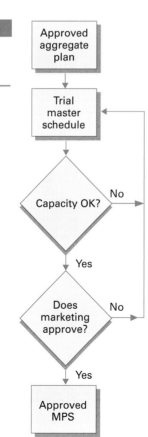

Freezing the Master Schedule

An important point that must be stressed is that the plans we have been discussing are not something a company can do once a year and then put away in a drawer. Planning is a continuous process that can be thought of as rolling out a scroll. As time passes, the scroll keeps getting rolled up on the end closest to us and unrolled at the other end, so that new material is always coming into view. This idea has been referred to as **"rolling through time."**

Obviously, forecasts far into the future will be less accurate than nearer term forecasts. Thus, it may be necessary to make changes in planned production as the planning horizon draws nearer. For instance, a company might find that demand for one of its products is far exceeding the company's forecasts. This organization would be foolish not to alter its production plans to meet the increased demand. Thus, both the aggregate plan and the master schedule will change as time passes. But, too much change can be disruptive. For example, a company might have already hired employees and bought materials to meet its production plan. Altering that plan could mean idle employees or inventories of unused materials. To avoid such problems, many companies "freeze" their master schedule for a certain time into the future. **Freezing** the master schedule means that no further changes can be made after a certain time. For instance, a company may indicate that the master schedule will be frozen for one month into the future. Thus, no changes may be made once a plan gets within one month of its execution date. This is depicted in Exhibit 13.7. The master schedule is commonly frozen over several weeks or a month, although longer and shorter periods are possible, depending on how easily a company can change its plans. This period is often determined by the cumulative lead time to procure materials and produce the product.

The Demand Management Process

In developing a master production schedule for the Maine Woods Company, we took two approaches. The first was based on producing to inventory while the second was based on producing to customer orders. In actual practice, both sources of demand must be considered. There are also other sources of demand. For example, companies that operate multiple plants often have one plant producing parts for another plant. Such orders would be identified as interplant orders. Further, many companies produce replacement parts for their products, such as starter motors for automobiles or blades for lawnmowers. These service parts requirements must also be considered. **Demand management** is the process of recognizing all such sources of demand and reflecting them in the master schedule. Such a process is depicted in Exhibit 13.8.

ROUGH-CUT CAPACITY PLANNING

The aggregate plan is a first step in ensuring that sufficient labor, capital, and machine time will be available to meet customer demand. But, the aggregate plan only looks at those

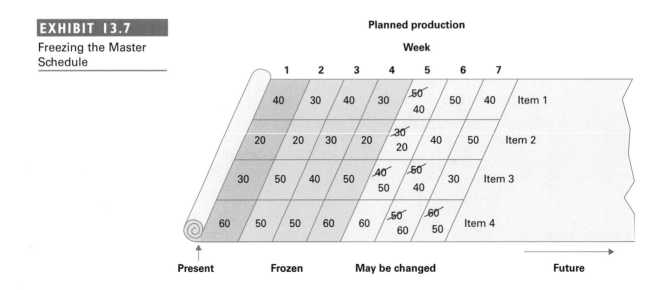

EXHIBIT 13.7

Freezing the Master Schedule

EXHIBIT 13.8

Recognizing all
Sources of Demand
through Demand
Management

	Week					
	1	**2**	**3**	**4**	**5**	**6**
Customer demand	100	125	75	150	200	100
Interplant orders	25		50			75
Service parts	5		10		5	
Branch warehouse orders	50	50	50	50	50	50
Research & development orders		5			5	
Marketing samples	15		20		15	
Total demand	195	180	205	200	275	225

resources in aggregate terms. The technique of rough-cut capacity planning is a means of determining whether sufficient capacity exists at specific work centers to execute the master schedule.

Calculating Requirements by Overall Factors

The purpose of **rough-cut capacity planning** is to determine whether approximately enough capacity will be available to meet the master production schedule. Thus, we will not be concerned with developing an exact figure. Many companies use the **method of overall factors** because of its simplicity and ease of calculation. This method relies primarily on historical accounting information to determine how many standard hours are required per unit of each product. By multiplying this figure by the number of units planned for production each week, an overall capacity requirement can be determined. This requirement can then be broken down by individual work centers, again based on historical data.

PROBLEM

Let's return to the production plan for Maine Woods' wheel goods. According to Exhibit 13.1, an aggregate production of 2,000 units has been planned for January.

In developing the master schedule of Exhibit 13.2, Maine Woods has converted that planned production into the detailed schedule for its three wheel-goods products—toy wagons, tricycles, and scooters.

Based on historical accounting information, each tricycle required .6 standard hour to produce, each toy wagon required .3 standard hour, and each scooter required .2 standard hour. This information can be used, as shown in Exhibit 13.9, to calculate capacity requirements for each product. By summing the weekly capacity requirements across all products, the total capacity requirements can be determined, as shown at the bottom of Exhibit 13.9.

Suppose Maine Woods is concerned about the high usage of its cutting and drilling operations. Again, based on historical accounting information, 40 percent of all standard hours are spent on cutting and 35 percent on drilling. The other 25 percent of standard hours is used for noncritical operations that are not of concern.

Tricycles

January

Week	1	2	3	4
Master Schedule	250	250	250	250
Capacity required	150	150	150	150

.6 standard hour per tricycle

Toy Wagon

January

Week	1	2	3	4
Master Schedule	250		250	
Capacity required	75		75	

.3 standard hour per wagon

Scooter

January

Week	1	2	3	4
Master Schedule		250		250
Capacity required		50		50

.2 standard hour per scooter

Total capacity required (standard hours)	225	200	225	200

This historical information can be used to estimate capacity requirements at each operation. For example, in week 1, a total of 225 standard hours is required. Of this, we would expect 90 hours (40 percent) to be required for cutting and 78.75 hours (35 percent) to be required for drilling. Exhibit 13.10 shows the estimated capacity requirements for each work center each week.

Handling Insufficient Capacity

Once a company has estimated capacity requirements at each work station or operation, those figures can be compared to capacity available. In some cases, excess capacity may be available, which would indicate the opportunity to either book more orders or decrease working hours. In other cases, however, requirements may exceed capacity available.

If insufficient capacity is available to meet the master schedule, the easiest approaches are for a company to try either to shift some scheduled production into an earlier time

EXHIBIT 13.10

Calculation of Estimated Capacity Requirements for Individual Work Stations

	Week			
	1	2	3	4
Total capacity required (standard hours)	225	200	225	200
Cutting—40% (standard hours)	90	80	90	80
Drilling—35% (standard hours)	78.75	70	78.75	70

period that has excess capacity or to schedule overtime, if possible. If neither of those approaches is possible, more major changes may have to be made in the master schedule.

PROBLEM

Maine Woods has 100 hours of cutting time available each week and 80 hours of drilling time. Thus, based on Exhibit 13.10, sufficient capacity is available to meet the master schedule. In fact, weeks 2 and 4 have considerable excess.

However, an important customer has just asked whether an order for seventy-five tricycles could be completed in week 3. Although week 3 falls within the master schedule's frozen time period, the vice-president of manufacturing has approved an override if capacity is available.

Seventy-five tricycles would require an additional forty-five standard hours (75 × .6) in week 3. Of these additional hours, we would expect 18 (40 percent) to be for cutting and 15.75 (35 percent) to be for drilling. Exhibit 13.11 indicates the capacity requirements for cutting and drilling if this new order is accommodated. Unfortunately, with only 100 hours of cutting time and 80 hours of drilling time, sufficient capacity will not be available.

Maine Woods has several options, including turning down the order for week 3. One option is to schedule overtime as necessary in week 3 for cutting and drilling. The customer might be charged a higher price to cover the added cost.

Another option is shown in Exhibit 13.12. In this case, the seventy-five tricycles have been spread among weeks 2, 3, and 4 (thirty-five in week 2, five in week 3, thirty-five in week 4) to utilize available regular-time capacity. In this case, all of the customer's order could not be completed in week 3, but perhaps enough could be finished to satisfy the customer.

MATERIAL REQUIREMENTS PLANNING

The medium-range (aggregate) plan and master schedule can be used to generate rough estimates of the labor and equipment that will be needed. But another important resource, materials, is not really accounted for. One approach that has been used in the past for material planning is to be sure that enough of everything the company uses is always in inventory (sometimes called Just in Case inventory control). This approach meant that huge inventories had to be maintained, resulting in extensive warehouse space and a large amount of money tied up in that inventory. Even then, many companies found that certain crucial items used in many of their products always seemed to run out at the wrong time. No matter how much inventory was kept, a large demand for certain parts could deplete their supply rather quickly.

EXHIBIT 13.11

Proposed Master Schedule Requiring Overtime in Week 3

	Week			
	1	2	3	4
Tricycles	250	250	325	250
Toy Wagons	250		250	
Scooters		250		250
Cutting capacity required (standard hours)	90	80	90 + 18 = 108	80
Drilling capacity required (standard hours)	78.75	70	78.75 + 15.75 = 94.5	70

EXHIBIT 13.12

Proposed Master Schedule with Changes to Avoid Overtime

	Week			
	1	2	3	4
Tricycles	250	(250 + 35) 285	(250 + 5) 255	(250 + 35) 285
Toy Wagons	250		250	
Scooters		250		250
Cutting capacity required (standard hours)	90	88.4	91.2	88.4
Drilling capacity required (standard hours)	78.75	77.35	79.80	77.35

Independent versus Dependent Demand

Inventory can also be classified according to the type of demand it is meant to serve. That type of demand determines the methods used to manage the inventory. Independent demand is demand that is not controlled directly by the company, such as demand from customers. **Independent demand** items usually include finished products, such as the completed tricycle or replacement parts sold to customers. Demand for such items is generally independent of a company's own production plans. Chapter 14 will discuss procedures for managing inventory of independent demand items.

Dependent demand is usually demand for an item that is generated by a company's own production process. One example would be the wheels for tricycles that a company produces. Each tricycle has three wheels so if the company plans to produce 200 tricycles in a given week, then it will need 600 (200 × 3) wheels that week. Thus the demand for wheels depends on the production of tricycles. To manage inventory for dependent demand items, companies often use material requirements planning (MRP), which is discussed in this section

The idea behind MRP is simple; you probably do it yourself in planning a special meal. A few days ahead of time, you figure out what you want to have, check the ingredients you need, and then go out and buy whatever you don't have enough of. The same approach is used in operations management.

The master schedule corresponds to your menu. Recall that the master schedule indicates precisely what end items, and in what quantities, the company plans to produce over some time horizon. By using the bills of materials, a company can determine what parts and materials, and how many of each, it needs to meet the master schedule. Inventory records will show how much is on hand. From this, it can be determined which parts or materials will come up short and how much more is needed of each.

The Data Files Used by MRP

For companies today, MRP is a computerized information system. As such, it requires data to provide the information needed for decision making. We have already mentioned the three most important data requirements of MRP—master production schedules, bills of material, and inventory records. Generally each of these is kept in a separate computer data file.

Master Schedule File

We have already discussed in great detail the master production schedule. For MRP purposes, the master schedule is what "drives" the system and generates material requirements. As mentioned earlier, this master schedule may be at the finished-products level for companies like Maine Woods that manufacture standard products. However, for companies making customized products, the master schedule may be at the level of components or subassemblies.

Bills of Materials File

Chapter 6 briefly discusses bills of materials. However, because MRP is a computerized system, some modifications are made to the bills of materials.

Indicating Product Structure   The bill of materials serves two purposes. First, it lists all the components of a product. Second, it shows the relationships among those components. For example, Exhibit 13.13 shows an exploded view of the tricycle produced by Maine Woods. One possible bill of materials would simply list all these component parts.

However, in manufacturing this tricycle, the front wheel, its supports, the axle, and the steering column are subassembled before the entire tricycle is put together. Likewise, the seat and rear axle supports are subassembled before final assembly.

One way to indicate these subassemblies is through a product structure tree diagram, as shown in Exhibit 13.14. Notice that all the parts brought together at final assembly are listed together on level 1. Any parts that are components of subassemblies are listed on level 2. Connecting lines indicate which parts go into which subassembly.

Indented Bills Of Materials   The tree diagram is useful for showing us relationships among components, but it cannot be read directly by the computer. Instead, an **indented bill of materials** is used by MRP to provide information about product structure. Each item is identified with a level, as shown in Exhibit 13.14. In an indented bill of materials, each level is indented from the one above it. Exhibit 13.15 is the indented bill of materials for Maine Woods' tricycle.

Low-Level Coding   Notice in Exhibit 13.15 that the same wheels are used on the front and back of the tricycle. However, the wheels at the rear are on level 1 because they are not part of a subassembly, while the front wheel is a level 2 item.

In a situation like this, there is the possibility of placing separate orders for the same part. To avoid this possibility, any part is always assigned the lowest level (highest level number) at which it appears. Thus, the wheels should always appear as a level 2 item. This is called **low-level coding.** Such coding also facilitates computer processing.

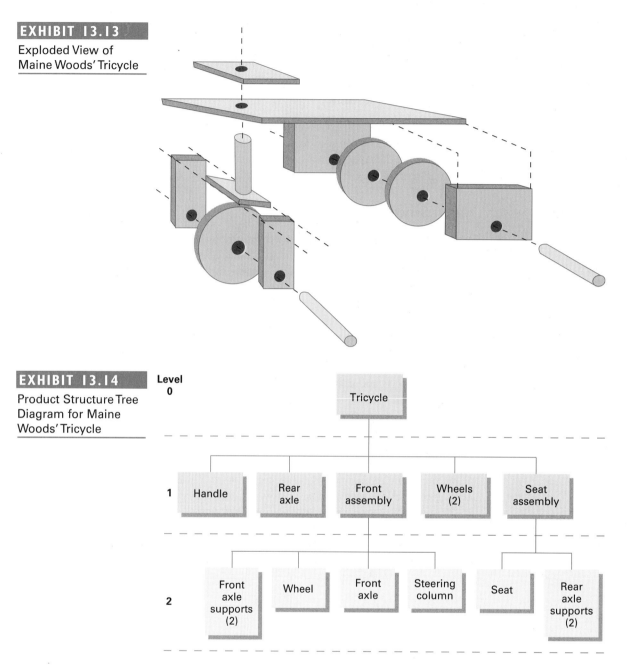

EXHIBIT 13.13

Exploded View of
Maine Woods' Tricycle

EXHIBIT 13.14

Product Structure Tree
Diagram for Maine
Woods' Tricycle

The Inventory File

In order for MRP to work, accurate inventory records must be kept. For most companies, this accuracy requires continually updating inventory records as items are withdrawn or added. To automate this function, many are using bar codes, which are similar to the universal product codes (UPCs) you see on items at the grocery store. Even then, mistakes can be made.

Cycle Counting. To reconcile inventory records and correct errors, many companies using MRP also employ what is called **cycle counting.** Using this method, a physical count

	Level	Part No.	Quantity	Description
EXHIBIT 13.15	0	127	1	Tricycle
	1	3417	1	Handle
Indented Bill of	1	2973	1	Rear axle
Materials for Maine	1	463	1	Front assembly
Woods' Tricycle	2	3987	2	Axle support (front)
	2	5917	1	Wheel
	2	2673	1	Front axle
	2	3875	1	Steering column
	1	5917	2	Wheel
	1	587	1	Seat assembly
	2	4673	1	Seat
	2	3965	2	Axle support (rear)

of each part is made at least once during its replenishment cycle, which is the period between orders to replenish inventory.

Determining Planned Order Releases for Level 1 Items

The objective of MRP is to ensure that the correct quantities of component parts are available at the proper time to produce finished products according to the master production schedule. In this section we describe how that is done for items that appear immediately below the finished product in the product structure tree diagram.

Displaying MRP Information

The information obtained from bills of materials, inventory records, and the master schedule can all be brought together in the diagram of Exhibit 13.16, which is the table commonly used to calculate and display MRP information.

You should notice that there are time periods across the top of the table. These represent time periods for planning purposes, or time buckets. The **time buckets** correspond to the master schedule, which, as we said previously, is usually drawn up in terms of weeks. The purpose of using these time periods is to state requirements for component parts and materials in terms of the total quantity needed during each time bucket. This process of stating requirements by time bucket is often called **time phasing.**

The first row in Exhibit 13.16 is labeled Gross requirements. **Gross requirements** represent the total quantity needed of a particular item in each time bucket, based on the master schedule and the bill of materials, regardless of current inventory of that item. The second row, **Scheduled receipts,** shows whether any orders for that item have been placed previously, but not yet received. Entries in this row indicate when that order should come in and how many units should be in it. Projected ending inventory shows the planned number of units that should be remaining at the end of each time bucket after all transactions of that period are complete. If the number of units available during a period (projected ending inventory from the previous period plus receipts) is not sufficient to cover gross requirements, then the row labeled **Net requirements** indicates the number of units the company is short. An entry in Net requirements indicates that a replenishment order will need to be placed. Thus, the last two rows show Planned receipts and Planned order releases. The **Planned receipts** row shows when orders must arrive in order to avoid a shortage of necessary parts or materials, as indicated by the Net requirements row. The **Planned order releases** row indicates the time periods in which those orders must be released (or placed) to arrive at the correct time. The difference between scheduled receipts and planned receipts is that scheduled receipts correspond to orders that have actually been placed some time in the past, but not yet received. Planned receipts correspond to orders planned for release, but not yet released. Both scheduled receipts and planned receipts are included as units available in the MRP record.

MRP Logic

The information in Exhibit 13.16 may be completed for each part or raw material as follows:

1. Obtain the bill of materials for the appropriate end product.
2. Begin with a level 1 item from the bill of materials.
3. Multiply the number of units of the level 1 item needed per unit of finished product (from the bill of materials) by the master schedule quantity for each time bucket. Insert this as gross requirements for the appropriate time bucket. Ordinarily the master schedule indicates the units of finished product to be produced in each time period, so the appropriate time bucket will be that same time period. In some cases, however, the master schedule indicates completion of production. If so, the time period when production begins would be the appropriate time bucket for gross requirements.
4. Enter any scheduled receipts of the item, based on lead time and orders previously released, in the appropriate time buckets.
5. Determine how many units should be in inventory at the start of the first time bucket. Enter this in the square to the left of that first time bucket.
6. Perform the following steps for each time bucket, beginning with the first, until the end of the planning horizon is reached. Add projected ending inventory from the preceding time bucket to scheduled receipts for the present period. If this total equals or exceeds gross requirements for the present period, go to step a. Otherwise, go to step b.

If gross requirements in the time bucket being planned are less than or equal to the projected ending inventory from the preceding time bucket plus scheduled receipts for the current period, enter the difference as projected ending inventory in the present period. Leave net requirements blank, and repeat this step for the next time bucket.

If gross requirements are greater than projected ending inventory from the preceding time period plus scheduled receipts for the time bucket being planned, enter the difference as net requirements. Leave projected ending inventory blank for the present time period until the following substeps have been performed:

EXHIBIT 13.16

Table for MRP

- Gross requirements
- Scheduled receipts
- Projected ending inventory
- Net requirements
- Planned receipts
- Planned order releases

1. For any period in which net requirements appear, plan an order release and corresponding receipt to cover the net requirements. (This ordering approach is termed "lot-for-lot." Net requirements from several periods may be combined into one planned order release using other lot-sizing methods.)

2. Subtract net requirements from planned receipts, and enter the total as projected ending inventory for the current time bucket. Proceed to step a for the next time bucket.

PROBLEM   Let's return to the Maine Woods Company. The bill of materials for tricycles, shown in Exhibit 13.15, indicates the front assembly (part #463) is a level 1 item. The inventory file for this item shows 100 units are expected to be in inventory at the end of December. Production lead time, the time it takes to receive front assemblies after more are ordered into production, is two weeks. An order for 500 front assemblies was released earlier and is scheduled for receipt during week 1 of January. Using the master schedule for tricycles of Exhibit 13.12, determine planned order releases for front assemblies.

Step 1. The bill of materials (Exhibit 13.15) indicates one front assembly is needed for each tricycle.

Step 2. Front assemblies are a level 1 item, so you may begin planning with them.

Step 3. The master schedule of production during weeks 1 through 6 is shown at the top of Exhibit 13.17. Because one front assembly is needed for each tricycle, and the master schedule shows units to be produced during each week, the gross requirements for front assemblies in each week will be the same as the master schedule quantities of tricycles.

Step 4. The scheduled receipt of 500 units is entered for week 1.

Step 5. The 100 front assemblies projected to be in inventory at the end of December are entered in the Projected ending inventory box to the left of week 1.

Step 6. *Week 1:* Gross requirements in week 1 are less than projected ending inventory from the previous week plus scheduled receipts for week 1. The difference,

$$(100 + 500) - 250 = 350,$$

is entered as projected ending inventory for week 1, as shown in Exhibit 13.17.

Week 2: Gross requirements in week 2 are less than projected ending inventory from week 1. Projected ending inventory for week 2 is

$$350 - 285 = 65,$$

as shown in Exhibit 13.18.

Week 3: Gross requirements in week 3 are greater than projected ending inventory from week 2 by 190 units. This difference is entered as net requirements for week 3.

1. An order for week 3 net requirements must be planned for receipt in week 3. Because the lead time is two weeks, the order must be planned for release in week 1 (week 3 – 2 weeks lead time = week 1).

2. The planned receipts for week 3 are 190 units, and net requirements are 190 units. Therefore, the projected ending inventory for week 3 will be zero.

Weeks 4 through 6 are completed in the same way, producing the results shown in Exhibit 13.19.

Determining Planned Order Releases for Lower Level Items

In the preceding example, we determine planned order releases for front assemblies, which are a level 1 item. The gross requirements for all level 1 items will be determined from the master schedule. But items that are level 2 in the bill of materials will be used in making level 1 items. Thus, their gross requirements will be determined from planned order releases for level 1 items, not from the master schedule.

PROBLEM

The front assemblies that were just planned using MRP are a level 1 item. However, the front axle supports used in that assembly are level 2. Therefore, the gross requirements for front axle supports will be determined by the planned order releases for front assemblies, as shown in Exhibit 13.20.

Combining Requirements

Many times, one particular part or subassembly will be used in more than one product. In such cases, the gross requirements for that part must take into account all planned production of products or subassemblies that use that part.

EXHIBIT 13.17

MRP for Front Assemblies

Master Schedule
Week

	1	2	3	4	5	6
	250	285	255	285	250	250

Front Assemblies
Week

		1	2	3	4	5	6
Gross requirements		250	285	255	285	250	250
Scheduled receipts		500					
Projected ending inventory	100	350					
Net requirements							
Planned receipts							
Planned order releases							

EXHIBIT 13.18

Partially Completed
MRP: Front Assemblies

		Week					
		1	2	3	4	5	6
Gross requirements		250	285	255	285	250	250
Scheduled receipts		500					
Projected ending inventory	100	350	65	0			
Net requirements				190			
Planned receipts				190			
Planned order releases		190					

EXHIBIT 13.19

Completed MRP: Front
Assemblies

		Week					
		1	2	3	4	5	6
Gross requirements		250	285	255	285	250	250
Scheduled receipts		500					
Projected ending inventory	100	350	65	0	0	0	0
Net requirements				190	285	250	250
Planned receipts				190	285	250	250
Planned order releases		190	285	250	250		

PROBLEM

The front wheel in the Maine Woods tricycle is exactly the same as the two rear wheels. However, the front wheel is part of a subassembly, while the rear wheels are not. Furthermore, the wheels on Maine Woods' scooter are also the same as the wheels used on its tricycle. Therefore, gross requirements for wheels (part #5917) will be the sum of planned order releases for tricycle front assemblies (Exhibit 13.19) plus the master schedule quantities for tricycles (Exhibit 13.12), multiplied by two, and scooters (Exhibit 13.12), also multiplied by two, as shown in Exhibit 13.21.

In this instance, you should note that low-level coding has been used, as the wheels are treated as a level 2 item even though the tricycle's rear wheels and both the scooter's wheels would ordinarily be level 1 items. By using low-level coding, we are able to combine all requirements for these wheels and plan all order releases at one time.

How MRP Coordinates Purchasing and Operations

The output from MRP is a schedule of planned order releases. If those are for component parts or subassemblies made by the company itself, then a **shop order**—an order that

EXHIBIT 13.20   MRP for a Level 2 Item: Front Axle Supports

Front Assemblies
Week

		1	2	3	4	5	6
Level 1	Planned order releases	190	285	250	250		

Front Axle Supports*

		1	2	3	4	5	6
Level 2	Gross requirements	380	570	500	500		
	Scheduled receipts	500					
	Projected ending inventory	40	160	0	0	0	
	Net requirements		410	500	500		
	Planned receipts		410	500	500		
	Planned order releases	410	500	500			

*2 axle supports per front assembly
Lead time = 1 week

authorizes production to make certain component parts or subassemblies—will be released. If the planned order release is for a part or raw material that is purchased from an outside vendor, then a **purchase order**—an authorization for a vendor to supply parts or materials—will be released.

The operations part of a company is usually the area responsible for running MRP. Thus, operations are aware that the release of a shop order means that a certain part or component should be started into production because a need will exist for it some time in the future. Since operations generated the shop order release, they will usually be aware that it is a valid order and should be produced in the quantity indicated.

However, purchase orders are usually handled by a purchasing or procurement department. If the order releases generated by MRP are to be carried out, then the purchasing department must be aware of what the MRP system is doing and trust in the output it generates. So, close coordination between the operations part of an organization and its purchasing arm is required.

CAPACITY REQUIREMENTS PLANNING

As was mentioned previously, the master schedule is developed, or disaggregated, from the aggregate plan. Thus, the master schedule can provide much more exact measures of the capacity requirements than the aggregate plan can. As the master schedule is developed, rough-cut capacity planning is used to check capacity requirements against capacity availability. But rough-cut capacity planning does not take into account lead-time

EXHIBIT 13.21   Combining Demand from Multiple Sources and Levels

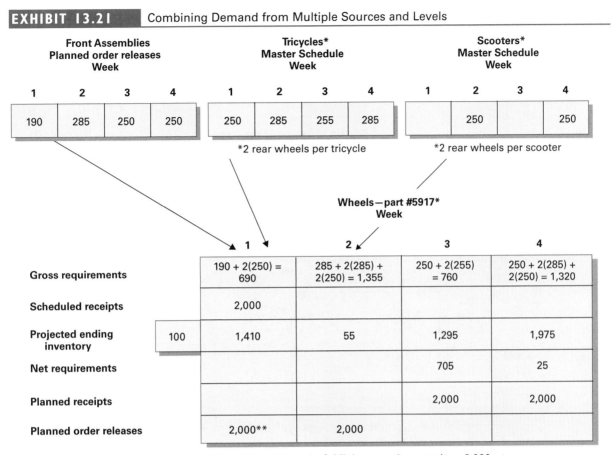

**Front Assemblies
Planned order releases
Week**

1	2	3	4
190	285	250	250

**Tricycles*
Master Schedule
Week**

1	2	3	4
250	285	255	285

*2 rear wheels per tricycle

**Scooters*
Master Schedule
Week**

1	2	3	4
	250		250

*2 rear wheels per scooter

**Wheels—part #5917*
Week**

		1	2	3	4
Gross requirements		190 + 2(250) = 690	285 + 2(285) + 2(250) = 1,355	250 + 2(255) = 760	250 + 2(285) + 2(250) = 1,320
Scheduled receipts		2,000			
Projected ending inventory	100	1,410	55	1,295	1,975
Net requirements				705	25
Planned receipts				2,000	2,000
Planned order releases		2,000**	2,000		

**Lead time = 2 weeks & Minimum order quantity = 2,000

offsetting, or the amount ahead of time component parts must be made to meet the master schedule for end items. Because MRP performs lead-time offsetting when it generates planned order releases, MRP can form the basis for much more detailed capacity calculations. For parts made in-house, the planned order releases generated by MRP indicate exactly when certain parts must be made and in what quantity. Those order releases will touch off a series of capacity requirements on the machines and equipment that must be used in producing those parts and subassemblies. By using the **routing sheet,** which indicates the sequence of machines or work centers a part must go through during processing and the labor standards, it will be possible to determine capacity requirements at each operation.

Exhibit 13.22 shows planned order releases for tricycle axle supports, along with information contained in the routing sheet for that part. In each week, the run time on each machine is multiplied by the order quantity for that week and then added to setup time to get capacity requirements. This procedure is done for each work center and each week.

You should note that the information generated in Exhibit 13.22 is only for one part. Many other parts would also generate capacity requirements on the same work centers. By adding up all the capacity requirements for each work center in each week, a total figure for capacity requirements will be generated. The total capacity requirements placed on a work center during a given time period are called the **load.** The output of **capacity requirements planning** (CRP) is usually in the form of a **load report,** or **load profile,**

Capacity Requirements Planning for Tricycle Axle Supports

Tricycle Axle Supports

	Week			
	1	2	3	4
Planned order releases	410	500	500	

Routing Sheet and Labor Standards

Process	Setup Time	Run Time per Unit
Cut	.2 hr.	.1 hr.
Drill	.1 hr.	.02 hr.

Capacity Requirements (Standard Hours)

	Week			
	1	2	3	4
Cut	.2 + .1(410) = 41.2	.2 + .1(500) = 50.2	50.2	
Drill	.1 + .02(410) = 8.3	.1 + .02(500) = 10.1	10.1	

which is a graphical representation of the load on each work center by time period. An example of a load report is shown in Exhibit 13.23.

THE ETHICS OF MRP

An important aspect of the relationship between a company and its customers is delivery reliability. For make-to-order companies especially, customers depend on the delivery due dates agreed on. Before the development of MRP, a company had to use rough estimates to determine when it thought a customer order could be shipped. Unfortunately, this left a lot of room for unethical behavior. For example, a company might agree to a certain shipping date to win a customer order, knowing from past experience that it might not be able to meet that date.

With MRP and capacity planning, a company is able to determine within a reasonable level of doubt when it will be able to ship an order. Thus, a great deal of uncertainty is eliminated from the order-promising process. Further, MRP provides the visibility necessary to determine whether unforeseen events, such as machine breakdowns or late deliveries from suppliers, will delay a customer order. If such an event occurs, a company can then notify the customer involved so that the customer can plan accordingly. Such a capability can greatly increase the level of trust between a company and its customers.

EXTENSIONS OF MRP

Our discussion of MRP thus far has focused on the bare bones, often referred to as "little MRP" or mrp. We now proceed to discuss extensions of MRP that make it even more useful and applicable to areas of the business beyond operations.

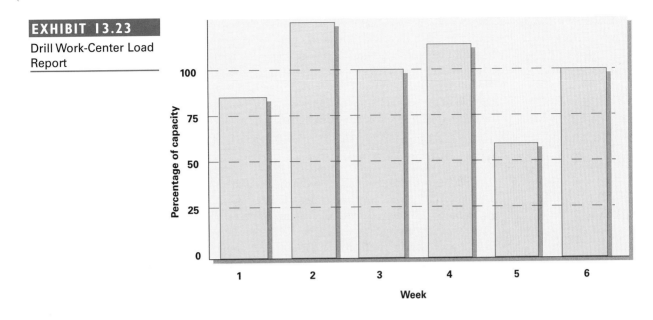

EXHIBIT 13.23

Drill Work-Center Load Report

Closed-Loop MRP

Capacity requirements planning is of significant benefit in ensuring that a company's plans are realistic and can be implemented. However, MRP, as we have discussed it so far, can only project what will happen. In reality, machines may break down, deliveries from suppliers may be delayed, or some other calamity may occur. If these events are not reflected back in the MRP plan, then that plan will be invalid.

Closed-loop MRP provides feedback about the execution of production plans. By tracking what actually happens on the shop floor and then reflecting that information in the MRP record, plans can be kept valid. Instead of just "launching" orders with no information about completion, closed-loop MRP provides the feedback loop necessary to keep information up to date.

Manufacturing Resource Planning

Many companies have found that material requirements planning can greatly improve their operations through better planning. MRP also forces companies to coordinate the activities of operations, marketing, and purchasing better. But what about other functional areas of an organization? Surely the master schedule will have implications for finance and personnel in terms of workforce requirements and purchases of materials. And how can a company be sure that its operations plan fits in appropriately with the business plan?

You should recall that in the preceding chapter we described how the strategic plan of an organization ties together all parts of that organization. But if that strategic plan is to be implemented, then all functional areas must base their activities on the plan. To do that, an extension of MRP has been developed called Manufacturing Resource Planning.

Manufacturing Resource Planning, or **MRP II,** as it is commonly called to differentiate it from Material Requirements Planning (MRP), is a way of tying all parts of an organization together with the operations activity to build on the strategic plan. As we discussed in Chapter 12, the strategic plan is an overall blueprint that specifies the company's objectives and how it plans to reach them. The operations function will develop its own goals and plans to help achieve the corporate objective, as will marketing, finance, and all other parts of the organization. The actions of one functional area, however, will have an impact on the other areas. For instance, if marketing plans a promotional effort that will greatly increase sales, then operations must be ready and able to turn out enough product to meet that increased demand. Hiring more employees or buying additional equipment, which will in turn have a major impact on the financial area, may be necessary. Because the operations activity is such an integral part of any organization, it can be especially vulnerable to the actions taken by other departments, and will itself have a major influence on other areas of the company through its actions.

Cost Control

The planned orders that MRP produces can also provide information about expected expenditures. Planned purchase order releases can be used to estimate future payments to suppliers. Shop order releases will generate needs for machine time and labor, so they can also be used to estimate future expenses. Before the development of MRP II, companies used cost accounting primarily as a means of keeping score after the fact. It was a way to find out what it had cost to do what was already done.

But MRP II can change the way companies operate. By generating cost projections, it is possible to plan for production costs ahead of time and then compare actual costs to these projections. Any major deviations can be spotted and investigated. A related advantage with MRP II is that it can be used to answer what-if kinds of questions. As we have said before, things may not always go according to plan. But one good way to be ready when Murphy's Law strikes is by trying out various possibilities. Using MRP II, a company can estimate the effect of a supplier cost increase and develop strategies to deal with it, instead of trying to react after the fact. Exhibit 13.24 shows how MRP II ties together all parts of the organization.

Simulation

Simulation is the use of some model of reality to predict the impact of certain changes. With MRP II, simulation can be used to answer the what-if questions mentioned above. Because MRP II generates cost figures, a company can immediately see how any projected changes will affect the organization's financial health. For instance, marketing might want to know what would happen if sales were increased by 10 percent. MRP II could be used to see how such a change would influence capacity utilization, labor costs, and cash flow. Or the operations area might want to know how a change in the production plan might influence its material costs. In each of these situations, MRP II could be used in "simulation mode" to project the impact of proposed changes.

MRP in Service Organizations

Although MRP was originally developed for manufacturing companies, it can also be applied to service organizations. Instead of the master schedule representing goods to be produced, it can represent services to be provided.

For example, an airline's master schedule could be the number of flights from different cities each week. In this case, the materials required to provide that service would be fuel for the airplanes, meals for the passengers, and so forth. Likewise, hospitals can develop a master schedule of the number of different types of surgeries each week. Materials required would be various surgical supplies. A variant of MRP, known as Hospital Requirements Planning (HRP) is now being explored.

EXHIBIT 13.24

MRP II

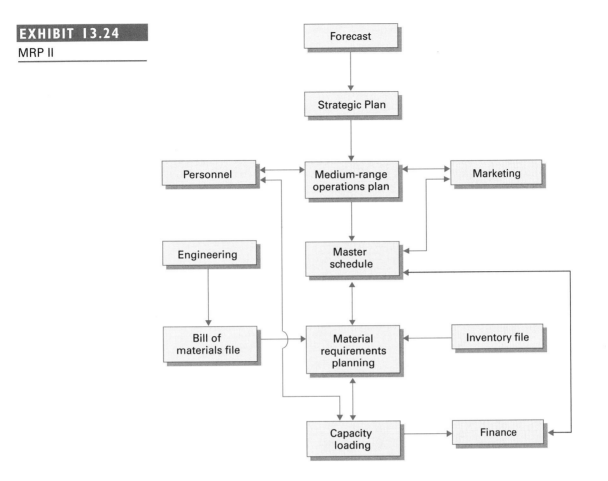

EXAMPLE

Although some surgeries are emergencies, many others are scheduled in advance. Historical information about emergency surgeries can be combined with scheduled ones to develop a master schedule. HRP can then be used to convert that master schedule into requirements for medical equipment, instruments, supplies, operating rooms, and staff. Houston's Park Plaza Hospital has used this approach to improve management of expensive inventory.

In the retail setting, the MRP approach has been applied so widely that a variant of MRP, called Distribution Requirements Planning (DRP), has been developed. In that case, the MRP planning logic is applied to requirements for retail outlets or warehouses.

Distribution Requirements Planning (DRP)

Distribution networks often consist of local outlets or service centers that are supplied from regional warehouses. In turn, these regional warehouses may be fed by a national distribution center. By thinking of each level in the distribution network as a level in a bill of materials, it is possible to see that orders placed by the service centers will generate gross requirements at the regional warehouses. Likewise, orders from the regional warehouses will produce gross requirements at the national distribution center. Exhibit 13.25 shows an example of **distribution requirements planning.**

Distribution Resource Planning

Just as manufacturing resource planning (MRP II) expands the role of MRP to generating requirements for personnel, capital, and so forth, distribution resource planning expands the role of DRP. Distribution resource planning generates requirements for warehouse space, workers, vehicles, and capital.

EXAMPLE

Giant Food Company, a supermarket chain, uses DRP as part of its ECR (Efficient Consumer Response) approach to supply chain management. DRP allows the company to connect its POS (Point of Sale) information from stores to inventory levels throughout the supply chain, making that information available to all supply chain partners. DRP then "pulls" items through the system based on customer demand, facilitating one of the basic ideas behind ECR.

EXHIBIT 13.25 Distribution Requirements Planning

Dallas Service Center

	Week			
	31	32	33	34
Forecast demand	600	300	400	400
Scheduled receipts		1,000		
Projected ending inventory (650)	50	750	350	950
Planned receipts				1,000
Planned order releases		1,000		

Phoenix Service Center

	Week			
	31	32	33	34
Forecast demand	250	300	350	450
Scheduled receipts	500			
Projected ending inventory (300)	550	250	400	450
Planned receipts			500	500
Planned order releases	500	500		

Southwest Regional Warehouse

	Week			
	31	32	33	34
Gross requirements	500	1,500		
Scheduled receipts	900			
Projected ending inventory (100)	500	0		
Planned receipts		1,000		
Planned order releases	1,000			

EXHIBIT 13.26   Information System for Managing and Controlling Operations

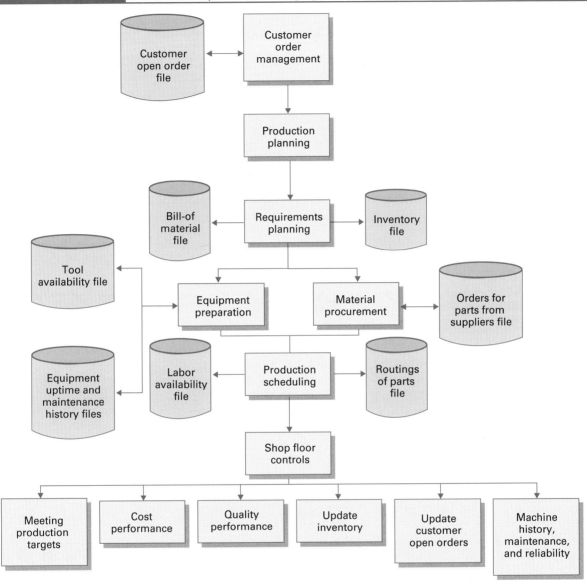

The Role of MIS in Planning

As was mentioned earlier, MRP is usually done on a computer because of the large volume of computations that must be performed and because much of the information, such as bills of material and inventory records, is kept on computerized databases. MRP II, by including more organizational functions within its scope, further increases the need for computerized information. As a result, companies very often use computerized information systems for operations planning and control activities. One such system and the data files that it works with are shown in Exhibit 13.26. As discussed in Chapter 5, Enterprise Resource Planning (ERP) extends this idea by using one database, which includes operations information, for the entire organization.

SUMMARY

- The production planning process leads from an aggregate plan to a master schedule to MRP.

- The master schedule is a more detailed version of the aggregate plan, usually by end products and weeks

- The method of overall factors uses historical information about capacity requirements to make a rough-cut capacity requirements estimate from the master schedule.

- Material requirements planning (MRP) uses the master schedule, bills of materials, and inventory records to plan orders for subassemblies and parts.

- Capacity requirements planning uses routing sheets and labor standards to develop time-phased estimates of capacity requirements based on planned order releases.

- Manufacturing resource planning (MRP II) provides simulation capabilities and cost information for other functional areas of the business.

 Visit our dynamic Web site, http://www.wiley.com/college/vonderembse, for extended chapter material, solved problems, mini-cases, computer software, and Web links.

KEY TERMS

available-to-promise
capacity requirements
    planning (CRP)
closed-loop MRP
cycle counting
demand management
dependent demand
distribution requirements
    planning
freezing
gross requirements
indented bill of materials

independent demand
load
load profile
load report
low-level coding
manufacturing resource
    planning
master production
    schedule (MPS)
method of overall factors
MRP II
net requirements

planned order releases
planned receipts
purchase order
rolling through time
rough-cut capacity
    planning
routing sheet
scheduled receipts
shop order
time buckets
time phasing

URLS

CIO magazine: www.cio.com

Giant Food: www.giantfood.com

Oliver Wight Companies: www.ollie.com

Park Plaza Hospital: www.parkplazahospital.com

SAP: www.sap.com

QUESTIONS

1. Define the following terms:
   a. Rough-cut capacity planning
   b. Time bucket
   c. Lead-time offsetting

      d. Freezing the master schedule

      e. Available-to-promise

2. Explain how a restaurant could use MRP. In what ways would its use in a restaurant differ from its use in a manufacturing organization?

3. Describe the information generated by MRP II and how it could be used by the following departments in a company:

      a. Personnel

      b. Finance

      c. Marketing

      d. Engineering

4. Explain how MRP can decrease a company's inventory while improving its customer service level.

5. Discuss the relationship between MRP and MRP II.

6. Why is it important for an organization to plan and allocate resources?

7. Define the following terms:

      a. Bill of materials

      b. Net requirements

      c. Gross requirements

      d. Scheduled receipts

      e. Planned receipts

8. Why are there separate lines for planned receipts and scheduled receipts in the MRP table?

9. Describe how capacity requirements planning differs from rough-cut capacity planning.

10. What information is needed for capacity requirements planning, and how is that information obtained?

11. The time you have available for studying is a limited resource. For the next week, develop a load profile that compares the time you have available (capacity) with time you should devote to studying for all your courses. What are your options if capacity is exceeded?

12. In what units might the capacity of a hotel be expressed, and what options are available if it is expected that capacity will be exceeded?

13. What are some things a company can do when rough-cut capacity planning indicates insufficient capacity to meet the master schedule?

14. How is the master production schedule modified for computerized MRP?

15. How does closed-loop MRP maintain the validity of a production plan?

16. How does MRP improve a company's ability to behave ethically toward its customers?

17. What are some advantages of ERP? What are some challenges of implementing it?

INTERNET QUESTIONS

18. Go to http://www.bicworld.com/inter_en/shavers/how_is_made/index.asp and use the information given to develop a bill of materials for a razor. Be sure to account for subassemblies and other steps in processing.

19. Visit the Web site for SAP (www.sap.com) and describe the approaches that SAP is taking to supply chain management.

20. Go to the Web site for CIO magazine (www.cio.com) and perform a search on the term "enterprise resource planning." Summarize the information you find there regarding ERP and MRP II.

21. Use the Internet to identify ways that companies may be combining MRP with just-in-time.

22. Visit the Web site for the Oliver Wight Companies (www.ollie.com) and determine what is meant by class A, B, C, and D.

PROBLEMS

1. The aggregate plan for Brookline Clothing Company indicates 3,750 men's pants are to be produced during March. Of these, 20 percent are style 493. Assuming there are five weeks of production in March, develop a master schedule for style 493 men's pants if they are produced in batches of 250 at a time.

2. A certain company has forecast demand during the first nine weeks of the year as 350 units per week for product A. Projected inventory of product A at the end of December is 800 units. If product A is produced in batches of 1,000, determine the master schedule and the available-to-promise quantities, based on the following customer orders booked:

				Week				
1	2	3	4	5	6	7	8	9
300	400	375	325	300	280	300	250	200

3. The Evans Sporting Goods Company has developed an aggregate plan that calls for producing 5,000 units of its wood-products group during April. Baseball bats make up 80 percent of this product group, based on past sales. At the end of March, the company expects to have 800 bats available in inventory. Customer orders booked in the five weeks of April are as follows:

	April Week			
1	2	3	4	5
900	875	850	745	720

If bats are produced in batches of 2,000, develop a master schedule, assuming forecast demand was expected to be uniformly distributed throughout the month.

4. A company has the following master schedules for two of its products:

			Product A Week				
1	2	3	4	5	6	7	8
240	300	350	350	400	300	300	400

Product B
Week

1	2	3	4	5	6	7	8
500	450	400	400	300	350	500	500

Both products must be processed on the same critical machine. Product A requires .2 hour of time on this machine per unit, and product B requires .1 hour per unit. The machine is available 120 hours per week. Use rough-cut capacity planning to determine whether sufficient capacity will be available on the machine. Suggest possible ways that any capacity shortage might be solved.

5. The Ernie and Winnie Public Accounting Company has just two employees (Ernie and Winnie). Ernie is available thirty hours per week for auditing and twenty hours per week for tax preparation. Winnie is available ten hours per week for auditing and thirty hours per week for tax preparation. Each audit takes five hours, and each tax preparation takes two hours. The company has received requests to perform the following audits and tax preparations each week during the next month.

	Week			
	1	2	3	4
Number of audits requested	5	8	10	9
Number of tax preparations requested	10	8	9	7

Identify possible problems that might occur if each employee's auditing and tax preparation times are fixed. What if excess time for one activity can be used for the other activity?

6. Referring to your answer in Problem 3, historical information shows that two standard hours are required to produce each baseball bat. Further, 60 percent of all standard hours for wood products have been for lathe time and 40 percent for finishing. Estimate the standard hours required in each operation to produce the bats scheduled in Problem 3.

7. Referring to Problem 6, suppose 2,000 standard hours of lathe time and 1,500 standard hours of finishing time are available each week. Determine whether sufficient capacity will be available each week. If not, suggest ways to meet demand with available capacity.

8. Central Eye Hospital has scheduled the following number of cataract surgeries during each of the next four weeks. Each cataract surgery requires the use of five pairs of surgical gloves. These gloves are ordered from a supplier in quantities of 1,000 pairs at a time. Ordering lead time is two weeks. Inventory records indicate that there will be 200 pairs of gloves in inventory at the start of week 1. An order for 1,000 more is expected to arrive during week 1.

	Week			
	1	2	3	4
Surgeries scheduled	30	60	55	60

Use MRP to schedule planned order releases for gloves.

9. A company that manufactures furniture produces a particular type of coffee table. As you might guess, each coffee table has four legs. The production lead time for these legs is two weeks. Inventory records show that 2,500 of these legs will be available as on-hand inventory at the beginning of week 32. An order for 2,500 legs has already been released and is scheduled to arrive in week 33. These legs may be produced in any quantity. Use MRP to schedule planned order releases.

Master Schedule—Coffee Tables

		Week			
32	33	34	35	36	37
500	400	450	300	450	400

10. A company that makes canned soups has developed the following master schedule for its 12-ounce cans of vegetable beef soup:

Master Schedule—12 oz. Vegetable Beef Soup

		Week			
12	13	14	15	16	17
1200	1500	600	900	200	1500

Each 12-ounce can of vegetable beef soup requires 7 ounces of beef broth. The company currently has 9,000 ounces of beef broth that will be available in week 12. Production lead time for beef broth is one week. Each ounce of beef broth requires 3 ounces of beef bones. These bones are ordered from a supplier in multiples of 32,000 ounces (2,000 pounds) and have a lead time of two weeks. There will be 30,000 ounces on hand at the beginning of week 12, and another 32,000 ounces are scheduled for receipt during week 13. Develop planned order releases for beef bones.

11. Referring to Problem 10, suppose that the supplier of beef bones has just called and indicated that the delivery of 32,000 ounces for week 13 has been delayed until week 14. How would you have to alter the master schedule for production of vegetable beef soup to compensate for this change if it is uneconomical to produce less than 100 cans of soup at a time?

12. An electronics manufacturer makes a product designated as 5400. Each 5400 is assembled from one of each of two subassemblies, A38 and B493.

Subassembly A38 requires two of part 1438 and two of component 1297. Component 1297 in turn is made from one of part 6438 and five fasteners numbered 4217. Subassembly B493 consists only of two units of part 1395 and four fasteners numbered 4217.

a. Draw a tree diagram indicating the structure of product 5400.

b. Using low-level coding, at what level would fastener 4217 be coded in the BOM?

c. Develop an indented bill of materials for product 5400.

13. Referring to Problem 12, the master schedule for product 5400 is as shown below.

Master Schedule—5400

	Week			
43	44	45	46	47
2,000	2,400	3,000	2,300	2,700

a. Determine gross requirements for A38 and B493 in each week.

b. Suppose that in addition to the information provided, the MRP system's item master file indicates the following lead times, and the inventory data file indicates the current amounts on hand and the scheduled receipts shown below. Develop planned order releases for parts 1438 and 1395.

Item	Lead Time (Weeks)	On-Hand Week 42	Scheduled Receipts	
			Quantity	Week
A38	2	3,000	3,000	44
B493	1	3,000		
1438	1	3,000		
1297	1	4,500		
1395	3	4,000	10,000	44
4217	2	60,000		
6438	1	5,000		

c. Using the preceding information, develop planned order releases for all parts and fasteners.

14. Referring to Problem 9, suppose the master schedule for coffee tables is altered, so 500 tables are planned for production in week 33. Change the planned order releases for table legs accordingly.

15. The Skillful Machining Company makes two different parts that both require milling. The planned order releases for these parts are shown below, along with the mill time required by each. If the milling machine is available sixty hours per week, develop a load profile for the milling machine in each week.

	Week					
	1	2	3	4	5	6
Planned order releases—Part A	100		50	300	50	100
Planned order releases—Part B	200	200	100	200	100	

	Setup (Hrs./Batch)	Run (Hrs./Unit)
Part A	1	.3
Part B	2	.2

16. The Davis Auto Center has scheduled the following numbers of transmission repairs on each day for the coming week. Each transmission repair requires two hours of transmission specialist time and four hours of general mechanic time. The company has one transmission specialist who works eight hours per day and two general mechanics who each work eight hours per day. Develop load profiles for the transmission specialist and the general mechanics.

Transmission Repairs Scheduled				
Mon.	Tues.	Wed.	Thurs.	Fri.
1	3	2	2	3

17. A furniture manufacturer operates two regional warehouses, both of which are supplied from the company's main factory distribution center. Shipping time from the

factory to each warehouse is one week. A particular model of sofa is shipped in standard quantities of fifty units, and production lead time is two weeks.

Given the following information, use DRP to determine planned order releases for each warehouse and for the factory.

Chicago Warehouse

	Week				
	31	32	33	34	35
Forecast demand		30	30	40	40
Scheduled receipts		50			
Projected ending inventory	10				

New Orleans Warehouse

	Week				
	31	32	33	34	35
Forecast demand		20	30	30	30
Scheduled receipts					
Projected ending inventory	40				

Factory Distribution Center

	Week				
	31	32	33	34	35
Scheduled receipts		100			
Projected ending inventory	20				

CHAPTER 14

Inventory Management

LEARNING OBJECTIVES

After completing this chapter, you should be able to:

1. List the purposes served by inventory.
2. Explain the differences between perpetual and periodic inventory systems.
3. Use the EOQ model to calculate a lot size.
4. Calculate economic order quantities under quantity discounts.
5. Determine the reorder point.

INTRODUCTION

As companies work to become more competitive, two areas they have focused on are productivity and time. Inventory can affect results in both those areas. Maintaining and replenishing inventory cost money so companies often seek to reduce inventory levels. But, inventory can also help a company respond to customers more quickly.

EXAMPLE The mail order company Lands' End must maintain an adequate inventory level of items to meet most customer orders. Items that are not in stock must be back ordered, incurring extra shipping and handling costs, and possibly alienating customers. For instance, one year Lands' End decided to try reducing its inventory, but the extra costs of backordering ate up 4.1 percent of the company's profits. Now the company seeks to be in stock on 90 percent of its customer orders.

In this chapter, we will be discussing methods for controlling independent demand inventory. You should recall from the discussion in Chapter 13 that independent demand is generated outside the company, usually from customers. We will discuss several different systems for controlling and monitoring independent demand inventory, especially with regard to using computers. We also present several different mathematical models that can help companies determine how much inventory should be ordered to minimize costs and also when to order that inventory so that a desired level of customer service can be provided.

PURPOSES AND TYPES OF INVENTORY

As the example of mail-order retailer Lands' End points out, inventory can be a valuable resource. In fact, inventory has many different purposes. Inventory can help companies:

- Meet expected demand
- Absorb demand fluctuations
- Protect against unexpected increases in demand
- Decouple stages in the production process
- Take advantage of quantity discounts
- Hedge against possible price increases
- Protect against disruption in delivery from suppliers

Types of Inventory

Several different types of inventory can be used to achieve the purposes listed above. The most commonly identified types of inventory are:

- *Raw materials inventory*—Parts and raw materials obtained from suppliers that are used in the production process
- *Work-in-process (WIP) inventory*—Partly-finished parts, components, sub-assemblies or modules that have been started into the production process but not yet finished
- *Finished goods inventory*—Finished products
- *Replacement parts inventory*—Parts maintained to replace other parts in machinery or equipment, either the company's own or that of its customer, as those parts wear out
- *Supplies inventory*—Parts or materials used to support the production process, but not usually a component of the product
- *Transportation (pipeline) inventory*—Items that are in the process of being shipped from suppliers or to customers through the distribution system

INFORMATION SYSTEMS FOR INVENTORY MANAGEMENT

Many different information systems exist for monitoring and controlling inventory. The purpose of any such system is to provide information so that sufficient inventory will exist to meet the company's objectives. Of course, too much inventory can mean extra costs. Thus, the inventory management system is designed to ensure that inventory levels are maintained within a desired range for each item.

With today's computer systems and the widespread use of bar codes (as shown in Exhibit 14.1), the job of inventory control has become somewhat easier and simpler. It may not, however, always be possible, or even desirable, to computerize all inventory control. This section describes several different systems and how they can be used, either with or without computers. All these systems focus on helping companies determine what, when, and how much to order.

EXAMPLE

A major problem in the toy industry is identifying when fads begin and end. For example, Furbies were a hot item a few years back, but are now passé. Toys "R" Us, with over 300 stores in the U.S. alone, carries 18,000 different items. To maximize profits, the company must be sure it maintains just the right amount of each item. One way it does this is by using computers to monitor sales data and to reorder (or stop reordering) as point-of-sale (POS) demand information indicates. This information is transmitted each day to the company's headquarters in New Jersey where it is automatically monitored. Thus, when demand for scooters started picking up recently, the computers caught the trend and began placing large orders; Toys "R" Us ended up selling over one million scooters. Likewise, drops in sales, when a fad has ended, can be caught and replenishment orders halted.

Perpetual Inventory Systems

A **perpetual inventory system** monitors changes in inventory levels on a continuous basis. For that reason it is also often known as a continuous review system. Under such a system, inventory transactions are recorded as they occur. If the number of transactions is small, this recording can be done by hand using index cards, which is what was done in the past. Computers, however, have made the process much easier and instantaneous. For example, grocery stores and retailers such as Wal-Mart use point-of-sale systems that record the transaction as each item is read by the bar code scanner. In fact, the ATM machine that you may use is a perpetual inventory system that updates the balance in your bank account as you make withdrawals. Companies have even started using bar codes on raw material and work-in-process inventories as a means of computerizing inventory records for those types of inventories. The bar codes shown in Exhibit 14.1 are used on a component part ordered from a supplier.

Using this type of system offers the advantage that we can constantly be aware of inventory level at any point in time. When inventory drops to a predetermined level (the **order point**), an order for more can be generated. Often, this ordering is done automatically by the same computer system that maintains the inventory records. The quantity ordered is usually a fixed amount, often the economic order quantity, which is discussed later in this chapter.

Periodic Inventory Systems

Many smaller organizations do not have the resources to maintain perpetual inventory systems. For example, small retailers often perform periodic counts of the inventory on hand of each item, then place an order based on that inventory and the level of demand expected. Such a system can work well if the supplier delivers only at fixed intervals, such as once per week, but it is also possible to run out of items because inventory level is not continually monitored.

Aggregate Performance Measures

You should realize that inventory represents a tremendous capital investment. In general, the companies that can operate with less inventory are the ones that operate more efficiently.

EXHIBIT 14.1

Bar Codes Used for
Inventory Management

Several aggregate performance measures can be used to judge how well a company is utilizing its inventory resources.

Average Inventory Investment

One of the most common measures, and one that is easy to interpret, is **average inventory investment**—the dollar value of a company's average level of inventory. This information is usually quite easy to obtain from a company's accounting data.

The primary disadvantage of this measure is that it makes comparisons of companies difficult. For example, larger companies will generally have more inventory than smaller companies. Thus, a large multinational company might have a larger average inventory investment than a small business, but could still be using its inventory more efficiently.

Inventory Turnover Ratio

Inventory turnover ratio is a measure that allows for better comparison among companies. This ratio is calculated by comparing a company's sales to its average inventory investment, as follows:

Inventory turnover = annual cost of goods sold / average inventory investment

The inventory turnover ratio indicates how many times during a year the inventory turns over, or is sold. Because it is a relative measure, companies of different sizes can be more easily compared. Thus, in general, a company with a higher turnover ratio will be using its inventory more efficiently. For example, automobile companies using JIT often have inventory turnover ratios of 60 or 70, while those not using JIT may be in the range of 6 to 25. One disadvantage of this ratio is that figures among industries may not be comparable. For example, grocery stores must carry much larger inventories than automobile manufacturers do.

Days of Inventory

A measure closely related to inventory turnover is days of inventory. The calculation procedure is as follows:

Days of Inventory = avg. inventory investment / (annual cost of goods sold / days per year)

The **days of inventory** indicate approximately how many days of sales can be supplied solely from inventory. Thus, the lower this value, the more efficiently inventory is being used. In general, inventory turnover can be converted to days of inventory by using the following calculation:

Days of inventory = days per year / inventory turnover rate

ABC Classification

As it turns out, companies often need not keep extremely accurate track of all inventory items. For instance, certain parts may have a relatively low value and be used infrequently; those items can often be monitored very loosely. On the other hand, high-value, high-usage items must be tracked carefully and continuously. To determine which inventory items should receive the highest level of control, a scheme called **ABC analysis** has been developed. The idea behind this scheme is that if we multiply the dollar value of each item by its annual usage, we will obtain a dollar usage value. As it turns out, dollar usage follows the Pareto Principle. Typically, only 20 percent of all the items account for 80 percent of the total dollar usage, while the remaining 80 percent of the items typically account for only 20 percent of the dollar usage. This truth leads to the ABC classification, which is based on focusing our efforts where the payoff is highest.

After calculating the dollar usage for each inventory item, the items are ranked by dollar usage, from highest to lowest. The first 20 percent of the items are assigned to class A, as shown in Exhibit 14.2. These are the items that warrant closest control and monitoring through a perpetual inventory system. Accurate inventory records are important, and there is a high potential for cutting costs through careful buying and close scrutiny of safety stocks.

The next 30 percent of the items are classified as B items. These deserve less attention than A items. Finally, the last 50 percent of items are C items. These have the lowest dollar usage and can be monitored loosely, with larger safety stocks maintained to avoid stock-outs. Often a periodic review system is used to control class C items.

THE ECONOMIC ORDER QUANTITY MODEL

At the beginning of this chapter we mentioned that inventory can have a significant impact on both a company's productivity and its delivery time. Productivity is largely influenced by the costs associated with inventory. One model that seeks to minimize those costs is the **economic order quantity (EOQ).** The EOQ model is concerned primarily with the cost of ordering and the cost of holding inventory.

Cost of Ordering

One major component of cost associated with inventory is the cost of replenishing it, usually called **ordering cost.** If a part or raw material is ordered from outside suppliers, then this really is an ordering cost. On the other hand, parts, subassemblies, or finished products may be produced in-house. In this case, ordering cost is actually represented by the costs associated with changing over equipment from producing one item to producing another. This is usually referred to as setup cost. To simplify things, we will refer to both ordering costs and setup costs as ordering costs.

EXHIBIT 14.2			ABC Classification of Inventory Items			
Item	Annual Demand	Unit Cost	Annual Dollar Usage	% Annual Dollar Usage	Cumulative % Annual Dollar Usage	Classification
1	5,000	$ 30	$150,000	48.91	48.91	A
2	200	450	90,000	29.34	78.25	A
3	2,000	10	20,000	6.52	84.77	B
4	800	20	16,000	5.22	89.99	B
5	1,000	10	10,000	3.26	93.25	B
6	1,200	5	6,000	1.96	95.21	C
7	1,300	4	5,200	1.69	96.90	C
8	2,500	2	5,000	1.63	98.53	C
9	3,500	1	3,500	1.14	99.67	C
10	500	2	1,000	.33	100.00	C
			306,700			

Ordering costs may include many different items. Some of these will be relatively fixed, and others may vary. For our purposes, it will be important to differentiate between those ordering costs that do not change much and those that are incurred each time an order is placed. For example, suppose a company currently places orders for a given part with its supplier five times per year. If, instead, the company ordered six times per year, which costs would probably change (variable costs), and which would probably not (fixed costs)? The general breakdown between fixed and variable ordering costs is as follows:

Fixed Costs	Variable Costs
Staffing costs (payroll, benefits, etc.)	Shipping costs
Office furniture and equipment	Cost of placing an order (phone, postage, order forms)
	Cost of lost production during setup
	Cost of materials used during start after setup
	Receiving and inspection costs

Cost of Holding Inventory

Although it costs money to replenish inventory, it also, unfortunately, costs money to hold that inventory. Such inventory holding costs, also called **carrying costs,** may include costs paid for storage space, interest paid on borrowed money to finance the inventory, and any losses incurred due to damage or obsolescence. Once again, we must differentiate between fixed and variable costs of holding inventory. Suppose we maintain a certain inventory level of a finished product. What if that inventory level is increased by one unit? Which costs would not change (fixed costs), and which would change (variable costs)? The general breakdown for inventory holding follows:

Fixed Costs	Variable Costs
Capital costs of warehouse	Cost of capital in inventory
Taxes on warehouse and property	Insurance on inventory value
Costs of operating warehouse	Losses due to obsolescence, theft, spoilage
Personnel costs	Taxes on inventory value
	Cost of renting warehouse space

In the next section, we will discuss the most basic approach to determining lot sizes—the economic order quantity (EOQ) model. In developing the EOQ model, we will attempt to minimize total annual costs by varying the order quantity, or lot size. Because, over the short run, lot-size variations affect only variable costs, those are the only costs that we will consider. Before starting that section, you should be sure you understand the differences between the fixed and variable costs that are listed above. Also, you should realize that the division between fixed and variable costs may change depending on the context. If additional personnel must be hired, staffing costs may be considered variable. Ordering cost and holding cost can be thought of as two children on a seesaw. When one goes up, the other goes down, and vice versa. This trade-off appears to present somewhat of a quandary: if we attempt to decrease total annual variable holding costs, total annual variable ordering costs will increase—and vice versa. The way out of this dilemma is to combine the two costs as total annual variable costs and worry only about minimizing that cost. As Exhibit 14.3 indicates, there is just one point at which total costs are minimized. The order quantity associated with that point is called the economic order quantity (EOQ).

Exhibit 14.3 indicates, conceptually, where the economic order quantity point is, but we need more information to calculate that point mathematically. First, however, we need to discuss four assumptions underlying our discussion.

EXHIBIT 14.3

Total Annual Variable
Costs

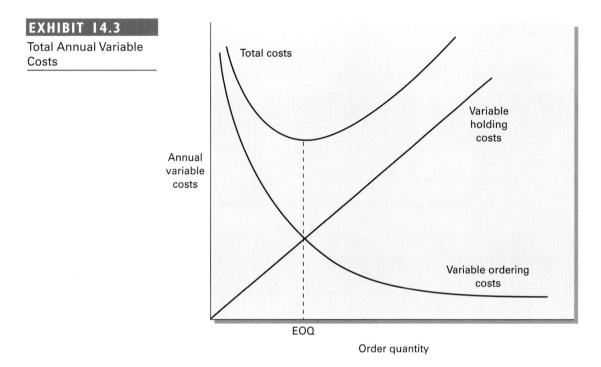

Assumptions of the EOQ Model

Because the EOQ model is a simplification of reality, we must make some simplifying assumptions. Those assumptions are described here. Later on, we will examine variations of the EOQ model in which some of these assumptions are not necessary.

Constant Known Demand

The first assumption we make in developing the EOQ model is that demand is fairly stable, or constant, and that we know reasonably well what that demand will be.

Cost Per Unit Not Dependent on Order Quantity

Most things can be purchased at a lower cost per unit if they are bought in larger quantities. For instance, large sizes of laundry detergent usually cost less per ounce than smaller sizes do. That situation, however, makes purchase cost a variable cost—something the EOQ model does not account for. Thus, we will also assume that purchase cost per unit remains the same, regardless of whether we are buying one, one hundred, or one thousand units each time.

Entire Order Delivered at One Time

This assumption relates to how inventory is replenished. One possibility would be to build inventory up gradually, as would happen in a clothing factory. As a particular model of jacket is produced, the inventory of that jacket builds up gradually. Another possibility is for all units in an order to arrive at one time, which is what happens when a clothing store orders from a factory. The factory ships an entire order of the jacket at one time; the store's inventory is replenished all at once. It is this latter, instantaneous replenishment, that we will assume occurs. This assumption, combined with the assumption of constant demand, results in the inventory pattern depicted in Exhibit 14.4.

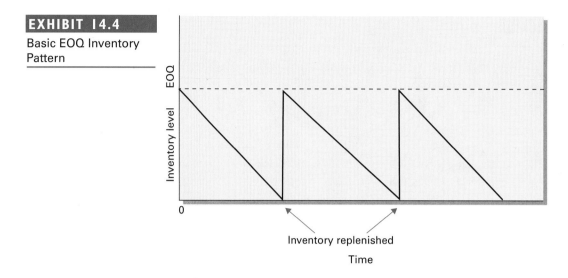

EXHIBIT 14.4

Basic EOQ Inventory
Pattern

Ordering and Carrying Costs Known and Independent

The final assumption is that we can determine the variable costs of ordering and carrying inventory. In many cases, such costs can be determined from company records or from the accounting department; however, they are sometimes not readily available and must be estimated. We also assume the two costs are not related in any way. Finally, we assume these are the only variable costs that are affected by the order quantity.

These assumptions may seem restrictive, and possibly unrealistic. Recall, however, that the EOQ model is the basic starting point. We will show that this particular model may be altered to relax some of these assumptions—and more closely match reality. But, we must begin with the basics.

Mathematical Statement of the Model

Variables to Be Used

Stating the EOQ formula in mathematical terms will require that we use variables to represent the important problem parameters. The variables of concern are:

$$D = \text{demand rate (units/year)}$$
$$Q = \text{order quantity or lot size (units)}$$
$$C_o = \text{variable ordering cost (\$/order)}$$
$$C_h = \text{variable holding cost (\$/unit/year)}$$

Once again, you should note that we are concerned only with variable costs. In this case, the variable ordering costs will represent any additional costs incurred when another order is placed and are stated as cost per order. Holding costs also include only the variable costs associated with keeping one more unit in inventory. Since we are concerned with annual costs, they are stated as cost per unit per year.

One other way of stating inventory holding costs is to break C_h into two components. If you think a minute about the variable holding costs, you will realize that they will depend on the number of units in inventory and the value of each unit.

In most instances, it is possible to state inventory holding cost, C_h, as a percentage of unit cost per year ($/$/year). The greatest part of this percentage is accounted for by capital tied up in the inventory. Since cost of capital is usually stated as a percentage, it is especially convenient to state holding cost in this form. To do so, we use the following variables.

v = cost or value of item ($/unit)

r = holding-cost percentage of unit value ($/$/year)

Then $C_h = vr$.

Annual Variable Ordering Costs

Regardless of how many units are ordered at a time, we can always determine how many orders must be placed by dividing annual demand, D, by the order quantity, Q. Thus,

$$\text{Orders placed per year} = \frac{D}{Q}$$

Since the cost per order is C_o, annual variable ordering costs can be easily calculated as follows:

$$\text{Annual variable ordering costs} = \frac{D}{Q}C_0$$

Annual Variable Holding Costs

Notice in Exhibit 14.4 that our theoretical inventory pattern fluctuates between the EOQ and zero when lot sizes equal to the EOQ are ordered each time. Suppose, instead, that we let the variable Q represent the quantity ordered each time. In that case, the maximum inventory level would be Q, assuming inventory is replenished just as it reaches zero. Minimum inventory would still be zero. This fluctuation in inventory level makes the calculation of annual holding costs somewhat difficult because we will have a different number of units in inventory at anyone time. To make matters worse, each unit will be in inventory for a different length of time—some for a very short period, others longer. The calculation of annual holding costs, therefore, requires the use of integral calculus. There is also an easier, but equivalent, way to determine annual holding costs.

The method we will use to determine annual holding costs is based on average inventory level. Because inventory follows a uniform pattern, with a maximum of Q and a minimum of zero, the average level will be halfway between the maximum and minimum values, or $Q/2$. In terms of the number of units in inventory, and the time each unit spends there, our fluctuating system is actually equivalent to maintaining $Q/2$ units at all times, as shown in Exhibit 14.5. This simplifies the calculation of annual variable holding costs to

$$\text{Annual variable holding costs} = \frac{Q}{2}C_h$$

Economic Order Quantity Formula

Total annual variable costs will be the sum of holding costs and ordering costs. Using the formulas developed above, this will be

EXHIBIT 14.5
Average Inventory

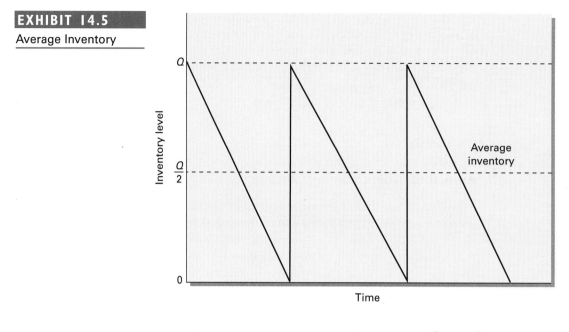

$$\text{Total annual variable costs} = \frac{Q}{2}C_h + \frac{D}{Q}C_o$$

The economic order quantity will be the point at which this total cost function is minimized. An easy way to find this point is by realizing that the EOQ occurs where annual holding costs and annual ordering costs are equal, as shown in Exhibit 14.3. In mathematical terms, this is

$$\frac{Q^*}{2}C_h = \frac{D}{Q^*}C_o$$

Note that we have used Q^* to designate the optimal value of Q, which is the economic order quantity. Solving the above equation for Q^*, we obtain

$$(Q^*)^2 = \frac{2DC_o}{C_h}$$

and by taking the square root of each side,

$$Q^* = \sqrt{\frac{2DC_o}{C_h}}$$

PROBLEM Bill Green, general manager for Poolco, a company that provides home pool maintenance services in the Los Angeles area, is responsible for developing inventory policies regarding all items the company stocks. One item that falls under his control is a clarifying agent that is added to pool water to improve its clarity. This item costs $5 per gallon. Variable costs of storing it in inventory amount to 25 percent of unit cost per year. Paperwork and shipping costs for placing an order are $10 per order. Each year the company uses an average of 500 gallons, a rate that is not expected to change. How many gallons should be ordered each time to minimize total annual variable costs?

$$C_h = 5(.25) = \$1.25\,\text{per unit/year}$$

$$EOQ = \sqrt{\frac{2DC_o}{C_h}} = \sqrt{\frac{2(500)(10)}{1.25}}$$

$$= 89.44\,\text{gallons}$$

Since an order must be placed for whole gallons, Bill would probably round this off to 89 gallons per order.

Sensitivity of the EOQ Value

The EOQ in the preceding example did not come out to an even value. In fact, rounding off to the nearest whole number still gave a result that was somewhat unusual. It would be far more likely that Bill Green could order 90 gallons at a time than 89. But suppose this clarifying agent comes in 55-gallon drums. In that case, the closest order quantity would be two drums, or 110 gallons. What impact will this have on total annual variable costs if Poolco must order 110 gallons of clarifying agent at a time?

As it turns out, the total annual variable cost function is rather "flat" around the EOQ, as shown in Exhibit 14.6. In other words, order quantities can be varied considerably from the EOQ, especially above it, without greatly increasing costs.

PROBLEM

Suppose Bill Green of Poolco wants to determine how much higher costs will be if he orders in lots of 110 gallons instead of the 89.44 gallons determined by the EOQ formula.

The total annual variable costs for the EOQ of the preceding example will be

$$\text{Total annual variable costs} = \frac{Q}{2}C_h + \frac{D}{Q}C_o$$

$$= \frac{89.44}{2}(\$1.25) + \frac{500}{89.44}(\$10)$$

$$= \$55.90 + \$55.90 = \$111.80$$

However, by changing Q to 110, the total annual variable costs will become

$$\frac{Q}{2}C_h + \frac{D}{Q}C_o = \frac{110}{2}(\$1.25) + \frac{500}{110}(\$10)$$

$$= \$68.75 + \$45.45$$

$$= \$114.20$$

Thus, the cost increase incurred by ordering in quantities of 110 gallons at a time is only \$2.40, or 2.15 percent more than the total annual variable costs of ordering EOQ quantities.

As this example indicates, the cost consequences of varying from the EOQ are not very great. The EOQ value should be thought of only as a ballpark figure that indicates approximate minimum-cost order quantities, not as a value that must be used exactly.

You may be wondering where holding and ordering cost figures for the EOQ formula can be obtained within an organization. Usually the operations function will not have such information itself, so the next most likely source is accounting. In some companies, accounting is responsible for determining inventory holding and ordering costs. Such costs are, however, often buried as part of overhead expenses and are not readily available for use in calculating the EOQ. Therefore, it is not uncommon for top management to set these values based on the organization's inventory policy. For example, an organization

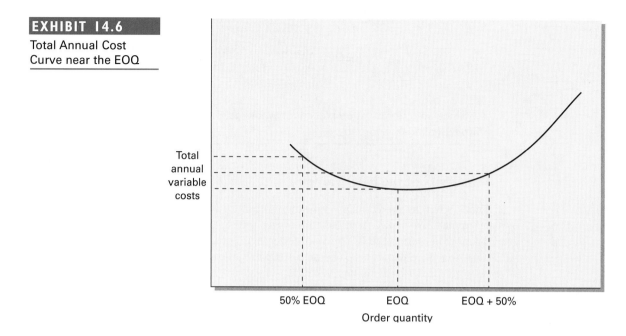

EXHIBIT 14.6

Total Annual Cost
Curve near the EOQ

that wants to minimize inventory might place a high value on holding cost. Because the cost of money tied up in inventory is often the largest part of inventory carrying cost, many companies also set holding cost based on their costs of capital.

Controversy Surrounding the EOQ Model

You should be aware that the EOQ model has attracted much criticism. Some of that criticism is based on the argument that the basic assumptions underlying the model are unrealistic and never exist in practice. Others argue that modern approaches to supply chain management, MRP and Just-in-Time manufacturing, make the EOQ model obsolete. Nonetheless, whether or not the EOQ model is actually applicable in practice, it is still important to learn because the underlying concepts are applicable in many other situations.

EXAMPLE   One of the products of Hewlett-Packard is integrated circuits. The demand for these items is highly variable, so there is always a high degree of uncertainty over how much inventory to maintain. Too much and inventory costs go up; too little and on-time delivery of orders suffers. However, HP was able to eliminate $1.6 million of finished goods inventory while also increasing on-time delivery performance from 93 percent to 97 percent by utilizing the Periodic Review inventory model, an approach discussed later in this chapter, which is based on the EOQ model!

A VARIATION OF THE EOQ MODEL

Starting from the basic EOQ model, it is possible to develop other models that either have less restrictive assumptions or are appropriate for other situations. In this section, we discuss one of the many possibilities that have been developed.

Quantity Discounts

One assumption in the basic EOQ model was that purchase price remained the same regardless of how many units were purchased. In reality, this is usually not true. For example, things usually cost less, per unit, when purchased by the case rather than individually. An entire truckload generally will cost even less per unit. Therefore, the order quantity directly influences the purchase price of an item.

Incorporating quantity discounts into the order quantity calculations requires that we modify the total-cost calculation to include purchase cost—which had not been included previously because it was a fixed cost. Now, however, the total annual cost of purchasing an item may vary due to quantity discounts. Unfortunately, this also means that we can no longer simply substitute numbers into a formula and get the correct answer, as we did for the EOQ. This situation occurs because quantity discounts occur in a stepwise manner, as shown in Exhibit 14.7. When this pattern of purchase costs is used to calculate total annual purchase cost and then combined with ordering and holding costs, the total-cost curve appears as shown in Exhibit 14.7. An iterative procedure is required to determine the order quantity that generates lowest total annual costs.

Procedure for Calculating Lot Size with Quantity Discounts

The procedure for calculating lot sizes with quantity discounts is based on using the unit cost, v, and holding-cost percentage, r, to calculate holding cost. In other words,

$$C_h = vr$$

Notice that as the unit purchase cost varies, so does the holding cost.

Step 1. Start with the lowest unit price. Calculate the holding cost, C_h, for this price, and then determine the EOQ. If this EOQ is "feasible"—in other words, if it falls in the range of order quantities required for that unit price—this is the optimal order quantity. Stop here.

EXHIBIT 14.7

Total Annual Cost with Quantity Discounts

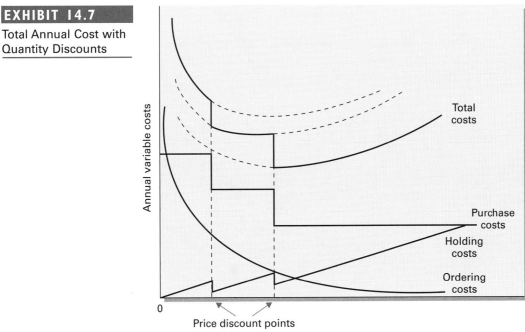

If the EOQ is not feasible, determine the minimum order quantity required for that unit price, and calculate the total annual variable costs (holding cost, ordering cost, and purchase cost) associated with that minimum order quantity. Proceed to step 2.

Step 2. For the next higher unit price, calculate holding cost, and determine EOQ. If the EOQ is feasible, then calculate its total annual variable costs, and compare this with the total annual variable costs for order quantities calculated previously. That order quantity with the lowest total annual variable costs will be optimal. Stop here.

If the EOQ is not feasible, repeat this step until a feasible EOQ is found; then calculate its associated total annual costs, and compare these costs with all total annual costs previously calculated. The order quantity with the lowest associated total annual variable costs will be optimal.

PROBLEM

Bill Green of Poolco has learned that the supplier of the clarifying agent will begin offering quantity discounts according to the following schedule:

Gallons Ordered	Unit Price
54 or less	$5.00
55–274	4.80
275–549	4.60
550 or more	4.50

Bill wonders whether he should change his lot size for ordering the clarifying agent. To answer his question, we will proceed through the steps described above.

Step 1. Calculate the holding cost and EOQ corresponding to the lowest unit price. This unit price will be $4.50, and its associated holding cost is (.25)($4.50) = $1.125/gallon/year.

$$EOQ = \sqrt{\frac{2(500)(10)}{1.125}}$$
$$= 94 \text{ gallons (rounding to the nearest whole number)}$$

However, this is not feasible because at least 550 gallons must be ordered each time to obtain the $4.50 unit price. Thus, we calculate the total annual variable costs, including purchase cost (Dv), associated with ordering 550 gallons each time.

$$\text{Total annual variable costs} = \frac{Q}{2}C_h + \frac{D}{Q}C_o + Dv$$
$$= \frac{550}{2}\$1.125 + \frac{500}{550}\$10 + 500(\$4.50)$$
$$= \$309.38 + \$9.09 + \$2,250.00$$
$$= \$2,568.47$$

Step 2. For the next higher unit price, calculate holding cost, and determine EOQ. This next higher unit price will be $4.60, obtained by ordering between 275 and 549 gallons each time. Holding cost will be (.25)($4.60) = $1.15/gallon/year and

$$EOQ = \sqrt{\frac{2(500)(10)}{1.15}}$$
$$= 93 \text{ gallons}$$

This also is not feasible since 93 is not in the range of 275 to 549 gallons required for the $4.60 unit price. Thus, taking the minimum value in that range of 275, we calculate associated total annual variable costs.

$$\text{Total annual variable} = \frac{Q}{2}C_h + \frac{D}{Q}C_o + Dv$$

$$= \frac{275}{2}\$1.15 + \frac{500}{275}\$10 + 500(\$4.60)$$

$$= \$158.13 + \$18.18 + \$2,300.00$$

$$= \$2,476.31$$

Since the EOQ for this unit price was not feasible, we proceed to the next higher price of $4.80 per gallon. Its holding cost will be $1.20/gallon/year, and the EOQ is 91 gallons.

This EOQ is feasible, so we calculate its total annual variable costs.

$$\text{Total annual variable} = \frac{Q}{2}C_h + \frac{D}{Q}C_o + Dv$$

$$= \frac{91}{2}\$1.20 + \frac{500}{91}\$10 + 500(\$4.60)$$

$$= \$54.60 + \$54.95 + \$2,400.00$$

$$= \$2,509.55$$

We then compare all the total annual variable costs calculated so far, as shown in the following table:

Order Quantity (Gallons)	Total Annual Variable Costs
550	$2,568.47
275	2,476.31
91	2,509.55

Thus, the lowest-cost order quantity will be 275 gallons, and Poolco should change its lot size for clarifying agent accordingly.

STOCKOUTS AND SAFETY STOCK

In the EOQ model, we assume that demand is constant and known. In reality, however, this is rarely true for independent demand. In this section we discuss ways of ensuring that uncertainty about actual demand does not result in lost sales. But we will begin by determining the point at which inventory must be replenished.

Order-Point Determination

In all of our calculations thus far, we have made the important assumption that inventory would somehow be replenished just as it hit zero. Thus, the minimum inventory level was treated as zero. In most situations, the replenishment of inventory requires some advance notice. For example, a company that orders materials from a supplier must account for the time it takes that order to reach the supplier's offices, the time to fill the order, and then the shipping time. This is called **lead time.**

Failing to account for lead time, or allowing an inadequate amount of lead time, can cause an organization to run out of inventory. This situation is known as a **stockout.** Any time a stockout occurs, the result is likely to be a disruption in production, idle employees, and unhappy customers. Most companies try to avoid stockouts if at all possible.

Doing so requires that inventory replenishment lead time be taken into account. Probably the easiest way to account for lead time is to use what is called an order point. An order point is simply a level of inventory at which an order should be placed, accounting for lead time and safety stock, so that the order will come in before a stockout occurs. Exhibit 14.8 shows how the order point is determined.

The concept depicted in Exhibit 14.8 is that the order point should be a level of inventory that will be sufficient to last throughout the lead time, with inventory reaching zero just as the order arrives. Mathematically, the order point can be determined as follows. We will use the following symbols:

$$d = \text{daily demand rate (units/day)}$$
$$L = \text{lead time (days)}$$

Then the order point, OP, can be determined by using the formula given below.

$$OP = dL$$

PROBLEM   Suppose that Poolco wants to determine the order point for its clarifying agent. We have already determined that daily demand would be 2 gallons per day (500 gallons per year/250 working days per year). Suppose we also learn that lead time for ordering the clarifying agent is ten working days. The order point is

$$OP = dL$$
$$= 2(10)$$
$$= 20 \text{ gallons}$$

EXHIBIT 14.8

Order-Point
Determination

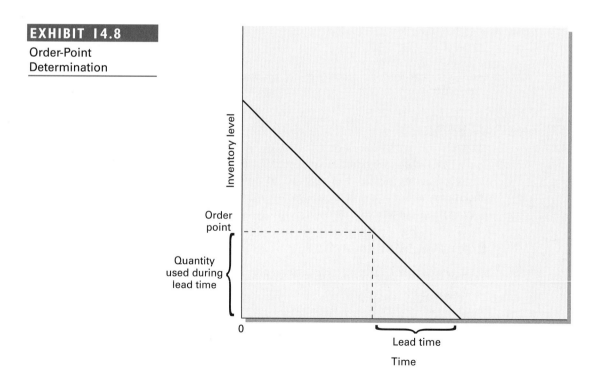

So, when only twenty gallons are left in inventory, an order for more should be placed. That order should arrive just as inventory reaches zero.

Safety Stock

The explanation of order-point determination given above works well in situations where demand rate and lead time are known and invariant. Unfortunately, it is much more common to find that demand and lead time are both variable. If either lead time or demand, or both, is less than expected, there will be no problem when the order arrives, some inventory will be left. But if either demand or lead time, or both, exceed our expected values, then a stockout will occur because inventory will hit zero before the order arrives, as shown in Exhibit 14.9. There is no margin of safety in the preceding order-point calculation.

To avoid stockouts, most companies add a **safety stock,** which is an extra amount of inventory, to the order-point calculation so that

$$OP = dL + s$$

where

$$s = \text{safety stock}$$

What this does is to add a buffer of inventory that can be expected to remain when an order is received. Instead of letting inventory hit zero when an order comes in, we only let it drop to *s*, the amount of safety stock, as shown in Exhibit 14.10. Of course, due to demand and lead time variability, more or less may remain at any given time. We hope, however, that this buffer of safety stock will be sufficient to prevent most stockouts.

EXHIBIT 14.9

Stockout Occurrence

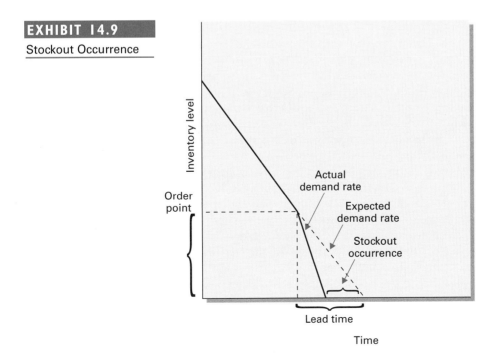

EXHIBIT 14.10

Inventory Level with
Safety Stock

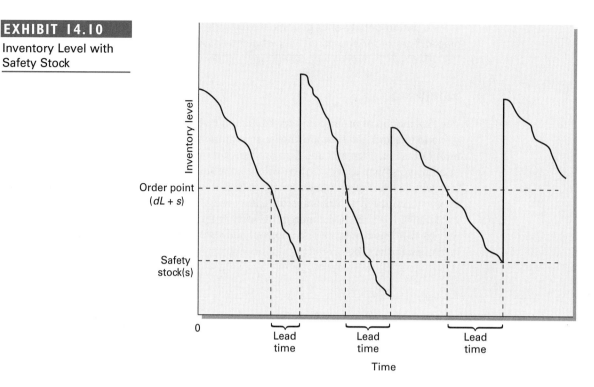

Service Level

No matter how much safety stock a company carries, there is always some chance that a stockout will occur due to unusually high demand or an extremely long lead time. It is just not possible for a company to avoid stockouts altogether. Instead, companies can select a level of stockouts that they are willing to accept. Several measures can be associated with stockouts, ranging from determining the expected time between stockouts (TBS) to minimizing total cost, including the cost of stockouts. The most common measure, and the one we will use here, is service level. **Service level,** for our purposes, is the percentage of times a replenishment order is received before a stockout occurs. For instance, a 95 percent service level would indicate that 95 percent of all orders placed to replenish inventory are received before a stockout occurs. But in 5 percent of the cases, inventory will hit zero before the order is received.

As was described in the vignette about Lands' End that began this chapter, inventory levels can greatly influence a company's ability to fulfill customer orders. For companies such as Lands' End, rapid delivery of customer orders can be so important that the extra cost incurred by carrying higher inventory is worthwhile. In other organizations, though, customers may not always expect the item they want to be in stock. For example, many people prefer to order an automobile with the precise features they want rather than take whatever is available on the auto dealership lot.

Because service level is so important, its determination must involve not only operations but also marketing, and possibly finance. By considering the role of rapid delivery in the organization's competitive strategy and balancing this role against the added costs of carrying extra inventory, an organization can determine the service level that will best meet its needs.

Determination of service level is a managerial decision that must be based on many factors. A company that competes on the basis of service may choose a service level of 99 percent or higher. Another company may be in an industry where meeting customer demand from inventory is not important. For the latter, a service level of 80 percent, or even lower, may be acceptable. Once the service level has been determined, a company may proceed to calculate its safety stock.

Calculating the Safety Stock

We will assume that demand during the lead time follows the normal probability distribution, which is often quite realistic and allows us to use commonly available normal probability tables. The normal probability distribution is described by a mean and a standard deviation. For our purposes, these values are

$$\bar{D}_L = \text{average demand during lead time}$$
$$\sigma_L = \text{standard deviation of demand during lead time}$$

The safety stock necessary to obtain a desired service level can be calculated as

$$\text{Safety stock} = z\sigma_L$$

where

$z =$ number of standard deviations from the mean required to obtain desired service level

The order point is then

$$OP = \bar{D}_L + \text{safety stock}$$
$$= \bar{D}_L + z\sigma_L$$

As Exhibit 14.11 indicates, the service level—or probability of no stockout—will be equal to the area under the normal curve up to $\bar{D}_L + z\sigma_L$. Thus, the value of z is determined on the basis of the desired service level.

PROBLEM A company has average demand during the reordering lead time that is normally distributed with a mean of thirty-five and a standard deviation of six. What safety stock and reorder point are necessary to obtain approximately a 90 percent service level?

EXHIBIT 14.11

Normal Probability Distribution

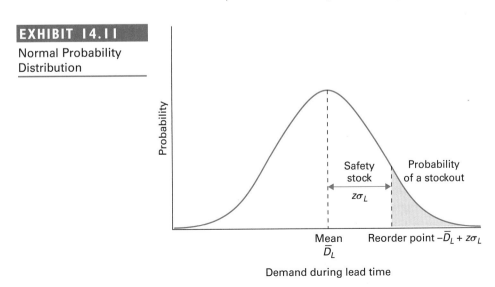

Referring to the normal distribution table in the Chapter 17 Appendix, we see that the probability closest to .90 is .8997, which is in the 1.2 row and .08 column. Thus, a z value of 1.28 is needed to obtain a 90 percent service level.

$$\text{Safety stock} = z\sigma_L$$
$$= 1.28(6)$$
$$= 7.692 \text{ or } 8$$
$$\text{Order point} = \bar{D}_L + \text{safety stock}$$
$$= 35 + 8$$
$$= 43$$

THE FIXED-ORDER-INTERVAL MODEL

The EOQ model that was discussed previously is most often used when a company can continuously monitor its inventory level to know when the order point is reached. In many cases, though, such continuous monitoring may not be reasonable or necessary. In such cases, orders are often placed at a fixed interval of time, which is when the inventory is reviewed. In spite of this difference, the EOQ model can be used to determine an optimum interval for reviewing and replenishing inventory. From any given review interval we can then develop a policy for determining how much to order each time.

Review Interval

Think for a minute back to the EOQ model and Exhibit 14.4. The time that elapses between replenishments really depends on the order quantity, or lot size. We used this idea to determine the number of replenishment orders placed per year. In a periodic review system, the opposite will occur. That is, the time between reviews, or the **review interval (R),** will determine average order quantity because the annual demand must be met during a year. If orders are placed frequently, then each order will be smaller. Infrequent ordering means large lot sizes.

Recall, though, that we still have the classic trade-off between variable ordering costs and variable inventory holding costs. Thus, the review interval that is chosen can directly affect total annual variable costs.

Fortunately, you have already learned most of what is needed to calculate that optimal interval, R, when you learned how to calculate EOQ. The reason why is that the relationship between order size and order interval means that an economic order quantity will also produce an economic order interval. In other words, the optimal review interval is simply the interval that would result in ordering an EOQ quantity each time. This order interval will be the EOQ divided by demand rate, D.

$$\text{Optimal review interval, } R = \frac{EOQ}{D}$$

PROBLEM   The Hunziker Hardware Store carries many different items, ranging from nails and screws to appliances and hot-water heaters. It doesn't make sense for them to maintain a continuous review system for the many small hardware items they carry. Instead, they would like to determine a review interval at which all items ordered from one regular supplier can be checked and ordered at one time.

One such group consists of brass items, such as screws, hinges, and cupboard handles. Because all such items are basically similar in terms of cost and demand level, they have been grouped together. Annual demand rate for these items is 10,000 units per year. Ordering cost is $25 per order, and holding cost is $.02 per unit per year. Using the above data, we can determine the EOQ as follows:

$$EOQ = \sqrt{\frac{2(10,000)(25)}{.02}}$$
$$= 5,000 \ units$$

Based on this, the review interval is

$$R = \frac{EOQ}{D}$$
$$= 5,000/10,000$$
$$= \frac{1}{2} \ year$$

Thus, the Hunziker Hardware Store should review its inventory levels of these small hardware items twice per year and order the required quantity of each.

Order-Up-to Level

The next question to be answered in a periodic review system is how much to order. Under continuous review, a replenishment order was always placed when inventory reached the order point. However, in a periodic review system, the inventory level at the time of review will vary, as depicted in Exhibit 14.12.

If a constant amount were ordered each time, it would be very difficult to recover from a low inventory level. Instead, the quantity ordered must bring inventory back up to a level sufficient to cover anticipated demand before the next order is received. This is called the **order-up-to level,** or *M*. A diagram of an order-up-to level is shown in Exhibit 14.12.

EXHIBIT 14.12

Order-Up-to Level in a Periodic Review System

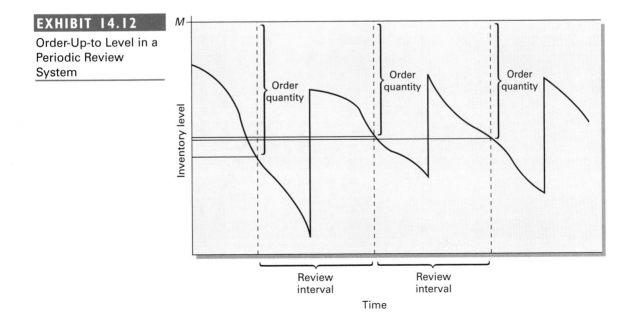

Another difference between continuous and periodic review systems relates to the period of time that must be covered by an order. Under continuous review, inventory level is monitored continuously and an order placed whenever that inventory reaches the order point. However, under a periodic review system, once an order has been placed, the inventory will not be checked again until the next review period. Thus, the amount ordered each time must be sufficient to cover expected demand during the review interval plus demand during the lead time, as shown in Exhibit 14.13, or a stockout will occur. If the review interval, R, and the lead time, L, are stated in terms of a year, then the order-up-to level to cover demand during the review interval plus the lead time must be

$$M = D(R + L).$$

PROBLEM

It was determined in the previous example that the review interval for the common group of brass hardware items will be 1/2 year for all items in that group. One of the hardware items in that group is a brass gate hinge that has a demand of 1,000 units per year. Lead-time is 1/10 year. What should the order-up-to level be for this hardware item? We can use the preceding formula to calculate this level as follows:

$$M = D(R + L)$$
$$= 1,000(.5 + .1)$$
$$= 600 \text{ units}$$

This means that whenever the hardware store reviews inventory of this group of items, it should order enough of the brass gate hinges to bring on-hand plus on-order inventory up to 600 units. For example, suppose that during the semi-annual inventory review, it is found that 100 brass gate hinges are in inventory. In that case, 500 brass gate hinges (600 − 100) should be ordered.

Safety Stock for the Fixed-Order Interval Model

In some ways, the order-up-to level developed above can be thought of as the order point in a continuous review system. As with the basic order-point calculation, the preceding

EXHIBIT 14.13

Period of Time an Order must Cover

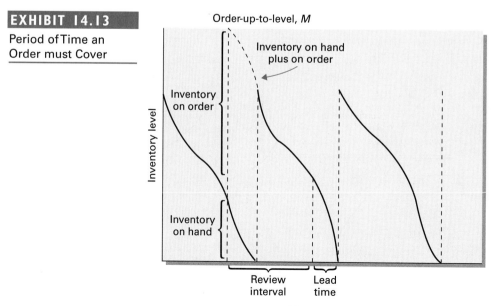

order-up-to formula does not include safety stock. Because of the nature of periodic review systems, safety stock is probably more important and necessary than in continuous review systems. It will also be larger, as you will see. Under a continuous review system, the lead time following an order was the period of time when a stockout could occur. Therefore, we calculated safety stock using the standard deviation of demand during the lead time. However, with a periodic review system, a stockout could theoretically occur at any time between review periods and during the lead time. Thus, safety stock for a periodic review system must be calculated based on the standard deviation of demand during the review interval plus the lead time. Except for this modification, the calculation is the same as for a continuous review system; safety stock will now be added to the order-up-to level.

PROBLEM

The brass gate hinge discussed in the previous example had an order-up-to level of 600 with no safety stock. Suppose that demand during the review interval plus the lead time has a standard deviation of 100 units. What must the order-up-to level be set at to obtain a 95 percent service level if we assume demand is normally distributed?

From the normal probability tables (Chapter 17 Appendix), a probability of 95 percent corresponds to a z value of 1.645. Therefore, the safety stock will be

$$\text{Safety stock} = z\sigma_{R+L}$$
$$= 1.645(100)$$
$$= 164.5 \text{ or } 165 \text{ hinges}$$

Adding this to the expected demand during the review interval plus the lead time (the M calculated in the preceding example), the new order-up-to level becomes

$$M = D(R + L) + \text{safety stock}$$
$$= 1,000(.5 + .1) + 165$$
$$= 765$$

SUMMARY

- The purposes served by inventory include meeting expected demand, absorbing demand fluctuations, decoupling production processes, hedging against price increases, and protecting against delivery disruptions, among others.

- The economic order quantity model is based on the assumptions that demand is constant and known with some certainty. Cost per unit does not depend on order quantity, and an entire order is delivered at one time.

- Quantity discounts mean that the total-cost curve is discontinuous, requiring an iterative procedure to find the minimum cost point.

- The order point is determined from expected demand during the lead time.

- If demand during the lead time is variable, then a safety stock may be added to the order point, based on a probability distribution.

- In a perpetual inventory system, inventory level is constantly monitored, and orders are placed whenever necessary.

- In a periodic system, inventory is checked at regular intervals, and enough is ordered to bring inventory up to a desired level.

 Visit our dynamic Web site, http://www.wiley.com/college/vonderembse, for extended chapter material, solved problems, mini-cases, computer software, and Web links.

KEY TERMS

ABC analysis	economic order quantity	order-up-to level
average inventory	(EOQ)	perpetual inventory system
investment	inventory turnover ratio	review interval (R)
carrying cost	lead time	safety stock
days of inventory	ordering cost	service level
	order point	stockout

URLS

Hewlett Packard www.hp.com

Lands' End: www.landsend.com/cd/frontdoor/

Stickley Furniture: www. Stickley.com

Toys "R" Us: www4.toysrus.com

INTERNET QUESTIONS

1. Visit the Web site for Stickley Furniture at www. Stickley.com and take the virtual tour of the factory. Identify the different types of inventory you see there.

2. At the Web site www.inventoryops.com read and summarize (but do not plagiarize) one of the "informational articles."

3. Read the ideas presented at http://www.urbanfox.com/costreduction/c03eoq.htm and present your own reaction regarding which might be the easiest to implement.

PROBLEMS

1. Fast-Mart is a discount retailer that uses a point-of-sale system to maintain continuous inventory records. A particular item has an average annual demand of 40,000 units. It costs $25 to replenish inventory of that item, which has a value of $10 per unit. If inventory carrying cost is 20 percent of unit value, how many should be ordered each time to minimize total annual variable costs?

2. Suppose Fast-Mart has found that the item described in Problem 1 has a lead time of two working days. If the company operates 250 days per year, determine the reorder point for that item.

3. The Fill-er-Up gas station has found that demand for its unleaded gasoline is fairly constant and uniform at the rate of 100,000 gallons per year. Fill-er-Up must pay $100 for shipping per order of gasoline, which it currently buys for $.75 per gallon. Inventory carrying cost is 10 percent of unit cost per year. How many gallons should be ordered at a time?

4. Suppose that in Problem 3, Fill-er-Up's underground storage tanks can hold only 10,000 gallons of unleaded gasoline. What is the extra cost incurred by ordering this quantity each time instead of the EOQ?

5. The Slick Oil Company buys crude oil from a supplier that has recently offered the following quantity discounts:

Barrels Ordered	Price per Barrel
1–999	$20.00
1,000–2,999	18.00
3,000 or more	17.50

If inventory holding cost is 25 percent of the unit price and it costs $100 for each order, regardless of order size, how many barrels should Slick order each time to satisfy its annual demand of 10,000 barrels?

6. Burger-Farm is a fast-food restaurant that buys hamburger buns from a local bakery. Those buns are used at the rate of 50,000 per year. The baker has just offered Burger-Farm the following quantity discounts:

Buns Ordered	Price per Bun
1–999	$.030
1,000–1,999	.028
2,000 or more	.027

If it costs Burger-Farm $1 for each order placed and the inventory holding cost is 25 percent of unit cost, determine how much should be ordered each time to minimize total annual variable costs.

7. Referring to Problem 6, suppose Burger-Farm is limited to ordering only one week's worth of buns at a time due to storage space limitations and spoilage problems. What impact will this have on total annual variable cost?

8. The Young Professionelle Shoppe is a boutique for professional women. A periodic system is used to control inventory. Suppose that a certain blazer has an average annual demand of 1,000 units. The ordering cost is $5, and the inventory carrying cost is $10 per unit per year. What should the review interval be for this blazer?

9. Suppose that the Young Professionelle Shoppe of Problem 8 prefers to review its inventory weekly. Estimate the effect on total annual variable costs of following this procedure.

10. A discount retail store uses a periodic inventory system under which each item's inventory level is reviewed twice monthly. Suppose it has been determined that a particular item has an average annual demand of 6,000 units, with a standard deviation of 100 units per month. If lead time is one-half month and the store wants a service level of 85 percent, determine the order-up-to level for this item.

11. The Goodstone Tire Store has been using a periodic review system to control its inventory. For one tire model, the annual demand averages 5,000 units. In the past, inventory was reviewed on a basis so that review interval plus lead time was one month. Standard deviation of demand during this period was fifty units. The company is now planning to use a continuous review system. Suppose lead time is one week and the standard deviation of demand during lead time is ten units. For a 90 percent service level, compare the safety stock necessary under periodic review with what would be necessary for continuous review.

12. An inventory clerk at the Fargo Machine Tool Company has just calculated the EOQ for one of the steel alloys used by this company as 500 pounds. However, the lead time for ordering this steel is four months, and the company uses 150 pounds per month, giving an order point of 600 pounds—which is greater than the EOQ! Can you help this inventory clerk figure out how to handle this case, in which order point exceeds the EOQ?

13. West Coast Furniture Distributors is a company that buys furniture in large quantities at low prices from manufacturers and then sells to the public at prices below what most furniture stores charge. To minimize costs, West Coast Furniture uses EOQ for ordering.

For one particular model of sofa, the manufacturer has now agreed to cover part of the shipping costs, reducing the ordering cost from $50 per order to $40. At the same time, West Coast Furniture has been able to obtain lower interest rates on borrowed money, reducing its inventory carrying cost from 25 percent of unit cost to 20 percent. The company expects to sell 1,225 of these sofas per year and pays $100 to purchase each one.

a. What effect will the preceding changes have on the EOQ?

b. What effect will the preceding changes have on the total annual costs of ordering and carrying inventory?

14. Referring to Problem 13, how many days' worth of demand will be covered by each order of sofas?

15. A company maintains inventories of the following nine items. Based on this information, determine which are A items, B items, and C items.

Item #	Value	Annual Usage
209	$14.76	2,000
4914	5.98	15,000
37	1.15	297,000
387	6.48	6,000
3290	2.17	6,000
235	75.00	300
48	23.95	7,000
576	4.32	5,000
14	932.00	1,000

CHAPTER 15

Just-In-Time and Theory of Constraints

LEARNING OBJECTIVES

After completing this chapter, you should be able to:

- Explain the basic concepts of just-in-time (JIT).
- Describe what is meant by the "pull" system.
- Describe the goal of Theory of Constraints (TOC).
- Show how to set up a drum-buffer-rope system.
- Explain how MRP, JIT, and TOC are similar and different.

INTRODUCTION

This chapter discusses two newer approaches to operations—**just-in-time (JIT)** and **Theory of Constraints (TOC).** Both can be viewed at various levels, ranging from a simple shop-floor scheduling system on up to an entire organizational philosophy of operation. Actual implementations of these approaches cover the entire range. In this chapter we will focus more on the organizational philosophy viewpoint, but will explain some of the narrower approaches to implementing JIT and TOC.

INTRODUCTION TO JUST-IN-TIME (JIT)

Originally pioneered by the Japanese automaker Toyota, JIT has now been used by many organizations throughout the world, including General Motors, Apple Computer, and IBM. In fact, the basic ideas underlying JIT have now evolved into a broader concept known as **lean systems.** Although many companies are just beginning to use the lean systems approach, the idea underlying it and JIT has been around for quite some time. In fact, Toyota has been using JIT for about forty-five years and claims that the original concept of JIT was put forth by none other than Henry Ford.

When the success of Japanese companies such as Toyota first brought attention to JIT, many people outside of Japan immediately classified it as an inventory control system. In fact, JIT was often referred to under other names, including stockless production and zero inventories. Although it is true that the low level of inventory carried by companies operating under JIT is one apparent aspect of the system and one possible approach to implementation, JIT can also be much more than just another system for controlling inventory. Some companies that are strong believers in the entire JIT philosophy find it really amounts to a totally different philosophy of how a company should operate. Thus, we will define JIT as a philosophy of operation that seeks to maximize efficiency and eliminate waste in any form. In its broadest sense, JIT influences all parts of a company, including purchasing, engineering, marketing, personnel, and quality control, and even determines the relationships among the company, its suppliers, and its customers. As you will learn, the benefits of JIT can go far beyond cost savings due to reduced inventories, even extending into a company's strategic planning. Today, this broader view of JIT is often referred to as lean manufacturing, lean thinking, lean systems, or even just lean.

EXAMPLE

The U.S. motorcycle manufacturer, Harley-Davidson is a good example of what can be achieved with JIT. In 1978, Harley-Davidson's motorcycle business was in big trouble when the company tried, but failed, to prove that Japanese companies were dumping motorcycles on the U.S. market at prices below manufacturing costs. The precariousness of Harley's position in the marketplace came to light when it was shown in court that operating costs of those Japanese manufacturers were a full 30 percent below Harley's costs. One of the primary reasons for those lower costs was the Japanese use of JIT. In 1982, Harley-Davidson decided that it, too, would have to use JIT if it was to survive.

In spite of some initial problems in getting suppliers to go along, Harley stuck by its plans for JIT, developing its own system called MAN (material as needed). The results for Harley have been dramatic. Today, the company is recognized as one of the outstanding U.S. users of JIT. The motorcycle business is highly profitable, largely due to decreases in manufacturing costs. For instance, the company has been able to reduce the cost of warranty work, scrap, and rework by 60 percent. Overall, setup time on machines has been reduced by 75 percent. The number of suppliers has also been reduced, enabling Harley to work out better contracts and reduce the distances from suppliers to its plant. This approach has meant a more reliable supply network and less need for large inventories of parts.

For Harley-Davidson, JIT has been a way to eliminate many problem areas in its production operations. Costs have been reduced, leading to greater profitability. A higher quality product also has meant more satisfied customers.

Fundamental Concepts of JIT

Because JIT implementation can range from a very narrow emphasis, focusing on inventory control or shop-floor scheduling, all the way to a broader organizational philosophy, experts have a difficult time agreeing on its components. The following items are ones that most experts generally accept as components of JIT. You should realize, though, that companies need not implement all of the following in order to be considered as JIT users.

Flow Manufacturing

Inventory represents a huge capital investment that ties up money a company could put to other uses. For instance, without large inventory investments, a company could buy better equipment, develop new product lines, or even give its employees raises. Any unnecessary inventory is actually robbing a company of other, more beneficial ways to use the money.

For an automobile manufacturer, eliminating unnecessary inventory might mean that no inventory of tires would be kept in stock. Instead, the four tires for a car would arrive just at the moment they must be mounted on the rims, just before being put on the car as it rolls down the assembly line. The result would be absolutely no inventory of tires. Carrying this idea further, there would be no inventory of the other parts that go on a car either. Instead, parts would be delivered from suppliers or from the manufacturing operation for those parts just when they were needed to be put on a car and only in the quantity needed for that car. Throughout the entire operation, there would be no unnecessary inventory—only work-in-process inventory destined for immediate use at the next processing operation.

Think of how this would work in theory. A worker finishes a radiator part and immediately hands it to another worker, who combines that part with others to produce an assembled radiator. As soon as the radiator is finished, it gets handed to another worker, who puts it on an automobile rolling down the assembly line. All along the way, the same thing happens as parts and subassemblies are produced only when needed and only in the quantities needed for immediate use.

Thinking back to Chapter 8, you might begin to realize that an objective of JIT is to make materials flow as they would in a continuous flow process, such as an oil refinery. In a refinery, work-in-process inventories are kept to a minimum, and material flows smoothly from one processing step to the next. The difference is that a company's objective with JIT is to make this smooth, uninterrupted flow run all the way from suppliers to final customers.

Exhibit 15.1 presents a useful analogy. Think of parts, materials, subassemblies, and final products as water. If there are many pools in which this water can collect as inventory, then the flow will not be smooth and swift, but will be like a series of quiet, stagnant ponds, as shown at the top of Exhibit 15.1. An objective of JIT is to eliminate these ponds and produce a smooth, rapid flow—like the mountain stream shown at the bottom of that exhibit.

Simplified Production Process

Eliminating inventory is often much more difficult than it might seem. For example, what if a certain machine takes five hours to readjust (setup time) whenever the company switches from making one part to making another? Obviously, if only one unit is made at a time, the machine will probably spend more time being readjusted than it will making parts. The answer to this problem is to simplify—either by buying a more general-purpose machine that can easily be changed from making one part to making another or by simplifying the readjustment process in some way. Companies that use JIT often have many general-purpose machines and have developed simple ways of switching them from making one part to making another. Often, this setup time can be reduced to less than a minute. In

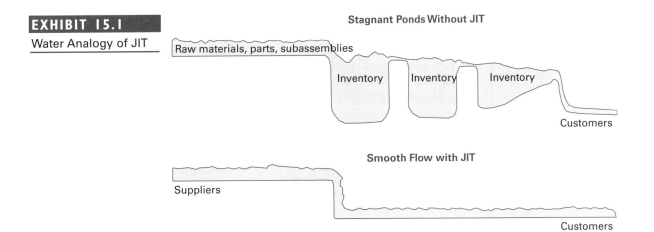

EXHIBIT 15.1

Water Analogy of JIT

fact, some companies have eliminated setup time altogether by using one simple machine for each part, instead of trying to do all parts on one complex, multipurpose machine.

Another problem encountered in using JIT has to do with the movement of materials. In the preceding section, we described how one worker might hand a radiator part to another worker, who assembles the finished radiator. But what if those workers are on opposite sides of the plant and an elaborate automated handling system has been used to move those parts in large batches? Once again, the answer is to simplify by getting rid of the automated handling system and moving the workers so they are in close proximity. Many companies implementing JIT have thrown out complex material-handling systems and rearranged the plant so workers could simply move parts by hand from one operation to the next. Most companies using traditional purchasing methods will buy large quantities from their suppliers once every month or every couple of months. These transactions usually involve much paperwork, such as purchase requisitions, packing slips, bills of lading, and invoices, for each order. A company using JIT, which sometimes places orders with suppliers several times per day, would be deluged in paperwork under this traditional approach to purchasing. To avoid such a problem, many companies have used blanket purchase requisitions, which authorize a vendor to supply a certain total quantity spread out over a certain time. Individual orders may be initiated by phone calls or by some other method.

Uncovering Problems Buried by Inventory

While inventory reduction is the most obvious aspect of JIT, its most valuable benefit is that it forces a company to uncover problems and inefficiencies in its operations. To see why, consider the electric power supplied to your home. The actual flow of electricity occurs only in response to a need for power, such as when you turn on a light. There is no inventory of electricity anywhere between your home and the generating plant. In essence, your electricity is supplied just in time. Now suppose that something occurs between the generating plant and your home—maybe a wire goes down or a transformer burns out. No matter what the problem, you'll be aware that something is wrong when you have no electricity. If this happens to enough other people, the electric company will be deluged with calls; a crew will be dispatched immediately to find the problem and remedy it. The situation is very similar for a company operating under JIT. With little or no inventory, any problem that disrupts the flow of work will become immediately obvious to everyone as work centers must shut down for lack of materials. Attention will immediately focus on the problem, and all effort will be devoted to solving that problem. In addition, because it is realized that production will again be disrupted if the problem reoccurs, effort will be devoted to providing a long-term problem solution, not just a quick fix.

The water analogy used in Exhibit 15.1 also illustrates this point. As before, parts and materials are represented by water. But this time, we can think of problems as rocks below the water, as shown in Exhibit 15.2. Some of these rocks may be just visible from the surface of the water, but may be difficult to remove due, at least in part, to the water. Other rocks may be totally obscured by the water. These rocks may represent quality problems, machine-breakdown problems, or any other problem that can disrupt production. When the water levels lowered, the rocks can be clearly identified and removed.

An Emphasis on Quality

One problem that can be especially disruptive in a JIT system has to do with quality. Think again of the radiator assembly operation in an automobile factory. Suppose the worker making radiator parts turns out a defective one. When the next worker tries to assemble that part on the radiator, it won't fit. This immediately causes a problem because there will

EXHIBIT 15.2

Problems Hidden by
Inventory

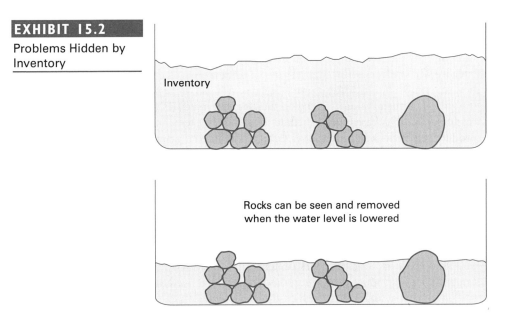

now be no assembled radiator to put on the next car. Everything will come to a halt because of that one bad part. And all eyes will be turned on the worker who made that bad part. You can probably bet that person will take steps to ensure that the same thing does not happen again.

But what if these parts were produced in large batches? The worker assembling radiators could just toss the bad part onto a pile with other bad parts and reach into the batch for a good part. There would be no incentive to change anything or to improve, especially on behalf of the worker making parts—who probably doesn't even know a bad part was made. By producing in batches, with large inventories, a company could chug along like this and never realize a problem existed—and also not realize how much better and more efficiently it could be operating.

To achieve the high level of quality required for JIT, many companies are also implementing a total quality management (TQM) program. TQM was discussed in Chapter 4.

Improvement as an Organizational Philosophy

The objective of eliminating waste in any form is difficult to achieve. Companies such as Toyota, which has been using JIT for many years, still have not reached that goal. But, it remains a goal toward which they are constantly striving. A company operating under JIT is constantly working to improve efficiency, reduce waste, and smooth the flow of materials. In working toward those ends, the company uncovers many problems and finds better ways to do practically everything.

Companies that have been extremely successful with JIT have not stopped trying to improve. These companies, once their own systems have been put in place, extend some aspects of JIT to their suppliers—and even to their customers. For example, Toyota has worked to get its suppliers to use JIT and to tie into Toyota's JIT system. At the other end, efforts have been undertaken to keep demand at the constant, uniform rate that is needed for a smooth flow from supplier to customer. Continuous improvement is also a component of Total Quality Management. You may wish to review that discussion in Chapter 4 to see how the continuous improvement philosophy is applied in that context.

The JIT "Pull" System

Although the differences and similarities between MRP and JIT will be discussed in detail later, we will briefly describe one very important difference here. Most traditional production systems, including MRP, use what is called a "push" system to move materials through the system. A **push system** is based on the idea that materials get pushed through the processing operations based on a schedule. Under this system, an order to produce a part or product gets "launched" into the system at a scheduled time and is pushed from one work center to another according to that schedule.

MRP is a slightly improved push system in the sense that each order release is based on requirements generated by the master schedule. Thus, materials are pushed through the system in an effort to meet that schedule. Everything is based on what has been planned to happen at some time in the future.

JIT uses a "pull" system to move parts and materials. Instead of pushing materials through processing based on a preplanned schedule, a **pull system** moves materials based on actual needs at successive work centers. Thus, if work center A provides parts to work center B, A will produce only in response to an actual need for more parts at B. This pull system concept actually starts with customer demand, which pulls finished products from the company. As those finished products are made, they pull the appropriate materials through processing. Materials and parts are also pulled from vendors and suppliers.

One way of comparing a push system and a pull system is based on the idea of a rope. Suppose we think of material moving through the various production processes as a rope. Under MRP, coils of rope (batches) are created at various machines and work centers throughout the plant. The MRP logic is used to ensure that all coils of the rope are moved forward through the processes at the appropriate time, preventing the coils from building up at any one spot. With JIT, the rope is not coiled, but remains as one long piece running through all processes. To move the rope forward, one has to simply pull on the end; there is no need to coordinate movement of coils because there are no coils, as shown in Exhibit 15.3. The key element of a pull system is some means for communicating backward through the production process whenever more parts or materials are needed at "downstream" work centers. In some instances, workers can determine visually when the next work center needs to be supplied. Work centers, however, are often too far apart physically for direct visual communication, and visual communication will not work with suppliers whose plants are at least several miles away.

EXAMPLE

Toys"R"Us, the well-known toy retailer, recently changed its inventory ordering process to a just-in-time approach. In the past, toys for the busy Christmas season would usually be ordered in February so that production could begin, with delivery scheduled for some time around August or September. But, that has meant that retailers like Toys"R"Us must pay for the toys, then keep them in inventory for at least several months. Because of the financial problems that Toys"R"Us has been encountering lately, the company decided it could do without that extra cost. So, it decided to shift the whole process to later in the year. Toys are now scheduled to arrive much closer to the actual Christmas selling season.

Kanban Systems

Within a JIT system, there are several ways that pull signals can be communicated. One of the best known is a method developed by Toyota based on cards, or kanban (con-bon), as they are called in Japan. **Kanban** is a Japanese word that can refer to a sign or a marker and literally means "visible record." In the operations context, the word "kanban" refers strictly

EXHIBIT 15.3

Push System with MRP

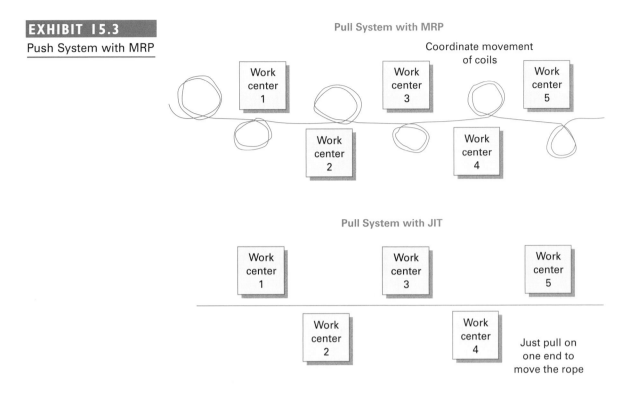

Pull System with MRP

Coordinate movement of coils

Pull System with JIT

Just pull on one end to move the rope

to a card that is used to signal the need for more materials, parts, or subassemblies at downstream operations (see Exhibit 15.4). Note that the word "kanban" is like the word "sheep:" the plural has no letter *s* on the end.

Standard Containers of Parts   Theoretically, the ideal situation with JIT would be to produce one unit at a time. However, this usually is not possible. For instance, the travel time to and from a supplier may be much longer than the time between requirements for the part from that supplier, or there may be an imbalance in the production rate between a particular work center and the preceding work center that supplies it. In these and other cases, it is necessary to move containers of parts rather than single units. A kanban is most often associated either with the movement of a container of parts or with the production of parts to fill an empty container. Accordingly, two types of kanban are generally used, the conveyance kanban and the production kanban.

Conveyance Kanban   The **conveyance kanban,** or **C-kanban,** is an authorization to move a container of parts or materials. Without it, nothing can be moved. The way a C-kanban works is depicted in Exhibit 15.5. As the exhibit shows, any container with parts in it cannot be moved without the C-kanban attached.

Many companies, notably Kawasaki in the United States, use only the C-kanban. This **single-card kanban system** is still an effective means of controlling inventory. The number of full containers is limited by the number of C-kanban, and inventory at the using work center (work center 2 in Exhibit 15.5) can be replenished only when a container is emptied. Thus, that work center cannot possibly hoard extra parts. The feeding work center (work center 1) usually produces to some sort of schedule, which may be generated through MRP. This schedule is generally based on the expected day's requirements for work center 2. However, limited storage space at work center 1 is generally used to shut off production at that work center if parts are not being used up at the expected rate (for instance, if work center 2 is shut down for some reason). In order for the single-card kanban system to work, the following rules must be observed:

1. Containers holding parts can be moved only when a card is attached.
2. Standard containers must always be used.

EXHIBIT 15.4

Example of a Kanban Card

M.A.N.   SHIPPING AUTHORIZATION

PART NUMBER	DESCRIPTION	DELIVERY TO
17389—83A	**ROCKER ARM**	**903**

CONTAINER	QUANTITY
PALLETAINER	**800**

Ship To:

HARLEY-DAVIDSON MOTOR CO. INC.
11700 W. Capitol Drive
Milwaukee, WI 53201

Card Seq.   **3**

EXHIBIT 15.5

Single Kanban System

Step 1. Worker at work center 2 opens container of parts, removes C-kanban and places it in a box.

Step 2. Material handler takes C-kanban to work center 1 and puts it on a full container of parts.

Step 3. Material handler moves container with C-kanban to work center 2.

Step 4. When work center 2 empties a container, the empty container is taken back to work center 1 and step 1 is performed again.

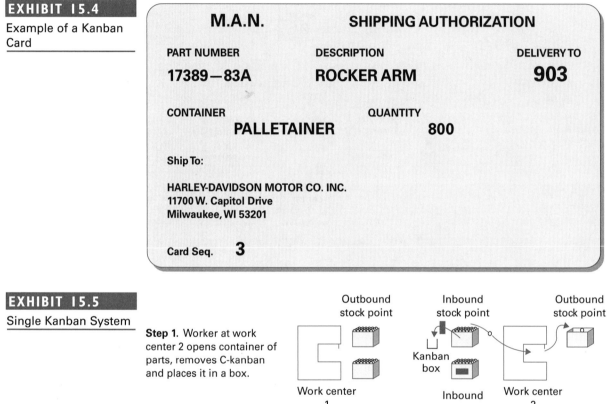

3. Each standard container can be filled only with the standard number of units.

Production Kanban   Some companies, primarily Toyota in Japan, use a two-kanban system that combines the conveyance kanban with a production kanban. The **production kanban,** or **P-kanban,** is used to authorize the production of parts or subassemblies. The two-kanban system, which combines the C-kanban and the P-kanban, is known as a **dual-card kanban system.** Its major advantage over single-card kanban is that it allows greater control over production, as well as over inventory, because both production and withdrawal of inventory are tied directly to need. In contrast, a single-card system bases production on a plan, which may lead to excess inventory if actual need does not match the plan.

Simplifying the Production Process

Earlier we used several analogies involving water to describe JIT. Such analogies have been used by many others before us, but they provide a useful way of thinking about JIT. Remember that the objective of JIT is to eliminate the pools of inventory and obtain a smooth, steady flow of materials all the way from supplier to customer.

Within a plant, we can think of that flow much like the creeks and rivulets that converge into streams—with those streams eventually converging into rivers. In this analogy, streams could be made up of processing operations for individual parts. Those parts flow together into subassemblies, which are then eventually joined together as finished products. The objective of JIT is to keep all those rivers and tributaries flowing smoothly without any pools of inventory. The following material describes some ways to achieve that objective.

Plant Layout

Notice, at the top of Exhibit 15.6, that each part must move from one machine area to another. This requires a lot of material handling and also encourages the production of each part in large batches. But when the machines are rearranged, as shown at the bottom of Exhibit 15.6, each part can flow directly from one processing step to the next. This type of layout also allows the production of small batches since each group of machines is dedicated to just one part. Also, there will not be interference between two parts that must both be processed on the same machine. It is this type of interference that leads to long queues of parts to be processed.

Reducing Setup Time

Setup time is the time it takes to readjust a machine or group of machines after making one particular part or product until acceptable units of another part or product are produced. Setup time may involve changing the tooling, adjusting the equipment, checking to be sure that the new part or product is being made to specifications, and then readjusting the equipment if it is not.

Setup time is an important consideration in JIT because it disrupts the smooth flow of materials. For example, a Group Technology (GT) cell may be used to make several different parts. Although each of those parts follows the same essential processing sequence, each may require different tooling in the machines or a different machine setting. If excessive time is taken for setup in changing from one part to another, then the flow of materials will be momentarily stopped—causing downstream processing operations to pause until the flow resumes. If "upstream" operations continue unchecked, unnecessary inventory will build up in the system, much as water builds up when a dam is placed across a river.

EXHIBIT 15.6

Rearranging Machine
Layout for Smoother
Flow

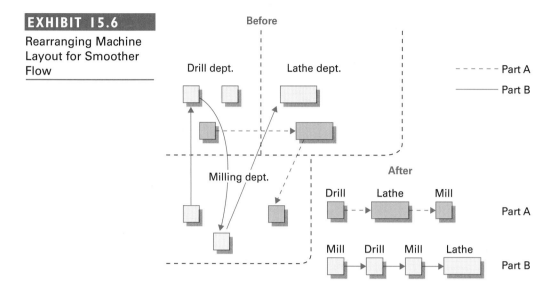

Thus, another objective in a JIT system is to reduce setup time as much as possible. The activities that can help reduce setup time follow:

■ Closely examine each setup to determine steps that can be eliminated or better ways of doing things.

■ Prepare as much ahead of time as possible. All tools and equipment should be readily available in predetermined locations.

■ Try to do as much setup as possible with the machine running. Stop the machine only when absolutely necessary.

■ Use special equipment to shorten downtime whenever possible.

■ Practice and refine the setup procedures.

■ Mark machine settings for quick adjustment.

Exhibit 15.7 indicates the setup time reductions that several companies have been able to achieve by using the procedures described above. As you can see, these changes did not occur overnight. In fact, companies often think it is not possible to reduce setup times on certain equipment. But Exhibit 15.7 shows what can be achieved with hard work and dedication.

As companies have sought ways to reduce setup times, one area they have focused on is product design. In the past, design engineers tended to worry little about actually making the product. But, as Chapter 6 explains, product design is now a team effort that includes individuals from the operations function.

As a result, issues concerning the ease of production have begun to attract the attention of design engineers. One such issue has to do with setup times. By reducing the number of different parts or making parts more similar, it is sometimes possible to reduce setup time or even eliminate setups altogether. For example, Motorola and other companies that manufacture electronic products have found that setups can be eliminated by using a common circuit board for different products. Previously, the automated equipment that inserts parts into the circuit boards would need an extensive setup every time it processed the board for a different product. By using one common board with different components, these companies need to change only the components and insertion pattern, both of which are easy to modify.

One question you might ask at this point is "How small must setup time be?" The answer is that it depends. Some operations may have enough slack that the existing setup

| | | | Original | | Reduced |
Company	Machine	Date	Setup Time	Date	Setup Time
Toyota	1,000-ton press	1945	4 hrs.	1971	3 min.
Toyo Kogyo	Ring-gear cutter	1975	6+ hrs.	1980	10 min.
Hitachi	Die-casting machine	1976	1.25 hrs.	1983	3 min.
Omark Industries	Punch press	1982	2+ hrs.	1983	3 min.
General Electric	45-ton press	1982	50 min.	1983	2 min.
Black & Decker	Punch press	1982	1 hr.	1984	1 min.

EXHIBIT 15.7
Setup Time Reductions

Source: Mehran Sepehri, *Just-in-Time, Not Just In Japan* (Falls Church, VA.: American Production and Inventory Control Society, 1986), pp. 4-11.

time is not disrupting material flow. In those cases, nothing needs to be done. But other operations may cause problems. As we discussed before, the idea is to remove inventory from the system and see what problems surface. If those problems involve setup time on a machine, then that setup time should be reduced. In general, if setup time is less than or equal to cycle time, then disruptions will be minimal. Recall that cycle time is the time it takes to perform a specified activity. In this instance, cycle time is the processing time required for each unit of a given part on a given machine. Thus, if setup time does not exceed cycle time, the disruption of flow will be limited to only one unit. This effect can be further minimized if it is arranged so that each machine performs its setup just ahead of a new part as that part flows from one machine to another. For example, if a company switches from making one product to making another, then each successive operation can perform its setup as the new parts flow through the system, causing the entire system to skip just one cycle.

Total Preventive Maintenance

Machine breakdowns are another possible source of disruptions to the smooth flow in a JIT system. In addition, machines that are not properly lubricated or maintained can produce defective parts without actually breaking down. To prevent either of these results from occurring, companies have adopted what is referred to as **total preventive maintenance (TPM),** also called total productive maintenance.

TPM involves three main components:

1. An emphasis on preventive maintenance. Efforts are undertaken to avoid equipment breakdowns by frequent inspection, lubrication, and the use of proper operating techniques.
2. The allocation of time each day for maintenance. Companies sometimes allow one entire shift for maintenance or set aside specific time during each shift.
3. Operator responsibility for maintenance. Instead of assigning this responsibility to a maintenance department, operators are trained to perform all but the most complicated maintenance on the machines they operate.

Employee Empowerment

Many companies, especially those that are highly unionized, find their workforce management procedures complicate the operations function. By empowering employees to take more responsibility and exercise more authority, many workforce management problems can be eliminated. For example, if employees are able to perform more than one job, resources can be shifted as needed or one employee can operate several machines. Many fast-food restaurants use this approach to meet shifting demand patterns.

Employee empowerment also means training employees to work in small problem-solving groups and allowing those groups to solve problems associated with the production process. If the employees who must produce a good or service are the same ones who work to improve the production process, then the process is greatly simplified and better problem solutions will result. Some basics of team problem solving are discussed in Chapter 4.

Planning in JIT Systems

You may have the feeling that JIT is a complete departure from all the planning concepts we discussed in the two preceding chapters. Actually, this is not true. Companies that use JIT successfully still follow most of the planning steps that we mentioned previously, from strategic planning to master scheduling. In fact, as you will see, it is even possible to combine JIT and MRP; but some changes must be made in the planning and scheduling process under JIT. Basically, those changes make the process easier.

Operations Planning and Master Scheduling

Planning and scheduling are so much easier with JIT because requirements for parts and materials can be tied directly to each unit of the end item. If fifty units of the end item will be made during a given day, then enough parts and subassemblies must be ordered for that day to make the fifty units. Since JIT is based on the idea of having just what is needed when it is needed, parts are usually not ordered in large batches. Instead, a steady stream of material in small batches is maintained at a rate that will match the production of end items.

The Aggregate Plan   The aggregate production plan for a company using JIT is basically the same as that for any other company, except that the JIT planning horizon may be somewhat shorter. Production is generally planned by product families on a monthly basis for about one year into the future. This plan is used for determining general workforce requirements and overall capacity needs and for ordering any parts or materials that have extremely long lead times.

The Master Schedule   In terms of its level of detail, the master schedule for a company using JIT will be the same as that for most other companies that follow a master schedule. That is, planning is usually done in weekly time buckets and by individual end items or product options. The master schedule is usually developed with a two to three-month planning horizon instead of the six to twelve-month horizon used for MRP. The master schedule is also frozen for about one month into the future under MRP, whereas this time fence may be less with JIT due to the shorter lead times.

In an MRP environment, the master schedule is usually what drives the MRP derivation of planned order releases. However, in JIT the pull system often eliminates this need for order release planning because parts and materials will be produced only in response to a downstream signal. The master schedule is used only when items with long lead times must be ordered. Thus, in a JIT system, the master schedule is primarily an intermediate step in reaching the final assembly schedule.

The Final Assembly Schedule

The final assembly schedule is an exact statement of the final products that are to be assembled. The final assembly schedule is stated on a daily basis, but most often goes only about a week into the future. Because lead times are usually so short in a JIT environment, it is the final assembly schedule that indicates which component parts, and their quantities, will be made each day.

The JIT philosophy of eliminating unnecessary inventory has a major impact on the final assembly schedule. So far, we have talked about eliminating work-in-process inventory. But it is important that any unnecessary finished-goods inventory also be eliminated. However, this is hard to do when a company makes more than one finished product.

The approach that has been followed in traditional manufacturing systems is to make a large number of one product before switching over to another. It means that the inventory of each finished product will build up when that item is being produced, but then drop back down when other products are being made, as shown in Exhibit 15.8.

This approach is inefficient because it leads to high levels of finished-goods inventory some times and very low levels—with the possibility of being unable to satisfy customer demand—other times. A better approach is to "level" the final assembly schedule. A **level assembly schedule** means simply that the number of units of each end product produced at a time is as small as possible, and that total daily production of each matches average daily demand during the scheduling horizon. In other words, if the scheduling horizon is twenty working days and demand during that period is expected to be 300 units, a level schedule would mean producing 15 units (300/20) each day.

The idea of a level assembly schedule is that the smallest reasonable number of units of each end product should be produced at a time. Thus, even if fifteen units of a product are to be made during a given day, those fifteen units should be spread throughout the day. This even spread is achieved through mixed-model sequencing.

Mixed-Model Sequencing **Mixed-model sequencing** is a procedure for maintaining the uniform production required by a level assembly schedule. If a company makes several different end items (different products or different models of the same product), it is desirable to spread the production of each evenly throughout each day. However, in order to keep the system running as smoothly as possible, there should be some continuity in the sequencing of those end items. For example, if four different products (A, B, C, and D) are produced, then the ideal schedule would be to produce them in some sequence such as A–B–C–D and to repeat that same sequence throughout the day for each day in the planning horizon. But sometimes demand for one product will be greater than for others. In that case, the sequence may have to be varied somewhat.

EXHIBIT 15.8

Finished-Goods Inventory with Long Production Runs

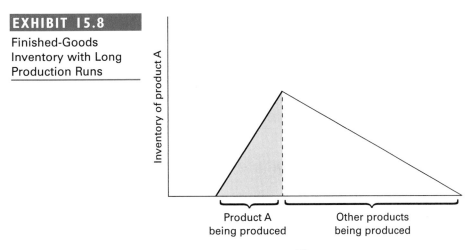

Inventory of product A

Product A being produced

Other products being produced

Time

PROBLEM

A company produces three products. Expected demand for each during the next twenty working days is as shown below.

Product	Expected Demand	Daily Requirements
A	420	420/20 = 21
B	280	280/20 = 14
C	140	140/20 = 7

The daily requirements are obtained by dividing expected demand over the planning horizon by the number of working days in the time horizon. To maintain a level schedule, the company needs to plan so that each product's daily requirements will be produced every day, evenly spread throughout the day if possible. It is also desirable that a set sequence of products be made, and that this sequence be repeated throughout the day.

The trick in solving this problem is to find the largest integer that divides evenly into each product's daily requirements. In this case, the number is 7. Thus, the company should develop a sequence that will be repeated seven times each working day.

Product	Daily Requirements/7
A	21/7 = 3
B	14/7 = 2
C	7/7 = 1

The result of dividing the daily requirements for each product by the largest integer that divides into each evenly is the number of times each product must be repeated in the sequence. Thus, product A should appear three times, product B twice, and product C once. Developing the sequence takes some trial and error, but the following is one possibility that would satisfy the company's objectives:

A–B–A–B–A–C

This sequence would be repeated seven times each day to produce the required twenty-one units of product A, fourteen units of B, and seven units of C, while still leveling the assembly schedule.

It should be noted in the above example that the mixed-model sequence produced is not the only one possible. Such a sequence would smooth out the production, but could also cause problems due to excessive changeovers. When the cycle time is short, it may be desirable to produce more than one unit of each end product at a time. Thus, the following sequence would also be acceptable for short cycle times:

A–A–A–B–B–C

In fact, there might be restrictions that would justify producing even more units of each product at a time. For example, these products might be packed ten per carton for final shipping. In such a case, it could make more sense to produce thirty of A, twenty of B, and ten of C at a time, instead of letting partially filled shipping cartons sit around. Regardless, the objective is to smooth out production by producing each item in the smallest quantities that are reasonable, given existing constraints.

Calculating Cycle Times The purpose of obtaining a level assembly schedule is to smooth out the production of each end item so that it will closely match demand. However, a level schedule also smoothes out the requirements for component parts that go into each finished product. This smoothing makes the pull system work better because demand for each part will be fairly uniform throughout the day, instead of occurring in batches, as it would if each finished product were made in large batches.

But, the flow of component parts must be adjusted to match the rate at which finished products will be produced. For example, if we make one product C every hour, it will do us no good to have a machine that makes parts for product C turning out one every two hours—or even one every half hour. What we would like is to match the production rate of all components to the final assembly schedule. This is done through cycle times.

Cycle time, as you learned in Chapter 11, is a measure of how often a particular product is made. For example, automobile assembly lines usually have a cycle time of about one minute. In other words, a new car rolls off the line every minute. The cycle time of any product can be calculated as follows:

Cycle time = working time per day/units required per day

PROBLEM

For the preceding example, the cycle time is calculated by using the formula given above. Suppose the plant is in production for seven hours (420 minutes) each day, and it must produce a total of forty-two units each day (twenty-one of A, fourteen of B, and seven of C) to match daily demand. Then the cycle time will be

420 minutes/42 units = 10 minutes/unit

This calculation can be extended to each of the individual products in order to determine how often each of these would be produced, based on a mixed-model sequence.

Product	Daily Requirements	Cycle Time
A	21	420/21 = 20 minutes
B	14	420/14 = 30 minutes
C	7	420/7 = 60 minutes

This means that one product A will be produced every twenty minutes, on the average, throughout the day by using the completely level sequence developed in the preceding example. In order to make this possible, the people and machines that supply parts and subassemblies for product A must also be balanced to produce with a cycle time of twenty minutes. Likewise, the entire system must be coordinated to produce one product—either A, B, or C—every ten minutes. In some cases, this may mean that ways must be found to reduce setup times or that more machines must be added. It can also mean that some machines will not produce at their capacity. It is much more desirable in a JIT system to have machines sitting idle than to have them producing inventory that is not needed. Ideally, though, all resources should be used as efficiently as possible, which may mean finding ways to use the same machine to make several different parts so it can be used efficiently without making excess inventory.

The Role of MIS in JIT

Implementation of JIT does not eliminate the need for information systems, although it does affect the way those systems must operate. For example, many companies have found after JIT implementation that they still need to use MRP for planning requirements of materials with longer lead times. MRP may, however, need to be modified to work correctly with JIT. One such modification might be shortening the length of each "time bucket" from one week to one day.

JIT also influences the accounting information system. Because the flow of materials is so rapid with JIT, the traditional cost-accounting procedures are not adequate. As a result, many companies have adopted activity-based costing (ABC), which develops accounting cost figures

388 PART III PLANNING AND MANAGING OPERATIONS

based on activities, called **cost drivers,** such as assembling components or performing a service. A related concept is **backflushing,** which calculates material usage for either a cost accounting or an MRP system based on the number of completed units produced and the materials required to produce that number of units.

From an operations viewpoint, the purpose of backflushing is to determine material usage. The information produced can also be useful for both the purchasing function and accounts payable. One responsibility of the purchasing department is to ensure that items ordered have actually been delivered. With JIT, however, deliveries are often so frequent that the purchasing department could be overburdened keeping up with them. Instead, backflushing provides the necessary information by indicating numbers of units actually used for each part. Because of JIT's minimal inventories, usage can indicate receipt.

The accounts payable function must also ensure that suppliers get paid for what they actually delivered. In traditional systems, that delivery would be signaled by the purchasing department. Through backflushing, though, usage can again indicate receipt and that information then generates the necessary documentation to pay suppliers.

JIT in Service Operations

Although JIT originated in manufacturing and most of the initial implementations occurred there, service organizations are now widely adopting many of the basic ideas from JIT. In fact, service organizations may have a head start because of their lack of work-in-process and finished goods inventories. For example, retailers are focusing on maintaining smaller inventories by being able to replenish that inventory more quickly and in smaller quantities. Insurance companies are finding ways to eliminate unnecessary steps in their claims processing procedures so that customer claims are processed more quickly. Airlines are using yield management (discussed in Chapter 12) to level the demand for their flights.

The JIT ideas that are probably most immediately relevant to services are that waste in any form should be eliminated and that efforts should be made to constantly improve. Specifically, we can focus on the following areas.

Simplified Production Process

Service operations often differ from manufacturing in that customers are more directly involved, and are often active participants, in the production process. For example, automated teller machines allow customers to enter transaction information formerly entered by bank tellers. Because most customers are not trained employees, the process must be as simple and obvious as possible.

Uncovering Problems Buried by Inventory

Even though services often have no finished-goods inventory, they still may have inventories of supplies or even work-in-process, as with loan applications in a bank. Those inventories can hide problems just as easily as inventory in a factory can. In fact, recent studies have shown that speed is becoming an important order winner for service operations. By uncovering problems through reduced inventory, service organizations can work toward providing the service when the customer wants it.

An Emphasis on Quality

Due to the direct contact between customers and service organizations, quality problems will be much more obvious to the customer. And, the definition of quality is often broadened in service organizations to include the helpfulness and friendliness of salespeople or even the pleasantness of the decor in a facility. For these reasons, service organizations must especially emphasize quality throughout their entire operation.

<table>
<tr><td>**EXAMPLE**</td><td>McDonald's employs a lot of part-time workers at all of its restaurants throughout the world. Many of these workers may have a low level of commitment to the organization. Consequently, the quality of McDonald's products and services could vary widely, depending upon the specific location or who happens to be working at a given time. To avoid such an outcome, McDonald's has institutionalized procedures that guarantee consistent quality. For example, the ketchup dispenser always puts the same amount of ketchup on each burger, no matter what.</td></tr>
</table>

Strategic Planning and JIT

We have already discussed strategic planning and its importance in Chapter 2. Any company must develop an organizational strategy based on its strengths and weaknesses, the competitive and economic environment, and the type of product it produces. However, JIT offers some very special competitive opportunities to the company that uses it. Robert Hall, an author who has visited many Japanese companies and studied JIT systems, lists the following major opportunities:

- Quality and reliability
- Product flexibility
- Volume flexibility
- Delivery dependability
- Productivity
- People utilization
- Cost minimization

Quality and Reliability

Total quality management is something that can have several payoffs. In a JIT system, the goal is to eliminate all defects, which means lower costs because scrap is virtually eliminated. At the same time, customers will be happier because they will be getting higher quality products that are likely to last longer. Producing higher quality products also means fewer returned items and fewer warranty repairs, which also will result in reduced costs. The goal of constant improvement will eventually lead to production of a product that gives the customer greater value at a lower price.

Product Flexibility

JIT production gives a company considerable flexibility in several ways. For one, producing to a level schedule means that each product is produced each day. Changes in customer demand can usually be accommodated rather quickly because the system is already designed to change from making one product to making another quite easily. Such is often not the case with companies that make long production runs of each product.

Low work-in-process inventories also provide added flexibility. With minimal inventories in the pipeline, companies can quickly switch to making different parts. There is less motivation to keep on producing a given product—even though demand has dropped—just to use up parts inventories.

Volume Flexibility

It may seem contrary to the goal of using a level assembly schedule to smooth production to argue that companies using JIT have more flexibility to change their volumes. But the results indicate that successful JIT implementation leads companies to a position in which they have greater capability to respond to sudden surges or drops in demand.

Part of this flexibility is related to low inventories. A company with very little work-in-process inventory can quickly cut off its production in response to a drop in demand. The ability to respond when demand increases is a result of the smooth material flows in a JIT system. Smooth flows generally mean that machines and people are being employed at a steady, uniform pace. When it is necessary to increase output, the ability is there to quicken that pace. It is like the difference between a marathon runner and a sprinter. Like the marathon runner, a JIT system is not going flat out all the time, so it has some extra capacity to sprint when necessary. A sprinter, on the other hand, is running flat out and has nothing left when a quick burst of speed is needed.

Delivery Dependability

All of the strategic aspects of JIT discussed so far help contribute to delivery dependability. Improved quality will mean that shipments to customers are not held up because of quality problems in the product or because of delays caused by defective parts. Product and volume flexibility means that the company is better able to respond when customers suddenly change the size or product mix of their orders.

Productivity

We have mentioned several times that part of the JIT philosophy is to use all resources efficiently. This efficiency extends to capital assets, such as plant and equipment. Because JIT requires less inventory, much less floor space is required. Plants using JIT often require less than half the space of traditional plants making the same product.

To obtain quick setups, many companies have found that buying simple, general-purpose equipment is better than buying more sophisticated, specialized equipment. Since general-purpose equipment usually costs less, the total investment in machinery will be less. In addition, this equipment is usually used more uniformly. The special-purpose machinery may sit idle until the one part it is designed to make is needed. General-purpose machinery can be kept busy making many different parts.

Maintenance is also an important aspect of JIT. To maintain the smooth flow of materials, it is essential that machine breakdowns be avoided. Companies using JIT concentrate heavily on strong preventive maintenance programs and on operating machines well below their rated maximum capacities. Equipment will last much longer, giving the companies a greater return on investment.

People Utilization

Companies using JIT depend heavily on their employees to solve problems, but utilization of people extends even further. For instance, maintaining the smooth flow of materials often means that one employee may have to operate several different machines. This cross-training leads to greater worker utilization. Likewise, companies using JIT tend to examine closely any areas where waste might be present. One such area in many companies is the office staff. Efforts are usually undertaken to find ways that managerial jobs can be combined or even eliminated—something few companies have done in the past.

Cost Minimization

The JIT philosophy of avoiding waste leads logically to cost minimization. Although the cost savings associated with inventory reduction have often received the most notice, other savings may be more substantial. For instance, total quality control can both cut material costs substantially and save on the labor costs that might have gone into making defective products. A level schedule avoids costly overtime by evenly loading the plant. Likewise, extensive machine maintenance means that downtime will be eliminated, repair costs will be lower, and equipment will last longer. Overall, companies using JIT have been able to achieve much lower costs than their competitors.

JIT II

The concept of **JIT II,** which was developed by Bose Corporation, is more appropriately related to vendor-managed inventory and supply chain management than it is to the broad philosophy of JIT. Thus, JIT II is discussed more fully in Chapter 5. JIT II does, however, tie in some with various components of JIT. Under JIT II, a supplier's representatives actually work within the customer company, taking responsibility for handling all orders from their own company. This approach can greatly reduce inventory, simplify processes, and promote a smooth flow of materials—all of which are objectives of JIT. Another possible reason behind the JIT II name is that companies using JIT often develop very close ties with their suppliers. Thus, the next logical step would be to actually have supplier representatives working within the customer company.

Lean Systems

The term "lean systems" is often used to describe many of the aspects of JIT. In fact, many people view JIT and lean systems as being interchangeable terms meaning the same thing. Others tend to view JIT as being a component of lean systems. One reason for this latter viewpoint is that JIT often is defined narrowly as consisting of only the pull (kanban) system described in this chapter. On the other hand, if one takes the broader view of JIT, as we have done, then it essentially covers most of the same ground as lean systems.

Current thinking tends to view lean systems as extending beyond JIT by encompassing the entire supply chain. While traditional JIT has been applied to a company and its immediate suppliers, lean systems tend to emphasize extending many of the basic concepts of JIT over the entire supply chain. Furthermore, lean systems focus even more extensively than JIT on eliminating any non-value added (NVA) activities from the entire supply chain. NVA activities would be anything that does not add value for the customer. The series of activities that add value, running through the entire supply chain from raw materials to the final consumer, are referred to as the value stream. Lean systems focus on applying the basic ideas of JIT to this entire value stream.

THEORY OF CONSTRAINTS

Theory of Constraints (TOC) began as a software package called OPT® (Optimized Production Technology). Aside from a set of OPT® Rules, not much was known about the inner workings of that software. Since then, the developer of OPT®, Dr. Eliyahu Goldratt, has expanded his OPT® Rules into TOC. This theory leads to an overall operating philosophy that is similar in some respects to JIT.

The Goal of Operations

Theory of Constraints begins by stating that the goal of a business organization is to make money. To measure how well a company is doing in achieving that goal we focus on three factors:

1. *Throughput*—The rate at which the system generates money through sales
2. *Inventory*—The money the system invests in purchasing things the system intends to sell
3. *Operating expenses*—The money the system spends in turning inventory into throughput

Using these three measures, the way to increase profits is to increase throughput while decreasing both inventory and operating expenses. These relationships are shown in Exhibit 15.9. Any action that does not move these measures in the desired directions will not move an organization toward its goal.

The Impact of Constraints

Theory of Constraints gets its name from the concept that a **constraint** is anything that prevents a system from achieving higher performance relative to its goal. For the preceding example, the constraint is the production process that limits how much may be produced. In general, there are three broad categories of constraints.

1. *Internal resource constraints*—A resource within the organization, such as capacity, that limits performance
2. *Market constraints*—Market demand for a product is less than an organization's capacity to produce that product
3. *Policy constraints*—Any policy that limits performance, such as a policy prohibiting the use of overtime

EXAMPLE

The Clowes Group, a printer in Northeast England, was faced with serious production problems that resulted in a severe drop in profitability. Before learning about Theory of Constraints, the company was able to solve those problems, but then found it had excess production capacity. After reading a copy of Goldratt's book, *The Goal*, the CEO realized the company was now faced with a market constraint. By applying TOC concepts to eliminating that constraint, the company was eventually able to increase sales so much that its printing presses were booked up three months in advance, even during the time of year when demand had historically been the lowest.

To see how these concepts are put into practice, consider the process indicated in Exhibit 15.10. As shown, products A and B are produced using the same process. The profit

EXHIBIT 15.9

Relationships between Throughput, Inventory, Operating Expenses, and Profit

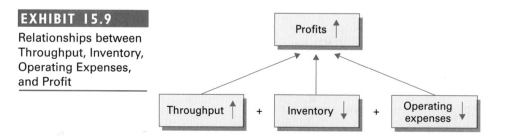

for product A is $80 per unit, and 100 units can be sold per week. For product B, the profit is $50 per unit, and 200 units can be sold per week. Unfortunately, because the process that produces these two products is available only sixty hours per week, we cannot satisfy all demand. How much of each product should be produced to maximize profits? Our initial reaction would probably be to produce as much as possible of product A because it provides the highest profit per unit. Therefore, we would produce 100 units of product A, requiring forty hours of production time but generating $8,000 profit per week. The remaining twenty hours of production time would be used to make 100 units of product B, generating another $5,000 profit per week for a total of $13,000.

To see how TOC can lead to a better solution than the one developed in the previous paragraph, refer again to Exhibit 15.10. In that example, the production process is an internal resource constraint because it limits the organization's ability to make a higher profit. That process is also often referred to as the bottleneck. Theory of Constraints proposes a series of steps to follow in dealing with any type of constraint.

1.   Identify the system's constraints.
2.   Determine how to exploit the system's constraints.
3.   Subordinate everything else to the decisions made in step 2.
4.   Elevate the constraint so a higher performance level can be reached.
5.   If the constraint is eliminated in step 4, go back to step 1. Do not let inertia become the new constraint.

In the example of Exhibit 15.10 we can perform the first three steps. We have already identified that the constraint is production capacity. However, we have not determined how to exploit that constraint. To do so, consider the ratio of profit to production time used for each product as shown in Exhibit 15.11. From that calculation, it is apparent that product B produces a higher *profit per hour* of the constrained resource used. Therefore, to exploit the constraint we should produce as much of product B as possible. That would mean producing 200 units of B for a total profit of $10,000 and utilizing forty hours of production time.

The third step is to subordinate everything else to the decision made in Step 2. Thus, we will produce product A only if time remains. With the remaining twenty hours, we could produce fifty units of product A, generating another $4,000 profit. Thus by exploiting the constraint we have produced a total profit of $14,000, an increase of $1,000 over what we achieved without considering the constrained resource.

EXHIBIT 15.10

A Constrained
Production Process

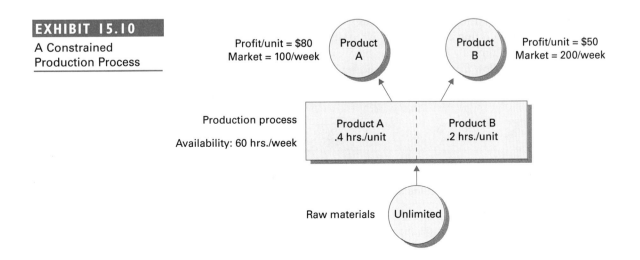

Applying TOC in Operations

The operations function does not usually deal with market constraints. Therefore, we will limit our discussion primarily to ways of handling internal resource constraints and policy constraints. Theory of Constraints suggests certain ways of managing operations so that such constraints can be exploited and elevated.

Bottlenecks

A **bottleneck** is defined as any department, work station, or operation that restricts the flow of product through the production system. Thus, a bottleneck is any resource that has capacity equal to or less than the demand placed on it. A nonbottleneck resource, on the other hand, is one that has capacity greater than the demand placed on it.

The reason TOC focuses on bottlenecks is that these determine output for the entire production process. For example, if machine A produces parts at the rate of fifty per hour and feeds them to machine B, which runs only ten per hour, the final output through these two machines will be only ten per hour. In this example, machine B is the bottleneck, and machine A is a nonbottleneck. Analysis of this example leads to the following two principles:

1. An hour of production time lost at a bottleneck subtracts one hour of output from the entire production system.
2. An hour of time saved at a nonbottleneck only adds an hour to its idle time.

These two principles have major implications for scheduling production of each type of resource, as you will see.

| EXAMPLE | The U.S. health care system has come under increasing pressure to decrease costs and also increase quality of care. One group that has felt that pressure is the U.S. Air Force's 366th Medical Group, which sought to provide its services to a larger group while also decreasing the waiting time for a routine appointment. The group used TOC to identify availability of routine appointment times as the constraint. It then found that routine appointment times could be exploited if other classes of nonroutine appointments were scheduled more effectively. As a result, the average waiting time for a routine appointment fell from 17 days to 4.5 days without additional cost. |

Process Batches and Transfer Batches

In discussing JIT, we mentioned that one objective is to eliminate any excess inventory. To do this, companies would ideally produce just one unit of each part or subassembly at a time. By reducing these batch sizes, it is possible to move toward the smooth, continuous flow that we mentioned earlier. However, it is possible to argue that reducing all batch sizes may produce undesirable results.

EXHIBIT 15.11

Constrained Resource Utilization for Each Product

Product	A	B
Profit	$80/unit	$50/unit
Resource utilization	.4 hrs./unit	.2 hrs./unit
Profit per hour of resource utilization	$\dfrac{\$80}{.4 \text{ hrs.}} = \dfrac{\$200}{\text{hour}}$	$\dfrac{\$50}{.2 \text{ hrs.}} = \dfrac{\$250}{\text{hour}}$

For example, consider the two situations shown in Exhibit 15.12. In the first case, batch sizes have been kept small, so that frequent setups are required between batches. Approximately half of the available time is used unproductively for setups. In the second case, however, batch sizes are larger, and less time is spent for setups. Therefore, more time is available to be producing.

For a bottleneck, any time spent in setups will be lost production. Therefore, it is desirable to give bottlenecks large batch sizes to process, minimizing their nonproductive setup time.

For nonbottlenecks, however, the situation is different. Excess capacity is available at nonbottleneck resources, so more time can be spent on setups without detrimental effects. Further, suppose a nonbottleneck work center must process parts and then feed them to a bottleneck. If the nonbottleneck produces in large batches, the bottleneck may be kept idle, waiting for that large batch to finish processing. Small batch sizes at the nonbottleneck work center, on the other hand, will tend to provide a continuous flow of materials for the bottleneck.

But suppose the nonbottleneck work center must process large batches. Is there any way to avoid delaying the bottleneck? The answer is that we must differentiate between the quantity processed and the quantity moved.

Process Batch versus Transfer Batch

Most companies have tended to operate under the philosophy that a batch being processed on one machine did not get moved to the next machine until the entire batch was completed. For example, if machine A is making a batch of 100 parts, the parts do not get moved to the next operation, machine B, until all 100 have been completed on A. But what if machine B is a bottleneck resource that must sit idle, waiting for parts from machine A? Surely it would be better to keep feeding parts to machine B as they are finished on machine A.

This is the idea of a transfer batch. While large batch sizes may be desirable for processing to reduce setups, they can also lead to idle time at operations farther along in the product flow. Thus, the **transfer batch,** the amount transferred from one operation to another, may not be the same as the **process batch,** which is the amount processed at one time on a machine. Exhibit 15.13 shows how a smaller transfer batch can reduce idle time and increase output.

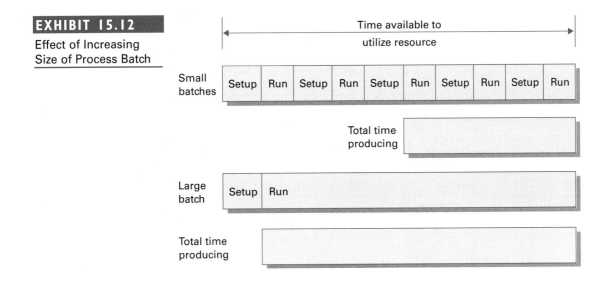

EXHIBIT 15.12

Effect of Increasing Size of Process Batch

The Drum, Buffer, and Rope

In TOC, three elements are of key importance. They are referred to as the drum, the buffer, and the rope.

The Drum

The **drum** is what determines the rate of production. In MRP, JIT, and TOC, that rate corresponds to the master production schedule (MPS). In MRP and JIT, the master schedule is determined primarily from market demand. For MRP, capacity requirements planning can determine when there will be insufficient capacity to meet the master schedule. Adjustments must then be made to the master schedule on an ad hoc basis.

With TOC, on the other hand, the constraints are used to develop the schedule. Thus, the constraint is the drum; it sets the rate of all other operations to match its own, which becomes the "drum beat" for the entire process.

[handwritten note: on Market Policy]

The Buffer

In spite of the carefully developed MPS, deviations will occur due to unforeseen events. In order to prevent such events from disrupting output of finished goods, buffers are placed at carefully selected locations. These buffers may be of two types—a stock buffer or a time buffer. Although both are actually inventory buffers, the amount of inventory in a **time buffer** is determined by the amount of output the system could produce during the period of time it takes to correct a disruption.

In general, the key location for time buffers will be before bottlenecks. That way, the bottlenecks can keep working even if the flow of material to them is disrupted. Time buffers before bottlenecks are often called constraint buffers.

EXHIBIT 15.13

Effect on Increasing Size of Process Batch

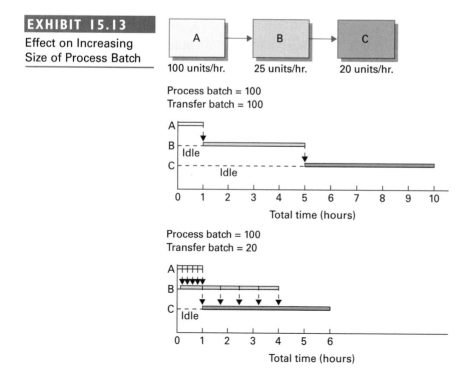

Process batch = 100
Transfer batch = 100

Process batch = 100
Transfer batch = 20

The other prime location for time buffer inventories will be at locations where parts from the bottleneck are combined with parts from other processes. They prevent those assembly or subassembly processes from having to shut down due to problems at nonbottleneck resources. If they did shut down, then the bottleneck process would also have to be stopped, losing production for the whole system or building up excess inventory. These are assembly buffers.

Stock buffers are inventories of finished goods held in anticipation of market demand. Their sizes are usually determined by forecasts of possible demand increases. Stock buffers are also called shipping buffers. The placement of both time buffers and stock buffers is shown in Exhibit 15.14.

WIP Buffer

The Rope

In Exhibit 15.3, we used a rope analogy to show how materials are pulled through a JIT system. That analogy is also useful for TOC because it shows how the rate at which processes operate must be linked together. We have already explained that a bottleneck operation will set the "drum beat" or production rate for the entire operation. For

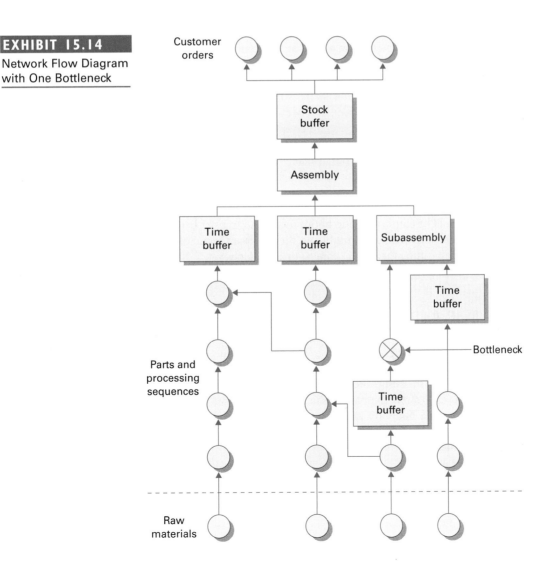

EXHIBIT 15.14

Network Flow Diagram with One Bottleneck

processes that come after the bottleneck, their rate of operation will be paced by what is produced from the bottleneck. Operations before the bottleneck have the potential of producing too fast for the bottleneck, thus creating excess inventory.

To prevent the buildup of excess inventory, there must be a linkage between a bottleneck and the first operation in the series of processes that feed it. This linkage is referred to as the rope. The **rope** can be a formal schedule of planned production or informal daily discussions between employees at the bottleneck and employees at another work station.

EXAMPLE

Valmont Industries produces steel light structures, such as highway and stadium light poles. Traditionally, the company had used MRP, but found that past-due orders kept growing while huge amounts of work-in-process inventory sat around the plant. After recognizing that its MRP system just was not producing the desired results, Valmont decided to implement a drum-buffer-rope (DBR) system. Almost immediately, the work-in-process inventory decreased and throughput increased. After using DBR for ten years, the company's shipments have increased by a factor of seven.

Comparing TOC, MRP, and JIT

All three techniques are aimed at the same goal—ensuring that production meets customer demand. Each simply goes about it in a slightly different way. As we have already mentioned, MRP works from the top down, beginning with an aggregate plan and then a master schedule, altering them as needed to stay within capacity limitations. But, MRP does not directly provide guidance about appropriate batch sizes and offers little guidance in terms of scheduling equipment.

While TOC also develops a master schedule, that schedule is developed more from the bottom up, working from available capacity at the bottleneck. When the master schedule is developed, there is no question about having sufficient capacity. Further, information can be obtained to determine appropriate process and transfer batch sizes.

JIT takes the approach of eliminating all forms of waste. Thus, buffer inventories would be eliminated, and both process and transfer batches would be as small as possible. If these changes cause problems, then ways are found of eliminating the problems, instead of exploiting them, as is done with TOC. However, TOC can also be used to reduce inventory by reducing the impact of constraints. Exhibit 15.15 makes other comparisons.

COMBINING TOC, MRP, AND JIT

The preceding discussion may leave you thinking that TOC, MRP, and JIT are independent choices. That conclusion would be incorrect because today many companies are finding that the best choice is to combine them by utilizing the strengths of each. For example, the great strength of MRP is in planning, especially for items that have long lead times. On the other hand, JIT excels as a shop floor control system for actually executing the plan. TOC is an excellent system for managing bottlenecks. Thus, we see Japanese companies that have used JIT for many years now implementing MRP as a front-end planning tool for use with JIT. Similarly, Valmont Industries, a long-time user of TOC, still uses MRP for planning starting and ending dates for production.

EXHIBIT 15.15   Comparison of MRP, JIT, and TOC

	MRP	JIT	TOC
Loading of operations	Checked by capacity requirements Planning afterward	Controlled by kanban system	Controlled by bottleneck operation
Batch sizes	One week or more	Small as possible	Variable to exploit constraint
Importance of data accuracy	Critical	Unnecessary	Critical for bottleneck and feeder operations
Speed of schedule development	Slow	Very fast	Fast
Flexibility	Lowest	Highest	Moderate
Cost	Highest	Lowest	Moderate
Goals	Meet demand Have doable plan	Meet demand Eliminate waste	Meet demand Maximize profits
Planning focus	Master schedule	Final assembly schedule	Bottleneck
Production basis	Plan	Need	Need and plan

SUMMARY

- JIT is a philosophy of constant effort to eliminate waste.

- JIT is classified as a "pull" system because materials are pulled through processing operations as they are needed.

- According to TOC, the goal of a business is to make money.

- TOC focuses on bottlenecks and schedules based on them. Buffers are used to maintain flow, and ropes are used to communicate.

- JIT II is a supply chain management approach to vendor-managed inventory that places supplier representatives within the customer company.

- Lean manufacturing extends the basic concepts of JIT throughout the entire supply chain.

 Visit our dynamic Web site, http://www.wiley.com/college/vonderembse, for extended chapter material, solved problems, mini-cases, computer software, and Web links.

KEY TERMS

backflushing	kanban	setup time
bottleneck	lean systems	single-card kanban system
c-kanban	level assembly schedule	stock buffer
constraint	mixed-model sequencing	Theory of Constraints
conveyance kanban	p-kanban	(TOC)
cost drivers	process batch	time buffer
drum	production kanban	total preventive
dual-card kanban system	pull system	maintenance (TPM)
JIT II	push system	transfer batch
just-in-time (JIT)	rope	

URLS

Clowes Group: www.clowes.co.uk

Goldratt Institute: www.goldratt.com

Harley-Davidson: www.harley-davidson.com

Kawasaki: www.kawasaki.com

McDonald's: www.mcdonalds.com

Toyota: www.toyota.com

Toys "R" Us: www4.toysrus.com

U.S. Air Force 366th Medical Group: www.mthome.med.osd.mil

Valmont Industries: www.valmont.com

QUESTIONS

1. List the aspects of JIT that result from elimination of excess inventory.

2. Which aspects of a fast-food restaurant are done just-in- time? Which are more similar to batch production?

3. In general, would you say that service organizations operate in a just-in-time mode? Why or why not?

4. Define what is meant by a pull system and a push system.

5. "The drumbeat of production" is a term frequently used to describe the coordinated movement of materials through a production process. What generates a "drumbeat" in an MRP system? In a JIT system? In TOC?

6. Explain why it is important to level the assembly schedule in JIT. Why isn't this so important with MRP?

7. Develop a list of companies or industries that might best benefit from the results that JIT produces.

8. Are there any companies or industries for which JIT would be totally inappropriate? Why?

9. Draw a chart that indicates the JIT planning process. How does this compare with a planning chart used in an MRP system?

10. Define the following terms:
    a. Drum
    b. Buffer
    c. Rope
    d. Throughput
    e. Inventory
    f. Operating expenses

11. Can TOC be used in a nonprofit organization?

12. In an MRP system, what might be thought of as serving the function of a rope?

13. Suppose you have a factory that is not using JIT, MRP, or TOC. How might you identify the bottlenecks?

14. Explain the use of the C-kanban in a single-card system and the use of the C-kanban and the P-kanban in a dual-card system.

15. What are some ways a production process can be simplified? Explain each.

16. Describe at least two ways that quality control is important in JIT.

17. Find an article about a company using JIT outside Japan, and determine whether any modifications have been made to fit local culture or business practices.

18. What is the difference between a process batch and a transfer batch? When are they most likely to be the same?

19. What are the similarities and differences among MRP, JIT, and TOC?

20. Discuss how the lean manufacturing concept of a value stream might relate to the water analogies of JIT.

21. The term lean manufacturing would appear to indicate that the ideas are not applicable to services. Is that true?

INTERNET QUESTIONS

22. Visit the Harley-Davidson Supplier Network Web site (www.h-dsn.com) and access the Public Menu. Go to the "Doing Business with Harley-Davidson" page; then scroll down to access the "Material Forecasting and Replenishment" document. This gives an excellent overview of H-D's use of JIT. Discuss how H-D combines the use of MRP and JIT.

23. Go to the Society of Manufacturing Engineers (SME) Lean Manufacturing Web page (www.sme.org/leanmanufacturing/lean_gateway_page.htm) and summarize what you learn there about lean manufacturing.

24. Visit the home page of the Goldratt Institute (named after the developer of TOC) at www.goldratt.com) and explain some TOC concepts not discussed in this chapter.

25. Go to the Toyota Web site (www.toyota.co.jp/Virtual_Factory). You do not need to install the Japanese language pack unless you want to—everything is in English. Click on "Smoothing the Flow," then explore buttons on the left to learn more about JIT at Toyota. Are there any ideas presented there that have not been discussed in this chapter?

PROBLEMS

1. A carpet cleaning service offers two types of cleaning, either steam cleaning or dry cleaning. The company finds that there are fifteen customers per week who would like the steam cleaning and ten per week who would like the dry cleaning. The average steam cleaning job requires three hours to do and produces a profit of $210. The average dry cleaning job requires two hours to perform and produces a profit of $100. The same crew does both types of cleaning, and that crew is available sixty hours per week. Use TOC to determine how the company can maximize its profits.

2. The Ota Toy Company produces two different toys using the processes shown here.

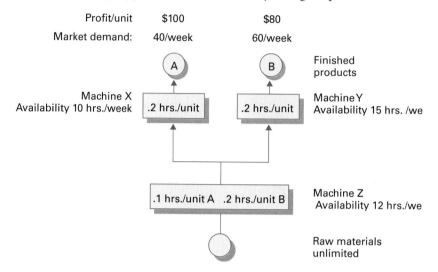

Determine what the constraint is and how to exploit that constraint.

3. A manufacturer of televisions produces three different models—X, Y, and Z. Demand over the next month is expected to be 400 units for model X, 200 units for model Y, and 100 for model Z. There will be twenty working days in the month. Develop a mixed-model sequence.

4. An automobile manufacturer makes two-door sedans, four-door sedans, convertibles, and station wagons. Customer demand for the next twenty-five production days is expected to be 400 two-door sedans, 300 four-door sedans, 300 convertibles, and 200 station wagons. Develop a mixed-model sequence that will level the assembly schedule and satisfy daily demand.

5. Refer to Problem 3. Suppose that the company has eight working hours each day. Calculate cycle times for the three different television models.

6. Refer to Problem 4. If the automobile manufacturer runs the plant seven hours each day, calculate cycle time for each type of car.

7. A company currently uses a job shop arrangement of equipment to make four parts that are used in its final products. The routings for these parts are shown below. Suggest how GT cells could be arranged to produce these parts.

Part #	Routing Sequence
3072	Lathe, mill, grind, drill
274	Shear, punch press, grind, deburr
2987	Mill, drill, grind
1075	Shear, punch press, punch press, deburr

8. The five parts listed below are all produced using a process layout consisting of a drill department with three drills, a lathe department with two lathes, one milling machine, and a heat treating department. Given the following routings, suggest some ways that machines could be rearranged to produce a smoother flow of parts. Unfortunately, heat treating must remain as one department.

Part #	Routing Sequence
1973	Lathe, mill, heat treat, drill
2075	Lathe, drill, heat treat
398	Lathe, drill
4098	Mill, heat treat, drill
298	Mill, drill, lathe

9. A company is trying to use JIT to make several different products. One of those products is assembled from the three parts listed below. Cycle time for that product is twenty-five minutes. Based on the following information, suggest some changes that must be made for JIT to work smoothly. (Note: Each part is made on different machines.)

Part #	Operation 1		Operation 2	
	Setup	Run	Setup	Run
298	5	2	10	6
1073	20	5	15	10
2987	60	10	15	2

	Operation 3		Operation 4	
298	30	10		
1073	20	5	24	1
2987	20	10	25	5

10. Product P1 is produced by processing material through operations A, B, C, and D, in that sequence. There are 480 minutes of processing time available per day, and each unit of product Pl requires fifteen minutes at A, thirty minutes at B, ten minutes at C, and twenty-three minutes at D. Market demand is twenty units per day. Categorize each operation as a nonbottleneck or bottleneck.

11. The process shown below produces a product with daily demand of fifty units and operates 480 minutes per day. Indicate which process should be the drum, where the buffers should go, and where the ropes should be.

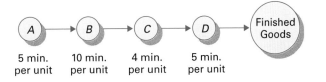

12. Referring to the preceding problem, suppose market demand drops to forty-five units per day. Now which process should be the drum, where should the buffers be located, and where should the ropes be?

13. Process A feeds process B, which in turn feeds process C. A particular part requires ten minutes per unit on A, twenty-five minutes per unit on B, and thirty minutes per unit on C.

    a. Indicate how long it would take to process a batch of 300 units if process batch and transfer batch are the same.

    b. Let process batch be 300 units and transfer batch be 50. Now how long would it take to process the entire batch through all three operations?

CHAPTER 16

Scheduling

LEARNING OBJECTIVES

After completing this chapter, you should be able to:

1. List the six possible criteria for scheduling and discuss the trade-offs involved with each.
2. Describe how scheduling for services differs from manufacturing.
3. Discuss issues of concern in scheduling an assembly line.
4. Use dispatching rules to schedule jobs and discuss each rule.
5. Discuss how priorities are determined in MRP systems.
6. Schedule employees for service operations.

INTRODUCTION

Scheduling is the last step in the planning process that began with strategic planning and proceeded through increasingly detailed planning activities. Recall that each successive stage of the planning process built on its preceding stage. In this chapter, we will describe how to schedule people, equipment, and facilities so that earlier steps in the planning process can be executed. For example, we will be concerned with such activities as sequencing different orders on a machine so that the delivery schedule can be met or scheduling employees for fast service.

In discussing scheduling, we are getting into one of the most challenging areas of operations management. As many companies have found, scheduling presents many day-to-day problems for operations managers because of changes in customer orders, equipment breakdowns, late deliveries from suppliers, and a myriad of other disruptions. At the same time, scheduling is one aspect of production planning for which few, if any, really satisfactory solution techniques have been developed due to the complexity of most scheduling problems. But scheduling is currently receiving considerable attention. In this chapter, we will discuss scheduling problems in various processes and present some methods for solving these problems.

Let us frame our discussion of scheduling by supposing that a company's master schedule calls for the production of two different products during a given time period. Using material requirements planning (MRP), it has been determined that certain parts for each of those finished products must be started into production during week 20, as shown by the circled figures in Exhibit 16.1.

EXHIBIT 16.1

Production Plan for
Two Products

Master Schedule—Product A
Week

19	20	21	22	23	24
500	200	300	400	200	300

Part # 103-B

		19	20	21	22	23	24
Gross requirements		500	200	300	400	200	300
Scheduled receipts							
Projected ending inventory	740	240	40	0	0	0	0
Net requirements				260	400	200	300
Planned receipts				260	400	200	300
Planned order releases			(260)	400	200	300	

Master Schedule—Product B
Week

19	20	21	22	23	24
100	400	300	450	200	300

Part # 2065

		19	20	21	22	23	24
Gross requirements		200	800	600	900	400	600
Scheduled receipts			1,400				
Projected ending inventory	200	0	600	0	0	0	0
Net requirements					900	400	600
Planned receipts					900	400	600
Planned order releases			(900)	400	600		

The routings for these two parts are shown in Exhibit 16.2. Capacity requirements planning (CRP) has been used to determine that insufficient capacity will exist in week 20 on the lathe, which is the "gateway," or first work center, for both parts. Management investigated both short-run and long-run solutions to this capacity problem, but has decided that it will follow a short-run strategy and schedule overtime to alleviate the capacity problem in the lathe department.

In this situation, two scheduling problems have been indicated. One has to do with scheduling employees and the other with scheduling the two parts. Since overtime will be used in the lathe department, it will be necessary to schedule an employee or employees to work during that overtime. The second scheduling problem, scheduling the parts, occurs because both parts will be released to the lathe department at the same time. This second scheduling problem is one of sequencing—determining which part to produce first.

EXHIBIT 16.2

Routing for Two Parts

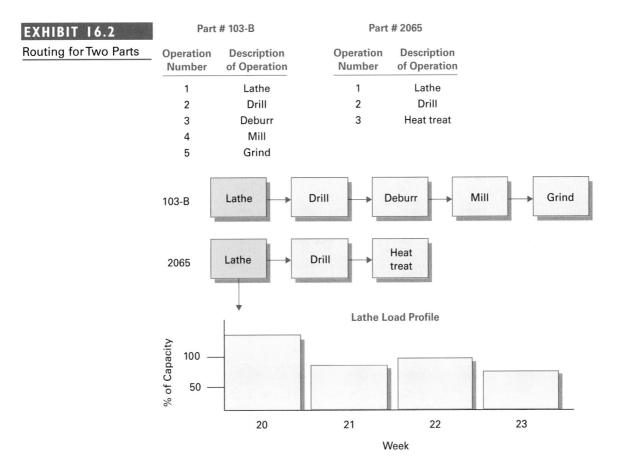

Part # 103-B	
Operation Number	Description of Operation
1	Lathe
2	Drill
3	Deburr
4	Mill
5	Grind

Part # 2065	
Operation Number	Description of Operation
1	Lathe
2	Drill
3	Heat treat

OVERVIEW OF THE SCHEDULING PROCESS

Scheduling is actually a complex process that involves many different steps. In this section we summarize those steps before going on to describe actual scheduling techniques.

Data Collection

Obviously, before scheduling can take place, there must be something to schedule. More importantly, sufficient information about the jobs, activities, employees, equipment, or facilities that are to be scheduled is needed. Depending on the scheduling situation, various types of data must be collected, as shown below.

1. Jobs
    a. Due dates
    b. Routings, with standard setup and processing times
    c. Material requirements
    d. Flexibility of due dates
    e. Importance of being completed by due date

2. Activities
   a. Expected duration
   b. Precedence relationships
   c. Desired time of completion
3. Employees
   a. Availability
   b. Job capabilities
   c. Efficiency at various jobs
   d. Wage rates
4. Equipment
   a. Machine or work center capacities
   b. Machine or work center capabilities
   c. Cost of operation
   d. Availability
5. Facilities
   a. Capacities
   b. Possible uses
   c. Cost of use
   d. Availability

Much of this information will be known and available within the organization. Other information must be gathered. In most instances, a great deal of important information must also come from customers themselves. That information is obtained when orders are entered, a process we discuss next.

Order Entry

The first step in obtaining information about orders involves entry of the order into a company's information system. For a **make-to-order company,** one that produces only to customer orders or that provides services, this could occur when a customer places an order. Given existing production schedules, capacity available, and the customer's desired due date, the particular order can be scheduled. This order scheduling will be a rough esti- mate based on capacity requirements to produce the customer's order. Actually producing that order will require further scheduling of the individual parts and components for a product or the employees and facilities for a service.

In a **make-to-stock company,** one that produces for inventory and meets customer orders from inventory, production orders will be entered by the company itself based on the inventory level of each item in its stock and the expected future demand of that item. In general, a make-to-stock company has a somewhat easier job of scheduling since it has some control over which products will be made. A make-to-order company usually must produce whatever is demanded by the customers.

In an MRP environment, the MRP system will generate planned order releases based on the master schedule. This is another form of order entry—in this case, for individual parts or subassemblies. Again, the process is similar except that the master schedule gener- ates requirements for materials and parts.

Orders Released for Production

As you learned in Chapter 12, the planning process involves a continual movement from strategic plans for the distant future toward more detailed plans for the less-distant future. As time gets closer to the present, plans become more precise and detailed until the time comes when each order is released for production. At that point, the schedule is implemented.

Because scheduling is the last step in production planning, it deals with the very near future. Plans are made to schedule a particular job, activity, or employee, but those plans are not converted into a detailed schedule until the last possible moment. The earlier planning stages dealt with determining what level of resources would be needed to meet the production plan. Scheduling allocates those resources.

When dealing with minute details, such as individual machines, parts, or employees, it is always possible that changes will occur. An employee may become ill or quit; a machine may break down; the raw materials for a part may not arrive on time. Because of these possibilities, scheduling must usually wait until the existing conditions are known with relative certainty. Even then, last minute changes must often be made. But this is what makes scheduling so challenging and so difficult.

As time moves forward and the scheduled starting time for a job or order is reached, that job or order is released for production. That step starts the job on its way through the processing operations. But that is not the last step.

Sequencing and Dispatching

The final steps in scheduling are the actual **sequencing** of activities, jobs, or parts in the order they should flow through processing and then the dispatching of those jobs. For our purposes, we will define **dispatching** as the assignment of priorities and the selection of jobs for processing at a work center or facility. For example, a customer order for a made-to-order product will have to be sequenced in with other orders. When the time comes for work to begin on that order, it will be dispatched at the first work center according to its priority at that time. In the following discussion of scheduling, we will concentrate primarily on ways of sequencing—whether of parts, orders, jobs, activities, or employees.

Managerial Considerations in Scheduling

Scheduling in P/OM is an attempt to allocate scarce resources. For example, machine time is a scarce resource that is allocated to different jobs, employee time is allocated to different activities, and facilities are scheduled for a given activity at a particular time period. In all of these scheduling tasks, different criteria may be used in deciding which of several schedules is best. Those criteria may relate to the amount of time equipment might sit idle, the importance of a certain order or a certain customer, or the level at which a resource is utilized.

The task of scheduling can be quite complex; what appears to be an optimal schedule from one viewpoint may be far from optimal from another. For example, a certain schedule may utilize one machine very efficiently, but may mean idle time for machines farther along in the processing operations. Another schedule might mean that an important customer's order will not be delivered on time. In general, there are six criteria that may be used in evaluating different possible schedules.

1.   Providing the good or service when the customer wants it

2. Minimizing the length of time it takes to produce that good or service (called flow time)

3. Minimizing the level of work-in-process (WIP) inventories

4. Minimizing the amount of time that equipment is idle

5. Minimizing the amount of time that employees are idle

6. Minimizing costs

Which of these criteria are most relevant will often depend on the product or service being produced, the particular industry a company is in, and especially the organization's competitive strategy. Different production processes will also incur different problems, and certain criteria will thus be more important. To make matters more difficult, it is usually impossible to satisfy all of the six criteria listed above at one time. Instead, management must choose among the various trade-offs:

■ *Providing the good or service when the customer wants it*—Requires flexibility. Can lead to large inventories and excess capacity during periods of low demand.

■ *Minimizing flow time*—Requires flexibility, short setup times, and fast production rates. Can require having excess capacity available.

■ *Minimizing WIP inventories*—May require excess capacity or the use of a pull system. Can lead to high machine or employee idle time.

■ *Minimizing machine idle time*—Often means keeping capacity low or accepting any customer orders. Can result in high inventories, the overloading of equipment, and late orders.

■ *Minimizing employee idle time*—Often means keeping workforce size low or accepting any orders. Can result in employee discontent, late orders, and high inventories.

■ *Minimizing costs*—Often requires compromises on the preceding criteria. The problem is to properly define and measure all relevant costs. Can result in poor customer service—a cost that is difficult to measure.

In determining which criteria to use, a company must carefully consider its corporate objectives, competitive strategy, and capabilities. The company's scheduling decisions will have a great impact on facility design, the type of equipment used, and the workforce requirements. Each of these will, in turn, influence its competitiveness in terms of cost, speed, and delivery reliability.

Ethical Issues in Scheduling

In Chapter 13, we discussed how master scheduling and MRP can help a company make due-date commitments to its customers with a high degree of certainty. Scheduling also plays an important role in ensuring that those due-date commitments are met. If jobs are scheduled without considering due dates, then many of the due dates may not be met.

To avoid that occurrence, companies must set scheduling priorities to meet customer due dates. One dispatching rule used in manufacturing, the critical ratio, takes due dates into account and compares them to remaining processing time. By using a procedure that sets priorities based on due dates, companies can be sure the due-date commitments they have made are kept visible throughout all operations

However, in service operations, there may be other considerations. For example, waiting lines at service facilities almost always operate on a first-come, first-served basis, especially in the United States where everyone wants to feel he or she is being treated equally. Many airlines, hotels, and car rental companies, however, have started offering special lines that require less waiting time for customers who have either purchased a more expensive service (e.g., a first class ticket on an airline) or who are frequent users of that service. Is it unethical to give some customers preferential treatment, or is it just good business practice?

There can also be ethical implications in the scheduling of employees. For example, nurses in a hospital are sometimes required to work a "double shift," meaning two eight-hour shifts in a row, if it is necessary to meet staffing needs. Can someone who must work such long hours provide care that is as good as someone who works only one shift? There have been cases in which a patient received the wrong medication because a health care employee was suffering from fatigue and made a mistake. Trucking companies that schedule drivers to work long hours without rest are also behaving unethically because overworked drivers may fall asleep at the wheel, causing serious accidents.

Obviously, some scheduling situations involve more ethical considerations than others. Still, all scheduling must take into account the organization's objectives, while treating customers and employees in an ethically responsible manner.

TECHNIQUES FOR SCHEDULING LINE-FLOW AND BATCH PROCESSES

In scheduling for manufacturing, we will be dealing primarily with two questions:

1. When should a given job, order, or product be processed?
2. How many units should be processed at a time?

The answers to these questions can have a great impact on the way a processing operation is run. For instance, a company that makes ice cream must decide which flavors should be made when. If chocolate is made before vanilla, there may be extensive time spent cleaning the equipment between runs. On the other hand, producing vanilla before vanilla-fudge marble may mean no cleanup between runs. In addition, the company must decide how many gallons of one flavor to make before it starts making another. The company does not want to produce so much of a given flavor that the ice cream deteriorates before it is sold. By the same token, producing small quantities at a time will mean excessive time spent cleaning and refilling the equipment between runs.

In this section, we will look at various techniques for scheduling. Because the scheduling problem is different for different types of processes, we will discuss the rules that are appropriate for each of the major process types—line flow, batch, and job shop.

Scheduling Continuous Flow Processes

A continuous flow process is one in which materials flow in a continuous, or nearly continuous, stream from beginning to end. A good example of a continuous flow process is an oil refinery. Such production processes are generally characterized by a few different finished products, only a few possible routings, and low work-in-process inventories.

Under such conditions, the relevant scheduling criteria become rather limited. For example, flow time is determined by the production process, rather than by a schedule. Work-in-process inventory is also not a major problem because it is generally quite low for continuous flow processes. Thus, the scheduling problem in a continuous flow process boils down to determining when to change over from making one product to making another. The relevant criterion is usually minimizing cost, although minimizing the time the facility is idle during changeover could also be important.

Scheduling an Assembly Line

An assembly-line process is similar to continuous flow, but instead of the products being continuous items, such as a stream of gasoline or a roll of paper, the products are discrete, individual items, such as automobiles.

One of the best examples of an assembly-line process is the automobile assembly line. In this example, the product follows a fixed path. Like the continuous flow process, an assembly-line process usually produces a limited number of products, and the routings are usually the same. Work-in-process inventory is also usually small. Thus, the same basic ideas used for scheduling in continuous flow can also be used for assembly line process scheduling. There are, however, two particular problems unique to assembly-line scheduling that we will discuss here.

Line Balancing

Chapter 11 presented assembly-line balancing in the context of facility layout. The emphasis there was on determining how many workstations would be needed to achieve a desired cycle time and which tasks should be assigned to each station to minimize "balance delay." Assembly-line balancing also provides the framework for scheduling. By assigning tasks to work stations, the material flow and job assignments have been specified by the line balance.

Keep in mind, however, that assembly-line balancing is not a perfect science. In actual practice, people with different abilities will be assigned to those stations. The result may be that even though a perfect balance was achieved theoretically, it will not be in practice. Some employees will complete their tasks in less than the average time. Others will take longer. The end result is that a line balanced in theory may be unbalanced in practice.

Scheduling is one approach to overcoming this problem. A skillful supervisor will know which employees can work faster and will assign those to the stations with more work. On a dynamic basis, tasks may even be shifted from one workstation to another as trouble spots appear. Thus, scheduling, in the sense of assigning employees to work stations or tasks to employees, is an integral part of fine-tuning the balance of a line.

Sequencing

Earlier we mentioned that sequencing was the problem of determining the order in which parts or products should be processed. That particular problem is relevant to an assembly-line process. Take, for example, an automobile assembly line. That line may be balanced for producing a particular make and model of car. But it will be out of balance for a different make or model. For instance, the work stations that install seats and interior padding will probably require a longer period to do a station wagon than they will a two-door sedan. If too many station wagons are sequenced in a row, those workstations will be **over cycled.** In other words, the amount of work will consistently exceed the cycle time.

Scheduling Batch Processes

In batch processes, the number of possible products is greater than in line-flow processes. Further, the production volume of each product is usually less than in a line-flow process. As a result, the same resources are used to produce at least several different products, producing a batch of each product at a time.

Because of this, how many units to produce in a batch and which product to produce become important questions. In answering them, the criterion of cost minimization is usually used to determine production quantity. Because each product is produced only intermittently, it must be produced often enough to avoid running out of inventory. Thus, the sequencing of products is often determined on the basis of which one is likely to run out of inventory first.

Batch Sizes

There are many different factors to consider in determining batch sizes. One approach is to attempt balancing the cost of setup for producing a batch against the cost of storing those units in inventory. Some basic ideas related to this approach were discussed in Chapter 14. Other considerations may include quantities in which a customer usually orders or shipping quantities, both of which may determine batch sizes. Finally, each product may be produced on some regular schedule, such as once per month. In that case, the batch size must be enough to satisfy demand until the next production run.

Run-Out Time

The question of batch size deals only with how much to produce; it does not indicate which product should be produced next. One method that can be used to answer this second question is called **run-out time.** This is simply a calculation of how long it will be before the company will run out of each product at current usage rates. It is determined as follows:

$$\text{Run-out time} = \frac{\text{current inventory}}{\text{usage rate}}$$

PROBLEM

Exhibit 16.3 indicates current inventory and demand rates for five different products made by a process. Run-out time calculations are shown for each of the five different products. Based on those calculations, product E should be produced next since it will run out first—in two weeks.

In actual practice, the order quantity and order sequence questions must be answered simultaneously. However, a discussion of that procedure is beyond the scope of this text.

Flexible Manufacturing Systems

It was mentioned before in discussing the use of the EPQ for production scheduling that the basic trade-off was between product changeover costs and inventory carrying costs. But, when the cost of changeover becomes extremely small, the question of how many to produce at a time is less important.

Flexible manufacturing systems (FMSs) have been able to reduce changeover costs to the point that it is economical to produce just one product or part at a time. The question

---

EXHIBIT 16.3

Run-Out Time Calculations

Product	Current Inventory	Demand Rate (Units per Week)	Run-Out Time (Weeks)
A	1,000	200	1,000/200 = 5
B	500	150	500/150 = 3.3
C	2,000	500	2,000/500 = 4
D	2,500	500	2,500/500 = 5
E	600	300	600/300 = 2

then becomes one of sequencing to keep this changeover time—and consequently the cost—low enough.

Group technology, which has been discussed in previous chapters, is an important aspect of any FMS. By grouping similar products into families, a GT cell within an FMS has to deal only with products that have similar characteristics, which tends to reduce the sequencing problem. Because computerized control is an important part of an FMS, the computer can be used to evaluate different possible sequences and determine the best one for each cell.

JOB SHOP SCHEDULING

One type of production process for which very few satisfactory scheduling techniques have been developed is the job shop. Unlike continuous flow or assembly-line processes, a job shop has many different and intersecting routings. Different jobs will be vying for time on the same machines. The decision about which job to process first on a given machine can have a major impact on what happens at other machines or work centers—possibly overloading some, while leaving others idle.

Sequencing Using Dispatching Rules

One of the earliest approaches to job shop scheduling was to focus on the criteria for scheduling that were mentioned earlier in this chapter. Those criteria could be used to generate dispatching rules to be used at an individual machine or work center. The five most common **dispatching rules** are described below.

Earliest Due Date

The earliest-due-date rule focuses on the criterion of providing the product when the customer wants it. The rationale is that whichever job is due first should be started first. The advantage of this approach is that some jobs may meet their due dates. This rule is popular with companies that are sensitive to due-date changes. However, finishing one job on time may make many more late. This method also does not consider how long it will take to process the job—which led to the next rule.

Shortest Processing Time

The rationale for the shortest-processing-time rule is to get the most work done as quickly as possible in order to minimize the level of WIP inventory. Unfortunately, jobs with long processing times may be made quite late as they wait for shorter jobs to be finished. Otherwise, this rule usually tends to work best on most measures.

Longest Processing Time

The longest-processing-time rule uses a different strategy—to get the jobs that will take longest done first, leaving time at the end to do the short-processing-time jobs. The rationale behind this rule is that jobs with long processing times may be more likely to miss their due dates than jobs with short processing times are. The great disadvantage of this approach is that many short jobs may also miss their due dates because of one long job.

This rule also tends to result in an increase in WIP inventory. It may be used when a critical job has a long lead time.

First-Come, First-Served

This rule is often used in service facilities because it is usually seen as the fairest one by customers. However, it totally ignores due date or processing time so it does not perform well on such measures.

Critical Ratio

The **critical-ratio rule** is an attempt to combine the preceding rules into one that considers both due date and processing time. It is based on calculating the critical ratio *(CR)*, which is

$$CR = \frac{\text{time until due date}}{\text{processing time remaining}}$$

This rule is implemented by scheduling first those jobs that have the lowest critical ratio. Values of *CR* below one mean the job will be past due. A negative value means it is already past due. Thus, an advantage is that those jobs scheduled first are the ones that have the greatest chance of missing their due dates.

It should be noted that the critical-ratio rule differs from the other dispatching rules in that it is dynamic. That is, a job's critical ratio will change over time as the number of days until the due date changes and the processing time remaining changes. Thus, the critical ratio must be updated constantly.

PROBLEM

The Hillside Machine Corporation has four jobs waiting to be run on its lathe. Exhibit 16.4 shows the days until due date and the processing time remaining for each job. Hillside wants to see what sequences will be generated by using each of the five dispatching rules. Exhibit I6.4 shows these sequences. It is interesting to note that in this

EXHIBIT 16.4

Comparison of Dispatching Rules

Job (Order Arrived)	Days Until Due Date	Processing Time Remaining
A	10	5 days
B	20	3 days
C	15	10 days
D	40	2 days

Earliest due date: A-C-B-D
Shortest processing time: D-B-A-C
Longest processing time: C-A-B-D
First-come, First-served: A-B-C-D
Critical ratio:

Job	A	B	C	D
CR	10/5 = 2	20/3 = 6.67	15/10 = 1.5	40/2 = 20
		C-A-B-D		

example, the longest-processing-time and critical-ratio rules happen to produce the same sequence of jobs—although such will not always be the case.

Sequencing Jobs on One Machine

As we have mentioned, flow time is the amount of time it takes to produce a product. If the product spends a large amount of time waiting to be processed, then its flow time will be long. By processing as many jobs as possible during a given period of time, average flow time will be minimized. The way to achieve this result is by using the shortest-processing-time rule, which has been proven to always minimize average flow time.

PROBLEM   Refer to the Hillside Machine Corporation data in the previous example. Suppose we keep track of how many days each job takes until it is done, using the critical-ratio and shortest-processing-time rules. As the results in Exhibit 16.5 indicate, all four jobs are finished within twenty days, regardless of which rule is used. However, with the critical-ratio rule, the average time each job spends before completion is 15.75 days. With the shortest-processing-time rule, the average time is only 9.25 days.

Sequencing Jobs Using Johnson's Rule

When there are two successive machines or work centers through which a group of jobs must all be sequenced, Johnson's Rule can be used to minimize total processing time for the group of jobs which is called the **makespan time.** The method utilizes the following steps:

1. List the jobs and the time each requires at each work center.
2. From the list, select the job with shortest time at either work center (break ties arbitrarily). If the time is for the first work center, proceed to step 2a. If it is for the second work center, proceed to step 2b.
   a. Place the job as close to the beginning of the sequence as possible without replacing other jobs. Go to step 3.
   b. Place the job as close to the end of the sequence as possible without replacing other jobs. Go to step 3.
3. Eliminate the job just scheduled from your list. Return to step 2.

EXHIBIT 16.5

Comparison of Average Flow Times for Two Sequencing Rules

Critical-Ratio Rule				Shortest-Processing-Time Rule		
Job	Start	End		Job	Start	End
C	0	10		D	0	2
A	10	15		B	2	5
B	15	18		A	5	10
D	18	20		C	10	20
	Total	63			Total	37

Average flow time = 63/4 = 15.75 days

Average flow time = 37/4 = 9.25 days

You should notice that this rule requires all jobs to follow the same sequence through both work centers. The sequence cannot change at the second work center.

PROBLEM

University Data Services has five computer payroll jobs waiting to be processed before Friday afternoon. Each job requires computing and then printing, in that order. Based on past experience, the company estimates each job will take the following time:

| | Processing Time (Hours) | |
Job	Computing	Printing
A	1.5	1.0
B	1.0	0.75
C	0.5	1.25
D	2.0	1.5
E	0.75	0.5

Using Johnson's Rule, we proceed as follows. Two jobs, C and E, have shortest processing time of .5 hours. We arbitrarily select C. Because its shortest time is for the first operation, we schedule job C at the beginning of the sequence.

$$\frac{C}{1} \quad \frac{\;}{2} \quad \frac{\;}{3} \quad \frac{\;}{4} \quad \frac{\;}{5}$$

We eliminate job C from further consideration and return to step 2. Now job E has shortest processing time. Because that time is for the second operation (printing), we schedule job E at the end of the sequence.

$$\frac{C}{1} \quad \frac{\;}{2} \quad \frac{\;}{3} \quad \frac{\;}{4} \quad \frac{E}{5}$$

Job E is now eliminated from the list. Therefore, job B has the shortest processing time, which is for the second operation. Job B is scheduled as close to the end of the sequence as possible.

$$\frac{C}{1} \quad \frac{\;}{2} \quad \frac{\;}{3} \quad \frac{B}{4} \quad \frac{E}{5}$$

After eliminating job B, of the remaining two jobs, A has the shortest processing time. Because that time is for the second process, we schedule A as close to the end as possible, which turns out to be the third position.

$$\frac{C}{1} \quad \frac{\;}{2} \quad \frac{A}{3} \quad \frac{B}{4} \quad \frac{E}{5}$$

The last remaining job is placed in the remaining slot in the schedule, producing the following sequence.

$$\frac{C}{1} \quad \frac{D}{2} \quad \frac{A}{3} \quad \frac{B}{4} \quad \frac{E}{5}$$

This sequence of jobs produces the processing sequence for each operation shown in Exhibit 16.6. As you can see, this method completes all jobs within 6.25 hours and leaves only .5 hour of idle time for the printer at the beginning of the sequence and .75 hour between jobs C and D.

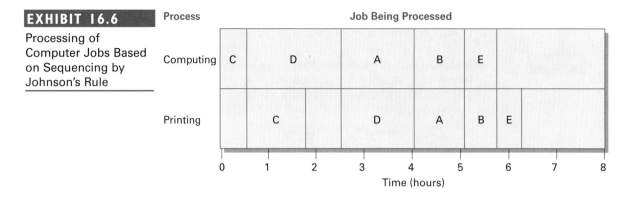

EXHIBIT 16.6

Processing of
Computer Jobs Based
on Sequencing by
Johnson's Rule

DISPATCHING IN MRP

The rules just mentioned are limited in the sense that they only consider the conditions that exist for a given point in time and a given work center. By and large, they ignore the fact that a given part may be part of a subassembly that must be made before the final product can be assembled.

But MRP takes those lead times into account. As long as the planning lead times used in MRP are valid, then the priority of each item should be based on the MRP lead times. Therefore, in an MRP system, priorities are determined by referring to the planned order releases and lead times. Thus, the dispatching rules are irrelevant to MRP systems. Instead, MRP works from the order due dates, scheduling order releases far enough ahead of time that these due dates should be met. Unfortunately, there may still be conflicts at machines and work centers. We now discuss ways of scheduling to avoid such conflicts.

Machine Loading

The dispatching rules previously described attempt to determine a schedule based on simply looking at the attributes, such as due date or processing time, of each job. But, the time it takes for a job actually to get processed consists of the following five components:

1. Wait time
2. Move time
3. Queue time
4. Setup time
5. Run time

Wait time is the time a job spends waiting before being moved to the next work center. **Move time** is the material-handling time between work centers. **Queue time** is the time spent waiting to be processed at a work center. **Setup time** is the time to get a machine ready to process that job, and **run time** is actual processing time.

In general, all of these components—except queue time—will be fairly fixed. Queue time really depends to a large extent on the workload that has been scheduled for each work center. If a machine's capacity is being used extensively, then it is more likely that many jobs will be waiting for processing at that machine. When the capacity of a work center is exceeded, it is a certainty that lines of work (queues) will build up in front of that work center.

Loading is an approach to scheduling that tries to take capacity utilization into account. There are several different approaches to loading, but loading begins with scheduling.

Forward Scheduling

Suppose we start from the present time and begin scheduling each job to start at the earliest possible moment. That is **forward scheduling.** As jobs progress through work centers, each work center will have a certain workload placed on it from the jobs that must be processed. Exhibit 16.7 indicates the schedule that would be generated by forward scheduling for four jobs (A, B, C, and D) and three work centers (lathe, mill, and drill), based on the following information and assuming six hours for wait/move time between machines.

Work Center Sequence and Processing Time
(Setup and Run Times in Hours)

Job	Operation 1		Operation 2		Operation 3	
A	Lathe	3	Drill	2	Mill	4
B	Mill	4	Drill	3		
C	Lathe	2	Mill	3	Drill	4
D	Drill	5	Lathe	4		

You should notice that in Exhibit 16.7, we begin each job as close to time zero as possible and schedule it through each of the successive operations, allowing six hours for wait/move time between machines. But, some jobs have been delayed (queue time) on certain work centers because another job had already started on that work center. For

---

EXHIBIT 16.7   Forward Schedule for Four Jobs with Finite Loading

example, job C had to wait three hours before it could start on the lathe because job A was still being processed on that machine. This approach of making one job wait if another has been scheduled on the same machine is called **finite loading** because it takes into consideration the limited capacity on each machine. Another approach uses **infinite loading,** which does not take capacity considerations into account. To demonstrate the other type of scheduling, we will use infinite loading.

Backward Scheduling

Backward scheduling is starting from a desired due date and working backward. We will use the information for the four jobs and three work centers presented previously, but add the following due dates:

Job	Due Date
A	Hour 24
B	Hour 16
C	Hour 24
D	Hour 16

In this case, we will use infinite loading, ignoring the problem of having more than one job at the same work center at the same time. The resulting schedule is shown in Exhibit 16.8.

Notice that in this case we began by scheduling the last operation for each job so that it would end at the time due, working backward through each operation. You should also notice that certain work centers have been scheduled to do more than one job at a time. This may not be a problem if more than one machine is available, or if sufficient slack capacity is available to get each job finished by its due date. For example, job A could be started at time 0.

EXHIBIT 16.8   Backward Schedule for Four Jobs with Infinite Loading

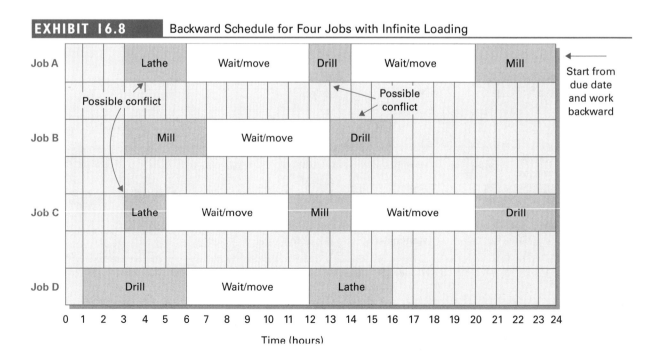

Actually, either finite or infinite loading can be used with either forward or backward scheduling. It is probably most common, however, for forward scheduling to use finite loading and backward scheduling to use infinite loading.

Either of the preceding schedules can also be used to generate a load profile for each work center. A **load profile,** as you should recall from our discussion in Chapter 13, indicates the workload being placed on that work center. Exhibit 16.9 shows the load profiles for the backward schedule of Exhibit 16.8 on an hourly basis. Those were obtained by adding up the number of jobs scheduled during each hour for each machine. Notice that any hour in which more than one hour of machine time is scheduled could present a problem if only one of each machine is available.

The reason we have discussed both forward and backward scheduling is that each is widely used—and many companies use both. Forward scheduling is useful for jobs that need to start right away. Backward scheduling works well when a desired due date is specified. We also discussed both finite and infinite loading. The problem with finite loading is that it requires much more effort for companies to keep track of which jobs are scheduled for which machines at what time. Unforeseen problems, variations in processing time, and other factors usually combine to make this a wasted effort. Therefore, most companies use infinite loading and then worry about how to deal with overloaded work centers after they have worked up the load profile.

This approach to scheduling helps to point up the importance of capacity requirements planning and its tie-in with both the medium-range production plan and the master schedule. While capacity requirements planning is only a rough estimation, it still helps to ensure that sufficient capacity will be available. If the master schedule is realistic from a capacity viewpoint, then infinite loading usually does not produce too many problems.

EXHIBIT 16.9   Load Profiles for Backward Schedule

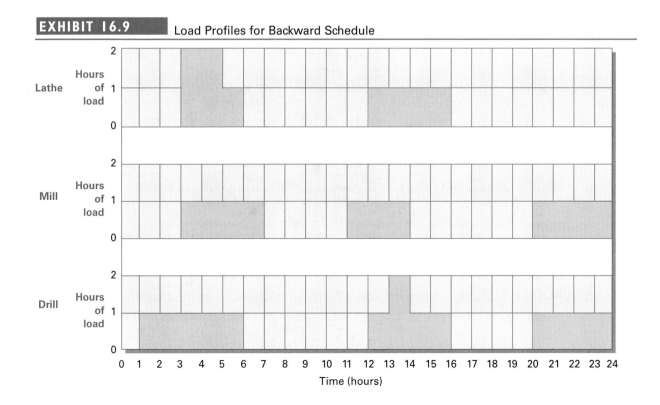

Sequencing

In presenting the forward schedule with finite loading, we did not allow two jobs to be in the same work center at the same time. Thus, if job 1 had been started at work center A, job 3 had to wait. But would it have been better to start job 3 on work center A first and make job 1 wait? To answer that question, we can use a device that allows us to schedule each work center—the Gantt load chart. The **Gantt load chart** has been around for many years, although it has not been widely used recently. This sequencing tool is now getting more use as companies realize the importance of their sequencing activities.

Each work center can be indicated by a bar of the Gantt load chart. The job being processed at each work center and its processing time can also be indicated. Exhibit 16.10 shows the Gantt load chart that corresponds to the forward finite load schedule of Exhibit 16.7.

The Gantt load chart is very useful for finite scheduling because it allows only one job to be run on each machine or work center at a time. Any conflicts will immediately become apparent. However, developing these charts and keeping them current for a large number of machines and many jobs can become tedious.

Finite Capacity Scheduling

Until recently, it was impractical for most companies to use finite loading simply because of the huge computational burden involved in the process. Advances in computers and software over the last five years have now made it possible for companies to schedule their jobs using finite loading. This approach is now being referred to as **finite capacity scheduling (FCS).** Quite a few software products for finite capacity scheduling are available on the market. Such products enable companies to schedule jobs very rapidly and easily, with capacity limitations and other constraints taken into account.

EXHIBIT 16.10   Gantt Load Chart for Forward Schedule

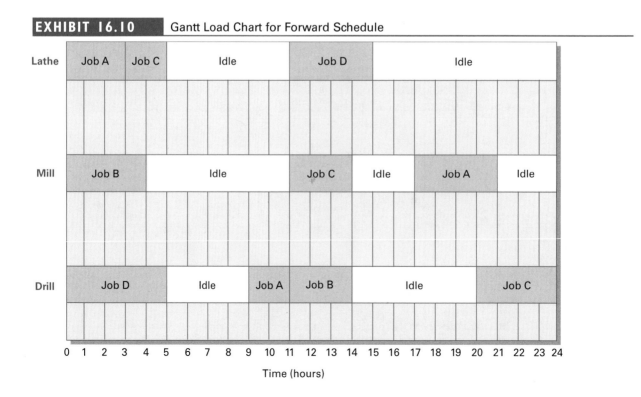

These FCS programs are so fast that they even overcome one traditional argument against using finite loading—that unknown future disruptions (Murphy's Law) would just lay waste to all the time and effort put into developing a finite capacity plan. Companies using FCS software now find that when disruptions do occur, the FCS software can be used to plan around those disruptions, minimizing their negative impact.

Input/Output Control

Input/output control is a method of managing work flow and queue lengths. The idea is simple. If work is put into a work center faster than it comes out, a queue will build up. If work is put in at a slower rate than it comes out, the work center may run out of work.

Exhibit 16.11 shows the input/output report for a work center. Notice that cumulative deviation of actual input from planned input and cumulative deviation of actual output from planned output are recorded each week. Further, the cumulative change in backlog is determined each week by comparing actual input to actual output. For example, in week 43, actual output exceeds actual input by thirty hours. Therefore, the cumulative backlog decreases by that amount. In week 45, actual inputs exceeds actual output by twenty hours, so backlog increases by twenty hours.

Simulation in Developing Schedules

By now, you should realize that scheduling and sequencing can be rather difficult in some situations. This is especially true in job shops where many different end products require different operations. Unfortunately, trying to develop schedules manually in such situations can be extremely time-consuming and difficult. There are just too many combinations to consider.

To help deal with this difficulty, computers have been employed. Using simulation techniques, it is possible to develop a trial schedule on the computer and then test that schedule without actually processing the jobs. Through this simulation, potential problems can be identified and an improved schedule developed. Today, more companies are developing computer simulation programs to help solve their scheduling problems. We will not discuss the details here, but some basic simulation concepts are presented in the supplement to this chapter.

EXHIBIT 16.11

Input/Output Report in Standard Hours

	Week					
	43	44	45	46	47	48
Planned input	400	380	410	370	375	360
Actual input	350	390	400	370	365	380
Cumulative deviation	−50	−40	−50	−50	−60	−40

	Week					
	43	44	45	46	47	48
Planned input	410	400	400	370	380	390
Actual input	380	400	380	400	380	370
Cumulative deviation	−30	−30	−50	−20	−20	−40

Backlog (hours)	80	50	40	60	30	15	25

SPECIAL PROBLEMS IN SCHEDULING SERVICES

One major difference between scheduling the production of goods and scheduling the production of services is that a service cannot be inventoried. For example, a company that manufactures air conditioners can build up its inventory during the winter months in preparation for peak summer demand. But a hospital cannot build up an inventory of emergency room services in advance. Unlike goods, services can be produced only at the time of demand, which means that the strategies for meeting that demand are more limited for services than for goods. In scheduling services, we are not so concerned with the question of sequencing. The scheduling problems in service industries usually have to do with determining what level of capacity should be made available at different times. For example, a hospital emergency room needs to know how many employees to schedule for weekends versus weekday mornings; a fast-food restaurant needs to determine how many employees it should schedule for lunch hour and how many for late evening.

When the Customer Is Waiting

Sequencing rules are usually applied to situations in which parts or products are waiting to be processed. But what if it is customers who are waiting? In general, companies tend to apply the first-come, first-served rule in such situations. Of course, that can be frustrating for those of us who, for example, simply want to just cash a check at the bank and must wait for someone with a time-consuming transaction.

Some companies have worked to find ways to route customers to faster lines if their processing time is less. For example, automated telephone lines or voice messaging systems let callers choose among a set of options depending on the nature of their transactions. The faster transactions are usually handled quickly by high-volume automated equipment.

Companies have even found ways to assuage those callers who must wait to speak with an employee. For example, frequent messages alert waiting customers that their calls have not been forgotten. One computer company even has a live disc jockey who plays records and periodically announces how many callers are waiting for various services. That DJ even intersperses sales messages for the company's products with the music.

Scheduling Strategies for Services

Services offer some unique challenges for scheduling. In this section we discuss some of the more common approaches to scheduling for services.

Schedule for Peak Demand

One possible approach to scheduling for services is to schedule for **peak demand.** That means that sufficient capacity will be available at any time to meet the peak expected demand. The advantage of this approach is that it allows for demand to be met at all times under normal conditions. Its greatest disadvantage is that a large portion of capacity may be idle a great percentage of the time.

Chase Demand

In discussing strategies for aggregate planning, we mentioned two strategies by which a company adjusts its production rate to match demand—varying the workforce and using overtime. Either of these strategies can be very useful for service companies if they can estimate expected demand with reasonable accuracy. For example, Burger King restaurants maintain extensive records of historical demand during various days of the week and hours of the day. This information is used by each restaurant to determine how many employees it should schedule during each hour.

This strategy works best if the employees are willing to work on a part-time basis. Fast food is one industry that is able to schedule its employees in this way. The primary advantage of the strategy is that it costs less than scheduling for peak demand, while still enabling the organization to meet its anticipated demand. The disadvantages are that it requires an extremely flexible workforce and demand forecasts must be fairly accurate.

Other Strategies

Some other possible strategies involve scheduling appointments or reservations for service, increasing consumer participation, creating adjustable capacity, sharing capacity, and cross-training employees.

The reservation strategy is commonly used by restaurants, hotels, and airlines. Reservations allow an organization to determine the advance demand for its service, while also limiting access to that service. Airlines, in particular, have used reservations to control access to their lowest fares. Those travelers who are willing to book their flights far in advance and satisfy certain length-of-stay criteria get the best fares; those who book only hours before the flight, when space may be limited, must pay the highest fares.

Fast-food restaurants have successfully used consumer participation, such as having customers serve themselves from the salad bar or draw their own drinks, as a way of reducing staffing requirements. This strategy reduces the workforce scheduling problems considerably because fewer people are needed. Self-service gas stations also use this principle. The one employee who takes the customers' money can usually handle any level of demand because the most labor-intensive part—pumping the gas—is done by the customers themselves. In fact, some gas stations have eliminated the employee altogether and replaced that person with a device that accepts credit cards!

Adjustable capacity involves the ability to use only part of the facilities or available employees at any given time. For example, restaurants can close off sections when demand is low. The wait staff who would serve those sections can fill saltshakers and perform other activities in preparation for peak demand. As the demand increases, those waiters and waitresses can be moved to waiting on tables as sections are opened.

Cross-training employees also provides similar advantages. If employees are trained to perform more than one activity, then they can be shifted from one to another as demand changes, as when employees in a supermarket stock shelves when not needed as checkers or baggers. Sharing capacity is a way that different organizations, or even different parts of the same organization, with different demand patterns can use the same facilities, and possibly the same employees. For example, many churches have found that their Sunday school facilities, which are normally idle during the week, can be put to good use for day-care centers. On the weekend, when day care is not in session, the church will use those facilities. Airlines have also been able to share gates, check-in facilities, and even ground crews.

Workforce Scheduling for Services

Assigning employees to work periods is a common scheduling problem in service operations. The objectives are to schedule enough employees to meet the projected needs during different time periods, but to also come up with a schedule that satisfies employees and avoids unnecessary overtime costs. For example, we may have employees who each work eight hours per day, but can each work different days per week. The Fair Labor Standards Act requires that employees receive overtime pay if they work more than forty hours per week so we want each employee to be scheduled only five days per week. Furthermore, employees usually prefer being off two days in a row, so we would like to schedule each employee to work five consecutive days, then be off for two. Using a procedure developed by Tibrewala, Philippe, and Browne, it is possible to easily develop such a schedule using the following steps.

Step 1. Find the two consecutive days that require the least total number of employees (realize that Sunday and Monday are consecutive days). In case of ties, make an arbitrary choice.

Step 2. Schedule an employee to be off the two days identified in step 1, and to work the other five consecutive days.

Step 3. For the five days just scheduled, reduce the number of employees required each day by one. Proceed to the next employee and return to step 1. Repeat the process until all employees are scheduled or all daily staffing needs have been met.

PROBLEM

Jack's Snack Shack is working out a workforce schedule for its employees Hack, Mack, and Yack. Each employee works five days and has two consecutive days off. Staffing needs each day are shown in the following.

	M	T	W	Th	F	S	Su
Requirements	1	2	2	2	3	3	3

Step 1. The two consecutive days requiring the least total number of workers are Monday and Tuesday (1 + 2 = 3 workers).

Step 2. We schedule Hack to work Wednesday through Sunday, and be off Monday and Tuesday.

Step 3. The revised requirements are shown in the following. We return to step 1 for Mack.

	M	T	W	Th	F	S	Su
Requirements	1	2	2	2	3	3	3
Hack			X	X	X	X	X
Revised req'ts	1	2	1	1	2	2	2

Step 1. In the preceding revised requirements row, the two consecutive days with the least total requirements are now Wednesday and Thursday.

Step 2. Mack is scheduled to be off the two days identified in step 1 (Wednesday and Thursday) and to work Friday through Tuesday.

Step 3. The revised requirements after scheduling Mack are shown in the following.

	M	T	W	Th	F	S	Su
Requirements	1	2	2	2	3	3	3
Hack			W	W	W	W	W
Revised req'ts	1	2	1	1	2	2	2
Mack	W	W			W	W	W
Revised req'ts	0	1	1	1	1	1	1

Step 1. After scheduling Mack, the two consecutive days with the least total requirements are now either Sunday and Monday or Monday and Tuesday. We could break the tie arbitrarily or ask Yack which consecutive days off she would prefer.

Step 2. Yack is scheduled to be off Monday and Tuesday and to work Wednesday through Sunday.

Step 3. The revised requirements after scheduling Yack are shown in the following.

	M	T	W	Th	F	S	Su
Requirements	1	2	2	2	3	3	3
Hack			W	W	W	W	W
Revised req'ts	1	2	1	1	2	2	2
Mack	W	W			W	W	W
Revised req'ts	0	1	1	1	1	1	1
Yack			W	W	W	W	W
Revised req'ts	0	1	0	0	0	0	0

We have now scheduled all employees, but one more employee is needed for Monday. One alternative would be to hire another employee to meet the requirement; but unless that person is willing to work only one day per week, it could mean paying the person to work days she or he is not needed. Another option would be for the owner (Jack) to fill in on Monday. Finally, one of the three existing employees might be willing to work an extra day each week. Of course, that person would receive overtime pay because he or she would be working more than 40 hours per week.

SUMMARY

- Criteria for scheduling include due date, flow time, WIP inventory, idle time, and costs. Doing well on some criteria can mean performing poorly on others. In scheduling manufacturing, we must ensure that due-date promises are kept. In services, first come, first served is usually the rule unless other factors are more important than fairness.

- The sequencing of products on an assembly line and line balancing are two issues of concern in scheduling.

- Dispatching rules include the earliest due date, shortest processing time, longest processing time, first come, first served, and critical ratio.

- Priorities are set in an MRP system by considering due dates and lead times of jobs.

- Employees can be scheduled for service operations using a simple procedure that is based on staffing requirements.

 Visit our dynamic Web site, http://www.wiley.com/college/vonderembse, for extended chapter material, solved problems, mini-cases, computer software, and Web links.

KEY TERMS

backward scheduling	infinite loading	peak demand
critical-ratio rule	input/output control	queue time
dispatching	loading	run-out time
dispatching rules	load profile	run time
finite capacity scheduling	makespan time	scheduling
(FCS)	make-to-order company	sequencing
finite loading	make-to-stock company	setup time
forward scheduling	move time	wait time
Gantt load chart	over cycled	

URLS

Allen-Bradley: www.ab.com

Burger King: www.burgerking.com/CompanyInfo/index.html

QUESTIONS

1. In describing JIT, the analogy of a stream is often used to represent material flow. Explain how this analogy could also be used when simulating material flow in a job shop.

2. Discuss the ways in which flexible manufacturing systems may alter the activities of production scheduling.

3. Allen-Bradley has developed a CIM system that is designed to produce the orders received in one day by the end of the next day. Would scheduling be easier or more difficult for Allen-Bradley, as compared with a company that has a one-month backlog of orders?

4. List the six criteria that can be used for scheduling.

5. Which scheduling criterion do you think is most relevant for a fast-food restaurant? For a physician's office? For a hospital emergency room?

6. Which of the dispatching rules do you use when deciding which homework assignment to do first?

7. Explain why scheduling a continuous flow production process involves different methods from those used for scheduling a job shop process.

8. What service operations might use the scheduling methods traditionally used for job shops?

9. For each of the dispatching rules, indicate which scheduling criteria will be satisfied and what the advantages and disadvantages of that rule would be.

10. List the data needed for scheduling, and indicate the usual sources.

11. How does dispatching differ from sequencing?

12. How are priorities set for jobs in an MRP system?

13. Explain the purpose of using input/output control.

14. How can computer simulation be used for scheduling?

15. Discuss different scheduling procedures that might be used for various types of service operations, such as a restaurant, a hospital, an airline, and so on.

16. The Internet has changed the way many companies sell products. In serving customers over the Internet, what might be some ways of handling customer waiting that are different than the traditional "bricks and mortar" retail outlet systems.

INTERNET QUESTIONS

17. Use a search engine to search on the term "dispatching rules." Summarize some of the ways you find that dispatching rules can be used.

18. Go to the Web site http://www.timetrade.com/solutions_small_testdrives.asp and test drive some of the examples of online scheduling for services. What are some advantages for a business to offer a service like this? Are there any disadvantages?

19. Perform a Web search on the term "workforce scheduling." List and describe some of the different approaches to workforce scheduling.

20. Visit the Web site http://www.pivotalz.com/html/scheduler.html and click on "screen shots" to see some actual computer screens for this job scheduling software. Can you think of some additional capabilities you would like to see in such software?

PROBLEMS

1. A company produces four types of paper in batches. Based on the following information, which product should be produced next according to the run-out time criterion?

Product	Demand Rate (1,000 Ft. per Month)	Current Inventory (1,000 Ft.)
Kraft paper	30,000	80,000
Duplicator bond	20,000	40,000
Regular bond	60,000	150,000
Carbon tissue	10,000	40,000

2. The David Harleyston Bicycle Company produces its two models of bicycles, the Avenger and the Hawk, in batches. Based on the following information, which model should be produced next?

Model	EOQ	Current Inventory	Monthly Sales
Avenger	2,000	10,000	30,000
Hawk	5,000	6,000	20,000

3. A consultant must complete four reports. She estimates that report A will take four hours, report B will take three hours, report C will take six hours, and report D will take two hours. In what sequence would she do the reports, using the shortest-processing-time rule?

4. A job shop has four jobs waiting to be processed on its computer numerically controlled (CNC) lathe. Determine the sequence of these jobs by using each of the five dispatching rules. Assume today is day 107, jobs arrived for processing in the order listed, and the following information is given:

Job	Due (Day)	Processing Time on CNC Lathe (Hours)	Total Processing Time Remaining (Days)
A	120	4	12
B	113	8	5
C	125	2	7
D	115	10	10

5. Late Wednesday afternoon, Data Processing Associates had four jobs waiting to be processed the next day. Each of these jobs requires keyboarding the data and then processing them on the company's minicomputer. The keyboarding is done by DPNs data

entry clerks who work from 8:00 A.M. to 5:00 P.M., with an hour for lunch at noon. The computer will be available continuously beginning at 9:00 A.M. on Thursday. Jobs may be either processed immediately after keyboarding or held for processing later.

Job	Keyboarding Time (Hours)	Processing Times (Hours)	Time Due
A	1	1	3:00 P.M.
B	1	2	12:00 Noon
C	2	0.5	2:00 P.M.
D	2	2	5:00 P.M.

    a. Develop schedules using the shortest-processing-time, longest-processing-time, and earliest-due-date rules, and draw Gantt load charts for keyboarding and processing, based on each rule.

    b. Evaluate each of the schedules in Part a with respect to customer service by calculating average past due hours per job for each scheduling rule.

6. Bill Berry, the heat treating department's second shift foreman at Ace Machine Tool Company, is bucking to become foreman on the first shift. To look good, Bill wants to keep queues in his department to a minimum, so he has been using the shortest-processing-time rule to schedule work. But, the assembly department, which usually receives jobs after they have been processed in Berry's department, is complaining they often do not get jobs early enough to meet the due dates.

    a. The following jobs are currently in queue at the heat treating department and must all be processed through the heat treating department and then through the assembly department. Develop a schedule based on the shortest-processing-time rule, and draw a Gantt chart for each department.

	Processing Time (Days)		
Job	Heat Treating	Assembly	Days Until Due
317	3	1	12
318	1	3	4
324	2	3	10
326	4	2	8

    b. Determine whether there is a schedule that can meet all the due dates.

    c. Comment on the implications of allowing each machine or work center to schedule its own work.

7. Dr. Houseworth, an orthopedic surgeon, likes to be kept busy during his office hours. All patients scheduled must first have X-rays before they see the doctor. On a certain Monday morning, Dr. Houseworth arrives at his office, and the following three patients are waiting to be X-rayed and then see him. Determine the sequence in which the patients should be X-rayed to minimize the time Dr. Houseworth is idle.

Patient	Time to X-Ray (Min.)	Time with Doctor (Min.)
Mrs. Green	5	10
Mr. White	15	20
Miss Gray	10	20

8. The following jobs are waiting to be processed on one machine. Determine the sequence that will minimize average flow time.

Job	Processing Time (Days)
A	4
B	2
C	6
D	3
E	5

9. The following jobs are waiting to be processed through two work centers.
   a. Use Johnson's Rule to determine a sequence.
   b. Draw a Gantt load chart for each work center.

	Processing Time (Hours)	
Job	Work Center 1	Work Center 2
A	3.0	2.0
B	2.4	3.2
C	1.8	4.0
D	2.2	3.5

10. A printer has six printing jobs. Each job requires typesetting and printing.
    a. Use Johnson's rule to sequence the jobs based on the following expected processing times.
    b. Draw Gantt load charts for printing and typesetting.

	Processing Time (Hours)	
Job	Typesetting	Printing
1	2.00	3.00
2	3.00	4.00
3	2.50	1.75
4	1.25	2.00
5	3.50	2.50
6	2.25	3.00

11. A city government requires that all new construction projects be reviewed by an architect, a city planner, and an environmental engineer (in that order). Four different construction projects are waiting to be reviewed, and the review time of each has been estimated as shown in the following.

Project	Architect	City Planner	Environmental Engineer
A	3 hrs.	2 hrs.	4 hrs.
B	2 hrs.	3 hrs.	2 hrs.
C	4 hrs.	1 hr.	3 hrs.
D	2 hrs.	1 hr.	3 hrs.

If the four projects must be processed in the order A, B, C, D by each person, use forward scheduling with finite loading to develop a Gantt load chart for each person.

12. Five parts must be processed through the following operations, and each has the due date shown. The following table shows the time required for each processing operation:

Part A	Part B	Part C
Lathe (2 days)	Lathe (1 day)	Mill (1 day)
Mill (3 days)	Grind (1 day)	Drill (1 day)
Drill (1 day)	Mill (2 days)	Due at end of day 5
Due at end of day 8	Due at end of day 6	

Part D	Part E
Mill (3 days)	Drill (1 day)
Grind (1 day)	Mill (3 days)
Lathe (2 days)	Grind (1 day)
Drill (1 day)	Drill (1 day)
Due at end of day 10	Due at end of day 6

Use backward scheduling with infinite loading to develop a schedule for each part.

13. Develop a load profile for the city planner in Problem 11.

14. Develop a load profile for the mill in Problem 12.

15. Suppose a restaurant has the following requirements for servers each day as shown in the following. Each server works five consecutive days and has two consecutive days off. How many servers will be required, and what will be the schedule for each server?

Day	M	T	W	Th	F	S	Su
Servers Required	3	5	7	6	10	12	8

16. In the preceding problem, the restaurant owner has found two employees who are willing to come in to work on Saturday only. Rework the schedule based on needing only ten regular employees for Saturday.

CHAPTER 17

Project Management

After completing this chapter, you should be able to:

1. List the planning steps for a project.
2. Draw a project network, using either activity-on-arc or activity-on-node representation.
3. Determine which activities are on the critical path.
4. Use PERT to calculate expected times and variances for activities.
5. Explain how resource requirements may be leveled.
6. Explain the concept and application of Critical Chain scheduling and Buffer Management.

INTRODUCTION

In Chapter 16, we discussed methods for scheduling different types of processes, from line flow to job shop. However, one type of process we did not mention was the project. That is because the procedures for planning and controlling projects are considerably different from those for the other types of processes and deserve an entire chapter unto themselves.

Projects such as building a facility or installing an information system represent another scheduling problem, although one that is often easier to deal with than job shop scheduling. The problem in project scheduling is to determine when each activity must begin or end so that the entire project can be completed on time. For example, in building a new facility, ground must be broken before the foundation can be poured, which must be done before the walls can be put up. Projects need not involve building activities. For example, many service organizations, such as British Airways, deal with projects on a regular basis. The development of an advertising campaign and the installation of a new management information system are other examples of nonbuilding projects.

Managing projects involves the usual managerial functions of planning, scheduling, and controlling. In order to ensure successful completion of the project, each of these activities must be performed. We will first briefly describe the planning process and then go on to discuss in more detail some common tools for carrying out the functions of scheduling and controlling.

EXAMPLE   Lucent Technologies' Outside Plant Fiber Optic Cable unit manufactures fiber optic cable for telecommunication uses. This area is one in which technology is constantly changing and customers frequently ask for new products. When such new products are requested, it can take a very long time to bring the new designs to market. A company's success in this competitive business arena requires getting new products to market faster than the competition. In the past, Lucent was no better than its competitors in this regard. But, after implementing Critical Chain project scheduling, Lucent was able to reduce its new product time to market by 50 percent, greatly increasing its competitiveness.

THE BEGINNINGS OF PROJECT MANAGEMENT

During the 1950s, three different organizations were faced with project management problems that were not easily solved by using techniques that existed at that time. Previously, projects had been managed using Gantt charts. Such charts, however, did not easily show precedence relationships and quickly became unwieldy for large projects.

The problem faced by the U.S. Navy was the coordination of some 3,000 contractors and suppliers involved in the Polaris missile project. Making matters worse, many activities that made up that project had never been done before, and estimates of the time they would take were uncertain.

At the same time, DuPont faced a different problem. It had to shut down its chemical processing plants on a regular basis to perform routine maintenance. Because these activities had been done before, excellent time estimates were available; but the company wanted to determine the shortest possible time to complete the maintenance and to identify the activities that were critical to that shortest completion time. For help in developing a method to solve this problem, the company hired Remington-Rand.

The method developed by the Navy was called the **program evaluation and review technique (PERT)** and allowed uncertain time estimates to be used. On the other hand, DuPont and Remington-Rand developed a technique that does not use probabilities and called it the **critical path method (CPM)**. Today, these techniques are referred to jointly as PERT/CPM, and the distinctions between them are minor. Both techniques can accommodate uncertain time estimates, and both can use either AOA or AON network representation.

PLANNING FOR PROJECTS

Before starting a project, the following steps must be carried out:

1. Develop a statement of work, describing the objectives to be achieved and the work to be done.
2. Proceed to a work breakdown structure that defines the individual activities or tasks that must be performed as part of the project and the precedence relationships among them.
3. List the resources, including money, personnel, equipment, and material—both internal and external—needed to complete the project.
4. Estimate the time required to perform each activity, and tie the resource requirements to that time frame.

NETWORK REPRESENTATION OF A PROJECT

As the saying goes, one picture is worth a thousand words. In managing a project, there are important relationships among various activities that are often better presented visually. For example, certain activities may not begin until others are completed. Other activities may be able to proceed simultaneously. One excellent way to visually represent these project activities is through a network. Two forms of project networks are discussed below.

Activities on Nodes

Because projects consist of activities that have certain precedence relationships, we can utilize the precedence diagrams from Chapters 6 and 9. In those chapters, the tasks were represented by circles (called **nodes**) and the relationships were indicated by arrows (called **arcs** or **branches**).

For example, suppose the College of Business at Middle Illinois State University is planning to install a computerized information system to maintain information about its students. Exhibit 17.1 is a list of the activities that have been identified for that project, the most likely duration of each activity, and the precedence relationships.

These relationships among activities are represented graphically in Exhibit 17.2. Notice that each node corresponds to an activity, indicating the letter designation of that activity and its duration. Arrows indicate the precedence relationships. For example, activity A (software selection) must be completed before activity B (software installation) can begin.

This type of network representation is referred to as **activity-on-node (AON) representation** because a node corresponds to each activity. An alternative representation in which activities are represented by arcs is also used frequently.

Dependency chart (Table) [handwritten annotation]

EXHIBIT 17.1

Work Breakdown Structure, Most Likely Durations, and Precedence Relationships for Information System Project

Activity	Most Likely Duration (Weeks)	Immediate Predecessor(s)
A. Select computer software	3	—
B. Install software	5	A
C. Install office network	7	A
D. Test software	6	B
E. Develop database	8	B
F. Train employees	3	C, D
G. Implement system	2	E, F

EXHIBIT 17.2

Activity-on-Node Network Representation of Information System Project

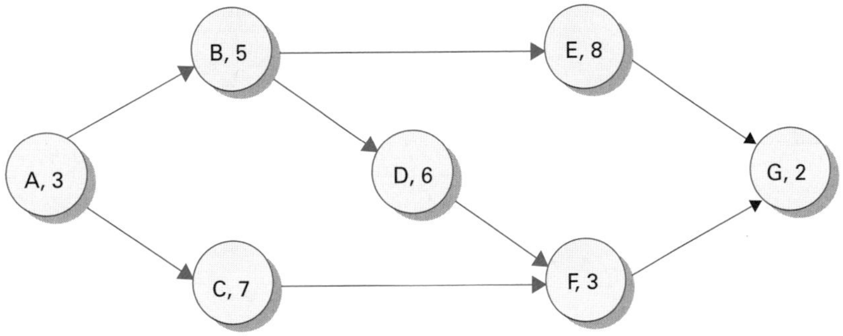

Activities on Arcs

We can also think of each activity as having a specific beginning and ending point. For example, activity A in the building project will have a point in time when it begins and a point in time when it ends. These beginning and ending points can be thought of as events, and nodes can be used to represent such events. Following this line of reasoning, if nodes represent the events that begin and end an activity, then the arrow connecting these two nodes can represent that activity, as shown in Exhibit 17.3. In fact, Exhibit 17.3 is the **activity-on-arc (AOA) network diagram** that corresponds to the information system project of Exhibit 17.2. In this case, notice that we have now assigned numbers to the nodes, designating them as events. Thus, each activity may be designated not only by the arc that represents it, but also by the events that begin and end it. For example, activity A can also be designated as 1–2, its beginning and ending nodes.

Dummy Activities

One additional requirement results from the fact that arcs are used in an AOA network to represent activities and precedence. In some cases, we may need to indicate precedence, but any relevant activity is already being used to indicate another precedence relation. In those cases, we use a dummy activity, represented by a dashed arrow. **Dummy activities** have duration of zero and are used only to show precedence. Exhibit 17.4 shows two AON networks and the corresponding AOA networks that require dummy activities.

In the top pair of networks in Exhibit 17.4, activity C is preceded by both A and B, but activity D is preceded only by B. Using the AOA network representation, a dummy activity is needed; otherwise, the diagram would imply D is also preceded by both A and B.

A second situation in which a dummy activity is useful is when each activity must have a unique pair of beginning and ending events. This is especially important when using computer programs that represent activities by their associated beginning and ending events. In the bottom pair of networks in Exhibit 17.4, activity D is preceded by both B and C. So that B and C can have different ending events, a dummy activity must be included.

In both cases shown, the dummy activity has been used strictly to show precedence and to clarify that precedence relation. Dummy activities are not needed in AON networks because arcs are used only to indicate precedence in that network representation.

In practice, both AON and AOA networks are used. Because AON networks are slightly easier to work with, they will be used in this chapter.

EXHIBIT 17.3

Activity-on-Arc
Representation of
Information System
Project

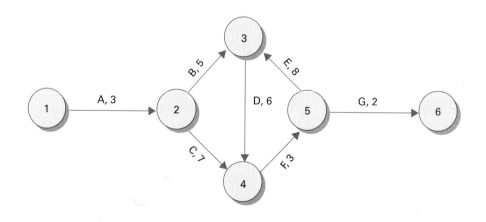

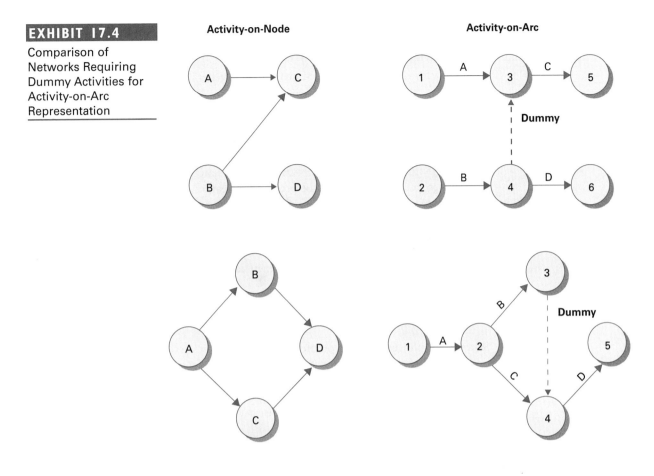

EXHIBIT 17.4

Comparison of Networks Requiring Dummy Activities for Activity-on-Arc Representation

THE CRITICAL PATH METHOD

The information provided by Exhibit 17.2 is useful in understanding relationships among activities, but it is possible to obtain much more information by using the critical path method (CPM). CPM provides a way for us to determine the earliest time each activity could start, based on expected durations and precedence relationships. Further, we can determine when the entire project is expected to be completed.

By working backward from a desired completion date for the project, it will also be possible to determine the latest time each activity could start and finish without delaying the entire project. Finally, we can calculate what is called the critical path, which will consist of those activities that determine how long it will take to complete the entire project.

Calculating Start and Finish Times

Earliest Times

If we let time zero represent the starting time for this project, then activity A can begin immediately at time zero. The expected finish time can be found by adding the expected duration to the starting time of zero. We will designate these starting and finish times as the **earliest start** (**ES**) and **earliest finish** (**EF**) because they are the earliest time the activity can start and finish, based on the starting time of zero and expected duration.

If the earliest finish time for activity A is 3 (0 + 3), then that also is the earliest time that C can start since activity C must be preceded by A. For any activity, its earliest start time will be the time at which all of its predecessor activities are completed. The earliest finish time for C can also be determined using the general rule

$$EF = ES + \text{activity duration}$$

The earliest start and earliest finish times for all activities in the project can be calculated the same way and are shown in Exhibit 17.5 by adding the earliest start and earliest finish information to the CPM diagram.

You should note that if an activity, such as F, has more than one predecessor, its earliest start time will be the latest of the predecessors' earliest finish times. This may sound a bit like double talk, but all it means is that no activity can start until all of its predecessors are finished.

Exhibit 17.5 indicates that we should expect the entire project to take nineteen weeks. We can also see the earliest time that each activity is expected to start. But one other question we might like to answer is how late each activity can be in order to meet a desired completion date.

Latest Times

Suppose the project must be completed within nineteen weeks. That represents the latest time that activity G (the last activity of the project) can finish without making the project late. The latest time that G can start will just be its duration, 2, subtracted from 19. Using this approach, we have determined the **latest finish (LF)** and **latest start (LS)** for activity G. At each node, the latest start time can be calculated using the general rule

$$LS = LF - \text{duration}$$

EXHIBIT 17.5   Calculation of Earliest Start and Finish Times

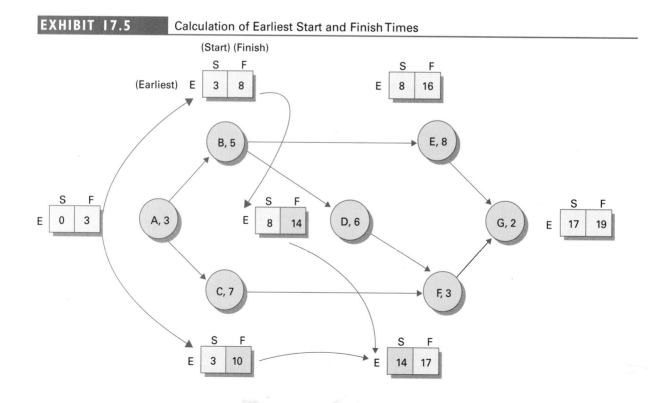

We can keep working backward from the desired completion date to determine latest finish and latest start times by realizing that all of an activity's predecessors must be completed by its latest start time. For instance, if G cannot wait past time 17 (19 - 2) to start, then the latest finish time for F will be 17. These latest start and latest finish times can be included on the CPM diagram, as shown in Exhibit 17.6. Again, you should notice that a choice must be made when one activity, such as B, is a predecessor to more than one other activity. In this case, B precedes both D and E. In such instances, the latest finish time of an activity will be the earliest of the latest start times of the activity it precedes. If this sounds like double talk again, don't worry—just remember that all of an activity's predecessors must be finished before it can start. Even though activity E could wait until time 9 to start, D must start by time 8. Thus, B must be done early enough for both to start on time, which is time 8.

Avoiding Late Completion

The information about earliest start, earliest finish, latest start, and latest finish can be used to keep a project on schedule. We know that *ES* and *EF* represent the earliest times we can expect each activity to start and finish. *LS* and *LF* are the latest times that each activity can start and finish without delaying the project past its desired completion date.

EXHIBIT 17.6   Calculation of Latest Start and Finish Times

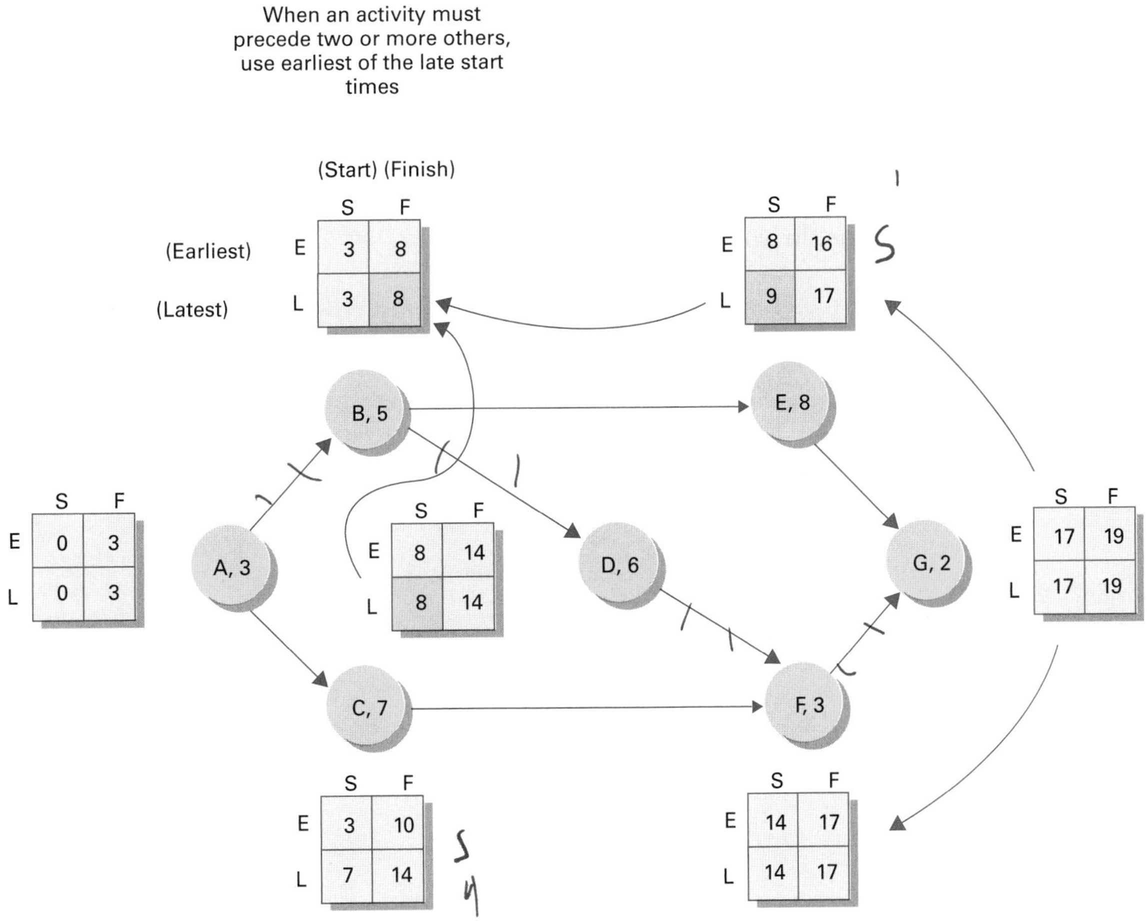

One more bit of information is useful. By comparing the earliest and latest times, we can determine the amount of slack for each activity. The slack is calculated as

$$Slack = LF - EF$$

or

$$Slack = LS - ES$$

Exhibit 17.7 indicates the slack for each activity in the project described above. The **slack time,** or slack, represents how much leeway each activity has in its starting time and duration. For instance, activity C has slack of four weeks. This means that C can wait four weeks beyond its earliest start time, or it can take four weeks longer than the expected duration—without delaying the project.

The Critical Path

Note that some activities have more slack than others. If we look at all the slack times, we will see that there is one lowest time that is common to several different activities. Those activities with the least slack will form a path through the CPM diagram from beginning to end. This path is called the **critical path,** and its associated activities are said to be **critical-path activities.** They are the activities that must be closely monitored if the project is to be completed on time. On the diagram in Exhibit 17.8, the critical path has been highlighted because the activities along that path (A, B, D, F, G) must start and finish on time, or the project will take longer than nineteen weeks. We can also tell that activities C and E can be delayed without delaying the project.

You should note that the least amount of slack does not necessarily have to be zero. For a desired completion time of twenty-two weeks, each activity would have at least three weeks of slack. However, those activities with the least amount of slack are still the critical-path activities. In fact, if a desired completion date is specified that is less than the earliest finish time, activities may have negative slack.

In this case, activity times must be shortened, a topic we will discuss later in this chapter. Regardless, the activities with the least amount of slack will still constitute the critical path.

Project Management Is Used Throughout Organizations

Although most of the concepts and techniques discussed in this book are used by the operations function, project management techniques are applicable to all areas of an organization. For example, the accounting department may undertake a project of installing a new accounting information system and use project management techniques to plan and control that installation. Similarly, marketing may develop plans for a new

EXHIBIT 17.7 Calculation of Slack and Determination of Critical-Path Activities		Start		Finish			
Activity	Duration	Earliest	Latest	Earliest	Latest	Slack	Critical Path?
A	3	0	0	3	3	0	Yes
B	5	3	3	8	8	0	Yes
C	7	3	7	10	14	4	No
D	6	8	8	14	14	0	Yes
E	8	8	9	16	17	1	No
F	3	14	14	17	17	0	Yes
G	2	17	17	19	19	0	Yes

EXHIBIT 17.8   Highlighted Critical Path in AON Network Diagram for the Information System Project

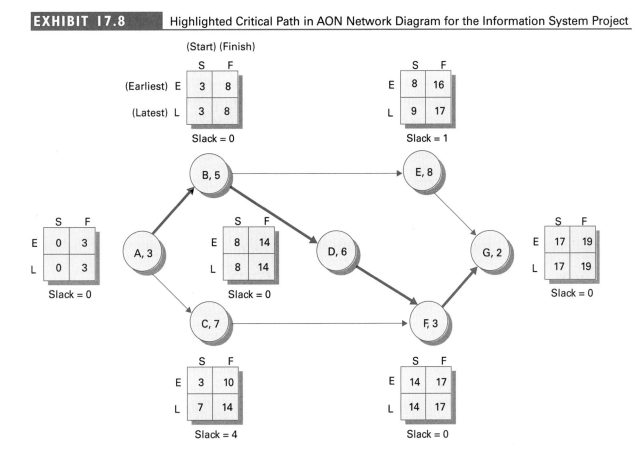

product promotion. That product promotion can also be placed in the framework of project management. In fact, any undertaking can be viewed as a project if it involves multiple activities with predetermined precedence relations.

INTRODUCING PROBABILITY WITH PERT

In our discussion of CPM, for each activity we used a duration that represented how much time the activity would probably take. Many factors may cause that time to vary. To deal with that possible variation, the program evaluation and review technique (PERT) uses the beta probability distribution. The beta distribution was chosen because its most likely value can fall anywhere between its end points. Unlike the normal probability distribution, which is symmetrical and must have the most likely value exactly in the middle, the beta distribution allows the most likely time estimate to be close to the pessimistic time, close to the optimistic time, or anywhere in between.

By obtaining three time estimates, instead of just one, for each activity, it is possible to calculate the expected duration of each activity and the standard deviation of that duration. Those values can then be used to determine an expected completion time for the project, as well as the probability of completing the project within a given time period.

Estimating Activity Time

The three time estimates used to calculate expected activity time are:

1. *Optimistic time (a)*—the shortest time the activity will reasonably take
2. *Most likely time (m)*—the time this activity would take most of the time
3. *Pessimistic time (b)*—the longest time the activity would be expected to take

Using these three values, it is possible to calculate the expected duration of an activity. You should note this expected time may not be the same as the most likely time *(m)*. Expected time represents an average time, while most likely time is the amount of time it takes most often. The formula for the expected time is

$$t_e = \frac{a+4m+b}{6}$$

The variance of activity duration is

$$\sigma^2 = \left(\frac{b-a}{6}\right)^2$$

PROBLEM

In the information system example of Exhibit 17.1, we used only one duration for each activity, the most likely time. Suppose, however, we want to take probabilities into account by including the optimistic and pessimistic times. Exhibit 17.9 shows those three time estimates for each activity.

Notice in some cases that all three time estimates are the same. Those are activities that will always take a set amount of time, without any variation.

The expected time for each activity is calculated, using the formula introduced previously. For example, the expected time for activity C will be

$$t_e = \frac{a+4m+b}{6}$$
$$= \frac{4+4(7)+16}{6} = 8\,\text{weeks}$$

The variance in that completion time will be

$$\sigma^2 = \left(\frac{b-a}{6}\right)^2$$
$$= \left(\frac{16-4}{6}\right)^2 = 4.00$$

Probability of Completion by a Given Time

The expected activity times and variances obtained from PERT allow us to estimate the probability of completing a project within a specified period of time. To do this, we must determine a variance for the critical path. This variance will be calculated by assuming that the durations of activities along the critical path are independent of one another. Thus, the variance of the critical-path time will be the sum of variances of activities on the path.

EXHIBIT 17.9

Expected Times and
Variances for Activities
in the Information
System Product

Activity	Optimistic Time (a)	Most Likely Time (m)	Pessimistic Time (b)	Expected Time (t_e)	Varience σ^2
A	2	3	4	3	0.11
B	5	5	5	5	0.00
C	4	7	16	8	4.00
D	4	6	20	8	7.11
E	6	8	10	8	0.44
F	3	3	3	3	0.00
G	2	2	2	2	0.00

To determine the probability of completing the critical-path activities within a certain time, we will assume the completion time is normally distributed. Although we had used the beta distribution for each activity's duration, we may now use the normal distribution for the sum of those durations based on the central limit theorem of statistics, which states that the sum of independent activity times follows a normal distribution as the number of activities becomes large. Although a large number of activities may not be on the critical path, the normal distribution is still a good approximation.

To determine the probability of completing the critical path by a given time, we use the z transformation formula:

$$z = \frac{T' - T}{\sqrt{\Sigma \sigma_{cp}^2}}$$

where

$$T' = \text{desired completion date}$$

$$T = \text{sum of } t_e \text{ for critical path activities}$$

$$\Sigma \sigma_{cp}^2 = \text{sum of variances for critical path activities}$$

The probability of completion by T' may be determined, then, by using the normal probability table in the appendix at the end of this chapter.

PROBLEM

Suppose we want to know the probability of completing the critical path of the information system project within twenty-three weeks. Using the expected activity times from Exhibit 17.9 and the precedence network from Exhibit 17.8, we can determine that the critical path consists of activities A, B, D, F, and G, which give an expected project completion time of twenty-one weeks. The sum of variances for activities on the critical path will be

$$\Sigma \sigma_{cp}^2 = 0.11 + 0 + 7.11 + 0 + 0 = 7.22$$

Then the z value will be

$$z = \frac{T' - T}{\sqrt{\Sigma \sigma_{cp}^2}}$$

$$= \frac{23 - 21}{\sqrt{7.22}} = .74$$

Referring to the normal probability distribution in the appendix at the end of this chapter, the probability corresponding to a z value of .74 is .7704 or 77 percent.

Joint Probabilities and Multiple Critical Paths

The procedure we have just described assumes only one critical path. However, there may be more than one. Further, a path that is not critical may have greater variance than the critical path does, making it possible for that path to end up being critical before the project is completed. Therefore, we need to consider the z values of all paths in the project. Using the same procedure as above, based on a desired completion time of twenty-three weeks, with the information in Exhibit 17.9, the z values for the non-critical paths are:

A–B–E–G	$z = 7.54$	probability greater than .999
A–C–F–G	$z = 3.45$	probability greater than .999

Thus, there is a very low probability that the other two paths would take longer than the critical path. However, this probability is non-zero. Therefore, the probability of completing the entire project within twenty-three weeks is actually less than 77 percent probability for the critical path. Calculation of a more accurate estimate can become very complex because the separate paths share some activities and, thus, are not independent of one another. Such calculations are beyond the scope of this text.

OTHER RESOURCE CONSIDERATIONS

Up to this point, we have been concerned only with time. Projects, however, invariably involve other resources, such as people, equipment, and money. In scheduling a project, it is important to consider the usage of these resources. Furthermore, there will be some trade-offs among the resources. In some instances, it will be possible to trade time for the other resources.

Balancing Resource Requirements

It should be remembered that time is not the only resource being scheduled for a project. Each activity of the project will also require certain other resources, such as people and equipment, for its completion. By scheduling activities, we are also scheduling those other resources. Based on the resource requirements associated with each activity, a diagram similar to the load profile discussed earlier can be developed. For example, Exhibit 17.10 indicates the workforce level that will be required for each activity that makes up a project. The top part of Exhibit 17.10 shows the expected start and finish times for each activity and the number of people needed for that activity. These requirements have been combined to develop the diagram at the bottom of Exhibit 17.10.

As you can see in Exhibit 17.10, the resource requirements will rise and fall as activities begin and end. Some activities may require more resources than others. Smoothing out these resource requirements to the extent possible is a problem in scheduling any project. For example, it would usually be undesirable to have the large workforce drop shown in weeks 7 and 8 of Exhibit 17.10 because this could mean having to lay off a large number of workers—an expensive proposition due to unemployment compensation and an action that could create poor labor-management relations.

Resource requirements can often be smoothed by shifting the start or finish of activities. If slack exists, then it can be put to use in this way. Other times, it may be necessary to delay the project finish or even replan the project in order to avoid large fluctuations in resource requirements. For the project indicated in Exhibit 17.10, activity B, which has large workforce requirements, can be delayed two weeks, resulting in a smoother workforce level, as shown in Exhibit 17.11.

EXHIBIT 17.10

Resource
Requirements

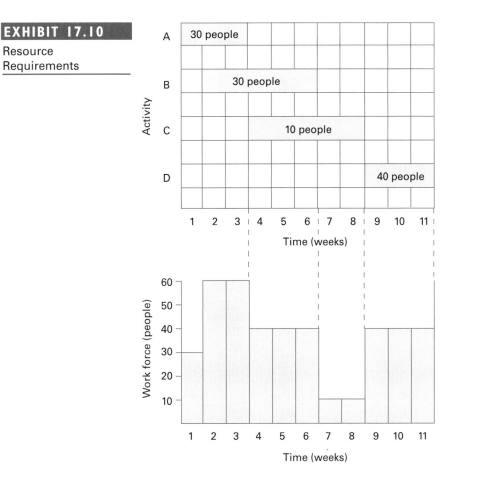

Crashing the Critical Path: Time/Cost Trade-Offs

In some instances, it may be necessary to shorten the time for a project. Shortening a project can often be done, but at the cost of incurring higher expenses. For example, activity times may be shortened by hiring more employees, scheduling overtime, or adding an extra shift. All of these strategies will shorten the overall activity time—but they will also mean higher labor costs. In cases where a project's duration must be shortened, the question becomes one of determining how to do so for the least additional cost.

Consider the project depicted in Exhibit 17.12. The earliest expected completion time for this project is nineteen weeks. Suppose that the completion time must be shortened by reducing the time for certain activities.

The activity times indicated in Exhibit 17.12 are usually called normal times. The **normal time** represents the time an activity will take under normal conditions. But, it may be possible to shorten the time for some activities. The shortest possible time in which an activity can be completed is called its **crash time.** The cost associated with doing an activity in its normal time is called **normal cost,** and the cost incurred when an activity's duration is shortened to the crash time is called **crash cost.** The normal time and cost and the crash time and cost for the project of Exhibit 17.12 are listed in Exhibit 17.13.

It is usually assumed that the cost increase per time reduction will be proportional. For example, activity E can be shortened by two weeks for an additional cost of $1,800. If

EXHIBIT 17.11

Smoothed Workforce
Requirements

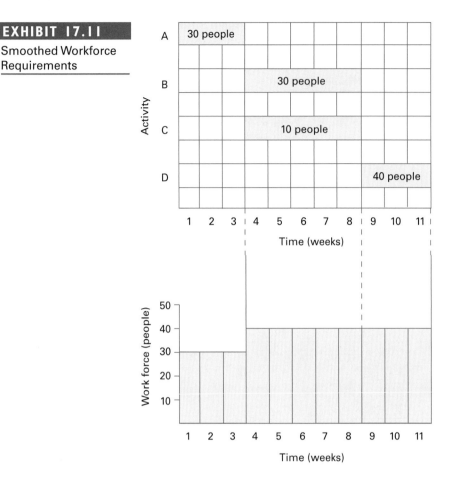

we wanted to reduce the time for E by only one week, we will assume that would cost us
an extra $900. The additional cost incurred per week of time reduction is shown as the last
column in Exhibit 17.13. Note that some activities, such as B, cannot be shortened. We
indicate that with a dash in the Cost/Week column.

Determining Which Activities to Crash

Suppose we want to complete the project of Exhibit 17.12 in eighteen weeks instead of the
nineteen it would normally take. Which activity or activities should be shortened? To
answer that question, first consider which activities influence the project duration. Can
you tell which activities are the ones that determine how long the project will take?

Recall from our earlier discussion that slack time indicates how much leeway a certain activity has in its starting and finishing times. Some activities have more slack than
others, but those that have the lowest slack values are called critical-path activities.
Those activities on the critical path are the ones that will determine a project's duration.
In this case, the critical path consists of activities with zero slack—namely, A, B, D, F, and
G. At least one of those activities must be shortened before the project can be completed
in less time.

To determine which of the critical-path activities to shorten, we refer to the
Cost/Week column of Exhibit 17.13. Shortening the duration of any critical-path activity
will shorten the project duration. But since it costs more to shorten some activities than

EXHIBIT 17.12   CPM Diagram for a Project

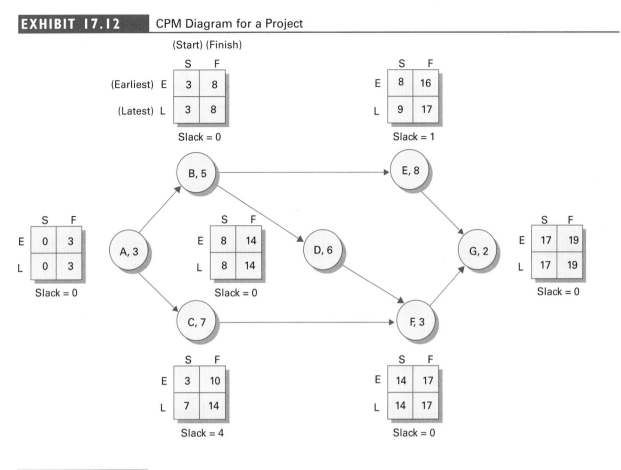

EXHIBIT 17.13

Normal Times and
Costs and Crash Times
and Costs

Activity	Normal		Crash		
	Time	Cost	Time	Cost	Cost/Week
A	3	$1,000	2	$2,000	$1,000/1 = $1,000
B	5	2,000	5	2,000	—
C	7	1,500	4	1,800	$300/3 = $100
D	6	5,000	4	6,000	$1,000/2 = $500
E	8	3,000	6	4,800	$1,800/2 = $900
F	3	1,200	3	1,200	—
G	2	500	2	500	—

others, it makes sense to pick the critical-path activity with the lowest cost/time value. That would be activity D. Thus, we choose to shorten activity D by one week for an additional cost of $500. The entire project will now take only eighteen weeks, as shown in Exhibit 17.14.

More Than One Critical Path

Suppose we want to reduce the project duration even further—to seventeen weeks. Once again, the key is to reduce the duration of at least one activity on the critical path. But the problem now is that there is more than one critical path (you can easily verify this for yourself by looking at the slack values in Exhibit 17.14). There are three paths through the

EXHIBIT 17.14   CPM Diagram for Project with Reduced Time

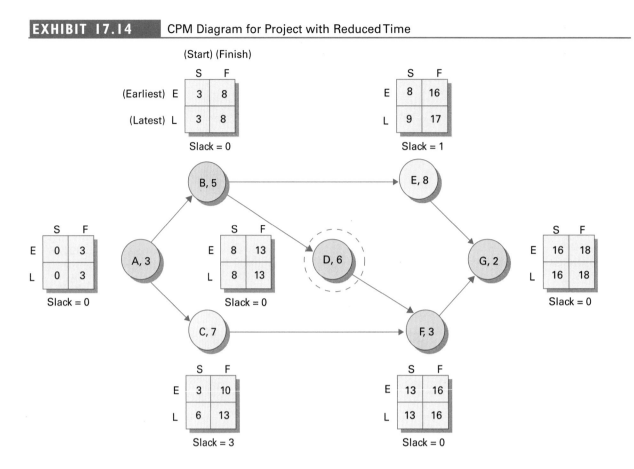

diagram of Exhibit 17.14, from beginning to end. They, and the sums of their activity times, are listed below.

A–B–E–G	18 weeks
A–B–D–F–G	18 weeks
A–C–F–G	15 weeks

Before activity D was shortened, the path A–B–D–F–G took nineteen weeks and was the only critical path. But now two paths are critical—A–B–D–F–G and A–B–E–G. The problem here is that if an activity on only one critical path is shortened, then those activities on the other critical path will not take any less time, and the project duration will not be shortened. This means that activities on both critical paths must be reduced before the project duration will decrease. There are several options here. First, one activity on each critical path could be selected. Again, we would select the lowest cost/time activity. On path A–B–E–G, that would be activity E, while the lowest cost/time activity on path A–B–D–F–G would be activity D, which would be shortened an additional week from five to four. The total cost of this option would be:

Reduce activity E by 1 week	$900
Reduce activity D by 1 week	500
Total additional cost	$1,400

The second option involves shortening the duration of an activity common to both paths. The common activities are A, B, and G. That is, those activities lie on both critical paths. Of those, only A can be reduced, at a cost of $1,000 per week. Since reducing activity A's duration will shorten both critical paths—this second option is the one we will choose.

To summarize, when shortening the duration of a project, it is important to check for multiple critical paths. If more than one exists, then either an activity on each critical path or an activity common to the critical paths must be reduced. Whichever option produces the least cost is the one to choose.

CRITICAL CHAIN SCHEDULING AND BUFFER MANAGEMENT

Eli Goldratt, the developer of Theory of Constraints (TOC), discussed in Chapter 15, has applied many of his TOC ideas to scheduling projects. The term used for that application is **Critical Chain scheduling and Buffer Management (CC/BM).** Goldratt argues, and as we mentioned earlier in this chapter, that some non-critical path may actually end up taking longer than the critical path, thus delaying a project beyond the desired completion time. Furthermore, a non-critical path activity may delay the start of an activity on the critical path, again delaying project completion. To avoid these problems, CC/BM uses buffers in ways very similar to their use in TOC.

CC/BM defines the critical chain as those activities that determine overall duration of the project, considering both precedence and resource requirements. Consistent with this view, there are three ways that a project can be delayed:

1. Activities on the critical path can fall behind schedule.
2. A non-critical path activity can delay start of a critical path activity, causing it to fall behind schedule.
3. A resource may be required on more than one activity at the same time, delaying at least one of those activities, causing it to fall behind schedule.

Three Types of Buffers

Corresponding to the three ways a project can be delayed, there are three types of buffers used to ensure on-time project completion. Each buffer prevents the project from being delayed by absorbing the corresponding delay listed above.

The Project Buffer

In discussing activity durations, we indicated that these are always estimates. Given human nature, each of these estimates will usually include some sort of safety factor. For example, if a manager knows that a particular critical-path activity generally takes seven days to complete, he or she will probably say it will take ten to avoid looking bad if the activity is delayed. But, when it comes time to carry out that activity, the "student syndrome" will probably set in. In other words, knowing that the activity should take only seven days, but that ten days are available, the manager will waste the three-day safety factor by waiting until seven days before the activity must be completed before starting it. Then, if a delay occurs, the activity completion will be delayed, making the entire project late.

To avoid the student syndrome, CC/BM removes any safety factors from all critical-path activities and places them together in the project buffer. Thus, the **project buffer** is placed at the end of the project and includes all safety factors for critical path activities, as shown in Exhibit 17.15. Thus, if completion of any activity on the critical path is delayed, that delay is absorbed by the project buffer.

Feeding Buffers

While the project buffer prevents a critical-path activity from taking longer than expected and delaying the project, it is still possible that a non-critical path activity could cause further delay of a critical-path activity and end up delaying the entire project. Thus, a second set of buffers are added. **Feeding buffers** are inserted whenever a non-critical path activity must precede an activity on the critical path. Again, these represent a safety factor that can be used to absorb delays. Note that they are placed at the end of the non-critical path activity, as shown in Exhibit 17.16. Thus, feeding buffers not only prevent the project from being delayed, but also may allow critical-path activities to start early in case things are going well.

Resource Buffers

The last way a project can be delayed is through problems with resources. One such problem occurs if a single resource is scheduled to be used on more than one activity during the same time period. This problem can be avoided by checking for such conflicts and rescheduling activities to start earlier, as necessary.

To ensure that resources needed for use on critical-path activities are available when needed, a **resource buffer** is a kind of early warning system. If a different resource was used

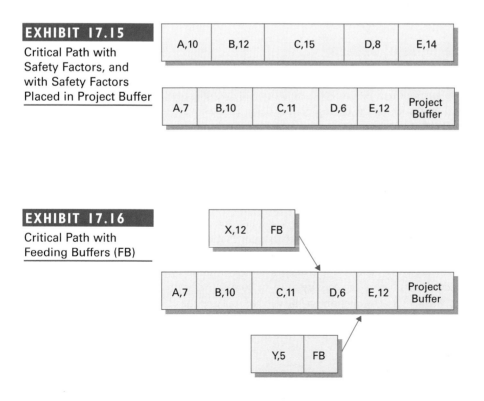

EXHIBIT 17.15

Critical Path with Safety Factors, and with Safety Factors Placed in Project Buffer

EXHIBIT 17.16

Critical Path with Feeding Buffers (FB)

on the preceding critical-path activity, then a resource buffer is inserted to ensure that the resource needed for the next critical path activity will be available at the time the next activity is scheduled to start.

Buffer Management

The use of buffers in CC/BM is designed to avoid project delays. Still, if all buffers are used up, then the project could end up being delayed. Therefore, it is important that buffers be monitored during the project. As activities are completed, managers update how much buffer time was used and track how much is remaining. If that level of remaining buffer time falls below some predetermined amount, then a warning is issued. Further decreases in remaining buffer will trigger corrective action.

SUMMARY

- The planning steps for a project are to develop a statement of work, define the work breakdown structure, list the resources, and estimate activity times.
- The activity-on-node (AON) network diagram is similar to a precedence diagram.
- The critical path consists of those activities with the least slack.
- PERT uses an optimistic time, a most likely time, and a pessimistic time to calculate expected time for each activity.
- Resource requirements may be leveled by shifting activities with slack time.
- Critical Chain scheduling and Buffer Management uses a project buffer, feeding buffers, and resource buffers to ensure that delays for individual activities do not delay the entire project. Buffer management monitors the remaining buffer available.

 Visit our dynamic Web site, http://www.wiley.com/college/vonderembse, for extended chapter material, solved problems, mini-cases, computer software, and Web links.

KEY TERMS

activity-on-arc (AOA) network diagram	critical path	nodes
activity-on-node (AON) representation	critical-path activities	normal cost
	critical path method (CPM)	normal time
arcs	dummy activities	optimistic time *(a)*
branches	earliest finish (EF)	pessimistic time *(b)*
crash cost	earliest start (ES)	program evaluation and review technique
crash time	feeding buffer	(PERT)
Critical Chain scheduling and Buffer Management (CC/BM)	latest finish (LF)	project buffer
	latest start (LS)	resource buffer
	most likely time *(m)*	slack time

URLS

Avraham Y. Goldratt Institute: www.goldratt.com

DuPont: www.dupont.com

Lucent Technologies: www.lucent.com

Microsoft: www.microsoft.com

QUESTIONS

1. What are the planning steps for a project?
2. What is the purpose of a statement of work?
3. What is a work breakdown structure?
4. Explain the difference between an activity-on-node diagram and an activity-on-arc diagram.
5. Why are dummy activities used?
6. Define the critical path.
7. What probability distribution is used for PERT?
8. Which activities are examined first in reducing the duration of a project?
9. Explain how resource usage can be leveled for a project.
10. Discuss some ways in which PERT/CPM is similar to MRP.
11. How could a Gantt load chart be used for project scheduling?
12. What is the role of computers in project planning and control?
13. Explain how the Critical Chain/Buffer Management approach to projects differs from the usual approach of PERT/CPM.

INTERNET QUESTIONS

14. Go to the Web site for Microsoft's project management software (http://www.microsoft.com/office/project/evaluation/tours.asp). Take the software "tours" and identify some capabilities the computer software provides over and above the pencil and paper approach discussed in this chapter.
15. One of the software tours you can take in Question 1 is for "Enterprise Project Management." How does this differ from project management?
16. The Web site http://www.aptconcepts.com/Articles/BuildingNetwork.html explains details about Critical Chain scheduling and Buffer Management. Write a summary of how those ideas extend the basic ideas of project management.
17. Another Web site for CC/BM is http://www.pdinstitute.com/tutorial/contents.html. Visit that site, and discuss how the method for identifying the critical chain there might differ from the usual method for identifying a critical path.

PROBLEMS

1. A project has the following activities, activity durations, and predecessors. Draw the AON diagram, and calculate the earliest start and earliest finish times. Assume the project must be completed within twenty days. Calculate the latest start and latest finish times and the slack for each activity.

Activity	Duration (Days)	Predecessor(s)
A	5	—
B	8	A
C	4	A
D	3	B
E	5	C
F	3	D, E

2. For Problem 1, draw the AOA network.

3. The AON diagram for a project is shown below. Using the precedence relationships and task times given, do the following:

    a. List all paths through the network and indicate the time for each path.

    b. Indicate which path is the critical path.

    c. Calculate the earliest start, earliest finish, latest start, latest finish, and slack times for each activity.

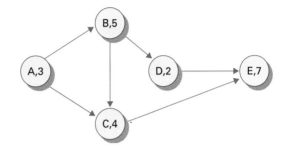

4. The AON diagram for a project is shown below. Determine the earliest start, latest start, earliest finish, latest finish, and slack times for each activity, based on a desired completion time of twenty-eight days. Find the critical path.

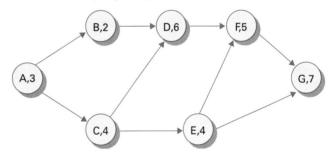

5. MadAve Advertising Agency is developing a magazine advertising campaign for a new client. The following activities have been identified as necessary in order to complete the project:

Activity	Duration (Weeks)	Immediate Predecessor(s)
A. Develop ad concept	2	—
B. Plan photo layout	1	A
C. Hire models	1	B
D. Take photographs	1	C
E. Write ad copy	3	A
F. Develop camera-ready copy	1	D, E
G. Select publications for ad	2	A
H. Send ad to publications	1	F, G

    a. Draw an AON diagram for this project.

    b. Calculate the earliest start, earliest finish, latest start, latest finish, and slack times for each activity.

    c. Identify the critical path.

6. Associated Technologies Company has been working on a new product—a laser oven—through its well-known division that already markets microwave ovens.

Unfortunately, the company has just learned that an overseas competitor is also developing a laser oven and plans to bring it to market in six months. If Associated Technologies is to capture a large share of the market first, its product must be out within ninety days. Fortunately, Associated has been taking an integrated approach to new-product development, and most pieces are already in place. After considering every possible reduction in time, the company came up with the following activities that must be completed and their respective times:

Activity	Duration (Days)	Immediate Predecessor(s)
A. Finalize distribution channels	30	—
B. Complete prototype testing	15	—
C. Finalize product design	30	B
D. Complete BOM files	15	C
E. Finalize production process	10	C
F. Complete employee training	14	E
G. Distribute sales literature	7	A, C
H. Produce and distribute product	14	D, F, G

a. Draw an AON diagram for this project.

b. Calculate the earliest start and earliest finish times for each activity.

c. Based on the desired completion time of ninety days, determine the latest start, latest finish, and slack times for each activity.

d. Identify the critical path.

7. The Compu-Form Company provides computer services to business and industry. The company is planning to replace one of its computers and has identified the following activities that will make up that project:

Activity	Duration (Hours)	Immediate Predecessor(s)
A. Shut down old machine	1	—
B. Disconnect wiring from computer	1	A
C. Remove old computer	3	B
D. Remove old wiring	2	B
E. Connect new wiring to peripherals	2	D
F. Test wiring connections	1	E
G. Move in new computer	3	C
H. Connect wiring to computer	2	E, F, G
I. Install operating system	1	H
J. Check memory	1	I
K. Check operating system	1	I
L. Check peripherals	1	J, K

Determine the shortest time it will take to complete this project and which activities are on the critical path.

8. A project consists of the following activities:

Activity	Optimistic Time	Most Likely Time	Pessimistic Time
A	4	6	10
B	3	3	3
C	8	11	14
D	3	15	17
E	3	5	12

Determine the expected time and the variance for each activity.

9. A project is made up of the following activities:

Activity	Optimistic Time	Most Likely Time	Pessimistic Time
A	2	6	12
B	3	7	9
C	8	14	16
D	3	10	18
E	3	10	12
F	10	12	20
G	12	19	27
H	9	10	15

Determine the expected time and the variance for each one.

10. Referring to the network diagram in Problem 3, use the following information to determine the probability of completing the project by time 22:

Activity	Optimistic Time	Most Likely Time	Pessimistic Time
A	2	3	6
B	1	5	7
C	3	4	9
D	2	2	2
E	2	7	9

11. Referring to the network diagram of Problem 4, determine the probability of completing the project by time 26, based on the following information:

Activity	Optimistic Time	Most Likely Time	Pessimistic Time
A	1	3	5
B	2	2	2
C	2	4	6
D	2	6	8
E	3	4	9
F	2	5	12
G	3	7	8

12. A project has been planned with the following activities, expected start and finish dates, and cash expenditures. Develop a load profile that will indicate cash requirements during the project.

Activity	Start	Finish	Cash Expenditure
A	0	3	$6,000
B	0	5	2,000
C	3	8	4,000
D	2	8	5,000
E	5	6	2,000

13. A project consists of the following activities, with the normal times and crash times listed. Based on the cost information, determine how much additional money must be spent to reduce the project duration by one day from its normal time and which activity should be shortened.

Activity	Normal Time (Days)	Cost	Immediate Predecessor(s)
A	5	$500	—
B	3	600	A
C	8	1,000	A
D	8	400	B
E	6	700	C
F	3	600	D, E

Activity	Crash Time (Days)	Cost
A	3	$800
B	2	700
C	5	1,600
D	8	400
E	5	800
F	1	900

14. The Able Construction Company must complete the following activities as part of a building project. This project must be completed in the shortest time possible. Determine what that time is, which activities should be shortened, and the total project cost.

Activity	Normal Time (Days)	Cost	Immediate Predecessor(s)
A	6	$1,000	—
B	10	1,200	A
C	9	600	A
D	9	800	B, C
E	8	1,500	C
F	5	500	D, E

Activity	Crash Time (Days)	Cost
A	5	$1,300
B	9	1,300
C	8	1,200
D	7	1,200
E	6	2,000
F	5	500

APPENDIX

AREAS UNDER THE STANDARDIZED NORMAL CURVE FROM $-\infty$ TO $+z$

z	.00	.01	.02	.03	.04	.05	.06	.07	.08	.09
.0	.5000	.5040	.5080	.512	.5160	.5199	.5239	.5279	.5319	.5359
.1	.5398	.5438	.5478	.5517	.5557	.5596	.5636	.5675	.5714	.5753
.2	.5793	.5832	.5871	.5910	.5948	.5987	.6026	.6064	.6103	.6141
.3	.6179	.6217	.6255	.6293	.6331	.6368	.6406	.6443	.6480	.6517
.4	.6554	.6591	.6628	.6664	.6700	.6736	.6772	.6808	.6844	.6879
.5	.6915	.6950	.6985	.7019	.7054	.7088	.7123	.7157	.7190	.7224
.6	.7257	.7291	.7324	.7357	.7389	.7422	.7454	.7486	.7517	.7549
.7	.7580	.7611	.7642	.7673	.7704	.7734	.7764	.7794	.7823	.7852
.8	.7881	.7910	.7939	.7967	.7995	.8023	.8051	.8078	.8106	.8133
.9	.8159	.8186	.8212	.8238	.8264	.8289	.8315	.8340	.8365	.8389
1.0	.8413	.8438	.8461	.8485	.8508	.8531	.8554	.8577	.8599	.8621
1.1	.8643	.8665	.8686	.8708	.8729	.8749	.8770	.8790	.8810	.8830
1.2	.8849	.8869	.8888	.8907	.8925	.8944	.8962	.8980	.8997	.9015
1.3	.9032	.9049	.9066	.9082	.9099	.9115	.9131	.9147	.9162	.9177
1.4	.9192	.9207	.9222	.9236	.9251	.9265	.9279	.9292	.9306	.9319
1.5	.9332	.9345	.9357	.9370	.9382	.9394	.9406	.9418	.9429	.9441
1.6	.9452	.9463	.9474	.9484	.9495	.9505	.9515	.9525	.9535	.9545
1.7	.9554	.9564	.9573	.9582	.9591	.9599	.9608	.9616	.9625	.9633
1.8	.9641	.9649	.9656	.9664	.9671	.9678	.9686	.9693	.9699	.9706
1.9	.9713	.9719	.9726	.9732	.9738	.9744	.9750	.9756	.9761	.9767
2.0	.9772	.9778	.9783	.9788	.9793	.9798	.9803	.9808	.9812	.9817
2.1	.9821	.9826	.9830	.9834	.9838	.9842	.9846	.9850	.9854	.9857
2.2	.9861	.9864	.9868	.9871	.9875	.9878	.9881	.9884	.9887	.9890
2.3	.9893	.9896	.9898	.9901	.9904	.9906	.9909	.9911	.9913	.9916
2.4	.9918	.9920	.9922	.9925	.9927	.9929	.9931	.9932	.9934	.9936
2.5	.9938	.9940	.9941	.9943	.9945	.9946	.9948	.9949	.9951	.9952
2.6	.9953	.9955	.9956	.9957	.9959	.9960	.9961	.9962	.9963	.9964
2.7	.9965	.9966	.9967	.9968	.9969	.9970	.9971	.9972	.9973	.9974
2.8	.9974	.9975	.9976	.9977	.9977	.9978	.9979	.9979	.9980	.9981
2.9	.9981	.9982	.9982	.9983	.9984	.9984	.9985	.9985	.9986	.9986
3.0	.9987	.9987	.9987	.9988	.9988	.9989	.9989	.9989	.9990	.9990

GLOSSARY

A

ABC analysis   A classification scheme for inventory items so that those 20 percent of items (A items) that account for the top 80 percent of dollar usage receive the most attention.

acceptable quality level (AQL)   The percentage of defective units that would be acceptable in a batch.

acceptance number   In acceptance sampling using MIL-STD-105D, the maximum number nonconforming allowed in a sample for acceptance of the entire lot.

acceptance sampling   A statistical procedure in which samples are used to determine whether an entire lot meets acceptable quality standards.

activity matrix   Organizes and displays the movement of people, parts, or other factors between departments.

activity-on-arc (AOA)   network diagram A method for representing project networks in which each arc corresponds to an activity.

activity-on-node (AON)   representation A method for representing project networks in which each node corresponds to an activity.

aggregate planning   A term used to mean medium-range operations planning. A first rough-cut approximation at determining how existing resources of people and facilities should be used to meet projected demand.

aggregation   Refers to the combining of products into groups or families for planning purposes.

allowance   Time required for personal time, rest, and delays as a percentage of normal time.

alpha (α)   The probability in acceptance sampling of committing a Type I error.

analysis   A step in design that separates the whole into its parts in order to determine their nature, proportion, function, and relationship.

annual fixed costs   Costs that do not vary with volume. These costs are incurred during the year and can include supervisory labor, utilities, and support staff.

appraisal costs   The costs incurred to measure quality, assess customer satisfaction, inspect and test products.

arc   An arrow in a precedence diagram or project network that connects two nodes.

assembly line   A process where discrete parts are put together to make a finished product. It is a high volume operation that produces products that are very similar in features and performance.

assignable causes   Causes of variation in the output of a process that can be assigned to factors such as tool wear, material from different suppliers, etc.

automated guided vehicle systems (AGVS)   Driverless and flexible transportation devices resembling a forklift truck, which can transport parts between manufacturing cells.

automated storage and retrieval system (ASRS)   A computerized system for storing and retrieving parts or tools.

available to promise   The number of units in a master schedule not yet committed to customer orders.

average inventory investment   The dollar value of a company's average level of inventory.

B

B2B   Business to business Internet transactions.

B2C   Business to consumer Internet transactions.

backflushing   Calculates material usage for either a cost accounting or an MRP system based on the number of completed units produced and the materials required to produce that number of units.

backward scheduling   An approach to scheduling that starts from a desired due date and works backward.

backward vertical integration   The situation in which a company owns organizations that perform activities in the upstream supply chain.

batch   A term used to describe a production process that does not have sufficient volume from a single product to fully use the facility. The facility must produce several products to have sufficient volume to achieve economies of scale. There is an equipment changeover prior to making each product.

benchmarking   A process by which a company compares its performance and methods for a certain activity against that of a recognized leader or an outstanding competitor.

benefit/cost ratio A productivity measure sometimes used for services, based on calculating benefits produced divided by the cost of providing those benefits.

beta (β) The probability in acceptance sampling of committing a Type II error.

bill-of-materials (BOM) Describes the type and quantity of each component part needed to build one unit of a product.

blanket purchase requisition A document authorizing a vendor to provide a specified quantity or number of parts or raw materials over a specified period of time.

bottleneck The department, work station, or operation that restricts the flow of product through the production system. A bottleneck department restricts the flow of product from upstream departments and starves downstream departments.

branch An arrow in a precedence diagram or project network that connects two nodes.

break-even point (BEP) The volume of a good or service that must be produced and sold so that profit is zero. This is the zero profit point in the cost-volume profit model.

buffer Any backlog that is used purposely to avoid running out of parts or material.

build-up method An approach to forecasting that starts at the bottom of an organization and makes an overall estimate by adding together estimates from each element.

bullwhip effect An example of what can happen when information is not shared in a supply chain. It occurs when a slight increase in demand at the retailer level gets magnified into a huge jump in demand at the raw material supplier level.

business plan A medium-range statement of planned sales, production, and inventory levels, usually in terms of dollars, on a monthly basis.

business process A set of work activities with a preferred order, an identifiable beginning and end, inputs, and clearly defined outputs that add value to the customer. A business process is usually cross-functional.

business-to-business (B2B) Refers to transactions between organizations. These organizations are usually part of a supply chain such as IBM selling services to Priceline.com.

business-to-consumer (B2C) Refers to transactions between an organization and its final customers such as Amazon.com selling products to consumers via the Internet.

C

C-kanban A kanban that authorizes the movement of materials from one location to another.

capacity A measure of the organization's ability to provide customers with the demanded services or goods, in the amount requested and in a timely manner. Capacity is the maximum rate of production.

capacity requirements planning (CRP) The process of estimating total capacity that will be required at each work center or machine, based on the master schedule and MRP.

capital budget Indicates planned expenditures for plant and equipment.

capital productivity The output achieved from an activity divided by the capital inputs.

carrying costs The variable costs associated with keeping inventory.

cause-and-effect diagram A diagram that is used in problem solving to list all the possible causes of a problem, usually divided into materials, equipment, methods, and personnel.

cellular manufacturing *See manufacturing cell.*

central tendency A measure of the average output from a process.

certified The designation a company receives after it has successfully met the standards of ISO 9000:2000.

chance causes of variation Sources of process variation that are inherent in a process, also known as common causes or random causes.

changeover time The time required to change the facility/equipment from making one product to making the next product.

closed-loop MRP A variation of MRP in which feedback about execution of production plans is provided so MRP can be updated to reflect reality.

coding and classification A method used to determine a family of parts in a group technology study. Each part is assigned a code which defines the size, shape, metal type, machining operations and other factors.

coefficient of correlation A measure of the strength of a relationship between variables. If there is no relationship, the coefficient of correlation will be zero. A perfect positive correlation is 1.0 and a perfect negative correlation is −1.0.

collaborative planning forecasting and replenishment (CPFR) A supply chain approach that seeks to enable collaboration among supply chain partners to jointly develop a plan that specifies what is to be sold, how it will be marketed and promoted, where, and during what time period. Furthermore, sharing of information is facilitated by utilizing a common set of communication standards.

common causes of variation Sources of process variation that are inherent in a process, also known as random causes or chance causes.

competitive advantage An organization's special abilities, such as shorter delivery lead-times or higher quality products, which customers value and which gives it an edge on its competition.

computer aided design (CAD) The effective use of the computer to create or modify an engineering design. An interactive CAD terminal can be used for dimensional analysis, interference checking between two or more objects, stress analysis, and examining cross-sections of the part.

computer aided manufacturing (CAM) The effective use of computer technology in the management, control, and operations of the production facility through either direct or indirect computer interface with the physical and human resources. (This definition of CAM was given by Computer Aided

Manufacturing International.) CAM systems include monitoring the production process and the operation of machines by machines.

computer aided process planning (CAPP) An expert system that can generate routings and machining instructions for parts.

computer integrated manufacturing (CIM) Blends recent developments in manufacturing with information technology to achieve a competitive advantage.

computer numerically control (CNC) A machining system that utilizes a dedicated computer to store programs. The programs control the machine so it can shape the finished part.

concurrent engineering When product design and process design are done simultaneously by the same group of people working in close collaboration.

constraint Anything that limits our choice of actions.

consumer's risk In acceptance sampling, the probability of accepting an unacceptable lot of material.

continuous flow process A process for mass producing products that does not identify individual units. The products are mixed and flow together in a continuous stream. Oil refining is a good example of a continuous flow process.

continuous improvement The concept that no matter how good a company is it must always work to do better. The Japanese term is "kaizen."

contribution per unit The selling price of a unit minus the variable cost of producing the unit. It is the amount that each unit of sales contributes towards covering overhead costs and meeting profit objectives.

conveyance kanban A kanban that authorizes the movement of materials from one location to another.

corner point The intersection of constraint lines in graphical solution of a linear programming problem.

correlation analysis Measures the degree of relationship between two variables.

cost drivers Any activity in activity-based costing that is used to generate costs.

cost-volume-profit (CVP) model A simple model of an organization that uses estimates of costs, revenues, volume sold, and volume produced in order to estimate profit.

cost of quality Includes the three categories of costs associated with quality: failure costs (internal or external); appraisal costs; and prevention costs.

crash cost The cost of completing a project activity in its crash time.

crash time The shortest possible time in which a project activity can be completed.

critical chain scheduling and buffer management (CC/BM) An approach to project management that utilizes concepts from Theory of Constraints to promote on-time completion of the project.

critical path A path in a CPM diagram that consists of all activities with the least slack. These are activities that must be watched the closest.

critical-path activities Those activities in a project that have the least amount of slack.

critical path method (CPM) An approach to project management that identifies those activities with the least amount of slack.

critical ratio A measure of the ratio between time until an order is due and the processing time remaining.

cross docking Seeks to coordinate inbound and outbound shipments so that little, if any, inventory must be kept at the distribution center.

CRP (capacity requirements planning) The process of estimating total capacity that will be required at each work center or machine, based on the master schedule and MRP.

customer The buyer of a service or good.

customer relationship management (CRM) A process to create, maintain, and enhance strong, value laden associations with people and organizations that buy products.

cycle counting A procedure in which inventory of an item is counted at least once during an order cycle.

cycle time The average time it took a worker being observed in a time study to perform the task.

D

days of inventory Indicates approximately how many days of sales can be supplied solely from inventory.

decision support systems (DDS) Are systems that allow managers to easily access information stored in a database and provide easy-to-use tools for analysis.

defective Items of product that do not conform to specifications, and are thus unacceptable.

Delphi Technique Use a panel of experts and surveys to build consensus regarding future events.

demand management The process of identifying all sources of demand and reflecting them in the master schedule.

Deming Prize Japan's highest quality award.

Deming Wheel A problem solving process used for continuous improvement, also called Plan-Do-Check-Act Cycle or Shewhart Cycle.

dependent demand Demand (usually for components or raw materials) that depends upon production of a finished product.

dependent variable The variable in regression analysis that is being predicted.

design for manufacture and assembly (DFMA) Designing products so they are easy to manufacture and/or assemble, resulting in high quality and low cost.

design for operations (DFO) Designing services so the operations function can provide high quality and low cost.

design of experiments (DOE) Using experimental methods in determining how to minimize the effects of random variation on process output.

designing the system Includes all the decisions necessary to establish the facilities and information systems required to produce the service or good.

deterministic simulation A simulation in which every change that occurs is according to fixed values, not random.

digital loyalty networks Links between a company's supply chain and its customer management operations such that the supply chain is customized to meet the needs of a company's most important customers or market segments.

disintermediation Eliminating some functions in a supply chain to improve its efficiency, such as when a manufacturer sells directly to the final consumer.

dispatching Assigning priorities and selection of jobs for processing at a work center.

dispatching rules Rules used for assigning processing priorities to jobs for scheduling.

dispersion A measure of the variability of process output.

distribution requirements planning (DRP) A system for determining the quantity of products needed within the distribution system. DRP uses forecasts of customers' orders to estimate the quantity of materials to have available at the distribution centers. Demands at the distribution centers, in turn, are aggregated to determine requirements at regional warehouses, which influence requirements at supplying facilities.

distribution resources planning A modification of distribution requirements planning that resembles MRP II.

distribution system Material handling between suppliers and customers. It involves moving materials between facilities and has a physical and an informational component. Distribution systems weave together customers and suppliers in a chain that takes the most basic materials, like iron ore, crude oil, and lumber, and transforms them into consumer products like power boats, toasters, and furniture.

dollar usage The unit value of an item multiplied by its annual usage, in units.

double sampling A procedure in acceptance sampling in which a second sample may be taken from a lot before a final decision is made.

downstream A designation for that part of the supply chain through which a company's products are sold, such as distributors, retailers, dealers, or even final consumers.

drum A term used in theory of constraints to identify the resource that will determine production rate for the entire production system.

dual-card kanban system A pull system that uses both C-kanbans and P-kanbans to carefully control WIP inventory.

dummy activity An imaginary activity that must be used in AOA project network diagrams to clarify precedence relationships.

durability The ability of a product to function when subjected to hard and frequent use.

E

earliest finish (EF) The earliest time a project activity can be expected to be completed.

earliest start (ES) The earliest time a project activity can be expected to start based on preceding activities.

early involvement An upstream investment in time by people involved in an activity or process that facilitates the identification and solution of downstream problems that would otherwise increase time or costs or decrease quality.

e-business Involves the use of electronic platforms to conduct company business. It has two types of transactions: business-to-business and business-to-consumer.

echelon 1 The part of a downstream supply chain, such as a distributor, that receives products directly from the company that makes those products.

echelon 2 The part of the downstream supply chain, such as a retailer, that receives products from echelon 1 organizations.

economic order quantity (EOQ) An amount to order at one time that theoretically minimizes total annual cost of ordering and holding inventory.

economies of scale This doctrine states that there is a most efficient size for a facility and there is a most efficient size for the firm. This implies building sufficient sales/production volume to take advantage of the fixed costs of the organization.

economies of scope Economies of scale across products. Economies of

scope implies building the volume necessary to cover fixed costs by producing a variety of products on the same equipment. It needs flexibility within the organization.

effective Means the system achieves the desired results.

efficient Means the system uses a "reasonable" amount of effort (inputs) to achieve the desired outputs.

efficient consumer response (ECR) An approach to supply chain management that emphasizes everyday low pricing and efficiently matching inventory replenishment to consumer demand.

efficient supply chain A type of supply chain that emphasizes cost minimization and efficiency.

electronic data interchange (EDI) The use of electronic means, such as telephone lines or the Internet, to share data among members of a supply chain.

employee empowerment Giving employees authority and responsibility to solve problems and make decisions related to their jobs.

enterprise resource planning (ERP) The use of one common database for all functions of an organization, or even all members of a supply chain.

ethics Sets of standards that guide behavior. These standards are usually higher than what is legal.

event In a project network, an event is the beginning or end of an activity.

event-oriented simulation A simulation in which time is incremented only as events occur.

expediting The monitoring of supplier deliveries of materials which have become critical for the customer.

expert system (ES) A computer-based approach that uses knowledge and inference procedures to solve problems that are difficult enough to require significant human expertise for their solution. The knowledge and the inference procedures are attempts to create a model of the best practitioners in the field.

external failure costs Costs of quality incurred after a product has reached the customer.

extreme point   The intersection of constraint lines in graphical solution of a linear programming problem.

F

facility layout   The physical arrangement of the work space including the position of departments or work groups with respect to one another and how the work space within a department is arranged.

facility location   The placement of a facility with respect to customers, suppliers, and other facilities with which it interfaces.

failure costs   Costs incurred whenever any product or component of a product fails to meet requirements.

family of parts   A group of parts that require similar machining operations.

feasible region   The area that satisfies all constraints in graphical solution of a linear programming problem.

feeding buffer   Extra time allowed in critical chain scheduling and buffer management when a non-critical path activity must precede one on the critical path.

final assembly schedule (FAS)   Like a master schedule except that it is usually done only a week ahead of time and it indicates exact option combinations for each finished product to be produced.

finished goods inventories   Final products awaiting customer acceptance and delivery.

finite capacity scheduling   A computerized approach to scheduling that uses advanced software to schedule jobs while taking capacity limitations into account.

finite loading   An approach to machine loading that considers available capacity.

fishbone chart   A diagram that is used in problem-solving to list all the possible causes of a problem, usually divided into materials, equipment, methods, and personnel.

flexibility   The ability to change between products or customers with minimal costs and delays.

flexible manufacturing systems (FMS)   Use computer and information technology, flexible automation, computer aided process planning, and manufac-

turing cell layout to produce families of parts.

flow process chart   Used for analyzing the movements of a worker or the flow of materials through a process.

flow time   The total time it takes to produce a good or service.

focused factory   Smaller operations producing fewer products. A focused factory does not attempt to achieve low costs through economies of scale (i.e., spreading fixed costs over a large volume). It achieves low costs through better control (i.e., eliminating waste), and ease of managing a smaller operation (i.e., fewer people involved).

forecast   An estimate of future events.

forecasting   An attempt to predict the future.

forward scheduling   An approach to scheduling that starts from the present time and schedules each job to start at the earliest possible moment.

forward vertical integration   The situation in which a company owns the organizations that constitute the downstream side of the supply chain.

freezing the master schedule   A policy that prevents changes in the master schedule within a certain time period from the present.

functional areas   The parts or subsystems of an organization such as accounting, marketing, finance, and engineering.

G

gainsharing   The process of awarding bonuses or extra compensation because of productivity improvements made by a group.

Gantt load chart   A graphic device for indicating the schedule of jobs on equipment or facilities.

go/no-go gages   Inspection tools that can be used to quickly determine whether a part meets specifications.

goods   Physical products.

grand mean   The overall mean of sample means.

graphical approach   A method of aggregate planning that uses a graph to indicate cumulative demand for the product versus cumulative production.

gross requirements   In MRP, the total demand for an item during a time bucket.

group technology (GT)   The grouping together of parts or products into families by processing operations so that all members of a family are processed in a miniature factory, called a GT cell, to maximize efficiency.

GT cell   A group of machines, usually arranged in a U-shaped layout, used to process a family of parts requiring similar operations.

H

hard automation   Used to describe processes which have very limited flexibility.

hierarchical production planning (HPP)   An approach to aggregate planning that breaks a large problem down into smaller ones, with each smaller problem being solved at the appropriate organizational level.

high process capability   Characteristic of a process that has a high probability of producing acceptable products when random variation is considered.

hiring costs   Include expenses associated with finding qualified personnel, interviewing and training them, and then any productivity losses involved before they become proficient at the job.

historical data in work measurement   The use of data about past worker performance to develop time standards.

holding costs   The variable costs associated with keeping inventory.

horizontal expansion of work   Giving a person more tasks or more jobs to perform.

house of quality   A diagram used to convert customer attributes desired in a product to engineering characteristics, parts characteristics, and process details.

I

ISO 9000:2000   An updated series of the ISO 9000 international standards for the quality management procedures and documentation used by a company in producing its product.

in control   The state when a process is influenced only by random variation.

indented bill of materials   A bill of materials in which components are indented from the item they go into.

independent demand   Demand (usually from the consumer) for a part or product that is not dependent upon a production plan.

independent variable   A variable in regression analysis which is used to predict the dependent variable.

infinite loading   An approach to machine loading that does not take capacity considerations into account.

input/output control   A method for managing work flow and queue lengths by comparing input to a machine with output from it.

insourced   When a company itself produces the goods or services that it uses in its own operations.

internal failure costs   Those costs of quality associated with defects found before the product reaches the customer.

internal supply chain   That part of the supply chain that is within a company, usually the manufacturer of the finished product. This can include purchasing, materials management, and production.

inventory   Material that is stored in anticipation of some future use. Inventory can be used as an alternative to future production. It is created when production (procurement in the case of purchased parts) exceeds consumption.

inventory control   The effort to maintain inventory levels and costs within acceptable limits. It includes models that determine how much and when to order inventory as well as systems for monitoring inventory levels for management evaluation and decision making.

inventory turnover ratio   Indicates how many times during a year the inventory turns over, or is sold.

Ishikawa chart   A diagram that is used in problem solving to list all the possible causes of a problem, usually divided into materials, equipment, methods, and personnel.

J

JIT II   Employees of major suppliers work right in the purchasing depart-

ment of a customer company to which they sell products, handling all purchases from their companies.

job enlargement   An employee's job is expanded to include several tasks.

job enrichment   Providing a person with more decision-making authority to increase job satisfaction.

job rotation   To periodically shift workers from one job to another.

job shop   A facility capable of producing a wide variety of products in very small volumes. The production facility is general purpose and flexible enough to meet a variety of needs.

job specialization   A job design in which each employee performs only a particular narrowly defined task.

just-in-time (JIT)   Can be used as a basis for planning and scheduling, yet is more properly viewed as a strategy for designing manufacturing systems that are responsive to customer requirements. Applying JIT forces a reexamination of operating philosophy. The JIT philosophy focuses on reducing lead times, reducing set-up times and improving product quality to minimize raw material, work-in-process and finished goods inventory.

K

kaizen   A Japanese term referring to continuous improvement.

kanban   A Japanese word meaning "visible record." In manufacturing, it is a card that is used to indicate when more materials are needed in a pull system.

key policies   Methods or guidelines for achieving an organization's goals.

knowledge engineers   Build expert systems. They help human experts structure the problem by interpreting and integrating human answers, drawing analogies, posing examples and bringing out conceptual differences.

L

labor productivity   The output achieved from an activity divided by the labor inputs. It is often measured as the number of units produced per labor hour.

latest finish (LF)   The latest time a project activity can be completed without delaying the project past a desired completion date.

latest start (LS)   The latest time a project activity can start without delaying project completion past a desired date.

layoff costs   Include any severance pay or state-mandated payments into an unemployment compensation fund when employees are terminated or laid off.

lead time   The difference between the time the order is placed and the delivery of the product.

lead-time offsetting   The process of taking lead time into account for planning purposes.

lean systems   An approach to operations that expands JIT concepts to the entire value chain.

learning curve   Indicates how the time required per unit of product decreases as the cumulative number of units produced increases.

learning factor   Indicates the percentage of time required to produce unit number $2n$ compared to the time for unit n.

level assembly schedule   A final assembly schedule that involves producing a specified sequence of products so that production of each is matched with expected daily demand.

leverage   When referring to operations and productivity it means to make the work force more productive through the use of better tools.

life cycle costing   Considering the cost of a product over its useful life not just the purchase price. When two alternatives are compared, which one has the lower total cost? Total cost includes purchase price, maintenance costs, and operating expense.

line balancing   The procedure in which tasks along an assembly line are assigned to work stations so each has approximately the same amount of work.

line flow processes   High volume operations. Two examples of line flow processes are continuous flow processes and assembly lines.

linear programming   A mathematical technique that can solve any resource allocation problem so long as that problem can be stated in terms of linear functions.

load The total capacity requirements placed on a machine or work center during a specified period of time.

load profile A diagram that indicates the work load being placed on each work center.

load report A graphical representation of the load on a machine or work center over time.

loading An approach to scheduling that tries to take capacity utilization into account.

logistics That part of a supply chain that includes companies that move or store items, such as trucking companies, railroads, and shipping companies, as well as warehouses or distribution centers.

long-range operations planning Involves activities that are planned to occur eighteen months or more in the future.

loss function In quality management, the measure of loss to society associated with deviation of a process from its target output value.

lot A quantity of material or number of units produced or processed at one time (a batch).

lot-for-lot A lot sizing rule used in MRP in which planned order releases are equated to net requirements by time bucket.

lot sizing The process of determining how much of an item should be ordered or produced at one time.

lot tolerance percent defective (LTPD) The percentage of non-conforming units in a batch that would definitely be unacceptable.

lower control limit (LCL) The lower limit of a control chart indicating the minimum value above which sample values would normally be expected to fall under random variation.

lower specification limit The lower limit on acceptability for some measure specified in the design of a product.

lower tolerance limit Same as lower specification limit.

lowest final cost The lowest total cost of the product, including the purchase price, shipping and receiving costs, costs to rework defective products, and costs for special processing that would not be necessary if another supplier were used.

low-level coding A procedure in which level numbers are assigned to parts in the bill of materials, starting at level 0 for the finished product. A part that appears at more than one level would be assigned the lowest level (highest number) at which it appears.

low process capability Describes a process that will have a high probability of producing nonconforming product due to random variation.

M

machine constrained The machine is holding back production. The equipment is operating for all the available time at its best speed while the operator has some idle time.

makespan time The total time required to complete a set of jobs.

make-to-order company A company that produces only to customer orders.

make-to-stock company A company that produces for inventory and meets customer orders from inventory.

Malcolm Baldrige National Quality Award (MBNQA) The highest quality award given by the United States, currently awarded to a maximum of two companies in each category of large manufacturer, large service, or small business, with plans to add categories for health care and education.

manufacturing A production process that produces goods.

manufacturing cell The physical layout of the facility into compact groups of machines that are responsible for producing families of parts. *See also cellular manufacturing.*

manufacturing resource planning (MRP II) An integrated decision support system that ties together departments such as engineering, finance, personnel, manufacturing and marketing via a computer-based dynamic simulation model. MRP II works within the limits of an organiza-

tion's present production system and with known orders and demand forecasts.

market research The study of consumer needs so the organization can determine new markets for existing products and discover demand for new products.

market share An organization's sales in a market divided by the total sales.

master production schedule (MPS) A specific statement of exactly what, usually in terms of individual end items or product models, will be produced in each time period. Usually these time periods are weeks, although they may be days or even hours.

mass customization The ability to quickly design, produce, and deliver products that meet specific customer needs at close to mass-production prices. From an operations perspective, it is the low-cost, high-quality, large volume delivery of customized products.

material handling Includes systems for moving materials within the facility. It implies a physical component (equipment to perform the task) and an information component (decisions about when and how much should be moved).

material management Includes decisions regarding the procurement, control, handling, storage, and distribution of materials.

material productivity The output achieved from an activity divided by the material inputs.

material requirements planning (MRP) A way of scheduling the ordering or production of parts or raw materials so they will be available when needed to meet the master schedule.

materials The physical items that are necessary to produce the goods and services we consume.

mean absolute deviation (MAD) The average of absolute error. The differences between the actual value of a variable and the forecasted value are added after the plus and minus signs are removed. This total is divided by the number of observations.

mean squared error (MSE) The average of all the squared errors. The differences between the actual value of a variable and the forecasted value are squared, added together and divided by the number of observations.

medium-range planning Concerned with the time between six months and eighteen months ahead.

method or overall factors A procedure for rough-cut capacity planning that uses historical accounting data to estimate the number of standard hours required per unit.

methods analysis Methods and techniques concerned only with the physiological aspects of a job—how easy the job is to do, how quickly the person can work.

methods improvement Methods and techniques for improving the physiological aspects of a job.

methods-time measurement (MTM) A system of predetermined time standards. Standard motions require a predetermined number of time measurement units (TMUs).

mixed-model sequencing The production of different products in small batches on the same equipment following a repeating cycle.

mixed strategy An aggregate planning strategy that combines two or more of the pure strategies.

model An abstraction from the real problem of the key variables and relationships in order to simplify the problem. The purpose of modeling is to provide the user with a better understanding of the problem, and with a means of manipulating the results for "what if" analysis.

Monte Carlo simulation The use of random numbers to simulate a real system.

MOST Stands for Maynard Operation Sequence Technique. MOST is based on MTM, but is much faster and easier to use.

most likely time In PERT, the most frequent amount of time an activity will take.

move time The material handling time between work centers.

MRP *See material requirements planning.*

MRP II Another name for Manufacturing Resource Planning.

MTM Stands for Methods Time Measurement and was developed by Dr. H. B. Maynard. Under this system, each movement has been determined to take a certain number of Time Measurement Units (TMUs).

multiple factor productivity Includes all of the input factors such as labor, material, and capital as well as the possibility of more than one output factor.

multiple regression analysis Regression analysis that uses two or more (independent variables) to predict one dependent variable.

multiple sampling A process in acceptance sampling in which successive samples may be required before a final decision can be reached.

N

natural variation The values over which most process output will fall under random variation (equal to 6σ).

net requirements The additional number of units required in MRP during a time bucket after inventory and scheduled receipts have been considered.

node A circle in a precedence diagram or project network.

nonconforming Items of product that do not conform to specifications, and thus are unacceptable.

normal cost The cost of completing a project activity in its normal time.

normal time The time that a project or an activity takes under normal conditions.

O

objective function The function in a linear programming problem that includes the variables and indicates what is to be achieved.

off-loading Involves taking a part that would ordinarily be processed on one machine and processing it on another machine that has available capacity.

operating characteristic curve (OC curve) A graph indicating the proba-

bility of accepting a batch as a function of the percentage of defective units in the batch.

operating leverage Replacing variable costs of production, usually labor, with fixed costs. This action causes profits to rise rapidly as volume increases because the incremental costs (variable costs/unit) are low.

operations The processes by which people, capital, and material (inputs) are combined to produce the services and goods we consume (outputs). Operations employ labor and management (people), and use facilities and equipment (capital) to change materials into finished good (farm tractors) or to provide services (computer software development).

operations management Decision-making involving the many factors that affect operations. Decisions that need to be made might include which products to produce, how large a facility to build, and how many people to hire on first shift.

optimistic time (a) The shortest time an activity would normally take.

ordering cost The variable costs associated with replenishing inventory.

order point The level of inventory at which a company should order more to avoid a possible stockout.

order status The ability to query the customer orders to determine if the order has been completed, scheduled, or is waiting to be produced and the reasons the order is waiting.

order-up-to level In a periodic review inventory control system, the level to which a replenishment order should bring on-hand plus on-order inventory.

order-winning criteria Criteria such as cost, quality, etc. that are used by a company to win orders from customers.

organizational structure The formal relationship between different function areas or subsystems.

out of control The condition when a process is being influenced by assignable causes of variation.

outsourcing Contracting with another company to do work that was once done by the organization itself.

over cycled   The situation on an assembly line when the amount of work assigned to a work station exceeds the cycle time.

P

P-kanban   A kanban that authorizes the production of more parts in a pull system.

panel of experts   An approach to forecasting that involves people who are knowledgeable about the subject. This group attempts to make a forecast by building consensus.

Pareto analysis   A procedure for identifying which problems are most important.

peak demand   The highest level of demand that can be expected during a specific time period.

PERT   A procedure for analyzing projects when activity durations may vary randomly.

periodic inventory system   A system in which inventory level is checked only at certain regular intervals. Orders are usually placed to bring inventory back up to a predetermined level.

perpetual inventory system   A system in which inventory level is continuously monitored and a replenishment order placed when inventory reaches a predetermined level.

pessimistic time (b)   The longest time a project activity would normally take.

piece-rate plan   An employee compensation plan in which pay is based on the number of units produced.

plan   A list of actions that management expects to take. A plan is a basis for allocating the organization's resources to deal with opportunities and problems present in the environment.

plan-do-check-act cycle   A problem solving process used for continuous improvement, also called Deming Wheel or Shewhart Cycle.

planned order release   An order to either the shop or a supplier, planned to be released for a given amount during a time bucket in MRP.

planned receipts   In MRP, a quantity expected to be received in a given time bucket based on an order that is planned, but not yet released.

planning horizon   A length of time into the future for which plans are developed.

planning the system   Defines the way in which an organization expects its physical facilities, people, and materials to meet projected customer demand and the organization's objectives.

point-of-sale (POS)   Data coming directly from the cash registers in a store.

poka-yoke   An approach adopted by many companies to prevent defects. The term is a rough approximation of Japanese words that mean mistake proofing.

postindustrial   Characterized by increasing global, complex, and uncertain markets and the rapid development and spread of technology world-wide.

precedence diagram   A series of nodes that represent activities and arcs or lines which indicate the sequence of operations.

preemptive pricing   A strategy based on the learning curve that involves short-term losses but long-term gains.

prevention costs   Quality costs that result from activities to prevent defects from occurring, such as employee training, quality control procedures, special efforts in designing products, or administrative systems to prevent defects.

proactive strategy   A strategy that emphasizes efforts to modify the environment, rather than simply reacting to it.

probability-based simulation   Simulation in which values of certain variables vary randomly according to some probability distribution.

process   Describes "how to."

process batch   The number of units of a given part that are processed consecutively on a given machine or work center.

process capability   A measure of the ability of a process to consistently maintain specifications.

process capability index, C_p   A value that indicates process capability.

process design   Describes how the product will be made.

process generator   A mathematical function that generates random numbers according to a given probability distribution.

process layout   Equipment is grouped or arranged by the type of process that the machine performs such as all drilling equipment in one location.

process postponement   Certain steps in the production process are delayed until the last possible moment such that the finished product will be produced only after customer orders have been received.

process selection   A series of decisions that include technical or engineering issues and volume or scale issues. The result determines how the services and/or goods will be produced.

process technology   The application of knowledge to improve the process.

producer's risk   In acceptance sampling, the probability of rejecting a lot of acceptable material.

product   Can be either a good or a service.

product design   The determination of the characteristics and features of the product, i.e., how does it function?

product development   A process to generate concepts, designs, and plans for services and goods that an organization can provide for its customers.

product facility strategy   One facility is responsible for producing one product or product line and shipping that product all over the country and around the world.

product flow analysis (PFA)   A method for determining families of parts. In this systematic analysis, the production sequence for each part, the machining operations for each part, and the characteristics of the material are used. From these data, similarities can be determined and parts can be divided into families.

product layout   The physical arrangement of facilities so that products move along one path. Resources are arranged around this path to minimize material movement, reduce material handling costs, and eliminate delays in production.

product life cycle A series of stages that products pass through. They include development, growth, maturity/saturation, and decline.

product mix Is the percent of total demand or output that is devoted to each product.

product postponement A generic product is produced at the central manufacturing facility, then specific components needed to customize the product for the final consumer are added at the latest possible point in the distribution system.

product technology The application of knowledge to improve the product.

production kanban A kanban that authorizes the production of more parts in a pull system.

production scheduling *See scheduling.*

productivity Output from an activity divided by total input to the activity.

profit point The number of units that must be produced and sold at a given contribution per unit in order to cover fixed costs plus profit. The break-even point is a special case of the profit point where target profit is zero.

program evaluation and review technique (PERT) A procedure for analyzing projects when activity durations may vary randomly.

project Is a process for making one-of-a-kind products. Most large construction jobs are projects. Many service jobs can be categorized as projects. Installing new computer hardware, adding major new computer software, or implementing a new management planning and control system all could qualify as projects.

project buffer Extra time allowed at the end of a project in Critical Chain Scheduling and Buffer Management to ensure the project is completed on time even if delays occur.

projected ending inventory In MRP, the inventory level expected to be on hand at the end of a time bucket.

prototype A model of a product. It could be a working model, a model

reduced in scale, or a mock-up of the product.

pull system An approach to manufacturing in which materials are pulled through processing based on actual requirements for those materials.

purchasing The activity of acquiring services and goods for the organization. It includes all the activities necessary for filling the organization's long and short-term needs.

purchase order An authorization for a vendor to supply parts or materials.

pure strategies Three strategies for medium-range operations planning: vary the workforce, vary workforce utilization, and use inventory to absorb demand fluctuations.

push system An approach to manufacturing that forces materials through processing based on a schedule.

Q

quality May have definitions that are either internal or external to a company, but defined most often today as consistently meeting or exceeding customer needs and expectations.

quality function deployment A procedure for spreading the voice of the customer throughout a company in determining how products should be designed and processes operated.

queue A waiting line.

queue time The time a job spends waiting to be processed at a work center.

quick response (QR) An approach to supply chain management that focuses on emphasizing the ability to respond quickly to changes in demand or consumer preferences.

R

random causes of variation Sources of process variation that are inherent in a process, also known as common causes or chance causes.

rating factor How fast or slow the worker being observed in a time study performed the task in relation to an average worker.

raw materials inventories Goods purchased and stored for later use in the production process.

reactive strategy A planning strategy that merely responds to the environment.

regional facility strategy Each facility is assigned a market area and each facility produces a complete line of products for that area.

registered The next step after a company is certified under ISO 9000:2000, in which it is listed in a directory of certified companies.

registrar A company that is accredited to audit companies for possible ISO 9000:2000 certification.

regression analysis A method to predict the value of one variable based on the value of one or more variables. It is based on minimizing squared distances from the data points to the estimated regression line.

rejection number In acceptance sampling using MIL-STD-105D, the minimum number nonconforming in the sample that are required for rejection of the lot.

relative advantage The difference between the lowest-cost producer and the next-lowest-cost producer.

reliability The length of time that a product will function before it fails.

request for quotes A notice that indicates that an organization wants to gather price information for the purpose of making a purchase.

revenue sharing A supply chain approach in which the retailer's revenue is shared between it and its supplier, in return for the supplier providing the product at a lower cost.

reverse logistics The functions in a supply chain that return defective products to the manufacturer for repair or replacement.

resource buffer A procedure used in Critical Chain Scheduling and Buffer Management to ensure a resource needed for a critical path activity will be available when that activity begins.

responsive supply chain A type of supply chain that focuses on quickly responding to changes in demand for various products.

review interval (R) The time between one review of inventory and the next in a periodic review inventory control system.

robot A reprogrammable, multifunctional manipulator designed to move materials, parts, tools or specialized devices through variable programmed motions for the performance of a variety of tasks.

robust design Product design that guarantees high quality regardless of variations that might occur in the processes that produce the product and provide it to the customer.

rolling through time A planning concept that conceptualizes time as a scroll. As time passes, the scroll keeps getting rolled up on the end closest to us and unrolled at the other end

rope A term used in theory of constraints to indicate methods of communication between the drum and other machines or work centers.

rough-cut capacity planning Used to determine whether sufficient overall production capacity will exist to meet the master production schedule.

rounding out capacity Adding capacity to a bottleneck department to increase the capacity of a system by bringing the capacity of the bottleneck department into balance with the other departments.

routing A sequence of machines or processes in which a part travels in order to be properly finished.

routing sheet A document used in manufacturing to indicate the sequence of operations, machines, or work centers that a part or product must follow.

run-out time The period of time before a company will run out of a particular product.

run time Actual processing time for a job.

S

safety stock An extra amount added to the order point as a buffer against stockout possibilities.

sales and operations planning An aggregate planning approach that coor-

dinates the plans of both marketing and operations, attempting to meet the objectives of both.

Scanlon plan Employees are rewarded for their cost reduction efforts. Any reduction in the labor cost per unit of output is reflected in an employee bonus, which is based on a ratio of total labor costs to the value of output.

scheduled receipts In MRP, a quantity for which an order has already been released and which is planned for receipt during a given time bucket.

scheduling A final, detailed determination of the times employees will work, the sequence in which goods or services will be provided, and the operating times for machines.

selected time The average time it took the worker being observed in a time study to perform the task.

sequencing A step in the scheduling process in which the ordering of jobs or work is determined.

service level The percentage of inventory replenishment orders that are received before a stockout occurs.

service parts Parts that are ordered and produced as replacement parts in units already sold.

services Intangible products.

setup The preparation of a machine to perform the required operations on a part.

setup time The time to get a machine ready to process a job.

seven basic quality control tools Used to control processes, collect and analyze data. These include control charts, check sheets, histograms and graphs, Pareto charts, cause-effect diagrams, and scatter diagrams.

short-range planning Goes up to about six months into the future.

shop order An order for more parts to be produced in a company's own fabrication facilities.

simple regression analysis Regression analysis that uses only one variable (independent variable) to predict a single dependent variable.

sigma (Σ) A value that describes the dispersion (variability) of a variable.

simplex method A mathematical procedure, usually programmed on a computer, for solving linear programming problems.

simulation The use of mathematical procedures to represent a real system.

single-card kanban system A pull system that uses only the C-kanban. Actual production may be scheduled using MRP.

single-sample plan An approach to acceptance sampling in which a decision is made regarding a lot based only on a single sample from that lot.

six sigma quality A measure of process performance that means only 3.4 defects will occur in every million units produced, or 99.9997% error free. However, the term six sigma actually refers to a broader range of defect prevention strategies.

slack time A figure representing how much leeway each activity in a project has in its starting time or duration.

sociopsychological factors Includes more than just how a job is done, but also how the employee feels about that job.

special causes of variation Causes of variation in the output of a process that can be assigned to factors such as tool wear, material from different suppliers, etc.

specification limits The limits placed on output from a process so that items falling between the limits are considered acceptable while ones outside are unacceptable.

stakeholders Groups of people that are affected by a decision; that is, they have a stake in the decision. In a business organization, stakeholders would include stockholders, management, labor, consumers, and the general public.

standard container A container used in pull systems to control inventory. Each standard container holds a specified number of units.

standard error of the coefficient A standard deviation for a coefficient estimated by regression analysis.

standard error of the estimate A measure of the amount of scatter around the regression line. It is the difference between each observed value, Y_o, and the estimated value, Y_e.

standard-hour system   In an incentive plan, each job has a standard time. Whenever an employee performs that job, they are paid based on the standard time—regardless of how long it actually took them to do the job.

standard time   Expressed in terms of time per unit (e.g., 3.75 minutes per part) or units per time period (e.g., 16 parts per hour). This represents the time it should take to perform a task under ordinary conditions, allowing for rest periods, fatigue, and other unavoidable delays.

statistical control   A condition in which a process is influenced only by random causes of variation.

statistical process control (SPC)   The use of statistical methods to determine when a process is out of control before defects are produced.

statistical quality control (SQC)   The use of statistical methods to avoid accepting or producing defects.

steady-state conditions   Conditions that prevail in a system after any start-up variations have disappeared.

stock buffer   Inventory maintained in a drum-buffer-rope system to ensure that material flow is not disrupted.

stockout   A condition that occurs when no more inventory of an item is left.

strategic profit model   An approach to performance measurement in a supply chain that relates activities to return on assets.

strategy   Consists of the organizational goals and the methods for implementing the goals, called key policies. Strategy defines how an organization chooses to compete within the framework dictated by the external environment.

sub-contracting   Buying parts or sub-assemblies from outside suppliers.

supplier   The seller of a service or good. A supplier is sometimes referred to as a vendor.

supplier certification   The verification of supplier performance in various categories such as quality, lead time, and reliability in meeting promised delivery dates.

supply chain   Includes all activities associated with the flow and transfer of goods and services from raw material extraction through use by the organization that sells to the final consumer.

supply chain management   The integration of supply chain activities through improved supplier relationships to achieve sustainable competitive advantage for all members in the supply chain

supply inventories   Materials that are not part of the finished product but are consumed either in production or in tasks in other departments.

survey   A systematic effort to elicit information from specific groups and is usually conducted via a written questionnaire or phone interview.

synergy   Cooperative (teamwork) actions where the actions taken together have a greater effect than the sum of the individual effects. The whole is greater than the sum of its parts.

synthesis   Putting the parts or elements together to form a whole. In analysis, each part is examined and answers to questions are determined. In synthesis, the parts are combined in a way that addresses the interaction between those parts. The concept behind synthesis is to make the best decision for overall performance of a system, not to optimize one part.

system   A group of items, events, or actions in which no item, event, or action occurs independently of at least one other. Accordingly, no item that is studied in isolation will act in the same way it would in the normal environment.

system cycle time   Refers to a series of operations or departments linked in a line flow process. It is the time between the nth unit and the $n + 1$ unit existing the line. It is determined by the department with the longest cycle time.

systematic layout planning   Use codes that describe the importance of having two departments close together to arrive at an appropriate job shop layout.

T

t-value   The calculated t-statistic used in hypothesis testing.

tabular method   A method for aggregate planning that utilizes a table based on the transportation method.

tacit judgment   A method for determining families of parts. It involves the visual review of design drawings and specifications for similarities. This process is usually easy to do and can result in good families of parts, if relatively few parts are involved.

Taguchi methods   Experimental design techniques used to identify those factors that cause output from a process to deviate from a target value.

tariff   Extra charges placed on goods or services that are imported into the home country.

task   A clearly defined activity that makes up a job.

technology   The application of knowledge, usually in the form of recently developed tools, processes, and procedures, to solve problems.

test market   Is a special kind of survey. The forecaster arranges for the placement of a new product or an existing product that has been modified. Data on actual sales are collected.

theory of constraints (TOC)   A manufacturing philosophy that identifies the most constrained resources and then plans production to optimize utilization of those resources.

third party logistics (3PL)   An outside supplier handles all the logistics activities between supplier and customer.

throughput time   Is the time from the receipt of a customer's order until the order is shipped.

tier 1 suppliers   Companies in a supply chain that sell component parts to the manufacturer that makes the finished product.

tier 2 suppliers   Companies in a supply chain that sell component parts or raw materials to a tier 1 supplier.

tier 3 suppliers   Companies in a supply chain that usually sell raw materials to a tier 2 supplier.

time-based competition   A strategy of seeking competitive advantage by quickening the tempo of critical organizational processes such as product development and order fulfillment.

time bucket   A period of time, usually a week, in which demand and requirements are grouped for master scheduling and material requirements planning.

time buffer   Inventory maintained in a drum-buffer-rope system to ensure that the bottleneck is not shut down for lack of materials if feeding work centers shut down.

time measurement unit (TMU)   Equal to .00001 hour, or .036 seconds.

time standard   Same as standard time.

time phasing   The process used in material requirements planning of determining requirements by time period.

TMU (time measurement unit)   Equal to .00001 hour, or .036 seconds.

tolerance limits   The limits placed on output from a process so that items falling between the limits are considered acceptable while ones outside are unacceptable.

total factor productivity   Productivity calculated based on all inputs of labor, capital, materials, and services.

total preventive maintenance   An approach to equipment maintenance that emphasizes prevention of breakdowns, maintenance each day, and operator responsibility for maintenance.

total quality management (TQM)   An organizational commitment to continuously improve in meeting or exceeding customer needs and expectations.

trade embargoes   Eliminate trade between two countries for a period of time. Trade could be eliminated entirely or in a specific product or product line.

transfer batch The number of units of a given part that are transferred at one time from one machine or work center to another.

transfer line   A sophisticated set of machines that are able to perform a complex set of operations without human operators. Transfer lines have very limited flexibility. A transfer line in the automotive industry can take a raw casting of an engine block in one end

and produce a machined engine block from the other without operator intervention. However, the same transfer line cannot produce eight, six, and four cylinder engines.

Type I error   An error in acceptance sampling in which a good lot is rejected.

Type II   error An error in acceptance sampling in which a bad lot is accepted.

U

upper control limit (UCL)   The upper limit of a control chart indicating the maximum value below which sample values would normally be expected to fall under random variation.

U-shaped layout   A layout of facilities or equipment in the shape of a U. This layout improves teamwork, reduces material handling, and provides better flow of materials.

upper specification limit   Same as upper tolerance limit.

upper tolerance limit   The upper limit of acceptability for some measure specified in a product design.

upstream   A designation for that part of the supply chain that includes suppliers, production planning, and purchasing.

V

vendor   The seller or supplier of a service or good.

vendor managed inventory (VMI)   A supplier manages inventory management decisions of the products it sells for the company that buys those products.

vertical expansion of the job   Giving workers responsibility for planning many of their own activities and, to some extent, allowing them to make decisions related to the job they are performing.

vertical loading   Giving workers responsibility for planning many of their own activities and, to some extent, allowing them to make decisions related to the job they are performing.

virtual corporation   A company that provides only coordination activities,

outsourcing all other activities involved in producing and distributing a product.

visual inspection   When referring to group technology see the definition for tacit judgment.

voice of the customer   A concept in product design to determine what the customer wants, likes, and doesn't like in the product.

W

wait time   The time a job spends waiting before being moved to the next work center.

WIP   A term used to denote work-in-process inventory.

work centers   *See workstations.*

work cycle   One repetition of a repetitive job task.

work improvement   Methods and techniques concerned only with the physiological aspects of a job—how easy the job is to do, how quickly the person can work.

work-in-process inventories   Products that the organization has partially completed.

work measurement   A tool that is used to determine the amount of time a work activity, or task, should take under ordinary conditions.

work sampling   Used in developing an estimate of the percentage of time a worker spends on different activities.

workstations   Places where individuals perform tasks on a product.

worker-customer chart   A chart used in methods analysis to study the interactions of workers and customers.

worker-machine chart   A chart used in methods analysis to study the interactions of workers and machines.

Y

yield   The ratio of the quantity of output to the quantity of input.

yield management   A proactive strategy that varies price in response to demand so as to maximize revenue.

INDEX

A

ABC inventory analysis, 350–351
activity-based costing (ABC), 387–388
activity matrices, 245, 261–263, 266, 269, 270
activity-on-arc (AOA) network diagrams, 436–437
activity-on-node (AON) representations, 435–437
activity times, estimating, 442
aggregate planning
  overview, 286–287
  cost considerations, 293–294
  global issues, 291–292
  graphs and, 300–302
  inventory issues, 290, 297
  JIT and, 384
  mathematical procedures and, 302–304
  medium-range operations planning, 287–292
  MPS and, 313–315
  order-winning criteria, 290–291
  in organizational contexts, 288–289, 291
  process selection and, 289–290
  in service organizations, 294–295, 298–300
  strategies for meeting demand, 292–295
  workforce strategies, 296–298
Air-Temp Corporation, 6
Alabama, state of, 226
Alber, Karen L., 110
Allen-Bradley, 46, 165
Allied Waste Industries, 107
Amazon.com, 45
American Airlines, 43, 295
analyses
  ABC inventory, 350–351
  correlation, 144–151

economic, 123
location, 233
market, 121–122
product flow, 259
regression, 144–151
SWOT, 29, 38
system capacity, 199–208
AOA (activity-on-arc), 436–437
AON (activity-on-node), 435–437
appraisal costs, 75
arcs. *See activity*-on-arc (AOA) network diagrams
Armour 269–270
asbestos litigation, 17
assembly lines
  balancing, 247–257, 412
  facility layout, 246–258
  process, 172–176
  scheduling, 412
assembly schedules, 384–385
automation, 46, 52, 65, 180
  See also information technology; technology
available-to-promise quantities, 317–318
average inventory investment, 350

B

B2B (business-to-business), 36–37, 105–106
B2C (business-to-consumer), 36, 37–38, 104–105
backflushing, 388
backlogs, 294, 298–300
backward scheduling, 420–421
backward vertical integration, 97–98
Badger Meters, 178
Baldrige Award, 86–87, 88
bar codes and scanners, 100, 101–102, 348–349
batch flow processes, 172, 176–177, 258, 394–395, 396, 412–413
benchmarking, 83–84

BEP (break-even point), 166
Berry, Leonard, 72–73
Best Buy, 163–164
Biema 55
bill of materials files, 325, 327
Blockbuster, 103–104
blue-collar workforce, 54
Boeing, 222
Bose, 101
bottlenecks, 201–208, 394–395, 397
branches. See activity-on-arc (AOA) network diagrams
break-even point (BEP), 166
British Standards Institute (BSI), 88–89
  See also International Organization for Standardization (ISO)
Browne, Jim, 426
BSI (British Standards Institute), 88–89
Buffa 269–270
buffers, 396–398, 448–451
buildup method of forecasting, 138
bullwhip effect, 94–95
Burger King, 424–425
business function, 18, 20–22
business plan, 18
business processes, 18, 20–22, 29–30, 38–39, 65
business-to-business (B2B), 36–37, 105–106
business-to-consumer (B2C), 36, 37–38, 104–105

C

CAD (computer-aided design), 46
Campbell Soup Company, 292
capacity
  definition and overview, 192–193
  adding, 208–211
  adjusting, 211–212, 425
  bottlenecks, 201–208, 394–395, 397
  for competitive advantage, 208–212
  determined by cycle time, 252–253

estimating, 193–199
finite capacity scheduling, 422–423
improving, 194–199
process selection and product design, 160–164
rough-cut capacity planning, 320–323, 324, 332–334
in service operations, 206–208
system analysis, 199–208
capacity requirements planning (CRP), 320–323, 324, 332–334
See also capacity
capital productivity, 57
carrying costs, 352, 353, 355
CC/BM (Critical Chain scheduling and Buffer Management), 448–451
cellular manufacturing, 174, 177–179, 259–261
certification process, ISO, 88–89
See also International Organization for Standardization (ISO)
changeover time, 172, 176–177, 394–395, 396
See also setup time
chase demand, 424–425
Chrysler Corp., 11, 36–37
Ciba, 16
CIM (computer-integrated manufacturing), 46
Cisco, 105
Citibank, 164
classification and coding schemes, 260
closed-loop MRP, 335
See also material requirements planning (MRP)
coding and classification schemes, 260
coefficient of correlation, 144–151
Cognitive Systems, Inc., 44
collaborative planning forecasting and replenishment (CPFR), 96
competitive advantage
overview, 28–30
business processes, 29–30, 38–39
capabilities, 31–38
capacity and, 208–212
customer requirements and, 30–31
customer service and , 121
facility layout and , 271–272
global issues, 11–12, 43, 94
information technology and, 43–48
strategy development and operations, 39–42
SWOT analysis, 29, 38
teamwork and, 38
Composite Container Corporation, 258

computer-aided design (CAD), 46
computer-based production planning and control systems, 46
computer-integrated manufacturing (CIM), 46
Computer Method of Sequencing Operations for Assembly Lines (COMSOAL), 257
Computerized Relative Allocation of Facilities Technique (CRAFT), 269–270
computers, use of. See information technology
COMSOAL (Computer Method of Sequencing Operations for Assembly Lines), 257
concurrent engineering, 10
concurrent processes, 125–127
constraints, impact of, 392–393
See also theory of constraints
continuous flow processes, 172–176, 245–246, 246, 411
continuous improvement, 84–85
continuous review system, 349
contribution per unit, 166
corporate strategy and operations strategy, 39–42
correlation analysis, 144–151
cost, revenue and time model, 227–228
cost drivers, 388
cost-volume-profit (C-V-P) model, 165–172
costs
aggregate planning and, 293–294
crash time and, 445–448
determinants of, 121, 123, 128–130
the ideal product, 34–35
international labor, 61–62
inventory, 351–358
location, impact on, 223–225
mass customization and, 184–185
minimization of, using JIT, 391
normal time and, 445–448
ordering, 351–358
projections using MRP II, 336
trade-offs, 160, 445–448
volume, impact on, 161–163
costs of quality, 74–76
CPFR (collaborative planning forecasting and replenishment), 96
CPM. See critical path method (CPM)
CRAFT (Computerized Relative Allocation of Facilities Technique), 269–270
crash time/costs, 445–448

Critical Chain scheduling and Buffer Management (CC/BM), 448–451
critical path method (CPM), 434, 437–441, 444, 445–448
critical ratio rule, 415
CRM. See customer relationship management (CRM)
Crosby, Philip, 76–77
cross docking, 100, 104
CRP. See capacity requirements planning (CRP)
currency fluctuations and labor costs, 62
customer relationship management (CRM), 36, 37–38
customer requirements, 20–22, 29, 30–31, 36, 37–38, 78–81, 121
customer service, 121
customization, mass, 174, 182–186
cycle counting, 326–327
cycle time, 249–253, 386–387

D

DaimlerChrysler, 11, 36–37, 226
Dataglove, 45–46
days of inventory, 350
decision support systems (DSS), 44
decline stage, mature products, 118
delayed differentiation (product postponement), 102
delivery dependability, 390
Dell Computer Company, 38, 75, 104, 105, 184, 271
Delphi Technique, 139
demand
dependent versus independent, 324–325
strategies for meeting, 292–295, 424–427
demand forecasts 288–289
demand management process 320, 321
Deming, W. Edwards, 76, 77
Deming Prize, 76, 86
Deming Wheel, 85
dependent demand inventory 324
dependent variable 144
design for manufacture and assembly (DFMA), 78
design for operations (DFO), 78
designing products for goods and services, 7
developing countries, productivity and labor costs, 61–62
development and testing phase
See also product development
development and testing phase of

product development, 117, 124
Devilbiss Corporation, 43
DFMA (design for manufacture and assembly), 78
DFO (design for operations), 78
differentiated products, 30
digital loyalty networks, 96
disintermediation, 98–99
Disney Cruise Line, 65
dispatching, 409, 418–423
dispatching rules, 414–415
distribution requirements planning (DRP), 337–338
distribution resource planning, 338
documentation and standardization procedures, 84–85
dot-com companies, 105
    See also e-commerce
Downey Carpet Cleaning, 198
downsizing, 20–22
downstream supply chain 97
Dresser, 17
DRP (distribution requirements planning), 337–338
drum, buffer, and rope 396–398
DSS (decision support systems), 44
dummy activities, 436–437
DuPont, 434

E

e-commerce, 36–38, 104–107
    See also dot-com companies; information technology; Internet
earliest due date rule, 414
earliest start/finish times, 437–440
eBay, 10, 127
EC (European Community), 43
echelons, supply chain 97
economic analysis 123
economic order quantity (EOQ)
    assumptions of model, 353–354
    carrying (holding) costs, 352, 353, 355
    controversy surrounding model, 358
    mathematical statement of model, 354–358
    ordering costs, 351–352, 355
    variation of model, 358–361
    See also fixed-order-interval model
economic systems 13–18
economy of scale 65, 129, 164–165, 172–174, 182, 211
economy of scope 165, 172, 174, 182
ECR (efficient consumer response), 101–104, 338

EDI (electronic data interchange), 95, 100, 101
efficient consumer response (ECR) 101–104, 338
efficient supply chains 99–100, 109–110
electronic data interchange (EDI), 95, 100, 101
EMC Corporation, 176
employees
    empowerment of, 10–11, 15, 197, 257, 383–384
    training of, 83, 185–186, 390, 425
    See also teamwork; workforce
engineering, concurrent, 10
engineering of new products, 123
engineers, knowledge, 44
enterprise resource planning (ERP), 106–107, 339
environmental issues, 15–16, 233–234
    See also ethics issues; legal issues
EOQ. See economic order quantity (EOQ)
equipment, impact on productivity, 64
Eroski, 96
ERP (enterprise resource planning), 106–107, 339
ethics issues
    in location decisions, 232–234
    in MRP, 334
    in operations, 14–18
    in process selection, 181
    in scheduling, 410–411
    See also environmental issues; legal issues
European Community (EC), 43
European Union (EU), 86
Excelsior Award, 86
exchanges, B2B 105
experience and learning, organizational, 65
expert systems, 44
exponential smoothing, 143–144, 145
external failure costs, 74–75
external supply chains 93

F

facility layout
    definition and overview, 242–244
    for assembly line processes, 246–258
    for batch processes, 258
    for competitive advantage, 271–272
    for continuous flow processes, 245–246
    JIT and, 381, 382
    for job shops, 261–271

for manufacturing cells and flexible manufacturing systems, 259–261
    for service operations, 246
facility location
    overview, 220–221
    ethics issues, 232–234
    global issues, 230–233
    qualitative factors, 222, 228–229, 238–241
    quantitative factors, 222–228
    for service operations, 222, 233
    socially responsible opportunities, 233–234
    as a strategic decision, 221–230
fact-based management, 83
failure costs, 74–75
Fair Labor Standards Act, 425–426
families of parts, 177–179, 259–261
FCS (finite capacity scheduling), 422–423
FedEx, 71, 116–117
feeding buffers 450
final assembly schedules 384–385
finish times, project, 437–440
finite capacity scheduling (FCS), 422–423
    See also capacity
finite loading, 420–421
Firestone, 75
first-come, first-served rule, 415
First National Bank of Oakland, 139
fixed inventory costs, 352, 353
fixed-order-interval model, 365–369
    See also economic order quantity (EOQ)
flexibility
    capacity requirements and, 193, 196–197
    in mass customization, 182–183
    of the operation, 31–33
    of the product, 389
    of volume, 390
flexible manufacturing systems (FMS), 46, 177–180, 259–261, 413–414
Flint Auto Stamping, 32–33
flow manufacturing, 374–375
FMS. See flexible manufacturing systems (FMS)
focused factories, 42, 181–182
Ford Motor Company, 12, 17, 75, 98, 104, 120
forecasting
    definition and overview, 132, 135–137
    accuracy and errors, 95–96, 151–152

CPFR, 96
demand forecasts, 288–289
qualitative methods, 138–139
regression and correlation analysis, 144–151
time-series methods, 139–144
See also formulas; models
foreign countries. *See* global issues
formulas
adjacent departments, 267
available-to-promise quantity, 318
capacity, 194
cost-volume-profit, 165–166
critical ratio, 415
cycle time, 252
expected time, 442
exponential smoothing, 143
inventory management
annual variable holding costs, 355
annual variable ordering costs, 355
days of inventory, 350
economic order quantity, 355–356
inventory turnover ratio, 350
lot size with quantity discounts, 359
optimal review interval, 366
order point, 362
order-up-to level, 367
projected on-hand inventory, 315–316
safety stock, 365
labor productivity, 57
method of overall factors, 321
multiple-factor productivity, 559
multiple regression, 150
operating ratio, 194
production rate, 194
production rates for assembly lines, 252
productivity, 51
profit, 165
simple moving average, 140–141
simple regression, 144–145
standard error of the estimate, 148
total cost, 162, 223
total revenue, 165, 226
volume, 166
weighted contribution, 168
weighted moving average, 142–143
yield, 198
z transformation, 443–444
See also forecasting; models; rules
forward buying, 101
forward scheduling, 419–422
forward vertical integration 98
Four Seasons Hotels, 71

14 Points for the Transformation of Management (Deming), 77
freezing the master schedule, 319–320
French food industry, environmental issues 16
function *versus* process, 20–22
functional areas, 18
functional (efficient) supply chains 99–100, 109–110

G

G-7 countries, productivity and labor costs 61–62
Gantt charts, 422, 434
Garvin, David, 73–74
GATT (General Agreement on Tariffs and Trade), 11–12
See also global issues; NAFTA
General Electric, 75–76
Genoa Ford, 40
Giant Food Company, 338
global issues
in aggregate planning, 291–292
expansion, building volume through, 164
labor costs and currency fluctuations, 61–62
in location decisions, 230–233
performance measures, 83–84, 108–109, 111
in product development, 119–120
in supply chain management, 94, 109–110
trade and competition, 11–12, 43, 94
See also GATT; NAFTA
Goldratt, Eliyahu, 391, 448
goods
defined, 4–7
dimensions of quality, 73–74
government incentives, 225–226
government organization and operations, 13–18
graphs, use of, 300–302
Greenwald 55
gross requirements, 327
group technology 177–178, 259–261, 414
growth rates, productivity, 60
growth stage, product development, 118

H

Halliburton, 17
Harley-Davidson, 374
Hayes, Robert, 172
health care industry, 179, 212

Henkel, 96
Hershey Chocolate, 107
Hewlett-Packard, 35–36, 185, 358
hierarchical production planning (HPP), 291, 292
holding costs 352, 353, 355
hospital requirements planning (HRP), 336–337
house of quality, 79–81, 130
HPP (hierarchical production planning), 291
HRP (hospital requirements planning), 336–337
human resources 66
See also employees

I

the ideal product, 34–35
idle time, 250
indented bill of materials files, 325, 327
independent demand inventory, 324, 347
independent variable, 144
infinite loading, 420–421
information technology
assembly line balancing, 257
competitive advantage through, 43–48
job shop layouts, 269–270
manufacturing, 45, 46
operations, 9–10, 43–46
productivity improvements, 65, 66–67
service operations, 9–10, 47–48
supply chain management, 36–38, 94–96, 104–107
See also Internet; technology
initial assessment phase, 121–122
See also product development
innovative (responsive) supply chains, 99–100, 110
input
defined, 4
measurement of, 55–59
See also input/output reports
input/output reports, 423
insourcing, 97
inspection
family of parts, 259
product, 130
intangible products *versus* tangible products, 4, 6
Intel, 129, 199
intellectual workforce, 54
interest groups, 13–14

intermediaries, 98–99
internal failure costs, 74–75
internal supply chains, 93, 97
International Labor Organization, 181, 232
International Organization for Standardization (ISO), 84, 86, 87–89
Internet
    productivity, impact on, 66–67
    service and manufacturing operations and, 44–46, 47
    supply chain and, 36–38, 104–107
    See also Amazon.com; eBay; information technology
inventory
    overview, 347–348
    aggregate planning and, 290, 297
    costs, 351–358
    demand fluctuations and, 297, 298, 299
    economic order quantity model, 351–361
    fixed-order-interval model, 365–369
    information systems for, 326–327, 348–351
    just-in-case, 323
    make-to-order versus make-to-stock, 290
    material requirements planning, 323–332
    on-hand, 315–317
    operations problems hidden by, 376, 377, 388
    in service operations, 6–7, 294–295
    stockouts and safety stock, 361–365
    in supply chains, 111
    turnover ratio, 350
    See also formulas, inventory management; material requirements planning (MRP)
inventory file, 326–327
ISO 9000:2000, 84, 86, 87–89
    See also International Organization for Standardization (ISO)

J

Japanese automotive industry in North America, 231–232
Japanese plant, pollution prevention, 16
Jeep, 11
JIT. See just-in-time (JIT)
JIT II, 101, 391
job design and work measurement, 66
job shops, 173, 179–180, 261–271, 269–270, 414–418

Johnson's Rule, 416–418
Juran, Joseph M., 76
just-in-case inventory control, 323
just-in-time (JIT)
    definition and overview, 373–374
    combined/compared with MRP and TOC, 398–399
    fundamental concepts, 374–377
    JIT II, 101, 391
    lean systems, 391
    planning, 384–387
    production and, 375–376, 381–384, 388
    pull system, 378–381
    role of MIS, 387–388
    in service operations, 388–389

K

kaizen, 84–85
kanban systems, 378–381
key policies, 18
knowledge engineers, 44
Kroger Supermarkets, 47

L

labor costs and currency fluctuations, global issues, 61–62
labor laws and organizations, 181, 232, 425–426
labor productivity, 56–57
labor relations, 10–11, 15, 257
    See also unions, labor
LaCourtier expert system, 44
Lands' End, 105, 347
late completion of projects, 439–440
latest start/finish times, 438–440
launch phase, product development, 124
layout decisions. See facility layout
lead time, 361–365
lean systems, 373, 391
learning and experience, corporate, 65
legal issues, 14–18, 127
    See also environmental issues; ethics issues
leisure time, 63
level assembly schedules 385
leverage, 159, 169–172
liability, product, 127
Lima (Ohio) Fire Department, 6
line flow 172–176, 411–414
L.L. Bean, 83
load profiles/reports, 333, 335, 421
    See also capacity requirements planning (CRP)
loading, 418–422
location decisions. See facility location
logistics, 93, 97, 104, 110–111

long-range operations planning, 287
longest processing time rule, 414–415
lot-for-lot, 329
low-level coding, 325, 327
Lucas County, Ohio, 226
Lucent Technologies, 434

M

machine constrained operations, 197–198
machine loading, 418–422
MAD (mean absolute deviation), 152
Maine Woods Company, 313–318, 321–323, 325–327, 329–335
make-to-order versus make-to-stock, 290, 408
makespan time, 416–418
Malcolm Baldrige National Quality Award (MBNQA) 86–87, 88
manufactured goods. See goods
manufacturing cells 174, 177–179, 259–261
manufacturing operations, 4, 5–7, 43–46, 54–55
    See also operations
manufacturing resource planning (MRP II), 335–336, 337
Marco's Pizza, 175–176
market analysis, 121–122
market changes, 33
market research, 20
market share, 28–29
market surveys, 124
marketing
    aggregate planning, 288
    interface with operations, 19–20
    research and analysis, 20, 28–29, 33, 121–122, 124, 139
Marriott Hotels, 75
mass customization, 174, 182–186
mass production, 164–165, 172–174, 176, 182
    See also process selection
Massachusetts Institute of Technology, 45–46
master production schedules (MPS)
    overview, 312–313
    aggregate plan and, 312–315
    capacity requirements planning, 320–323, 324, 332–334
    customer orders and, 315–318
    demand management, 320
    development of, 313–314
    freezing, 319–320
    integration with other functional

areas, 319
iterative process, 319
JIT and, 384
in service organizations, 318
time horizon, 313
See also scheduling
master schedule files, 325
material productivity, 57
material requirements planning (MRP)
overview, 323
capacity and, 332–334
closed-loop MRP, 335
combined/compared with JIT and TOC, 398–399
data files used, 325–327
dependent *versus* independent demand, 324–325
dispatching rules, 418–423
ethics issues, 334
logic, 328–329
planned order releases, 327–330
purchasing and operations coordination, 331–332
in service organizations, 336–337
tables for, 328, 330–331
See also inventory
materials, movement of, 376
mathematical procedures, 302–304, 354–358
See also formulas
matrices. *See* activity matrices
maturity/saturation stage, product development, 118
MBNQA (Malcolm Baldrige National Quality Award), 86–87, 88
McDonald's, 78, 110, 129, 389
mean absolute deviation (MAD), 152
mean squared error (MSE), 151–152
medium-range operations planning. *See* aggregate planning
Meijer, 192–193
Mellon Bank, 48
Merck & Company, 48, 172–173
Microsoft, 8, 61, 106
Midas, 40
Minnesota Mining and Manufacturing Company, 16
MIS
JIT and, 387–388
planning and, 339
mixed aggregate planning strategies, 298, 299, 300–301
mixed-model sequencing, 385–386
models
definition and overview, 132–135

cost, revenue and time, 227–228
cost-volume-profit, 165–172
economic order quantity, 351–361
fixed-order-interval, 365–369
moving averages, 140–144, 145
multiple regression, 150–151
objective function, 263
regression analysis, 144–151
simple regression, 145–150
strategic profit, 108–109
See also forecasting; formulas; rules
Modine Manufacturing Company, 37
modular design, 128
money and productivity, 53–54
Montgomery County, Pennsylvania, 47
mortality, product, 124–125
motivation, 197, 257
See also employees
Motorola, 71, 75–76, 82–83
move time, 418
moving averages, 140–144, 145
MPS. *See* master production schedules (MPS)
Mr. Coffee Concepts, 98
MRO hubs (B2B), 106
MRP. *See* material requirements planning (MRP)
MRP II. *See* manufacturing resource planning (MRP II)
MSE (mean squared error), 151
multiple factor productivity, 59–60
multiple-product companies, 167–169
multiple regression model, 150

N

NAFTA (North American Free Trade Agreement), 11–12, 43, 211, 232
See also GATT; global issues
National Park Service, 64
net requirements, 327–329
network representations of project management, 435–437
New York Telephone, 55
nodes. *See* activity-on-node (AON) representations
normal time and costs, 445–448
North American Free Trade Agreement (NAFTA). *See* NAFTA
Northwestern Mutual, 55

O

objective function model, 263
Ohio, State of, 226
on-hand inventory, 315–317
on-site *versus* off-site expansions, 230
operations

definition and overview, 3–5, 7–11
flexibility, 31–33
information technology and, 9–10, 43–46
legal and ethics issues, 14–18
manufacturing *versus* service, 5–7
marketing interface with, 19–20
part of the organization, 4, 7–8, 12–13, 18–23
purchasing and, 331–332
systems approach to, 12–13, 22–23
teamwork and, 10–11
TOC and, 394–395
operations management, 5, 22–23
operations strategy and corporate strategy, 39–42
OPT® (Optimized Production Technology). *See* theory of constraints (TOC)
Oracle, 105
Orbitz, 99
order entry, 408
order fulfillment, 39
order point, 349, 361–362
order releases, 327–330
order-up-to level, 367–368, 369
order-winning criteria, 290–291
ordering costs, 351–352, 355
orders released for production, 409
organizational learning, 65–66, 185–186
organizational structure, 19
organizations
defined, 3
manufacturing *versus* service, 5–7
as part of economic and government systems, 13–18
role of, 52–55
output
defined, 4
measurement of, 55–59, 61
See also input/output reports
outsourcing, 97, 127, 296
overall factors, method of, 321
overtime, 296, 298
Owens Corning, 17, 107

P

Pacific Bell, 271–272
panel of experts forecasts (Delphi Technique), 139
paper industry, 234
Parasuraman, A., 72–73
Pareto Principle, 351
Park Plaza Hospital, 337
peak demand, 424

Penske, 104
performance measurement, 83–84, 108–109, 111
periodic inventory systems, 349
perpetual inventory systems, 349
PERT/CPM. *See* critical path method (CPM); program evaluation and review technique (PERT)
PFA. *See* product flow analysis (PFA)
Philippe, D., 426
Plan-Do-Check-Act Cycle, 85
planned order releases, 327, 328
planned receipts, 327–329
planning
    JIT and, 384–387, 389–391
    MIS and, 339
    project, 434
    See also aggregate planning; capacity requirements planning (CRP); distribution requirements planning (DRP); enterprise resource planning (ERP); hierarchical production planning (HPP); manufacturing resource planning (MRP II); material requirements planning (MRP); scheduling; strategic planning
point-of-sale (POS) systems, 96, 100, 101–102
poka-yoke, 75
postponement, product and process, 102–103
prevention costs, 75
proactive strategies for meeting demand, 292–293, 294
probability in project management, 441–444
process batch, 394–395, 396
process design, 9, 123–130
process layout, 200, 204–206
process postponement, 102–103
process redesign, 53
process selection
    definition and overview, 159–160, 173, 175
    aggregate planning and, 289–290
    alternatives
    batch flow, 172, 176–177, 258, 394–395, 396, 412–413
    focused factories, 181–182
    job shops, 173, 179–180
    line flow, 172–176
    manufacturing cells and FMSs, 174, 177–179
    mass customization, 174, 182–186

projects, 173, 180–181
    capacity and product design decisions, 160–164
    cost-volume-profit model, 165–172
    economies of scale and scope, 164–165, 172–174
    ethics issues, 181
process *versus* function, 9, 20–22
Procter & Gamble, 53, 102
product. *See* goods; services
product design, 9, 121, 123–130, 128–129, 160–164, 258
product development
    definition and overview, 38, 116, 121–127
    cost decisions, 121, 128–130
    customer service decisions, 121
    global issues, 119–120
    increasing importance of, 118–119
    product life cycles, 94, 117–118
    quality decisions, 121, 128–130
    safety and liability issues, 127
    suppliers, role of, 127–128
    teamwork, using, 120, 125–127
product facility strategy, 221–222
product flexibility, 389
product flow analysis (PFA), 259
product layout, 174, 199–204
product life cycles, 94, 117–118
product mix, 167–169, 195–196, 205–206
product mortality, 124–125
product postponement, 102
product quality, 73–74, 121, 128–130
product safety, 16–17
production process, simplifying, 375–376, 381–384, 388
production proposal components, 123
production rate, 194–199, 250
productivity
    definition and overview, 33–34, 51–55
    assessing, 55–60
    enhancing, 63–66
    JIT and, 390
    nature of work and, 54
    technology, use of, 65, 66–67
    in the U.S. and overseas, 60–63
profit point, 166–167
profits, 8
program evaluation and review technique (PERT), 434, 441–444
project buffers, 449–450
project management
    definition and overview, 173–174,

180–181, 433–434
    crashing the critical path, 445–448
    Critical Chain scheduling and Buffer Management, 448–451
    critical path method, 437–441
    network representation of project, 435–437
    planning for projects, 434
    probability with PERT, 434, 441–444
    resource requirements, balancing, 444–445
prototypes, 124
pull systems, 378–381
purchase orders, 331–332
purchasing and operations in MRP, 331–332
pure strategies for aggregate planning, 296–299
push systems, 378

Q

QFD (quality function deployment), 79–81, 130
Quadrum Corporation, 260–261
qualitative factors in the location decision, 228–229, 238–241
qualitative forecasts, 138–139
quality
    definition and overview, 71–72
    awards and standards, 86–89
    capacity increases, 198
    costs of, 74–76
    dimensions of, 72–76
    emphasis on, 376, 388–389
    the ideal product, 34–35
    of manufactured goods, 73–74
    in mass customization, 176, 182
    pioneers of quality management, 76–78
    product development decisions, 121, 128–130
    productivity and, 55
    of services, 72–73
    six sigma, 75–76
    total quality management, 78–86
quality function deployment (QFD), 79–81, 130
Quality is Free (Crosby), 76–77
quantitative factors in the location decision, 222–228
quantity discounts, 359–361
queue time, 418
quick response manufacturing, 100–101
quick response (QR) programs, 95, 100–101

R

Raghunathan, T.S., 81
reactive strategies for meeting demand, 293, 294
receipts, planned/scheduled, 327–329
regional facility strategy, 221
registrars, 88–89
    See also International Organization for Standardization (ISO)
regression analysis, 144–151
relative advantage, 11
reliability, product, 73, 74, 129, 334, 389
    See also quality
Remington-Rand, 434
requirements, gross/net, 327–329
resource buffers, 450–451
resource considerations in project management, 444–448
responsive (innovative) supply chains, 99–100, 110
revenue, cost and time model, 227–228
revenue sharing, 103
reverse logistics, 93
review interval, 366–367
revolutions in productivity, 33–34
rightsizing, 20
Ritz-Carlton Hotels, 37, 81–82
robust design, 77–78
"rolling through time," 319
rope analogy, 378–381, 396–398
rough-cut capacity planning, 320–323, 324, 332–334
rounding out capacity, 203–204
routing sheets, 333
rules
    critical ratio, 415
    dispatching, 414–415
    earliest due date, 414
    first-come, first-served, 415
    Johnson's Rule, 416–418
    longest processing time, 414–415
    shortest processing time, 414
    See also formulas; models
run-out time, 413
run time, 418
Ryder, 110–111

S

safety, product, 16–17, 127
safety stock, 362–365, 368–369
sales and operating planning, 291
SAP AG, 107
Saturn Corporation, 110–111
Sauder Woodworking Company, 16
scale factors, in process selection, 164–165, 172–174
scanners, bar code, 101–102, 348–349
scheduled receipts, 327–329
scheduling
    definition and introduction, 405–407
    dispatching in MRP, 418–423
    ethics issues, 410–411
    job shop process, 414–418
    line-flow and batch processes, 412–413
    managerial considerations, 409–410
    process overview, 407–411
    project, 433–451
    in service operations, 318, 425–427
    workforce, 425–427, 444–446
    See also master production schedules (MPS)
Segway Human Transporter, 64
Seibel Systems, 181
sequencing, 409, 412, 414–418, 422
sequential processes, 125–127
service level, 363
service operations
    defined, 4
    aggregate planning for, 294–295, 298–300
    flexibility in, 183
    information technology and, 9–10, 47–48
    inventory and, 6–7, 294–295
    JIT and, 388–389
    layout analysis, 246
    location analysis, 233
    manufacturing cells/flexible manufacturing systems, 178–179
    versus manufacturing operations, 5–7
    MRP for, 336–338
    productivity in, *versus* manufacturing operations, 54–55
    quality of, 72–73
    scheduling, 318, 425–427
    system capacity, 206–208
services and goods, compared, 4–7
setup costs. *See* ordering costs
setup time, 375–376, 381–383, 418
    See also changeover time
Shenandoah Life Insurance Company, 15
Shewhart, Walter, 76
Shewhart Cycle, 85
shop orders, 331–332
short-range operations planning, 288
shortest processing time rule, 414
Shouldice Hospital, 64
silicone breast implants, product safety issues, 17
simple moving averages, 140–142
simple regression model, 144–147
simulation, 205–206, 336, 423
six sigma, 75–76
    See also quality
slack time, 440, 446
socially responsible companies, 14–18, 233–234
Southwest Airlines, 10–11, 73, 110
spatial relationships, 229–230
specialization, 52, 53, 63–64
Sport Obermeyer, 100
stakeholders, 13–14
standard error of the coefficient, 150
standard error of the estimate, 149
standardization and documentation procedures, 84–85
Stanley Works, 232–233
start times, project, 437–440
stock buffer, 396
stockouts, 361–364
strategic planning, 38, 86–87, 286–287, 335, 374, 384, 389–391
strategic profit model, 108–109
strategy, corporate, 18–19, 39–42
subcontracting, 296, 297, 298
subsystems, defined, 12–13, 18, 22–23
suppliers, 97, 127–128
supply chain management
    definition and overview, 36–37, 92–94
    e-commerce, 36–38, 104–107
    global issues, 94, 109–110
    information sharing, 94–96, 106–107
    performance measurement, 83–84, 108–109, 111
    principles of, 110–111
    strategies, 100–104
    structure, 97–100
supply chains
    definition and overview, 36–37, 92–93
    types of, 99–100, 109–110
survey method of forecasting, 138–139
SWOT analysis, 29, 38
synergy, 38, 46
synthesis, 123
system, defined, 12–13, 18
system capacity analysis, 199–208
    See also capacity
systematic layout planning (SLP), 270
systems approach to operations, 12–13, 22–23
systems development, 38–39

T

t-values, 150
tacit judgment, 259
Taguchi, Genichi, 77–78
Taguchi Methods, 77
tangible products *versus* intangible products, 4, 6
teamwork
    competitive advantage and, 38
    operations and, 10–11, 15
    problem solving, 78, 82–83, 84, 89, 384
    product design and process selection decision-making, 161
    in product development, 120, 125–127
    See also employees; workforce
technology
    defined, 9
    to achieve the ideal product, 34–35
    automation and , 46, 52, 65, 180
    group, 177–178, 259–261, 414
    manufacturing and, 45, 46
    operations and, 9–10, 43–46
    process design and, 9
    product design and, 9
    productivity, impact on, 65, 66–67
    service operations and, 9–10, 47–48
    supply chain management and, 94–96, 104–107
    See also information technology
test marketing, 139
testing, product, 130
theoretical capacity, 193
theory of constraints (TOC)
    overview, 391–393
    Critical Chain scheduling and Buffer Management, 448–451
    drum, buffer, and rope, 396–398
    impact of constraints, 392–393, 394
    MRP and JIT, combined/compared with, 398–399
    operations applications, 394–395, 396
third-party logistics (3PL) partnerships, 104
Tibrewala, Rajendra, 426
tiers, supply chain, 93, 97
time, revenue, and cost model, 227–228
time-based competition, 35–36

time buckets, 327–329
time buffer, 396
time/cost tradeoffs, 445–448
time phasing, 327
time-series methods of forecasting, 139–144
Timken, 119
TOC. *See* theory of constraints (TOC)
Toledo, Ohio, 226
Toledo Edison Company, 16
Toledo Zoo, 65
total preventive maintenance (TPM), 383
total quality management (TQM), 78–86, 376–377, 389
Toyota, 373
Toys "R" Us, 348–349, 378
TPM. *See* total preventive maintenance (TPM)
TQM. *See* total quality management (TQM)
trade and competition, 11–12, 43, 94
    See also GATT, global issues, NAFTA
trade-offs
    efficiency/cost in process selection, 160
    inputs/outputs of productivity, 57–59
    time/cost in project management, 445–448
transfer batch, 394–395, 396
Travelocity, 99
tree diagrams, 325, 326
trial and error method, 207

U

Underwriters Laboratories (UL), 89
    See also International Organization for Standardization (ISO)
undifferentiated products, 30
unions, labor, 15, 231, 296, 301, 383
UPC codes and scanners, 100, 101–102, 348–349
upstream supply chain, 97
U.S. Air Force 366th Medical Group, 394
U.S. economy, 60–61
U.S. Navy, 434
U.S. Postal Service, 47, 64–65
U.S. West, 55
USA Today, 47

V

Valmont Industries, 398

value added by operations, 8
Van Fossen, Tom, 81
variable inventory costs, 352, 353, 355–358
vendor managed inventory (VMI), 101
vertical integration, 97–98
virtual corporations, 98
virtual reality, 45
visual inspection, 259
VMI (vendor managed inventory), 101
voice of the customer, 78–81
volume
    flexibility, 390
    process selection decisions and, 161–163, 169–172
    unit costs, impact on, 161–163
    See also capacity
volume and global expansion, 164
Vonderembse, Mark, 81

W

wages and productivity, 61–62
wait time, 418
Wal-Mart, 53, 101, 104
Walker, William T., 110
weighted moving averages, 142–143
what-if questions, 135
Wheelwright, Steven, 172
Whirlpool Corporation, 258
work execution, 129
workforce
    aggregate planning and, 296–300
    increasing or decreasing, 196–197
    productivity improvements and, 62–63
    roles, 54
    scheduling, 425–427, 444–446
    See also employees; teamwork
workstations/work centers, 246

X

Xerox, 83–84

Y

yield, product, 198–199
yield management, 294–295
yield managers, B2B, 106

Z

z transformation formula, 443–444
Zeithaml, Valarie, 72–73